Life
Applications
from
Every Chapter
of the
BIBLE

Life
Applications
from
Every Chapter
of the
BIBLE

G. Campbell Morgan

Fleming H. Revell
A Division of Baker Book House Co
Grand Rapids, Michigan 49516

Published by Fleming H. Revell
a division of Baker Book House Company
P.O. Box 6287, Grand Rapids, MI 49516-6287

Originally published as Searchlights from the Word by Fleming H. Revell

First paperback edition 1994

ISBN: 0-8007-5535-9

FOREWORD

THESE notes were written over a period of three and a half years, and published in a weekly religious journal. During that time I constantly received messages from ministers, missionaries, and lay preachers, in many fields, telling me of their helpfulness in suggesting themes for sermons. This gave me great satisfaction, for I know of no service that I would rather render than that of being helpful to just such men. Multitudes of them are rendering heroic service in out-of-the-way, and oftentimes lonely places, cut off from libraries, and not able to procure many books. Moreover, my own experience has taught me that more detail-work, with its drain upon one's strength, devolves upon the pastor of the small church, than upon those in the larger ones. Anything that can be done to help such men is more than worth while. It is in the hope that I may be rendering such help that I publish these notes.

The word I have employed in the sub-title is intended to indicate the specific character of the notes. They are sermon-suggestions; they are not sermons. Not one of them is complete. They are not sermon-outlines. No attempt is made in any of them at systematic arrangement of a sermon. Moreover, I have resolutely refrained from heading the notes with suggested "subjects," preferring to let the text of Scripture be their only caption.

On every page of the "Holy Letters"—the "God-breathed Writings"—there are many thoughts, which stretch out like long, clear arms of light across the darkness, discovering things which otherwise were hidden, and often illuminating wider areas than those of the immediate context. They are searchlights.

From a multitude of these, I have selected one in each chapter of the Bible. Perhaps the work will also serve to illustrate a method of showing how focal points of radiating light gather their radiance from the context.

Thus, with a strong desire only to help by suggestion, I commit this work to book form, praying that some of my brethren who are gloriously toiling in difficult corners of the Field may find it to be of some value to them, in the prosecution of their labours.

G. CAMPBELL MORGAN

WESTMINSTER CHAPEL
LONDON, S.W.1

LIFE APPLICATIONS FROM EVERY CHAPTER OF THE BIBLE

GENESIS

The Spirit of God moved upon the face of the waters.—*Gen. 1. 2.*

That is the key-note of the music of the Biblical Literature. It is preceded by two brief but pregnant declarations. They are concerned with creation and catastrophe. In a simple and majestic sentence, all the order in the midst of which man lives is declared to be Divine origin. Nothing is said as to how God wrought, or how many ages were employed in the process. The one fact is stated that the beginning of the heaven and earth was by His creation. In an equally simple, but most graphic declaration a picture is presented of confusion. Nothing is said of how it was brought about. The picture is such that we know at once that the condition described resulted from some great upheaval. Thus we have suggested immediately, two opposing ideas, those of godliness and order, and lawlessness and disorder. The prevailing condition is that of disorder. The riddle of the universe as to its being, is solved. It is a creation of God. The problem of evil as to its being, is not solved, but it is recognized. Then follows the statement that the condition of disorder is not final. The earth is waste and void, but it is not abandoned. The Spirit of God brooded—for such is the force of the word—upon the face of the waters. Thus the original creation is conserved; and thus evil is limited. Over the waste and void earth, thus conserved, the Word of God sounds forth, uttering His will. That Word is never void of power, and therefore there is reconstruction, accompanied by new acts of creation. That is the whole theme of the Bible.

And the Lord God formed man of the dust of the ground, and breathed into his nostrils the breath of life; and man became a living soul.—*Gen. 2. 7.*

That statement contains an account of the nature of man, from which no Biblical teaching ever departs. In the previous chapter we were told the fact of his creation, and that he was created in the image of God, and placed in dominion over the restored order. Here we are distinctly told how God did the work. Glance for a moment at the last sentence: "Man became a living soul." The Hebrew verb rendered "became" (HAYAH) is always emphatic, and means came to be, or came into existence. The statement is not that man, already existing, was by some act of God,

changed into a living soul. The words "a living soul" describe man as God created him. The sentence would perhaps be clearer if written thus: Man became—a living soul. In his creation God employed dust, and the Breath of lives. Thus man is composed of the material and spiritual. The physical is not all of him; neither is he complete as a disembodied spirit. His body is of the dust. His spirit is of the Breath of God. Nothing is told us here as to the condition of the dust when God breathed into it. What processes were included in the forming, are not declared. It is a simple statement as to this original material of the physical. Let it be remembered that dust is also a Divine creation, and no particle of it is ever lost, though it may pass through many changes, as did the body of our Lord in resurrection.

The man and his wife hid themselves from the presence of the Lord God amongst the trees of the garden. —*Gen. 3. 8.*

That is the first revelation of the sense of the soul towards God, resulting from distrust and rebellion. It is the sense of sin. They hid because they were afraid. Their fear was not the outcome of any change in God. The change was in themselves. They had yet to learn that there can be no hiding from God. And, moreover, they had yet to learn that their only chance of restoration lay in that fact that there could be no hiding from Him. They had cut themselves off from the possibility of communion with Him, but they had not escaped either from His law or His love. These are the supreme revelations of this story. How true all human experience is to this first picture! The fear of God which prompts men to desire to escape Him, and to hide from Him, is as potent to-day as ever. The hiding may take the form of denial of His existence, of rebellion against His law, of indifference to His claim. It is always the same, a dislike of God, born of fear, and it is always caused, not by what God is, but because of what man is. The fear of God is ever a witness to the holiness of God, even though it be a proof of ignorance of His love. In so far, therefore, it is a principle of real value. In that sense the fear of the Lord is the beginning of wisdom. But it is only the beginning. If when, in spite of our hiding, He find us and make known to us His love, we yet persist in fleeing His presence, and refusing His claims, then we commit the sin that has no pardon nor can have. That is what Jesus described as eternal sin. The only safe hiding-place from the holy wrath of God, is in the wounded heart of God. There is a Tree which will hide us, but that is the Tree where we find God in Christ, reconciling the world unto Himself.

God hath appointed me another seed instead of Abel; for Cain slew him.—*Gen. 4. 25.*

What tragedy and triumph merge in these words! It was the cry of a mother's heart. This is the chapter telling the story of the first children born to man. The names tell the story of hopes and fears. Cain, meaning Acquired, revealed her hope that in him the Divine promise of a seed to triumph over evil was fulfilled. Abel, meaning Vanity, revealed her disappointment, not first in him, but in her firstborn; and so perhaps in him also. Then came the tragedy. The boy she named Vanity grew up to know God, and lived according to His will. Then Cain, the Acquired, slew him. Then the mother heart had learned some deeper lesson, for the third boy was named Seth, which meant Substitution. That was a note of hope. If the Divine promise tarried, it was not broken. It could not be fulfilled in Cain. It might have been, to her thinking, in the boy who bore the name revealing her disappointment, but he was dead. The story is not over. Another boy is given by God, and so she learns the great word. What simple things, and what sublime, are suggested by all this! It has something to say to us about our children. We do not know all about them. Each one of them must work out its own destiny apart from our hopes and fears. It has much to say to us about the ways of God. In His dealing with all the problem of human sin, there can be no hurrying.

This is the book of the generations of Adam.—*Gen. 5. 1.*

Only twice in the Bible do we find this exact formula; here, and in the first verse of the New Testament; in the one case the reference is to the first man, the first Adam; in the other it is to the second Man, the last Adam. This in itself is a suggestive fact. Here in Genesis the words constitute the title of the scroll which immediately follows, on which the posterity of Adam, through Seth, is given, up to Noah and his three sons. It covers the history of the first period, or age of human history after the Fall; that is the period from the Fall to the Deluge. In the previous chapter the history of the posterity of Adam through Cain is given, up to Lamech, who was contemporary with Enoch. The period covered lasted for fifteen hundred years, and this chapter is of importance because it is the only Biblical history of those centuries. That history is arresting in its brevity and baldness. In the main it is the story of the continuity of the race under the penalty of death resulting from the Fall. Man had distrusted God, and rebelled against His government, because he had believed the word of the enemy, who had said, "Ye shall not surely die." Through these centuries the tolling of the bell of death is persistent; we read it again and again, eight times: "and he died." Thus history was proving the word of the enemy to be a lie, and that of God to be the truth. This is what history always does. Yet the principle of triumph over sin and death is illustrated in the story. Once the death-knell is not heard. Of one man's passing from the earth, the description is different. Of Enoch it is written: "He was not, for God took him." And the explanation is found in the fact that in life he found his way into fellowship with God.

The Lord saw that the wickedness of man was great in the earth, and that every imagination of the thoughts of his heart was only evil continually. *Gen. 6. 5.*

These words give the reason for the Deluge. We come at this point in the record of human history, to the first activity of the punitive judgment of God. A crisis was reached, which made it necessary, in order to the carrying on of the Divine purpose for humanity, that there should be such action; and in these words the nature of the crisis is revealed. They are very emphatic, and show the utter moral depravity which prevailed. To read them carefully is to discover that fact. When evil choices and courses have thus wrought themselves out, God ever acts in judgment in this way. Over and over again has He done so. We have lived through a period of such Divine activity. And so it will continue until the final victory is gained, and evil is completely banished from the earth. Two matters are revealed which are of the greatest importance. First, God never acts in such judgment until it is necessary in order to the fulfilling of His highest purposes for humanity. Second, God always does so act, when it is necessary. They are the facts of His patience and His persistence. Evil never escapes Him. He presses upon it, and compels it to go on to the uttermost expression; and that, in order that He may destroy it. The flood, the blood and fire and vapour of smoke, all are the instruments of His judgment, and are employed in order to the realization of His high ideals for humanity.

And the Lord shut him in.—*Gen. 7. 16.*

In wrath, God ever remembers mercy; He always keeps alive His work; in the midst of the years He ever makes it known. In this history we are looking out upon an awful desolation resulting from the act of God made necessary by the sin of man. Everywhere the destroying and cleansing waters prevail, but riding upon them, in absolute security, is the ark. Within it are eight souls. They constitute the link between the first Divine purpose, and the ultimate realization thereof. They are safe, for God has shut them in. They are there because they have listened to Him, have believed in Him, have obeyed His word. Therefore are they safe; and much more, the purpose of God is safe, for through them He will move on toward the final triumph. Again we see the first illustration of a principle and method which have obtained in all human history. God's judgments are always discriminative in their exercise, and beneficent in their issue. The darkness has never completely mastered or extinguished the light. He has always found a remnant of faithful souls, through whom He has been able to move onward to the goal; and they have ever been safe in His keeping. Surely this old story should speak with searching and comforting power to our hearts. It searches us as it compels us to define our own relation to Him. Are we such men and women as He can shut in the ark of His preserving Grace, and through whom therefore He can work for the fulfilling of His purposes?

While the earth remaineth, seedtime and harvest, and cold and heat, and summer and winter, and day and night shall not cease.—Gen. 8. 22.

These words are part of the new covenant which God made with man after the Flood. In that judgment of a corrupt race the order of Nature had been set aside. One whole lunar year had been a year of judgment (compare Gen. 7. 11 with Gen. 8. 13, 14), and during that time there had been neither seedtime nor harvest, nor cold nor heat, nor summer nor winter, nor day nor night, so far as the experience of man and the condition of the earth were concerned. The purpose of that particular judgment being accomplished, God reinstated man in his relationship to the earth, putting him under a new order of life, that of the government of man by man (see 9. 1-6). In doing so He restored, and abidingly confirmed, the natural order. The next judgment of the earth will be its final fire-cleansing (see 2 Peter 3. 7 and 12). Until then this order abides. It is well that we remember that this covenant has never failed, and that the continuity and regularity of the seasons is due to the faithfulness of God. Through the ages man has lived by seedtime and harvest, by cold and heat, by summer and winter, by day and night; and this because God has been faithful and patient. The sorrows of humanity are all due to man's misuse of these things. If they were properly used under the Divine government, there would be neither pain nor poverty, but perfect human conditions. All earthly blessings flow from these Divine arrangements. All earthly curses result from human misuse of them.

I do set My bow in the cloud, and it shall be for a token of a covenant between Me and the earth.—Gen. 9, 13.

Thus God selected one of the already existing and most beautiful of natural phenomena, and made it the abiding sign of the covenant He had made with man. Apart from clouds and rain there can be no bow. But the bow is never seen on the clouds, except when the sun is shining. In view of the instrument of the judgment through which the earth had just passed, that of the rain and the flood, this was an exquisitely fitting symbol of that covenant made with man by the God of mercy and of grace. The context shows us the use to be made of it. Necessarily when seen in the cloud it would speak to man of this covenant, and without any doubt that was within the mind of God. But that is not the purpose for its adoption as a sign which is stated in the story. It is rather that God said: "The bow shall be seen in the cloud, and I will remember My covenant" (verses 14, 15); and that is still further emphasized by the words, "The bow shall be in the cloud; and I will look upon it, that I may remember" (verse 16). The full value of the bow in the cloud, then, was not so much that when man looked at it he remembered the covenant; but rather that he remembered that God was looking and remembering. That touches a deeper note, and creates a profounder sense of peace. When next we see the rainbow, let us remind ourselves that we are looking at something at which God is looking, and that as He looks He remembers.

These are the families of the sons of Noah, after their generation, in their nations; and of these were the nations divided in the earth after the flood.— Gen. 10. 32.

The reader will observe that in this tenth chapter we have an account of how the nations were "divided in the earth." It precedes the story of the occasion of this division, which is found in the next chapter. It is here that the national idea emerges in the Bible story. Up to now there had been one race. There would still be one race, but henceforth in its growth and development, it would consist of different branches, families, nations, each having peculiar characteristics, which in the Divine economy are intended to be held in trust for the commonwealth, that so the race, being communal, might be the richer. Babel was an attempt to evade this wider purpose of God. Thus the writer describes the division, which followed Babel first, because it was the first

Divine purpose. All this should be very carefully pondered. The national idea is Divine, but its principle is co-operation, and its purpose communion. Man has made its principle competition, and its experience has become conflict. When the nations are last seen in the Biblical Revelation, they are walking in the light of the City of God (Rev. 21. 24); and then the commonwealth of man will be realized in the Kingdom of God, and all conflict will have ended for ever. The last glory of the race will not be monotony, but harmony, the cultivation by every nation of its own peculiar powers and resources, in the interest of all the other nations. That is the far-off Divine event, to which the whole creation moves; and that the glory of the vision which inspires to all sacrifice and service till it be realized.

Therefore was the name of it called Babel.—Gen. 11. 9.

So a name is given to the Mystery of Lawlessness as it operates in human society. From here, the evil thing is seen running on through all succeeding ages of the history of man, until it comes to final expression, and is destroyed (Rev. 18. 21). This story of Babel is that of man's attempt to realize a social order in defiance of a Divine purpose. The purpose of God was the full realization of the race, and that necessitated the replenishing of the whole earth by the scattering of men over all its face. Man took counsel against this scattering, and attempted to realize a State at Shinar, "lest we be scattered abroad." In order to the fulfilment of the larger purpose, God confused their language and drove the nations into separation. The purpose of the scattering was that of the larger gathering which should fulfil His purpose. He confused their schemes that His plan might be realized. This is not only an ancient story, it is the story of a perpetual process. Over and over again men have sought to establish themselves either in rebellion against, or without reference to, the Divine plans. The result has always been confusion. God has never permitted humanity to realize a social order from which He is excluded, nor will He do so to the end. Such an order would mean the limiting and ultimate destruction of humanity. Therefore He confuses all such attempts, and, compelling men to work out their own false conceptions to their logical issue, destroys them.

I will make of thee a great nation, and I will bless thee, and make thy name great; and be thou a blessing.— Gen. 12. 2.

In this chapter we have the beginning of the history of the people through whom God has acted in human history, in order to the redemption of the race and the restoration of the Divine order. From this point the Biblical literature is concerned

with that people, until of its stock the Deliverer appeared. Then it is concerned with Him and the elect race resulting from His work. While this is so, we must never imagine that the nations or the world are excluded from the Divine thought and purpose. The nation now to be called into being; the One Who, after the flesh, would be of that nation; and the new race created by His work—all, in the purpose of God, are called into co-operation with Him on behalf of the world and of all the nations. The recognition of this fact is fundamental to any correct interpretation of the Biblical Revelation. This is the vital matter in these words spoken to Abram. The last words, "Be thou a blessing," give the reason of the former, "I will make of thee a great nation, and I will bless thee, and make thy name great." In calling Abram, God did not reject other men; in making his name great, He did not degrade other names; in blessing him, He did not hand others over to a curse. When at last this nation was for a season cast out from privilege and responsibility it was because it had become self-centred, and forgotten its high responsibility for the nations of the world. When that nation is restored to its true place, it will be to fulfil that office. The truth abides. The Church exists in order to be a blessing. For that, she is blessed of God. To forget this, is to fail utterly, and to be cast away.

Lift up now thine eyes, and look from the place where thou art.— Gen. 13. 14.

These words were spoken to Abram when he was in a place of peculiar difficulty. He was now in the land to which he had been sent by God. Moreover he was there after a deflection from the pathway of faith, in which deflection he had gone down into Egypt. An hour had come when domestic difficulties had arisen between him and his kinsman, Lot. It had become necessary for them to separate from each other. With the magnanimity of a great soul, Abram had given to Lot the right to choose the place where he would dwell in the land, and Lot had chosen. The result was that Abram, on that level of human arrangement, was excluded from the best of the country. It was at this juncture that God communed with him, and gave him this command. The words are seen in their true suggestiveness when they are put into contrast with those found in the tenth verse, "Lot lifted up his eyes." In doing so, Lot had chosen upon the ground of personal advantage. When he had gone, God said to the man who had chosen not to choose, "Lift up now thine eyes," and directed him to look "northward and southward and eastward and westward"; that was to every point of the compass and consequently over all the land, including that which Lot had chosen for himself. All he thus looked upon was then secured to him by the covenant of God. The teaching of the story is patent. Man has no final rights in any possessions other than those which are his by the gift of God. The man who, by faith, leaves the choices of his life to God, is the man who finds his way into possessions of which he cannot be robbed.

I will not take a thread nor a shoe-latchet nor aught that is thine, lest thou shouldest say, I have made Abram rich.—Gen. 14. 23.

These words show how high an order of faith was that of this man Abram. He had rendered a great service to the King of Sodom, in the victory he had gained over the five kings, even though he had entered into the conflict, not on his behalf, but for the sake of Lot. To a man of less keen perception it would have seemed perfectly natural, and quite harmless, to receive from this king a gift of the material substance which he had rescued. But true faith always sees beyond the immediate, and refuses to compromise its future by any action in the present. Abram saw at once, and saw clearly, what might eventuate; and he refused to put himself in any way under obligation to one who might at some later period take advantage of his action in such a way as to bring discredit upon his God. How wide in its application is the principle here revealed; and how much stronger men of faith in all ages would have been had they acted upon it! How often has the Church, or a church, found its spiritual influence limited, and in many cases destroyed, because she has received gifts from those who in all the facts of their lives were in rebellion against God. Moreover, Abram had no need of such gifts, nor was he impoverished by refusing them. The next chapter begins with the words: "After these things the word of the Lord came unto Abram in a vision, saying, Fear not, Abram, I am thy shield, and thy exceeding great reward." Such a man needed no reward which the King of Sodom had to offer him.

He believed in the Lord; and He counted it to him for righteousness.— Gen. 15. 6.

That this is a statement of central importance is self-evident, and this is corroborated by the fact that Paul and James both quote it, in letters which some have thought to be contradictory, but which are equally complementary; Paul in his letters to the Romans (4. 3), and the Galatians (3. 6), and James in the one which he wrote (2. 23). Reference to these passages will be found helpful. Let us consider the statement as it stands. What belief on the part of Abram is referred to? That in which he believed that God would actually do for him that which, on the level of the human, seemed impossible. This he believed, and thus he believed God. That belief God counted to him for righteousness. It is of the utmost importance that we make no mistake as to the simple meaning of that statement. Let us therefore at once say that it does not mean that God put something down to his account which he did not possess. His belief was right, therefore it was righteousness. His belief was the reason of all the activities of his life subsequent to his exercise of it. Therefore it was the inspiration of righteous activity. Thus we see how Paul and James agree. Paul argued that only faith can make righteous. James claimed that the only proof of faith is righteousness. Jesus said, "This is the work of God, that ye believe on Him Whom He hath sent" (John 6. 29); and the same great truth is confirmed by that saying. The first act of righteousness is belief. The man who believes God has righteousness counted to him, because by so doing he does the right, and makes possible the realization of righteousness in his character and conduct.

Beer-lahai-roi.—Gen. 16. 14.

This was the name given to the well by the side of which Hagar, the bondwoman in Abram's household, and the mother of Ishmael, had been visited and comforted by the Angel of Jehovah. It is significant as revealing her experience. It has been variously translated: "Well of a living, my seer"; "The well of living after seeing"; "The well of him that liveth and seeth me." These renderings are all of the nature of interpretation. The actual translation must recognize the combination of three words: Beer—a well; lahai—life; roi—a seer or a vision. To understand the suggestiveness we need the context. The previous verse shows that she had seen God as the One Who saw her. He therefore was the living One, Who cared for her life and comforted her. These, then, were surely the ideas giving rise to the name. God was discovered as the living One Who sees. That vision brought life to Hagar. This whole incident is most illuminative, showing us that God is not unmindful of those who are outside the covenants made with the people called to carry out His purposes. He is always the God Who sees; and He is ever the living God, Who acts according to what He sees. In many ways, which are beyond those of His special covenants with His chosen, He is giving life to those who see Him, however dimly. This name of a well, then, seems to stand out upon the page of the ancient story, like a shaft of light in darkness, suggesting great thoughts about God, and His ways with men, and filling the heart with confidence in His justice and goodness.

I am God Almighty; walk before Me, and be thou perfect.—Gen. 17. 1.

In this word Jehovah revealed Himself in a new way to Abram, and called him to a yet completer devotion. The name or title, El-Shaddai, is peculiarly suggestive, meaning quite literally, the mighty One of Resource or Sufficiency. We miss much of its beauty by our rendering God Almighty. The idea of Almightiness is present, but it is fully expressed by the word El. The word Shaddai goes further, and suggests perfect supply, and perfect comfort. We should reach the idea better by rendering God All-bountiful, or even better still, God All-sufficient. This was the new revelation, and it was in connection with its making that Abram was called to walk before this God, and to be perfect. This is ever God's way with His own. He reveals the perfection of their resources in Himself, and then calls them to a walk which is made possible by these very resources. Who can walk before God and be perfect in his own wisdom or strength? Surely none! But, on the other hand, who need fail to do so, if depending upon Him for all He, in tender and mighty strength, is able and willing to supply. To gather sustenance and consolation from the bosom of God, is to be made strong for all the pilgrimage, however long the march, or difficult the route. For us, the revelation of this truth about God is perfected in our Lord, for "The only begotten Son, Who is in the bosom of the Father, He hath declared Him." And more: "Of His fulness we all received, and grace for grace."

I will speak yet but this once; peradventure ten shall be found there.— Gen. 18. 32.

This is one of the greatest chapters in all the Bible in its revelation of the possibilities open to the man of faith in communion with God. Abraham is seen as concerned for the honour of his God. To him it seemed that if in the judgment of the wicked, the righteous should be involved, justice would be violated; and in that view he was right. His conviction was the direct result of his knowledge of God. Under stress of this concern he talked to his God, and was answered. Accepting his suggestion as to a number, God declared that if fifty were found in Sodom He would spare the city. Encouraged by this assurance, Abraham applied his principle to forty-five, forty, thirty, twenty, and in every case the Divine response ratified his conviction. Then once more he ventured, suggested ten, and being again answered, stopped there. The statement is illuminated by the sequel. Abraham stopped at ten, but God carried out the principle in that He delivered the one, as He compelled Lot to leave before the judgment fell upon the city. The lesson for us is patent. God is not only, as we sometimes say, better than our fears; He is better than our hopes. If we are concerned for His honour, He is ever willing to commune with us, and to lead us as far as our faith will travel, ever giving

us assurance of His faithfulness to the highest things we think of Him. Then we may know, that when we dare go no further in suggestion, He will go beyond our daring.

I cannot do anything till thou be come thither.—Gen. 19. 22.

In these words we find the carrying out to the uttermost of the principle for which Abraham had contended in his communing with God. They reveal to us the fact that it is impossible for God to be untrue to His own character of righteousness. His judgments can never be inconsistent with His justice. All this is emphasized when, reading this whole story, we see the reluctance of Lot. He was a righteous man, vexed with the lawless deeds of the men of Sodom (2 Peter 2. 7, 8); but his associations with the city, and doubtless his possessions therein, were such that he lingered, and could hardly be persuaded to leave. While he was there God could not do anything, because to do so would have been to destroy that man, righteous, though reluctant to leave; and that would have been to deny Himself, and to undermine the very foundations upon which His throne is built. That is the truth which gives us confidence at all times. However terrible the judgments of God are, they are always discriminative; and even when to our limited vision it may appear that the righteous are involved with the wicked, we know it is not so. Amos had that conviction when he said: "I will sift the house of Israel among all the nations, like as corn is sifted in a sieve, *yet shall not the least grain fall upon the earth*" (Amos 9. 9). This does not mean that the righteous never suffer as the result of the sin of others. They may suffer, and even die; it does mean that such suffering and death have another meaning.

What sawest thou, that thou hast done this thing?—Gen. 20. 10.

These were the words of Abimelech to Abraham; of the King of Gerar to the father of the chosen people. In the chapter we have the account of a deflection from the pathway of faith on the part of the man of faith. In such departure he was reduced to the expedient of making arrangements for his own safety by deceitful practices, in that he hid the truth that Sarai was his wife, and told the half-truth that she was his sister, she being his half-sister, the daughter of his father, Terah, by another wife. The astounding thing is that he had done this before in the case of his visit to Egypt. This question of Abimelech was an inquiry as to what motive had prompted Abraham, and it brought this answer: "Because I thought, Surely the fear of God is not in this place." What a revelation we have here of blundering!

Abraham thought that among a people who lacked the fear of God, he must act for himself, and without God. God taught him by this experience, first, that His fear existed where he did not think it did; and therefore that it was not only unnecessary, but also wholly wrong, for him to act as he had done. By such action he had placed the whole purpose of God in jeopardy, and but for the intervention of God it would have been made impossible of realization through Abraham. What unutterable folly it is ever to limit God in our thinking, and so to have to fall back upon our own policies! To do so is always to turn aside from the high ways of His purpose, and to imperil the possibility of working together with Him.

God hath heard the voice of the lad where he is.—Gen. 21. 17.

This was the word of the Angel of God about Ishmael, and it is one which we do well to ponder. Ishmael was the son of the bond-woman, the offspring of a failure of faith. When Isaac, the child of faith, was born, the bond-woman mocked. That is a suggestive statement. It was necessary that Hagar and Ishmael should be sent forth. They could have no part in the purposes of God, which were being wrought out through the chosen people. But when thus sent out, they had not passed out of the sight of God, nor beyond His care and government. God provided for him what he needed at the moment to preserve his life; God was with the lad, and he grew; God made of him a great nation. This story, rightly apprehended, will help us to that view of all history which is necessary to intelligent understanding thereof. God's elections never mean His abandonment of those not elected. There is no nation which He has not made. There is no people which He has excluded from the purposes of His goodness. Those elected are elected to serve the others. When at last His city is built, all the nations shall walk in the light thereof. When the seed, called in Isaac, has won the final triumph, Ishmael will share in the glorious results. A remembrance of that fact will purge our hearts from the possibility of all contempt for any "less-favoured" peoples. We shall see in them those whom God sees, for whom God cares, and for whose ultimate recovery and blessedness God is ever working.

Because thou hast done this thing.— Gen. 22. 16.

These six words have no meaning thus removed from their context, but in relation thereto are full of value, as they fasten attention upon an act of Abraham, and upon what that act made possible in the activity of God. In this act, the faith of Abraham rose to its highest level, and its most wonderful expression. In obedience to a Divine call, Abraham took an action which by all human calculation would prevent the fulfilment of a Divine Promise, knowing that the Word of God could not be broken. Because he did so, God was able to make him the instrument through whom all the nations of the earth should be blessed. That is the whole of this story, the details of which are so graphically given in this wonderful chapter. The one word which clings to the mind is that word, "Because." God is able to do things when we dare to trust Him. How much is involved in any hour when our faith is put to the test! Not our own character alone; nor merely the question of our personal relationship with Him; but issues and results much larger than, at the moment, we can see. It is perfectly true and clearly revealed by this story, that God does prove us by calling us to great ventures of faith, ventures which often run counter to our intellectual ability and emotional life, ventures which call us to poignant suffering. But He never does so, save to prepare us for co-operation with Himself in some great purpose of His wisdom and His love.

And the field, and the cave that is therein, were made sure unto Abraham, for a possession of a burying-place by the children of Heth.—Gen. 23. 20.

This field and its cave as a burying-place constituted the only holding which this man Abraham ever had, in the land which was given to him as a possession by a covenant with God. How insecure this making sure to him by the children of Heth was, is revealed by the fact that eighty years later his grandson Jacob regained possession of it by re-purchase (see Gen. 33. 19 and Acts 7. 16). How constantly faith possesses in a covenant with God what cannot be secured by a covenant with man. Never, even yet, has the seed of Abraham finally and perfectly possessed that land; but it is equally true that no other race has possessed it. It is reserved in the purpose and power of God for His ancient people, and they will possess it. Faith knows this, and thus persistently possesses what it does not seem to hold. This is the perpetual victory of the man of faith. He receives the promises as promises, and dies, not having received the promises as realizations. He dies triumphantly, knowing that the promise will be fulfilled. Thus, all the realizations of the high things of human life are held in the consciousness of faith; and are made sure, by its activity in fellowship with God. Faith is the power to do without what God has promised, until the time comes when He in His infinite wisdom provides the thing promised. Yet all the while faith possesses, and enters into all the joys of the gift. God's gaining earth and our gaining heaven are assured by Divine covenant.

Thou shalt go unto my country, and to my kindred, and take a wife for my son Isaac.—Gen. 24. 4.

On the part of Abraham this sending of his servant to seek a wife for Isaac was an act of obedient and intelligent faith. He was now about a hundred and forty years old, and Isaac was forty. The record declares that "Jehovah had blessed Abraham in all things" (verse 1); and the chief blessing granted was this son. Through him the promises made to Abraham were to be fulfilled; the promised Seed was to come. The certainty of this promise made it incumbent upon Abraham to co-operate with God intelligently. Therefore he took this method of securing the seed of his son from contamination with the people of the land. It was an activity of faith. This is seen in the answer Abraham gave to his servant when he suggested that the woman he might find might not be willing to follow him. He declared that Jehovah would snd His angel before him. The sequel shows how wonderfully this man was guided through the ordinary circumstances of everyday life. The principle suggested and illustrated by this whole story is that faith is to act reasonably. To believe in the promises of God is to act in accordance with them, in the sense of intelligent co-operation. Faith does not sit down and say: God has promised, therefore I have nothing to do. It rather says: God has promised, therefore I must do everything in the line of His promise; and so far as in me lies, see to it that nothing interferes with His purpose.

Abraham gave up the ghost, and died in a good old age, an old man, and full.—Gen. 25. 8.

That is a great word, especially if we leave it as it is in the Hebrew Bible, without the addition of the words, "of years." Abraham died full, not of years only, or principally, but of life, of experience, of all the great things. By faith he had abandoned much, but he had gained far more. He had come to know God; to walk with Him, to talk with Him; to enter into a true fellowship with Him in all the great processes of His heart. "He was called the friend of God" (Jas. 2. 23). Such life is full whatever it seems to lack. The man whose vision is bounded by the things of time and sense might well say that Abraham died singularly empty. As the writer of the letter to the Hebrews said, he "died in faith, not having received the promises." For a hundred years he had sojourned in a land given to him in a covenant, but he had not possessed it according to the standards of human possession. Surely he had little of earthly gain in which to boast, and he had given up very much when he left Ur of the Chaldees. Nevertheless, he died full, for in his fellowship with God he had learned to measure time by eternity,

to value the things of sense by those of spirit. To such a man death is but passing on to wait the accomplishment of the Divine purposes, and the fulfilment of the promises of God on the other side. So the fulness of Abraham was that of a wealth which death could not touch. The fulness which men gain who live by sight and not by faith, is a fulness of which they are emptied in death. They leave their possessions behind them. The men of faith carry their fulness with them. It is a great thing thus to die—full.

And he removed from thence, and digged another well.—Gen. 26. 22.

In these words we have a revelation of the character of Isaac, and an indication of the nature of his faith. He was a quiet, placid man, not given to making any great ventures, not given to restlessness. His was the pastoral habit, that loved to dwell peaceably, digging wells and so providing for the needs of those of his people and his cattle who were dependent upon him as the head of his tribe. But he was a man of persistence. He would not engage in strife with those who stole his wells, but he would quietly go on digging until they were tired of stealing. When his persistence found its reward in a well which his enemies did not appropriate, he called it Rehoboth, and attributed his victory to Jehovah, saying: "Jehovah hath made room for us, and we shall be fruitful in the land." All this is very valuable, as it helps us to see that faith expresses itself in different ways, according to differing temperaments. The faith of Abraham was ever of the high, adventurous order, and was the means by which God could lead him to great experiences. The faith of Jacob was always that of restlessness, but it was faith, and so was the vantage ground which God found for the perfecting of the man, and for using him. That of Isaac was restful, persistent devotion to immediate duty, and it was the principle which made it possible for God to give room in the land to the people He had chosen. God needs, and will honour and use, the adventurous faith of Abraham, the restless faith of Jacob, and the patient, persistent faith of Isaac.

Tarry with him a few days.—Gen. 27. 44.

This was Rebekah's conception of the measure of the wrong she had done to Esau by her duplicity, and it was the proof of her misunderstanding of her own children. She had acted in harmony with her conviction that the purpose of God was to carry out His purposes through Jacob rather than Esau, but her action was none the less wrong. She did not know the strength of Esau's hatred and anger. She thought it would expend itself in "a few days." Those few days multiplied into twenty years; and while we have no account of Rebekah's death, it is at least more than probable that she never saw Jacob again. The whole story shows how God overrules the blunders of men; but it none the less illustrates the folly of wrong-doing, and teaches us how human cleverness, acting apart from Divine guidance, falls into the most complete miscalculations. How constantly, when we turn aside from the pathway of a simple obedience, we count up the cost, and how again and again we have to learn that we were wrong in our estimates! The few days become twenty long years; the comparatively trivial disadvantage is found to be a lifelong disability: the negligible quantity becomes the permanent pain. It is well for us if we learn that our cleverness is always at fault when it attempts to arrive at the Divine goal in any other way than by travelling along the Divinely marked pathway. What constant pain should we be spared if we really believed that God ever works for them that wait for Him! That is true faith.

Surely the Lord is in this place; and I knew it not.—Gen. 28. 16.

These were the words of Jacob when he awoke from his sleep, and they record the result of the revelation which had been granted to him through the dream of the ladder and the ascending and descending angels. Their deepest significance is discovered when we notice particularly the tenses of the verbs he employed: "Jehovah *is* in this place ... I *knew* it not." The first tense is present; the second is past. Through the experience of the night he had come to the consciousness of an abiding fact—"Jehovah *is* in this place," of which he had been ignorant when he had gone to sleep—"I *knew* it not." The fact was that of the abiding presence, the constant nearness of God. He did not say, "Jehovah *was* in this place," as though he had received a visit from God. The revelation which had come to him was far more wonderful and better than that. Those ascending and descending angels had shown him the perpetual nearness of Heaven to earth, and the voice of God which he had heard was the voice of One very nigh at hand. He had travelled away from home, and from the place of the altar, but he had not travelled away from God, notwithstanding the fact that his journey had been made necessary by his own wrongdoing. Seeking a stone for a pillow, in utter loneliness, he had lain him down to rest, not knowing that the God of his fathers was with him yet. He woke to the realization of the fact, and that very place became to him Bethel, the house of God.

Tell me, what shall thy wages be.— Gen. 29. 15.

That was Laban's question, and in the light of the whole story it is a revealing question. The name of Jacob has become almost the synonym for crafty cleverness, and there may be, and doubtless is, a great deal of justification for that fact. Nevertheless, it is impossible for any one who loves straight dealing between man and man to study this whole narrative without prejudice, and not to feel satisfaction in the fact that Jacob was one too many for this man Laban. Jacob was clever, but he was honourable in his dealings; he broke no contract, he fulfilled his obligations. This cannot be said for Laban at any point. He deceived Jacob, and that most cruelly; and every time he offered him some apparent benefit it was with an ulterior motive which was wholly selfish. Laban was the type of man who without scruple makes use of his fellows, squeezing every advantage out of them, and then throwing them aside without compunction. It is a mean and dastardly type. This is a story to which one's mind constantly recurs when one hears people speaking contemptuously of the Hebrew people. Let it be granted that they have outwitted, and still do succeed in outwitting, many of those who would oppress them; it is nevertheless true that for every Jacob among them a Laban is found whose methods are those of rank injustice. Indeed, it is not very far from the final truth to say that it is Laban's unscrupulous methods which have developed Jacob's craftiness. At least, it is proven beyond fear of contradiction that those who have treated the Jew with justice and consideration have found in him a response of fidelity and faithfulness which has been irreproachable.

The man increased exceedingly, and had large flocks, and maidservants and menservants, and camels and asses.— Gen. 30. 43.

And that in spite of Laban, or perhaps rather as the result of the unjust pressure which Laban had brought to bear upon him through the years. There was nothing unjust or dishonourable in the methods of Jacob. They were clever, astute, perhaps not those which the Christian ethic would warrant. But this man did not know that ethic, nor could he. He had desired at this time to depart from Laban. Laban, however, on his own confession had profited by the service which Jacob had rendered him, and so had a strong desire to retain him. Therefore he consented to an arrangement which Jacob proposed (verses 31, 32). This compact he immediately broke (verses 35, 36). It was then, when deceived again by Laban, that Jacob commenced the method which resulted in his enrichment. Here it should be said that most expositors refer the statements in verses 35 and 36 to Jacob, supposing that it was he who separated the ring-straked and spotted to himself. But such a view can only be maintained by the strangest forcing of the story, which goes on distinctly to declare that Jacob fed the rest of Laban's flocks. Here then we have another instance of the unscrupulous methods of Laban, and of how Jacob played his part against them successfully. All this is interesting, but there are deeper things than those appearing yet upon the surface.

The Lord watch between me and thee, when we are absent one from another.—*Gen*. 31. 49.

In this chapter we part company with Laban, and that not with any regret. These particular words are selected today because of the incidental light they throw upon superficial and false methods of using the Bible. They constitute a revelation of the reason why the heap of stones erected by Jacob when he left Laban was called Mizpah, that is, a watch-tower. It was Laban who uttered them, and they were the words of suspicion rather than of confidence. As these men parted, they were conscious of mutual distrust. The heap of stones was a boundary of separation. It was a witness that neither was to pass it in order to harm the other, and God was called upon as the Watcher Who should see to it that the compact was observed. That helps us to see how false is the use made of the word oftentimes. Not many years ago, it was the fashion to give and wear rings engraved with the word Mizpah, which were supposed to indicate a friendship cemented in the watchfulness of God. Perhaps it was all very harmless, but it was certainly very ignorant. To set this simple thing to the test of the Scriptures themselves is at least to be warned as to the danger of slipshod reading and careless interpretation, the results of which are not always harmless, but may lead to entirely false ideas and actions, not only out of harmony with truth, but destructive thereof. God is the Watcher Who never loses sight of the ancient landmarks, and woe be to the man who removes them, or wrongs his neighbour. But where justice is guarded by mutual love, no Mizpah is required, a watch-tower reminding us of the vigilance of God in this way.

Thy name shall be called no more Jacob, but Israel.—*Gen*. 32. 28.

The centrality of this chapter to the story of Jacob is recognized. In these words we have a revelation of the real meaning and issue of the night of struggle through which he had passed. Everything depends upon a right understanding of the contrast between these names. Jacob literally meant heel-catcher, and so supplanter. Israel is a compound of two words, Isra, which means ruled, and El, the name of God, and so means Ruled-by-God. This

was the discovery made to him that night, and that discovery constituted God's victory. Jacob had contended with men and had prevailed. That had been the story all through, and the effect of his successes upon his character had been that of making him self-reliant, and in that measure forgetful that these very successes had resulted from the fact that all his life was arranged and ruled by God. That was the lesson he had to learn in order that he might be delivered from a self-sufficiency which must inevitably have ruined him. That explains all the story of that night. God crippled him to crown him, revealed his weakness to teach him the secret of strength, defeated him that he might find victory. His cry, "I will not let Thee go except Thou bless me," was not the strident cry of a man compelling a reluctant God to yield to him; it was the sobbing wail of a man casting himself at last at the feet of a God seeking to heal him (see Hosea 12. 4). From that day he halted in his walk, and that halt was the patent of his nobility. Whatever others thought of it, he knew it was the abiding sign of God's victory, and that he was a man ruled by God. How often apparent disabilities are the signs of royalty, and so of ability!

El-Elohe-Israel.—*Gen*. 33. 20.

The naming of this altar was certainly significant. It will be observed that the name God occurs thrice therein. "El-Elohe-Israel." It means God—the God of Israel, or if we further translate God—the God of the one ruled by God. Dr. Scofield has an illuminative note on this name. He says that this naming of this altar was "Jacob's act of faith appropriating his new name, but also claiming Elohim in this new sense as the God through Whom alone he could walk according to his new name." Whether Jacob at this time had understood this may be doubted, but that it is a vital truth there is no question. The fundamental lesson of all true life is that we must be ruled by God; but the further lesson needs to be learned, namely, that it is only possible for us to walk, according to the Divine rule, in the Divine strength. Yielding to God is far more than an act; it is an attitude. As the act of yielding is ever that of response to the Divine call, and often the Divine pressure, so also the attitude of yielding is only maintained in the measure in which we depend constantly and entirely upon God. Happy indeed is the soul who is completely at the end of self-confidence. Then, and only then, is man safe, when he can and does truthfully pray—

Grant me now my soul's petition,
None of self and all of Thee.

It is never quite safe to sing that last line without the preceding one. It is when dedication is expressed as a prayer rather than as an act of will, that it becomes complete.

Simeon and Levi, Dinah's brethren, took each man his sword, and came upon the city unawares, and slew all the males.—*Gen.* 34. 25.

This is a dark page in the history. The story of the wrong done to and by Dinah is a tragedy, and there is a sense in which we cannot wonder at the anger of her brothers. Nevertheless the words we have chosen for emphasis reveal a greater wrong. These men had discussed the situation and had entered into a compact with Hamor and Shechem. They in their turn kept the pact. Then, in spite of that arrangement, the sons of Jacob slew the men of the city. The wrong of it weighed heavily on the soul of their father, and in his final charge to them ere he died, he reverted to the matter, and severely reprobated their action. (See Gen. 49. 5, 6.) In this story is seen something which is constantly emphasized in the Bible, and it is a matter that we do well to ponder. The principle involved may thus be broadly stated. Man has no right to act unrighteously in a righteous cause. God never does so, and He is eternally opposed to such action. Moses was finally excluded from the Promised Land because his spirit was unrighteously moved in a righteous cause, and he spake unadvisedly with his lips. We must not do evil that good may come, neither must we employ evil methods for the punishment of evil. It is a hard lesson, and one which the heart of man is slow to learn. It does seem to be such an excellent thing to visit the wrong-doers with vengeance; but it is wholly reprehensible to do so, when the act involves infidelity to a covenant made. God never needs that wrong shall be done in order to the vindication of right.

She called his name Benoni, but his father called him Benjamin.—*Gen.* 35. 18.

The human elements in these words are very suggestive and full of pathos. Rachel was Jacob's one love. For her, during the years of his exile, he had served fourteen years, seven while waiting for her, and seven in comradeship with her. Now they were back in his own country, and in giving birth to her second boy she died. Ere she passed, she expressed her soul as she named him Benoni, son of sorrow. What did she mean? The question is an open one, and there may be different answers. Among the rest, one that is at least as probable as any other, and perfectly suits the story of the love which existed between her and Jacob, is that she was thinking, not of herself, but of him. He would have the son, but at the cost of the mother, and so he would be to him the son of sorrow. Jacob changed the name to Benjamin, son of my right hand; and here there seems to be his agreement with Rachel rather than disagreement, only he emphasized the other side of the

truth. If he was to be bereft of his loved one, Rachel, yet the son born to her would be his comfort and consolation. Thus read, the verse is an idyll. The story is that of sorrow, but it is sorrow transfigured by love. Two who have journeyed together in the joy of true love are about to be separated; but amid the deep shadows of death, there is the light of this new life. Rachel expresses her understanding of what the boy will ever be to his father, the son of sorrow; Jacob, understanding also, and desiring to give her comfort as she passed on, reminded her that the boy would be to him a strength in his sorrow—the son of his right hand. Doubtless the story may have deeper values, but this human touch, of its first natural meaning, is full of beauty.

Esau (the same is Edom).—*Gen.* 36. 1.

This is the special chapter about Esau's descendants. He is now to pass out of the story. We shall read no more about him. But his descendants will remain, the people of Edom, persistently in opposition to the descendants of Jacob. They appear again and again, especially in the prophetic writings. One brief but revealing book deals with Edom. It is the prophecy of Obadiah. In it, the judgment of God upon Edom is declared, and the peculiar nature of its sin is described. It is chiefly remarkable, however, for its closing movement, which foretells a day of ultimate redemption even for the mount of Esau, a day when saviours shall come up on Mount Zion to judge it, a day when the kingdom shall be Jehovah's (Obadiah 21). It is good thus in our reading sometimes to glance ahead, for by so doing we may be guided and helped in our attitudes toward much that may be happening around us. Esau was a profane person, who sold his birthright; from his loins there sprang a profane nation, which filled the cup of iniquity to the brim. Therefore their judgment was inevitable. That is not the last word, however. The last word is one of saviours and salvation, within the one and only kingdom of Jehovah. Those who watch with God, see this always. Sin must work itself out. Punishment is inherent in sin. But God is greater than sin, and His eyes are ever fixed upon the issue, and toward that He is ever working. Those who watch with Him, therefore, work with Him; and they wait with Him, enduring the travail, but assured of the triumph.

I will go down to the grave to my son mourning.—*Gen.* 37. 35.

Thus Jacob spoke when his son Joseph was lost to him. It was the language of a perfectly honest man. He saw nothing before him for the rest of his days other than sorrow, seeing that the eldest boy of his beloved Rachel had been slain by a wild beast, as he believed. Moreover, there was the wilfulness of a strong man in the declaration. His sons and his daughters rose up to comfort him, and he refused to be comforted. He chose to abide in sorrow. He would not accept comfort. Such was the desolation created by the loss of Joseph, that he had no desire to escape the sense of it. He was in that mood which the human heart often experiences, when it would seem a wicked thing to be comforted. Yet he was wrong. His outlook was wrong, and his wilfulness was wrong. He did not go down to the grave sorrowing. That son he mourned was alive, and brought joy to his father, illuminating for him the way to the grave. We may say he was not to be blamed, because he did not, nor could he, foresee this fact. But that is exactly where faith comes in. Faith, moreover, is not foresight. It is confidence in God, which means certainty that, however dark the way, it is leading us to sunlit places. Sorrow is not wrong; but waywardness in it, and refusal to be comforted, is always wrong. The man of faith can never consent to judge any circumstances as constituting the whole of things. He must reckon with God, and venture upon Him. To do so, is never to be overcome by sorrow.

She is more righteous than I.—Gen. 38. 26.

Like chapter 34, this is a dark page in the history. It constitutes a digression from the main story, but it is necessary in order to an understanding of the frailties of these men, and because of its bearing upon subsequent history (compare Matt. 1. 3 and Luke 3. 33). It is, first, the story of the sin of Judah, which was not only carnal, but spiritual, in that the wrong was wrought with the daughter of a Canaanite, the race with which the chosen people were strictly forbidden to intermarry. Then it becomes the story of a breach of contract. Judah had covenanted with Tamar that she should have Shelah as her husband. Necessarily we must understand such a covenant in the place it occupied at that time and among those people. This promise he broke, and Tamar took drastic and evil means to avenge herself. This brought home his guilt to him, and called forth these words: "She is more righteous than I." There is no doubt that he was right. The method which Tamar adopted may have been, even in the light of those times, entirely evil, but the motive was that of a passion for the right, which Judah lacked. The story inserted here has this value—that it once more, as in chapter 34, reveals the Biblical conception of the heinousness of the sin of breaking a contract.

And Joseph was brought down to Egypt. . . . And the Lord was with Joseph.—Gen. 39. 1, 2.

The nearness of these two statements to each other in the story is full of suggestiveness. They bring before us the two matters which affect us all, those, namely, of circumstances and God, and they set the first in the light of the second. For Joseph, circumstances were certainly adverse. He had had his dreams, but the experiences through which he had passed were of such a nature that there seemed to be no possibility of their realization. Here he was, exiled from his own land, in a strange country, cut off from the father who loved him so fondly, in the midst of utter strangers; and having lost his freedom, he was a slave. For the moment everything looked dark indeed. The other fact was that Jehovah was with him. We, writing the story, might have introduced the statements with the word "but"—expressing it thus—"But Jehovah was with Joseph." It is at least significant that the writer did not do so. He said: "And Jehovah was with Joseph." This very method was in itself a recognition of a sequence, and so of a relationship. His being brought to Egypt was no accident. Joseph himself came to recognize that clearly, as we shall see presently (Gen. 45. 5). Indeed, his whole bearing during these trying days would lead us to believe that he knew all through that Jehovah was with him. The lesson for us surely is that circumstances always demand God, if they are to be explained. If we live wholly occupied by the things seen, we shall know perpetual unrest. If we ever see Him who is invisible, we shall surely endure.

Yet did not the chief butler remember Joseph, but forgat him.—Gen. 40. 23.

It is now fully fifty years ago since I heard that quaint and forceful preacher, Thomas Champness, read this chapter as a Lesson. Through the reading he made no comment, but as he finished this verse he closed his Bible, and said: "And his name isn't always Butler!" It was an unconventional, humorous, almost startling remark, but it left an impression upon me which has never departed. It has helped me often to remember. This forgetfulness on the part of this man cost Joseph two more years of prison. It is perfectly true that he was safe in the will of God, and quietly preserved for the hour when he would be needed to be the deliverer; but that does not excuse the butler. How true are the words which we have often quoted:

"Evil is wrought by want of thought
As well as want of heart!"

We bear no malice; we really desire to help; but we forget. Our own good fortune drives out of mind the evil fortunes of those whom we would serve, and sometimes those to whom we have pledged our word. It is wholly wrong. To forget may be as evil in its effects upon others as the doing of some positive harm to them. Good intentions and sincere promises are of no value until they are carried out, fulfilled. There are many things we have done to-day. Have we forgotten something?

Can we find such a one as this, a man in whom the spirit of God is?— Gen. 41. 38.

This was the impression which Joseph made upon Pharaoh. It goes without saying that we must not read it in the full light of the age of the Holy Spirit in which we live. That fact, however, does not make it less remarkable, but more so. We need not be concerned with the exact conception of God which was in the mind of Pharaoh. Whatever that conception was, he felt that this man was the instrument of God to him, that through him the wisdom of God was made known. That is the fact which is arresting in the story. Joseph had passed through much trial, but through it all it is evident that he had maintained his loyalty to the God of his fathers. Through all the varied and trying experiences, Jehovah had been with him. Now in the hour of opportunity He was still with him; and this, Joseph recognized and confessed. When he appeared before Pharaoh he at once declared, as to the interpretation of dreams; "It is not in me; God shall give Pharaoh an answer of peace." In his interpretation he attributed the dreams of the king to God, and gave them their meaning. The notable fact is that in the heart of this king there was that which recognized the truth of these claims, and in these words he confessed that recognition. This is a persistent fact which we do well to ponder. There is that in human nature which recognizes and responds to true godliness. Whether men obey or not, they know what is of God, and what is not.

We thy servants are twelve brethren, . . . and one is not.—Gen. 42. 13.

How constantly wickedness and deceit break down within their own borders. Just at the moment when evil should be most careful, it breaks down by its own methods, and puts itself in danger of discovery and defeat. To say that "murder will out," is really to say that truth will be made known, however desirable it may seem, in the interest of unrighteousness, that it should be hidden. In that sense also it is seen that truth is mighty and will prevail. In some unguarded moment something is said which gives up a secret which there is no wish to reveal. In this story, of course, Joseph was the one who "was not" of that family circle, and sooner or later these men would be confronted again with their sin. But from the standpoint of their desire to hide the past—seeing that, so far as they knew, this high official with whom they were dealing could have no knowledge of them—why did they not say: We thy servants are *eleven* brethren? There is no answer save that suggested. Evil is ulti-

mately foolishness, and is overcome by the truth. The whole fact was now given away; and by their own confession as to the twelve, they must sooner or later account for the one. Thus has God created man. He cannot wholly escape from the truth. However he try to conceal it, he himself will sooner or later utter it to his own condemnation. "The lip of truth shall be established for ever; But a lying tongue is but for a moment." To do the right thing is to be able to speak the true word; and that is to live the life free from fear. The way of truth is the way of simplicity and liberty.

And Joseph made haste; for his bowels did yearn upon his brother.— Gen. 43. 30.

This is a very human touch, and is another revelation of how wondrously this man Joseph had been preserved by his loyalty to God through the years of his varied experiences. When at last his own brother Benjamin was before him, the son of his own mother Rachel, all the memories of the past crowded upon him, and his strong nature was moved to its very depths. It may be said that this was very natural; but the fact remains that natural affection is often destroyed by adversity, and by prosperity. This man had passed through experiences of suffering which might have hardened and embittered him. Moreover, he had risen to such a position of eminence and authority as often renders a man callous and makes him forget old ties and associations, however sacred. Human history is full of instances in which this has happened. It was not so with Joseph. He had passed through the long years of suffering; he had attained the place of highest authority in all the land of Egypt. Yet his heart was true to his kindred, and at the sight of Benjamin he could with difficulty restrain himself from manifestations of emotion, even in the presence of the men whom for the moment it was necessary to conceal them. Thus it ever is to those who live in fellowship with God. To such, adversity brings no destructive bitterness; and prosperity no proud or arrogant forgetfulness. The Divine comradeship ever keeps the heart young and tender, and all the finest things of the soul in being, and in health. Joseph's love for Benjamin was natural, but it had been maintained by his loyalty to his God.

Let thy servant, I pray thee, abide instead of the lad a bondman to my lord.—Gen. 44. 33.

Here Judah said the finest thing of his life. It would seem as though this strain of a true nobility was always present in this man in spite of his failures. When in the days of long ago, these men were stirred up against Joseph, it was Judah who saved his life. The story of chapter 36 reveals him as acting with his brethren and possibly feeling resentment against Joseph, but even there the better side of him manifested itself. While to these hard and cruel men he appealed on the ground of profit, suggesting that they would make nothing out of the business if they slew their brother, the real motive of his interference was manifested in his words, "for he is our brother, our flesh." Now he saw the life of the other son of Rachel—Benjamin—in jeopardy, and he was concerned for his father, whose grief for the loss of Joseph he had known. His appeal was full of real and genuine eloquence and anxiety, and here it reached its highest note as he declared his readiness to enter into slavery if his brother might be set free. The next chapter shows that it was that appeal which made it impossible for Joseph any longer to refrain himself, or conceal his identity from these men. In the light of this incident it is interesting to remember that the tribe of Judah, together with that of Benjamin, remained longer loyal to Jehovah than any of the others.

God did send me before you to preserve life.—*Gen.* 45. 5.

Thus, in the hour when Joseph made himself known to his brethren, did he account for all the events of the years. It was not merely a magnanimous way of forgiving them, and attempting to put them at their ease. It was his reading of his life's story, and it was the true reading. He was quite emphatic about the matter, for he repeated it again (verse 7), and yet again (verse 8). This did not exonerate them for their past action, but it did show that God had overruled their evil deeds, not for their sakes personally, but in the interest of His purposes through them as His chosen instruments. For this reason, Joseph could afford to forgive them, and he did so magnificently. This outlook on life is that which ever comes to a man sooner or later who maintains his loyalty to God amid circumstances of trial and of testing. Faith looks up, and believes in God, however dark the day; it looks on, and is assured that the Divine purposes will be realized, however adverse the circumstances. Then the day comes when it can look back, and understand the reason of all the strange experience through which it has passed. We all believe that the hour will come when we shall look over all life's troubled and devious ways and say: "Right was the pathway leading to this!" It is good to antedate that hour of realization by faith, and so to sing upon the way: "Right is the pathway leading to that!" As we shall know one day by clear sight that God has ordered our goings, let us live as those who know it now by faith.

I will go down with thee into Egypt; and I will also surely bring thee up again.—*Gen.* 46. 4.

It is not difficult to imagine the strangeness of the emotional experiences of Jacob at this time. He had long mourned Joseph as dead, and now the astonishing news was brought to him that he was not only alive, but that he was "ruler over all the land of Egypt." How natural the story that "his heart fainted, for he believed them not"! When the evidences were forthcoming in the laden wagons, he started on his journey to see him, halting on the way to offer sacrifices at Beersheba. Then in the visions of the night God communed with him, and spake these words of strength and of comfort. It is a beautiful illustration of the ways of God. He is infinite in His patience with His own; and in hours of special need, ever makes Himself known anew to them in order to their strengthening, for whatever may be in His will for them. The measure in which Jacob at this juncture was conscious of the purposes of God, as they had been made known to his fathers and to himself, was the measure in which it must have appeared as though departure with all his seed from the land appointed of God was fatal to the fulfilment of the Divine purpose. To go into Egypt was to leave the region of appointment. Then came the word that assured him of two things: first, that God would be with them in Egypt; and secondly, that there should be a return to that land. In the strength of that assurance he went on his way. He knew nothing of the details, nor was it necessary that he should. It is enough for the men of faith at any time to know that their God is with them, and that He will fulfil all His covenant with them. The details are always unimportant.

Bury me not, I pray thee, in Egypt.—*Gen.* 47. 29.

"Jacob lived in the land of Egypt seventeen years"—long enough to see his seed greatly prospering in all material things; and not long enough to see any of the trials and tribulations through which they would have to pass ere they would be returned to the Land of Promise. So prosperous were they, that there appeared no reason at the moment why they should not permanently settle in that land of Goshen. Moreover, they were not in danger of any contamination by inter-mixture of seed with the Egyptians. They were separated more effectually than they would have been in the land of Canaan. In spite of all this, Jacob knew that in the purpose of God this was not to be their final resting-place; and so, as he came to the end of the pilgrimage, his heart was still in the land of the Divine Covenant. Hence his request to Joseph that he should not be buried in the strange land. While it is true that natural sentiment may have had its part in the request, it is certain that it would not wholly account for it. The tombs of Abraham and Isaac, of Rebekah and Rachel were in Canaan, but all his children were with him in Goshen, and everything pointed to their remaining there. Why should he not be buried there? Simply because, whatever the appearances of the hour were, he had the Word of God to rely on, and, believing God, he saw them all return. The faith of Jacob was always more or less restless, but it was real faith; and never was it more quietly and definitely manifested than when he made Joseph both promise and swear, that he should be laid to rest in the Land of Promise.

Behold, I die; but God shall be with you.—Gen. 48. 21.

Here again the faith of Jacob is manifest. These were the words of calm and satisfied assurance, the words of a man who, through the patience and persistence of God, had learned the lesson of life. The quiet declaration, "Behold, I die," is remarkable in the light of all his history. He had been a singularly self-reliant man. Indeed, his self-reliance had been the one element of real danger in his character. It had never destroyed his faith in God, but it had often made it difficult for God to deal with him. He had secured the birthright from Esau; obtained the blessing of Isaac; outwitted the unscrupulous Laban—and all by his own cleverness. Then had come the night of wrestling and the great discovery of the might of God. From that time his own schemes had never been so successful. With real understanding, he had known the pre-eminence of Joseph among all his sons, but his methods with him had resulted in apparently disastrous failure. Yet he had now lived long enough to know that God was overruling everything, and moving on toward the accomplishment of His own purposes. To-day he was weak and blind, and of no practical use. There was only one act remaining to him, and that one from which he could not escape. He named it—"Behold, I die!" The statement was not one of despair. It really did not matter. The only thing that mattered was that God would not die. And so he added: "But God will be with you." It is a great thing to come to the end of life strong in the conviction that we are not indispensable. There is so much we have not done. It is of no importance. We die; but God remaineth. Then may we pass in peace.

Gather yourselves together, that I may tell you that which shall befall you in the latter days.—Gen. 49. 1.

These final words of Jacob about his sons are very full of beauty. They may be read from the purely human standpoint, as revealing what he felt concerning these sons of his. In such a reading we discover the notes which show how their actions had impressed him; how he had not forgotten their deeds of heroism, or those of their shame. He had observed them carefully, and knew both the elements of strength and of weakness which were resident within them. On this level we are impressed with his evident sense of helplessness. He knew his children but he could do nothing for them. He clearly saw them as having to work out their own lives, without any aid from him, save that which they might receive as the result of these descriptions of them. But that is not the profoundest note, nor the chief value of these words of Jacob. That is to be discovered, in his realization, that these human lives were within the government of God Most notably that is seen in all he had to say about Judah and Joseph. The things he said concerning them were not descriptions of natural developments of what they were in themselves. They were the things of the Divine counsel concerning them. Thus at the last there was granted to this man to have a wonderful vision of the plan and power of God. It was the crowning reward of his faith.

God will surely visit you, and ye shall carry up my bones from hence.—Gen. 50. 25.

This was the last charge of Joseph to his brethren. It was characterized by the same faith which in the case of his father Jacob had requested that he should not be buried in Egypt. There are some senses in which perhaps it was even more remarkable. When Jacob had passed on, there were no evidences of any trouble threatening his seed. It is almost certain that Joseph, thoroughly acquainted as he was with all the State affairs of Egypt, would be conscious of the possibility of danger to his people when both he and the Pharaoh who had known him should have passed on. That consciousness is at least suggested by his declaration that God would visit them and bring them into the land which He had promised to Abraham, to Isaac, and to Jacob. As he looked on, he had no doubt as to the issue. Whatever the difficulties ahead, there could be but one final result, and that the accomplishment of the Divine purpose, the fulfilment of the Divine promise. His request that, when that day of visitation should come, his bones should be carried up from Egypt, reveals his choice to be identified with his own people in their Divine destiny. He had served Egypt well, and Egypt had treated him well, but he belonged to God and to his people. Thus, in a word of true faith, ended the life of one of the very greatest of the men presented to us in the pages of the whole of the Old Testament. He is the one man on whose escutcheon no stain rests; and in very many respects he is the most wonderful type of the coming Son and Servant of God to be found in the history of Israel.

EXODUS

The more they afflicted them, the more they multiplied, and the more they spread abroad.—*Ex.* 1. 12.

This book of Exodus takes up the history of the children of Israel, and carries it on from the point where Genesis left it. Its opening word "Now" is exactly equivalent to "And," thus marking the continuity. It has a character all its own. It is the story of how God rooted the national life of this people in His own redeeming love and power. In their days of quiet and prosperity in the land of Goshen, they had never come to national constitution. They were a subject race. The first pages of this book introduce us to them in circumstances of darkness and difficulty. They were now not subjects, merely; they were slaves; and most unjustly and cruelly oppressed and afflicted. The hopes of Jacob and Joseph concerning a going back into their own land seemed to have no chance of realization. They were absolutely powerless, and if simply left to themselves they were positively threatened with extermination. It was to that end that the power of Egypt was working. If there were still any hope in their hearts, it was set on God. This was His hour. In the words we emphasize to-day, we have the first evidence of His presence and His blessing. On the level of the physical, they could not be destroyed, because God had chosen them for the fulfilment of His purposes. The principle is of perpetual application. Every successive age in the history of men has seen it working. The more the forces antagonistic to the will of God operate against the people of God, the more do these people rise and gain strength. It is not persecution, but patronage, that they have most to fear.

When she saw him that he was a goodly child, she hid him three months. —*Ex.* 2. 2.

Necessarily the outstanding figure in this book is Moses. He was the chosen instrument of God for carrying out the purposes of His will. Prepared by remarkable experiences, he was brought to that faith in God which made possible his employment in this way. It is well for us to recognize at once that the faith of Moses was preceded, and so made possible, by the faith of his parents. This is explicitly stated by the writer of the letter to the Hebrews (11. 23): "By faith Moses, when he was born, was hid three months by his parents, because they saw he was a goodly child; and they were not afraid of the king's commandment." The picture of that mother, hiding the baby-boy, because she believed in God, is a very suggestive one. When one day, the eleventh chapter of Hebrews is elaborated and completed, and in the light of God's ultimate victories we read the splendid record of how His city has been built by faith, how many stories like this shall we find? We shall certainly have stories of men of conspicuous ability and adventure, who have led and directed the movements of the hosts of God. But we shall surely then also discover that these men were often provided and preserved, begotten and nurtured, by men and women of faith. What the whole world owes to the strong and simple fathers and mothers who have wrought with God by faith, will then be known. It is surely a great thing thus to see, at the back of all the subsequent story, this mother hiding a baby, her heart free from the fear of the king, because she believed in God.

Moses was keeping the flock.—*Ex.* 3. 1.

Eighty years had passed away since Jochebed had hidden her baby-boy. Nothing of any apparent value had transpired. The children of Israel still sighed by reason of their bondage. Once, half-way through the period—that is forty years before this—there had been a flame, a flash, a commotion. This young Hebrew, who had lived at the Court of Pharaoh, had broken loose upon an Egyptian, and had slain him, for oppressing a Hebrew. He had also endeavoured to readjust differences between two contending Hebrews, but his interference had been resented. The actions had brought him into danger at the Court, and by faith he had renounced all his earthly advantages and fled. And so the second forty years had run their course, and we see him now keeping the flock of his father-in-law in the wilderness. Yet as we read the story of these years, in the light of Divine overruling, how wonderfully they were preparing the way for the future, in their preparation of this man for his work! Forty years he had spent at the Court of Pharaoh, and there had received an education which made him, on that level, an accomplished man. Then, in the crisis referred to, he had learned how inadequate he was to deliver his people. The second period of forty years had been spent in the quiet splendours of the wilderness, and his shepherd occupation had prepared him for the meekness necessary to the leadership of the people of God. Now, in the midst of that work, God appeared to him, and called him to His task.

Moses answered and said, But . . .
—*Ex. 4. 1.*

The eyes of Moses had beheld the mystic wonder of the Bush that burned with fire, but was not consumed. The ears of Moses had heard the voice of God. In a strange and wonderful communion he had talked with God. There had been made known to him the ways of Jehovah, the secrets of His compassion and His purposes. Yet he "answered and said, But . . ." It is a very natural human story. That this man should be filled with misgivings when he thought of the condition of his people, of the power of Egypt, and of his own disabilities, is not to be wondered at. Nevertheless this attitude of hesitancy and of fear was wrong. This is proven by the fact which this chapter reveals. When Moses persisted, "the anger of Jehovah was kindled against him, and He said, Is there not Aaron, thy brother, the Levite?" As we read this story, the natural mind feels full sympathy with the tremors of the soul of Moses; but it is surely written that we may learn the deeper lesson of the wrong of such failure. We are ever prone, when God is calling us to some high service, to say "But," and thus to introduce our statement of the difficulties as we see them. Presently Moses learned to use his "But" in another way. In presence of difficulties he came to the habit of considering them, and then of saying "But God"! The whole difference between faith and fear is that of the difference of putting our "Buts" before or after God. God commands, *but* there are difficulties. That is paralysis. There are difficulties, *but* God commands. That is power.

Moses and Aaron came, and said unto Pharaoh, Thus saith the Lord.— *Ex. 5. 1.*

Thus began the dealing of God with Pharaoh, in order to the deliverance of His people. His servants came to the proud monarch, and in his person faced all the power of Egypt, with no other authority and no other resource than the word of Jehovah. Even they had yet to prove the finality of that authority, and the fulness of that resource. In the case of Pharaoh, we begin here a wonderful story, in which the patience and power of God are equally patent. The acts of God in judgment throughout were but the ratification of the acts and attitudes of the man himself. To this we shall return in a subsequent chapter. The first result of the delivery of the Divine word was that of the challenge and flat refusal of Pharaoh, and the consequently increased hardship and suffering of the Hebrew people. It was not to be wondered at that the people should murmur against Moses. His plan for delivering them must have seemed to them to have disastrously failed already. Moses himself was perplexed and troubled; but his action was that of faith—he took his trouble and perplexity immediately to God. Thus it ever is. Those who face men, having the right to say to them, "Thus saith Jehovah" have also the right to return to Jehovah and state the difficulties, and expose openly their own doubts and fears. Such action always brings the answer of His patience and His power.

I am Jehovah.—*Ex. 6. 2.*

This was the great word of God's answer to the cry of Moses, in presence of the difficulty created by the refusal of Pharaoh, and the consequent sufferings and complaint of the Hebrew people. First, He declared that He would so deal with Pharaoh as to compel him to let the people go. Then, in a remarkable passage, He assured His servant by a message of Self-assertion. The force is gathered if we glance over it, noticing the repetition of this declaration, and of the recurrence of the personal pronoun. It may be good to set these out. "*I am Jehovah.*" "I appeared." "I was not known." "I have established." "I have heard." "I have remembered." "*I am Jehovah.*" "I will bring you out." "I will rid you." "I will redeem you." "I will take you." "I will be to you." "*I am Jehovah.*" "I will bring you in." "I lifted up My hand." "I will give it you." "*I am Jehovah.*" This incomplete reading is of value, as it emphasizes for us all the practical values of the name, Jehovah. It was the name which supremely stood for the grace of God. All the activities of the past, referred to, and all those of the future, promised, reveal Him as acting on behalf of His people. This was the Divine declaration made in answer to the statement of human difficulty. Even then Moses did not, could not, grasp its full significance; but its statement gave him surer ground upon which to stand, as he waited for the interpretation of experience. The children of Israel were so full of sorrow that they "hearkened not," but Moses had heard for them.

I have made thee a god to Pharaoh. —*Ex. 7. 1.*

This was the word of Jehovah to His servant in view of his further hesitation. When Moses had received the declaration concerning God in connection with the revelation of Himself as Jehovah, he had proclaimed it to the children of Israel, and they had not hearkened; that is, they had not received it, had not believed it, or had not felt the power of it. Very naturally he argued that if they had failed to realize its value, it was not probable that Pharaoh would be impressed by it. Then Jehovah made this arresting assertion. This man should be as *Elohim* to Pharaoh. He should stand before Pharaoh in the place of God, not only delivering His messages, but accompanying them with such actions of power as should demonstrate the authority of those messages. And this is exactly what happened, through all those processes which eventuated in the breaking of Pharaoh's power, and the deliverance of the people of God. How full of beauty all this story is, in its revelation of the patient method of God with those whom He calls to serve Him! He constantly calls men to do things for which they are totally unfit in their own natural powers, even though those powers also are of Divine origin. In such hours they naturally shrink and are afraid. He never loses patience, so long as they remain loyal to Him in heart. On the contrary, He hears their expression of fear, explains His method, and thus step by step leads and strengthens them, till they accomplish all His will, notwithstanding their fears.

Then the magicians said unto Pharaoh, This is the finger of God.— Ex. 8. 19.

As the story runs on, of God's dealings with Pharaoh and the power of Egypt, we watch the process with the deepest interest and that from many standpoints. As to Pharaoh, it is the story of a strong will, making itself stupid, while all the way, until the condition was utterly beyond hope of remedy, God gave him opportunities to use that strong will in surrender. Before the first plague fell, he was warned, and thus given the chance of escape. He refused, and then, under the pressure of the plague, relented. At once respite was given, and again he made his heart stubborn, with the result that the second plague fell. Perhaps his obstinacy was partially accounted for by the fact that his magicians had been able to produce wonders similar to the first and second plagues. When the third fell, they were powerless, and were constrained to recognize "the finger of God." In consequence of his continued stubbornness, after the confession of his magicians, Pharaoh had to face a new element, that of the information given that Israel would be immune. Thus in many ways did God seek to impress the heart of this man. It is well to observe Moses through these events. Evidently his preparation by Jehovah had been sufficient, for he moved through all these experiences with singular calm and dignity. It is permissible to wonder whether the success of the magicians in the first two plagues did not challenge his faith. If so, he remained faithful, and in the third he saw that their power was limited by God. There were things they could not do.

He that feared the word of the Lord among the servants of Pharaoh.— Ex. 9. 20.

Here is a very interesting and suggestive gleam of light amid the prevailing darkness. A fifth and a sixth plague had fallen

upon Egypt, and still Pharaoh pursued his way of stubborn resistance. A new cycle was about to commence, and the warning given was more explicit and careful than on any previous occasion. It is in connection with this warning of the coming of the plague of hail, that we read that some of the servants of Pharaoh feared the word of Jehovah, and acted in accordance with it, with the result that they also escaped the devastating hail. Thus God is seen, as He ever is, acting with strict and impartial justice. No man or nation ever yet perished by the act of God, of whom or of which it might not truthfully be said that their blood was upon their own head. He never desires to destroy; He ever seeks to save. No matter how long the rebellion continues, if it give place to a true repentance, He is ready to forgive. His benefits are never confined to the people of one nation. "In every nation he that feareth Him, and worketh righteousness, is acceptable to Him." This is what Peter perceived in the house of Cornelius, and in these words we have an early illustration of the truth. Fear may have been the first impulse, but it was the fear of Jehovah, and that is in itself of the essence of faith. Acting in accordance therewith, they found deliverance.

There shall not an hoof be left behind.—Ex. 10. 26.

This was the final word of Moses in a persistent conflict against anything in the nature of compromise. Pharaoh had attempted to bring this about since after the fourth plague. Note the stages of these attempts. At the beginning he had declared that these people should not go to sacrifice to Jehovah their God. After the plague of flies, the fourth, he suggested that they might sacrifice, but they could do it without going away from the land (8. 25). This Moses at once refused. Then Pharaoh suggested that if they must go, it should not be very far away (8. 28). On this Moses entreated for him, and the plague was removed, but he would not let them go. He proposed later, after the eighth plague (that of locusts), that they should leave the women and children behind (10. 8–11). Moses refused. After the ninth plague (that of the darkness), he suggested that the cattle be left (10. 24). Then Moses spoke this final word: "There shall not an hoof be left behind." That is the true attitude of the man of faith. Evil is always suggesting some compromise. To listen to it, is to remain enslaved. The only way into liberty is to leave the land of evil; to go accompanied by the women and the children; and to take all property also. It is when that attitude is assumed, that men pass out from all bondage, and find the liberty which is in the purpose of God for them. The truth may be applied in individual and national life. It is equally true in each case.

The Lord hardened Pharaoh's heart, and he did not let the children of Israel go out of his land.—*Ex.* 11. 10.

This is the last declaration of this kind in connection with the plagues, prefacing the story of the slaying of the firstborn. The same idea is found again in chapter 14, verses 4, 8, 17. In a previous note (on chapter 5. 1), we said that the acts of God in judgment were the ratification of the acts and attitudes of this man. We may at this point consider that fact. In the course of the story the words *harden* and *hardened* often occur. By marginal readings the Revised Version has sought to show a difference in meaning. As a matter of fact, three Hebrew words are all translated in the same way. To understand the story they must be distinguished. The first of these (*châzaq*) means to *make strong*. This the Revisers have always indicated in the margin. The second (*kâbad*) means to *make heavy*, with the idea of stupidity. The third (*qâshâh*) means to *make hard*, in the sense of cruelty. Throughout the story, the first is used to described the action of God (4. 21; 7. 13, 22; 8. 19; 9. 12, 35; 10. 20, 27; 11. 10; 14. 4, 8, 17). It is never employed to describe the act of Pharaoh. It is once used to describe the anxiety of the Egyptians that the Israelites should go (12. 33), and there is rendered *urgent*. The second occurs first as God's description of Pharaoh's condition (7. 14); then twice of Pharaoh's act (8. 15, 32); then as the historian's description of Pharaoh's condition (9. 7); then again of Pharaoh's act (9. 34); and finally to describe the act of God (10. 1). The third is only found twice; once it describes the act of God (7. 3); and once to describe the method of Pharaoh's refusal (13. 15). A careful examination will show that God's activity was that of strengthening this man, and so leaving him to act. He never hardened him in the sense of rendering him stupid, until he had persisted in that action himself beyond remedy. These distinctions are of the utmost importance.

This month shall be unto you the beginning of months; it shall be the first month of the year to you.—*Ex.* 12. 2.

These words constitute the record of a change of calendar at the command of God. This change was introduced in the hour when these people were passing into national constitution as a Theocracy, a people under the direct and immediate government of God, having no king except Him. It was directly connected with the institution of the Passover Feast. Thus the beginning of the year was changed from Tishri, the month of harvest, to Abib, the month of green ears, or of springtime, known after the captivity as Nisan. Thus the new year henceforth was to begin with the celebration of the feast which empha-sized the relation of the people to God, and brought constantly to their memory the redemptive basis of that relation. God is ever the God of new beginnings in the history of failure. The ultimate statement is found in the Apocalypse in the words: "Behold, I make all things new." All such new beginnings are founded on plenteous Redemption, conditioned in persistent Righteousness, and issue in perfect Realization. God had redeemed His people from slavery. The dawn of their new year was ever to be radiant with the glory of His bringing of them forth from cruel bondage. God had brought them to Himself, that under His law they might realize the meaning of life, and fulfil its highest purposes. God had admitted them to a fellowship with Himself, which meant, for them, the supply of all need; and for Him, an instrument in the world for carrying out the programme of His infinite grace.

God led them not by the way of the land of the Philistines, although that was near.—*Ex.* 13. 17.

A great principle of the Divine government emerges in these words, an understanding of which will explain many experiences through which His people are called to pass. These people were but now released from slavery, and were undisciplined and untrained. Before they could be ready to withstand the opposition of new enemies, they had much to learn, and many experiences through which to pass. The near way geographically to their destination lay through the land of the Philistines, but to pass that way would inevitably have involved them in conflict. For this they were not in any way prepared. To have been thus plunged into it, would necessarily have filled them with despair, producing a change of mind which would have sent them back to Egypt. Therefore God led them round about, by a longer way, having its own difficulties as the sequel will show, but delivering them from this first peril. How constantly God does this with His people! He leads us by ways which seem to us to be long and tedious, when there are ways apparently so much more direct to the goal where we know He wills we should be. Let us ever know that when He does so, He is avoiding for us perils of which we may not be conscious, but which are far graver than those through which we pass as we travel the pathway He marks out for us. The nearest way is not always the shortest. Our God never permits us, as long as we obey Him, to meet any danger unprepared. The length of the way, and the slowness of the method, are really making for quick and sure arrival.

Thus the Lord saved Israel.—*Ex.* 14. 30.

The little word "Thus" summarizes all the narrative. Some years ago, a Scotch minister was talking to the children in the Sunday-school, and he asked if any of them could tell him how God brought the children out of Egypt. Many hands were held up, but the bright and eager eyes of one wee bit lassie attracted him, and he asked her to tell him. With radiant face and great eagerness she said: "Just fine"! Was ever better answer given? What a wonderful story it is, of His wisdom, His might, His tenderness, His patience! As we read it, we are impressed with that wisdom as it was manifested in His perfect understanding of the hearts of all those who were involved, and in His methods with them. His power had been witnessed in His dealings with Egypt, and in His cleaving of the sea. His tenderness had been proven by all His words, and by every arrangement He had made. His patience had been seen in His dealing with Pharaoh, to whom He had given every chance to set this people free without suffering to himself or his people. Thus had He saved them. They had nothing of which to boast, except their God. They were not free as the result of their own cleverness or strength. They owed everything to Him. And so it ever is. We also have nothing of which to be proud, except that we have such a God. In that, we may at all times make our boast; and all such boasting is wholly good, for it sets forth His praise, and keeps us free from the self-confidence which ever weakens and destroys.

Then sang Moses and the children of Israel.—*Ex.* 15. 1.

That was natural, inevitable. There are moods of the soul that can only be expressed in poetry and in music. They are the great moods, whether of joy or of sorrow, of gleam or of gloom. This was a moment of high experience. The hour was full of the sense of the greatness of life. The shackles were gone, the enemies were destroyed; freedom was theirs, and opportunities were before them. This sense of the greatness of life was created by the sense of the greatness of God. What could they do other than sing? In such experiences prose becomes useless, poetry is the only method of expression; monotone is insufficient, harmony is necessary. An examination of the song will show that it was a glorious celebration of their King, on the part of this newborn nation. It had its backward and its forward look, and in each case the supreme fact was God. He had triumphed gloriously. All the power opposed to Him, and so to them, had proved weak in His mighty grasp. Moreover, He would fulfil all His purposes, bringing them in and planting them in the mountain of His inheritance. When, looking back, God is seen, and forward, His purposes and power are recognized, the soul can sing, even though the threatening dukes of Edom, men of Moab, and inhabitants of Canaan

are all about it. Such moments of high vision and glorious praise are full of value, even though presently there may be much of darkness and declension. Whenever they come, let us avail ourselves of them to the full.

The whole congregation of the children of Israel murmured.—*Ex.* 16. 2.

What a startling change from the song of yesterday! Therein the human heart is revealed. It seems incredible that so soon they should have descended from the height of glorious song, to the level of mean murmuring. Yet so it was, and so often still it is. What had happened? Had God changed? Was He not still the glorious King? Or had they encountered some enemy more powerful than Pharaoh, some obstacle more impossible to overcome than the sea? No, none of these things had happened. They were hungry! That was all. It is very mean and unworthy. Had they forgotten God? No, not wholly, but they were allowing the near, and the trivial, to make them for the moment unmindful of Him. This is a very revealing story. Again and again, indeed almost invariably, when the people of God are found murmuring, it is over some experience through which they are called to pass, which is of the most trivial nature by comparison with the great things of life. This kind of thing spreads. Notice that the whole congregation joined in the unworthy business. Unanimity is not always proof of wisdom or of rightness. In an hour when the prevailing mood is that of dissatisfaction, it is a good thing if some lonely singer celebrates the Lord in song. We may at least be perfectly assured that unanimous murmuring, whenever we hear it, is wholly wrong. Therefore let each one refuse to join therein. If singing is impossible, let there at least be silence. That is always better than murmuring. The sequel shows how unnecessary the murmuring was. It always is.

They tempted the Lord, saying, Is the Lord among us, or not?—*Ex.* 17. 7.

There are two things to be specially noted here. The first is the nature of the suggestion made by the people; and the second is the effect which is produced upon God. As to the first. Under stress of an immediate lack, these people doubted the one fact of which they had overwhelming evidence. The whole of the experiences through which they had passed, and which had brought them where they were, were directly due to the presence and power of God. Had He not been with them, they had yet been in slavery. Yet, lack of water made them either question that fact, or imagine that God had abandoned them. To us it seems utterly unreasonable, and yet it is of constant recurrence. The question persists. In hours of lack, of stress, of difficulty, we are constantly prone to imagine that God has left us, or even to imagine that we have been wrong in believing that He has ever been with us. It is not only unworthy, it is wicked. This is shown by the language used to describe the effect produced upon God—"they tempted Jehovah"; that is, they gave Him cause to abandon them, as they suggested that perchance He had done so. Necessarily the statement is an attempt to express a Divine truth through human analogy. He provided for them, but that was wholly of His mercy and grace. Such questioning of God merits punishment. They tempted God, even though He was not moved to such response as they deserved. We should ever strive against the suggestion that He can act in any way which contradicts our past experiences of His presence and power.

And Moses' father-in-law said unto him, The thing that thou doest is not good.—Ex. 18. 17.

This is an arresting story. It is almost certainly quite out of its chronological place here. It most probably happened later, as the people were about to depart from Sinai. Compare Num. 11. 14–17 and Deut. 1. 7–14. It has been suggested that it was inserted here in order to show that while Jethro lived among the Amalekites he was not under the curse pronounced upon them (see chapter 17. 16). The arresting thing is that this advice as to the administration of the affairs of the people came from a man outside their borders, and that Moses acted upon it. A well-known expositor, writing of this story, says: "Jehovah entirely ignored this worldly-wise organization, substituting His own order." I think that is hardly warranted. It would be nearer the mark to say that Jehovah approved the principle, and instituted His own order. Two matters strike us as being significant. The first is that the principle is a good one. No man is warranted in attempting to carry more than he is able to carry. One of the greatest signs of capacity for leadership is the ability to call others into fellowship in responsibility and service. The second is that God has many ways of making known His will to His servants. He at times speaks through a Jethro to a Moses, as surely as through a Moses to His people. Perhaps to these two, we should add a third, namely, that all advice which we receive from men should be tested by remitting the same to God for ratification or amendment.

All that the Lord hath spoken we will do.—Ex. 19. 8.

These words should be most carefully pondered, because they are vital to an understanding of this whole story. The words of Jehovah to the people, to which these words of the people constituted a reply, were the words of infinite grace. He reminded them of His dealings with them in redemption from slavery, and in bringing them to Himself; He also declared His purpose for them, that they should be a kingdom of priests and a holy nation. Let it be observed that these are the very terms which describe His purpose for His Church, so far as the earthly calling of that Church is concerned. Their response to that word of grace was a declaration that they would do everything necessary on their part to be worthy of that redemption, and to fulfil that purpose. How little they knew themselves! Their answer was sincere, but it was ignorant. The very next words of Jehovah were, "Lo, I come unto thee in a thick cloud," and these prepared the way for the Law and the priesthood. These were provided then for a people who, however sincere their desire, were yet not able to realize the high ideals and purposes of God. Thus began the period of Law which continued until Calvary and Pentecost. It was a period of the persistent failure of these people, and of the persistent patience and victory of God. Even so with us. We say, "All that Jehovah hath spoken we will do," and we fail. But God never fails. He waits and pursues His own way of grace and government. We may truthfully say, both for Israel and for the Church, All that Jehovah hath spoken they will do finally; but it will be by His grace, and not by their own wisdom or strength.

I am the Lord thy God, who brought thee out of the land of Egypt, out of the house of bondage.—Ex. 20. 2.

These are the words which introduce the Law. They constitute the immediate prelude to the Ten inclusive Words; and have their bearing on all the applications and elaborations thereof, both with regard to conduct and to worship. This we should never forget. God's law was for His ransomed people. Every requirement is rooted in this fact of relationship. God did not promulgate a code of laws for the children of Israel, while they were in bondage, telling them that if they would obey it, He would deliver them. He brought them out of the land of Egypt, out of the house of bondage, and then gave them His law. From all responsibility to the proud despotism of Egypt He liberated them, by bringing them under His immediate government; from all the shackles of the house of bondage He set them free, by bringing them into the liberty of His love. Then He gave them the words which revealed His will. Thus Law in itself was an expression of Love. This is ever God's way. In this special dispensation of His grace it is still true. Now, however, it is perhaps more necessary to remind ourselves that grace does not set aside ethical requirement. He still gives us laws which condition conduct and worship, and because in Christ Jesus grace has had its most perfect outshining, and its most powerful operation, the terms of law have become severer and more exacting. Nevertheless, the thought of strength and comfort for us is ever that every requirement of His law is rooted in His love.

I will not go out free. . . . Then . . .—Ex. 21. 5, 6.

Among the first of the "judgments" following the enunciation of the Ten Words of the Law, were those which regulated slavery. A careful consideration of them will show that they abolished slavery, and substituted for it, covenanted labour. A man might buy a servant, but only for a period of six years' service. In the seventh year he must go out free. No man was allowed to hold men or women as his property in perpetuity. Here, however, was an exception. There were certain circumstances under which one man could become the servant of another for the whole period of his life. That, however, could not be by the compulsion of the master, but by the deliberate choice of the servant. It has been said that no man ought to yield himself up thus to the service of another, that such a choice could only issue in the degradation of life. There is an element of truth in the contention. Some men won't face life. They prefer the ease of service in which there is no necessity for responsibility, to the strenuous activities which freedom ever demands. Such choosing of bondage is always ignoble. It should, however, be carefully noted that this is not the choice here indicated. It is rather that of a yielding to the claims of love. The servant has gained wife and children from his master. His master has earned his love. Rather than go out into personal freedom, he chooses to abide with his loved ones, and to serve a master whom he loves. There is nothing ignoble in such action. Then service becomes noble. There is no higher exercise of freedom than that of choosing to serve in love.

Thou shalt not suffer a sorceress to live.—Ex. 22. 18.

Thus with blunt directness and complete finality, the law of God against all traffic with the world of evil spirits was promulgated. The enactment reveals the possibility of such communications; and by punishing with the death penalty, makes perfectly clear the heinousness of all such action. Christian people have often made the mistake of denying the possibility of such communications; they have treated witchcraft, sorcery, spiritism, as unreal things, to be laughed at, or denied. No graver blunder can be made. There are very real dealings with spirits. The Biblical revelation recognizes this everywhere; and the evidences of the possibility abound on all hands in human history and experience. But it is equally true that the whole Biblical teaching is opposed to the practice; it views it as essentially evil, it strictly forbids it; and all human experience shows the evil effects of all such traffic. Wherever it is indulged in, sooner or later it produces terrible results, physically, mentally, or morally, and generally in every way. It is clearly against the will of God that in this life men should hold any communication with the spirit world, save that of direct fellowship with Himself, through His Son, by the Holy Spirit. Wherever it is done, we may rest assured that those with whom communication is gained are evil and impure spirits; for the good and pure, abiding in the perfect love of God, would neither wish nor be able to break His law.

Thou shalt not follow a multitude to do evil.—Ex. 23. 2.

The first application of these words was to the subject of the administration of justice. The possibility in mind, is that of popular prejudice being allowed to influence judgment against an individual. How needful the command, we know full well. It is the danger of miscarriage of justice from such cause, which has made English law hold it a misdemeanour for newspapers to discuss any case which is still *sub judice*. Involved within the command there are much wider applications. It reminds us that popular opinion is not always right. A very false catchword has had great vogue, namely, *vox populi vox Dei*. The voice of the people is by no means always the voice of God. Indeed, majorities have so often been wrong, that it is only with caution that one can consent to be counted as among them. The history of all right movements has been in the first place the history of lonely souls, who, having heard the authentic voice of God, have stood alone or in small minorities. Therein is the reason for the greatness of Lloyd Garrison's epigram: "One with God is a majority." Of course it is always easy to move with the current, to drift with the tide, to shout with the multitude. But ease is not the condition either of righteousness or of true progress. In the home, in society, in business, in the national life, and sometimes in the Church, the multitude may be wrong. Then the soul must refuse to follow, must stand alone. To do so will bring strain and stress; but it will always discover strength, for it will find God.

They beheld God, and did eat and drink.—Ex. 24. 11.

Three verses here (9, 10, and 11) give the account of one of the most wonderful events in connection with the giving of the Law. It is the story of a great communion.

Seventy-four men were gathered together around the manifested presence of God, and in that Presence they did eat and drink. The account of this experience is reverently reticent. No description is given us of the form which the manifestation took. All the description attempted is that of the footstool of Deity, which is mysteriously referred to as "a paved work of sapphire stone, and as it were the very heaven for clearness." The declaration that they saw God is arresting. We know that in so far as the material sense of sight is concerned, no man hath seen God at any time. Subsequently Moses was told, "Thou canst not see My face; for man shall not see Me and live" (Ex. 33. 20). How then are we to explain this statement? It is important that we should remember that two different Hebrew words are employed in this story to describe the experience. The word *saw* in verse 10 is the common word for seeing, and is used in a great variety of ways. The word *beheld* in verse 11 is one which is almost invariably used of mental perception or discernment. Here there is very little doubt that the second word interprets the first. These men in an exalted moment of communion were given a sensible vision of glory through which they rose to a spiritual vision of God. It was a great experience, and the supreme wonder was that in such an hour "they did eat and drink"; that is, they lived their natural lives in all fulness.

Of every man whose heart maketh him willing, ye shall take My offering. —Ex. 25. 2.

An abiding principle is revealed in these words. It is that the one value to God of gifts presented to Him by His people, is that of the willingness of heart which prompts them. All the materials for the building of the Tabernacle were to be supplied by the people themselves. This was not because God could not have provided everything in some other way. At Athens, speaking on the subject of Temple-building, Paul declared that God is not "served by men's hands as though He needed anything." Nevertheless, He asks men to provide the necessary materials, but lays down the one condition that their offerings must come out of their willing hearts. When this is so, the simplest gift becomes of real value to Him, for it is the sacramental symbol of loyalty and devotion. The truth finds most explicit statement in the New Testament: "Let each man do according as he hath purposed in his heart; not grudgingly or of necessity; for God loveth a cheerful giver" (2 Cor. 9. 7). It is a healthy exercise to test our gifts by this standard. To do so will be to reveal the meanness and worthlessness of many which men may count munificent; but it will be also to reveal the beauty and the value of some which intrinsically seem to be very small.

The veil shall divide unto you between the holy place and the most holy.—Ex. 26. 33.

That beautiful veil was the solemn symbol of inclusion and exclusion. It is well to notice where it hung; not between the camp and the courts; not even between the courts and the Holy Place; but between the Holy Place and the Most Holy. It did not divide between the secular and the sacred; it did not distinguish between service and worship; it separated between all high things, and the highest, between relative purity and absolute holiness, between all human interrelationships, and the place of fellowship with God, between every other exercise of life, and its highest function, that of worship. Every detail of its "blue and purple and scarlet, and fine twined linen with cherubim" in gold, was symbolic to the mind of those people of the perfections in man which were necessary to such communion with God. Every detail therefore was eloquent of the exclusion of imperfect man. Only once in the year was man represented there by the high priest, and that only for a brief period by the grace of God, and upon the ground of atonement. It is when all this is apprehended that the full significance of the words in Matt. 27. 51 is recognized: "And behold, the veil of the temple was rent in twain from the top to the bottom." When at last the Man in whom all perfections were realized, had made full atonement for human sins, the symbol of separation was destroyed. Now, through Him, but through Him alone, we may draw near to God, and realize the highest of life, as in fellowship we fulfil its highest functions.

Pure olive oil beaten for the light, to cause a lamp to burn continually. —Ex. 27. 20.

Within the veil, that is in the Holy of Holies, there was no light other than that created by the glory of the Lord, shining above the mercy-seat. The Holy Place, outside that veil, was illuminated by the seven-branched lampstand. It was for this that the oil was to be provided (Lev. 24. 1–4). This lamp was the sacred symbol of the light-bearing function of Israel. She was the lamp-stand. The light of this symbolic lamp in the Holy Place was to be derived from pure olive oil, burning continuously, and this was to be attended to ceaselessly by the priests. The conception was apprehended by prophets, seers, and psalmists, and emerged constantly in their messages and songs; and its meaning was understood. A notable exposition is found in the prophecy of Zechariah (4. 1–14), of which paragraph the central statement is, "Not by might, nor by power, but by My Spirit, saith Jehovah of hosts." Oil is uniformly the symbol of the Holy Spirit of God. Here, then, is the true value and meaning of this sacred oil. The elect light-bearers of the world are only able to fulfil their function by the Holy Spirit. This was so in the case of Him Who said: "I am the light of the world." He was conceived of the Holy Spirit, full of the Spirit, anointed of the Holy Spirit, wrought in the power of the Holy Spirit, offered Himself through the Holy Spirit, was raised through the Holy Spirit, took up His abode in the Church by the Holy Spirit. Therefore it is ever so in the case of those of whom He said: "Ye are the light of the world." It is only as they are baptized in the Spirit, filled with the Spirit, anointed with the Spirit, that they can shine as lights in the world.

Anoint them, and consecrate them, and sanctify them.—*Ex. 28. 41.*

These words indicate the method by which the priests were prepared to minister to God, and a study of them is full of suggestiveness. There is no tautology here. Each of the three words has its own particular value, and the three in sequence cover the whole ground of preparation. The first, *anoint*, is quite simple, and describes the actual putting of the sacred oil upon the head (see *29. 7*), the symbol of the communication of the Holy Spirit to the one to exercise priestly ministry. The second, *consecrate*, is the translation of two Hebrew words, meaning the filling of the open hand, and signifies the perfect equipment of the anointed one for the discharge of that ministry. The third, *sanctify*, means literally, to make clean, and refers to the spiritual and moral separation of the priest from all defilement. Thus all priestly ministry is made possible by the anointing of the Holy Spirit. That anointing communicates the power, and ensures the purity, apart from which there can be no priestly ministry before God. Thus we see how the Divinely arranged ritual of the Hebrew economy was intended to convey to these people truths of fundamental importance. This ritual is done away in Christ, because all the things it typifies are realized in and through Him. If we are priests unto God, it is because in Him we have the anointing of the Spirit, and so the power for our ministry, and the cleansing, apart from which there can be no exercise thereof. Anointed, consecrated, sanctified souls, may minister before the Lord as priests.

And the Tent shall be sanctified by My glory.—*Ex. 29. 43.*

Neither in himself, nor in his works, even though they be done under Divine direction, can man attain unto sanctification. It may indeed be said that it is obtained rather than attained. It is always the outcome of the coming of the cleansing, purifying glory of God. The Tent of the Israelites was to be made according to the Divine pattern. That pattern was detailed, accurate, and in every smallest detail suggestive of holy facts and forces. Those preparing it were called to devotion to the will of God. Nevertheless it needed sanctification, separation to its ultimate intention by cleansing; and that sanctification was communicated by the coming of God, and by the purifying splendour of His glory. Our minds almost inevitably travel on as we read these words to those of John in the prologue of his Gospel: "The Word became flesh and tabernacled among us (and we beheld His glory, glory as of the only begotten from the Father), full of grace and truth." It was by that becoming, that God sanctified a place of meeting between Himself and man. We may make our places of assembly beautiful, as we should; we may do all the work of preparation with true devotion, as we must; but neither the devotion of the doing, nor the beauty of the deed, has any sanctifying power. It is the glory of God, effective through His coming near, which sanctifies a place of meeting, and so creates the possibility of our fellowship with Him. The perpetual joy of our life should be that He has sanctified for us a Tabernacle of meeting by His glory.

The rich shall not give more, and the poor shall not give less, than the half-shekel.—*Ex. 30. 15.*

That is not the law of giving. It is certainly not so for us in this Christian dispensation. Each of us is to give "as he may prosper" (*1 Cor. 16. 2*). It was not so for the Hebrew. The devotion of the tenth was proportional within limits, but the gifts of the rich were more than those of the poor in amount, though less, in relation to their own possessions after the giving. The half-shekel was not a gift in the sense of a free-will offering. It was a recognition of redemption, a sign of atonement, made and received. Here the rich and the poor stood upon a perfect equality. Nothing that a man has, can procure him access to God, or exclude him from that access. Nothing that he lacks, can exclude him from that access, or admit him thereto. Such access results from an atonement which God makes, and not man. Therefore the ransom that a man gave was to be of the same amount in every case; and it was given in connection with the numbering, that is, with the enrolment of the host. It was, therefore, a sign of the complete dedication of personality. Each half-shekel represented one person. It was not a gift from the amount of possessions. It was a symbol of the fact that the person representing it was wholly the Lord's by the grace of the atonement which He had provided. The necessity for the symbol is done away in Christ, but the thing symbolized has been brought to its fulfilment. Our numbering among the redeemed is a fact; and one, the obligations of which, in complete devotion to the Lord, we should ever realize and discharge.

I have filled him with the Spirit of God, in wisdom, and in understanding, and in knowledge, and in all manner of workmanship.—*Ex.* 31. 3.

This is a radiantly beautiful word in its revelation of how God equips those whom He appoints to service. It must not be forgotten that these people had been in slavery for centuries, and therefore in all probability were devoid of that artistic fineness which was necessary for the construction of the Tabernacle according to the Divine pattern. Then it was that God called Bezalel, and prepared him for his work. The description of the fitness conferred is very careful. Each word has a special significance, and a sequence is revealed. *Wisdom* is capacity; *understanding* suggests progress, the capacity acting in apprehension of the idea presented; *knowledge* is the ultimate attainment of skill resulting from this intelligent action of capacity. The result was "all manner of workmanship," the doing of the things appointed according to the pattern given. All this resulted from a man being filled with the Spirit of God. Thus a man was made the instrument of Divine action. To do His work, the Spirit of God needed a man. To do his work, the man needed the Spirit of God. This is perfect co-operation. The story is all the more valuable when it is remembered that this was co-operation, not for priestly or prophetic work, but for work in gold, in silver, in brass, in stones, in wood. Surely there is only one thing we need to be careful about, and that is that the work we do is that appointed for us by God. If that is so, we need have no anxiety, for He will give us perfect equipment.

. . . Thy people, which Thou hast brought forth out of the land of Egypt. —*Ex.* 32. 11.

These were the words of Moses to God in an hour of grave peril. The people had fallen into grievous sin. They had deliberately broken the second commandment. The making of the golden calf was not an attempt on their part to substitute another god for Jehovah. It was rather an attempt to make a likeness of God. Their choice of a calf was at least suggestive. In the East the ox is ever the type of service and sacrifice, and in choosing it they had some glimmer of the truth about God. Nevertheless the attempt in itself was an actual sin, as it was an act of definite disobedience. The anger of the Lord was stirred against them, and He threatened to consume them. Then it was that Moses became the intercessor. These particular words reveal the ground of his plea. Observe the contrast between his description of the people and that of Jehovah. God said:

"*Thy* people which *thou* broughtest up out of the land of Egypt." Moses replied: "*Thy* people which *Thou* hast brought forth out of the land of Egypt." Moses was swayed by pity for the people, but the deepest concern of his heart was a passion for the honour of God. Thus did Jehovah lead His servant into fellowship with the deepest things of His own heart. Therefore his intercession prevailed. It is well that we realize the importance of this.

If Thy presence go not with me, carry us not up hence.—*Ex.* 33. 15.

These words were the answer of Moses to the promise of Jehovah. The whole story is very full of light. It is the account of a very intimate and wonderful communion between God and His servant; "Jehovah spake unto Moses face to face, as a man speaketh unto his friend" (verse 11). In that holy atmosphere of sacred intimacy, Moses was able to say all that was in his heart. All the sin of the people was on his heart, and about that he talked with God. Realizing his responsibility as leader of this people, he first pleaded for a fuller knowledge of the ways of God, and of God Himself. To this plea the gracious promise was returned: "My presence shall go with thee, and I will give thee rest." The very relief which that promise brought to his heart set free this great outburst: "If Thy presence go not with me, carry us not up hence"! He knew that no substitute could take the place of that actual Presence. He recognized that it would be better for them all to perish in the wilderness, than to attempt to possess the promised land without that Presence. This is a great truth. The very gifts of God are liable to curse us, if we lose fellowship with the Giver. We may make the land of plenty the occasion of our poverty, if we enter it without God. He alone understands us, and He alone can give us true possession of whatever He bestows upon us. The portion of goods received from the Father, spent without the Father, in the far country, is the instrument of the undoing of the son. So, whether for life or service, our prayer should be that of Moses.

He was there with the Lord forty days and forty nights; he did neither eat bread, nor drink water.—*Ex.* 34. 28.

It is impossible to exaggerate the stupendous things suggested in that simple statement. It was a period during which to this man there came the clearest of light. He was with God. That was the supreme consciousness and certainty. Yet let us carefully remember that this was not a period of ecstasy in which Moses was separated from the consciousness of all the things of earth. On the contrary, it was a time in which, because of his sense of God, he saw the things of earth in the true light. In that communion, he saw the people, understood their need, realized their weakness, and discovered the deepest things of their safety and their strength. During that forty days and nights, he received the law for their government, and the order for their worship. From that experience he returned, not to be a dreamer, for ever thinking and talking of a past rapture; but to be, as never before, the man of affairs, directing, controlling all the earthly life according to the standards received in the mount. It would seem as though the only thing he forgot was himself. During the period, "he did neither eat bread nor drink water." In that forgetfulness, however, he found himself, though all unconsciously. When he descended to men, he came, not thin, emaciated, weak, but strong and glorious in beauty, for his face shone with a brilliant radiance. All this is full of instruction. High experiences of fellowship with God are often granted to His servants, and they always result in fresh power for service.

Every one whose heart stirred him up, and every one whom his spirit made willing . . . brought the Lord's offering.—*Ex. 35. 21.*

When God provided a system of worship for His chosen people, He did so according to His own mind and heart and will. There was no detail neglected, but in the smallest detail there was nothing of triviality. This a later singer recognized when he said, "In His temple everything saith Glory!" (Psa. 29. 9). Nevertheless, He needed the human instrument through which to communicate, He found it in Moses. And now He also needed that men should provide earthly materials for carrying out the heavenly purpose. Yet the gifts must be sanctified by the Giver in every case, and in these words we are informed as to the true inspirations of all such giving. They must be the expressions of a true devotion. This we have noted before (Ex. 25. 2). Here the matter is yet more fully stated. Two stages are marked. First, the stirring of the heart. That goes to the deepest thing in human personality. Desire is the fundamental factor in life, and that is of the heart. When the heart is stirred, it is because the soul supremely desires something. When gifts are contributions toward the realization of desire, they are acceptable. If a man desire the worship of God according to Divine arrangement, and gives to realize it, his gift is of value. The second stage is the constraint of the will by the spirit-life. That completes the perfection. It is possible to desire, and even to give, when the will is not in harmony. Then giving is the discharge of duty. God asks for more than that. When the spirit is so in fellowship with God, as to constrain the will, then giving is a delight.

So the people were restrained from bringing.—*Ex. 36. 6.*

This is a wonderful chapter in its revelation of how these people were moved to high and holy things at this time. It is almost impossible to read these particular words without a sense of surprise, so rarely has it happened that it has been necessary, in the case of work for God, to restrain His people from giving. And yet this is the natural result of those inspirations which we were considering in our previous note. When the heart is truly stirred, and the spirit makes willing, giving is robbed of all meanness; indeed, it ceases to be calculating. Nothing is too precious to be given, no amount is too great. Everything is poured out in glad and generous abandonment. When this is so, the work of God never languishes for lack of means. All this is a matter for serious thought. In the presence of the claims of the work of God, how is it that the heart is ever devoid of that stirring which produces such giving? Why is it that there is ever unwillingness to bring our offerings to God? Is it not always because for some cause the vision of the glory of the work is dim? If the enterprises of the Kingdom of God were clearly seen, there could hardly fail to be a perpetual stirring of heart, an unceasing willingness of spirit, to give. And that leads the inquiry further. Why has the vision become dim? Are answers to be found in some words of Jesus in the parables of the Kingdom? "Persecution," "tribulation," "the care of the age," "the deceitfulness of riches" (Matt. 13. 21, 22)?

Toward the mercy-seat were the faces of the cherubim.—*Ex. 37. 9.*

Of the ranks and orders of the celestial beings we have no clear revelation in Scripture, save that it is patent that there are such ranks and orders. The term *angels*, meaning messengers, is applied to all of them. What is the particular office of the cherubim, we are not told. The references to them in Scripture would lead us to the conclusion that in some way they are the especial servants of the holiness of God, its guardians in creation. We first meet them in the Biblical revelation at the gate of Eden after human sin, guarding the way to the tree of life. That makes this reference to them the more suggestive. Here they are seen bending over, and ever gazing at the mercy-seat. The suggestion is that of the guardians of the Divine holiness considering the mystery of the Divine mercy. Those who represent that holiness are observing how it is guarded and realized in the operation of the grace of God. The symbolism of their watching suggests that very truth, that in the exercise of mercy, God violates nothing of His holiness. Surely Peter was thinking of these overshadowing, watching cherubim when, writing of "salvation," of "the sufferings of

Christ, and the glories that should follow them," he said: "which things angels desire to look into." Than this holy mercy of God, there is nothing more wonderful in all the majesty and mystery of His ways and works. It is a subject worthy the consideration of the highest intelligence. What reverent, earnest, and persistent attention we should give to it! We can never fathom its depths, scale its heights, or encompass its reaches; but we can find in it the ultimate of joy and gladness.

And he made the laver of brass, and the base thereof of brass, of the mirrors of the serving women which served at the door of the tent of meeting.— Ex. 38. 8.

It will be noted that, later on in this chapter (verses 29–31), we find the account of the amount of the brass offering, and also a list of the articles made from it. In that list there is no reference to this laver. The bearing of that fact on this particular verse is, that it shows that the suggestion that the meaning is that the laver was provided with mirrors, is erroneous. Quite patently our rendering is correct. It was made of the brass of the mirrors of these serving women. The idea of service here is that of worship, and the women referred to are those who gathered about the door of the Tent of Meeting to worship God. Their dedication of the mirrors to the work of making the laver was a very suggestive one. These mirrors were among the most precious possessions of these women, and were related to their personal adornment. Moreover, they were used by Egyptian women in their acts of worship. Here then we see the Hebrew women renouncing the things precious for personal adornment, and at the same time abandoning a false habit in worship. The act was a testimony to their spiritual discernment, and their realization of the true adorning of life which is found in a true worship. It was highly significant that the brass of these mirrors was employed to construct that laver in which the priests must wash on approaching the altar or entering the Tabernacle. It is in the beauty of holiness men must worship, and by the surrender of everything of the flesh.

And Moses saw all the work, and behold, they had done it; as the Lord had commanded, even so had they done it: and Moses blessed them.— Ex. 39. 43.

The fact that the work of making the Tabernacle was done according to pattern, is emphasized by the repetition of the words: "As Jehovah commanded Moses" seven times in this chapter (verses 1, 5, 7, 21, 26, 29, 31). The same emphasis is found in the next chapter, in the sevenfold repetition of the same formula in the description of the setting up of the Tabernacle (verses 19, 21, 23, 25, 27, 29, 32). This is a very simple and yet a most important matter, as it reminds us that Divine work must always be done according to the Divine pattern, and most strictly in the Divine way. The truth is so self-evident, that it would seem needless to stress it. Yet a perpetual temptation to the mind of man is to endeavour to improve upon a Divine plan. It is an utterly foolish conceit to imagine that this can be done. "As for God, His way is perfect" (Psa. 18. 30), is a truth of universal application. In His plan, every detail is absolutely and finally perfect in wisdom and in power. There can be no improvement; and wherever man interferes and changes, by so doing he is destroying the perfection. It is a truth which we need to have ever in mind in all our work for Him, whether that of evangelism or edification. He has given us the pattern of His House, whether it be that of the individual soul, or that of the catholic Church.

The glory of the Lord filled the Tabernacle.—Ex. 40. 34.

That was God's answer to man's obedience. Apart from that obedience there could have been no filling of the House with the Divine glory. Apart from that filling, the House would have had no value. This coming of the glory of Jehovah to the Tabernacle was the foreshadowing of the hour when the Holy Spirit came to the Church at Pentecost, and of the hour when that same Spirit takes up His abode in the heart of the believer. Therefore it is also true that whatever building we erect for the worship and work of God, it lacks completion until it is consecrated by the coming of the glory of Jehovah. If ever the hour comes when the glory of Jehovah departs from Tabernacle or Temple, then the structure is useless, however ornate and beautiful it may be as to its material appointments. These things cannot ensure the glory of Jehovah. On the other hand, however plain or poor a structure may be, if the glory of Jehovah be there, it is made beautiful indeed. It is by the presence of that glory, moreover, that the people of God are to be guided in their goings by day, and kept and comforted in the night seasons. In that glory there ever merge the things of the Divine holiness and mercy, the things of God's government and grace, the things of love and light and life. When these are present, the trivial becomes sublime, and the small becomes great. When they are absent, everything tends to weariness and death. Nothing is worth while if the glory of God be missing. Everything is fruitful where that glory is found.

LEVITICUS

Without blemish.—*Lev.* 1. 3.

Leviticus was the hand-book of the priests. It contains the laws governing the whole system of worship. In Exodus we have the record of the words God spake to Moses from the Mount. They are the fundamental words of moral order. In Leviticus we have words God spake to Moses from the midst of the Tabernacle. They are the words of His administration of the affairs of His people in holiness and in grace. Throughout, God is seen as the God of all perfection, making it possible for imperfect man to draw nigh to Himself through sacrifice. The sacrifices and offerings were all to be provided by the worshippers, but they were to be the symbols of an Offering and Sacrifice which the worshippers could not provide, but which would be provided by God. Because they were thus to symbolize perfection, they must be, so far as man could make sure of it, perfect in themselves. That is the significance of this phrase "without blemish." Nothing offered to God must be imperfect. The principle abides, even though we are looking back to the one perfect Offering, rather than onward in expectation of its coming. Our only right to offer anything to God, in any form, is created by the one Offering through which we are sanctified. Every offering is a symbol still of the One. Therefore only of the best we have, have we any right to offer to Him. He is worthy to receive the most precious, and we do wrong to the perfection of His Sacrifice when we give to Him in kind, or in effort, that which is second-rate or imperfect. Our best is but poor, but that which we do give, must be our best.

No meal offering which ye shall offer unto the Lord, shall be made with leaven.—*Lev.* 2. 11.

As the burnt offering was to be "without blemish" so the meal offering was to be without leaven. This meal offering was the work of men's hands, of the fruits of the ground, the result of cultivation, manufacture, and preparation; and it was the symbol of service offered. Therefore it was not to be mixed with leaven. Why not? Because leaven in its very nature is corruption, and its influence is corrupting. Whenever it is introduced, it sets up the work of disintegration and break-up. Nothing of that kind must be permitted in the symbol of service, because God demands a perfect service as well as a perfect offering. Not only the gift, but also the deed must be without corruption. The application of the principle to ourselves is found when we turn to the New Testament, and find what leaven sym-bolizes for us. Our Lord warned His disciples against the leaven of the Pharisees and Sadducees (Matt. 16. 6). The leaven of the Pharisees was hypocrisy; that is, of ritualism without spiritual and moral content. The leaven of the Sadducees was rationalism; that is, Herodianism or wordliness; the elimination of the super-natural. Paul speaks of the leaven of "malice and wickedness," as the opposite of "sincerity and truth." These then are the corrupting influences which are not to be mixed with our service. In all the work we do for God, there is to be an absence of hypocrisy, of materialism, of the spirit which is contrary to love and truth.

An offering made by fire, of a sweet savour unto the Lord.—*Lev.* 3. 5.

These words, "of a sweet savour," are used with reference to the first three offerings, the Burnt Offering, the Meal Offering, the Peace Offering. They are not used of the Sin Offering or of the Trespass Offering. Every one of these offerings was made by fire. In the case of the first three the fire brings out the savour; in that of the last two it destroys. The suggestiveness of all this, it is impossible to escape. Fire is pre-eminently a symbol of God, and of certain facts about His character and activities. Invariably it speaks of some aspect or activity of His holiness. It is a symbol of what He is as the Holy One, in that only things which are in conformity with that nature can live in His presence. It is therefore a symbol of His wrath as He consumes that which is contrary to His nature. It is also a symbol of cleansing in that He purifies from all alloy those things which do conform to His character. Therefore, the offerings which represented sin and trespass, the fire destroyed; but those which represented devotion, service, fellowship, it affected so as to bring out the savour pleasing to God. The God of holiness is a God of fire, and He is to man what man is in regard to Himself. If man be in rebellion, a sinner persisting in his sin, the fire destroys him. If he be yielded, the fire brings out the beauty of character. Christ knew the fire bringing out sweet savour in His absolute perfections; He knew it as consuming, as He represented the sinner, and was made sin.

If anyone shall sin unwittingly.—*Lev.* 4. 2.

These words recognize an aspect of sin which we are at least in danger of thinking of lightly. There is a great tendency to imagine that sin is only in the will. There is a sense in which this is true. Guilt never attaches to sin until it is an act of the will. But imperfection and pollution exclude from God, even though there be no responsibility for them. God is "of purer eyes than to behold evil." This aspect of sin demands cleansing, while wilful sin needs forgiveness. I need not ask the forgiveness of God for sins which I have committed unwittingly, for pollution for which I have no responsibility. But I do need cleansing from them also. I need that "sanctification without which no man shall see the Lord." This is what was suggested by the sin-offering, the dealing with sin which sets the soul free from its pollution and paralysis. The trespass-offering suggested the dealing with sin which makes it possible for God to forgive the soul the wrong of wilful disobedience. Nothing is more clearly stamped upon these pages of Leviticus than the fact that sin must not be lightly treated. Jehovah is the God of holiness, and can make no terms with sin. But He is also the God of grace, Who provides a plenteous and perfect redemption for the sinner. All this is most perfectly emphasized in the fact that this great system was done away because it made nothing perfect. It revealed a need and promised deliverance, but nothing more. In Christ the promise was fulfilled and the need met.

If his means suffice not for a lamb.— Lev. 5. 7.

A great principle of the method of God with man in grace is revealed in these words. The appointed offering was "a lamb or a goat." But it might be that some man would not be able to provide one —his means might not suffice for it. Then was he to be excluded from the benefit of the priest and the altar? By no means. Let him bring "two turtle doves or two young pigeons." Or if he could not provide these, then let him bring "the tenth part of an ephah of fine flour." The right of access was not created by the intrinsic value of the guilt-offering, but by a gift of such relation to a man's means, as should show his appreciation of the principle upon which it was possible for him to be received and forgiven. This negative word necessarily has a positive value. If a man's means sufficed for the appointed lamb or a goat, and he brought two turtle doves or pigeons, or a tenth part of an ephah of fine flour, such action would show that he had no adequate sense, either of his own sin, or of the Divine grace. Is there not some light here on the whole question of "the means of grace"? The supreme thing is grace. The means may vary. Nevertheless, in every case they must be an adequate representation of the soul's apprehension of grace. Where they are so, grace comes through them, whether ornate or simple. Where they are not so, they are never its channels.

Fire shall be kept burning upon the altar continually; it shall not go out.— Lev. 6. 13.

A reference ahead to the account of the consecration of Aaron and his first exercise of the priestly office will show that this fire was originally supernatural (9. 24). It came out from before Jehovah. This was the fire which was to be kept burning, by being constantly provided with fuel. Thus, the fire was from God, but it was maintained by man. The responsibility for the carrying out of this instruction rested upon the priests. A glance back at a previous note (3. 5) will remind us that fire was the symbol of the holiness of God in different activities, making possible life in His presence, consuming all contrary to Himself in nature, and so purifying all like Himself from alloy. Here then we are reminded of the necessity for the perpetual maintenance of the action of that holiness. It comes from God. Man has no holiness other than the holiness he receives from Him. But in order that its flame may burn continually, and its heat accomplish the Divine purpose, the fire must be fed. That demands ceaseless vigilance. The unworthy things must be handed over for destruction. The things of worth in service and fellowship must be yielded up to the fire for purification. Neither day nor hour nor minute passes which has no need of this cleansing fire. We may be comforted by the certainty that, as we bring the fuel, the fire will continue to burn, accomplishing all its purposes, whether of destruction or purifying.

With cakes of leavened bread.— Lev. 7. 13.

We noted that no leaven was to be mixed in the Meal Offering, because leaven is in itself corrupting, and is perpetually the symbol of corruption. This makes us pause when we find that leaven was now commanded to be mixed with the Peace Offering. In order to understand it, let the reader note carefully that in the previous verse (12) the worshipper is commanded to offer with the Peace Offering *unleavened* cakes, and *unleavened* wafers. Then also *leavened* cakes. Surely the suggestion is quite patent. The Peace Offering is supremely the symbol of communion based on reconciliation. It is the offering which symbolizes two sides to a great transaction; one of those is that of God, the other is that of man. God and man are at peace. The Godward side can only be symbolized by that which is unleavened, free from all evil, separated from everything that tends to corruption. On the other hand, there remains in man much of imperfection. This is symbolized by the leavened cakes. Our unworthiness in and of ourselves abides. In our thanksgiving and our praise there is no room for boastfulness. Of this we need to be constantly reminded. The truth is brought out in the lines of a great hymn of worship:—

> Unworthy is thanksgiving,
> A service stained with sin,
> Except as He is living,
> Our Priest, to bear it in.

Aaron and his sons did all the things which the Lord commanded.—Lev. 8. 36.

These concluding words of a chapter make us look back over it. It is the account of the consecration of Aaron and his sons; that is, of the High Priest and the priests. Let us remind ourselves of the sequence of ceremonies. First Aaron and his sons were washed. Then the High Priest was robed in his garments of beauty and glory. This was followed by his anointing with the holy oil. After that his sons were robed. Before there could be exercise of their priestly function, two offerings were sacrificed to Jehovah; first, the sin offering for pollution; and then, the burnt offering as a sign of complete dedication. Then on the right ear and right thumb, and great toe of right foot, of Aaron and each of his sons, blood was put; the symbol of cleansing of sin, in order to the fulfilment of priestly functions. Next the wave-offering signified the rights and privileges of the priests, all offered to God. Again they were anointed with blood and oil. Their sustenance was provided, and they were completely separated to God and His service. Every detail was suggestive. Into the spiritual significance the reader will enter. We desire only to stress the teaching that the way of entrance to service in holy things is the way of obedience to the Divine ordinance. Nothing must be omitted which Jehovah commands. His priests must be washed, robed, anointed, sustained, separated, and all in His way, or they cannot exercise their functions in His service. To neglect anything, is to invalidate ministry.

Moses and Aaron went into the Tent of Meeting, and came out, and blessed the people.—Lev. 9. 23.

Thus when all things were done in accordance with the Divine plan, Moses and Aaron had access to the Tent of Meeting, and by that access were enabled to pass out and bless the people. In the Chaldee Version of the Pentateuch the words of the blessing are thus reported: "May the Word of Jehovah accept your sacrifice with favour, and remit and pardon your sins." Whether these were the actual words or no, the truth remains that these men pronounced a blessing upon the people which was of Divine authority. The principle is abiding. The servants of God, whether prophets or priests, have no power to bless men save as they receive it in direct communion with God. Before we

can go out and bless the people, we must go in to the Place of Meeting with God. This is so self-evident that it seems hardly necessary to state it. Yet we are perpetually in danger of allowing our very eagerness to serve men, to interfere with our communion with God. To do so, is to fail disastrously. It is only as we serve in the Holy Place, in worship, in silence, in reception from God, that we are able to serve in the camp in work, in speech, in giving to men. Forgetfulness of this is the secret of much futility in Christian work, of much fussiness, of much feverishness. It is the souls who are strengthened, enlightened, quieted in the Tent of Meeting, that pass out to the places and ways of men, carrying blessings with them.

Strange fire.—Lev. 10. 1.

This was, quite simply, fire which Nadab and Abihu kindled themselves. Everything else seems to have been in order. They were duly appointed priests, being sons of Aaron. They employed the proper censers. They put incense on them. And finally they offered before Jehovah. The one failure was that they touched that incense with fire they had kindled rather than with the fire from the altar which had been kindled directly by the Lord (see 9. 24). Apparently it was an unimportant matter; at least, the fact that they did it, proves that they considered it to be so. That it was not unimportant, is proved by the further fact that "there came forth fire from before Jehovah, and devoured them." That sacred fire, kept perpetually burning, was the one central symbol of the holiness of God, and any offering unsanctified thereby was polluted. The lesson is evident. The fire in which all our service must be rendered is that of the Spirit of God, Who is the Spirit of Holiness. To seek to make our work effectual and acceptable by any agent other than the Holy Spirit, is to burn "strange fire." The energy of the flesh, and the cleverness of the mind, unbaptized in the Holy Spirit, are polluted; and however pleasing the results may be to human minds and hearts, such forces are ineffectual in the service of God, and unacceptable to Him. To offer "strange fire"—is a deadly business. We may be in true orders, doing God-appointed work, but if we attempt these things in any energy other than that of the Holy Spirit, we are in danger of being cast away.

To make a difference between the unclean and the clean.—Lev. 11. 47.

These words refer to the food of the people of God. Here we come to the laws which touch the ordinary and everyday life of the people. Those already enunciated have had to do with worship, the whole subject of the people's approach to God. The people for whom such rights and privileges are created are never away, either from God's thought and will for them, or from their obligations to Him. He is interested in every detail of their lives. He issues His commands as to what they may eat, and what they may not eat. They are not permitted to choose for themselves in the matter of that food which is to sustain their physical strength. There is no doubt at all that these regulations were all fundamentally sanitary. They were by no means capricious. We may not be able to discover the scientific reasons for the classification. Moreover, they may have been regulated largely by the climate, and the particular period in which men were living. Possibly, therefore, some of them may not apply to those living in other lands and in other times. All that being granted, the permanent value of these enactments consists in their revelation of the fact of the Divine interest in, and care for, all these details. If to-day we are not to be governed by the actual rules of this Hebrew law, the principle involved in it finds expression for us in the words of Paul: "Whether therefore ye eat, or drink, or whatsoever ye do, do all to the glory of God" (1 Cor. 10. 31). To eat or drink anything which harms the body, which is the instrument of the spirit, is not to glorify God. Therefore into this whole question of food, the fact of our relationship with God enters, and each is called upon to act for himself or herself accordingly.

The priest shall make atonement for her, and she shall be clean.—Lev. 12. 8.

This is a brief chapter in our Bibles, as it was a brief section in the Hebrew laws. It is none the less one full of suggestiveness. It is the law of Motherhood, and it fences it round in the most sacred way, physically and spiritually. On the purely physical side it will bear close and reverent consideration, providing as it did for the perfect repose of the new mother; and it has been suggested that in the difference of time in the case of male and female children, it had an important bearing on the regulation of the sexes. On the spiritual side, its requirements are very full of importance. Motherhood is one of the most sacred and beautiful things in the whole realm of human experience. This needs no argument. But motherhood is exercised in a race which is defiled. When the great singer of Israel, in his penitential psalm, said: "Behold, I was shapen in iniquity, and in sin did my mother conceive me" (Psa. 51. 5), he was casting no reflection upon his own mother, but rather stating a racial fact, from which no human being escapes. Here then is the value of this law. God provided that Motherhood should be sanctified by sacrifice. To us, Motherhood has been for ever made holy by the Seed of the woman, through Whom woman is saved in child-bearing. It is always a sad thing, to say nothing stronger, when mothers forget to remember this, and

to recognize it in the sacred service of the sanctuary.

The priest shall look.—Lev. 13. 10.

Even until to-day leprosy is so dire a disease that it completely baffles the skill of the physician. Much may be done to alleviate the distress which it causes, but there is no cure for it. In countries where sanitary laws obtain, it is almost eliminated, but that is done by removing causes, not by curing those suffering from it. In Eastern countries, and under the conditions obtaining in many of them, it is still prevalent. In these laws it is dealt with at great length comparatively, and that undoubtedly because of its dire nature. We cannot wonder that it became, and still continues to be, the very symbol of sin. It is a disease in the blood itself, which is the life; its manifestations are most terrible and loathsome; and—as we have said—it is incurable. In these two chapters we have the laws for dealing with it; and in the brief words, "The priest shall look," we have revealed the utmost that could be done for those suffering from it. The whole fact may thus be stated, that the only thing that the priest could do, was to discover whether or no the disease was actual leprosy. If it were not, then there might be a period of separation, and presently a restoration to the community. If it were leprosy, nothing could be done other than to separate the sufferer completely from others. In the light of these considerations, we remember that there came in the fulness of time One Who could not only look at, but touch the leper—One Who could cure. That is also the story of His dealing with sin.

He shall break down the house.— Lev. 14. 45.

That is, the house affected by leprosy. There was a time when it was suggested that this law was due to superstition. Modern science has proved its beneficence. A house may be infected with many forms of disease. This now needs no argument. All our present methods of dealing with disease from the standpoint of the welfare of the community are based upon it. It is made a criminal offence to-day not to notify cases of certain diseases. This attitude is entirely warranted by this law. A house which is likely to communicate disease must either be cleansed completely or destroyed. No man has any property rights which are superior to the rights of the health of the community. What we really need to-day, is a more drastic application of the principle. When we turn to the spiritual suggestiveness, we at once realize its importance. In the letter of Jude, the principle suddenly flames out in his words: "Hating even the garment spotted by the flesh" (verse 23). Whatever in our life has been associated with and contaminated by the leprosy of past sin, it is good to destroy without compromise or pity. How often where this is not done, even those who have known personal deliverance have been infected anew! Old haunts, old associations, should be left, abandoned, without compromise, or else the last state may be worse than the first.

Thus shall ye separate the children of Israel from their uncleanness.— Lev. 15. 31.

This chapter contains the laws governing the whole experience of issues from the flesh as they are involved in uncleanness. It is a strange and solemn chapter in which, once again, as in the one dealing with the subject of motherhood and childhood (12), there is brought before the mind, with dread and forceful solemnity, the fact of the defilement of the race. A simple and yet careful consideration of these requirements will serve to remind us that the procreative powers of humanity are all under the curse, as the result of race-pollution. Whether the exercise of such powers be natural or unnatural, within the restraint of law or beyond such restraint, they are tainted with the same virus of sin in the sight of a God of absolute holiness. Therefore for these people of God who were to be preserved from all contamination physically with other races, in connection with the activity of these powers, stringent laws were enacted for cleansing. The chapter, therefore, has a solemn message to all of us concerning the fact of the pollution of human nature at its fountain-head, and the consequent perpetual necessity for cleansing. This view of human nature is not flattering, and the human mind is often in rebellion against it. To deny it, is to deny a fact which is constantly proven true in human experience. We should, therefore, sedulously observe the spiritual significance, and apply it resolutely in the physical realm. For us the way of perpetual cleansing is provided in Christ.

To make atonement for the children of Israel because of all their sins once in the year.—Lev. 16. 34.

This chapter contains the instructions which were given concerning the observance of the Day of Atonement. This was in many ways the greatest day in the religious year of the Hebrew people, for this was the most important religious rite in the whole economy. In this rite provision was made for dealing with the whole question of sin, known and unknown. We noticed in an earlier note, when dealing with the difference between the sin-offering and the trespass-offering (chapter 4), that the element of accountability was conditioned in knowledge, but that sin, in the sight of God, is sin, even though committed in ignorance. All sin, therefore, was dealt with on the day. Every arrangement

was intended to impress upon the mind the solemnity of the approach of the soul to God, and to stress the truth that the sinner has no right of access save that which is provided for him through sacrifice. As these arrangements are pondered, one can easily realize that their necessary imperfection could not produce anything like perfect rest in the conscience. Indeed, the more sensitive the spirit, the more that imperfection would be realized. For us there is no waiting for an annual day of atonement. We need not wait, with sin undealt-with for an hour. Our Priest abides in the holiest, and we have access there through Him at all times. This should not make us less reverent in our coming, but more so. The cleansed conscience is never rude, irreverent. It is ever subdued, chastened, sensitive. It rejoices in freedom, but never loses the sense of debt.

And they shall no more sacrifice their sacrifices unto the he-goats.— Lev. 17. 7.

This is a startling interpolation. It occurs in the midst of instructions concerning sacrifices. It is first provided that all sacrifices must·be brought to the door of the Tent of Meeting. There must be no other place of worship through sacrifice. This provision recognized the fact of the unification of the nation around the Divine Presence; reminding the people that there could be no access to God on the part of any person in self-willed isolation; and so made difficult, if not impossible, the worship of false gods. It was in this connection that these words were uttered. The Authorized Version reads: "They shall no more offer their sacrifices unto devils." Perhaps that was too strong a rendering. The Hebrew word literally is "hairy-ones." In Isa. 13. 21 and 34. 14 it is rendered "satyr" in the Authorized Version, and "wild-goats" in the American Standard Version. The satyr was an imaginary being, half-goat, half-man, of demon nature. In Egypt the goat-man, Pan, was worshipped. It would seem as though this word recognized the fact that these people had in Egypt probably worshipped that false god. It is but a reference, and we may not dogmatize as to the actual meaning. The one truth of value for us is that when man worships God in the right way, according to the Divine provision and law, all false worship becomes unnecessary and impossible. To be deflected from the true method, even of the worship of God, is ever to be in danger of turning to other gods.

After the doings of the land of Egypt, wherein ye dwelt, shall ye not do; and after the doings of the land of Canaan, whither I bring you, shall ye not do.—Lev. 18. 3.

The particular application of these words was to all the corrupt social practices of Egypt and Canaan, those very practices which had resulted in a corrupt and degenerate race; so corrupt and degenerate that it was necessary, in the interest of the human race, that they should be swept out. All that promiscuous intercourse between the sexes which inevitably tends to disease and degeneracy, was contrary to the mind of God, because destructive of humanity. Therefore, His people were safeguarded against those things by this general command, and by detailed particularity of statement. In the interests of the health and strength of national life these enactments are still of force. To break them, is to bring about inevitable deterioration and ultimate destruction. The principle involved in the words has much wider application. The people of God are called upon to conform in all the ways and habits of life, not to the customs of the world, but to the mind and will of God as made known in His law. The full force of the principle is found in Paul's injunction: "Be not fashioned according to this world; but be ye transformed by the renewing of your mind" (Rom. 12. 2). It is a requirement of which we need to remind ourselves constantly. It is so easy to be lured from our loyalty by the customs of the men and women by whom we are surrounded. Such requirement is not capricious. It is based upon God's loving purpose for His own, and His determination to preserve them from all destructive practices.

Thou shalt not wholly reap the corners of thy field.—*Lev.* 19. 9.

This is a remarkable chapter. It consists largely of the repetition of laws already given, with one reiterated emphasis, namely, that of the fact that JEHOVAH was the God of His people. It opens with a general call to holiness, based upon its ultimate reason: "Ye shall be holy, for I Jehovah your God am holy." This is the ultimate reason for holiness. The holiness of Jehovah must be exemplified in His people. This formula, "I am Jehovah," is repeated in this one chapter no less than fourteen times. Every commandment here repeated is set in relation to this fact. In the words we are specially noting, there is a gleam of light, full of beauty. In the reaping of their harvests they were forbidden to reap the corners of the fields. These were to be left for the poor and the stranger, and this because "I am Jehovah your God." An essential quality of the holiness of God is His beneficence, His tender concern for the needy. The people who are called to exemplify His holiness, are to observe that fact. The exactitude and thoroughness in dealing with one's own harvests, which leaves no room for those who are in need, is strictly forbidden. Happy indeed are those who in all their business enterprises retain a consciousness of human need, and such consideration for it as will make them leave something which of strict justice belongs to themselves, that this need may be ministered to. This is holiness according to the Divine standard, which ever has this element of compassion.

That the land, whither I bring you to dwell therein, vomit you not out.—*Lev.* 20. 22.

This is an arresting word. The whole Biblical revelation insists upon the close relationship between the earth and man. At the beginning it is written, in view of man's sin: "Cursed is the ground for thy sake" (Gen. 3. 17). In the Roman letter, Paul declares, again as the consequence of human sin, that: "the whole creation groaneth and travaileth in pain together until now" (Rom. 8. 22). The prophets repeatedly emphasized the truth that the earth becomes polluted by man's pollution. The measure in which the land is dealt with by corrupt man, is the measure in which it becomes barren, and at last refuses to support man. In that sense it vomits him out. The very land referred to in this word of the law of God, stands to-day at the centre of the earth, a standing witness to the truth. There it has been for ages, fruitless and barren, and yet naturally there is no land more fertile. Men corrupted it, and it vomited them out. When presently the people of God are finally restored to their land in faith and loyalty, it will become again the garden of the Lord, full of fruit and full of beauty. Again the principle is of the widest application. Whatever the territory man reigns over, it is affected by his character. If he be polluted and corrupt, then all that is under his sway becomes polluted and corrupt, and so fails to supply him with the very things he seeks therefrom; it vomits him out, and that by the desolation which he has himself produced. Thus has God conditioned His whole creation within laws which ever operate with Himself and His holiness and against evil.

No man of the seed of Aaron the priest, that hath a blemish, shall come nigh to offer the offerings of the Lord.—*Lev.* 21. 21.

In this chapter the subject is that of the behaviour and condition of life, necessary in the case of the priests. The absolute necessity for their strictest separation from all possibility of defilement is carefully set forth. They stood in a place of special nearness to God as the Divinely-appointed mediators of the people; therefore they must of all men manifest, in all the externals of life and conduct, the necessity for that holiness without which no man may see the Lord. They were strictly forbidden to defile themselves by contact with the dead in any form. The only exceptions permitted were in the cases of those who were their next of kin. Even these exceptions were not made for the High Priest. He must never touch a dead person, even though it were father or mother. Moreover, his family must be most strictly guarded. This was revealed in the one flaming declaration that if the daughter of a priest defiled herself, she profaned her father, and was to be burned with fire. Finally, in the words we have selected, it was provided that no cripple of any sort should exercise the priestly office. Approach to God necessitated perfection, and so far as it was possible to emphasize this by the external symbols, it was done in the case of the priests. There followed a recognition of the fact that blame may not attach to a man in the matter of physical defect. Therefore he was permitted to eat the bread of God, but not to offer it. All this should at least emphasize for us the truth that we ought to seek that those who minister in holy things should be of the strongest rather than the weakest.

Speak unto Aaron and to his sons, that they separate themselves from the holy things of the children of Israel.— Lev. 22. 2.

In this chapter we have the further enforcement and wider application of the necessity for the complete separation of the priests from all defilement. They were to abstain from the exercise of their office, to "separate themselves from the holy things of the children of Israel," under certain conditions which were described. If from natural cause, or from disease, or from contact with defiling things, the priest were for the time defiled, he was to abstain from his service, until such time as he had been actually and ceremonially cleansed. Not only must he himself be free from blemish and defilement, he was charged to see to it that all he offered was of the same character. And yet further, he was not to extend any hospitality to those who were unclean, or strangers to the covenant, of the things which appertained to the house of his God. These stringent instructions close with a reaffirmation of the reason which had been given in other connections: "I will be hallowed among the children of Israel" . . . "I am Jehovah." These people were constantly reminded that the deepest purpose of their existence was that of their call to manifest the things of God. Thus, such requirements under the Hebrew economy, have a very direct bearing upon the Christian Church. All the degradation existing among the nations is due to the false ideas of God which characterize their life and worship. To know the true God, is life for the nations, as surely as for individuals.

The set feasts of the Lord.—Lev. 23. 2.

This is a wonderful chapter, as it shows how the whole year, that is, the passing of

time, was for this people marked by great religious festivals, which were at once national signs and symbols of the relation of the people to God, and means of keeping ever before them the real secrets of strength. Eight set feasts are named. The first was the Sabbath. It was to be a perpetually recurring feast every seventh day, thus persistently reminding them of these relationships between God and the national life. Then seven were established which created the calendar. First came Passover, which merged into Unleavened Bread. With these the year commenced, reminding them of their redemption from slavery and their separation to God. Then came the Feast of First-fruits, and seven weeks later the Feast of Pentecost, reminding them of their dependence upon God for sustenance, and of their responsibility to Him for the culture of the land. The seventh month was most sacred of all, for therein three connected Feasts were observed, those of Trumpets, of Atonement, of Tabernacles. The Trumpets called them to cease from servile work in order to worship. Atonement reminded them of the way of access to God by sacrifices and the putting away of sin. Tabernacles was the feast of joy in which they remembered their deliverance, His guidance of them, and His law for them. Thus by these set feasts the year was made sacred, and their symbolism emphasized the sanctity of the secular in the Kingdom of God.

Ye shall have one manner of law, as well for the stranger, as for the home-born.—Lev. 24. 22.

This is an interesting chapter, in that it seems to break in on the continuity of the Book. In the first section some laws are repeated. Then follows a fragment of history. It is the story of a blasphemer upon whom punishment fell. This man was the son of an Egyptian father and an Israelitish mother. Seeing that he was not of pure Hebrew blood, the people were not sure as to how to deal with him when he committed the heinous offence of blaspheming the Name. It was under these circumstances that the principle was laid down that there should be one manner of law for the stranger and for the home-born. It was a principle of justice and of mercy. Its first emphasis is upon the fact that those who enter the Kingdom of God, and enjoy its privileges, must be governed by its laws. No man within that Kingdom can claim the rights of other citizenship as giving him freedom to break its laws. To enter that Kingdom is to renounce all other lordships, and to accept its laws. The principle has another value, in that it protects the stranger from the possible injustice of the home-born. Those who, for any reason have birth-rights in the Kingdom of God, are not permitted to impose upon the strangers who desire to enter any other obligations than such as are binding upon themselves. To-day there are no "home-born" members of that Kingdom. All are "strangers," who enter by a New Birth. Yet the principle needs remembering, for it is not always easy for those who have had the privileges of the Kingdom longest, to be just and impartial to those newly entering.

It shall be a jubilee unto you.— Lev. 25. 10.

The provision for the year of jubilee was a method by which the people were perpetually reminded that all human inter-relations were dependent upon the deeper things of Divine authority and possession. The first part of this chapter gives the law of the land-sabbath. Every seventh year the land was to have rest from cultivation. Thus the Divine ownership was recognized, as men were forbidden to treat the land as their absolute property. There is no doubt that this requirement, in common with all others, was based upon the true method of dealing with the land. Every fiftieth year was one in which all sorts of human arrangements were interfered with. In that year, men dispossessed through adversity were restored to possession. In that year the slave was to be set free, and all men released from toil. The laws for this year were clearly set out, as they affected the land, dwelling-houses, and persons. They should be carefully pondered, for in them the foundations of the social order were firmly laid. By them we see how all human inter-relationships, both as to property and person, are conditioned by the fact that the fundamental ownership, both of property and persons, is that of God. The only right a man has in land is that of his own labour therein. The liberation of the slave proved that no one human being can have the right to possess, absolutely and finally, any other human being. The master has only a right in the work of his slave. The readjustment of the year of jubilee re-called men to the realization of the sovereignty of Jehovah, and of the limitations within which they lived.

Because they walked contrary unto Me, I also walked contrary unto them. —Lev. 26. 40, 41.

In this chapter two gracious promises and solemn warnings are set forth. It opens with the reiteration of fundamental laws. There is to be no idolatry. There must be a constant observance of the Sabbath. The reverence of the Sanctuary must be maintained. Then follow the promises showing that conditions of well-being are entirely dependent upon obedience to the government of God. In like manner the warnings show that disobedience will always be followed by calamity. It is most suggestive to notice how, even in the giving of the Law, the declension and wandering of the people were known to the King, and yet, notwithstanding this fact, that these promises of final restoration were made. Thus human responsibility was solemnly enforced; and yet the whole chapter cannot be read without the conviction being created that the love of God will prove finally victorious over all failure. The words we stress reveal the law of the soul's relation to God perpetually. God is faithful and unchangeable. We may change our experience of His government by a change of attitude toward it. If we walk with Him, He walks with us, and all His infinite resources of wisdom and power and love are at our disposal. If we change our course, and walk contrary to Him, He pursues His way of wisdom, love, and power, but His goings are against us, and we experience the contradiction of His opposition. He remaineth faithful. He cannot deny Himself. Therefore we know His government as strength, helping or opposing, according to whether we walk with Him or contrary to Him.

None devoted, which shall be devoted of men, shall be ransomed.— Lev. 27. 29.

This last chapter has to do with vows. A vow is a promise made voluntarily to God. It is an undertaking to do something which is not commanded, that is, something in some way beyond the requirements of the actual law. That is not to say that a vow is wrong. It is by no means so. It expresses devotion to the service of God, in a degree beyond that which is demanded in the terms of the Divine statutes. It is not necessary that such vows should be made; but if they are made, they must be religiously observed. The careful reader of this chapter will note a distinction between things "sanctified" and things "devoted." Throughout, the word *sanctify* is used in the simplest sense of setting apart; while the word *devoted* is used in reference to complete and final giving. The things sanctified by vow, that is, set apart to Divine uses, may be redeemed by the payment of their full value and something beyond. The things devoted, that is, once completely given, cannot be redeemed. All this has much to say to us. Our devotion to our Lord should be complete, because for that He asks. We need add no vow of extra devotion, because we have no extras to offer. Then let us ever remember that we cannot ransom ourselves from our bondage to Him. There is no sin more despicable than that of taking back anything given. Children in their play all recognize this. Let us live by the truth, in its application to our devotion to our Lord.

NUMBERS

As the Lord commanded Moses, so he numbered them in the wilderness of Sinai.—*Num.* 1. 19.

The Book of Numbers records the wilderness experiences of the people of God. It resolves itself into the account of a long discipline due to disobedience. In the Divine programme, these people should now have gone up and possessed the land promised to them. Their entry was postponed for forty years through their failure, and this Book is occupied largely with matters pertaining to that period. It records two numberings of the people, one of the beginning, and the other at the close of the forty years. This first numbering was that of the men of war, and it was undertaken at the direct command of God. Those to be enrolled were the men of twenty years and upward. The numbering yielded an army of 603,550. This was the first movement in preparation for the coming of the people into the land. The nation had been created an instrument for the carrying out of Divine purposes for the world. Its first mission was punitive. The peoples occupying the land of Canaan had become utterly corrupt, and it was necessary in the interests of purity that they should be swept out. The chosen people were to be the instruments of this purifying process. They must be prepared for warfare, and this was the reason of the taking of this census. The reason for the preparation of this army must never be lost sight of. The story of the conquest of Canaan is not that of the spoliation of feeble peoples by a stronger, in order to possess territory. It is that of the purification of a land, in order that there might be planted in it a people from whose history blessing would come to all the nations.

The children of Israel shall pitch every man by his own standard.— *Num.* 2. 2.

This whole chapter is very full of interest as revealing the orderliness of the Divine arrangements. This host of God was not a mob, lacking order. It was a disciplined company, and in these provisions for its encampment this fact was emphasized. At the centre of everything was the Tent of Meeting, for ever reminding the people that they constituted a Theocracy, and that all their national life was centred in the God Who had called them to Himself. Nearest to this sacred centre—that is, around the enclosure of the courts—the Levites encamped; and thus the nation was kept in the consciousness of the fact that its first obligation was the service and worship of God. Beyond this encampment of priests and Levites came the tribes, and these again were in a Divinely-arranged order. On the east—that is, fronting the entrance—the standard-bearing tribe was Judah, with its symbol of a lion of gold on a field of scarlet. With Judah were Zebulun and Issachar. On the west, Ephraim's standard was a black ox on a field of gold. Associated with Ephraim were Manasseh and Benjamin. On the south, Reuben bore the standard on which was a man on a field of gold. Simeon and Gad were grouped with Reuben. On the north, Dan was the standard-bearing tribe, his synbol being an eagle of gold on a field of blue. With Dan were Naphtali and Asher. Thus the whole encamping of the people was beautifully symbolic of the nature of the national life, and of the presence and purpose of God therein.

I have taken the Levites from among the children of Israel instead of all the firstborn.—*Num.* 3. 12.

In this, and the following chapters, the service of the Levites is dealt with in detail. In the taking of the census for the men of war, the Levites were exempted from military service. This was a clear indication of the mind of God as to the true value of directly religious and spiritual work in national service. A fact which is sometimes overlooked in our thinking of the Levitical order is brought out in the words we have selected from this chapter. It is that the Levites were representatives. The first Divine arrangement was that the firstborn male in every family was to be consecrated to the service of God in the priesthood. Now, in all probability for the sake of cohesion and order, one tribe was set apart to represent the firstborn sons of the nation. In this first carrying out of the arrangement, the number of the tribe of Levi available was 22,000, while there were 22,273 firstborn sons. This company of 273 unrepresented by Levites had to pay a redemption price of five shekels each, which was devoted to the service of the sanctuary. In the light of these things it is interesting to remember that our Lord was the First-born, and so was a Priest according to the original Divine arrangement, and not according to the Levitical order. All those who are redeemed by Him, exercise a priesthood which results from their birthright in Him, and so have no need of any order of men to represent them in priestly work. In this way also the order of Levitical priesthood is done away in Christ.

Every one according to his service, and according to his burden.—*Num. 4. 49.*

In this chapter we have a continuation of the instructions concerning the Levites. It gives a minute account of their work in connection with the marching of the people. The duty of carrying all the holy furniture was that of the Kohathites. This furniture, however, they were not permitted to look upon, or touch. Aaron and his sons first entered the Holy Place and covered each sacred piece, affixing the staves which were to rest upon the shoulders of the Levites. On the march these holy vessels were in charge of Eleazar, who carried also the anointing oil and the sweet incense. The curtains and the tents which constituted the Tabernacle itself were carried by the Gershonites. They were under the charge of Ithamar. To the Merarites were committed the boards and bars and pillars, and other things which formed the foundations upon which the sacred hangings rested. These also were under the charge of Ithamar. All this is instructive, as it reveals the Divine thought and care for every detail of the life and worship of His people. It is of particular value, too, as it teaches us that in the thought of God every detail is sacred. These men were in this regard the "caretakers" of the House of God. How often we are prone to think meanly of "caretakers" in these modern times! Such thinking is utterly wrong. The men and women who have charge of the houses of our worship are rendering holy service.

The priest shall take holy water in an earthen vessel; and of the dust that is on the floor of the tabernacle the priest shall take, and put it into the water.—*Num. 5. 17.*

These words occur in a section which emphasizes the necessity for the purity of the camp. All that were in any way unclean were to be put outside that camp. This does not mean that they were left to perish as the people continued their march, but that they were not permitted to retain their proper place with the tribes of their people. They were, for the time being, camp-followers only, shut out, until their purification was ensured, according to the provision made in the laws already given. It was also insisted upon that there must be moral rectitude among the people in their inter-relationships, and to this end restitution was constantly to be made by all such as had in any way sinned against their fellows. It is in this atmosphere that we find the careful, and to us at first, strange instructions as to the peril of jealousy between husband and wife. The very fact of these instructions shows how important it is, in the mind of God, that, in the interest of true national strength,

family life should be maintained at its strongest and purest. It is well that we remind ourselves that this ordeal of drinking bitter water has no similarity to the ordeals by fire and poison of which we read in the history of the Dark Ages, and of barbarous peoples. The drinking of this water was perfectly harmless in itself. It only became proof of guilt by the act of God. If a woman, guilty of infidelity, consented to this ordeal, the tokens of her guilt were manifested, not by any action of the water, but by the act of God.

So shall they put My Name upon the children of Israel.—*Num. 6. 27.*

The solemn act of pronouncing this blessing was a distinct part of the worship of the Hebrew people. A reference to Leviticus 9. 22 will show that it followed upon the completion of the presentation of the offerings. It consisted of a placing of the Name of Jehovah upon the people, that is, a declaration of His relationship to them. The formula was definitely fixed. That is the significance of the word "SO" which the Revised Version gives us. It was to be done in this way and in no other. The Name in itself was JEHOVAH, the Name signifying the infinite grace of God, wherein He bends to meet the need of His people, becoming to them at all times, exactly what they really need. The sentences of this benediction were interpretative of the values of that Name. The first sentence, "Jehovah bless thee, and keep thee," does not describe the way nor the nature of the blessing, but fixes attention upon the fact that God is its source. The second sentence, "Jehovah make His face to shine upon thee, and be gracious unto thee," declares, not only that God is the source of blessing, but that He is its channel, that through His activity it reaches men. The final sentence, "Jehovah lift up His countenance upon thee, and give thee peace," is a declaration that the experience of the blessing in the soul is that of Jehovah Himself creating that experience. For us these words must ever speak of the Trinity. The Father is Jehovah the Source of blessing; the Son is Jehovah the Channel of blessing; the Spirit is Jehovah the Creator of the experience of blessing. "So," He has put His name upon us; so He has blessed us indeed.

He heard the Voice speaking unto him from above the Mercy-seat.—*Num. 7. 89.*

This is a brief statement of something that happened after the dedication and anointing of the altar. It was a great day, and all this longest chapter in the book is occupied with the account of it, and of the offerings of the princes. These offerings had been twelve days in course of presentation. They were purely voluntary. Not in answer to any compulsion or Divine requirement, but out of the consciousness of the importance of worship did the princes of the people offer willingly. Seeing that they were giving thus willingly, it was Divinely arranged that the giving in each case should be equal, thus precluding the possibility of any spirit of rivalry. When all was done, Moses entered the Tabernacle. The Revised Version here helps us, in that it renders very literally. Instead of attempting interpretation, as in the King James version by rendering, "he heard the voice of One," it translates directly, "he heard the Voice." This is perhaps the one instance in which we have a clear statement that in his communing with God, Moses did actually hear a voice. The communications which he received were more than subjective impressions; they were objective expressions. The place of the voice is definitely and carefully stated. It came "from above the mercy-seat, that was upon the ark of the testimony, from between the two cherubim." This is emphasized by the last statement, "and He spake unto him," which Rotherham has rendered: "So He spake unto him," with undoubted accuracy.

The seven lamps shall give light in front of the candlestick.—*Num. 8. 2.*

A reference to Exodus 25. 31–37 will explain the "seven lamps" and the one "candlestick." The word "candlestick" would certainly be better rendered "lampstand." The word first occurs in Genesis 1. 4, where it is used of sun, moon, and stars. These are light-holders. So also was this golden stand, which occupied a place in the Holy Place opposite the table of shewbread. This light was given by the seven lamps which it held. Thus one light was shining, but it was sevenfold, coming from these seven lamps in the one light-holder. The statement that this light was to shine in front of the lampstand raises the inquiry as to what it fell upon within that Holy Place. As we have already said, opposite to the lampstand was the table of shewbread. Upon that table the priests placed twelve cakes every Sabbath day, having frankincense on them. These were the symbols of the fellowship of the people with God. Upon that table the light from the golden lampstand ever fell. Thus were typified the great principles of the life of fellowship with God, which have their fulfilment for us in Christ. We have a table of communion, but it is well to remember that upon it the light is ever shining. We only have right to that table as we dwell in that light. The light for us comes from the Holy Spirit; but we are responsible for the reception of His indwelling; we have to keep the lamps trimmed.

At the commandment of the Lord the children of Israel journeyed, and at the commandment of the Lord they encamped.—*Num. 9. 18.*

Our chapter brings us to the moment when everything was ready, so far as Divine provision was concerned, for the march to the promised land. The hosts of God waited only for the Divine will. This was to be made known through the cloud. The first appearing of this cloud was in connection with the actual exodus, and from henceforth it was the appointed symbol and token of the Divine presence. It was a remarkably suggestive one, at once mystic and revealing. There has been a good deal of speculation as to the nature of this cloud. It is surely best, reverently to consider it as a supernatural manifestation, indicating the presence and guidance of God. The instructions given were most definite, that the people were only to move in obedience to the movement of the cloud. It was at once a beneficent and drastic provision. It lifted all responsibility from them, except that of simple obedience. They were not called upon to consider the time or direction of their march, but they were not allowed to object or delay. We have no longer any such visible means of guidance, but the guidance is as sure for us as for them; and it is given to us to know it by the life of maintained fellowship with the Father through the Son by the Holy Spirit. In proportion as that is maintained by our fulfilling of the true conditions, there need be no place or time in which we may not discover what is the will of God for us.

Thou shalt be to us instead of eyes.—*Num. 10. 31.*

This is a very suggestive story. Reuel was the father of Zipporah, and so he was Moses' father-in-law (Exod. 2. 18–21). Hobab, therefore, was his brother-in-law. Just as they were on the eve of departure from Sinai to go into the promised land, Moses sought to persuade him to accompany them. His first appeal was made in the words: "Come with us and we will do thee good." Hobab declined this invitation. Then Moses used another method as he said: "Thou shalt be to us instead of eyes." The words immediately following this appeal, "And they set forward from the mount of Jehovah," leaves no room for doubt that Hobab went. Wherein lay the difference between the argument which failed and that which succeeded? However good the intention, and however true the statement, the first appeal was to selfishness. It promised the man that he should gain something by going. The second was an appeal for help. It suggested that his knowledge of the wilderness would be of service, that he could do something for others which would be of real value to them. The first failed. The second succeeded. Is there not something here that we do well to consider? We are very prone to make our appeal to selfishness—granted, on a high level, but still to selfishness. Would not the appeal that calls to service and sacrifice to the heroic be far more forceful? One thing is certain, and that is that this was the supreme note in Christ's. call to men in the days of His flesh. He certainly desires us to come to Him that He may do us good; but He ever calls us as those whom He needs to serve Him, by serving others.

The mixed multitude that was among them fell a lusting.—*Num.* 11. 4.

The mixed multitude was a perpetual source of trouble to Israel. For an explanation of this multitude we must refer to Exodus 12. 38. There the statement is simply made that such a multitude accompanied them on their journeys. They were merely camp-followers. The fact of their presence was apparently innocent and harmless. The issue proves that it was far otherwise. The influence on the children of Israel of these people was that of making them dissatisfied. The statement in Exodus shows that they were wealthy, having "flocks and herds, even very much cattle." Perhaps that accounted for the willingness of the people of God to permit them to accompany them. The fact that they had such possessions would seem also to suggest that they were more than adventurers. They had a certain interest in the migration—one of curiosity, perhaps. The only thing that is certain is that they were not of the Theocracy; and not having true part or lot in the Divine movement, they fell a-lusting after the things of Egypt, and infected the people of God with the same unholy desire. What significant teaching there is in this story for the Church of God! How often she has been defiled and weakened by the influence of camp-followers! The mixed multitude which have no vital relation with Christ, but who follow out of curiosity and interest that is less than absolute, are a perpetual menace to the people of God. Better far, a fellowship of souls all actually sharing the life of Christ, and loyal to His enterprise, though it be small in numbers, than a crowd of those who follow outwardly, but in whose heart there is yet the lusting for the things of evil.

The Lord spake suddenly unto Moses.—*Num.* 12. 4.

That is an arresting statement. It marks an action on the part of God, so definite and immediate, that to Moses His speech was that of suddenness. It lends emphasis to the importance of this story. It is the story of rebellion against Moses, the God-appointed leader of the people, on the part of Miriam his sister, and Aaron his brother. The occasion was that of Moses' marriage with a Cushite woman. This was not the reason of it. It gave Miriam and Aaron an opportunity of acting upon a deeper feeling of jealousy which was present in their hearts. They resented the exercise of Moses' authority, evidently desiring to share it with him in a larger degree. The story illustrates a great truth in human experience. Sooner or later, if there be hidden evil, circumstances will occur in which it will be outwardly manifested. Stern and majestic was the Divine method of dealing with this outbreak. The sudden summons of God brought these three people out from the host, and into the immediate presence of God. Then in the plainest terms Jehovah vindicated His servant. Thus are we taught that God will not permit any interference with His appointments. To question the authority of those whom He appoints is to question His authority. There is great beauty in the end of the story. Aaron pleaded with Moses on behalf of his sister. Moses pleaded with God on her behalf. The cry was heard, and after seven days Miriam was restored. Surely He is ever a God ready to pardon. Nevertheless, the warning was solemn and severe, showing that rebellion is most reprehensible when it is manifested by the most highly placed.

Howbeit.—*Num.* 13. 28.

This is the revealing word as to the report of the majority of the spies. The Hebrew word means *cessation*, an end; and when used adverbially it signifies, no further! It suggests that what has already been said is all that can be said in that direction; and therefore that now other things are to be said, which will have a corrective effect on the things already said. The report of these men so far has been entirely favourable concerning the land. They were convinced of its desirability. They had clearly seen its excellencies. "Howbeit," they had also seen the difficulties, the strength of the inhabitants, the fenced cities, and the compactness of the enemies they would have to encounter. They had seen themselves also in comparison with these enemies, and they were but as grasshoppers. The remarkable fact is that in their report there was no reference to God. They would seem to have lost sight of Him completely for the time being. In that lay the secret of their failure. Human calculations are not wrong. They are wrong when they do not take account of all the quantities; and unutterably wrong when they omit the chief quantity. What a revealing story it is! How constantly we are all in danger of making the same mistake! The way of God is revealed to us; we see it, and recognize all its advantages; "howbeit," we see the difficulties, and become so occupied with them as to lose sight of God. Then our hearts fail us, and fear paralyses us, and quite naturally. The foes massed against the people of God are always mightier than are they, if they are called upon to act alone.

If the Lord delight in us, then . . . —*Num.* 14. 8.

These are the outstanding words of the minority report. They reveal the difference in viewpoint between the minority and the majority. These men saw all the others saw, and more. They had clear apprehension of the goodness of the land; they were by no means blind to the formidable nature of the difficulties that stood between them and possession. But they saw God. They started with that vision, and saw everything else in its light. Therefore the enemies were "as bread" for them; their defences were removed, if indeed Jehovah were with them. Yet these men also saw that there was a condition and they named it in the words: "If Jehovah delight in us." In these words there was surely the recognition of a fact, and the statement of a responsibility. The fact was patent. Jehovah did delight in them. He had ransomed them from slavery, brought them to Himself, provided for all their need, promised them this very land. What further proofs could they have of His delight in them? Nevertheless, they were in danger of placing themselves outside the benefits of that delight, by their rebellion and their unworthy fear. These things were surely written for our learning. Every call of God to His people is a call to those in whom He delights. Therefore they should know that no difficulties need daunt them. They are not called to meet them in their own strength. He will be with them in the path of obedience.

. . . That they put upon the fringe of each border a cord of blue.— *Num.* 15. 38.

This was a sign for the coming days of wilderness wanderings. The first part of the chapter is occupied with the repetition of certain laws already given, and their enforcement as binding. This repetition and enforcement are explained by the opening words: "When ye be come into the land." In the Divine discipline of the people for their failure in faith, they were about to turn their faces from the land which they might at once have possessed; and in this reiteration of certain laws for their dwelling within that land, there was at once a prophecy of the ultimate fulfilment of Divine intention, and a means of preserving in their minds the principles of the law by which they were to be governed. It would also serve to remind them that even in the wilderness they were to live as those belonging to the land, even though for the time being they were excluded from it. The purpose of this cord of blue was distinctly declared. It was a symbol of the deepest truth concerning their national life. The colour blue was always the symbol of heavenly beauty, and thus they were constantly reminded that they were under the direct government of God. It was to help them to remember the one great fact which they had forgotten, when they had permitted the difficulties of the way to fill them with fear. In the fuller light and glory of our fellowship with the Father, through the Son, by the Holy Spirit, such material signs should not be necessary, but it would be a daring thing to say that they are wholly wrong. If some outward sign helps us to remember, then let us use it; only let us ever fear lest we become so accustomed to it, that we forget its true significance.

The Lord will show who are His, and who is holy.—*Num.* 16. 5.

This chapter gives the account of a strong and organized opposition to Moses and Aaron; and in these words we have the appeal which Moses made for a Divine decision. The attitude taken up by those who organized the movement was plausible and popular. It was democratic in its expression: "All the congregation are holy, every one of them, and Jehovah is among them." It was a plea for equal rights, and for independence of action. Moses chose the only method of reply to such an attitude. It was that of calling for the submission of the case to God, Whose authority was called in question. The answer was immediate. When presently the censers of the offending men were beaten out into a covering for the altar, a provision was made for a perpetual witness to the danger of intruding upon service in any other way than that of the Divine appointment. The whole story serves to show how false may be the most apparently popular movements. The voice of the people is by no means always the voice of God. The declaration that all men have equal rights may be entirely false. It is fundamentally true that all men have an equal right to direct dealings with God, and to receive the law of life from Him. But within that law are provisions which give to each man his service, and no man has any right to serve in any way not directly appointed by God. We have no right to choose the place or character of what we shall do. Therefore we sin against God when we rebel against the exercise by any man of an authority which has been given him by God.

The man whom I shall choose, his rod shall bud.—*Num.* 17. 5.

Thus a supernatural sign was given to the people in vindication of Aaron's right to the position which he held. The reason for this was clearly stated in the words: "I will make to cease from Me the murmurings of the children of Israel which they murmur against you." Mark well the form of this statement. The murmuring of the people was against Moses and Aaron, but God saw that it was murmuring against Himself. The sign was efficacious; for while the spirit of rebellion manifested itself subsequently in other ways, it may safely be said that any complaint against the rights of the God-appointed priesthood ceased from this time. The blossoming and fruitbearing of Aaron's rod undoubtedly resulted from the direct and supernatural action of God, but it was in itself a most suggestive sign. It taught both the people and the priests that their prevailing mediation was due, not to anything inherent in themselves, but to the direct action of Jehovah through them. As the rods of the other princes were unable to bud or blossom or bear fruit of themselves, so also was that of Aaron, apart from this Divine action. The proof of authority was this manifestation of Divine appointment in life. The principle still obtains. All our fruit is from God. Its absence proves that we have no authority. Its presence proves that we have, but also that the authority is finally His, and not our own. Fruitbearing will ever give us a sense of authority and deep humility of spirit.

I give you the priesthood as a service of gift.—*Num.* 18. 7.

This chapter moves in the same realm of thought, that of the Divine appointment of the priesthood. The reason for these repetitions and re-emphases is explicitly stated in the words: "That there be wrath no more upon the children of Israel" (verse 5). A reference to the closing verses of the previous chapter (12 and 13) will show how the recent events had produced a spirit of dejection almost amounting to despair in the minds of the people. Such a mental mood was wholly healthy, for it proved that the people had profited by the severe judgment that had fallen upon them. To this troubled condition of mind these words were now spoken, and through them there runs the repeated affirmation of the fact of the Divine appointment of the service of the priesthood. Among the rest these words, "I give you the priesthood as a service of gift," emphasized again the fact that these priests, and these people had done nothing to merit the provision. It was wholly one of grace, a gift from God. Therefore it was not less, but more, important that they should recognize its sanctity. This is ever so. Love demands a loyalty more thorough than anything else. To hold in contempt any provision of the Divine Love, is a most heinous sin. Whatever service is ours as a result of the giving of grace, is the most holy and sacred service, and therefore to be rendered with the uttermost devotion.

A water of separation.—*Num.* 19. 9.

This is a very interesting chapter, because it gives us the account of a new and special provision made for these people during the time they would be moving about from place to place. When in the course of such movement the camp was not pitched, and therefore the ordinary methods of the ceremonial law could not be observed, provision was made for ceremonial cleansing. This water of impurity was water with which ashes, specially provided, were mixed. With solemn ceremony and most minute carefulness, a red heifer was sacrificed. The whole of it was to be burned, and as it burned, cedar wood and hyssop and scarlet were mingled with it. The ashes from this burning were those appointed for mixture with water in order to prepare this special "water of impurity." Without attempting to deal with all the details of the suggestiveness of the sacrifice and the burning, we note this special provision. It emphasized the need for constant cleansing, but it also revealed the fact that there need be no postponement of such cleansing in times when the duly appointed place and method were not available. In the course of our reading it reminds us of the wonder of God's fulfilment in Christ of all thus typified. For us, there are, or should be definitely appointed times and places for confession and the claiming of cleansing; but we need not carry the burden and pollution when, for any reason, we are unable to avail ourselves of these. The infinite worth and merit of our Lord's redeeming work are available to us at all times, and in all places. Let us never fail to apprehend this truth, or to appropriate this grace.

Because ye believed not in Me, to sanctify Me in the eyes of the children of Israel, therefore ye shall not bring this assembly into the land which I have given them.—*Num.* 20. 12.

Perhaps there is no story in all the Old Testament more searching for all who are called to lead the people of God, than this of the failure of Moses. There is no honest heart which can fail to understand the action of Moses. What he did was most natural. Therein lay the wrong of it. If that sounds a hard thing to say, let the story be considered. The people murmured against Moses because they were without water; and that, in spite of all the evidences they had received of the Divine care and provision. Moses and Aaron went to Jehovah, and received instructions what to do. These instructions had in them no note of rebuke. Thus assured, Moses went before the people, and, as the Psalmist said, "spake unadvisedly with his lips" (Psa. 106. 33). By this manifestation of anger, which as we have said was so very natural, the servant of God misrepresented God to the people. His failure was due to the fact that for the moment his faith failed to reach the highest level of activity. He still believed in God, and in His power; but he did not believe in Him *to sanctify Him in the eyes of His people.* The lesson is indeed a very searching one. Right things may be done in so wrong a way as to produce evil results. There is a hymn in which in the first two lines we may miss the deep meaning, if we are not thoughtful—

Lord, speak to me that I may speak
In living echoes of Thy tone.

That is far more than a prayer that we may be able to deliver the Lord's message. It is rather that we may do so in His tone, with His temper. This is where Moses failed, and for this failure he was excluded from the Land.

Any man, when he looked unto the serpent of brass, he lived.—*Num.* 21. 9.

And that, not because there was any healing virtue in the brazen serpent, but because the look was one of obedience to the Divine command. It was a simple provision, but it touched the deepest facts of life. These people had sinned in their rebellion against the government of God. They were suffering through the Divine action consequent upon their sin, for "Jehovah sent fiery serpents among the people"; and that as punishment. The serpent on the pole was there by the command of God, and for their healing they were told to look at it. In doing so, they bowed to the Divine will, and thus made it possible for God to restore them and heal them. The principles revealed are of abiding application. Rebellion always issues in suffering and disaster. Repentance and return ever lead to healing itself. Thus we see how the sanctions of God's righteousness are preserved in the exercise of His mercy. It is so in regard to man's salvation by Christ. The benefit of His atoning work may only be appropriated by return to the government of God. This return consists in repentance and faith, whereby men turn to God from idols, and commit themselves to Him through the One Whom He has appointed. Thus in infinite grace He has made a way back to Himself, and so to healing for all men, which is of the simplest nature as to human action, but which is of the very essence of His righteous requirements.

I cannot go beyond the word of the Lord my God, to do less or more.—*Num.* 22. 18.

These words record a truth which Balaam knew. If he acted in accordance with them all would have been well with him. He tried to act in response to the base motive of greed. Hence his disaster. We have no knowledge of who he was,

save that he was the son of Beor, and dwelt at Pethor—by the river. He appears first as a man of understanding, and one who realized his limitation by the Divine government, as these words reveal. The story is startling. He was first forbidden, and afterwards commanded to go. The only explanation that is satisfactory is that, while attempting to maintain an external obedience to this supreme will of God, his heart was lusting after the riches offered to him by Balak. That is revealed to us in the words of Peter: "Balaam the son of Beor, who loved the hire of wrongdoing." In all this we see the working of a perpetual principle. Man is ever compelled to work out what is deepest within him, while all the time God, by that very compulsion, is making possible the change of that deepest thing, if it be evil. Circumstances are ever overruled by God, for the development to outward manifestation of the inward facts of life. This man loved the hire of wrongdoing, and therefore he was compelled to go forward, even though the sin of his action was revealed by the Divine interventions. He was attempting to compromise between loyalty to the Divine government and love of hire, greed, and the deepest motive was this very greed. Thus in the fullest sense, he could not go beyond the word of Jehovah. By that he was held and compelled.

I took thee to curse mine enemies, and, behold, thou hast blessed them altogether.—*Num.* 23. 11.

This was Balak's word about the prophesying of Balaam; and how true it was is evident as his four messages are considered. They constitute a remarkable unfolding of truth concerning the people of God. The first consisted of a vision of the nation as separated from all others, and its central words are: "Lo, it is a people that dwell alone." It ended with a sigh which shows how profound was this man's conviction of the high privilege of Israel: "Let me die the death of the righteous: And let my last end be like his!" The second prophecy celebrated the fact that the people, being God-governed and God-guided must be victorious. Its central statement is: "Jehovah his God is with him; And the shout of a king is among them." It was after the first of these that Balak used these particular words. After the second he asked that nothing more should be said: but now Balaam insisted that he must utter all Jehovah had to say. The story is a remarkable revelation of how completely a man is in the grasp of God. While Balaam was being compelled to carry out his deepest desires, he was absolutely prevented from uttering a word, which could in any wise harm the people of God. How unutterably futile is that pride of will, which makes men imagine that they can escape the will of

God! They may change their experience of the power of God, but they cannot escape from it.

And the Spirit of God came upon him.—*Num.* 24. 2.

In this chapter we have the third and fourth of Balaam's prophecies. After the first and second, he was taken to yet another place of vision, and from the top of Peor looked out over the wilderness. Knowing that it was the purpose of God to bless Israel, he used no enchantments this time. But he did not seek the word of Jehovah as on the two previous occasions. It would appear as though there was an attempt on his part to speak from himself, and this perchance in the interest of the greed that was in his heart. He could not thus escape. When he did not seek God, the Spirit of God came upon him, and again he spoke only the things which God would have him speak. This third prophecy consisted of a vision of a people victorious and prosperous, a glorious forecast of ultimate conditions. The central words were: "How goodly are thy tents, O Jacob, Thy tabernacles, O Israel." This message aroused Balak's anger, and he bade Balaam be gone. But if he would, he could not. There was yet another word of God to be proclaimed. Its keynote was: "There shall come forth a Star out of Jacob," and it foretold the ultimate victory of God and therefore of His people. While the story of Balaam is full of solemn warning, the account of God's dealings with him and Balak is full of encouragement. The fact that those who desired to curse were compelled to utter only words of blessing, is significant; but even more wonderful were the messages thus delivered, as showing the Divine purpose for His people.

I give unto him My covenant of peace—*Num.* 25. 12.

In the letter to the church at Pergamum we learn that "Balaam . . . taught Balak to cast a stumbling-block before the children of Israel, to eat things sacrificed to idols, and to commit fornication" (Rev. 2. 14). This chapter opens with the declaration that: "The people began to play the harlot with the daughters of Moab; for they called the people unto the sacrifices of their gods; and the people did eat, and bowed down to their gods." This, then, was the work of Balaam. When he could not utter a curse against Israel, he taught Balak how to seduce them from their loyalty. The action appeared to be one of pure neighbourliness, but it was a corrupting of the covenant. The story of Phinehas is that of one man, loyal to God, and jealous for his honour, daring to violate these false conventionalities, and visiting with swift and terrible punishment one daring wrongdoer. That action stayed the plague, and saved Israel. Action like that of Phine-

has is not easy. It brings the man who dare take it into the place of grave peril, especially when it is directed against some popular movement. Yet to that man is given God's covenant of peace. That is the only peace which is worth while for man or nation. The price of it may be stern conflict, and a hazarding of all ease and quietness: but it is peace indeed, for it is right relationship with the principles of righteousness, and so with God.

There was not left a man of them, save Caleb the son of Jephunneh, and Joshua the son of Nun.—*Num.* 26. 65.

With this chapter we begin what is really the third and last section of this Book of Numbers. In it we have the account of the second numbering of the people, and their preparation for coming into possession of the land from which they had been excluded for forty years. In the census many of the names occurring in the first are omitted, and others have taken their place. Two men only of those who had come to the margin of the land were now to pass over into its possession. These were Caleb and Joshua, the men who constituted the minority, the men who had seen much more than enemies and walled cities, because their vision of God had been unclouded. Loyal in heart to their God and their faith they had shared the discipline of the nation, and had seen the whole generation of unbelieving men pass away. They had been preserved, an elect remnant, and a living link with the great deliverance wrought by the Exodus. Thus we see God's continuity of purpose, notwithstanding the change of persons. It is always so. I may fail to enter in because of unbelief and disobedience, but the day of entry will come. Happy are those who being of another spirit, walk with God, not only through the processes, but into the accomplishment, of His purposes. The secret of such life is always the same, that of a clear vision of God. To lose that, is to see all other things in a false light, and to be either lured by the deceitfulness of sin, or filled with unworthy fears. To see God, is to see everything in the true light, and so to be able to walk without stumbling.

When thou hast seen it, thou also shalt be gathered unto thy people.— *Num.* 27 13.

There is something inexpressibly solemn in the story of Moses. In the plan of God the time was come when it was necessary that the people should go in and possess the land from which they had been excluded so long. Moses was not permitted to enter with them. In a sad hour he had failed to represent God truthfully to the people (chapter 20); and this was the punishment of that failure. There was no relaxing of this discipline even in the case of this man. Nevertheless there was great tenderness in God's dealings with him in these closing scenes, and the evidence of his greatness is marked by his perfect acquiescence in the will of God. When this command to ascend the mountain, and look upon the land he could not enter, was given to him, his one anxiety was for the flock of God, that it might have a shepherd. He knew, as no other man knew, their weakness, and the necessity for one to lead them according to the will of God. The request was granted, and to him was given the joy and satisfaction of knowing that the appointed man was one of God's own choosing. The account of his going is given at the end of Deuteronomy, but these words bring the facts before us in this book, which is the book revealing the Divine discipline of failing people; and it serves to keep before us the fact that the most faithful servants of God cannot escape the results of their failures in this life. The compensations of grace are found afterwards, and to this man it was given to

. . . stand with glory wrapt around
On the hills he never trod,
And speak of the strife which won
  our life,
With the incarnate Son of God.

My oblation, My food for My offerings, made by fire, of a sweet savour unto Me, shall ye observe to offer unto Me in their due season.— Num. 28. 2.

In this and the next chapter we have a repetition of the laws concerning the great religious observances of the nation. This repetition is an orderly statement covering the whole year, and thus showing its relationship throughout to spiritual things. It was thus set forth anew on the eve of their entering upon possession of the land, in order that the arrangements for worship might be duly carried out. First we find the religious rites connected with the smaller time divisions, those of the days, and the weeks, and the months (28. 1–15). Then we have those associated with the year, those of the Spring-time, Passover, and Pentecost (28. 16–31), and finally those of the Autumn, Trumpets, Atonement, Tabernacles (29). The words we have emphasized are those which, introducing this section, reveal the value of these rites. The first word, "My oblation," covers the whole ground; the rest interpret. The word here rendered *oblation* by our revisers is the Hebrew word Korban. It always refers to the present which secures admittance. To-day in the East it is called the Face-offering. Thus we see the meaning of these religious rites. They recognized the relation of men to God, and their need of Him for all life. They need Him every day, every week, every month, every year. Because all time is

thus arranged for in Divine relationship so also is all activity. If the time be redeemed, all activity is sanctified.

These ye shall offer unto the Lord in your set feasts, beside your vows, and your freewill offerings—Num. 29. 39.

Thus, as at the beginning of this section (see previous note), the real value of these religious rites was declared; at its close, stress is now laid upon the fact that all these things are to be done as to Jehovah. The observances which sanctified the year were far more than a recognition of certain religious principles; they were means of positive and direct dealing with God Himself. For that reason all were sacrificial. Not only must the worshippers bring gifts —they must bring gifts which were ordained, and in which the necessity for expiation of sin was perpetually recognized. A glance over the whole ground again will show how an increase in the number of sacrifices, and a growing importance in the religious rites, is marked in the growth of the time divisions. Daily, one lamb in the morning, and one in the evening, was offered. Weekly, that is on the Sabbath, two he-lambs were offered, in addition to the continual burnt-offering. Monthly, two young bullocks, one ram, and seven he-lambs were offered, again in addition to the continual burnt-offering. That increase is most marked in the great yearly feasts. All this is very full of significance. We need God; and to gain what we need, we must condition all our days by approach to Him through the putting away of sin. The one perfect sacrifice is provided in Christ. We must never begin a day, a week, a month, a year, apart from the appropriation by faith of the value of that Sacrifice. Only thus have we right of access to God; only thus, any hope that life will be what it ought to be.

These are the statutes which the Lord commanded Moses, between a man and his wife, between a father and his daughter.—Num. 30. 16.

This is really a very arresting chapter. At first it may seem to have very little application to our modern civilization. But if it be carefully considered, it will be seen that it consists of a series of enactments based upon a fundamental principle of human society. The chapter is concerned with vows; and principally those of women. Let us state these provisions in other words. The vow of a man is declared to be absolutely binding; from it there is no release. In the case of women this is not so. If a woman dwelling in her father's house take a vow upon her, her father has the power to forbid, and so to release her. If he do not so, then the vow is binding. In the case of a woman dwelling with her husband, the husband has a like power. If he do not exercise it, then her vow is also binding. In the case of a widow, or one divorced, if her vow is made in her widowhood or while she is divorced, it is absolutely binding. If it was made while she dwelt with her husband, and he forbade it, she is released. If he did not forbid it, then it is binding upon her. Now what did these careful enactments mean? They are of the utmost importance, as they reveal the Divine conception of the necessity for the maintenance of the unity of the family. In no family must there be two supreme authorities; and here, as always in the Divine arrangement, the headship is vested in the husband and father. It can easily be seen how, were this otherwise, through religious vows discord and probably disruption in family life would ensue. The measure in which modern society has departed from this ideal, is the measure of its insecurity.

Moses was wroth with the officers of the host.—*Num.* 31. 14.

This is a chapter of terror, recording an avenging, by the order of God, which was terrible indeed. We have stressed these particular words because they emphasize all the rest. Moses was wroth with the officers, not because of the severity of the judgment they had executed on Midian, but rather because they had failed to carry out the judgment completely. In order to understand this we must recognize the cause of the wrath. Here we touch again the history of Balaam. He was still living, and from the fact that he was numbered among the slain, we may safely infer that he was still exerting his evil influence. This man, who under Divine compulsion had been compelled to bless when he intended to curse, had yet wrought the most terrible evil in Israel, in that he had been the means of causing the nation to commit fornication with the corrupt people of Midian. The words of Moses show that this had been definite and dreadful (see verses 15, 16). The holy seed was polluted. Therefore the judgment upon the polluting people was drastic. Again we say, this is a chapter of terror; but it is well that we recognize that there is a false pity which is of the essence of cruelty. That is true love which makes no terms with evil, and which is able, in circumstances of stern necessity, to adopt stern measures and carry them out without relenting.

Shall your brethren go to the war, and shall ye sit here!—*Num.* 32. 6.

In these words Moses revealed the wrong principle actuating Reuben, Gad, and the half-tribe of Manasseh. They desired to settle and prosper on the wrong side of Jordan in order to escape the responsibilities of war. Moses, by his speech and action, brought them to a confession of willingness to share that responsibility with the rest of the tribes, but the whole story is one of failure. It was a wrong desire on the part of the tribes. The distinctly avowed purpose of Jehovah was that they should go over Jordan. They desired to compromise, and indeed succeeded in doing so. In the case of Moses it is noticeable that we have no account of his seeking Divine guidance, as he had so constantly done in other matters. His own first conviction was against granting the request. He pointed out that in essence it was of the same spirit which their fathers had manifested forty years before, and which had resulted in the long and weary discipline. Urging their plea and promising to cross the Jordan to help in the coming conflict, the desire of these people triumphed, and Moses permitted their settlement. Subsequent events proved the wrong of that decision. The whole event should teach us that no merely selfish desire for early and easy realization of peace and prosperity should ever be permitted to interfere with the declared will of God. No policy of compromise can ever justify a coming short of Divine purpose. Peaceable settlements on the wrong side of the river are the inspiration and causes of conflict in subsequent days.

Ye shall drive out all the inhabitants of the land from before you, and destroy all their figured stones . . . and demolish all their high places.—*Num.* 33. 52.

This was the distinct command of God to a people whom He had wondrously led and prepared, by delivering them from Egypt's slavery, and disciplining them for forty years in the wilderness. They were now to come into the possession of the land which He had appointed to them. They were His people, and the purpose of their coming into that land was that of the manifestation of Himself, and that of the carrying out of His programme. While their possession was to be in order to the preservation of the nation until the Deliverer of all the nations should come, it was in the first place in order to the cleansing of that land from a people utterly polluted and corrupt. It was necessary that the latter should be utterly dispossessed, and every trace of their worship swept away, wherever found. This charge was accompanied by warnings, uttered in simple terms, and yet of the most solemn nature. No false pity or selfish motive was to operate in such fashion as to leave any corrupting influence behind. The unequivocal command to drive out all, was based upon the tenderest regard of God for the well-being of the chosen people, and through them, the whole race. To tolerate what God has condemned to destruction, is to retain what in itself will prove to be a source of continual difficulty and suffering. The most solemn words of all are those with which the chapter ends: "And it shall come to pass, that as I thought to do unto them, so will I do unto you." God's elections to blessing are dependent upon obedience to His will.

This is the land which ye shall inherit by lot.—*Num.* 34. 13.

In this chapter we have the arrangements Divinely made for the positive side of the purpose for which the people were to be brought into this land. They were really to take possession of it, and so, to realize its resources and their own national life. Again the Divine care is manifested, in that the division was made by Divine choice and arrangement. A careful examination will show how, as to amount of territory, that division was based upon the comparative needs of the tribes; and as to position, it was based upon the will of Jehovah, which unquestionably was based upon His perfect knowledge of the characteristics of the different tribes. The divisions given were for those who were about to pass over into the land beyond Jordan. Reuben and Gad and the half-tribe of Manasseh had no part in this inheritance. Thrice over it is said: "They have received." They had made their own choice, and it was now ratified. Long after, they were the first to be captured and carried away. While the arrangement for division was Divine, human instruments were appointed to see them carried out. They were the priest Eleazar; the leader, Joshua; and the princes of the tribes. Among these, one name arrests our attention. It is that of Caleb. Thus he reaped the reward of his fidelity. How wonderfully this story illustrates the order and beauty of the Divine government, and of the principles of obedience through which we may derive the blessing and benefit thereof.

Ye shall appoint you cities to be cities of refuge for you.—*Num.* 35. 11.

The provision of these cities of refuge was a proof of the mercy and justice of God. These people were naturally fierce and vindictive. The law of God had made life sacred, and the punishment of taking it had been solemnly declared in the words: "Whoso sheddeth man's blood, by man shall his blood be shed." Yet it was quite possible that in connection with the taking of human life there might be extenuating circumstances. For premeditated murder there was no forgiveness, and for the murderer in such case, no city of refuge was provided. For killing in haste, under sudden impulse of passion, such provision was made. These cities were not provided that men might evade justice, but that justice might be ensured. It is quite possible to do unjust things in the name of justice. It was against such a possibility that these cities were provided. Further, the fact that a man-slayer reached one of these cities did not ensure him against enquiry and investigation. It provided for the possibility thereof, and indeed made it obligatory. Thus the man had an opportunity of explanation, and the nation the certainty of just action. The wrong of taking human life was marked in the case of the man-slayer who was not found worthy of the death-penalty, in that it was provided that he must remain in the city until the death of the high priest. It is a wonderful illustration of the strict and impartial justice of God in all His dealings with sin. While it cannot be excused, the sinner is never punished unjustly.

The children of Israel shall cleave every one to the inheritance of the tribe of his fathers.—*Num.* 36. 7.

This word was uttered in connection with the question of the inheritance of women, which had already been raised through the application of the daughters of Zelophehad. It was now opened again by the heads of the tribes. It was possible that these women might marry men out of other tribes. In that case their inheritance would pass over to another tribe. Therefore it was now enacted that they must only marry within their own tribe. By this law, the Divine purpose that the settlement in the land should be orderly and sustained, was ensured of realization. Thus closes the Book of Numbers. It is essentially the Book of the Wilderness. The nation was on the eve of entering the land. The actual history is resumed in the last chapter of Deuteronomy. It is impossible to have studied this book without having been impressed, first, with the failure of the people. It is a record of long-continued stubbornness and folly. Yet we are prevented from thinking hardly of this people by the fact that the book is a record of the unwearying patience and perpetual faithfulness of God. Throughout, the progress of a Divine movement is manifest. It is not of man, but of Jehovah. Indeed, it is hardly a history of the Hebrew people, being far more a revelation of the sure procedure of God toward the final working out into human history of the redemptive purpose of His heart; the first movements of which were recorded in Genesis, the central work of which was accomplished by the Son of God, and the final victories of which are not yet.

DEUTERONOMY

. . . the Lord your God, Who went before you in the way, to seek you out a place to pitch your tents in.—Deut. 1. 32, 33.

This Book of Deuteronomy is didactic rather than historical. Its actual history covers a very brief period, probably not many days. It consists of a collection of the final discourses of Moses. The first of these (1. 6–4. 43) is retrospective. In it, Moses dealt with the three stages of their wanderings—from Horeb to Kadesh-Barnea (1. 6–46); from Kadesh-Barnea to Heshbon (2); and from Heshbon to Beth-peor (3)—and then exhorted them to obedience (4. 1–43). In dealing with the first stage, he reminded them of the Divine call which caused them to leave Horeb, and recalled their rebellion in the matter of the spies. The purpose of the review was that of setting all the facts of their experience in the light of God's government. Their disturbance at Horeb was that of the direct command of God. The way of the wilderness was a terrible one, but they had not been left to grope their way through it alone. In this connection the words quoted above were used, and they are very full of revealing beauty. Through them we learn that in the government of God nothing is haphazard. How often life is a wilderness way! As we journey, there seems no map, no plan, no time-table. The truth is that our God is not only accompanying us on the march; He is ever going before us, selecting the places of our pausing. Wherever at night we pitch our tents, the place is chosen by God. That is all we need to know.

Ye have compassed this mountain long enough.—Deut. 2. 3.

After the failure of faith at Kadesh-Barnea, the people had turned back into the wilderness, and had tarried long in the neighbourhood of Mount Seir. Then again the command came to them to move northward. All that Moses told this people, they already knew—as to the actual facts of the long and tedious processes of these forty years. The great burden of his message was that of reminding them how, even amid such sorrowful and suffering discipline they had still been remembered and guided by God. This government of God is a fact which breaks in upon our consciousness in many ways. Over and over again, when we have reached some place of comparative quietness, He upsets all our plans and purposes, and we find ourselves commanded to new journeyings, and those often not by ways we would have chosen for ourselves. He is constantly disturbing us. These disturbances are never capricious. He is always leading us toward the fulfilment of His own purposes, and that means that He is leading us toward the realization of our highest good. And yet again, it is not only true that the end to which He leads us is good; it is equally true that He leads us by no unnecessary pathways. There are a meaning and a value in every stretch of the road, however rough and tortuous it may be. We learn lessons in the region of Mount Seir which can be learned nowhere else; we discover God in the country of Moab as we could do in no other region. Let us, then, ever rejoice in His commands, however much they disturb us. His will is always "good and acceptable and perfect."

Ye shall not fear them: for the Lord your God, He it is that fighteth for you.—Deut. 3. 22.

To these people fearlessness was a duty. Over and over again this command was laid upon them. They had no right to be afraid. Moses now argued for this by reminding them of how in the cases where already they had been at war, they had been victorious. But the supreme note in his argument was that contained in these words. The reason for these victories, and the reason therefore why they should be without fear, was that it was Jehovah their God Who fought for them. This needs to be understood. We must be careful to recognize that it does not so much mean that God was on their side, as that they were on the side of God. God would not have fought for them, if their cause had been unrighteous. It was because in their warfare they were carrying out His will, that He fought for them. This is an important distinction of perpetual application. Lincoln was once asked if he thought God was on his side, to which he replied that it had never occurred to him to ask such a question, but that he was persistently anxious to discover whether he were on the side of God. In no conflict have we any right to ask or expect that God will fight for us, save as we know we are with Him. When we do know that, we have equally no right to be afraid. Fear is disloyalty; it questions the supremacy of righteousness and the power of God. Fear is paralysis; it cuts us off from contact with the forces of righteousness, for it cuts us off from fellowship with God.

Lest thou forget.—Deut. 4. 9.

Having surveyed the history of the Divine guidance and governance of the people from Horeb to Beth-peor, Moses exhorted them to obedience. He based his appeal upon the greatness of their God, and the perfection of His law. He challenged them to put their God and His commandments into comparison with all others. He reminded them that their existence` and history as a nation were centred in a spiritual ideal. No visible form of God had been granted to them, even amid the solemn and majestic manifestations of Sinai. In the midst of this discourse he warned them, as indeed he did upon more than one occasion, not to forget. What a necessary warning this ever is! It is most strange how prone man is to forget. It is true that, while some things can never be actually forgotten, they nevertheless are constantly forgotten in the sense of being of any value. We forget the law of God, we forget the deliverances of God, we forget the disciplines of God, we forget the very love of God, in so far as memory serves us as an inspiration to true conduct, to trust, to amended life, to the loyalty which love demands. Such forgetfulness is not an aberration of intellect; it is a definite wrong done to God, a sin against Him. Memory is a non-moral function of the soul. If it is either to help or hinder it must be trained and used. When it is employed to keep certain great facts in the mind, so that they may influence the will, it is one of the greatest forces for good.

They have well said all that they have spoken. Oh, that there were such an heart in them!—Deut. 5. 28, 29.

These were the words of God to Moses, concerning what the nation had said, through the heads of the tribes and the elders, in answer to the giving of the Law; and Moses reminded the people of them as he began his second discourse, which consisted of a résumé of the laws already given. They had confessed their sense that these were indeed laws from God, had expressed their fear of God, and had asked that Moses would mediate between them and God. Of all this God said that they had spoken well, but He added: "Oh, that there were such an heart in them!" In these words we have the recognition of a persistent difficulty in human experience. The mind of man recognizes the beauty of the Divine ideal, realizes human weakness, understands the necessity for intermediation; and yet the heart of man breaks down. This touches a very deep note in human nature. The deepest fact therein, and the one most powerful in producing results, is not that of the intelligence or the mind; it is that of the desire or heart. A man becomes what he really desires. That also is the significance of the declaration: "With the heart man believeth unto righteousness." A man may be intellectually convinced that righteousness is good, but he only arrives at righteousness when his desires put confidence in the Lord of righteousness. All this shows how supremely right the great evangelists have always been, when they have represented Christ as asking for the human heart.

Thou shalt teach them diligently unto thy children.—Deut. 6. 7.

God's thought of the children, and care for them, is evidenced throughout all the enactments of the Law, and indeed in all the ceremonies of worship. A careful study of these writings from that viewpoint will show how constantly arrangements were made which would appeal to the natural curiosity of a child, inspiring it to ask questions. It was the business of parents to answer such questions, and so to instruct each successive generation in the matter of the national history in its relationship to the Divine government. So with the Law. It was the duty of parents to teach "the commandments, the statutes, and the judgments" to their children. Moreover, it is well that we remember that the fathers were principally responsible for the giving of this religious instruction. Sometimes it seems as though Christian people have lost something of this ideal, and especially Christian fathers. There is a great tendency to trust the religious teaching of our children to others than ourselves, such as preachers, Sunday-school teachers, and those who specialize in that work in one form or another. For the work of all such we cannot be too thankful; but we ought to remember that the first responsibility for the diligent teaching of the children belongs to those to whom they are entrusted as the most sacred and blessed gift of God. The teaching of the things of God by fathers and mothers has a value and a virtue which can be supplied by none other.

The Lord did not set His love upon you, nor choose you, because ye were more in number than any people.—Deut. 7. 7.

Here at the entrance to the land of their possession, the people were warned against that most persistent peril of a passion for statistics and pride of numbers. By this time they were comparatively a great nation, having an army of over six hundred thousand. They would be tempted to trust in numbers, and to fall into the gross error of imagining that God had chosen them because of their numerical strength; in other words—as Napoleon said—that God is on the side of the big battalions. Let them guard against this utterly false idea by remembering that from which they had sprung, that they "were the fewest of all peoples," and that they had multiplied under His guardian care. God is never seeking for numbers, for the sake of numbers. He is always seeking for such as "love Him, and keep His commandments." It would be entirely false to say that God cannot use great companies, but it is certainly true that quality is more than quantity with Him. If God were in need of big battalions, He could create them. That fact John the Baptist declared with a fine touch of satire when he said: "God is able of these stones to raise up children unto Abraham!" And yet how the false idea persists! Our annual reports are always in danger of giving the impression that our work is only successful in the measure in which it is capable of being expressed in impressive figures, and by "impressive" we generally mean *big*. Figures are only really impressive as they stand for those who are true, loyal, devoted. With two or three of such God can do great things anywhere.

That He might make thee know.— Deut. 8. 3.

The methods of God with His own are always those which have as their object the bringing of them to knowledge of the deepest facts of life. If we once grasp that truth, we shall have discovered a secret which will guide us continuously and rightly. The one question we should ever be asking is, what God is intending to teach us by the circumstances through which we are passing at any given time. God humbled these people, suffered them to hunger, and fed them, all for the same purpose; that they might know that their life depended, not upon position, or bread, or hunger, but upon Himself. Note carefully that they were not to learn through hunger only, but also through bread. This is very important. We are sometimes strangely prone to think that God only speaks to us through limitation and suffering. It is not so. He speaks through prosperity and through joy. In the day of adversity He certainly speaks, and we generally listen. But He also is intending to teach us in the day of abounding gladness. Let us listen then also. To the soul who realizes this, all life becomes sacramental. Every experience through which He leads us, is a sign. How often we have eyes and see not, ears and hear not; and therefore we pass through the days learning nothing, while all the time our Father is overruling all the details of them, so that we may come to fuller knowledge of life in all its deepest meaning, because we gain profounder and fuller knowledge of Himself.

Know, therefore, that the Lord thy God giveth thee not this good land to possess it for thy righteousness.— Deut. 9. 6.

In these words another peril, constantly threatening the people of God, is revealed, that, namely, of interpreting His goodness to them as resulting from their own righteousness. In the case of these very people, in process of time this was the peculiar sin that wrought their undoing. They came to look with contempt upon others, a sure sign of self-righteous pride. The result was that national exclusivism which prevented their fulfilment of pur-

pose and ensured their downfall. The matter may be stated most powerfully perhaps by a personal application. It is well, therefore, that we constantly remind ourselves that when at last life's probationary experiences are done, and we pass on to the Father's home and the greater things beyond, our right of entrance there will be that of His abounding grace alone. As to service, we must never forget our Lord's words, that having done everything, we have but done our duty, and remain unprofitable servants. As to life itself, no long triumph over temptation, or realization of the character of holiness, can be thought of as creating our claim on God. Pride in our own righteousness, satisfaction with our own goodness, trust in our own holiness, are alike foolish and reprehensible. To the soul that knows itself, it is a growing wonder that God should love us at all. That He does so, is our only confidence.

He wrote on the tables, according to the first writing.—Deut. 10. 4.

Moses now told the people again the story of how God gave him the writing of the great words of the Law a second time, and distinctly affirmed that the second tables were also written by the finger of God. In the previous chapter we read how he told them that he had broken the first two tables in the hour of his consternation in the presence of their sin in making the golden calf. What an experience this must have been to Moses! We can understand with what fulness of heart he would remember it, and refer to it in these last discourses ere he left the people. That breaking of the first tables was natural; and unintentionally, it was symbolic. That is what man has ever done with the law of God. Here then is the impressive fact about the writing of the second tables. That is what God is ever doing. The whole Bible is full of the truth that He finds a way for His banished ones to return, gives to failing man his second chance; writes again the broken law, restores the years the canker-worm has eaten, makes the marred vessel over anew, seeks and saves the lost. Upon the basis of that grace, men may hope, and start anew. In a passage of great beauty, thrilling with earnestness, Moses summarized the requirements of God in view of His grace. Let these be considered with care. The people were to fear Him, that is reverence; to walk in His ways, that is obedience; to love Him, that is worship; to serve Him, that is co-operation; to keep His commandments, that is fidelity.

A land which the Lord thy God careth for.—Deut. 11. 12.

This is an arresting description of the Holy Land, and the place it occupies in the world geographically and historically is equally remarkable. As to location, it is central. Granted the realization of completed civilization in all the other lands, with accompanying perfected means of inter-communication, it would be better suited than any other place on earth for the seat of world-wide government. Under such conditions, thither would the tribes go up easily; and in the intellectual and spiritual light of its capital city, all the nations of the earth might walk; and into it, send their glory and their honour. Its history is covered by the naming of three names. Abraham, Moses, Jesus; these three forming a sequence in the Divine movements therein. Its climate varies from Alpine cold on Hermon, to tropical heats in the region of the Dead Sea. It is a land of abounding water. Its soil is fertile, especially in Bashan and Sharon, and is capable of supporting a large population if properly cultivated. The vicissitudes of its conditions have been very varied, and have had distinct relationships with the spiritual condition of its inhabitants. In the light of Biblical reference, and of its own history interpreted by such reference, it is impossible to think of it without reverence. It is the land for which God careth. He makes it fruitful or barren. That is its story in the past. There can be no doubt in the mind of the student of these Holy Writings that it will yet be the earthly centre of the Kingdom of God. On the slopes of Olivet the feet of the King shall yet actually stand, and from the City of the great King, the law shall yet go forth, in obedience to which man shall realize the highest of life.

Ye shall rejoice in all that ye put your hand unto, ye and your households, wherein the Lord thy God hath blessed thee.—*Deut.* 12. 7.

These words occur amid the most careful and urgent instructions on the matter of worship, as it was to be observed by these people when they came into the land. All the false places of worship which they would find in the land, were to be utterly destroyed. In that land, God would appoint them a place of worship; attendance at which was to be obligatory. That is to say, that they must go and worship at this place; and that they must not set up any other place of worship. The particular value of these words is that they reveal the Divine thought of worship. It is an exercise of rejoicing, resulting from blessedness. God blesses men, and in that blessedness they rejoice before Him. It is well that we remember this. Solemnity, reverence, awe, there must ever be, when men draw near to God in worship; but solemnity is not sadness, reverence is not cringing fear, awe is not dulness. All our worship should have the note of joy, of gladness. It should be full of song. It should be of such a glad nature that all our households, children and servants, should

find happiness therein. If when we worship, we do, in special sense, come into the presence of God, then let us remember that in His presence is fulness of joy, and at His right hand are pleasures for evermore. There is a place for sadness, for contrition, for penitence before God; but that is the place of preparation for worship. When that preparation is fulfilled, worship becomes a joy and a gladness.

If thy brother, the son of thy mother, or thy son, or thy daughter, or the wife of thy bosom, or thy friend, which is as thine own soul, entice thee secretly. . . .—*Deut.* 13. 6.

The section of this discourse of Moses in which these words are found begins in the previous chapter at verse twenty-nine, and runs through this whole chapter. It consists of express warnings against idolatry. It is a very valuable chapter, because it reveals the ways by which men may be seduced from the pure worship of God to the false worship of idols. The first is that of curiosity. The people were charged not to indulge such curiosity by inquiring after false methods of worship (12. 29-32). The second is that of being influenced by signs and wonders wrought by false prophets. No such sign or wonder must draw the soul away from the worship of God. Moreover, all working such signs are pronounced worthy of death (13. 1-5). The third temptation is that referred to in the words which we have chosen for our emphasis. It is that of the enticement of human affection. It is always a powerful temptation, but it is to be sternly guarded against. However near to the heart another human being may be, the place which God occupies must be supreme, and all human affection refused when it threatens loyalty to Him (13. 6-11). Finally there is a peril which arises from looseness of discipline. Therefore the people were charged to take drastic measures against seducers and seduced. The necessity for this severe note is recognized when we remember that worship determines character and conduct. To us also comes the emphatic word: "Little children, guard yourselves from idols."

Ye are the children of the Lord your God; ye shall not cut yourselves, nor make any baldness between your eyes for the dead.—*Deut.* 14. 1.

This was a command not to conform to pagan customs in the presence of death. Notice that it was based upon the declaration that these people were the children of Jehovah their God. Whereas it is most probable that the Hebrew people never came to any clear certainty about personal immortality, it was given them to know that their attitude toward death, and so toward sorrow, could not be that of people whose gods were not real. They were children of the living God. Therefore there must be nothing of hopelessness or despair, in the presence of death, or in the sorrow arising from it. For Christian men and women this is far more urgent. Christ has brought life and immortality to light. Therefore we can never think of death as final, and we can never sorrow as those who have no hope. Is there not a very practical application of this, which we do well to consider? In the reflected light of Christianity, even worldly people no longer cut themselves, or mutilate themselves, in their sorrow in the presence of death. But all the heavy, sombre, desolation-suggesting trappings of mourning are entirely pagan. They should never be employed by Christians. For them the sackcloth is transfigured; the departed are not lost, but gone before. They will know sorrow; but upon all of their tears there will rest the glory that creates the rainbow. Let there be flowers and brightness in the death-chamber. We are children of God, and as our Master said, He is not the God of the dead, but of the living.

Beware that there be not a base thought in thine heart.—*Deut.* 15. 9.

The words flash like a light into the inner places of the life. We are warned against entertaining a base conception in the region of desire. To read them apart from their context is to realize what God is ever seeking in us. It is not enough that we abstain from base deeds. The heart must be free from baseness in thought. But the words become far more searching when they are interpreted by the context. Considering them alone, we might limit their application to things counted vulgar by men—to thoughts of murder, of impurity, of fraud. Examining them in their setting, we discover that the base thought referred to is that of a man who would refuse to help a fellow-man in immediate need, because the legal year of release was near at hand. That is a word, not of light alone, but also of fire. How perpetually prone we all are to this very kind of baseness! The need is patent, we do not deny it, but relief will come presently of necessity; therefore there is no urgency laid upon us to help. That is a base thought. To the people of God, immediate need calls for immediate help. We have no right to take refuge in our selfishness, under the plea of relief which will come presently. We are to give at once, and that not with grief in our hearts. Reluctance in giving sterilizes the gift. God is ever calling us to such vital fellowship with Himself that we give gladly, generously, immediately. Happy shall we be, if this world of light and fire from the old economy shall in us

Burn up the dross of base desire,
And make the mountains flow.

They shall not appear before the Lord empty.—*Deut.* 16. 16.

This command had application to the three great feasts of the year, those, namely, of Passover, with which it opened; of Pentecost, connected with harvest; and of Tabernacles, the great feast of remembrance and of joy. The observance of each of these feasts was a recognition of what the people owed to God. At Passover, they were reminded that their national existence was the result of their deliverance by God out of Egypt's bondage. At Pentecost, they recognized that not only their existence as a nation, but their perpetual sustenance also, was dependent upon His crowning of their toil. At Tabernacles, they recalled all the way in which He had led them, especially in the wilderness, and confessed that their possession of the land was the result of His gift. Nevertheless, in every one of them, they were called upon to bring gifts to God. This is an ever-increasing wonder to the truly devout heart. It seems incredible that man can offer anything to God that can possibly be worth His acceptance. And there is a sense in which it is true that He needs nothing. But He does value the spirit of devotion and love which prompts the gift. Where the full hands of worshippers are the results of hearts full of love, however poor intrinsically our gifts may be, they are very precious to Him. It is all very wonderful in its revelation of the fact that our eternal, almighty, infinite God, is no cold impassive Deity, but a God Whose heart is a very real fact.

He shall write him a copy of this law in a book.—*Deut.* 17. 18.

In this chapter, at verse fourteen, we commence a section which ends at the close of the next chapter. It deals with the threefold medium through which the will of God would be interpreted to the people, that of the king, the priest, the prophet. In this chapter the subject is that of the king. In dealing with it, Moses was speaking in the light of prophetic foresight. He foresaw what would happen after they came into the land. He knew how they would clamour for a king, and how God would grant them their request, and so teach them, ultimately, the folly of their desire. In the light of this, the principles of the appointment were declared. The king must be chosen of God, and be of their own nation. He was forbidden to multiply horses, wives, silver and gold. Perhaps the most striking requirement was this, that he, the king, should write a copy of the law in a book. Necessarily the purpose was that he should be a student of the law, but *this* requirement gave special emphasis to *that* requirement. One wonders how many of the kings carried out this wise instruction. This whole paragraph is a remarkable revelation of God's ideal of a king. It would be an interesting exercise to place the kings of all time by the side of it for measurement. Such a procedure would inevitably result in a twofold consciousness. First, we should surely discover that the measure in which kings have approximated to this ideal, is the measure in which they have contributed to national strength. Second, we should as surely find that one King only fulfils the conditions.

The Lord thy God will raise up unto thee a prophet from the midst of thee, of thy brethren, like unto me; unto him ye shall hearken.—Deut. 18. 15.

In this chapter priest and prophet are dealt with. The priest was already among the people by the appointment of God. The provisions that he was to have no inheritance in the land, and that his material needs must be supplied by the people, were restated. Special provision was now made for any priest whose heart prompted him to special service. In dealing with the prophet, Moses enjoined the people to beware of the false, and to know the true. He described the methods of false prophets. They are those of the dark arts, of dealing with the spiritual forces of evil, in a professed attempt to discover the will of God. The true prophet was then described briefly, but graphically. It is impossible to read this description without realizing that it was a prophecy which only found its fulfilment in One, and that the One Who was Himself the Word of God. All the true prophets approximated to the ideal; but in Him it was filled to the full. This section in our readings is of special interest as we realize how perfectly Moses was guided to set forth the true ideals of king, priest, and prophet; and how completely they were realized in our Lord! He was the true King; of His brethren, appointed by God, knowing, doing, and administering the law. He was the true Priest; of His brethren, without inheritance in His own land, abiding in the service of God, ministered to by the people of God. He was the true Prophet; of His brethren, uttering the Word of God in purity and in fulness.

One witness shall not rise up against a man for any iniquity.—Deut. 19. 15.

This chapter contains certain applications of laws already given. It deals with the sacredness of life, the importance of the land, the necessity for truth, the obligation of justice in all human interrelationships. The particular words which we have taken set up a principle which has been recognized and acted upon wherever laws have been based upon a passion for justice. They provided that no man could be condemned upon the testimony of one witness. There must be corroboration at the mouth of another. Moreover, every witness must be put to inquisition by the judges. If in the course of that investigation a man was found guilty of bearing false witness, he was to be severely punished. This spirit of strict and impartial justice breathes through all these laws, and helps us to understand God's ways of dealing with men. Only, we are safer in the hands of God than we can ever be in the hands of man. In spite of all precautions, justice does miscarry at times, in the best human courts; and that because there are things which the eye cannot see, or the ear hear, and it is only upon these evidences that man can bear witness. Our final judgments are with Him Who judgeth, not by the seeing of the eye, or the hearing of the ear, but with righteous judgment, which is based upon perfect knowledge of all the facts. That is a truth which comforts and warns us. With men we may be punished, or we may escape punishment, because all the facts are not known. It is never so with God.

The officers shall speak unto the people saying . . .—Deut. 20. 5.

These words introduce a paragraph, and they are chosen to draw attention to it. Let us first note the whole chapter. It contains that section of this discourse of Moses in which most particular instructions were given for the guidance of the people in the wars which they must inevitably be engaged in. They were being led, not merely to find a land for their own possession, but as a scourge of God against a corrupt and corrupting people. They were charged, first, that in the day of battle they must keep before them the vision of God, for that alone would free them from fear in the presence of the foe. Before actual conflict the priest was authoritatively to announce the fact of the presence, and authority, and power of God. Then we read our words, and the connected paragraph. It has to do with the grounds upon which men were to be exempt from military service. First, men who had duties and obligations, the fulfilment of which were necessary to the home-life of the nation were not to go to war. Men who had unfinished houses, ungathered vineyards, and men newly married, were to remain at home, at least until such times as they had discharged their obligations. Then also, men who lacked courage were to remain behind, because fear is contagious. It is impossible to read all this in view of much modern history without furious thinking! At least, we are driven to the conclusion that armies thus sifted would have a quality that is lacking entirely when they are made up of all sorts and conditions.

He that is hanged is accursed of God.—Deut. 21. 23.

The reference was to a man who for sin had been put to death, and whose body had been impaled on a tree or a stake, and thus exposed as a warning to other evil-doers. The command was that such exposure was not to outlast the day. By night the body must be buried, and so the whole fact of his sin, now expiated as to human society, put completely away. This parenthetical statement—for such it is—gives the reason for the burial. The man was not accursed of God because he was hanged on a tree. He was hanged on the tree because he was accursed of God. The hanging was the outward sign of the curse upon him, the curse of death for sin. When that curse was accomplished and witnessed, the sign was to cease; then let the man be buried, and that burial be the sign that the curse was sufficient. The understanding of this helps us when the mind travels on in solemn thought to the One Who hung upon the Tree on Calvary. He was there because He was "made sin," and so accursed of God. Such blunt statement gives the soul a shock; but it is the very shock we need, if we are ever to come to anything like a true apprehension of the way of our saving. In His case this law was fulfilled. He did not remain on the Tree through the night. The curse on sin was borne, and witnessed; the sin was expiated before God, because the One Who suffered its penalty was sinless. His burial was the sign that sin was put away. His resurrection was the beginning of a new life for Himself, as Redeemer; and for us, as redeemed.

Thou shalt not see thy brother's ox or his sheep go astray, and hide thyself from them.—*Deut. 22. 1.*

In these words we discover an element of responsibility which outruns all ordinary standards of righteousness. According to it, we are not only responsible that we do no harm to our fellow-men; we are also responsible to prevent harm being done to them when it is in our power to do so. The very simplicity of the illustration makes it all the more powerful. If I should see an animal belonging to my neighbour straying away, it would be in perfect keeping with human ideas of justice if I should say that it was no business of mine. Indeed, I might even argue that if he should lose that animal, it would be a just punishment for his carelessness concerning his own property. He certainly would have no claim on me that could be enforced in any human court of law. But in the court of Eternal Justice, I am counted as violating justice when I claim exemption from responsibility on such grounds. The reason for this is that, in the righteousness of God, there is always the element of compassion, and such concern for absolute right, that it must be maintained at all costs:—Because my neighbour is impoverished by the straying of his animal, whether through his own fault or no, I must intervene to save him from such

impoverishment if it be in my power to do so. What a wonderful world this will be when that is the law of life! And it will come, because God has anointed as King the One Who, to fulfil all righteousness, took the sinner's place in the baptism of death.

Thou shalt not abhor an Edomite; for he is thy brother; thou shalt not abhor an Egyptian; because thou wast a stranger in his land.—*Deut. 23. 7.*

Here, again we are brought face to face with this same element of compassion and mercy in the righteousness of God. It is wonderful how constantly it emerges in these laws. We are sometimes in danger of thinking of them as characterized by a cold negative justice, which fills the soul with fear. Nothing can be further from the truth. Here are two illustrations of the one principle. The first is that of the command that these people were not to abhor an Edomite. The Edomite was the descendant of Esau, as the Israelite was of Jacob. There were reasons why there should be separation from them, but there was to be no hatred, no contempt. The second is that of the Egyptian, with whom the Israelite had no race relationship. But Israel had been a stranger in the land of Egypt, and at one time had been given real hospitality there. This was never to be forgotten. Again, there were the most cogent reasons why Israel should make no political affinity with Egypt, but she was not to harbour abhorrence in her heart against the Egyptian people. Again, in these commandments to His people, what a revelation we have of God! There are evils with which He will make no compromise, there are peoples with whom He can have no communion; but in His heart there is nothing of hatred or contempt, even though there may be holy wrath. To be like Him is to be devoid of all bitterness, which is the outcome of selfishness.

And thou shalt remember that thou wast a bondman in the land of Egypt: therefore I command thee to do this thing.—*Deut. 24. 22.*

The thing immediately commanded was that at harvest-time the people should remember the stranger, the fatherless, the widow. In their reaping of their corn, their beating of their olive-trees, their gathering of their grapes, they were to remember those less privileged than themselves; and remembering, they were to relax the strict measure of their own rights, as they left something behind them for others. The argument used was that they were to remember the days of their own adversity. That such an argument should be necessary, seems at first to be strange, and yet a stranger fact is that people do so easily forget their own adversity in days of prosperity. Over and over again one sees a man, who in early life knew the pinch of poverty, having come to ease and comfort of circumstance, hard and callous in the presence of the trials of others. It is not always so, but it should never be so; and to those who live according to this law of God, it will never be so. Again, through this law of God for man, we have an unveiling of God Himself. In all His unsearchable riches, He thinks of the poor, and not only arranges that they may glean, but places all His wealth at their disposal. When then we yield up some gleanings of our possession for the relief of the needy, we have nothing of which to be proud. It is poor action as compared with the Divine. Verily there is only room for humility in the life of those who know God.

Thou shalt not muzzle the ox when he treadeth out the corn.—*Deut.* 25. 4.

Twice Paul quoted these words in his letters; once to the Corinthians (1 Cor. 9. 9, 10), and once to Timothy (1 Tim. 5. 18); and in both cases with reference to the duty of those who receive ministry in spiritual things to care for the material needs of those who minister. In the former case, he asked: "Is it for the oxen that God careth, or saith He it assuredly for our sake?" To his question, he replied: "Yea, for our sake it was written." Undoubtedly he was right. When this command was laid upon the people of God, it was in order that in all their life there might be the recognition of a principle. That, however, does not mean that God does not care for oxen. It does mean that if He cares for oxen, His care for men is necessarily greater. The principle had clear statement in the words of Jesus when He said of the birds: "Your heavenly Father feedeth them. Are not ye of much more value than they?" (Matt. 6. 26). In God, love acts toward all. Nothing He has made is outside that love. His provisions for all are perfect. His children are to be like Him in this. We do not minimize the application of this command to men, when we insist upon its application to animals. The Wise Man uttered a great truth when he said: "A righteous man regardeth the life of his beast" (Prov. 12. 10). If I see a man ill-treat a horse or a dog, I know he is capable of being brutal to a man. I would trust no child to a human being who showed cruelty to any dumb animal. If that is recognized, the applications in higher realms is patent.

I have brought the first of the fruit of the ground, which Thou, O Lord, hast given me.—*Deut.* 26. 10.

In this chapter we read the end of the second discourse of Moses. The great leader lifts his eyes, and looks out over the land to be possessed; and he proceeds to charge the people as to their worship therein, as it will have special regard to that fact of possession. The first act of worship is to be that of a recognition of their rights as vested in God. The people were to go up to the appointed place of worship, and there a formal confession was to be made. This was to be threefold: first, the fact of possession was to be stated; second, the origin of the nation was to be remembered, "A Syrian ready to perish was my father"; and finally, the fact that their possession was due to the act of Jehovah was to be acknowledged. With such confessions, offerings were to be presented to Jehovah, and then the people were to rejoice together. The true method of giving is that of bringing Him the first-fruits. We are ever in danger of thinking of Him last. When we are planning the expenditure of income, how often we arrange for things, perfectly proper and necessary, but purely personal, first; and then, when our list is completed, we begin to consider what we have left to offer to our Lord! If such lists are to be made, the first expenditure should be our giving to Him. The true principle of life for the Christian should be that of first recognizing that, not a tenth, but ten-tenths of our incomes belong to Him. Then every part should be expended for His glory. Even in that case, the first gifts should be His, specifically devoted to His work.

Keep silence, and hearken, O Israel; this day thou art become the people of the Lord thy God.—*Deut.* 27. 9.

This chapter consists of a historic interlude, and the commencement of Moses' third discourse. Immediately upon the conclusion of the second discourse, Moses and the elders of the people commanded them concerning the erection of great stones and an altar on Mount Ebal. On the stones were to be inscribed the words of the Law. The action was to be suggestive. The law thus inscribed and exhibited indicated the necessity for obedience, while the altar spoke of the provided method of approach to God because of disobedience. Upon entrance to the land there was to be a formal pronouncement of blessing and cursing. The blessings were to be pronounced from Mount Gerizim by the children of Leah and Rachel; Simeon, Levi, Judah, Issachar, Joseph, Benjamin; the cursings from Mount Ebal by two sons of Leah, Reuben and Zebulun, and the children of the bond-women, Gad, Asher, Dan, Naphtali. These arrangements having been made, Moses uttered his third discourse, the dominant note of which was that of warning. It consisted of the cursings and the blessings, together with appeal. He first called upon them to keep silence and hearken because they had become the people of Jehovah. The people of Jehovah have a law and an altar. Their cursing or their blessing results from their attitude to that law and that altar. Because of disobedience, the law can only curse. Because of the altar, there may be obedience. Thus the people of Jehovah ever live between their own failure and the Divine Grace. Grace is no excuse for failure, but in failure there is no reason for despair.

The Lord thy God will set thee on high above all the nations of the earth. —Deut. 28. 1.

That was the purpose of God for His people. Its fulfilment was conditional upon their obedience. They were to act above the nations of the earth; "If thou shalt hearken diligently unto the voice of Jehovah thy God, to observe to do all His commandments." Having made this general declaration. Moses proceeded to describe the blessings which would follow obedience; and then to declare the evils which would overtake them, if the law of God should be disregarded. In the light of the subsequent history of these people we see how literally all these things were fulfilled. How solemn and searching all this old-time story is for us. In Christ the law as given to Moses is done away, because He has given us a higher law, which far transcends the former in its standards of purity. In Christ the prophetic altar has been superseded by the one altar, by which men may draw near to God, and appropriate all the resources of His grace for the keeping of this higher law. The principles abide. Disobedience still issues in disaster; and obedience, in realization of Divine purpose. We blaspheme the name of God, and desecrate the final altar, when we become careless about the will of God as it has been revealed to us in the perfections of the Son of Man. It is still when we hearken diligently unto the voice of God, to observe to do His commandments, that we are set above the nations of the earth. With us, also, as with the people of Israel, the Divine intention of our exaltation is not that we should tyrannize over the nations of the earth, and hold them in contempt; but that we should serve them, and lead them into blessedness.

The secret things belong unto the Lord our God: but the things that are revealed belong unto us and to our children for ever, that we may do all the words of this law.—Deut. 29. 29.

The fourth discourse of Moses was concerned with the covenant, and urged the nation to be true to it. Here we should notice that the first verse of chapter 29 in our version is the last verse of chapter 28 in the Hebrew Bible. The statement "These are the words of the covenant," refers to what has already been uttered. Moses based his appeal on Jehovah's deliverances, from Egypt, through the wilderness, and

in the day of battle. The appeal was made to all classes of the community; to the rulers, and the people; to men, women, and children; and also to servants. In graphic and burning words he again described the results of breaking the covenant. Then, recognizing the limitations of the people, and their inability to understand all the ways of God, he enunciated this great principle of life. It is of far-reaching application and of perpetual importance. To the mind of man, in all life there are secret things, things veiled, things which cannot be explained. These things are not veiled to God. He knows them. To the mind of man there are things revealed, that is unveiled, things which are known. If man will obey them, he will be brought into right relation with the secret things, and progressively pass to apprehension of them, while all the time they, the secret things, co-operate with him for his perfecting. In the apprehension and practice of this law of life, man finds his way into strength.

This commandment which I command thee this day, it is not too hard for thee, neither is it far off.—Deut. 30. 11.

Continuing his discourse concerning the covenant, Moses uttered words thrilling with tenderness, and urgent in their appeal. In the first ten verses of this chapter we have the long look ahead of love. He seems to have seen the people in the conditions which he had told them would result from their disobedience. He looked on, and saw them scattered, far off from the land which they were then about to enter. Yet he saw them returning to God as the result of the sore discipline through which they would pass. But, best of all, he saw God ready to receive and pardon them. It was a great prophetic evangel, the value of which Israel has even yet not learned, but the message of which is true for her to-day. Then, renewing his appeal, he uttered these particular words. They constitute a statement of the reasonableness of the commandments of God. His law is never too hard for man. It is based upon God's knowledge of human nature. He asks of man nothing other than the true realization of his own nature. Every word of the Divine law is an interpretation of human life. When a man breaks the law of God, he is not sinning against a requirement superimposed upon him, and for the doing of which he is not fitted. He is sinning against his own life. Moreover, the law of God is easy because it is made known. Man is not left to grope in the dark mysteries of his own being, seeking for it. Over against those mysteries, God has made the light of His revealed will to shine. As a man walks in that light, he is walking according to his deepest powers and possibilities.

Write ye this song—*Deut.* 31. 19.

For forty years Moses had led the people. During that time he had constantly communed with God, and in the course of that communion had received many changes. This was one of the last things he was told to do. He was to write a song, and the purpose of it was distinctly stated. A great song once embodied in the life of a people will remain from generation to generation. In days of disaster it will be a haunting memory testifying to truth concerning God. In days of difficulty it will be a messenger of new courage. In days of victory it will be a means of expression. Songs often remain after commandments are forgotten. Therefore Moses was commanded to write a song and teach it to the people. The song itself is found in our next chapter. This is a very suggestive story, bringing to our hearts anew a sense of the value of poetic expression, and showing that it is also a gift of God. There are people who seem to imagine that if we speak of poetry, we are referring to something speculative, imaginative, probably untrue. As a matter of fact, poetry is the highest method of human language, giving expression, as prose never can, to the deepest and truest things of the soul. The Church is more enriched in her catholic songs, than in all her systematic theologies. In the former she realizes her unity, whereas in the latter she too often creates her divisions. The Wesleys did more for experimental Christianity in their hymns, than in all their printed explanations. A great song is a great possession, and not for Israel only, but for us also this song of Moses is among the most beautiful and most strong.

It is no vain thing for you: because it is your life—*Deut.* 32. 47.

These words were addressed by Moses to the people after he had repeated the song to them. He referred to the law as it was interpreted by the song. Let us then glance at the song. It opens with a call to attention and a statement concerning its nature. It is a song concerning the name of Jehovah (verses 1–3a). Then, in brief but pregnant sentences, the song sets forth the glories of the name as it celebrates the greatness, the perfection, the justice, the faithfulness of God (3b, 4). Then in sudden contrast, and in short, sharp fashion, it describes the people in their unworthiness (5). It then becomes an appeal, calling upon the people to remember, and merges into a description, full of beauty, of the tender government of God. It is a wonderful revelation of the fact that love is the inspiration of law (6–14). In strange contrast again the song becomes a wail as the unfaithfulness of the people is described, beginning with the words, "But Jeshurun waxed fat and kicked" (15–18). Such unfaithfulness had resulted

in discipline which the song describes (19–28). Then it breaks out into lament. "Oh, that they were wise," and describes the blessings which follow obedience (29–43). That is merely an analysis. Let the song be studied by its simple aid, and it will be found how wonderfully it was calculated to teach men that the will of God for them is indeed no vain thing, but their very life.

Happy art thou, O Israel; who is like unto thee, a people saved by the Lord.—*Deut.* 33. 29.

These sentences are taken from the last discourse of Moses. This also was a poem. It is described as a blessing. Often he had set before the people cursing and blessing. His last words to them were of blessing only. In stately and majestic language he first affirmed anew the majesty of Jehovah, and declared His love for the peoples, that is for the tribes of Israel. He then pronounced the words of blessing upon these tribes, Simeon only being omitted (why, we do not know). Reuben and Judah are referred to in terms which suggest that they were saved so as by fire. Levi, having lost all earthly possessions for the special honour of bearing the Word of Jehovah, receives the reward of such sacrifice. The reference to Benjamin shows the safety of frailty in the Divine government. The choicest things of all are said of Joseph. His are all "precious things and the good-will of Him that dwelt in the bush." His, therefore, is the portion of government. Issachar and Zebulun are seen triumphing over disability. Gad, overcoming at last, is appointed a judge. Dan becomes typical of conquest. Naphtali is satisfied. Asher is sustained. Thus in his final benediction Moses makes the varied realization of blessing by the tribes unfold the all-sufficiency of God. The concluding words again celebrate the greatness of God as finally manifested in His tenderness and strength toward His people. Verily, happy are the people who are saved by Jehovah.

There hath not arisen a prophet since in Israel like unto Moses, whom the Lord knew face to face.—*Deut.* 34. 10.

In this last chapter of Deuteronomy we have the writing of another hand. It contains the story of the death of Moses, the equipment of Joshua for his work, and a last tender reference to the great leader and law-giver, beginning with these particular words. For the man who wrote them, they were true words; and they remained true through all the history of that wonderful people until One was born of the seed of David, Who was greater far than Moses. In his second discourse Moses had foretold his coming in the words: "I will raise them up a prophet from among their brethren like unto thee." Long centuries elapsed, but at last He came, and in His coming fulfilled all Moses had initiated under the Divine government; absorbed and abolished the law which came through him, in the grace and truth which He brought to men. All this does not detract from, but rather enhances our sense of the greatness of this servant of God. His passing was full of beauty. In the fact of his exclusion from the land toward which he had led the people, it was a punishment; but, like all the chastisements of God, it was wonderfully tempered with mercy. There had been no weakening of his force. Everything ended in full strength. He went up to die. Jehovah gave him a vision of the land, and then buried him in that unknown grave. It was an august and glorious ending to a great and dignified life. Thus ends the last book of the Pentateuch, the final section of the Law. Its supreme value is its revelation of the need for the Priest and the Gospel.

JOSHUA

Moses my servant is dead; now therefore arise, go over this Jordan.— *Josh.* 1. 2.

As these words are read, we are reminded of John Wesley's saying: "God buries His workmen, but carries on His work." Joshua was called, equipped, appointed to carry the purpose of God a step further; but all he was about to do was made possible by what Moses had already done. The first great leader of the people had completed his task; he had done what God had appointed him to do, but there were things he could not do. He came to the end of his service knowing the greater things yet to be done. The second leader was now to take up his task; he also must do what God had appointed, knowing that there were things which he could not have done. He came to the beginning of his service knowing his dependence upon the things already done. Thus it ever is with regard to God's enterprises in this world. He is supreme in plan, in purpose, in power. He alone is the One Who worketh continuously, and without cessation, until the work is completed. His instruments are men, and high indeed is the honour of being such. Each will take up a work already begun, and will leave it unfinished. Each is debtor to those who have gone before, and creditor to those who are to follow. Therefore it behoves us to be filled with humility and restfulness. We must be humble as we remember that no service we render is wholly ours. The conditions which make it possible have been created by others; and indeed in itself it is part of their work. But we must be restful also. None of us can finish anything. The work we do is part of a larger whole, and when our "twelve hours" have run their course, it will not be completed. God will still continue it, and find other instruments. That is the joy of working together with Him.

The Lord your God, He is God in heaven above, and on earth beneath.— *Josh.* 2. 11.

These words constituted the confession of Rahab. They are remarkable, first, as showing the effect which these people, God-governed, were already producing upon the peoples of the land to which they were coming; and further as revealing the capacity of the human soul for coming to right conclusions in the presence of manifestations of the Divine power. As to the first. The effect was not that of a sense of the greatness of the Hebrew people, but of the greatness of their God. The heathen had heard of the deliverance from Egypt, and of the victory over powerful enemies. They knew that these things had not been done by the Israelites, but for them, through their God. They recognized Him in His Almightiness, for this is the full meaning of the declaration that "He is God in heaven above, and on earth beneath." As to the second. This woman's language all through shows her power of discernment. She had heard of the past wonders, and so she knew the issue. She stands out in separation from her people because she made her knowledge the inspiration of her faith. The men of Jericho shared her conviction, but rebelled against it. She recognized the act of God and yielded to it. The one really valuable influence exerted by the people of God is that of a revelation of His power. They render true service to men, not as they make a name for themselves, but as they make His name great among men.

Sanctify yourselves; for to-morrow the Lord will do wonders among you.— *Josh.* 3. 5.

This was the command which indicated the conditions upon which God covenanted with His people to lead them in. Thus their first movement forward under Joshua was of such a nature as to impress them as the chosen people with the truth of their positive relation to God. There was nothing in this first advance calculated to give them any cause for personal glorying. They came on to the actual soil of Canaan, not by deflecting the course of the intervening river, nor by bridging it, but by Divine intervention. His might was exercised as He laid arrest upon the rushing river, and so made a highway for His people to the other side. But His power operated when they fulfilled these conditions. The wonders of God are performed for His people when they sanctify themselves, that is when, so far as they have light, they walk in it. The call to sanctification, as an act on the part of the people of God, is a call to separation from everything which they know He disapproves, and of dedication to Him completely, in mind and heart and will. The attitude is more than activity. That is to say, in proportion as in our deepest life we yield to His will we place ourselves in line with His work. The application is personal and social. It is true of the individual and of the Church, that all our progress is the result of the putting forth of His power; but it is equally true that He works when there is response to His call, and when our sanctification to Him is unquestioned and complete.

When your children ask in time to come.—*Josh.* 4. 6.

The people of God had sanctified themselves as He had commanded, and He had wrought the wonder of bringing them across Jordan by the putting forth of His power. Now, before there could be any forward march, they were commanded to halt for worship, and the performance of a ceremony which was in itself a recognition of the Divine presence and activity. Stones were to be gathered out of the river-bed by representatives of the tribes, and these stones were to be erected as a memorial-pile on the side of the Jordan to which they had now come. We miss the real beauty of this arrangement if we fail carefully to note the true reason of this pause and erection of a pillar. That reason is declared in these words: "That this may be a sign among you, that when your children ask in time to come." It is repeated later (verses 21, 22). The ultimate purpose of God lay far on, and out of sight. Ere it was reached, many generations would come and go. None of the lessons learned by the way must be lost. They must be perpetuated in the national memory throughout the coming days. In order that this might be so, Jehovah definitely arranged for such things as would appeal to the natural curiosity of children. Thus in answer to their questionings the story of the Divine deliverance was to be repeated to each succeeding generation. This is the true value of all monuments and memorials. They are erected to make children inquire, and it is the business of those who have charge of them, to answer their questions. Thus the child is instructed as to the things of real significance in national life; and thus the nation is preserved from forgetfulness of those things.

The manna ceased.—*Josh.* 5. 12.

The manna had been God's supernatural provision for the needs of His people during the time of their journeyings in a wilderness where cultivation of the soil was impossible. They were now in a land already cultivated, and capable of cultivation. They were now fed with the corn of the land, and their future supply would depend upon their own labour. They would be as surely fed by God in the land as they had been in the wilderness; but they would now be responsible for co-operation with Him in the labour of their own hands. This is ever so. For the needs of His people God always provides. When they are in such circumstances, under His direction, as to be unable to provide for themselves, He cares for them without any action on their part. When it is possible for them to act and to work, He provides for them through that activity. God never employs supernatural methods of supplying needs which can be met by natural means. In other words, He puts no premium upon indolence by His provisions for men. If for any reason within the compass of His government of our lives, we are unable by our own effort to obtain what is necessary for our life and service, we may count upon Him to provide for us. When the hour comes in which that inability no longer exists—when we are able by thought and toil to secure necessary things—He demands that we use the strength He has provided, and in such use. He works together with us. The manna always ceases when by industry we are able to produce bread.

Only Rahab the harlot shall live, she and all that are with her in the house, because she hid the messengers that we sent.—*Josh.* 6. 17.

The writer of the letter to the Hebrews cites this as an illustration of the activity of faith: "By faith Rahab, the harlot, perished not with them that were disobedient, having received the spies with peace" (11. 31). This is very interesting, as it helps us to understand the true nature of faith. In this Christian writing her faith is placed in direct contrast with disobedience. She was obedient, and that was faith. Her obedience was not, in the first place, that of doing what the spies told her. It was that of receiving them. She was obedient to conviction. In a previous chapter (2), we have her own account of that conviction. She told the men that she knew the power of their God, and that the people of the land knew it also. They were disobedient; that is, they did not act in accordance with their convictions. She had faith; that is, she did act in accordance therewith. That is of the very essence of faith. It is far more than a creed intellectually held. It is always volitional surrender to intellectual conviction. Not every one who saith Lord, Lord—even though the confession may be a perfectly honest statement of real conviction—but he that doeth the will, enters into the Kingdom.

The light which Rahab had, was not particularly brilliant—her advantages had been very few—but she followed the gleam, she believed actively, and was thus delivered. Thus is clearly revealed the true principle of life.

Therefore the children of Israel cannot stand before their enemies.—Josh. 7. 12.

This chapter opens with a significant and ominous "but." So far the people of God had been completely victorious. We now see them defeated and flying before their enemies. Joshua was filled with the profoundest consternation, and poured out his soul before God. The central word of his agony was that in which he cried: "O Lord, what shall I say, after that Israel hath turned their backs before their enemies!" The answer was given him at once. Israel had sinned; therefore they were unable to stand before their enemies. The sin was that of a man, but Israel was now a nation, and therefore no one person could act alone. This is a striking revelation of the Divine conception of the solidarity of human society. The sin of the one is the sin of the community. All the hosts of God were defeated, and His enterprises checked, because one man had disobeyed. The story of Achan's sin, as he himself confessed it, is full of warning. Mark carefully the progress of it. "I saw." "I coveted." "I took." Every one sees. The danger begins when the sight lingers until desire is generated. The next stage is almost inevitable. Swift and terrible, and yet necessary for the strength of the national life, was the judgment which fell upon this man. The confession he made was complete, but it was worthless because it was not made until there was no escape from detection. Confession, and being found out, are two things. The ultimate teaching of the incident is undoubtedly that of its revelation of the fact that any one member of the hosts of the Lord may bring disaster upon those hosts by personal sin.

As well the stranger as the home-born.—Josh. 8. 33.

Among the final instructions given to the people by Moses, were those which provided for the setting up of great stones upon which the words of the law were to be written; the erection of an altar on Mount Ebal; the offering of sacrifices; and the uttering of the blessings and cursings as appointed (Deut. 27). These words occur in connection with the account of the carrying out of these instructions. The principle involved we have observed before (Lev. 24. 22) in its application to the law. There was to be one law as well for the sojourner as for the home-born. That emphasized the rights of the sojourner. Here it stresses equality of privilege and also of responsibility. It is to be observed that from the beginning, the door was open to others to enter this Theocracy, this Kingdom of God. The claims of blood and birthright were not exclusive. But it was insisted upon, that such as entered must accept the law, and abide by the blessings and cursings as provided. They could claim no exemption from responsibility, and the home-born could exercise no exclusivism against them, on the ground that they were not of the actual Israelitish blood. To-day that door of entrance to the Kingdom of God, through Jesus Christ the Lord, stands wide open to men of every nation. There is a sense in which there are no longer any home-born, and that because all who enter are born anew of the Spirit. That, therefore, is the one necessity both as right and responsibility which must be insisted upon. Any desire for comprehension, which suggests the admission into the fellowship of the Christian communion of those who are not completely yielded to Christ, and so share His very life, is dangerous, because it threatens to destroy that fellowship, and make impossible the realization of its true functions.

We have sworn unto them by the Lord, the God of Israel; now therefore we may not touch them.—Josh. 9. 19.

These words were spoken concerning the Gibeonites through whose strategy a new peril threatened the people of God. The whole story is suggestive. The fame and dread of the Israelites were spreading far and wide throughout the land. Indeed, the kings of Canaan conscious of their danger, had formed a league against the oncoming hosts. Before they had time to take action, this trouble with the Gibeonites arose. They sought to secure their own safety by deceit. The fundamental mistake made by the princes of Israel in this matter was that they acted on their own account, instead of remitting what was a new situation to God for counsel and guidance. They "asked not counsel at the mouth of Jehovah." Moreover, they had been straitly charged to make no covenant with the people of the land, and though it is possible that in doing so with these people, they thought they were people from a great distance, it is yet clear that they approached perilously near to disobedience, if indeed they were not actually guilty of it. But the covenant being made and ratified by the use of the Name of God, they would not break it. In this is a revelation of what these people felt as to the sacredness of a covenant, made, and there is no doubt that they were right. Joshua, strictly bound by the letter of the covenant, condemned the Gibeonites to perpetual servitude. In all the subsequent history we see that this treaty was recognized.

All these kings and their land did Joshua take at one time, because the Lord, the God of Israel, fought for Israel.—*Josh*. 10. 42.

That statement is to be carefully noted All the way through this history of the conquest of the land, we must bear in mind that the record treats it as a Divine movement by which a corrupt people were cleared out of possession, and so a new era in the history of the whole race was created. Joshua took the kings and their land, because Jehovah the God of Israel fought for Israel. Joshua and Israel, as leader and people, constituted God's instrument for this cleansing and purifying work. Those who read the story without this recognition miss its supreme note. It is well to remember, too, all the great spiritual and moral benefit which has accrued to humanity through this people of God. True, to-day they are a people scattered and peeled over the face of the whole earth, but that fact is a further witness to the same activities of God. When these people failed to fulfil the Divine purpose, and themselves became degenerate and corrupt, God cast them out of the land, as He had done with the previous dwellers therein. "Jehovah is a Man of war" in very deed, but He is always on the side of "truth and meekness and righteousness"; because of these things. He in His majesty rides on prosperously; and for them His right hand teaches terrible things (see Psa. 44). In the strength of this Divine passion and power, Joshua fought on, until the whole of Southern Canaan was cleared of the corrupt peoples, and in possession of Israel.

And the land had rest from war.— *Josh*. 11. 23.

But that rest did not come quickly, nor was it realized until war had achieved the high purposes of God. After the conquest of Southern Canaan, a new confederacy had to be faced and fought. The northern kings, conscious of their peril, joined together in an attempt to break the power of the conquering hosts. Turning north, Joshua attacked, and utterly routed them. He then turned back to Hazor with like results. As we have said, all this did not happen immediately. Indeed, we are told in the text that it occupied "a long time" (verse 18). In all probability, from the death of Moses to this period, five years had elapsed. Thus ended the unity of the action of the hosts of God. There was still much to be done in the way of conquest, and afterwards there was much fighting as occasion demanded, but the preliminary campaign of conquest was complete. The statement that the land had rest from war does not mean, therefore, that there was to be no more war, for in the settlement of the land the separate tribes were involved

in war. It rather declares that rest was reached through war. It has often been so in the history of man. Through blood and fire and vapour of smoke, the signs and symbols of conflict, God cleanses the land, and the heart of man, from those evil things which produce human feverishness and restlessness; and thus, through the terrible ordeal, leads men to quietness and rest. When passions are purified, and evil thoughts are no more, war will cease. Till then God makes it the awful instrument of cleansing and renewal.

All the kings thirty and one.— *Josh*. 12. 24.

This chapter contains no new matter. It is rather a concise summary of the extent of the conquest; first, that under Moses (verses 1–6); and then, that under Joshua (verses 7–24). These words refer to the extent of Joshua's victory on the west side of Jordan, and in their bald simplicity help us to realize at once the difficulty and greatness of what he accomplished. That comparatively small strip of country was occupied by these many peoples, living among its mountains, at perpetual and cruel strife, united only in their utter degeneration and corruption. Six races are named—Hittites, Amorites, Canaanites, Perizzites, Hivites, and Jebusites. Every considerable city had its king. There was no true cohesion among the nations, but there were confederacies formed against Joshua, as we have seen. When he had completed his great campaign, these all were subdued, and the land passed under the rule of God through His people. Thus ends the first section of this Book. The destructive part of the Divine work is potentially completed. The constructive work of God may now go forward. The whole story recalls Whittier's lines:—

All grim and soiled and brown with tan
  I saw a strong One in His wrath,
Smiting the godless shrines of man
  Along His path.

I looked; aside the dust-cloud rolled—
  The Waster seemed the Builder too;
Upspringing from the ruined old,
  I saw the New.

There remaineth yet very much land to be possessed.—*Josh*. 13. 1.

With this chapter the second part of the Book of Joshua commences, which gives the account of the settlement of the people in the conquered land. Joshua was now probably about ninety years of age, and the word of Jehovah reminded him that there was still much to be done. Of the land which God had chosen for His people, there was very much even yet unsubdued; and within the area of that conquered, strong cities such as Jerusalem, Gezer and others, were still held by the otherwise defeated Canaanites. The people of God were called upon to complete this work; and now, in order that it might be accomplished, Joshua was commanded to proceed forthwith to the division of the land among the tribes. The danger was recognized that these people might rest content with victories already gained, and so fail to realize all the purposes of God for them. As a matter of fact this did happen, as we shall see subsequently. The words have a message for us. In whatever realm we think of the Divine purpose for us, we have to say: "There remaineth very much land to be possessed." We have never occupied all the territory provided for us in the Divine intention, and we are ever terribly prone to be satisfied with less than that which is in the will of God for us. It is true in the realm of spiritual experience; it is true in the matter of missionary enterprise.

Give me this mountain.—*Josh*. 14. 12.

This was the petition of Caleb, and it is characteristic. He was now eighty-five years of age, and was still in possession of full vigour. He it was who, with Joshua, forty-five years before, had seen the truth about the land, for he had not only seen the difficulties, he had seen God. The whole history of the man is full of interest and instruction. The victory of his faith at Kadesh-Barnea had been that of a man who "wholly followed Jehovah." For forty years he had shared the wanderings and discipline of those who had not shared his faith. For five years undoubtedly he had taken part in the conflict which had resulted in their coming into the land. During all that period he had never been uncertain of the issue. He had apparently occupied a comparatively quiet and obscure position among his people, while his friend Joshua had been called into the place of conspicuous and powerful leadership. Very beautiful is this story of the converse of the two men. Caleb came while there was still much to be done; and urging his unabated vigour as constituting fitness for the work, he asked for a possession in the land, which would make stern demands upon him in order to make it his own. On that mountain the Anakim had dwelt; on it there had been great and fortified cities in the day when his faith had triumphed. They were still there, and he asked for the privilege of demonstrating and vindicating faith by works. Joshua's recognition of his friend and of his right to this choice was quick and generous. He granted him the mountain he asked, and blessed him. In the history of Caleb three things are illustrated concerning faith. Faith sees and dares in the day of overwhelming difficulty. Faith waits patiently through delays caused by failure in others. Faith acts with courage in the day of opportunity.

As for the Jebusites, the inhabitants of Jerusalem, the children of Judah could not drive them out.—*Josh*. 15. 63.

This is a very interesting statement. because it is the first made about Jerusalem in the Bible. The city has been named before. It was the King of Jerusalem, Adonizedek, who called together four others to join him against Joshua and the people of Israel (chapter 10). This, however, is the first thing we are told about it, and it is very suggestive. The children of Israel could not dislodge those who possessed it. In David's time it was taken, and in some senses was held by the people of God for centuries—how imperfectly, the whole history reveals. Subsequently it was lost to them, because they were never able to drive out their enemies. The last references to Jerusalem in the Sacred Writings are to it as a city coming out of heaven from God. All which things may be treated as an allegory. God's high purposes for men will never be achieved by man. They will come to men from God. Man is a Divine creation, but he is devilishly fallen, and he cannot recover himself. His recovery can only come by redemption, and he cannot redeem himself. God alone can redeem him. All this is true of the city of Mansoul, it is true of the whole social order. Both the one and the other are possessed by enemies too strong for us to deal with them, or drive them out. But our hope is in God. He has perfected the work, and will carry it out to the ultimate realization. The City of God is yet to come, and it will come, not by earth's activities, but out of heaven, from God, and not from man.

And the children of Joseph, Manasseh and Ephraim, took their inheritance.—*Josh*. 16. 4.

This is the account of the portion allotted to Joseph, as it was divided between his two sons, Ephraim and Manasseh, with special reference to the lot which fell to Ephraim. It was a fertile and beautiful district, perhaps in many respects the most desirable in the whole country. It was nevertheless a possession of peculiar difficulty, in that it still lay largely in the power of the Canaanites. The history of Ephraim—which later on became the dominant tribe, as Hosea's prophecy shows—was a sad one. The failure of the tribe began at this time, and is recorded in the words: "They drave not out the Canaanites that dwelt in Gezer; but the Canaanites dwell in the midst of Ephraim." They took their inheritance, but they did not take possession of it. In the will of God, and by the consent of Ephraim, it belonged to them; but they failed to appropriate it in all its fulness, because they left these Canaanites in possession. The gifts of God to His people belong to them because

He bestows them; but they can only be really possessed by conflict, and thus by the action of those upon whom they are bestowed. Moreover, the richer the gifts, the stronger the foes which have to be dealt with, and therefore the sterner the conflict to be waged. How constantly the people of God fail as did Ephraim! They take their inheritance in the sense of recognizing the Divine gift, and speaking of it as belonging to them; but they fail to dispossess those who hold it from them by their presence and power. To fail to appropriate Divine gifts by conflict against enemies, is to lose them. The things that are ours by Divine grace, we must make ours by our own devotion.

If thou be a great people, get thee up to the forest, and cut down for thyself there.—*Josh.* 17. 15.

The territory of Manasseh is indicated in this chapter. It is interesting to notice that some of the cities of Ephraim were within that territory; and moreover, that some of the cities of Manasseh were within the territory of Asher and Issachar. The reason for this, as to the first, may be that it was intended to mark the unity existing between Ephraim and Manasseh as sons of Joseph; and, as to the second, that Asher and Issachar were not strong enough to subdue the territory committed to them. The overlapping emphasized the unity of the tribes in one national life. Of Manasseh it is also true, as of Ephraim, that they did not drive out the Canaanites. Yet these children of Joseph were discontented with their portions, and complained to Joshua. They said they were a great people, and that the lot given to them was not adequate The answer of Joshua was characteristic of him, and evidenced the greatness of his statesmanship. He manifested a clear understanding of the weakness of these tribes, and of the way by which alone they could become strong. He did not deny that they were a great people, but—surely with a touch of irony—he charged them to demonstrate their greatness by taking possession of what they had. He instructed them to go up to the mountains, and cut down the trees and drive out their foes, and so to enlarge their borders by cultivating their possessions, rather than by seeking more ground.

How long are ye slack to go in to possess the land which the Lord, the God of your fathers, hath given you?—*Josh.* 18. 3.

These words were addressed to the whole of Israel, but had special application to seven tribes. It would seem as though, after the allotment of districts to Judah, Ephraim, and Manasseh, the nation slackened in its work. In view of this, Joshua first caused the erection in the midst of the land, at Shiloh, of that place of worship which was the perpetual symbol of the deepest truth of their nationality. Having done this, and having rebuked the seven tribes for slackness, he made arrangements by which the rest of the land should be divided into seven parts, and so the responsibility of taking possession would be shared by all the tribes. The arresting word in this question of Joshua is the word "slack," as it reveals a peril always threatening those who are called to carry out some Divine enterprise. How perpetually the work of God suffers because His people become slack! There is no weakening of the sense of the importance of the work, there is no intention of abandoning that work; but weariness creeps upon the soul, the enthusiasm which characterized the beginning cools; things lose their grip upon the mind, and effort grows sluggish. Against that tendency we should strenuously guard ourselves. If we do not, slackness will become paralysis, and the work will wholly cease. Inertia is one of the most deadly foes of all campaigns. That is the truth recognized in Paul's word: "Let us not be weary in welldoing." The reaping is only sure "if we faint not."

So they made an end of dividing the land.—*Josh.* 19. 51.

This chapter gives us the record of the division of the remainder of the land among the six tribes—Benjamin's portion being described at the close of the last chapter. When all had been provided for, Joshua was given a special portion. It was the portion for which he asked. The time and nature of his choice are alike revelations of the character of the man. He did not ask for a possession for himself until all had been supplied. He was content to wait, taking only when all others had received, and then taking his portion as the gift of the nation. His choice in itself was suggestive. He asked for Timnath-serah. Thus he chose a city in the rough and uncultivated hill district which was part of the lot of Ephraim. When the children of Joseph had complained that the lot appointed to them was not worthy of their greatness, Joshua had charged them to go up to the mountain, and prove their greatness by taking possession actually of what was theirs in the appointment of God. Now, at last, when his opportunity came, he proved that he was prepared to act himself upon his advice to others. Thus, as a member of these very tribes, he proved his greatness. There is a splendid ring of the resoluteness of his character in the statement that "he built the city and dwelt therein."

"So they made an end of dividing the land." The work had been done by Joshua the leader, Eleazar the priest, and the heads of the tribes; and all had been done at the door of the Tent of Meeting, and thus in relation to those great facts which lay at the foundation of the national life.

These were the appointed cities.—Josh. 20. 9.

The reference is to the cities of refuge. Now that the people had come into the land, these were provided according to the arrangements already made (see Num. 35). Three were on the west of the Jordan, and three on the east; and they were so placed as to be available to the whole of the land. They were all Levitical cities. Maclear says that "Jewish commentators tell us how in later times, in order that the asylum offered to the involuntary homicide might be more secure—(a) the roads leading to the cities of refuge were always kept in thorough repair, and required to be at least 32 cubits (about 48 ft. broad; (b) all obstructions were removed that might stay the flier's foot or hinder his speed; (c) no hillock was left, no river was allowed over which there was not a bridge; (d) at every turning there were posts erected bearing the words 'Refuge,' 'Refuge,' to guide the unhappy man in his flight; (e) when once settled in such a city the man-slayer had a convenient habitation assigned to him, and the citizens were to teach him some trade that he might support himself." In this method of dealing with the most heinous of all sins, as between man and man, certain principles are revealed; (1) God does make distinction as between sin and sin, showing that there are degrees of guilt. Premeditated murder was to find no sanctuary, even in the city of refuge. (2) Man must not punish man, except his guilt be established after the fullest investigation. (3) All deliverance is closely connected with the priesthood, which stands for sacrificial mediation. The first two are observed in all human courts of law. Deliverance from sin, in any degree, can only come through the act of God.

There failed not aught of any good thing which the Lord had spoken unto the house of Israel; all came to pass.—Josh. 21. 45.

This chapter records the last things in the settlement of the land, and they had to do with the appointment to the Levites of their cities and pasturage in Israel. These men who, in place of the first-born, were devoted to the specific service of the nation in spiritual things were to live among the people, not in isolation and separation from them. Their presence everywhere was intended to serve as a perpetual witness to the relation of the nation to God, and of its consequent responsibilities. Thus the second division of this Book of Joshua, dealing with the settlement of the people in the land comes to an end. It concludes with the declaration that Jehovah gave them the land, and they possessed it. His every promise to them had been fulfilled. No man had been able to stand before them, as they had been obedient to Him. He had delivered their enemies into their hands. And yet, those enemies had not all been driven out, and so they had not fully possessed their possessions. As a matter of fact, they never did completely realize the purpose of God in this matter. The failure, however, was wholly due to their own disobedience, and so the record at this point fittingly closes with this delaration of the faithfulness of God to all His covenant with them.

Let us now prepare to build us an altar, not for burnt-offering, nor for sacrifice; but it shall be a witness between us and you.—Josh. 22. 26, 27.

The two and a half tribes now returned to their possessions on the other side of Jordan. As they did so, they builded an altar to the west of the river. To this the nine and a half tribes objected, not because they had any fear of their brethren possessing within the central borders of the land so recently divided, but because this act of erecting an altar seemed to indicate the setting up of a new centre of worship. In these words they replied to that fear, declaring that the altar was not raised for purpose of worship, but for a witness that they remained an integral part of the nation. It was a recognition of God, born of a fear of man. They were afraid that subsequent generations of those dwelling in the land might repudiate those dwelling on the other side of Jordan. It is all a very humiliating story, as it shows how suspicions and misunderstandings may exist between different tribes of the one nation. Its value to us is that it does indicate the true way of realizing unity. It is that of recognizing and testifying to our common allegiance to the one Lord. That is the bed-rock of our unity. There may be many temperaments, many dialects, many modes of expression, but there is "one Lord, one faith, one baptism," and in proportion as each recognizes this, and yields wholly to it, all come to the realization of true unity, which is ever that of harmony—not monotony, but concordant difference.

Take good heed, therefore, unto yourselves, that ye love the Lord your God.—Josh. 23. 11.

As the time of Joshua's passing approached, he twice gathered the people together, and delivered farewell messages to them. The first of these is contained in this chapter. Its burden is that of the power and faithfulness of God, and the consequent earnest desire of the great leader for the faithfulness of the people to Him. The references which Joshua made to himself were very few and brief; the principal ones being: "I am old and well stricken in years," "I am going the way of all the earth." Only incidentally did he refer to his own work. After having declared that Jehovah had brought them in, he said: "I have allotted unto you these nations that remain." His references to Jehovah were constant: "Jehovah your God hath done"; "Jehovah your God, He it is that fought for you," and so on. Earnestly and urgently he charged them to be "courageous to keep and to do" the law, to "cleave unto Jehovah"; closing with the most solemn warning as to what would happen to them if they departed from their allegiance. Of all the wonderful address, the words we have chosen constituted the supreme note. Everything else is assured if men love Jehovah. Failure to keep the law is always the outcome of failure in love to the Law-giver. For such failure in love, men are responsible. In order that love may be maintained, they need to take heed to themselves. That is the meaning of the charge of Jude: "Keep yourselves in the love of God." To cease to discipline the life, is to cool in devotion.

If it seem evil unto you to serve the Lord, choose you this day whom ye will serve.—*Josh. 24. 15.*

These were the words of a fine irony. In spite of a constant use of them, they did not constitute an appeal to choose between God and idols. Joshua was supposing that they had decided not to serve God, and he called them then to choose between the gods their fathers had abandoned, and those which they had found in the land. He had traced their history from the call of Abraham to that time. This history he had expressed in the form of the speech of Jehovah; and in the compass of eleven verses the Divine pronoun "I" occurs no less than seventeen times. It was a great statement of the truth that everything of greatness in their history was of God. From that fact, Joshua made the natural deduction: "Now therefore fear Jehovah, and serve Him." But if not—then let them choose between these other gods. The implicate of the appeal was the recognition of a great necessity in all human life. Man must worship, he must have a god. That is universally true. If men will not serve the Lord, then let them choose whom they will serve, only let them make their decision in the clear light of what the kingship of God really means of light, and love and life and liberty. This is a great method of appeal. If to-day men say of God's annointed and appointed King. "We will not have this Man to reign over us," then let us urge them to choose as between the alternatives which are offered them; only let them compare the results of the reign of Christ over human life with those of any other authority to which loyalty may be yielded. Such comparison compels us to Joshua's decision: "As for me and my house, we will serve Jehovah."

JUDGES

After the death of Joshua.—*Judges 1. 1.*

The Book of Joshua began with the words: "After the death of Moses," and recorded the story of the people of God under the leadership of his successor. Now the story is continued as to what followed his death. These beginnings keep us reminded of the persistence of the Divine purpose, in spite of the frailty of the human instruments. After the death of any servant of God, the service of God goes forward, and the work of God is carried on. Yet the other side of that truth is not to be lost sight of. God carries on His purpose and His work through human instruments. Moses made possible the work of Joshua. Joshua had made possible the work of all who were to follow. The period covered in this Book is that from the death of Joshua to the judgeship of Samuel, and the movement toward monarchy. On the human side, it is a story of disobedience and disaster; and on the Divine side, of continued direction and deliverance. Therefore in its light the servant of God may always find encouragement. When the appointed task is done, he will ever be conscious of the incompleteness of it, of the things desired but not done, of the perils threatening the ultimate realization which he must leave unattained; but he will know by all this history that God never abandons His purpose, cannot be finally defeated, will always find those to take up and continue the service which is unfinished. Happy is the man who in his little hour works with God. He may be at rest about the issues.

The Lord raised up judges.—*Judges 2. 16.*

This brief sentence records the method of God during this period. It was a method made necessary by the repeated failure of the people. That should be clearly understood. These men were not judges in our sense of the word. Neither were they appointed to rule in the normal way. The nation was a Theocracy, having God as King. Its life was conditioned by His law, and His will was made known through His worship, and the teaching of the priests. The first sentences of the previous chapter reveal the nation inquiring of Jehovah on a matter of national importance. The answer was direct. It was sought and obtained by the use of Urim and Thummim by the priest (Exod. 28. 30). The people had no need of any other administrators in times of obedience. When through disobedience they passed into circumstances of difficulty and suffering, God raised up judges who became the instruments of Divine deliverance. The Hebrew word *Shophetim* is derived from a word meaning to put right, and so to rule, and this is exactly what these men did. In the earlier cases, when they had accomplished deliverance they retired again into private life. Gradually they came to retain office. Samuel judged Israel forty years. The need for them arose out of human failure: the provision was of Divine Grace. This principle runs through all the history of man. Man persistently fails, but God persistently overcomes man's failure in order to man's wellbeing. Priests, judges, kings, prophets, are all means by which God stoops to man's level in order to recover him.

The Spirit of the Lord came upon him, and he judged Israel.—*Judges* 3. 10.

Othniel was the first of the judges. The circumstances which made his appointment necessary were those of the oppression of the people of God by the king of Mesopotamia. For eight years they had been subject to him. That subjection was due to their sin. They "forgat Jehovah their God, and served the Baalim and the Asheroth." The method of the statement suggests a gradual deterioration, ending in complete degeneracy. The stern discipline of the eight years brought them back to remembrance of God, and they cried unto Him. Then He raised up Othniel, who was to them a saviour, judging them, and leading them to victory over their enemies. The words we have emphasized are those which reveal his equipment for this work. Here the phrase, "The Spirit of Jehovah," occurs for the first time in the Bible story. We have read before of "the Spirit of God"; we have heard Moses say: "Would . . . that Jehovah would put His Spirit upon them." But now it is said that "The Spirit of Jehovah came upon" this man. There is no doubt that the reference is to the Holy Spirit; but the suggestion is not so much that of the might of God, as in the phrase "the Spirit of God" or *Elohim*, as of the grace and condescension of God. It was "the Spirit of *Jehovah*," that is, of the One Who was ever pledged to the need of His people, and Who became to them exactly what they needed in order to rescue them. This Spirit came upon a man, whose relationship to Caleb at least suggests that he was a man loyal to God amidst the prevalent declension of the people. By that enduement of love and power, he was perfectly equipped for his work.

Now Deborah, a prophetess . . . she judged Israel at that time.—*Judges* 4. 4.

In the light of subsequent Jewish prejudice against women as leaders, the story of Deborah is full of interest, as it reveals the fact that there never was any such prejudice in the mind of God. Whereas motherhood in all the sanctity and beauty of that great word, is the special function and glory of womanhood, yet when a woman is specially gifted for the exercise of prophetic and administrative work, she is not barred by any Divine law from such work. Deborah was a prophetess in the full sense of that word; that is, she was the inspired mouthpiece of the Word of God to her people. She also judged Israel, and whatever that meant in the case of the men who exercised that office, it also meant in her case. She was a saviour, a deliverer; she administered the affairs of the people, and led them out of the circumstances of difficulty into which their sin had brought them. One can imagine how this daughter of her people, true child of faith, had suffered under the consciousness of the degradation of the people. There is a touch of poetry and romance in the story which is full of fascination. Ever and anon in the long history of God's patient dealing with men, we find Him raising up some woman to lead, to guide, to inspire; and always there is this same element of enthusiasm and force. The one great message of the story seems to be that it warns us to take heed that we do not imagine ourselves to be wiser than God. When He calls and equips a woman to high service, let us beware lest we dishonour Him by refusing to recognize her, or co-operate with her.

Curse ye Meroz. . . . Because they came not to the help of the Lord.—*Judges* 5. 23.

The words are taken from the great song of Deborah in celebration of victory. It is full of fire and passion throughout, and is a remarkable revelation of the character of the woman. Its first part is a chant of confidence, telling the secret of the victories won. Everything is attributed to the direct government and activity of God. The second part celebrates the victory. Those who, hearing the call for help, responded, are spoken of with approval. Those who remained behind, taking no part in the conflict, are the objects of her fierce scorn. These particular words constituted her curse on neutrality. Meroz had not joined the enemies of the nation in open hostility. It had held aloof. Its sin was that it had not helped. There are hours and situations when neutrality becomes criminal. It is always so when the principles of righteousness, justice, and compassion are involved. In such hours, to stand aloof is to range oneself on the side of evil things. In the case of the enterprise of God in human history, as that enterprise is centred in Christ, it is always so. To this Christ bore unequivocal witness when He said: "He that is not with Me is against Me; he that gathereth not with Me, scattereth abroad." This is a clarion note which needs to be sounded abroad. There are multitudes of people who are in the condition of Meroz. They would protest that they do not desire to hinder; but they do nothing to help. So superlative is the claim of Christ, and so fundamental to all human well-being His work that neutrality is impossible. The curse of Deborah rests upon all such attitudes.

The Lord is with thee, thou mighty man of valour.—*Judges* 6. 12.

The story of Gideon is one of the most fascinating in this Book. Forty years' rest followed the work of Deborah. Then the people fell again into evil ways, and for seven years suffered the most cruel oppression at the hands of Midian. They were driven to hide in dens and caves and strongholds. From that terrible situation Gideon was raised up to deliver them. These words were addressed to him by the Angel of Jehovah. They reveal the secrets of the strength which gave him the victory presently over Midian; and those secrets were two. First, there was the one supreme fact that Jehovah was with him; but there was also what he was in himself—"a mighty man of valour." Wherein did that valour consist? Apparently he was a simple man living a very ordinary life. The Angel found him about his daily duty, "beating out wheat in the wine-press." He had given no sign of military disposition or ability. We shall discover the answer to the inquiry as we listen to what he said to the Angel. To the heavenly visitor he confessed his double consciousness. This may be stated in two sentences which he uttered: "Did not Jehovah bring us up?" "Jehovah hath cast us off." He was thus revealed as a man conscious of the true relation of the people to Jehovah; and of the fact that their sufferings were the result of the Divine judgment. It is ever the man who has this double vision of Divine intention and human failure, who is the man of might and valour. With that man the Lord can work.

By the three hundred men that lapped will I save you.—*Judges* 7. 7.

This is a wonderful illustration of the kind of men that God needs in order to carry out His enterprises in the world. This company of three hundred was an elect remnant, carefully separated from an army of thirty-two thousand. It becomes valuable when we observe the principles of selection. Two were applied. The first was stated in the words: "Whosoever is fearful, and trembling, let him return." On this test, twenty-two thousand retired. Those who were left were devoid of fear. The second was stated in the words: "Every one that boweth down upon his knees to drink." All such were to be sent home. The test was peculiarly military. Men in such a position were not on guard against sudden surprise. Those who took unnecessary time over necessary things were sent back. On this test nine thousand seven hundred were retired. Those who were left were full of caution. It is an old story, and full of Eastern colour, but the central values abide. God needs, to do His work, those who know no fear; and those whose devotion forbids them taking any risks. Courage and caution are the essentials of victorious campaigning. If all those to-day who are fearful about the issue of God's work would retire from the ranks, the armies of the Lord would be much stronger. If those who lack the uttermost devotion, which watches as well as prays, would stand aside, the sacramental hosts would do better work. The work of God needs quality more than quantity. This is the death-warrant of statistics.

I will not rule over you, neither shall my son rule over you; the Lord shall rule over you.—*Judges* 8. 23.

Here was clearly manifested the decline of the people from the high ideal and central glory of their national life. They were a Theocracy, needing (and so far having) no king other than Jehovah. Their creation as a nation by God was in order that this true conception of life should have its manifestation among other nations. Their peculiarity was their distinctive feature, and their secret of power among the nations surrounding them. All the recurring discipline through which they passed resulted from their rebellion against the rule of God, and constituted His method of restoring them to that rule. They found relief in the judges who were raised up of God, and began to hanker after some ruler, visible, and of their own number. They thought that, by securing this, they would preserve themselves from the recurrence of these troubles. So they proposed establishing an hereditary rulership, that is, kingship, and they asked Gideon to accept the position. He declined in these words, and by so doing revealed his clear understanding of the truth about the nation. That is the true attitude of all those whom God raised up to lead and deliver His people. Their leadership must ever stop short of sovereignty. Their business is never that of superseding the Divine rule; but of interpreting it, and of leading the people to recognition of it, and submission to it. This is true, not only of kings, but also of priests, prophets, and preachers.

Hearken unto me, ye men of Shechem, that God may hearken unto you.—*Judges* 9. 7.

Thus did Jotham introduce his parable. He saw that the action which the men of Shechem were contemplating was one which could only result in their cutting off from the right of approach to God. God can only hearken to men when they walk in the way of His commandments. If they rebel against His rule, and break His laws, He cannot receive them, or attend to their prayers. Gideon had refused to be made king; but when he passed on, Abimelech, his natural son—a man unprincipled and brutal, but of great personal force—secured to himself the allegiance of the men of Shechem, and practically usurped the position of king. In order to make his position secure, he encompassed the massacre of all the sons of Gideon, except Jotham. He, escaping, uttered a parabolic prophecy from the height of Mount Gerizim. It was full of a fine scorn for Abimelech, whom he compared to the bramble accepting a position declined by the olive, the fig-tree, and the vine. It is noticeable that these were the three symbols of the national life of Israel. In the course of his parable, he indicated the line along which judgment would fall upon them, if they committed this wrong. Abimelech would be the destruction of the men of Shechem, and the men of Shechem would be the destruction of Abimelech. That prophecy was literally fulfilled. The nation was chosen to reign over nations, under the rule of God. It lost its power to reign, when it ceased to yield its allegiance to its one and only King. Had it then hearkened to Jotham, it would have been possible for God to hearken to it.

His soul was grieved for the misery of Israel.—*Judges* 10. 16.

These are wonderful words about God, especially when considered in the light of the circumstances concerning which they were written. The people of God seem for a period to have given themselves up with an appalling abandonment to almost every form of idolatry which presented itself to them. Notice the list: the Baalim, the Ashtaroth, the gods of Syria, the gods of Zidon, the gods of Moab, the gods of the children of Ammon, the gods of the Philistines. The anger of Jehovah against them proceeded in judgment through the Philistines and the men of Ammon, and it continued for eighteen years. Then, in their sore distress, they cried to God, and for the first time it is recorded that He refused to save them, reminding them of how repeatedly He had delivered them, and yet they had turned back to their evil courses. In the message of His anger there was clearly evident a purpose of love. He would recall them to a recognition of His

power by bidding them seek deliverance from the gods whom they had worshipped. The method produced the result. They put away the strange gods and returned to Jehovah. Then, these words admit us to the deep fact underlying all the Divine activity: "His soul was grieved for the misery of Israel." The Hebrew word literally means "impatient." It suggests God's restlessness in the presence of suffering. It is the restlessness of His love, and that is the cause of His anger, and the governing principle in all its activities.

Jephthah fled from his brethren.—*Judges* 11. 3.

To those who are willing to see it, the story of Jephthah affords a solemn warning as to the wrong of treating a child born out of wedlock with contempt. It is constantly done, even by excellent people, and it is wholly unjust. Here we see God raising up such a man to be a judge of his people, and to deliver them in time of grave difficulty. Jephthah was the son of a harlot, and had been thrust out from his inheritance by the legitimate sons of his father. The iron had entered into his soul, and he had gathered to himself a band of men, and had become a kind of outlawed freebooter. He was a man of courage and heroic daring, and it is impossible to read the story of the approach of the men of Gilead to him in the time of distress without recognizing the excellencies of his character. He can hardly be measured by the standards of Israel, for he had lived outside the national ideal. Yet it is evident that he was a man of clear religious convictions. All of which should be remembered when the question of his vow is discussed. The picture of this man, defrauded by his brethren of his rightful inheritance, fleeing from them with the sense of wrong burning its way into his soul, is very natural and very sad. The one thing which we emphasize is that God did not count the wrong for which he was not responsible, a disqualification. He raised him up; He gave him His Spirit; He employed him to deliver His people in the hour of their need. Let us ever refrain from the sin of being unjust to men by holding them disqualified for service or friendship by sins for which they are not to blame.

We will burn thine house upon thee with fire.—*Judges* 12. 1.

We draw attention to these words in the story because they illustrate the arrogance with which injustice often speaks, and the sequel shows the utter futility and folly of such boasting. The men of Ephraim could have had no reason for this complaint and threat, other than that of hatred of Jephthah. They complained that he had not called upon them to help as he went forth to war with Ammon. The folly of that complaint is evidenced by the fact that he had gained a complete victory without their aid. If he had failed, they might have had some reason for complaint. The answer of Jephthah to the complaint and threat was logical and final. He first told them why he had not called them. When he and his people had been at strife with Ammon, he had asked the help of Ephraim, and it had been withheld. Why then should he appeal to them again? Having thus given an answer to the complaint, he replied to the threat by severe punishment. It may safely be affirmed that behind arrogance and threatening, there is invariably injustice; and further, that these things are the sure signs of incompetence. A frantic boast is proof positive of fundamental weakness. To threaten frightfulness is to declare the consciousness of wrong. Those who are strong in the sense of the justice of their cause, are never arrogant in their speech; they do not threaten, they act. When we are tempted to loud protestations of ability, we may well seek for the weakness which inspired us to such wordiness. When we are inclined to threaten, we are wise if we ask ourselves what injustice prompts such action.

Wherefore asketh thou after My name, seeing it is Wonderful?—*Judges* 13. 18.

This answer of the heavenly Visitor to Manoah is very interesting. Whereas the answer was in itself in the form of a question, it was nevertheless a declaration. He told him that His name was Wonderful. All this opens out a line of study which may be followed with profit. The reading of this reply almost inevitably calls to mind two other passages of Scripture, far apart in the books of the Bible. The first is in Genesis 32. 29, "Wherefore it is that thou dost ask after My name?" The other is in Isaiah 9. 6, "His name shall be called Wonderful." The question was addressed to Jacob by one who was described as "A man"; (Gen. 32. 24), and concerning Whom Jacob said in the morning. "I have seen God face to face" (Gen. 32. 30). The prophecy was concerned with the Child, the Son upon Whose shoulder government is to rest, and Whose name is also "Mighty God." The visitor to Manoah is described as "The Angel of Jehovah," and Manoah's wife described Him as "A Man of God." A careful study of the Old Testament Scriptures will show that there is a distinction between the phrases, "an angel" and "the Angel of Jehovah." "The Man of God," Whose name was "Wonderful," was none other than the Son of God. Here then we have a Christophany, and so wherever this august title "the Angel of Jehovah" appears. I repeat: all this opens out a profitable line of study. This note is only intended to suggest it.

And the Spirit of the Lord came mightily upon him.—*Judges* 14. 6.

The story of Samson is one of the strangest in the Old Testament. It is surely that of a great opportunity and a disastrous failure. Everything would seem to have been in his favour. The story of beginnings is full of tragic pathos in the light of the after years. His birth was foretold, and the method of his training indicated by the Angel of Jehovah, whose name was given as Wonderful. Of his earlier years it is said that "the Spirit of Jehovah began to move him." Had he but yielded wholly to the impulses of the Spirit, how different a story might have been recorded! In this chapter the boy is seen, having grown to manhood's estate. full of strength and of passion. Going to Timnah, he saw a woman of the Philistines, and desired to take her to wife. His parents attempted to dissuade him, but he determined to follow his own inclination. This action was a direct violation of the law of God. There is nothing to admire in this man in these transactions. In the course of the reading, two statements arrest our attention. The first is in verse 4: "His father and mother knew not that it was of Jehovah"; and the second in verse 6: "The Spirit of Jehovah came mightily upon him." They both reveal God overruling the life of this man, and giving him renewed opportunities, in spite of his failure. The phrase, "It was of Jehovah," is used in the same sense as in Joshua 11.20. God makes the folly of man to contribute finally to the fulfilment of His own purpose.

We are come down to bind thee.—*Judges* 15. 12.

What a contemptible action is recorded here on the part of the men of Judah. Three thousand of them went down to bind Samson, in order to hand him over to the Philistines. Their words revealed their meanness of spirit. They said: "Knowest thou not that. the Philistines are rulers over us?" What terrible abjectness was this on the part of the people who had been made a nation having God as their one and only Ruler! So low had they sunk at this time that they were willing to bind, and hand over, the one man who was a menace to their enemies. There is no situation more tragic than that in which the people of God, in cringing fear of their enemies, are prepared to sacrifice a man who alone among them has the courage and the ability to oppose those enemies. And yet the same kind of thing has often been done in the long process of the enterprise of faith. As we see Samson, the Spirit of Jehovah again coming upon him mightily, breaking the bonds, and then with terrific onslaught, armed only with the jawbone of an ass, slaying a thousand of their number, we are conscious of what he might have been and done, had he been wholly yielded to that "Spirit of Jehovah," instead of governed so largely by the fires of his own passion. No force employed against him, whether that of the direct hostility of his enemies, or that of the treachery of his kinsmen, could have overcome him. In him was powerfully illustrated the truth of Shakespeare's words:

The fault, dear Brutus, is not in our stars,
But in ourselves, that we are underlings.

But he wist not that the Lord was departed from him.—*Judges* 16. 20.

Than this, there is no more tragic sentence in the whole Bible. It reveals a most appalling condition, that of the unconscious loss of the one essential to success in the work of God. At last the hour had come in which God no longer co-operated with Samson; and the man did not know it! It is impossible to believe that this unconsciousness was a sudden thing. That is to say, this man had lost the keen consciousness of the presence of God, or else he would have been conscious of His absence. Having yielded to his own passions, rather than to the Spirit of God, he had come to the condition in which his knowledge of the power of that Spirit was intellectual rather than experimental. He had had great experiences of that power, and he went on expecting them, even when he was making them impossible by his manner of life. In the hour of need, he said: "I will go out as at other times."; but he could not. The expected experience did not come. He was caught, and blinded, and made the bond-slave of his foes. The story is one to fill the soul with holy fear. The possibility of going on in an attempt to do the work of God after God has withdrawn Himself, is an appalling one. The issue is always that of defeat and the uttermost shame. The value of the whole story for us is that it ought to teach us that if we yield ourselves to those desires of the flesh and spirit which are out of harmony with the will of God, He must withdraw from us the power in which to do His work. The only way to be sure that we have not lost the fellowship of enablement, is to maintain a conscious fellowship in complete obedience.

In those days there was no king in Israel: every man did that which was right in his own eyes.—*Judges* 17. 6.

These words constitute a commentary on the conditions obtaining in this particular period; and they were doubtless written at a later time, when the nation was brought to a more orderly state under the rule of its kings. Whether the writer intended to or no, there is a deeper note in them than that. The nation had turned away from its one true King. He had not abandoned them utterly. That He had never done. But they had flung off restraint, and were acting according to their own desires. This chapter, and the next four, do not continue a consecutive history. That ended with the story of Samson. In these five chapters we have illustrations of the internal conditions of the national life, and it is most probable that they were written with that intention. The strange and deadly mixture of motive is set forth in the story of Micah. His act was a violation of the second Commandment. When he made images to himself and to his household, he was not adopting the idolatries of the heathen. His mother's words reveal her recognition of Jehovah, "Blessed be my son of Jehovah." So also do his own words to the Levite: "Now know I that Jehovah will do me good." Micah was desirous of maintaining his relations with God, but he attempted to do so by violating the commands of God. When in full and practical loyalty the King is dethroned, it is impossible to maintain relationship with Him.

So they set them up Micah's graven image which he made, all the time that the house of God was in Shiloh.—*Judges* 18. 31.

Whether intentionally on the part of the writer or no, there is a touch of satire in this declaration. There, at Shiloh, was the true centre of the national life, the house of God. In connection with its worship, all the resources of national strength were to be found. Nevertheless, at Dan they gathered about the false, and rendered a worship which was destructive. The terrible decadence of the religious idea is very startlingly revealed in this whole story. The consciousness of the importance of religion was deeply embedded in the mind of the people. Micah must worship, and the Danites felt the necessity of maintaining some kind of relationship with God. Then why did they turn from the true, to a perversion which was utterly false? The answer is found in the revelation of motive. In each case there was a prostitution of religion to purposes of personal prosperity. Micah hoped by the maintenance of some form of worship, and the presence of a priest, that Jehovah would do him good, by which he evidently meant that material prosperity would come to him. The Danites, going forth on the enterprise of providing more territory for themselves, were anxious for the maintenance of religion. Whenever religion is acknowledged and adopted merely in order to ensure material prosperity, it suffers degradation. Thus do men try to serve God and Mammon. It cannot be done. The attempt always fails. All history proves the folly of leaving the true God for the false, in the ruin which results to those who do so. God is not mocked.

Consider of it; take counsel, and speak.—*Judges* 19. 30.

This, and the next two chapters, tell the story of a Levite, and in them again a clear mirror is held up to the times, revealing the most startling moral conditions, and showing how good and evil conflicted during the period. These particular words reveal the effect produced upon the people by the terrible message conveyed by the portions of this dead woman. In the story there are several things we do well to note. First, we must recognize the imperfection of the times as revealed in the practice of polygamy and concubinage among the chosen people. And yet, even in these matters, we see how far they were in advance of the peoples of the land. There is evidenced a moral sense, and an ideal of virtue which stands in striking contrast to the practices of the other nations. The fact that a Levite took to himself a concubine shows a low level of morality, but this must be considered in the light of the times. When this is done, we notice the sacredness which characterized his thought of his relation to her. This was entirely distinct from the loose conceptions of the Canaanitish people. Then again, the terrible degeneracy of a section of the chosen people is seen in the action of the men of Gibeah, which was nothing less than that of the men of Sodom of long before. And once more, on the other hand, the method of the Levite, drastic and terrible, by which he drew the attention of Israel to the sin of these men, is a revelation of the conscience of the better part of the people concerning purity. All this portrays the results of the loss of the keen sense of the Kingship of God.

And the Lord smote Benjamin before Israel.—*Judges* 20. 35.

These words briefly recall the real meaning of the awful judgment that fell upon Benjamin. It was the stroke of God. The chapter gives the result of the consideration, taking counsel, and speaking, of the nation in answer to the call of the Levite. His action served its purpose. The nation was stirred to its centre. A great moral passion flamed out. Underneath all the degeneracy there was a very definite stratum of religious conviction, and it was this which, in the presence of the iniquity of the men of Gibeah, sprang to life and action. It is very remarkable how, in the case of nations backsliding from religious ideals, this is ever so. In the midst of the most soiled and debased times, in the presence of some more than usually violent manifestation of evil, the slumbering convictions of a people will flame into new sensitiveness and demand recognition. In response to the ghastly and bloody appeal of the Levite, Israel gathered itself together before God, seeking to know how to act. The low level of morality which had manifested itself in so fearful a form, could only be dealt with by general suffering. The men who were in the wrong were brutally defiant. Moreover, they were strong enough at first to defeat the army of Israel. This fact at least suggests that Israel was not clean enough herself to punish wrongdoers. Again the people gathered before God, and this time in weeping and lamentation. After this, they again went forward, this time to victory and the sore punishment of the sinning people, and those who had condoned their sin. Thus not Israel, but God, smote Benjamin.

Why is this come to pass in Israel, that there should be to-day one tribe lacking in Israel?—*Judges* 21. 3.

This is a very sad chapter, and gives us the last of the illustrations of the conditions obtaining when there was no king in Israel. As we have seen, more than once the writer drew attention to the fact, and so traced the lawlessness to the lack of authority. The truth is that Israel had lost its living relation to its one and only King. Uninstructed zeal, even in the cause of righteousness, often goes beyond its proper limits, and does harm rather than good. The terrible slaughter of the men of Benjamin continued until not more than six hundred of the tribe were left. Then another of those sudden revulsions which characterize the action of inflamed peoples occurred. Israel is seen suddenly filled with pity for the tribe so nearly exterminated. They realized that the unity and completeness of the family of Jacob was threatened by their action. The sad part of the story is that, to remedy the threatened evil, they resorted to means which were utterly unrighteous. Wives were provided for the men of Benjamin by further unholy slaughter at Jabesh-Gilead, and by the vilest iniquity at Shiloh. It is impossible to read these last five chapters without realizing how perilous is the condition of any people who act without some clearly defined principle. Passion moves to high purpose only as it is governed by principle. If it lacks that, at one moment it will march in heroic determination to establish high ideals, and purity of life; and almost immediately, by some change of mood, will act in brutality and all manner of evil. Humanity without its one King, is cursed by lawlessness.

RUTH

Thy people shall be my people, and thy God my God.—*Ruth* 1. 16.

The Book of Ruth stands in striking contrast to the Book of Judges, and especially to the last five chapters thereof. The story which it tells illustrates the truth that God has never left Himself without witness. It is an idyll of faithfulness amid infidelity. It has, moreover, the value of being a link in the chain of history, showing how God moved forward to the central things of His redeeming purpose through faithful souls. The choice of Ruth, here recorded, in its devotion and in the very manner in which she expressed it, has become enshrined in the heart of humanity. With constant recurrence her language has been employed to express the fidelity of love. The younger woman found her heart closely knit to the older one, and she declined to be severed from her in the pathway that lay before her, choosing to share whatever the future might have in store for the one upon whom her love was set. While all this is true, it does not touch the deepest note. It is patent that Ruth's love for Naomi was created by the new faith which she had learned from her. The deepest note in her expression of devotion was: "Thy God, my God." It is a beautiful illustration of how a quiet, strong fidelity to God produces faith in Him on the part of others. Happy indeed are we, if our life is such as to compel some soul to say, "Thy God shall be my God." This is what Naomi had done for Ruth. This result is never obtained by the witness of the lips, save as that is vindicated and reinforced by the witness of life.

Her hap was to light on the portion of the field belonging unto Boaz.—*Ruth* 2. 3.

The home-coming of Naomi and Ruth was to poverty, and they were faced by very practical problems. These were rendered more difficult by the fact that Ruth was a Moabitess. Yet, she it was who faced the fight, and went forth as a gleaner to gather what would suffice for immediate sustenance. The human side of things is expressed in these words. But the statement is by no means a pagan one. The Hebrew word rendered "hap" does not necessarily mean that the thing that occurred was accidental, although often used in that way. It literally means, *that which she met with*, and the statement is that it was that portion of the field which belonged to Boaz. All the issues reveal the Divine overruling. That which she met with, was that to which she was guided by God—if all unconsciously, yet none the less definitely. God led this woman, who

had given up everything on the principle of faith, to a man, completely actuated by the same faith. The lines of his portrait are few, but they are strong, and a man of the finest quality is revealed. It is a radiant illustration of the truth that God does guide those who confide in Him and in the most definite way. Some experience is often so simple that we are tempted to say it happened, and to mean that it was a sort of accident. Yet the long issues make it certain that it was no accident, but part of a covenant, ordered in all things and sure. When in loyalty we make the venture of faith in God, we are ever choosing the path that is safe and sure. There are no accidents in the life of faith. In its music, the accidentals perfect the harmony.

Then will I do the part of a kinsman to thee.—*Ruth* 3. 13.

In these words the nobility and faithfulness of Boaz are manifested. It is hardly possible to read the story without seeing that he loved Ruth, and that therefore he was perfectly ready to take the responsibility of the next-of-kin. There was, however another who had a prior right, and in loyalty to the law of his people, he gave that one his opportunity. The action of Naomi in this matter can hardly be characterized as other than doubtful, and on the basis of faith alone, it is difficult to justify it. Nevertheless, the expedient to which she resorted must be judged in the light of her own age. We must recognize that at the lowest it was an error of judgment, rather than a wilful disobedience; and the overruling love of God carried it to a beneficent issue. One element, and perhaps the strongest, in her action, was that of her confidence in Boaz. Her appeal should have been made to the next-of-kin, but the whole attitude of Boaz toward Ruth had made it natural for her to look to him. He, however, fulfilled his first obligation to the law, as he gave the first opportunity to the true kinsman. This next-of-kin had a perfect right lawfully to abandon his claim, seeing that another was ready to assume it. Thus again the Divine, overruling to highest ends is seen in the case of those who walk by faith, and in strict obedience to the known law of God.

They called his name Obed; he is the father of Jesse, the father of David.—*Ruth* 4. 17.

The story ends with poetic simplicity and beauty. "Boaz took Ruth, and she became his wife." Naomi at last was comforted indeed. The women of her own people spoke words of cheer to her which unquestionably were full of comfort, as they set forth the praises of the one who had chosen to share her affliction, and had become the medium of her succour. There is a stately simplicity in this story of the issue. It constitutes a record of the Divine movement in the history of the chosen people, for thus the kingly line is ordained, in the midst of infidelity, through faithful souls. All the period of the Judges was characterized by the failure of the people to realize the great ideal of the Theocracy. They had no king because they were disobedient to the One King. Presently we shall hear them clamouring for a king "like the nations," and one will be appointed by whose reign of forty years they

will learn the difference between earthly rule and the direct government of God. Then the man after God's own heart will succeed him; and that man will be David, descended from these souls who, in dark and difficult days, realized in their own lives the Divine ideal, as they walked humbly with God. But this Book flings its light much further on. After centuries had run their course, there sprang from this union of Boaz and Ruth in faith and love, the Man of Nazareth, Jesus, the One and only King of men, because He was not only a Child born to Mary, descended from these, but also the Son of God in all the fulness of that title. God, in love and might, ever moves on through human failure, in co-operation with human faith.

FIRST SAMUEL

If Thou wilt . . . give . . . I will give.—1 *Sam.* 1. 11.

These words constitute the central terms of the vow which Hannah vowed to Jehovah. The story is full of human interest, but there is much Divine light upon it. The proper and beautiful passion for motherhood drove this devout woman of the Hebrew people to Jehovah in prayer; and He made it His way of raising up for His people one who was to be their leader in strangely difficult times. Whatever may have been the motive of Hannah's desire, the method she followed is one which is very full of suggestiveness. This pre-natal dedication of a life to the service of God, was an act of faith; and it was one which, by the working of wonderful and mysterious laws, produced definite results in the life of the child. The question is still sometimes asked as to when we should begin to deal with our children as to their relationship with God. Does not this story afford a somewhat startling answer to the inquiry? Here was a woman who by an act of solemn faith deliberately dedicated her child to God, not only before he was born, but while he was not yet conceived. In such an act what remarkable dedication of motherhood was manifested! With all the spiritual influence of such a vow upon her, how carefully Hannah would guard, first herself and then her child, in order that he might be worthy of the high service to which he was thus dedicated! The old-fashioned mothers who still believe that "children are a heritage of Jehovah" are those who give them— the children—opportunities in life which are denied to those who are thought of in other wise. Such dedications of children by mothers, cannot ensure the dedication of themselves by the children, but it makes it very difficult for the children to go wrong ultimately. This is a great subject, and worthy of careful pondering.

Samuel ministered before the Lord, being a child, girded with a linen ephod.—1 *Sam.* 2. 18.

The words "being a child" are inscribed by the chronicler to emphasize the fact that Samuel at this time was quite a young boy. He is placed in contrast quite definitely with the sons of Eli. They, the appointed priests of Jehovah as sons of Eli, were desecrating their office, and bringing the whole religious life into contempt by their evil courses. Here in the Tabernacle precincts was a lad being prepared for such high service as would restore these religious facts to their true place in the thought of the people. We must remember that at this time the boy was by no means conscious of the ultimate meaning of his life. So far he had no knowledge of God based upon personal and first-hand communion with Him. His service of Jehovah was that of his natural and simple waiting upon Eli in all the details of everyday life, under the inspiration of his love for his mother. This is the true line of religious life and activity for children. The Boy of Nazareth, long afterwards, surely ministered before Jehovah, when He went down with His parents and was subject unto them. It should ever be the aim of parents, and all who have charge of the little ones, to help them to understand the sacred beauty of doing all the natural everyday things as to the Lord. It is by such devotion in the ordinary things, that they are being prepared for some hour when the call of God will come to them directly, and so the way be opened for direct communion and co-operation with Him on their part.

Speak; for Thy servant heareth.— 1 *Sam.* 3. 10.

These were the words in which Samuel yielded himself to God, for the reception of

His word, on behalf of Israel. The boy, dedicated to the service of God before his birth, and having ministered to Jehovah simply and naturally by serving Eli, was now brought into a closer relation with Jehovah. He was still very young— Josephus says about twelve years of age. That was the age at which the Hebrew boy came to be a son of the Law, that is, began to be directly responsible. At this juncture God spoke to him. Instructed by Eli, he answered the call, and thus submitted himself of his own will to God. Thus yielded, he became the instrument of Divine action in a remarkable way, for, like Moses, he was not judge only, he was prophet and priest. Simple as these words are, they reveal the one true attitude of those who are called of God to deliver His word to men. That attitude must ever be that of the wholly-surrendered life, and that of waiting to hear the word of God. Too often we fail because we do not listen before we speak. With all best intentions we attempt to interpret the will of God by a general knowledge, and the observation of the circumstances of the hour. It is ever a mistake. God still waits to speak to those through whom He would make known His will; and it is for them to wait until His revelation comes. Only thus can there be anything like authority in the message delivered.

The glory is departed from Israel; for the ark of God is taken.—1 Sam. 4. 22.

It was indeed a dark hour for Israel when the Philistines routed them in battle. There fell of Israel thirty thousand footmen; the two sons of Eli were slain; and the Ark of God was captured. A woman in the anguish of child-birth understood the central tragedy. Her husband was slain, but the more terrible fact was that the Ark was taken. The glory had departed from Israel. That Ark had been at once the symbol and pledge of the Presence of Jehovah in the midst of His people To that Presence they owed everything. If that was gone, Israel had no glory, for she had neither might nor wisdom apart from her relationship to God. The perpetual spiritual significance of this is patent. The people of God, in every age, have no glory save that of the actual and manifested Presence of the Lord in their midst. If that is lacking, they are poor indeed. They may be, as to earthly matters, rich and increased with goods, and having need of nothing; but they are poor, blind, naked, miserable, when the living Lord is not patently present among them. And there is no mistaking the absence. Men of the world know when the elaborate and spectacular organization is devoid of the power of the living Presence; and when it is so, they hold it in contempt. The sense of the Presence of the Lord to-day may be mystic, defying our explanation, but it is the one and only thing which gives us distinction, and creates our power in the affairs of men. When it is absent, there is no glory—we are Ichabod.

Send away the ark of the God of Israel, and let it go again to its own place.—1 Sam. 5. 11.

This short chapter is full of interest, in that it shows how God is able to become His own witness when His people fail in their testimony to Him among the nations. All that is essential in this story is of abiding application. To Israel the ark was the centre and symbol of their national life. In itself it was devoid of power. In the hour of peril from Philistine attack, and hoping to save themselves, the people had brought this Ark into the midst of the fight. That was an entirely superstitious use thereof, and had proved utterly unavailing. The Ark was not a charm equal to delivering disobedient Israel. But God would not permit the enemies of His people to trifle with it. If men hold their peace, stones will cry out; and if chosen witnesses are unfaithful to God, then He will make the Ark, which is the symbol of His presence, the occasion of His judgment upon His enemies. Thus Philistia was made to feel that if she had been able for the moment to conquer and break the power of Israel, she had still to deal with the God of Israel, and that was a different matter. This cry of the people to the Philistine lords to send the Ark away was the result of this conviction. Thus God constantly breaks through on human consciousness directly, not always in ways which we describe as supernatural, but always with certainty and conviction. This fact may give us encouragement, but it must not be used as an excuse for the infidelity of those who should be His witnesses. Had Israel been obedient, Philistia had never taken the Ark of God.

And the kine took the straight way by the way to Beth-shemesh.—1 Sam. 6. 12.

These words constitute the record of a remarkable fact, which to Philistia was a conclusive proof of the action and power of God. As the result of the clamour of the people that the Ark should be sent away, a council was called; and the help of the diviners was asked. It is intensely interesting to see how definitely they recognized the·Divine action. Whatever the long years had done for Israel, it is certain that the fear and dread of Jehovah had been implanted in the heart of the surrounding nations. The counsellors advised the sending back of the Ark, accompanied by offerings which would indicate their recognition of the fact that the plagues which had fallen upon them had come by the act of God. The method of sending the Ark was of the nature of an experiment, and the sequel shows how their own test must have conclusively proved to them that God was at work. That the kine took their way directly to Beth-shemesh was clear evidence of His overruling. That they should go quietly, lowing as they went, was a most remarkable fact, for they were "milch kine," not trained to draw loads. That they should travel away from their calves was the more remarkable. That they should take their way to the first city of Israel was conclusive. To those who have eyes to see, God constantly bears witness to Himself by turning the natural courses of men and things into extraordinary and unnatural lines of activity.

Hitherto hath the Lord helped us.— 1 Sam. 7. 12.

A dark period of twenty years is passed over without detailed record. It would seem that for all that time Israel was suffering oppression under the power of Philistia. There was no definite centre of worship; for while the Ark was resting in the house of an individual, the Tabernacle was probably dismantled. During this period Samuel passed from youth to manhood, and now approached the hour of his definite leadership. This was ushered in by the lamenting of the people after God. Of this Samuel took advantage, calling them to return to Him and put away all strange gods. At Mizpeh by a direct Divine intervention the power of Philistia was broken, and her cities were restored to Israel. Samuel erected an altar, and called it Ebenezer. In connection with this, he uttered this great word: "Hitherto hath Jehovah helped us." The significant word is "Hitherto." It included all the experiences through which they had passed, not the victories only, but the discipline and suffering also. This man of clear vision recognized the government of God, and its beneficent purpose and method. Through chastisement God had brought them to lamentation after Himself; through such lamentation, to the condition in which it was possible for Him to deliver them. This is ever so. To look back honestly, is to see that God has always been acting for our highest welfare, even through the dispensations which have been those of calamity and sorrow. The light of that backward look should be allowed to fall upon the present, and give us confidence for the future.

Make us a king to judge us like all the nations.—1 Sam. 8. 5.

In this chapter we come to the dividing-line in the national history of the children of Israel. They had been created by God a Theocracy. That was the peculiar character and glory of their national life. They had no king other than Jehovah. In proportion as they had realized the ideal, they had witnessed to other nations as to the perfection of His government. Their realiza-tion had been, so far as they were concerned, most imperfect. Through persistent deflections, they had created the necessity for the raising up of the judges, and thus had approximated towards a human king. Now the hour came when they definitely asked for such a king. The very terms of their request revealed the evil of it. They asked for a king *like the nations*. Their glory and their power had consisted in their unlikeness to the nations in this very fact. By reason of their failure to submit themselves completely to the rule of God, they had failed, themselves, to realize all the breadth and beneficence of that rule. And so they sought conformity to the ways of the nations. It was a sad fall. There is but one King who is able to govern humanity perfectly, and that is God. Man's only hope of realizing all freedom and all fulness of life is that of return to the Kingdom of God. Never will there be final peace and prosperity on earth, until humanity has rid itself of all human kings, and yielded to God as the one and only King. God has appeared in human history as Man, and He has appointed a day in which He will govern the world in righteousness through that Man. That is the fact which makes it certain that men will find liberty and life in all strength and fulness.

I have looked upon My people, because their cry is come unto Me.— 1 Sam. 9. 16.

These words were spoken by Jehovah to Samuel in explanation of His action in giving them a king. His perfect counsel for them was that they should have no king other than Himself. They had failed to realize this high possibility. Their God knew them; He had looked upon them. Their cry for a king had come up to Him. That cry should be answered. He would give them a king, in order that, in the long processes of experience, they might learn the folly of their choice. In this is revealed a constant method of the Divine government. When men fail to rise to the height of the purpose of God, and clamour for something lower, He gives them what they ask, and then watches over them and guards them as they work out their low choice to its ultimate conclusion, and thus are eventually brought back to His purpose with a full understanding of its perfection. The grace of the method is discovered in the fact that, while God gave them up to the discipline of their choice, He selected the king. If there be one thing more important than any other in our lives, it surely is that we should begin all our praying by petitions which ask that we may be taught to desire only what God desires for us. When desire is out of harmony with the will of God, He constantly grants its petitions, and then in justice and mercy watches over us until we have discovered in experience how much better is His way.

God save the King.—1 Sam. 10. 24

This was the cry of the people when Saul was presented to them as the chosen of Jehovah. The literal translation would be, "Let the king live." It was simply an expression of desire for the long life of the one thus appointed. This first expression of the Hebrew people has passed into the current speech of all peoples who live under monarchic government. In this earliest use of it, it expressed the satisfaction of the people that their request was granted, their recognition of God in the appointment, and their submission to the authority of the appointed one. Such submission was wholly right. If men desire a king, their first duty is to obey the king. Paul recognized this when he clearly enjoined obedience to kings and all in authority. On the side of the king it was, and is, necessary that he recognize the fact that his authority is a delegated authority, that the powers that be are ordained of God. If he fail to do so, and govern without righteousness and justice, then the time will inevitably come when God will act through the people for his dethronement, and if necessary for his death. Not only this Bible history, but all human history testifies to the truth of these things. In them we discover the persistence of the Divine government. Man with all his choosing and planning never escapes from that final authority and power. This is the one and only ground for confidence in human affairs, and it is a rock foundation.

There shall not a man be put to death this day; for to-day the Lord hath wrought deliverance in Israel.—1 Sam. 11. 13.

It would seem as though Saul, going down to his house at Gibeah, did not take up the active responsibilities of his kingship until the Ammonite invasion stirred within him, as the Spirit of God came upon him, a sense of responsibility. He, at once, in the presence of danger, and under the constraint of the Spirit, gathered the people and led them to victory. The closing sentences of the previous chapter reveal the fact that there were certain men who did not agree to his appointment. In the day of his victory the people suggested the punishment of these men. The possibility of greatness in Saul is manifested in that he refused thus to mar the days of God's victory. When we contrast this attitude of the man with that of the days when, the evil spirit being upon him, he sought by every means in his power to destroy David, we realize how great was his fall. At this time he had a true outlook. He took no credit to himself for his victory. He knew that deliverance had come by the act of God. Therefore what right had he to put men to death because they were not loyal to him? The sense of God

corrects all the things of a human life. Where it is acute, there is no room for the passion of revenge. There is not even a care to fight for one's own rights. To realize the Divine government is always to be patient and magnanimous in one's dealings with other men; and let it never be forgotten that such magnanimity will do more to make a throne secure than all the methods of oppressive tyranny.

As for me, God forbid that I should sin against the Lord in ceasing to pray for you.—1 Sam. 12. 23.

Let us be very careful not to misread these words of Samuel, for rightly apprehended they are most arresting and revealing. Samuel did not say: "Far be it from me that I should sin against you, in ceasing to pray for you." There is a secondary sense in which he might have said that, for we do certainly sin against men when we cease to pray for them. But that is so for the very reason which is revealed in what Samuel did actually say, namely: "Far be it from me that I should sin against Jehovah in ceasing to pray for you." His thought was that if he ceased to pray for Israel he would be sinning against God. What a remarkable truth is involved in that conception concerning prayer. Quite simply stated, it is that in prayer we create conditions which make it possible for God to act in ways otherwise impossible to Him. When we cease to pray we limit God. When we pray we open His way to act. We may not be able to account for this philosophically. It may seem to us as though our praying could not possibly make any difference to the putting forth of the Divine power, even though it might possibly affect His will. As a matter of fact, the reverse is true. No prayer of mine can change the will of God, which is ever "good and acceptable and perfect." But my prayer can and does make it possible for His power to operate in ways impossible apart from it. When I cease to pray for men, I sin against God first, because I hinder Him in that I do not help Him. Therefore I grievously sin against men when I cease to pray for them.

Thou hast done foolishly.—1 Sam. 13. 13.

What had this man done? A reference to a previous statement (10. 8) will show that in the day of his anointing Saul had been implicitly instructed by Samuel as to what would take place at Gilgal, and as to what line of action he was to follow. Many years had passed, but undoubtedly that command had been the revelation of a rule of conduct for the king, viz. that he was to undertake no enterprise, apart from the making known of the Divine Will through the prophet, in connection with the offering of burnt-offerings and peace-offerings. The circumstances in which Saul found himself were particularly trying. The people were filled with fear in the presence of the Philistines and were scattering. Saul waited seven days, according to instructions, and then, in order to stop the rout, he arrogated to himself the function which was that of the prophet only. This was his foolishness. It is an arresting story. The action seems plausible; judged by ordinary political standards, it was justifiable. As a matter of fact, it was an action which denied the root principle of theocratic monarchy. It was an act of insubordination to the one King, Jehovah. It cost this man his kingship. We may learn from it that plausibility is no justification for disobedience. However dark the day, or difficult the circumstances, we are never justified in following our own reasonings, when they bring us into conflict with the Divine order. That order is always that of the utmost wisdom, and anything which controverts it is foolishness, however much it may seem to be in harmony with reason.

The people rescued Jonathan, that he died not.—1 Sam. 14. 45.

In this act the true Theocracy, that is, the people God-governed, and so the true democracy, asserted their will against that of the king, and setting aside his ruling, prevented a great wrong. Saul's oath was one of rashness, and was wholly wrong. As Dr. Kirkpatrick has pointed out, it led to three evil results, viz.: It hindered rather than helped the pursuit of the enemy; it involved Jonathan in involuntary trespass; it indirectly occasioned the sin of the people. When the result threatened was the death of Jonathan, all the deepest things in national life found expression, and the king was gloriously disobeyed. It is an arresting and assuring fact that this has often happened in human history. Deep down in the human heart there is that which understands the right; and over and over again, under stress of circumstances, that understanding becomes active. When it does, it is invincible. Nothing can stand before it. Kings, rulers, parliaments, are swept aside, and the right is done. Those who desire to lead men in right ways may always appeal to this deepest fact in human consciousness. That is not to say that the appeal will always be obeyed. There are times when the voice of the people is by no means the voice of God. In such cases however we may know that the voice of the people is contradicting the deepest knowledge of the people. God has never left Himself without witness in the human soul, and whenever we appeal for righteousness and truth, we may know that there is an answering appeal within the human conscience.

Thou hast rejected the word of the Lord; He hath also rejected thee from being king.—1 Sam. 15. 23.

The appointments of God are always conditional. If the conditions upon which they are made are not fulfilled, they cease. Saul was surely chosen of God, and by Him appointed to the office of king over this people. But that position had been clearly defined for him from the beginning. If the people had rejected Jehovah from being their King (see 8. 7), He had not given them up, nor resigned His position as their King. Granting them their request for a king, He had not for a moment ceased to reign. From the first, Saul had been instructed by Samuel that he was but to reveal and exercise the Divine authority. His one law in all his exercise of the Kingly office must be the word of Jehovah. When, leaning to his own understanding, he failed to act according to that word, he forfeited his right to rule. Therefore God rejected him from being king. It is ever so. In His grace God calls men to positions of high responsibility and authority; and in doing so, ever makes clear the conditions upon which they will be able to discharge that responsibility and exercise that authority. If they fail in any degree to fulfil those conditions, they are unable to do the work to which they are appointed. Then without any compromise they are rejected of God from the position. There are no appointments in the economy of the Kingdom of God which are perpetual, save as those holding them are carrying out the appointed work by fulfilling the revealed conditions. However successful in the higher senses a servant of God may be, if he or she depart from the law of God conditioning that service, they will become "castaway" from that service.

There remaineth yet the youngest, and, behold, he keepeth the sheep.—1 Sam. 16. 11.

In these words Jesse expressed what he considered the disqualifications of David for the kingly office. The fact that he was the youngest removed him furthest from the possibilities of responsibility; and the fact that he was doing the most menial work of the family made it most unlikely that he should in any sense be fitted for such responsibility. So completely was David out of the running in his father's thought, that he had not even been sent for. Yet he was the chosen of Jehovah. The deepest reason is given earlier (verse 7), "Jehovah looketh on the heart." Thus even here in these olden times we are brought face to face with a matter which even yet men have hardly come to realize. All the things which men count as privileges, and therefore as creating fitness for position and high service, are in themselves of no value in the sight of God. He looketh on the heart. He considers the deepest fact in personality, the inner and hidden impulse, desire, affection. Perhaps there is a yet deeper note in the story. The very supposed disadvantages in the case of David were advantages. The youngest son would naturally, from the discipline of those earlier years, be more free from arrogance than Eliab the first-born. The shepherd-boy was, in the very work of that position, learning the true art of kingship. Homer said: "All kings are shepherds of the people," and that certainly is the Biblical conception. God's choices and appointments are ever based upon the highest wisdom.

Thou comest to me with a sword, and with a spear, and with a javelin: but I come to thee in the name of the Lord of hosts, the God of the armies of Israel, which thou hast defied.—1 Sam. 17. 45.

The contrast in these words is between the equipment of the two men. Looking at them apart from this equipment, the contrast between them proved the inequality of the combat. Goliath stood somewhere in the neighbourhood of ten feet high, and was massive in proportion. David was by comparison a stripling. On that level of observation an onlooker would say that this was not war, it was murder. The youth could have no chance. This was not his own conception of things, as these words show; and the reason was, that he took account of the equipment of each. The man came armed with offensive weapons, all in the realm of the physical. The youth had also material weapons of a simple, primitive nature, but he did not name them. He was armed with the profound sense of the righteousness of his cause. The armies defied, were the armies of Jehovah of hosts. In His name then, he went forth to conflict. The sequel we know. The material weapons of David were needed, and on that level, they were superior to those of the giant, for they operated ere the sword, the spear, or the javelin could be brought into use. But it was the sense of the righteousness of his cause which gave inerrancy and strength to the slinging of David. The truth is of abiding application.

And Saul eyed David from that day and forward.—1 Sam. 18. 9.

Saul became suspicious and jealous of David. The reason is given later (verse 12): "Saul was afraid of David, because Jehovah was with him, and was departed from Saul." This is an inexpressibly sad and tragic story. This man was set aside from a position of trust, through his own sin, and now was filled with hatred of the man who was called to assume the position, and fulfil the responsibilities from which

he had been rejected. The processes of sin are terrible indeed. Out of the first act, others inevitably grow, until the whole nature becomes corrupted. Saul stooped to the basest acts in his hatred of David, and sought every method to rid himself of the man whom he considered his rival. In all this, we see the blindness which results from sin. Saul seems to have had no consciousness that in his persecution of David he was still fighting against God. Here we need to watch and pray. If through our failure, the Divine discipline operates, we deepen our sin by fighting against it. Our true attitude should be that of accepting it, and yielding to it. What a different story would that of Saul have been if he had submitted to the chastisement of God, and received David as the appointed king! Through such acquiescence in the chastening of the Lord the soul may be restored to fulness of life. Even though the opportunity of some special service is lost for ever through disobedience, the life of fellowship may be restored and maintained; and in some other way God may still make use of those who, thus having failed, are yet responsive to the deepest intentions of His discipline.

An evil spirit from the Lord was upon Saul.—1 Sam. 19. 9.

This evil spirit came upon Saul when the Spirit of Jehovah departed from him (see 16. 14). There is no doubt that Saul suffered through all this period from a mental disorder. His actions were those of a madman, over and over again. What is remarkable in the narrative is, first, that this malady is attributed to the action of an evil spirit, who found its opportunity when the Spirit of the Lord was withdrawn; and secondly, that this evil spirit is declared to have been under the government of God also, in that it is described as "from Jehovah." This is all very suggestive The tendency of modern thinking, to deny the actuality of the influence of spirits on human life, is entirely out of harmony with Scripture teaching. Therein, the fact is always recognized. Two things, however, are illustrated in this story, and the whole Biblical revelation corroborates them. The first is, that the spirits that have access to the soul of man are all evil; they are the spirits of lawlessness. There is but one Spirit Who brings to the soul influences of purity and wisdom and strength, and that is the Spirit of God. The second fact is, that these evil spirits are also under the control of God. They are permitted to act, but ever only within His government. Satan must seek permission to tempt Job; he must obtain the Apostles by asking, if he would sift them as wheat. The messenger of Satan may buffet, but only within the limitations fixed by God. Finally, no created being, whether angelic or human, escapes the government of God.

For he loved him as he loved his own soul.—1 Sam. 20. 17.

The story of David and Jonathan is one of the most beautiful idylls in the Bible, and so also in all literature. Its beauty is enhanced in the sacred Scriptures because it is set in relation to an exceedingly dark background. Love is always beautiful, but the full richness of its colours is only discovered in the presence of suffering and of adversity. From the account of the beginnings of this friendship (chapter 18) it would seem that Jonathan's love for David was earlier than (and the inspiring cause of) David's love for Jonathan. Indeed, the whole story seems to warrant us in saying that love had an even finer expression in Jonathan than in David. There was less, perhaps, of selfishness in it. He was heir-apparent to the throne, but he knew that God had chosen David for that position, and without any pang of regret he acquiesced in the Divine will, and remained the friend of David, loving him more rather than less because he was the anointed of Jehovah. Jonathan loved David as he loved his own soul. That is the basis of real friendship. It is the love of complete selflessness, which substitutes the interests of the loved one for those of self. Such love is not common. It is, however, often manifested, and it shines with all beauty. Experience does not find, in all life's course, many such friends. Happy is the man or woman who has found one such. And yet, perhaps, there is a higher happiness, that, namely, of being such a friend to someone else. David was blessed in Jonathan, but in the deep experience of his own soul Jonathan was supremely blessed in such love for David.

David . . . was sore afraid of Achish. —1 Sam. 21. 12.

This is a strange story about David; and yet it is not strange, in that it is so true to human experience. Fear and faith are constantly antagonistic. The triumph of the one is always the defeat of the other. This is the record of a period in the life of David when fear triumphed over faith. In fear of Saul he fled to Achish, the enemy of the people of God. There he was filled with fear of Achish, and we have the sad picture of God's anointed man feigning madness in order to protect himself. There can be no question that these were days of great strain for David; and judging simply on the ground of what man is able to endure in his own strength, we cannot wonder that the tension reacted upon him. But there was no need for him to depend upon himself. Faith might have triumphed over fear of Saul. Had it done so, he would never have sought refuge with Achish, and would not have been reduced to such unworthy expedients for securing safety. Surely all these things were written for our learning; and while the experience of David calls

out our sympathy, because we have so often yielded to fear, and then resorted to foolish methods to find escape from danger, nevertheless the lesson which is patent is that we have no right to take refuge from any peril among those who are the enemies of the Divine purpose. That means, finally, that fear is wrong. Faith in God is the strength of righteous action, and there is no reason for any other attitude of mind than that of perfect confidence in Him.

Every one that was in distress, and every one that was in debt, and every one that was discontented, gathered themselves unto him.—1 Sam. 22. 2.

The story of Adullam is a great story. Thither David went when he left Achish. Whether his going there was the final act of his fear, or the return to faith perhaps, it is hard to decide. In any case, he had now abandoned the attempt to seek safety among the enemies of his people. The cave became a rallying ground, and the result is found later in the character of the mighty men who were gathered about him. In many ways it was a sorry crowd that went down to join him there. Men in distress, in debt, and discontented, gathered about him. From the view-point of Saul they were the unfit men, who were a menace to the existing order of things. The probability is that they were what they were as a result of the chaotic condition of the kingdom; their distress resulting from the false method of government; their debt due to oppressive taxation; their discontent a righteous discontent with the prevailing wrongs. The true kingliness of David is seen in the effect he produced upon these men. They became an orderly company of mighty men, filled with the high heroic spirit which is capable of splendid loyalty and glorious deeds. It is almost impossible to escape from the parabolic value of this story. Our King is still rejected of men, though appointed by God. In His rejection He is gathering about Him those in distress, in debt, discontented; and He is changing them by His rule into the men of might, who will stand by Him until the day of His earthly coronation. The phrase "cave of Adullam" has become the description of all sorts of associations of discontented men. Well, if these men are gathering about God's King, their discontent is being made the dynamic of human deliverance.

Saul sought him every day, but God delivered him not into his hand.— 1 Sam. 23. 14.

Thus the historian declares a great fact about the history of David. He was the object of Saul's bitter hatred, but he was perfectly safe in the keeping of God. The scores of happenings recorded in the chapter reveal the difficulty of David's position. Saul, still nominally king, was devoting all his strength to the persecution of this man, while the affairs of the kingdom were in the most hopeless confusion. While David in exile was most certainly the popular idol of the people, their fickleness was manifested in the despicable treachery of both the Keilites and the Ziphites. David, with the true spirit of patriotism, waged war against the Philistines. It is yet evident that his exile and persecution were telling upon him, and nervous fear was at work in his heart. Nevertheless, his trust in God triumphed at this time, and to Him he made his appeal in this hour of trial. In that hour of communion he learned that the Divine government would not mean that he would be free from persecution, but it did mean that he would be delivered therefrom. To be in the will of God among men who disobey that will, is inevitably to be persecuted. They will ruthlessly seek to harm and destroy. But they are powerless. God will never deliver His servants ultimately into the hands of His enemies. There came the hour when great David's greater Son was delivered up by the determinate counsel and foreknowledge of God, but that deliverance was into the pathway that led to final victory.

The Lord avenge me of thee: but mine hand shall not be upon thee.—1 Sam. 24. 12.

In this chapter we have the account of how circumstances suddenly put Saul in the power of David. It would have been perfectly easy for him to take the life of his enemy, and so put an end to the bitter experiences through which that enemy was compelling him to pass. From the standpoint of worldly wisdom, he missed his opportunity, and so prolonged his own suffering. From the standpoint of the true wisdom, that which results from faith in God, he acted rightly. To have slain Saul would have been to have taken things into his own hands, and to do that is always to bring disaster. It is ever better to wait for God than to attempt to hurry His purposes by actions dictated only by the appearance of fortuitous circumstances. It is perhaps one of the hardest lessons for the human heart to learn, and yet more harm than we think is done in the enterprises of the Divine Kingdom by the zeal which is without knowledge. The hour comes when we have such a chance of getting level with our foes, of wiping out old scores, of ending our suffering by some swift act in the dark. Let us be very much afraid of such hours. They almost always conceal perils far greater than those from which they seem to afford opportunity of escape. It is ever better to wait for God. He sees all. We see but a part. We are always safer waiting for Him.

The soul of my lord shall be bound in the bundle of life with the Lord thy God.—1 Sam. 25. 29.

Thus Abigail gave expression to her understanding of the place of David in the will and power of God. The first and simple meaning of the declaration was that the life of the man chosen of God to be king, was safe in His keeping. The truth was beautifully expressed. The phrase, "the bundle of life," described the sum total of things precious to God, and therefore held together in His preserving power. Very suggestive is the idea of close fellowship with God expressed in the statement that Jehovah God Himself is included in that bundle of life. The soul of David was bound up in that bundle with *Jehovah God*. How perfectly safe is any soul when it is thus bound up together with God Himself. The strength of that bundle of life is not that of bindings or tackling superimposed. It is that of the identification of God with all included in the bundle. In these words there flashes through, on the page of the Old Testament, that great conception of fellowship with God, which finds its full exposition in the New Testament. In Christ, God has identified Himself with man; in Christ, God has identified man with Himself. That is the meaning of eternal life. Those who have that life are indeed bound up in the bundle of life with God. They live one life with Him. In that is their safety. Because of that union, no bitterness in the heart of Saul, no churlishness in the attitude of Nabal, can harm those who are included; neither can any force of evil prevent such from coming ultimately to the realization of all that is in the will of God for them.

Behold, I have played the fool.—1 Sam. 26. 21.

Saul said this in a moment of mental and spiritual illumination. Once again his life had been in the hands of David, and David had refused to slay him. Moreover, he had expostulated with Saul as to the unreasonableness and wickedness of his persistent persecution. Then suddenly the whole truth flamed out upon this man. He saw himself and his actions in the light of actual truth, and under the impulse of the revelation, he told the truth about himself as he said: "I have played the fool." In these words we have a perfect autobiography. In them, the complete life-story of this man is told. Their interpretation is found in the whole narrative, and the explanation of that narrative is contained in them. From the very beginning Saul had failed. To him there had been given the greatest of opportunities; and his way had been made easy for him by all the resources placed at his disposal. There had been given to him the Spirit of God, the friendship of Samuel, and the devotion of men whose hearts God had touched. He had so acted that the Spirit had departed from him: Samuel had been unable to help him; and the hearts of his people had been turned away from him. The whole secret was that he had leaned to his own understanding, had failed to obey, and so had become the evil-tempered man he was, mastered by hatred, and fighting against God. He verily had played the fool. And so every man plays the fool when he forgets that the fear of Jehovah is the beginning of wisdom. The very gifts of God are of no value, when they are not received and held in that holy cleansing fear.

David said in his heart, I shall now perish one day by the hand of Saul.— I Sam. 27. 1.

Once more we see David possessed by fear, and passing over to dwell for a time among the Philistines. Again we have to say that we can understand his action. Long and weary indeed had been his period of suffering. There came upon him the sense of depression. For the moment he forgot that his soul was bound up in the bundle of life with Jehovah God. It is easy to forget this, "when all around tumultuous seems." Looking at circumstances, there seemed to David no hope. And so he went to live in Gath. It was a sorry period. He made occasional raids upon other ancient enemies of his race, and with success. In order to hide this from those among whom he dwelt, he was driven to telling untruths. When a man is mastered by fear through failure of faith, and consequently occupies a false position, he is always in grave danger of violating some principle of his loyalty. It is impossible to see David taking refuge in Gath, without recognizing that he had lost for the time being the clear vision of God which made him strong against Goliath. The reading of this story inevitably suggests a contrast between David and his greater Son. David was the anointed king, and he was persecuted by the rejecting king. All this was repeated in the history of Jesus. The contrast, however, is marked. No fear ever made the Anointed One quail. He never crossed over to the enemy to find personal safety. He often spoke of the fact that men would kill Him, but always ended such foretelling with the prophecy of His ultimate triumph.

The Lord is departed from thee, and is become thine adversary.—I Sam. 28. 16.

Perhaps there is no chapter in Old Testament history more tragic than this. Saul's visit in the day of his trouble to the witch of Endor, was the last manifestation of his degradation. Yet what a testimony it affords to that inherent capacity of man for the spiritual! In the day of his direst calamity, he knew the insufficiency of his own wisdom, the uselessness of human advice, and he longed for a voice from the spirit world. In order to secure it, he turned to a woman whose practices were condemned by the law of God. This is the history of spiritism always. It is more than strange how this story has been quoted in defence of things occult. As a matter of fact it condemns them. Let it be carefully read, and it becomes perfectly evident that this woman had nothing to do with the bringing up of Samuel. Still practising her black art, she commenced to practise the deceptions with which she was familiar. When Samuel appeared, she was startled beyond measure. That he did appear to Saul, there can be no question, but he did not come in response to her call. He was sent of God, for the express purpose of rebuking Saul for his unholy traffic with these evil things, and to pronounce his doom. The words are full of solemn import. God, departed from a man, becomes his adversary, and that in the necessity of the case. God never departs from a man until the man has departed from Him. Then, in the interest of righteousness, God is against that man.

The princes of the Philistines were wroth with him.—I Sam. 29. 4.

These princes were wroth with Achish for allowing David to accompany the Philistines in their campaign against Israel. David's sojourn with Achish had resulted in his being compelled to join the Philistine army in its preparation for attacking the Israelites. The Philistine lords seemed suddenly to have realized the danger of this proceeding. They were familiar with the song which had celebrated his prowess, and his victories over them; and they felt that they dared not trust him in the day of battle. It is perhaps idle for us to speculate as to what the result would have been, had he been allowed to remain. On the basis of policy their objection was probably justified. Achish seems to have formed a high estimate of him, and a strong affection for him, but he was compelled to yield to the majority. There can be no doubt that it was not in the purpose of God that His anointed king should be placed in circumstances of such difficulty. Here, then, along the line of perfectly natural emotions, God is seen acting on behalf of His servant. He made the wrath of the princes praise Him, in that it accomplished His purpose. When once we have seen the fact of the Divine government, it seems impossible not to see it. It operates everywhere. It controls all circumstances, and all men, in spite of themselves, and often unknowingly to them, so that they contribute to the realization of the will of God, and the accomplishment of His purposes.

As his share is that goeth down to the battle, so shall his share be that tarrieth by the stuff; they shall share alike.—1 Sam. 30. 24.

David, delivered by the overruling of God from his relation with the Philistine army, returned to Ziklag. In his absence it had been sacked by the Amalekites. The true spirit of patriotism flamed within him, and he moved forward, after seeking counsel of God, to punish the wrong-doers. He was completely successful, punishing his foes, and rescuing all his own. In the course of his action, which was rapid and strenuous, two hundred of his company of six hundred men were exhausted, and so were compelled to remain at Besor, while the rest went forward. When the four hundred returned victorious, there were those among them who would have withheld any portion of the spoils from those who had been unable to accompany them all the way. This David sternly forbade, and laid down a law which was to apply for all time. The rectitude of the decision is unquestionable. The measure of personal responsibility in the campaign of righteousness is ever that of the putting forth of the whole of one's strength. That, these men had done. They were "dead-beat" ere they paused. They had done their utmost. Those who went all the way had done no more. Therefore they were to share the spoils. The story has warning and comfort in it. If a man shall tarry and rest at Besor while he have any strength to go forward, he is renegade; and no share of the spoils should come to him. If a man put all his strength into the enterprise, and stop at Besor, because he has no more that he can do, he has done all; and honourably may share in the triumph.

So Saul died.—1 Sam. 31. 6.

This closing · chapter of the Book is draped in sackcloth, and covered with ashes. It tells the tragic story of the last act in the career of a man who was a ghastly failure. Defeat at the hands of the Philistines drove Saul to uttermost desperation. Wounded in the final fight, and fearing that the last blow might be struck by an enemy, he called upon his armour-bearer to slay him. Upon his refusing to do so, Saul died by his own hand physically, as he had already perished as to purpose and possibility by his own sin and his own folly. Suicide is always the ultimate action of cowardice. In the case of Saul, and in many similar cases, it is perfectly natural; but let it never be glorified as heroic. It is the last resort of the man who dare not stand up to life. Schopenhauer once said that suicide is not the result of hatred of life, but rather of love of it. A man loves life and because he cannot live, as he considers, full life, he will not live at all. There is a great element of truth in that; but still it leaves the brand of the coward upon the suicide. It ever seems to me that the chief spiritual value of this first Book of Samuel lies in the solemn lessons taught by the story of the life and failure of this man Saul. It proclaims in clarion tones the arresting and searching truth, that great advantages and remarkable opportunities are in themselves no guarantees of success. Unless the heart be firm and steady in its allegiance to principle and its loyalty to God, these things will only be weights and burdens, crushing the soul, and assuring the uttermost ruin of the man to whom they come.

SECOND SAMUEL

Thy glory, O Israel, is slain upon thy high places.—2 Sam. 1. 19.

These are the opening words of the song which David wrote after the death of Saul and Jonathan, and which he commanded to be taught to the people. It is a singularly beautiful song. Its references to Saul and Jonathan are full of stately dignity, and it merges into extreme tenderness when it refers to Jonathan only. As the song proceeds, it unquestionably has to do with Saul and Jonathan personally; but these opening words are capable of an interpretation which would suggest that David was conscious of much more than the merely personal matters. The term, "thy glory," is almost invariably treated as having reference to Saul and Jonathan as constituting the chief glory of Israel. There are senses in which that is so.

But it may be that in this very description of them there was a note of spiritual satire. The people had clamoured for a king like the nations. They had obtained such a king, and had gloried in him. This was the result. He, and his son as heir to the throne, were slain upon the high places. Presently the song refers to "the shield of Saul, not anointed with oil." This indeed was the deepest meaning of all that had happened. Jehovah was the true glory of His people Israel. They had turned from Him, and had boasted in Saul and his kingly house. That self-chosen glory was slain. The true glory of the nation, that of their one and only King, was not slain. Whenever the people of God, under that old dispensation or in the new, have· made anything their chief glory, other than God Himself, sooner or later the day of disaster has come, the idol has been shattered, and, for the time being, they have been put to shame and confusion among their enemies. It is they who look to Him who are lightened; it is they whose faces are not confounded.

David inquired of the Lord.—2 Sam. 2. 1.

David knew that the hour was come for him to enter upon the work to which he had been called of God, that of reigning over the people of God. He knew intimately all the story of Saul, and he knew that in the very fact of a human kingship in any form the people had lost their chief glory. Therefore it was that at the very beginning he recognized the true King Jehovah; and took no step of any kind without inquiring the will of that King. He asked, first, whether he should go into any of the cities of Judah; and when commanded to do so, he asked, which. This was a true beginning, and so long as David continued thus to inquire he made no mistakes. Whatever blunders he made subsequently were due to his acting upon his own initiative. The principle is fundamental and perpetual. The fact that a man is certainly called of God to a definite work, never sets that man free from the necessity of consulting the will of God as to the next move. We are not anointed to serve and then left to find out for ourselves the way of service. God is ever available to those whom He calls to work for Him in any way. Therefore that time is never wasted in which a man stops to pray, to inquire of Jehovah as to His will. That time is worse than wasted in which any man tries to serve God without having first, in the smallest detail, sought from God the making known of His will.

David waxed stronger and stronger, but the house of Saul waxed weaker and weaker.—2 Sam. 3. 1.

How much is involved in this statement! Quite simply, it is a statement that the king chosen and anointed of God, under the guidance of God, moved quietly forward to the full realization of the Divine purpose for him. But the fact that a man, so chosen and anointed, was not able to come at once to the position for which he was elected, reveals the effect produced by past failure. The Kingdom of God had become the kingdom of Saul, and was seething with all the elements of strife and consequent weakness. The spirit of Saul, which was that of antagonism to David, was perpetuated in Abner, who was Saul's cousin and the captain of his host. He was actively opposed to David, and sought to perpetuate the line of Saul in securing the crown to Ishbosheth. Thus the kingdom was not yet David's as to actual possession. It had to be gained, and seven years passed before he was crowned as king of the whole nation. Nevertheless, he gradually gained ground; he "waxed

stronger and stronger, but the house of Saul waxed weaker and weaker." Two lessons for us emerge from the consideration. The first is that the Divine purpose is always making headway, however much circumstances may seem to give reason for a contrary opinion. The second is that we need the patience which is able to endure, knowing that the way to victory is the way of conflict, and of persistent faith.

As the Lord liveth, Who hath redeemed my soul out of all adversity.—2 Sam. 4. 9.

In this chapter we see the weakness of the house of Saul. Abner was dead, slain by Joab; Ishbosheth, in any case a weak man, was robbed of his only strength by this fact, and his hands were weakened. The chronicler here inserted a paragraph to emphasize this picture of weakness, in which he pointed out that the only remaining scion of Saul's house was a cripple, Mephibosheth. Two men, Baanah and Rechab, who had served under Ishbosheth, undoubtedly prompted by the desire to gain favour with David, cruelly murdered their master, and brought his head to him. It was under these circumstances that David made use of these words. In them he revealed his profound sense of the ways of God with him, and that he, having received the kingdom as a gift from God, had so far been led through all the troublous experiences of the years by God. For this reason he would have no part in the activities of subterfuge and injustice in order to secure the realization of those ends appointed by God. This is the true attitude of faith. The Jesuitical doctrine that the end justifies the means, is a doctrine of devils. While it is true that God overrules all the doings of men, and compels them ultimately to serve His high purposes, it is equally true that no servant of His can ever consent to do evil that good may come. It is an arresting truth that our Lord in the days of His earthly life would not accept the testimony of demons, and that He explicitly declared that Satan cannot cast out Satan. It is a truth we do well to remember, and to apply in the smallest particulars of our life and service.

David took the stronghold of Zion; the same is the city of David.—2 Sam. 5. 7.

This was the first act of David after he was crowned king of the whole nation. Thus Jerusalem became the capital, and the great centre of the religious and national life of the people of God. The stronghold was considered impregnable by those who held it, and up to this time they had been able to resist successfully every attempt to capture it (see Josh. 15. 63, and Judges 1. 21). So sure were they that it could not be overcome, that in taunt they declared that it was defended by the blind and lame. To the taunt David replied with taunt, as he commanded the assault to be made, and the "blind and lame" to be smitten. The fortress was captured, and David took up his abode therein. What strange vicissitudes the city has passed through in the centuries! To it, in the fulness of time, the true King came. He came to His own, and His own received Him not. Then with tears He pronounced its doom, and until this day it has been trodden under foot of the Gentiles. As we write, it is held by a Gentile Power, on trust for the ancient people of God. What lines its settlement by man's arrangements will take, we cannot tell. The one certainty is that, in His own time, the King will come to His City again, and it will be the earthly centre of His reign. There is a sense in which, though David took it from the Jebusites, it has never yet been possessed as the City of God. There have ever been forces which men could not cast out. The Man of Nazareth will yet actually dispossess these forces and reign there in righteousness.

He died by the ark of God.—2 Sam. 6. 7.

The king was mindful of the central truth of that national life over which he was called to reign. The nation was still, in the deepest fact of its being, a Theocracy, and the ark of God was the central symbol of that fact. Believing this, David made arrangements to bring that ark into the capital. In connection with this a startling thing happened. Contrary to the instructions given long before by Moses, the ark was placed upon a cart for conveyance. The oxen drawing it stumbled, and one man, daring to stretch forth his hand in an attempt to steady the sacred symbol, was immediately smitten with death. The effect of this vindication of the will of the Divine Majesty was that David was not only displeased, but wholesomely afraid, so that for the moment he dared not go forward with his purpose, and for three months the ark rested in the house of Obed-edom. Of that fact the chronicler says: "Jehovah blessed Obed-edom and all his house." What an arresting contrast this is! A man daring to lay a hand upon the ark of God contrary to the law of God, was smitten to death; a man reverently receiving it, and living in right relationship with all that it represented, was blessed in himself, and in all his affairs! The ark was the instrument of death or of life, according to the attitude taken up towards it. This is true of every Divine matter. The messengers of the Gospel of Christ are to men either "a savour from death unto death," or "a savour from life unto life" (2 Cor. 2. 16). All the "means of grace" bless or curse men, according

to whether their attitude toward them be according to the will of God or contrary thereto.

What can David say more unto thee? For Thou knowest Thy servant, O Lord God.—2 Sam. 7. 20.

In these words David submitted himself finally to God. His desire to build the house of God was perfectly natural. So much was this the case that it appealed to Nathan, who advised him to do all that was in his heart. It was not, however, in the will of God that he should carry out the work; and consequently the prophet was sent to deliver a message which was neither agreement with David's desire, nor with his own opinion. The story reveals the triumph both of Nathan and David in their ready submission to the declared will of God. The prophet unhesitatingly delivered his message, even though it contradicted his own expressed view. It takes much courage on the part of a prophet to do this kind of thing. David immediately acquiesced in the will of God, and worshipped. The desire in itself was not necessarily wrong. Solomon, when referring to this matter at the Dedication of the Temple, said: "Jehovah said unto David my father, Whereas it was in thine heart to build an house for My name, thou didst well that it was in thine heart" (1 Kings 8. 18). Yet it was not God's will that he should do it, and his submission to that will was of the essence of wisdom. It is of the utmost importance that we should ever test our desires, even the highest and the holiest of them, by His will. Work, excellent in itself, should never be undertaken, save at the express command of God. The passing of time will always vindicate the wisdom of the Divine will.

David executed judgment and justice unto all his people.—2 Sam. 8. 15.

This short chapter constitutes a sort of summary of the way in which the kingdom was developed and consolidated under the reign of David. It first records some of the victories he gained over the enemies of his people, the Philistines, and the Moabites, and then the Syrians. By these victories he strengthened his own position, and that of his people. It is to be noted that the house of Jehovah was still in his mind for though he knew he would not be permitted to build, he gathered treasure in preparation for the work of his son. The chapter ends with a brief account of certain officers of State, and thus shows how the internal condition of the kingdom was strengthened. The central words of the record are those which we have chosen. They disclose the deepest truth about his reign, as they state the principles of his government. He did not exercise authority in order to secure safety or privilege for himself; he sought the well-being of the people, and served them as he "executed judgment and justice" among them. Thus he fulfilled the true function of the kingly office, for thus he acted as the representative and agent of their one and only King. So long as he thus reigned, he was able to strengthen the nation in all the highest senses. The measure of his ultimate failure as king, was the measure in which he departed from these principles, and exercised authority from selfish motives. This Bible literature and all human experience persistently teach that authority is finally vested in God. In proportion as appointed rulers recognize that, and rule as executing the will of God, they achieve the true ends of their rule. When they forget it, they bring disaster to those under them, and eventually destroy themselves.

Is there yet any that is left of the house of Saul, that I may shew him kindness for Jonathan's sake?—2 Sam. 9. 1.

There is an exquisite tenderness about the story of this chapter. David's love for Jonathan was still fresh. One can easily imagine how, in the days of his growing prosperity, the king would often think of the old strenuous times, and of his friend's loyalty to him under circumstances so full of stress and peril. For David, the house of Saul, which had caused him so much suffering, was redeemed by his love for Jonathan; and therefore he instituted inquiry as to whether there were any left of that house, to whom he might show kindness for the sake of his friend. This inquiry resulted in the finding of Mephibosheth, whose lameness was tragic and pathetic, in that it had been caused by a fall on the awful day of Jezreel, when his father and grandfather had fallen together. To him the king restored the lands of Saul, and he set him as an honoured guest at his own table. David's own account of this was that he desired to "show the kindness of God unto him." This declaration recalls the words of the covenant made between him and Jonathan long before, in which his friend had charged him to show him "the loving kindness of Jehovah," and also that he should show this same kindness to his house for ever. In this action David is seen as the man after God's own heart, keeping covenant and heaping benefits upon those who might be accounted enemies. The common attitude of human nature would not prompt such action. It was indeed the kindness of God.

Be of good courage, and let us play the men for our people, and for the cities of our God: and the Lord do that which seemeth Him good.—2 Sam. 10. 12.

This was the language of the highest patriotism. The difficulties had arisen as the result of another action of David which had been prompted by goodwill. He had sent to comfort Hanun, the new king of Ammon, upon the death of his father. The action had been replied to insultingly, with the result that Israel was forced into war with these children of Ammon, and the Syrians. As the battle was prepared for, Joab uttered these words to his brother Abishai. Observe the elements of patriotism as revealed in them. The first matter was personal to those called upon to fight. They were to be of good courage, and to play the men. All the arrangements for the conflict, and its issue, show how these men fulfilled this responsibility. But a deeper note is struck in what follows. They were to do all this for their people and for the cities of their God. There was to be nothing of the passion for personal aggrandisement in what they did. They were to act for the high purposes represented in the people of God, and the cities of God. Personal courage was to be inspired by relative considerations. Then came the deepest note of all. When, in view of the interests of the nation they had done all that was possible, then "Jehovah do what seemeth Him good." Men who thus prepare themselves for high enterprise, and then commit themselves wholly to the will of God are invincible.

But the thing that David had done displeased the Lord.—2 Sam. 11. 27.

The chronicler inserted this statement at the close of his account of the sad fall of David. The fact that he did so is arresting. It would seem to be so self-evident as to leave no room for stating it. It always seems to me that the statement is really rather a prelude to the next chapter with its account of the Divine forgiveness, than a close to the story of the wrong-doing. It was necessary thus emphatically to place on record the Divine displeasure. In the light of that statement we consider the tragic story. In doing so we notice the downward steps following in rapid succession. First, "David tarried at Jerusalem." It was the time of war, and the true place of the king was with his army. Instead of going with them he had remained behind, and so in the place of temptation. This is not to say that conditions of peace are more perilous than those of war, but rather that any place, other than that to which duty calls, is one of danger. From this, events moved rapidly, but surely downward. In briefest quotations we may indicate that movement "He saw"; "he sent and inquired"; "he took." The king had fallen from the level of purity to that of moral defilement. And then, because one sin ever leads on to another, he fell lower yet, and was guilty of base injustice to Uriah, Even more fittingly in his own case than in that of Saul and Jonathan might his words concerning their death have now been employed: "How are the mighty fallen!"

I have sinned against the Lord.— 2 Sam. 12. 13.

Evidently a year passed before Nathan was sent by God to David, for Bathsheba's child was born ere he came. We can imagine what that year had been to David, and that the message from God through His servant must have come as a relief to the troubled man. It was at this juncture that the best in David was apparent. He at once confessed. "I have sinned," and his whole bearing under the chastisement which fell upon him reveals him as a man who in the deepest facts of his life was true to God. Dr. Margoliouth, in his book, "Lines of Defence of the Biblical Revelation," argues with convincing clearness that in all this David was pre-eminently revealed as a man after God's own heart. Other men who had been guilty of such failure might have defended their actions, might have slain the prophet. Not so with this man. He knew God, and he knew the wrong of his action, and he confessed his sin. If we read Psa. 32 and 51, which are connected by common consent with these experiences, we shall know how deep was this sense of sin. The readiness of God to pardon, is radiantly set forth in the story, in that directly David said, "I have sinned," the prophet replied. "Jehovah also hath put away thy sin." Note the "also." A man puts away his own sin when in sincerity he confesses it. That makes it possible for God *also* to put it away. The Divine putting away of sin is always made possible potentially by the Divine atonement; but it can only become possible in the experience of the sinner, when the sinner confesses, and so judges and puts it away from himself.

And David mourned for his son every day. He was comforted concerning Amnon, seeing he was dead.— 2 Sam. 13. 37 and 39.

What tragedy there is in these two sentences. They are concerned with two sons of David. Amnon was his first-born. He had fallen into sin after the pattern of his father's. Absalom had secured the murder of his brother, and as a result was a fugitive. Thus in his family life David was reaping something of the harvest of those lower things of his own nature which had led him into sin. When the sin of Amnon had been made known to him, we are told he was wroth, but we are not told that he took any disciplinary action. How could he? Surely he had rendered his own arm nerveless by the sin of the past. A very solemn consideration arises out of all this. It is, that sin may be forgiven most surely, so as to restore to the sinner the possibility of the sense of reconciliation with God; but its results, on the level of

human relationship and experience in this life, run on. To the end of our earthly life we shall find how true it is that "God is not mocked; for whatsoever a man soweth, that shall he also reap." And is not this also a proof of the beneficent character of the government of God? If, in a world like this, forgiveness meant that men were released from all the results of sins committed in the past, even that blessing would become the occasion of yet more disastrous consequences.

God . . . deviseth means, that he that is banished be not an outcast from Him.—2 Sam. 14. 14.

This was the supreme argument employed by the wise woman of Tekoah, as, at the instigation of Joab, she sought to persuade David to recall Absalom. The story in itself is a somewhat perplexing one. Opinions widely differ as to why Joab thus set himself to bring back Absalom. These, however, need not concern us now. It is of great interest to observe that this woman knew God, and here uttered one of the most beautiful things, and the most true, ever said about Him. This is the whole of redemption revealed in a sentence. Man is banished from God by his own sin, and that most righteously; and, in the interest of the perfect order of all things, is necessarily banished. Nevertheless he, the banished one, is not abandoned by God. His love is unchanged toward the sinning man, even though His wrath is kindled against his sin. This is the love that will not let us go. But how can the banished one be saved from being an outcast? The answer is that "God . . . deviseth means." In all the fulness of human history we learn how much that statement is worth. Literally the statement is that God "thinketh thoughts." These must be thoughts of holiness; and they are thoughts of love. Then they are thoughts in which both these combine, and discover a way of rescue, of recall, of restoration for banished souls. The thoughts of God then become thoughts of self-emptying, of sacrifice, and of taking all the responsibility for the wrong of the banished one. Thus guilt is cancelled, and the way of return is made possible. It is a glorious word, this; and introduces us to the unfathomable mystery of the love of God, which in its working can never be interpreted; but in which the soul finds its healing and its perfect rest.

And David went up by the ascent of the Mount of Olives, and wept as he went up.—2 Sam. 15. 30.

These were days of poignant sorrow to David. He had brought Absalom back, but had not given him full pardon, and had not allowed him to see his face for two years. Then he had re-admitted him to favour, without any sign of repentance on the part of Absalom. Now at last open rebellion had broken out, and David for the moment was exiled from his city, and from his home. It is indeed a tragic picture, this, of David, Yet in it all, his greatness is manifested. Stanley says of this day in the life of the king that "There is none . . . that combines so many of David's characteristics—his patience. his high-spirited religion, his generosity, his calculation; we miss only his courage. Was it crushed for the moment by the weight of mental grief, or of bitter remorse?" In the light of all the facts it is almost certain that the tears David shed as he climbed Olivet, were rather those of humiliation and penitence, than those of self-centred regret. For Absalom there was no excuse, but David carried in his own heart ceaselessly the sense of his own past sin. To know more of what was passing in the mind of David in those days, some of the Psalms he then wrote may be consulted. Those which are by common consent connected with the period, are 3, 4, 26, 27, 28, 62, 63. They all breathe the spirit of perfect trust in God, and unbroken confidence in ultimate deliverance, even though they reveal the sense of his suffering. The soul-experience revealed is that which Fred. W. H. Myers expressed in his St. Paul:—

> Yes, Thou forgivest, but with all forgiving
> Canst not renew mine innocence again;
> Make Thou, O Christ, a dying of my living,
> Purge from the sin, but never from the pain!

Let him alone, and let him curse; for the Lord hath bidden him.—*2 Sam. 16. 11.*

Sorrows multiplied upon the head of David during these dark days. Ziba added to David's grief by traducing Mephibosheth, and suggesting that his kindness was ill-requited. It was all the more wicked in that it was untrue. Shimei struck at the king when he was in the dust. When Abishai would have taken speedy vengeance on him, David forbade him, and in these words showed how he was even then placing higher interpretations upon life than would have been possible to any man who was not, in the deepest of his life, in spite of all failure, a man after God's own heart. The action of Shimei was sinful, but David recognized the very hand of God in what he did, so far as his own soul was concerned. He received the cursing of this man as part of the discipline through which his God was bringing him. He expected that good would come out of it, as his next words reveal: "It may be that Jehovah will look on the wrong done unto me, and that Jehovah will requite me good for his cursing of me this day." This is a radiant illustration of the deep and inward peace given to any man who is living in fellowship with God in motive and desire. Such a man will receive all the sorrows which come to him as within the will of God for him, and therefore as intended ultimately to bring him good and not evil. This sense of Divine overruling will cleanse the spirit of all desire for revenge. He will pass on his way while curses and stones are showered upon him, realizing that they also are compelled under God, to minister to his perfecting, and the full realization of God's purposes for him.

The Lord had ordained to defeat the good counsel of Ahithopel, to the intent that the Lord might bring evil upon Absalom.—*2 Sam. 17. 14.*

These words stand out revealingly at the centre of a story of strange and complex intrigue. Absalom is seen listening to two counsellors. One the one hand, Ahithophel gave him the counsel which would undoubtedly have led to the success of his rebellion, at any rate for the moment. David had not yet had time to gather about him any large body of men. Let a company be set to capture him, and that immediately. Hushai, on the other hand, gave him counsel which appealed to his vanity. It would have been a far more spectacular thing to lead a great army in person, and gain a great victory. His vanity ensured his ruin. Thus amid the complexities of human cleverness, the will of God is seen moving inexorably forward to the accomplishment of His high purposes. The pressure of the Divine power compelled the true inwardness of the thought and vanity of Absalom to act in accordance with itself, and so to bring about his utter defeat. This is one of the great principles of life which every page of the Bible emphasizes and illustrates. Men cannot escape God. They go their own way, but that way never sets them free from the authority and invincible power of God. The very fact that they are compelled by God to carry out their own way, is the assurance of their ultimate discomfiture and defeat. Man's way for himself, as apart from God, is ever the wrong way, and cannot lead to success.

Would God I had died for thee, O Absolom, my son, my son!—*2 Sam. 18. 33.*

Following the advice of Hushai, Absalom delayed until he had gathered together a great army. That strategically was his undoing. It gave David time also to gather an army and set them in orderly array. The forces met and fought in the forest of Ephraim. Absalom was slain by Joab, in whose heart there was no pity for him. That his action was warranted from the standpoint of national safety, there can be no doubt. In this hour David's cup of sorrow was filled to the full. Everything in the story leads up to, and culminates in, this wail of anguish over his dead boy. It is very brief, but it thrills with agony. Five times he repeated the words, "my son." This surely had a deeper note in it than that of the merely half-conscious repetition of words occasioned by personal grief. The father recognized how much he was responsible for his son. It is as though he had said: He is indeed my son, his weaknesses are my weaknesses, his passions are my passions, his sins are my sins. Out of all that sense there came the deepest cry of all "Would I had died for thee!" Here surely David reached the profoundest moment of his suffering. May none of us ever experimentally enter into its awful consciousness! In order that we may not, we need to ponder all the story carefully, and learn the solemn lessons it teaches of parental responsibility.

Yea, let him take all, forasmuch as my lord the king is come in peace unto his own house.—2 Sam. 19. 30

This was the language of a glad heart. Mephibosheth had known the kindness of God through David in the days when he had been found and brought to the king's house and table. How he had suffered during the sad days of the king's absence from his own city! That suffering had been all the more acute because by treachery he had been prevented from accompanying his benefactor into exile, and had been slandered by Ziba. Now the trouble was over, the rebellion was at an end, the king was brought back to his own house. This was joy enough for the crippled son of Jonathan. In view of this, let his enemy have all the material things. This is a suggestive story in its revelation of the selflessness of true loyalty. For his own enrichment this man cared nothing at all. It was everything to him that his king should come into the possession of his kingdom in peace. How the incident talks to us! We have been given a place in the House of our King, and at His table, in infinite grace. Is our loyalty to Him as disinterested as that of Mephibosheth for David? Is it more to us that He should have His rightful place, than that we should have even the things which are our rightful possessions because they are the King's gifts to us? It is to be feared that too often we are more concerned about our rights than about His. It is a great and glorious thing when our loyalty and love make us far more concerned about the victories of our Lord, than about our own unquestioned rights. Yet that should be the normal attitude of all who sit at the King's Table.

We have no portion in David, neither have we inheritance in the son of Jesse: every man to his tents, O Israel.—2 Sam. 20. 1.

This was the cry raised by an evil man who sought to divide the kingdom and to create a position for himself. It was extremely clever, in that it was of the nature of a protest against a certainly unjustifiable action on the part of the men of Judah. The roots of the trouble are found in the preceding chapter. The tribes of Israel had been the first to propose the restoration of the king after the defeat of Absalom (19. 9, 10). The men of Judah had not invited them to take part in the great gathering at Gilgal. This had raised their anger. Occasion invariably finds a man for evil, as well as for good. This chapter opens with the words: "And there happened to be there a base fellow." He it was, who sought personal aggrandisement, and made this hour of tension his occasion. The movement was quickly defeated, as Joab, with relentless anger, quelled the insurrection. The story should teach us that popular and plausible catchwords ought to be received and acted upon with great caution. There may often be an element of truth in complaints which are made; but when they are made, careful attention should be paid to the character of the men who voice them. Too often evil men are thus allowed to make a just cause the occasion of seeking, not its rectification, but the bringing about of some evil design subversive of all that is highest in the interests of the people who complain. That Judah blunders, is no reason why the kingdom should be disrupted. Injustice is never corrected by a yet deeper wrong.

David waxed faint.—2 Sam. 21. 15.

In these closing chapters of this book several matters are dealt with, not in chronological order or relation, but as illustrating the times which have been under consideration. In these final records we have further revelations of the direct government of God; two psalms of David, which constitute an unveiling of his character; and some accounts of the deeds of his mighty men. That from which these words are taken unquestionably happened toward the end of his reign. Evidently at this time he was reigning over all Israel again. Fresh trouble arose from their old enemies the Philistines, and David went down to fight against them. He was no longer physically the man he had been, and in the process of the fray, his physical strength gave way, and had it not been for the timely aid of Abishai, he would have been slain. This manifestation of weakness drew forth an expression of love from his people, who declared that he should no more go out to battle with them, lest he "quench the lamp of Israel." Thus at last all the strongest servants of the Lord come to the days of failure in physical strength. They can no longer endure the campaign—the old energy is no more. Happy indeed are such when the consecration of strength, in the days of its fulness, has made such a place for them in the hearts of the people of God, that their love thus gathers around them in thoughtfulness and care. Let those who after long service find themselves waning in strength, be content to abide with the people of God, still shining for them as a lamp, and thus enabling them to carry on the same Divine enterprises. Such action in the last days of life is also great and high service.

The Lord is my Rock, and my Fortress, and my Deliverer, even mine.—2 Sam. 22. 2.

In this chapter and the next, we have two psalms of David, fittingly included in his life-story, for in them the true character of the man is strikingly revealed. In the first of these we find the deepest things. It is so fine a song that it may be well to note its main divisions with their varying notes. (1) Jehovah is declared to be the Source of all strength (verses 2-4). (2) All deliverances are attributed directly to Him (5-16). (3) Such deliverances are wrought upon the condition of right conduct on the part of His people (17-25). (4) The central principle of life is declared: God is to man what man is to God (26-28). (5) The psalm then becomes personal testimony to the truth of the things sung (29-46). (6) All ends with a doxology, setting forth the praise of Jehovah (47-51). Such convictions as these—of the absolute sovereignty of Jehovah, of His omnipotent power to deliver, of the necessity for obedience to His law, and of assurance that in the case of such obedience He ever acts for His people—constituted the underlying strength of David's character. In the opening sentence, which we have emphasized, the sense of truth is reinforced by the final words, *"even mine."* By them the singer revealed the fact that all he celebrated in song was more than theory, it was experience. He had found Jehovah to be at once Rock, that is foundation; Fortress, that is the place of refuge founded on the rock; and Deliverer, that is the One Who guarded the refuge.

An everlasting covenant, ordered in all things, and sure.—2 Sam. 23. 5.

According to the chronicler, in these words we have the last which the king uttered—that is to say it was undoubtedly the last psalm which he wrote. It is a wonderful song, in that it breathes the consciousness of his own failure. and yet sets forth with confidence the Divine faithfulness. In verses 1-4, he declares in most exquisite language the true ideal of the kingship. In verse 5, he recognizes that he has not realized the ideal, but declares that nevertheless God is faithful to His covenant. In verses 6 and 7, in words which must have been to him full of fire, he announces what the fate of the wicked must surely be. There is no doubt that when the man of faith reaches the bound of life where burdens are laid down, and looks back over the way he has come, he realizes that the covenant of God with him has not only been kept, but that it has been "ordered in all things and sure." In the Divine dealing with us, there is no mistake, no lapse. Nothing has been permitted which has not been made to serve the highest purpose. This is so even of our failures, if, like David, in true penitence we have forsaken them and confessed them. It is certainly so of all our sorrows and trials. Believing that our song at the end will celebrate this truth, happy are we in the measure in which we live in such confidence that it is so even now. As one day, reviewing the whole of the way, we expect to sing: "Right was the pathway leading to this," let us to-day sing: "Right is the pathway leading to that!" Thus we antedate heaven's joy, and strengthen earth's pilgrimage.

Let us fall now into the hand of the Lord; for His mercies are great: and let me not fall into the hand of man.—2 Sam. 24. 14.

The Book of Samuel closes with one other story, revealing the direct government of the people by God, in that he visited king and nation with punishment for the numbering of the people. That the act was wrong, is evident from David's consciousness that it was so. It is also evident that this numbering had resulted from a wrong motive, and this Joab knew, as his words show: "Now Jehovah thy God add unto the people, how many soever they may be, an hundredfold, and may the eyes of my lord the king see it; *but why doth my lord the king delight in this thing?"* A spirit of vainglory in numbers had taken possession of king and people, and there was a tendency to trust in these numbers, to the forgetfulness of God. It is a very persistent peril. The choice of David, as to punishment reveals his deep sense both of the righteousness and tenderness of Jehovah. He willed that the stroke which was to fall should come directly from the Divine hand, rather than through any intermediary. And how right he was! In the chastisements of God there is no trace of personal vindictiveness. They are all remedial in their purpose, and also beneficent in their execution. The tender mercies of the wicked are cruel, sometimes in their leniency, and sometimes in their brutality. The punishments of God are ever merciful, sometimes in their severity and always in their perfect justice.

FIRST KINGS

Amen: the Lord, the God of my lord the king say so too.—1 Kings 1. 36.

As the days of David ran out, trouble arose in the kingdom through his son Adonijah. A remarkable statement is made concerning the training, or lack of training, of this man, which throws light on his action: "His father had not displeased him at any time in saying, 'Why hast thou done so?'" He now sought to secure the kingdom for himself and was joined in his rebellion by Joab and Abiathar. David took prompt action, and Solomon was crowned king. When David gave his instructions to his loyal men, he said concerning Solomon: "I have appointed him to be prince over Israel and over Judah." To this Benaiah replied: "Amen: Jehovah, the God of my lord the king say so, too"; thus showing himself to be a man understanding the matters which are of real importance. This should be, not only the prayer we pray in connection with all the arrangements we make for our service, but the principle upon which we act in making those arrangements. In this case it certainly was so, for it was within the Divine purpose that Solomon should succeed David. According to Nathan, there were of the people who had already said, "Long live king Adonijah!" Now others of them would say, "Long live king Solomon!" In these words Benaiah appealed to the Divine arbitrament. His "Amen" signified his personal agreement; but he knew the importance of the Divine approval. No elections are really valid, and no choices of any lasting value, except the Lord say so too!

And the kingdom was established in the hand of Solomon.—1 Kings 2. 46.

Solomon's first action was characterized by the best side of his nature. In dealing with Adonijah, clemency and dignified authority were alike manifest. The charge which David gave him was one which revealed his understanding of the secrets of true success, in so far as he called him to absolute loyalty to God. That part of this charge which had to do with Joab and Shimei has been severely criticized. Much of this criticism is surely unwarranted. David knew these men by experience, and appreciated their danger to the State. He had kept his covenant with them and spared their lives. Moreover, it is to be carefully noted that in each case he left the matter of how to deal with them in the hands of Solomon, being assured of his wisdom. His words concerning the death of each were prophetic rather than vindictive. Events soon proved the accuracy of his forecast. Adonijah's request for Abishag, interpreted in the light of Eastern customs, was a movement toward rebellion. Joab and Abiathar were implicated in this movement. Solomon acted in the highest interests of the kingdom as, with clemency and yet with strict justice, he dealt with these treacherous impulses. Adonijah and Joab were slain, and Abiathar was deposed from the priesthood. To Shimei an opportunity of life was granted on certain well-defined conditions. He broke his parole, and paid the penalty. The words with which the story ends vindicate the action of the new king. There are times when, in the interest of the establishment of a true order, the sternest measures are the most kind.

Behold, I have done according to thy word.—1 Kings 3.12.

This was the answer of God to the request of Solomon, when appearing to him at Gibeon He commanded him to ask a gift. Only be it observed, that the context shows that God gave more than he asked. This appearing of God to the new king was all of grace. The first paragraph of the chapter reveals at once the strength and weakness of Solomon. He was strong in that he loved Jehovah, and walked in the statutes of his father David. The weak side of his nature was manifested in his affinity with Pharaoh and marriage with his daughter. Politically it seemed an astute move, but it was unutterably foolish. The perils of mixed motives and a divided heart are very grave. This appearing of God gave him a great opportunity, and his choice again was due to the triumph of the highest side of his character. Realizing his personal disability for the great work devolving upon him, he asked for an understanding heart. God's answer was full of gracious kindness. He gave him what he asked, and superadded the things he might have chosen, yet showed his wisdom in passing by. Long life, wealth, and victory are good things when they come as the direct gifts of God. Should a man from selfish motives choose them rather than ability to fulfil the Divine purpose, they would prove curses rather than blessings. In the case of Solomon, so long as he sought the highest, these lower things were means of blessing to his people.

And Judah and Israel dwelt safely, every man under his vine and under his fig-tree.—1 Kings 4. 25.

These were the golden days of the monarchy. For awhile the people had rest from war, and the king gave himself up to the careful organization of his kingdom.

He ruled with the understanding heart which he had received from Jehovah, and the system of government as set forth in this chapter is remarkable. The king was supreme, but he gathered around him a company of officers of state, each having his own department, for which he was responsible. The words which we emphasize pictorially set forth the peace and prosperity which characterized the period. Such a time is always one of peril to a nation. It is under circumstances of adversity, when a strain is put upon life, that man is most likely to realize and practise his dependence upon God. Circumstances of ease, when demands upon life are not severe, are always calculated to produce evil results, spiritually and morally. In saying that, have we not almost inadvertently revealed the secret of the peril? Life is not intended for ease, if by ease is meant anything approaching indolence. Days of prosperity should never be days when service ceases. Life is so rich potentially, that there is always room for fuller realization, and all enrichment should but create opportunities for more complete development. That was the meaning of the garden of Eden with its work, before man sinned. That will be the meaning of the Kingdom of God when fully established on earth, not laziness, but strenuous activity in the fulness of strength. Luxury, producing languor, destroys. Abundance, inspiring endeavour, makes for permanence.

Blessed be the Lord this day, which hath given unto David a wise son over this great people.—1 Kings 5. 7.

These words of the King of Tyre constitute one of the illustrations constantly, if incidentally, occurring in these Hebrew records of the fact that men outside the actual covenant people had some very definite knowledge of God. This man used the special name or title of God, which was that of the Hebrews, namely, JEHOVAH. Moreover, he recognized the coming of Solomon to the throne, as the appointment and gift of God. In this case almost certainly this knowledge was directly due to the influence of the people of God. David had obtained timber for the building of his own house from Hiram King of Tyre, and a friendship had existed between them. Whether this was the same man, or his son—for forty years had elapsed between these two events—he "was ever a lover of David." These stories all serve to remind us that men everywhere have capacity for receiving truth about God; and some of them at least suggest that God may make Himself known to men in other ways than those of the more self-evident lines of revelation. Perhaps the case of Melchizedek is the supreme example of this. In any case, all such stories as that of Hiram should serve to call us to the sense of opportunity and responsibility of revealing God to those with whom we are brought into contact in every walk of life. In these words of Hiram, we have not only a recognition of God, and of His government, but a definite act of worship in an ascription of praise to JEHOVAH.

So was he seven years in building it. —1 Kings 6. 38.

Directly Solomon had set the kingdom in order, he turned his attention to the building of the Temple, which work he evidently considered to be his by special appointment. The time was now opportune, for the nation was at peace, and his own words to Hiram had aptly described the conditions: "Jehovah my God hath given me rest on every side; there is neither adversary nor evil occurrent." In this chapter we have a comparatively brief, but very impressive account of the carrying out of the work. In all essentials this Temple was patterned after the Tabernacle as to its actual central building. It was, however, twice its size, and built of solid material, because intended to remain in permanent position, seeing that the nation was now settled in the land. The time occupied in its construction was seven years, during which the actual work of erection in the city went forward in impressive silence. Like the Tabernacle, its chief splendour was within, where everything was encased in gold, neither wood nor stone being visible. The magnificence of this small Temple—for small it was by comparison with temples erected to other gods—may be gathered from the fact that the amount of gold used was six hundred talents, the approximate value of which in English currency has been estimated at over three millions in gold. These must have been great years for Solomon. With loving devotion he was carrying out, as the one appointed by God, the dearest desire of his father's heart; and at the same time, by the work, establishing at the centre of the national life that which would be a persistent witness to the deepest secrets of national strength and prosperity.

And Solomon was building his own house thirteen years.—1 Kings 7. 1.

It is impossible to escape the contrast between these words and those of our last note. Moreover, the contrast was evidently intended by the chronicler, for in his writing there were no chapter divisions, and the two statements run right on thus: "So was he seven years in building it. And Solomon was building his own house thirteen years." This is not to suggest that the work of building the Temple was hurried. There is no doubt that it was done thoroughly. But it does show the place which his own personal comfort and luxurious tastes had come to occupy in the life of Solomon, that he should build for himself a palace which took nearly twice as long to build as the House of his God. It is often by such simple, and unexpected tests, that the deepest facts of a human life are revealed. However strong our zeal may be for the House of God, and however accurately we may discharge our obligations in regard to it, if the proportion of time and possessions devoted to the things of our own ease and comfort be greater than the proportion devoted to the service of God, our master-passion is surely proven thereby to be selfish rather than godly. In the case of the Christian campaign of witness, this is even more searching a test. Solomon did discharge his obligation so far as the Temple was concerned, even though the love of self played so large a part in his life's activities. We have never discharged our obligation while any region of the earth remains unevangelized, or any human soul is yet without the knowledge of Christ.

The cloud filled the house of the Lord.—1 Kings 8. 10.

This shining of the glory of Jehovah in the house which Solomon had built was a radiant manifestation of the grace of God. The thoughtful consideration of the whole account of the erection of this Temple will show that in permitting it, God was accommodating His methods to meet human frailty, as He had done in the appointment of the priesthood. and in the choice of a king. When David had desired to build, it had been pointed out to him that such a building was not by Divine request or command. Nevertheless God had permitted the building, and now filled the house with His glory. The one permanent and unchanged link between the Tabernacle and the Temple was the Ark of the Covenant; and it was when that sacred symbol of the Divine presence and authority found a resting-place in the Temple, that the mystic glory filled the building. Over all human failure grace triumphs; and this shining-forth of the Divine glory in the new Temple was an evidence of that truth. The human attitude which made this possible, was that of the loyalty of the king and people to the deepest truth of their national life, as this was expressed in the desire to give that Ark its proper place at the heart of the city of the king. When the heart is loyal, God acts in grace, even when the methods of expression are not in themselves of the highest. This explains many of the manifestations of Divine glory in the midst of systems and methods which are not in strict harmony with the simplicity which is in Christ.

The Lord appeared to Solomon the second time, as He had appeared unto him at Gibeon.—1 Kings 9. 2.

This second special appearance of Jehovah to Solomon was very significant. It came at a critical time. Solomon had finished all the work prompted by his desires, both godly and self-centred. He had completed the House of God, and his own house. It was the hour when the accomplishment of work means the relaxation of effort. That is always a perilous hour, and the greater the work done, the graver the peril. A life which has been full of activity, when that activity ceases, demands some new interest, and will find it, either high or low, noble or ignoble. It was at such a moment that Jehovah specially manifested Himself to His servant. He declared that his prayer had been heard and answered, but that in order to continued well-being there were conditions which must be fulfilled. Thus the king was called to a new sense of responsibility as to his own life, and as to the administration of his kingdom. Alas, the sequel is a very sad one. The conditions were not kept, either by king or people; and the ultimate issue was that of the destruction of the Temple, and the driving out of the nation. That sad sequel, however, does but serve to reveal more completely to us the importance of heeding all those tender and strong methods by which our God is ever seeking to deliver us from failure. When one task is accomplished, He never leaves us a prey to the perils which follow. For us, in Christ, He is always at hand and available, no longer needing to come in special ways; and it is for us to listen for His next word, that we may continue in His will.

The fame of Solomon concerning the name of the Lord.—1 Kings 10. 1.

It is well to notice these words, as they reveal the real reason of the visit of the queen of Sheba. Her coming shows how far the fame of this king of Israel had spread, and these words teach us the nature of that fame. The reports of him had evidently accounted for his greatness and his wisdom, by his relationship to Jehovah. It was not the story of his magnificence which attracted this Arabian queen. but his fame concerning the name of Jehovah. Her visit revealed to her what the government of God really meant. Arriving, as she did, in the time of the nation's peace and prosperity, she was constrained to employ words which set forth her sense of the greatness of all she saw, as exceeding all reports concerning the prosperity of the kingdom and the happiness of the people. She saw clearly that the secret of everything was that of the reign of God, This she expressed in words which revealed the clearness with which this had been manifested: "Blessed be Jehovah thy God, which delighted in thee, to set thee on the throne of Israel; because Jehovah loved Israel for ever, therefore made He thee king, to do judgment and justice." These were the great days in Solomon's reign. That is true fame for the servant of God, then people are attracted through him, not to him, but to the God whom he represents. It is an evil hour when, concerning the servants of God, men are attracted by them, and by what they are, rather than directed through them to God.

The Lord was angry with Solomon. —1 *Kings* 11. 9.

What a tragic sentence this is! In its setting, it is a revelation of the anger of God which we do well to ponder. The reasons for it are found in the story of Solomon contained in this chapter. Here we have the account of his degeneracy and doom. The nature of the man had ever a strong animal side. His commercial enterprises led him into alliance with surrounding nations, and following Oriental custom, he allowed his heart to go after strange women. The wrong thus began invaded higher realms, and he built temples for these women. Inevitably there followed the demoralization of king and people, until at last: "Jehovah was angry with Solomon." It is indeed a tragedy that the man who had built the Temple, and in priestly dignity had presided over its dedication, crying to God for His abiding presence, should, seduced by the lower side of his nature, turn from his loyalty, and break the covenant. This anger of Jehovah was not passive merely. "Jehovah raised up an adversary unto Solomon, Hadad the Edomite" (verse 14). "God raised up another adversary unto him, Rezon the son of Eliada" (verse 23). "And Jeroboam . . . he also lifted up his hand against the king" (verse 26). All this was Divine judgment, and yet it was but the natural outworking of the evil heart which had possessed the king and people. Man is never punished for sin but that in the midst of the punishment he may say: This is the stroke of Jehovah, but it is my own deed and act. The whole story of King Solomon is full of the most solemn value. His was a life full of promise, but it ended in failure and gloom, because his heart turned from loyalty to God, in response to the seductions of his sensual nature.

My father made your yoke heavy, but I will add to your yoke: my father chastised you with whips, but I will chastise you with scorpions.—1 *Kings* 12. 14.

In this and the four following chapters, we have the appalling story of the break-up and degradation of the nation. It covers a period of about sixty years, from the disruption after the death of Solomon, to the corruption under Ahab, and the coming of Elijah. The seeds of strife had long been growing. The occasion of the actual division arose with the accession of Rehoboam, and the rebellion of Jero-boam. Both these men were unworthy, as the folly of the one, and the sin of the other, prove. Jeroboam led a popular movement of protest against the burdens which had been imposed upon the people under the reign of Solomon. Rehoboam was proud and despotic, and answered the people in these words. They were foolish and empty. He had no right and no power to rule thus despotically. The terrible rending of the kingdom in twain was the result. The story remarkably illustrates the fact that despotic power is not hereditary. Solomon had gained such a position that his rule had become actually despotic. Rehoboam's will was to increase its grip and severity. He could not do so. The people will strangely submit to tyranny for a long time, if the tyrant has managed by some means to gain a personal influence over them. But there are limits. Stooping humanity has the persistent habit of lifting itself up after a time. Then kings are swept aside and revolutions result. Such revolutions are often wrong in their method; but, in their assertion of the greatness of humanity, they all contribute to the onward march of God.

It is the man of God, who was disobedient unto the mouth of the Lord. —1 *Kings* 13. 26.

The story of the "man of God out of Judah," and the "old prophet in Bethel" is a very strange one. We may rest assured that the prophet in Bethel was not a good man. It is quite evident, however, that he gained influence over the "man of God" by his claim to speak in the Name of Jehovah. That, however, was no sufficient excuse for the other's disobedience, and swift judgment fell upon him. The sentence is a very arresting one: "It is the man of God, who was disobedient to the mouth of Jehovah." It is possible to be called of God, sent of God, and yet to be disobedient. Moreover, the disobedience may be in some apparently minor detail. This man of God had faithfully delivered the message of God, and yet broke down in obedience. We are taught that no command of God must be disregarded by His messengers, even when, or if, an angel suggests a change of method. A Divine purpose directly communicated is never set aside by intermediation of any kind. How necessary, therefore, that those who are called of God should "prove the spirits whether they are of God!" When direct assault of evil would utterly fail to seduce the servants of God, the enemy constantly transforms his appearance into that of an angel of light, and claims to bring to the soul a Divine revelation. That is the most subtle of his methods. One thing may ever remain a certainty with us, and that is, that all suggested revelations may be tested by those already received. God never contradicts Himself in His dealings with His servants. Let us be true to His commands, refusing to be deflected from the path of obedience, even by an angel from heaven.

There was war between Rehoboam and Jeroboam continually.—1 *Kings* **14. 30.**

And the supreme tragedy of the situation was that neither the northern nation of Israel, nor the southern one of Judah, was right. In the north, a false system of worship had been set up in the interests of supposed political expediency, and the people were being swiftly corrupted thereby. In the south, the people were also doing that which was evil in the sight of Jehovah, and provoking Him to jealousy with their sins. Thus the whole nation was steeped in idolatry, and utterly failing to bear to the surrounding nations the testimony to the purity and power of the Divine government, for the bearing of which they had been created. Then God is revealed as acting in judgment. Unenlightened peoples—unenlightened through this very failure on the part of the chosen nation—become a scourge in the hands of God for the punishment of the chosen. This is seen in the invasion and spoliation of Judah by Shishak. Moreover, this long internecine strife was also a method of Divine retribution. When the life of the nation was not employed in fulfilment of Divine purpose, it expended itself in a process which was destructive. To fail to fulfil the Divine purpose is not only to be useless, it is to retard that purpose. Therefore the chosen instrument must itself pass under the destructive power of God.

Nevertheless, the heart of Asa was perfect with the Lord all his days.—1 *Kings* **15. 14.**

Rehoboam was succeeded as King of Judah by his son, Abijam, who for three years continued the evil courses of his father, and the process of national deterioration went forward. Then, with the accession and long reign (of fifty-one years) of Asa, there was in a measure a halt in the downward progress. The partial reform under his influence preserved Judah from the speedy spread of corruption which occurred in the case of Israel. The statement of the chronicler, that his heart "was perfect with Jehovah," is a revelation of the fact that his purpose and intention were right. His will and power were not equal to his purpose, and consequently the reforms were not radical. He went a long way when he removed his mother Maacah from being queen, and cut down the abominable image which she had erected; but he left the high places still standing. It is the record of a faulty life, but one in which the deepest thing, that of desire, was right; and so it is the record of a life, the influence of which was a blessing rather than a curse. It is a revealing story. While it is necessarily true that the higher form of life is that in which will completely answers desire, and at all costs carries out high purpose, it is a great source of encouragement thus to discover that God accepts, values, and makes use of those whose desires are in harmony with His will, even though they do not attain to the fulness of realization.

Ahab the son of Omri did that which was evil in the sight of the Lord above all that were before him.—1 *Kings* **16. 30.**

The uttermost corruption of the northern kingdom of Israel was reached in the reign of Ahab, and represented in him. He was a veritable incarnation of evil. The story of the kings of Israel is tragic in the extreme! The record of corruption runs on from Jeroboam through Nadab, Baasha, Elah, Zimri. Of these, two were murdered, and one committed suicide. Then further division was attempted, but Omri overcame Tibni and reigned in continued evil for six years. Then came Ahab. He united Jezebel with himself in the exercise of power, and gave himself and his people over to the most appalling forms of idolatry. This alliance with Jezebel was in itself contradictory to the law of God, and she became a terrible curse to the nation. Under the joint reign of Ahab and Jezebel, Israel sank to the same level as the surrounding nations. Its testimony as a nation was completely destroyed. The truth of the one God was denied by the multiplication within her borders of idols and idol-shrines. The call to purity was silenced by the awful corruption of the court and people. There was hardly a ray of light, for although, as subsequent declarations reveal, a remnant loyal to God still existed, their testimony was overwhelmed by the abounding pollution. It is a most searching history, giving the heart solemn pause, as it shows how complete may be the ruin of the most highly privileged peoples, if they are deflected from the way of absolute loyalty to the Throne of God. There is no safety for man or nation, apart from the liberty which results from complete bondage to the rule of God.

And Elijah the Tishbite.—1 *Kings* **17. 1.**

This sudden introduction of Elijah is in itself suggestive of the startling and dramatic way in which he broke in on the national life of the kingdom of Israel. To this day there are doubts as to his nationality and parentage. He came like a bolt from the blue; or, more accurately, he flamed like a lightning flash upon the prevailing darkness. His coming was the initiation of a new method in the Divine government, that of prophetic authority. There had been prophets before, but with the appearance of Elijah the office was elevated to one of supreme national importance. From that point onward the prophet was superior to the king. Presently kings arose whose hearts were set upon reform, but their work was directed by the prophets of God, through whom the Divine will was made known. The very first words of Elijah declared his authority. He affirmed that Jehovah the God of Israel lived; and he announced the fact that in the message he was about to deliver he spoke as the messenger of the enthroned Jehovah. The Divine action in thus sending Elijah was arresting. All earthly authority and protection were swept aside as being unnecessary. In simplest ways God protected His messenger, and provided for him. Thus God does break in upon human affairs, and assert Himself ever and anon, by some messenger. Men may refuse the message, and persecute the messenger; but the word he speaks is the word of Jehovah, and it is the word by which men live or die according to their response to it.

I have not troubled Israel; but thou, and thy father's house.—1 Kings 18. 18.

Ahab the corrupt king of Israel met Elijah the prophet of God for the first time under strange circumstances. For over two years there had been a drought in the land according to the word of the prophet. The judgment of God had rested upon the whole land. During that period Elijah had been preserved by God, away from the court of the king. Then, by the direct command of God, Elijah appeared to Ahab. The king greeted him with the words: "Is it thou, thou troubler of Israel?" They were a tacit confession that he knew that the judgment which had fallen upon the land was not due to natural causes, that it had come rather by the word of this strange messenger of the Divine authority. The question was one of resentment and anger. The reply of Elijah was immediate, direct, revealing: "I have not troubled Israel; but thou, and thy father's house." And that was so. Apart from the national sins resulting from the corrupt practices of the king, there would have been no judgment. The troubler of a nation is never the man who, in loyalty to righteousness, proceeds against wrongdoing, even though he be probably an outsider. It is rather he through whose corruption the nation becomes corrupt even though he be king. The men who stand for God, and protest against iniquity, are always troublers of those who are doing evil. But that is a very different thing from troubling the nation. The destroyers of the nation are these very evil-doers, and those who trouble *them* are rendering the highest service to the nation, even though they are persecuted, and their message, for the time being, refused.

Arise and eat.—1 Kings 19. 5.

The story of Elijah is very human, and appeals to us because it is so true to the experience of life. The account of his encounter with the prophets of Baal is full of majesty. With calm dignity he stood against the combined evils of a corrupt court and a pagan religion. His vindication by the fire of God was perfect. The slaughter of the prophets of Baal aroused the ire of Jezebel to such a degree, that she sent a direct message, full of fury, to Elijah, Then came reaction. The man who had stood erect, confronting all the forces of evil, now fled for his life. Full of beauty is the story of God's method with His overwrought and fearful servant. Before entering into that communion with him which was for the correction of his false attitude of fear, He commanded him to eat, thus ministering to his physical weakness. The words which are suggested by the story are those of the psalmist: "He knoweth our frame; He remembereth that we are dust." How often the way to spiritual strength and mental restoration is that of physical renewal! While we are serving our King in this sphere of earth there can be no divorce between physical and spiritual health. Over and over again the breakdown of spiritual vision is the result of physical weariness. Let us never forget that the word of Jehovah to His servant of old under these conditions was, first: "Arise and eat." He had much to say to Elijah afterwards, and much to reveal to him; but He prepared him by renewing his bodily strength. A wonderful, understanding God is ours!

As thy servant was busy here and there, he was gone.—1 Kings 20. 40.

These words constitute the central light in a parable which one of the sons of the prophets employed to rebuke Ahab for his failure in the matter of Benhadad. God had created for the king an opportunity of return to Himself. Benhadad, drunken, profligate, despotic, came in the pride of his arms against Samaria. By the prophets Jehovah spoke to Ahab, who acting under Divine direction, gained complete victory over his enemy. Then followed failure in the very hour of triumph. He made a covenant with the man whom God had devoted to destruction. He had one thing to do by the command of God, and while he did a hundred things he neglected the one. That was the meaning of the parable. What a revelation this of a perpetual reason and method of failure! We are given some one responsibility by God, some central definite thing to do. We start to do it with all good intention; and then other things, not necessarily wrong in themselves, come in our way. We get "busy here and there," doing many things, and neglect the one central thing. That is failure of the most definite kind. If a man is called to preach the Word, and becomes busy over a hundred things other than that of his central work and and so loses the opportunity to preach, his failure is complete. That which is our God-appointed work, we must do. If we fail in that, the fact that we have been "busy here and there," doing all sorts of other things, is of no avail. Concentration upon the work entrusted to us is a solemn obligation. Diffusion of energy over all sorts of things not appointed to us, is a waste, and a wrong.

Hast thou killed, and also taken possession?—1 Kings 21. 19.

Ahab had allowed the selfish and corrupt coveting of his evil heart to drive him to the murder of Naboth, in order to gain his vineyard. And now he had gone into the vineyard to take possession of it. But men do not so easily possess the things which they obtain by unrighteous methods. Right there, in the midst of the coveted garden, with startling abruptness, Elijah, the rough prophet of Horeb, stood before him. Thus God perpetually confronts the evil-doer, and spoils for him the gain of his wrong-doing. One can easily imagine the mixture of terror and of anger in the voice of the king as he exclaimed: "Hast thou found me, O mine enemy?" Elijah rose to the full dignity of the prophetic office. There was neither fear nor faltering in the awful message which he delivered. Men may outwit their fellowmen, may deceive and wrong them, may even murder them to rob them. The last word is always with God. He cannot be outwitted or deceived. This question which the prophet asked rings with holy satire. There is a taking possession which never results in possessing. Ahab never possessed the vineyard of Naboth. He held it, but that very fact became to him a torment. However fine the vintage, for him the grapes were acrid, poisonous. Nothing is ever possessed by any man, save that which is his by righteousness and truth and as the gift of God. Not the overlords of injustice, but the meek, inherit the earth. That which is gained by fraud is never possessed.

There is yet one man by whom we may inquire of the Lord, Micaiah the son of Imlah; but I hate him . . .—1 Kings 22. 8.

This was the hatred of an evil soul for the truth. Ahab knew in his heart that Micaiah would not fear or flatter him, but only declare the word of Jehovah. This he construed into personal hatred. Mark the following words: "He does not prophesy good concerning me but evil." What a revelation this is of the degradation of soul which follows upon evil courses! This man knew, none better, the true function of the prophet to be that of expressing the truth, as made known by God. With a superstitious dread, he still desired the supernatural interpretation which came from the prophetic word, only he wanted it to be in his favour. He was not seeking the truth, but such messages as would be for his own personal advantage. This is the lowest level to which a soul can sink. To rebel absolutely against the interference of the prophet, to decline to give any heed to the Divine thought or will, is a far less evil thing than to desire to make use of the prophet to minister to selfish desires. And yet how often this same appalling thing is seen at work! There are men who hate the prophet of God still, simply because he has no care other than to utter the very Word of God. Whenever this is so, it is because, in their deepest consciousness, men know that their courses are evil, and therefore can only be denounced. Hatred of the messenger of God is clear evidence of wilful wickedness.

SECOND KINGS

Is it because there is no God in Israel, that ye go to inquire of Baal-zebub, the god of Ekron?—2 Kings 1. 3.

Ahaziah the son of Ahab had succeeded his father upon the throne of Israel. He was not so strong a personality as was his father, but he gave himself wholly to the most abominable idolatry, in that he served and worshipped Baal. In the midst of difficulties created by the fact that Israel was at war with Moab, he sought counsel from Baal-zebub, the god of Ekron. It was then that Elijah, who had been in seclusion, suddenly appeared, and asked this question. Again it was a question vibrant with satire. Baal-zebub was no god. The God of Israel was God, and beside Him there was none else. And yet this man Ahaziah, excluded by his wickedness from the true God, sought counsel of one who was no god! And that is ever so. Men cannot live without some kind of traffic with powers supernatural, and so superior to themselves. When they are cut off from direct communication with God, they turn to the under-world, to those dark and sinister forces which are no gods. That is the meaning of all forms of spiritism. God is ever available to man, but if man by sin exclude himself from God, then he turns to false methods of dealing with the supernatural. Such methods are all, and always, destructive. Sooner or later, God breaks in again upon the soul, if not in healing revelation in response to penitence, then in swift judgment.

My father, my father, the chariots of Israel, and the horsemen thereof.— 2 Kings 2. 12.

There is something weirdly pathetic in the final movements of Elijah. Accompanied by Elisha, and watched by the prophets, he moved from place to place. It would seem as though he endeavoured to escape into complete loneliness for that translation which he knew was at hand. Elisha, upon whom his mantle had already been cast, followed him loyally, determined to stand by him to the last. It was permitted to him to do so, and to see the chariot and horses of fire, which parted them as Elijah was caught up to heaven by a whirlwind. Then this great cry escaped from the man who was left. That cry almost certainly took this particular form as the result of the vision, but its reference was not to the fiery chariot and horses upon which he had looked but to Elijah. Elisha saw that the strength of Israel had been that of the presence of the prophet of God. It is more than a coincidence that when presently Elisha himself passed away, Joash, the reigning king, uttered the same exclamation (13. 14). This is ever so. The last line of strength in national life is never that of munitions or money, nor even of men. It is that of the word of the living God, declared, interpreted, applied, by messengers whom He calls and sends. It is by this word that men live, are strong, and overcome. Without the guidance of this word, munitions, money, and men are employed to no purpose. Under the direction of this word, they all contribute to the reaching of true national strength and stability.

Were it not that I regard the presence of Jehoshaphat the king of Judah, I would not look toward thee nor see thee.—2 Kings 3. 14.

The ministry of Elisha stands in many respects in striking contrast to that of Elijah. There is a gentleness about it which inevitably reminds us of that of Jesus. Instead of suddenly appearing at critical moment, like thunder and flame, he seems to have moved about amongst his people, doing good wherever he came. It is the contrast between John and Jesus foreshadowed. That is not to suggest that his work and word lacked sternness where necessary. This sternness was manifested in his refusal on this occasion to deal with the king of Israel. In that refusal he stood for the righteousness of God in national

life. Jehoram was continuing in the ways of evil, and to him the prophet would have nothing to say. Jehoshaphat was still desirous of discovering the will of God, even though in this alliance with Jehoram and the king of Edom, he was acting foolishly. For his sake, and that of the nation of Judah, Elisha acted as the interpreter of the Divine will, and the instrument of the Divine beneficence. These words of his to Jehoram are full of solemn meaning, as they show us that there is an attitude of life which makes it impossible for God to speak to it. If a man turns from God to idols, from the messages of God to the words of the prophets of those idols, then let him seek counsel from them in the hour of his distress. To such a man the true prophet of God can have no message, other than that of denunciation. This refusal is never that of an angry resentment; it is always that of absolute justice. It is that of Divine consent to human choice.

According to the word of the Lord.— 2 Kings 4. 44.

In this chapter we have four instances in the ministry of Elisha, in which we see him carrying on his beneficent work among the people; his provision for the need of the widow, whose creditors were threatening her; his kindness to the Shunammite woman, who had shown him hospitality; his healing of the pottage at Gilgal; and his feeding of a hundred men with twenty loaves. The words we have noted are connected with the last of these incidents, and primarily have reference to it alone. But they apply with equal force to all the rest. The ministry of this man was wholly a ministry of the word of Jehovah. He had no other burden. Everything he did was in obedience to that word, and in interpretation of it in the life of the nation. By all this activity, he was demonstrating to those who had the spiritual capacity to apprehend, how good and beneficent were the thoughts and intentions of God concerning His people. During all this time Elisha was at the head of the prophetic schools, and, as he journeyed from place to place, was known as the messenger of God. His deeds were expositions of his message. His life was that of the utmost simplicity. This is evident from the provision made for his entertainment by the wealthy Shunammite woman. His apartment was a chamber on the wall, containing a bed, and a table, a stool, and a candlestick. Yet that life was full of dignity, as the attitude of the people toward him testifies. A ministry "according to the word of Jehovah," interpreting the will of God, and illustrating it by deeds of goodness, is independent of all save the simplest ways of life; but it is ever full of sublime influence.

The leprosy therefore of Naaman shall cleave unto thee.—2 Kings 5. 27.

This was the punishment of a man who in answer to selfish desire, obtained advantage to himself and lied to his master. The deepest wrong in the action of Gehazi was that it involved the Divine witness which had been borne to the Syrian, Naaman, by the action of the little serving maid in his house, and the prophet Elisha. Their action had been wholly disinterested, and for the glory of God. The child had witnessed to the power of her God through His prophet, and that in a desire to bring help to her suffering master. Here the motive and the method were right. Elisha's attitude throughout was that of dignified loyalty to God. Because of this, he had resolutely refused to accept anything in the nature of personal reward for that which had been wrought by the hand of God. To these, Gehazi stood in direct contrast. Governed by selfish desire, he made capital of the work of God, to seek personal enrichment. The judgment was swift and terrible. The story searches the soul like an acid. While we clearly see, and intellectually condemn, the sin of Gehazi, when we allow the whole of the facts, especially those of the motives which moved him, to investigate our deepest life, we surely realize how much we are in danger of falling into the same sin. To exploit a beneficent and healing act of God for our own material and personal advantage, is a grievous wrong, principally in that it devitalizes the testimony to the grace of God which such an act is intended to bear.

Open his eyes, that he may see.—2 Kings 6. 17.

Elisha, in company with his servant, was in Dothan. The city was compassed about by the hosts of the king of Syria. They were there for the express purpose of capturing the prophet of God. The servant of Elisha, going out in the morning early, saw these enveloping hosts, but he saw nothing else. Therefore his very love for his master filled him with fear. Then the prophet prayed for him, and God answered. How constantly we need to pray this prayer on behalf of ourselves: "O Jehovah, open our eyes that we may see!" To the servants of God there are often hours in which circumstances speak of defeat, forces in opposition are gathered round about in strength, and there seems no way of escape. All such seeming is false, for it is ever true, as Elisha said, that "They that be with us are more than they that be with them." It is always true that—

Hell is nigh, but God is nigher,
Circling us with hosts of fire.

It is such consciousness that maintains the heart in strength, and courage, and quietness, on the day when otherwise there might indeed be panic. That man always

endures, who sees Him Who is invisible. This is the true function of faith, and so faith becomes the secret of endurance, and the actual method by which we may take hold upon all the sources of strength. Faith is never the imagining of unreal things. It is the grip of things which cannot be demonstrated to the senses, but which are real. The chariots of horses and fire were actually there. God is not a myth.

Behold, if the Lord should make windows in heaven, might this thing be.—2 Kings 7. 2.

This was the language of incredulity, in spite of faith. That is a curious statement. Let us look carefully at the situation, for there is much to learn from it. Samaria was besieged by the Syrians, and reduced to a state of famine. When a woman in sore distress appealed to the king, he became angry with Elisha. Probably Josephus was right in saying that his anger was caused by the fact that the prophet did nothing to relieve the situation. In his anger he went to the prophet, and then Elisha uttered the word of Jehovah which proclaimed deliverance as at hand. On the morrow there should be abundance of food. Then it was that this military officer uttered these words. His faith was that of a belief in Jehovah. He knew that He was able to do what pleased Him. Yet faith failed to travel to logical conclusion. There was only one way in which there could be supply. From the earth it could not come. If it came, it must be supernaturally. If the windows of heaven were opened, it might be. But of course there would be no such interference, and so the words were those of mockery and derision. How often faith breaks down in this way! It knows that God is, and that He can act. But it only sees one way, and refuses to believe that such a way will be taken. The supply came without the opening of heaven's windows. It is good to rest in Jehovah, and to wait patiently for Him.

The man of God wept.—2 Kings 8. 11.

This is another evidence of the greatness of Elisha, and indeed still further emphasizes what we have previously remarked as to his foreshadowing of the spirit of Jesus. The incident was a very remarkable one. Elisha visited Damascus, and while there the king, Benhadad, sent Hazael to inquire whether he would recover from his sickness. Elisha's reply was a strange one. He declared that the king would recover, but that he would die; that is to say, he affirmed that his death would not come by his sickness but that it would come soon in another way. As a matter of fact, the death of Benhadad came by the hand of this man Hazael, and that almost immediately. This, it is evident, the prophet knew. He looked long and fixedly into the eyes of Hazael. He saw far more in the soul of the man than any other had seen, perhaps more than the man himself was conscious of. He gazed until Hazael was ashamed, and then the prophet broke into tears. He was conscious that this man would be the instrument of terrible chastisement to Israel in days to come, and he told him all the story. His tears were in themselves signs of his understanding of the necessity for those severe judgments which must fall upon the guilty nation; but they were the outcome of his deep love for his people. In those tears he was surely still in fullest sense the messenger of the word of Jehovah. By them he spoke for God as surely as he did in uttering the doom. The mind passes on inevitably to One Who bore the same double testimony to the truth about God, when He wept over Jerusalem, even as He pronounced its coming desolation.

What peace, so long as the whoredoms of thy mother Jezebel and her witchcrafts are so many.—2 Kings 9. 22.

The hour had struck for the carrying out of the sentence of God upon the house of Ahab. Of this judgment, Jehu was the instrument. He was a man of furious driving, and this was the symbol of his character. He halted at nothing, but swept like a relentless whirlwind from point to point until he had accomplished his purpose. In these words, uttered to Joram in answer to his question: "Is it peace?" Jehu showed that, so far, he understood the righteousness of the judgment he was called upon to execute. That is a truth of persistent application. Peace is not peace which is merely a cessation of hostilities on the basis of compromise with evil. The words of a later prophet are for all time: "There is no peace, saith my God, to the wicked." In the presence of widespread and deep-rooted corruption the activity of the Divine government is no longer that of tenderness and compassion, but that of scorching and destructive flame and fire. Evil men will seek for peace, as ease, quietness, the end of suffering; but God never seeks peace except through purity. And here once more it is necessary to remind ourselves of the reasonableness and justice and beneficence of this fact. It is because God is ever seeking the true peace of man, individually, socially, racially, that He smites their godless shrines and shrivels with devouring fire the things that tend to disintegration and disturbance.

Come with me, and see my zeal for the Lord.—2 Kings 10. 16.

Such were the words of Jehu to Jehonadab, as he invited him to accompany him on his mission of judgment. They are revealing words, showing, as in a sudden flash, the central pride of his spirit. That he was the instrument of the Divine judgment there is no question. With terrific speed and thoroughness he swept out the posterity of Ahab. Having accomplished this, he turned himself against Baalism. With a thoroughness which was terrific, he broke and destroyed it. It was while occupied in this very work that he spoke these words. He was proud of his own zeal. How subtle the peril! And it is a peril. Wherever it exists, it leads to other evil things. While this man was carrying out the judgments of God upon Israel, he was in his own life corrupt. It is written of him: "He departed not from the sins of Jeroboam," and "he took no heed to walk in the law of Jehovah." When the central fact of the life is that of self-glorying, even though there may be zeal for the doing of God's work in the destruction of certain evils, there will always be the toleration of others which appeal to personal desires; and that means there can be no fellowship with God. It is a story full of searching power, revealing as it does the fact that a man may be an instrument in the hands of God, for some purpose, while yet never being in personal communion with Him.

She arose and destroyed all the seed royal. But . . .—2 Kings 11. 1, 2.

The significant word here is the *"But."* It marks the futility of evil in its campaign against the purposes of God. Athaliah was the sister of Ahab, and was of his corrupt nature, and strong personality. When Jehu slew Ahaziah, she seized the throne, and made it sure by killing—as she thought—all the seed royal. For six years she swayed the sceptre of her terrible power over the kingdom of Judah. *But*—and there is always a "but." In the day when she was securing her position by slaying the seed royal, her own daughter—moved either by pity for the baby Joash, or by some higher motive, perhaps by both—took the child and hid it, and for six years nursed and cared for the young life within the Temple precincts. Thus evil always breaks down. It is extremely clever, it calculates on all the changes, and seems to leave no unguarded place; but with unvarying regularity it fails somewhere to cover up its tracks, or to insure its victory. God finds His forward highway in the pity of a woman's heart, in some perfectly simple and natural circumstance, and thus the continuity and ultimate realization of His purpose is insured. This is perfectly natural. Evil is always limited in its outlook. It cannot take in all the facts or possible contingencies. God alone sees everything, knows the end from the beginning. This is in itself one reason why we are certain of His final triumph. In the day when it seems as though the forces of evil have done everything, and that they must succeed, let us rest assured that somewhere there is a *but:* and God is finding His vantage ground, amid the events even of that dark hour.

And Jehoash did that which was right in the eyes of the Lord all his days, wherein Jehoiada the priest instructed him.—2 Kings 12. 2.

Jehoash was made king when he was seven years of age, and he occupied the throne of Judah for forty years. In the early days he was the symbol of the restoration of the true order, and the government of the people was really in the hands of the priest Jehoiada. As the years passed on, the responsibility necessarily devolved upon the king himself, but he had the great advantage of the friendship and guidance of this priest of God. So long as this continued, he did that which was right in the sight of Jehovah. During this period the Temple was rebuilt. In order to this, there was first the correction of official abuses, and then the institution of a voluntary system of giving. These reforms, however, were not complete, for the high places were not taken away, and the people still committed idolatry thereon. The story of good in this reign is the story of the power behind the throne. The king himself was not a strong personality, but under the influence of a good man his actions were right. When that influence was removed, the weakness of the man was manifested in the craven cowardice which, in an hour of threatened invasion by Hazael, gave up all the vessels and treasures of the House of God to secure safety. Men, naturally weak, prove their wisdom when they consent to be guided by some other person of stronger personality. The trouble too often is that weak men are too proud to do anything of the kind. Perhaps we can pray no more important prayer than that God will teach us our weakness, and make us willing to seek the help of those who are stronger.

The man of God was wroth with him, and said, Thou shouldest have smitten five or six times.—2 Kings 13. 19.

The story of corruption in Israel runs on in the account of the reign of Jehoahaz. He was succeeded by Joash, concerning whose reign the chief incident recorded is that of his visit to Elisha. The prophet was now sick and feeble, but evidently keenly alive to all the things of true national interest. It is interesting to notice here again, that the king used of Elisha the very words which Elisha had used of Elijah: "My father, my father, the chariots of Israel, and the horsemen thereof!" Joash recognized that the true strength of the nation was not that of its military equipment; but rather that of its possession of such as interpreted the will of God. In his intercourse with Elisha, the weakness of the king was manifested.

Following the prophetic signs, he lacked that passion and consecration which were necessary to the full accomplishment of his purpose. There was no heart in his striking on the ground with the arrows; "he smote thrice and stayed." It was a literal obedience, devoid of enthusiasm, and it revealed the whole nature of the man. For lack of that touch of flame and passion, he would fail in his enterprise, and this the prophet plainly told him. It is a story we do well to heed. A mechanical obedience will carry us so far; but it always breaks down short of the complete fulfilment of purpose. Willingness to do ever needs the reinforcement of passion, if the thing in hand is to be well done. Perhaps one of the chief reasons of the ineffectiveness of the Church of God oftentimes is to be found in her lack of fire.

And the Lord said not that He would blot out the name of Israel from under heaven: but He saved them by the hand of Jeroboam, the son of Joash.—2 Kings 14. 27.

The arresting fact about these words is that of the form in which the recorder made his statement. It seems to suggest amazement in his mind as he contemplated the patience of Jehovah with the sinning nation. It had continued persistently in its evil courses, with the necessary result that it knew affliction of the most bitter kind. In spite of this it showed no signs of returning to Jehovah. To the eyes of man it seemed that the only course left open to Jehovah was that of blotting the name of Israel from under heaven. Yet that, says the historian, is what He did not do. He saved them for a time from these very afflictions by the hand of Jeroboam. He restored to the people a measure of liberty, and regained for them some lost territory. In the process of the centuries the words have come to have a wider and fuller meaning than that of their immediate application to the deeds of Jeroboam. The ancient people of God are scattered and peeled over the face of the whole earth; they are a people largely despised and persecuted. Yet God has not blotted out their name from under heaven. He has not lost them, nor abandoned them. While they walk amid the deep shadows resulting from their own infidelities, He watches and guards; and in His own time, when affliction have accomplished His purposes, He will raise up for them their one Saviour, and bring them back to fulfil their true mission of making Him known among the nations.

In those days the Lord began to send against Judah, Rezin the king of Syria, and Pekah the son of Remaliah.—2 Kings 15. 37.

The sequence of these chapters deals with a period in some respects the most terrible in all the history of this people. To the throne of Israel man succeeded man by the way of murder. Can anything be more appalling than this fact? What a commentary it is upon that first clamour for a king, in which they had rejected God from the place of immediate government! Israel was under a military despotism, downtrodden and oppressed, and yet sinning still with a high hand. The state of affairs in Judah was very little better. Jotham had followed Azariah upon the throne; and he was followed by Ahaz, during whose reign the sin of Judah came to its head. At this time a confederacy was formed against Judah between Israel and Syria, under their respective kings, Pekah and Rezin. From Isaiah we learn that they planned to set up a king over Judah of their choosing, one there described as "the son of Tabeel" (Isaiah 7). The historian sees the hand of God in this confederacy. He says, "Jehovah began to send against Judah, Rezin . . . and Pekah . . ." This view of the Divine overruling of all the affairs of men is persistent in these sacred writings. The plans and policies of men, their hatreds and their intriguings, are all seen; but behind them all, holding them within the grasp of His own government, God is ever seen.

So Ahaz sent messengers to Tiglath-Pileser, king of Assyria, saying, I am thy servant and thy son.—2 Kings 16. 7.

In the hour of difficulty created by the confederacy of Syria and Israel against him, Ahaz turned to Assyria for help. From the standpoint of the policy which trusts to human wit, and shuts God out of its calculation, it was a perfectly natural thing to do. But the folly and weakness of such a policy is revealed in the method which it has to adopt. In these words Ahaz deliberately put his neck under the yoke of Tiglath-Pileser, offering to become his vassal. This led on to the blasphemy of setting up a heathen altar within the actual courts of the Temple of God. This is always so. Refusal to submit to God is acceptance of some destructive yoke. Those who are submitted to the rule of God, never bend the neck to any tyranny. Our reading of all this history needs the illumination of prophetic books. It would seem from this story as though the light of truth were wholly extinguished. It was not so, for Isaiah was uttering his message, as also was Micah. So far as the nation and its kings were concerned, the testimony of truth was indeed lost, and the very name of God was being blasphemed among the heathen. But that testimony was kept alive by the ministry of these prophets; and through it an elect remnant was held and instructed. At this period, when the king of Judah was content to describe himself as the servant and son of the king of Assyria, teaching was given to loyal souls about the coming of One Who should be Immanuel, the Servant and Son of God, through Whom the final freedom of His people should come.

The Lord removed Israel out of His sight.—2 Kings 17. 23.

In these words the historian refers to the carrying away into captivity of the people of the Northern kingdom of Israel. Necessarily they are not to be taken with too great literalness, for there is a sense in which His people are never out of His sight, even when, through disobedience, they are excluded from His fellowship. Nevertheless, they help us to realize how great was the disaster overtaking them. They were to exist for a period as though He had no care for them. They had refused Him, and now they were to pass to an experience in which they would have no communication from Him. This chapter is of great interest, from the fact that the historian seems to have been at great pains to declare the reasons for this exclusion of the people from the land, and from the consciousness of God's government. These reasons are very explicitly stated (verses 7–12). Disobedience to Jehovah; conformity to the nations from which they had been separated; secretly-practised abominations; and, eventually, public idolatry—these were the sins which finally brought the calamity upon them. These things, moreover, they did in spite of God's patience and warning: "Jehovah testified unto Israel and unto Judah, by every prophet, and every seer." These messages they would not hear. They rejected His statutes, they forsook His commandments, they practised all the abominations of the heathen. Their sin was first against law; but finally against love.

He trusted in the Lord, the God of Israel; so that after him was none like him among all the kings of Judah, nor among them that were before him.— 2. Kings 18. 5.

This is high praise, and there is no doubt that it was justified. The comparison is with the kings of Judah; that is, with all those from Rehoboam to Zedekiah. Among the whole of them, Hezekiah stands out as the one who approximated most nearly to the Divine ideal of kingship. This is a remarkable fact when we remember that he was the son of Ahaz, one of the most worthless of the kings of Judah. We must remember, however, that all his life, Hezekiah had been under the influence of the great prophet, Isaiah. The one secret of his greatness was that he trusted in Jehovah, the God of Israel. In that trust he lived, doing right in the sight of Jehovah in all his personal actions; and in that same trust he instituted reforms, more widespread and thorough than any that had been attempted by his predecessors. One simple but revealing illustration is given. So low had the people sunk spiritually that the serpent of brass, which Moses had made in the wilderness, and which had been carefully preserved, had positively been made an object of worship. Hezekiah called it by its right name, Nehushtan, a piece of brass, and broke it in pieces. The greater illustration is that of how he behaved in the presence of the invasion of Sennacherib. Through his obedience to the prophetic word, based upon his trust in Jehovah, the nation was delivered. But this obedience followed a period of vacillation and fear.

Save Thou us, I beseech Thee, out of his hand, that all the kingdoms of the earth may know that thou art the Lord God, even Thou only.—2 Kings 19. 19.

These were the closing words of the prayer of Hezekiah when confronted by the last threatening of Assyria. It reveals the deepest fact in his life. He was anxious that his people should be delivered from the oppressor, but the deeper concern of his heart was that of a zeal for the honour of Jehovah God. When the peril which he, in an hour of weakness, had attempted to buy off, was imminent, in penitence the king had turned to his old and trusted friend, the prophet Isaiah; who thereupon uttered a prophecy concerning the deliverance which was to be wrought. Said Isaiah of Sennacherib: "He shall hear tidings." This was exactly what happened, and because of the tidings the Assyrian king withdrew. Rabshakeh, finding his master departed, sent a letter to Hezekiah, which he at once spread before Jehovah, and offered his prayer. The prayer was heard and answered. The swift judgment of God passed upon the hosts of Assyria; and Sennacherib escaped to Nineveh, only to be slain in the house of his god. The one true passion of the human heart should ever be that of seeking the glory of God. It is when the heart is purged from selfish motives, that it reaches the true place of safety; for God is ever glorified in serving and saving such as put their trust in Him, and seek first His Kingdom. Here is the law of fellowship between man and God; man is ever and only to seek the glory of God; God is ever and only seeking the blessing of man. God in Christ empties Himself, and endures the Cross to save men; man denies himself, and takes up his cross to glorify God.

Hezekiah hearkened unto them, and shewed them all the house of his precious things.—2 Kings 20. 13.

In this chapter we have the account of the last things in the life of Hezekiah. From a severe sickness he was delivered in answer to prayer, and by the intervention of the prophet. Again he manifested weakness in his action in connection with the visit of the Babylonians. He showed them all the treasures of his house, and was sternly rebuked by Isaiah for so doing. The prophet told him that the things they had seen they would ultimately carry away. The reason for the Divine disapproval of this action needs to be sought by considering the story. The ostensible reason for the coming of the Babylonians was that of congratulating the king of Judah on his recovery from sickness. The real meaning of the visit was political; Babylon desired to throw off the yoke of Assyria. What nation was more likely to help them than the one at the hands of which Assyria had been so completely defeated? Babylon sought alliance with Judah against Assyria. When they came, Hezekiah, flattered and pleased, received them with all cordiality, showing them all his treasures. Evidently he was inclined to agree to the alliance they sought. The chronicler gives us an illuminating word about this action when he says: "His heart was lifted up" (2 Chron. 32. 25). He made answer to the impulse of pride as it appealed to his own judgment. In this he was not seeking the glory of God, not looking for His guidance. That was the secret of the failure. The story talks loudly to us of the need of persistent watchfulness.

Manasseh seduced them to do that which is evil, more than did the nations whom the Lord destroyed before the children of Israel.—2 Kings 21. 9.

In this chapter we have the story of reaction. It manifested itself in two reigns, both utterly evil. That of this man, Manasseh, lasted for fifty-two years, and that of his son Amon. Amon merely continued in the evil courses of his father, until his servants conspired against him, and slew him in his own house. The sin of Manasseh was not only that of personal wrongdoing; it was also that of deliberate undoing of what his father had been at such pains to accomplish. That which we have noted more than once as resulting from such failure, is here declared in so many words. Manasseh seduced the people of God to do that which was evil more than did the nations which Jehovah destroyed before them. Nothing can be clearer as a vindication of the absolute righteousness of the judgment which fell upon them, when presently they also were driven out from the land. The depravity of the people is marked in the fact that, when the servants of Amon slew him, so completely were they in sympathy with the evil ways of these evil kings, that they slew the men who had slain Amon. What a commentary all this is on the failure of human kingship! All that Hezekiah had done was on the surface of things only, in spite of his personal devotion to his God. Directly the opportunity was given, the corrupt heart of the people returned to all the evil courses which were bringing about their ruin. The Kingdom of God is the only kingdom in which man can be guarded from the things that destroy him, and enabled to come to the realization of his own possibilities.

I have found the book of the law in the house of the Lord.—2 Kings 22. 8.

With the accession of Josiah there came the last attempt at reformation before the final sweeping away of Judah into captivity, and the ending of the period of human kingship. His first act of reformation was that of the restoration of the Temple. All that followed resulted from that. In the course of the work came the discovery of the book of the law. The condition of affairs in Judah may be gathered from the fact of such a finding. The nation had become utterly corrupt during the fifty-four years covering the reigns of Manasseh and Amon. The Temple had been neglected and deserted, and it would seem that neither king nor priest knew of the whereabouts of this book. Of its existence there can be no doubt that they were aware; but so far had the people departed from recognition of the Divine government, or response thereto, that the sacred writings had been neglected, and the actual Temple copy lost. The effect of the reading of the book upon the king revealed his ignorance of its contents. Therein he discovered how far the nation had wandered from the Divine ideal, and how terrible were the curses pronounced upon them for such wandering. Having a quick and sensitive conscience, he at once realized both the danger threatening them, and its cause; and he turned for counsel to the prophetess Huldah. Speaking on Divine authority, she recognized the sincerity of the king, and the corruption of the people; and declared that the reformation would be unreal so far as the people were concerned. The suggestive and searching fact of the story is that of the book of the law was lost in the Temple of God. When that is so, nothing can save from ruin.

The king stood by the pillar, and made a covenant before the Lord, to walk after the Lord.—2 Kings 23. 3.

The figure of Josiah in this story is heroic and pathetic. From consultation with Huldah he knew that the people were so corrupt that there would be no deep note or lasting value in their reformation. That fact, however, did not give him the right to refuse to follow the light which had come to him. The description of what he did is graphic. He carried out his work with enthusiasm and energy. He first arranged for the public reading of the book of the law. Then he made this covenant. Immediately succeeding, the work went forward; the Temple was purged of all the vessels of false religions; from one end of the land to the other, idolatrous shrines and altars were swept away. Following this, the Passover Feast, long neglected, was observed with all its ancient glory. So far as Josiah was concerned, this whole procedure was the outcome of sincerity and loyalty. The people, however, were simply following the lead of the king, not under any sense of penitence, or return to Jehovah. Therefore there was no turning on the part of God from His necessary purpose of judgment. The action of Josiah the king, like that of Jeremiah the prophet, was heroic, in that both were loyal to the will and word of God, even though their action produced no results in the national life.

Surely at the commandment of the Lord came this upon Judah.—2 Kings 24. 3.

After the death of Josiah, the judgments of God fell upon the nation in rapid succession. Jehoahaz succeeded to the throne; but, notwithstanding all that had been done during the reign of Josiah, he turned immediately to evil courses in his brief reign of three months. The king of Egypt deposed him, and set Jehoiakim upon the throne. He reigned only as tributary to Pharaoh. The lesson of righteousness was not learned, and for eleven years this man, no longer king, but only the vassal of Israel's old enemy, Egypt, continued in evil courses. He became tributary to Babylon under Nebuchadnezzar. The continuity of evil made respite impossible, and the solemn words are written: "Jehovah would not pardon." Calamity upon calamity fell upon the people, until completely broken and spoiled, they were carried away into captivity. And the historian in these words records the solemn fact that all these evils came upon Judah at the commandment of Jehovah. In this whole story the abiding truth is illustrated. that men cannot escape from God. They are always under His control. They may create their own experience of that government, by their attitude toward it. If His throne be recognized and His law obeyed, He commands blessing. If, on the other hand, His throne be disregarded, and His law broken, He commands calamity. Moreover, in either case the inspiration of His action is that of love.

The captain of the guard left of the poorest of the land to be vinedressers and husbandmen.—2 Kings 25. 12.

What a record of the last things in the history of the kingdom! Jehoiachin, who had succeeded Jehoiakim, was carried away by Nebuchadnezzar, with the men of war and rulers, all who were at all likely to cause rebellion. Zedekiah was placed in authority by Nebuchadnezzar as his representative and vassal. He occupied his position for eleven years, during which he continued in courses of evil. Then he rebelled, but was captured and taken to Babylon. The picture of him is tragic. With eyes put out, and bound in fetters, he was carried to the court of the conqueror, the symbol of the people who had rebelled against God, and had been broken in pieces. The goodly and pleasant land, the God-appointed home of His chosen people—chosen to witness to Him—is seen occupied by the poorest of the people, whose life became nomadic and agricultural. Thus, on the human side, the record of the movement which began when the people clamoured for a king like the nations, ends in tragic and disastrous failure. To those whose eyes are fixed upon the eternal throne, it is certain that in spite of all such failure, the Divine purpose in and through these people must yet be accomplished. Into long years of servitude and suffering they had passed; but through them all, they would be watched over by their one and only King, and by these very sufferings prepared for co-operation according to the covenant of grace, in the forward march of the overruling God.

FIRST CHRONICLES

Adam, Seth, Enosh.—1 *Chron.* 1. 1.

That is a strange beginning for this book. The method is systematic. A principle underlies it, which is illustrated through the first ten chapters, and indeed throughout the history. It is that of Divine election. Let us first remind ourselves of certain facts concerning these books of the Chronicles. The history with which they deal has already been under review in the books of the Kings. Here, however, the history is confined to Judah. Israel is only referred to in cases where Judah is involved. Again, within the kingdom of Judah the history is that of the house of David, all other matters being referred to as they affected, or were affected by, the Davidic line. In the Kings we have seen the history of this period from the standpoint of the Divine overruling of human will; here we see it from that of the Divine choices and procedure. The actual history begins with the death of Saul, but the chronicler prefaces that history with these genealogical tables, which relate the particular period to all that had preceded. They are not exhaustive, but serve a clearly defined purpose, in that they indicate the Divine choice of channels for the accomplishment of the Divine purposes. Carefully observe the technical method of this first chapter. The only son of Adam mentioned is Seth. From him the line is traced through Enosh to Noah. Then an excursion gives the genealogies of Japheth and Ham, because of the relation of their descendants to the people of God. The direct line proceeds through Shem, and finds a new departure in Abram. Another digression traces the descent through Ishmael and the sons of Keturah. The direct procession continues through Isaac. A third, and elaborate aside, traces the descendants of Esau. The first words, then, suggest the value of the genealogies. Cain is omitted. There are men whom God excludes from the operation of His purpose. Follow this through, and it will be discovered that the choices of God are determined by the character of men.

The sons of Judah.—1 *Chron.* 2. 3.

In this chapter the same method is manifested, and still further illustrated. The twelve sons of Israel are first mentioned. All of them are subsequently referred to, with the exception of Dan and Zebulun, of whose descendants the chronicler gives no account. The direct line of the Divine movement centres in Judah. His sons are named, and once again we see the practice of selection operating upon the principle of character. Er, the firstborn, is slain because of his wickedness, and presently also Achar (*i.e.* Achan), the troubler of Israel. Some lines of the descent of those excluded are again traced, and for the same reason, that of their relation to the history of the chosen people. From Judah the main movement passes through Perez and Hezron to Ram, somewhat indirectly. Then it becomes very direct through Jesse to David, who is the one through whom the royal line is at last to reach the one appointed King. All this is very technical; but carefully observed, it reveals the fact that the elections of God constantly set aside the prejudices and plans of men. The law of primogeniture, for instance, has no place in the Divine reckoning. Of this the last illustration in the series of Divine choices before us is that of David, and he was the seventh son—the youngest of them all. So also the principle of choosing and appointing impressive men, that is, men who by outward appearance seem to be men of power, is entirely ignored. In the economy of the Divine government privilege is not hereditary, neither is it bestowed upon natural ability. Everything depends upon character. Jehovah looketh upon the heart.

The sons of David.—1 *Chron.* 3. 1.

In this chapter the genealogical tables continue to deal with Judah, and have special reference to David. The names of nineteen of his sons are given. Six of these were born in Hebron, and four were sons of Bathshua (*i.e.* Bath-sheba). There were nine others. From these nineteen, one, Solomon, was chosen, and the descent is traced through him, through the kings of Judah, and right on into the period of captivity. The peculiar character of this Book of Chronicles is very evidently marked in this chapter, in the fact that in referring to Solomon, and his three brothers, no reference whatever is made to the sin of David. They are simply spoken of as the sons of Bathshua. Indeed, nowhere in these books are any of the failures of David referred to save that of his numbering of the people. The standpoint of observation throughout is that of Divine government, and the continuity of the purpose of God in His activity. And is there not here a deeper note? In the election of Solomon we see that God does not allow wrong, for which a man is not in any sense responsible, to be a bar sinister in his life. If God does not count as advantages what man often does, neither does He reckon as disqualifications the things which man does. Everything depends upon the relation of the man to Himself, as to whether the man is a fit instrument for the Divine work. If a man be right with God, his lack of advantages can be supplied, and his disqualifications overcome.

The sons of Judah.—1 Chron. 4. 1.

These words were the key-note in chapter 2 also. Here another line from Judah is traced, and must be viewed in the light of the royalty manifested in David. It is the story of the multiplication and settlement of the people, who became workers in the great kingdom. Also in this section we have the account of one man and of how he, by prayer and obedience, obtained the favour of God. As to the people, we have the descent of such as became workers in fine linen, of the potters and of the king's workmen. The king of Judah ever needs the sons of Judah who are equipped by God for the work of the kingdom; and here we are reminded of the fact that such are also chosen and appointed by God to their work. Therefore all their work is as sacred as that of the king. The story of an individual is that of Jabez, in all probability a nephew of Caleb. For some reason his mother gave him this name, which means "bringeth sorrow." Perhaps this knowledge of the meaning of the name had cast a shadow over his life. In his prayer he asked "that it be not to my sorrow." For us, the beauty of the story consists in its revelation of God's interest in individuals. While through these genealogies, and indeed through all the history, we are occupied with matters of the government of the nation for the accomplishment of the Divine purpose in human affairs, it is refreshing and helpful thus to be halted by the story of one man, who took his need directly to God, and obtained an immediate answer of His grace.

Of him came the Prince.—1 Chron. 5. 2.

The section in which these words occur really begins at the twenty-fourth verse of chapter 4. It consists of the genealogies of Simeon, Reuben, Gad, and Manasseh. These words are found in connection with the name of Reuben, and here that of which we have been thinking through all these chapters, the principle of Divine election, flames out centrally. The Prince toward whose advent everything was moving, is named. Yet He is not to come through the line of the birthright. That birthright was taken from Reuben because of his sin, and given to Joseph. But the Prince was to come through Judah. In these occasional gleams of light upon the progress of events, nothing is more clear than the revelation of the God Whose selections are ever based upon His complete knowledge and undeviating justice. Such light is at once the occasion of joy and fear in the heart. The joy is begotten of the confidence that no mistakes are ever made in the Divine government. All the blunders and failures of men are overruled, and resolved into the harmony of the perfect wisdom and might of God. This very assurance, however, must have the effect of solemnizing the heart and filling it with wholesome fear, as it makes clear the fact that no supposed right obtains for one moment in the economy of God, if its conditions be violated by the disobedience of men.

The sons of Levi.—1 Chron. 6. 1.

This long chapter of eighty-one verses is wholly devoted to the priestly tribe. This is in harmony with the viewpoint from which the history is now written. Judah, the kingly tribe, is the only one which has more space devoted to it—one hundred and two verses. The tribe of Levi was God's chosen election for priestly service. The sons of Levi, Gershom, Kohath and Merari are named. Then a list of priests is given, doubtless with the intention of showing the proper priesthood of Joshua the son of Jehozadak in the days of the return under Ezra and Nehemiah. The chain is complete from Aaron to Jehozadak. Then follow lists and details of service. A careful distinction is drawn between the work of Aaron and his sons, and that of the Levites generally. While these latter had charge of the whole of the Tabernacle, and attended to the orderliness of its appointed services, the work of the high priests was specially that of attendance at the altar of burnt-offering, at the altar of incense in the Holy Place, and in connection with the Day of Atonement. The last part of the chapter gives an account of the arrangements made for the dwelling-places of priests and Levites. The distribution ensured the scattering of these men throughout all the land. As we read all this, we do so with the knowledge of the failure of the whole tribe, and indeed the whole system of the priesthood. Nevertheless, we recognize how very complete were the provisions made ideally. These men of God scattered everywhere, and all having vital connection in the discharge of their duties with the religious centre of the national life, ought to have exerted the highest influence. The failure was not in the system, but in the men. This is ever so.

And of the sons . . .—1 Chron. 7. 1.

"Of Issachar . . . Benjamin . . . Naphtali . . . Manasseh . . . Ephraim . . . Asher." So run the sub-headings of this chapter, the genealogies of six of the tribes being thus given. In this chapter again the matter of principal interest is its revelation of the purpose of the chronicler. His mind was dominated by his recognition of the choice of the tribe of Judah as the kingly tribe, and therefore those tribes most closely associated with Judah have much fuller treatment than others. In referring to Issachar, Benjamin, and Asher, both genealogies and the number of the fighting men are given. These numbers undoubtedly referred to the time of David, around whose reign the principal interest of the book revolves. The special help of these tribes is indicated. Of the men of Issachar it is said that they were mighty men of valour; and of their number, the chief men of the nation were found. All this was true also of the tribes of Benjamin and of Asher. Naphtali is dismissed in a verse. Concerning Manasseh some few names are given, and the possessions enumerated. All this is technical, and yet full of interest, as it reveals another side to the history. Here tribes, and individual men, are seen as gaining importance and value in proportion as they co-operated in the purpose of God. While His elections are sovereign, they ever have relation to the attitude of human choices in the pursuance of His purpose. Issachar, and Benjamin, and Asher were elect instruments so long as they walked in the way of the Divine Will; and no longer, as subsequent history will reveal.

And Benjamin.—1 Chron. 8. 1.

This whole chapter constitutes a fuller account of the house of Benjamin. It is really very little more than a list of names, the genealogy of Benjamin, and a list of the families of Benjamin which settled at Jerusalem. When, at the disruption of the kingdom, after the death of Solomon, the ten northern tribes revolted, Benjamin remained with Judah. This fact in itself would account for the giving of all these particulars by the chronicler. In the course of the reading of the chapter we come across two names, almost buried among the rest, and yet standing out conspicuously in the history of David. They are those of Saul and Jonathan. Of these, the father was his most implacable foe for many years, and the son his choicest friend throughout his whole career. The love of Jonathan very largely cancelled the cruelty of Saul for David—as his subsequent treatment of Mephibosheth revealed. It is an interesting illustration of much of human life, that this tribe, the tribe of the first king Saul, should eventually become the one tribe which remained loyal to the kingdom of David, as it persisted in Judah, when Israel broke away. Notwithstanding the fact that there were strong partisans of Saul who caused trouble, it would seem that the influence of Jonathan was stronger than that of his father among the people. How often as we look back over life we find that our Sauls and our Jonathans come from the same stock of some Benjamin; but in the long issues the force of love and friendship is mightier than that of hate and enmity. Happy indeed are those who in every "now" of stress, can count upon the "long issues" and God.

Very able men for the work of the service of the House of God.—1 Chron. 9. 13.

In this chapter the genealogies are completed; that is to say, they here reach the latest point in their history, as they refer to the dwellers in Jerusalem after the return from captivity. They are lists of the heads of the families of Judah, Benjamin, the priests, and the Levites. The words we notice are used in connection with the account of the attempt to restore the order and worship which had been lost through the carrying away into captivity. They refer to the company of the priests, upon whom the chief responsibility rested. Round these were grouped the Levites, both porters and singers, helping them in all their work. The phrase "very able men" means "mighty men of valour," and is so rendered in this historic connection in Nehemiah (11. 14). The description is usually employed with reference to military men, and that makes its use here the more arresting. Valour is always spiritual ultimately, and men who are not called to actual physical conflict need it, if they are to fulfil their true functions of leading the people of God in the way of His commandment. If the priests, whose work is ever that of maintaining a relationship between God and the people, lack valour, then the valour of the fighting men will be wrongly inspired, and sooner or later will fail. The valour of the priests must ever be that of courageous and often daring loyalty to righteousness and purity, and all the things which are in consonance with the Divine character.

Saul died for his trespass . . . and also for that he asked counsel of one that had a familiar spirit.—1 *Chron.* **10. 13.**

Before the chronicler proceeds to tell the story of the reign of David, he records the death of Saul. In sublime and graphic language he recounts the facts of the passing of the king chosen by men. It is a terrible picture of a man of magnificent capacity and opportunity going down in ruin. Magnificent indeed was the ruin, but it was ruin. Saul was a man who had great opportunities, but his failure was disastrous Of good standing in the nation; distinctly called and commissioned by God: honoured with the friendship of Samuel; surrounded by a band of men whose hearts God had touched; everything was in his favour. From the beginning he faltered and failed. Step by step he passed along a decline of character and conduct. At last, routed by his enemies, he died by his own hand, in the midst of the field of defeat. He went out of life, having failed himself, and dragging his nation into such confusion that its very existence was threatened. These words reveal the secrets of his failure. First and fundamentally, he trespassed against God. He went the way of the disobedient, Then finally, he sought counsel from the dark underworld of evil spirits. These two things constantly follow each other, in this order. When a human being is called of God to service, there is always given to such a one the guidance of God, in direct spiritual communication. If there be disobedience, this guidance is necessarily withdrawn. Then, the forsaken man or woman, craving for supernatural aid, turns to sorcery, witchcrafts, spiritism; and the issue is always destructive. Upon the whole subject of responsible service, the story of Saul throws the light of most solemn warning.

They anointed David king over Israel, according to the word of the Lord, by the hand of Samuel.—1 *Chron.* **11. 3.**

We now come to the particular period of history with which this book is concerned, that, namely, of the reign of David. It was undoubtedly in many ways the greatest time in the kingdom of Israel, using the word, kingdom, in its lower sense of describing the monarchy, rather than the theocracy. It is significant that the chronicler makes no reference to the seven years in which David reigned over Judah. He begins with the crowning at Hebron, when all Israel acknowledged his kingship. There may be two reasons for this. First, it is evident that the history is written from the standpoint of David's greatness, and therefore the years of the partial reign are omitted. Second, it was in connection with his crowning as king of the complete nation, that the activity of David concerning the ark and the Temple com-

menced and in the view of this writer these were the central things in the national life. The people for forty years had been under a king "like the nations" in Saul. Then for seven years there had been a divided kingdom. Now, over the united kingdom David, "the man after God's own heart," was to reign. The kingship of God was to be represented to them through this man, at once a statesman, a warrior, a poet, and a man of faith. His imperfections are patent; and also is his failure to represent that Divine kingship faithfully. Nevertheless, it was a wonderful period, during which the whole nation came nearer to the true ideal than at any other time in the monarchy.

These are they that came to David to Ziklag . . . and they were among the mighty men, his helpers in war.— 1 *Chron.* **12. 1.**

The story of David's mighty men is always full of fascination. It is principally interesting in view of what they were in the days of David's exile during the reign of Saul. There had then gathered to him in the mountain fastnesses, a company of men graphically described as those in debt, in danger, and discontented. His influence is seen in their devotion to him, and still more surprisingly in the heroic character which they developed. Some of the statements made concerning them in this chapter are full of suggestiveness. They "could use both the right hand and the left"; this speaks of careful training. They were "mighty men of valour . . . trained for war"; this reveals their disciplined strength. They "could handle shield and spear"; that is, they were able to act on the defensive and on the offensive. Their "faces were like the faces of lions"; they had become a kingly company. They were "as swift as the roes upon the mountains"; that describes their perfect fitness. They were, moreover, men of differing capacities, all of which were consecrated to David. Among the sons of Issachar were "men that had understanding of the times." Among the sons of Zebulun were those "not of double heart," that is, incapable of treachery. It was a great company of great men; and their greatness resulting from the influence of David, was consecrated to his interest. Every word of this chapter carries the mind on to great David's greater Son, and the men He gathers about Him.

Let us bring again the ark of our God to us.—1 *Chron.* **13. 3.**

David's consciousness of the true strength of the kingdom is clearly manifested in the fact of his anxiety concerning the Ark of God. This sacred symbol had been for long years at Kirjath-jearim, apparently neglected. He now set himself to bring it into the midst of the people, as a recognition of the nation's relationship to Jehovah. He knew that not he, but Jehovah, was their true King. His own rule must depend upon the will and counsel of God. This it was not only necessary for him to know, the fact must be recognized by the people. Hence his determination to bring in the Ark of God. In connection with this action a terrible event taught David a lesson of deep solemnity. If God's order is to be established, it must be done in His way. The long neglect of the Ark may have rendered these men unfamiliar with the very explicit commands concerning the method of its removal. Or they may have grown careless as to the importance of attending to such details. In any case, they arranged for its removal by a device of their own. The swift death of the man who stretched out the hand to save the Ark, was evidence at once of the presence of God among the people, and of the necessity for perfect conformity to His minutest instructions. David was angry and afraid. The whole movement was stayed, and the Ark was carried to the house of Obed-edom, where it remained for three months, and brought abundant blessing. Most graphically does this story set forth a truth, never to be forgotten by the people of God, that zeal for Him must be according to knowledge.

When thou hearest the sound of marching in the tops of the mulberry-trees, that then thou shalt go out to battle: for God is gone out before thee. —I Chron. 14. 15.

It is very remarkable how constantly these words have been made use of by the people of God. The spiritual instinct which has caused this is a true one. In this chapter David is seen taking counsel of God before going to battle against the Philistines. That is the fundamental note. It shows that he was conscious of his relation to the Throne of God, both for guidance and for strength. In the first case he was told to go, and victory resulted. The second time he was forbidden to go until there should be granted the supernatural indication of the sound of marching in the tops of the mulberry-trees. He obeyed, waited for the sign, went forward, and again to victory. In these days, signs of this particular kind are not given. They are no longer necessary to a people whose holy right it is to live in constant and close fellowship with God through His Son, by the communion of the Holy Spirit. And yet we use the words, and properly. In that very communion of the Holy Spirit, signs are given to the people of God by which they know the hour of their opportunity. They are mystic, but none the less definite. There are times when waiting for such signs is the only true attitude. When they are granted, there is no mistaking them. Their method can never be tabu-

lated or described, but the fact of them is one of the most real experiences of the life of fellowship.

She despised him in her heart.— I Chron. 15. 29.

This is a revealing word. The circumstances were those of the greatest joy to David. Michal, having no understanding of the reasons of that joy, despised her husband for the dancing which gave expression to it. The Ark was brought at last into the city. This account of how it was done shows that David had learned the lesson which the death of Uzzah was intended to teach. He declared that the work must be that of the Levites only. After careful preparation of the Tent for its reception, the ceremony of bearing it to its resting place was carried out. Companies of instrumentalists and singers were appointed, and with high jubilation the Ark was borne by the priests into the prepared Tent. David, full of holy gladness, accompanied the glad procession, playing and dancing. Michal looked at him and despised him. The incident illustrates the perpetual inability of the worldly-minded to appreciate the gladness of the spiritually minded. The external manifestations of the heart of joy of such as hold communion with God, cannot convey to the unenlightened the real meaning of that spiritual delight. A meeting for prayer and praise is still held in contempt by those who have no personal experience of the peace and joy of the secret place of the Most High. Out of such a consideration a somewhat disturbing thought arises. Perhaps we may best express it by asking ourselves whether there is ever anything in our outward demeanour, born of our inward experience, which provokes the contempt of the worldly.

On that day did David first ordain to give thanks unto the Lord, by the hand of Asaph and his brethren.— I Chron. 16. 7.

There is an ambiguity about this verse which admits of two interpretations. The first is that this was the day when Asaph and his brethren were first officially appointed to the service of praise. The other is that this was the first occasion on which this Psalm was employed in that service. Personally I lean to the second view. It is not a vital matter. That which is vital is the Psalm itself, sung in connection with the bringing of the Ark of God into the City of God. The Psalm is found in the Book of Psalms; its first movement (8–22) in Psa. 105. 1–15; its second movement (23–33) in Psa. 96. 1b–13a; its third movement (34–36) consisting of a quotation of the opening and closing sentences of Psa. 106, verses 1–47 and 48. It has been said that it consists of quotations from these Psalms. It may be that they contain quotations from it. The three movements indicate a growth in the experience of the glory of the Divine government of which the Ark was the symbol. The first is an ascription of praise, merging into a call to remembrance of the works of God, and of His covenant. In the second, the sacrifice of praise moves on to a higher level, as it expresses itself in adoration of God for what He is in Himself in majesty. This has been displayed, under differing circumstances, in their history. In the third, it reaches the highest level, as it utters thanksgiving for what He is in mercy. In the restoration of the Ark after a period of neglect, the people found a sure token of that mercy.

Who am I, O Lord God, and what is my house, that Thou hast brought me thus far?—1 Chron. 17. 16.

The presence of the Ark in the city would seem to have created, or at least to have renewed, the desire in the heart of David to provide for it a permanent and worthy resting place. The desire in itself was certainly not unworthy, but it was not in accordance with the Divine purpose. The method of Jehovah with David in this matter is very full of suggestiveness. He was brought into the conscious presence of Jehovah, and there was made to pass before his mind all that God had done for him. The man who desired to build a house for God, was reminded that God was building his house for him. David's desire to do something for Jehovah, was set in the light of what Jehovah had done for him. The response of David was full of beauty, and a radiant revelation of the deepest things in his character. He at once submitted to the will of God, and expressed the worship which was founded upon his sense of his own unworthiness, and of the consequent greatness of the Divine mercy and goodness. He poured out his heart in gratitude to God for all His goodness and His truth, and rested his soul in the blessing promised. In all this there is much of spiritual value for us. Our relationship with God is always based upon what He does for us, never upon what we do for Him. If He wills that we build a Temple, it is ours to do it, but the doing of it creates any merit by which we may claim anything from Him. Conversely, if He wills that we should not build, we have lost no merit by not doing it. Our relation with Him remains the same, sure founded upon His activity in grace.

These also did King David dedicate unto the Lord.—1 Chron. 18. 11.

With very slight variations, this chapter is identical with 2 Samuel 8. It tells the story of David's victories over surrounding foes, by which victories he made his position secure as to the boundaries of his kingdom, and with a view to increasing his trading facilities. In view of the desire of the king to build the Temple of God, the chapter is of special interest; it shows how in these wars he was amassing treasure with that purpose in view, not for himself, but for his son. The Moabites and the Syrians brought presents. Shields of gold and very much brass were gathered from the cities and servants of Hadarezer. Vessels of gold and silver and brass were sent by Tou. All these things were dedicated to Jehovah. Thus, through all the days of conflict, and notwithstanding the fact that he was not personally to be permitted to build, the desire for the accomplishment of the purpose burned in his heart. In all this his greatness was manifested. To be willing to do the work of preparation, when not permitted to undertake the principal service, is a proof of real devotion. The story reveals to us the possibility which is always open to us of serving the work of God in very real ways, even when we are not permitted to do those things which we desired to do. The passion of the heart may have moved us to dedicate ourselves to the foreign field for service, and for some reason our way is blocked within the will of God. The temptation which assails us then is that of imagining that we are excluded from the work altogether. It is not so. There are many ways in which we can serve the same high enterprise. If in no other way, we may do as David did; we may gather treasure for the work, and so help it.

I will show kindness unto Hanun the son of Nahash, because his father showed kindness to me.—1 Chron. 19. 2.

David's attempt to deal kindly with the new king of Ammon was misinterpreted and resented, and his messengers were treated with indignity. The issue was the utter rout of Ammon by the hosts of David under Joab and Abishai, notwithstanding the confederacy with the Syrians. The attitude of Ammon does not detract from the nobleness of the action of David. In that action he proved that he had not forgotten the kindness which had been shown to him by Nahash. Perhaps it was an impolitic thing to do, using that word "politic" in its lower sense. But David acted in obedience to the higher sanctions of nobility and gratitude. This is the true way of living. That man is always richer in the best things of character who is big enough to act in accord with the promptings of a generous nature, even though such action be misinterpreted and resented. A more cautious man, actuated by suspicion, will silence the higher suggestions in the interest of his own safety or dignity, and by so doing lose irreparably in his character. It is a great thing to hold one's own life true to the highest ideals, even though, in doing so, risks be taken of being thus slandered. The man who has been true to the highest things is never weakened, but rather strengthened. In the subsequent conflict, provoked by the unworthy suspicions of the princes of Ammon, not they, but David, was victorious.

David tarried at Jerusalem.—1 Chron. 20. 1.

That is the only reference made in this book to the greatest sin and failure in the history of David. The insertion of the full story, as given in 2 Samuel, would not have served the purpose of the writer of this book, but we ought not to allow ourselves to forget the warning it affords. The story in Samuel is introduced by exactly the same statement concerning the tarrying of David at Jerusalem at the times when kings go out to battle. That was the first stage in that swift passage of shameful sin. There is nothing more full of subtle danger in the life of any servant of God than that he should remain inactive when the enterprises of God demand that he be out on the fields of conflict. How many have found the peace of ease to be that of deadly peril, when the demands of the Divine service were calling for strenuous endeavour! There is a very old adage, and very simple, at which perhaps we are inclined to smile; but it is well to remember it, not only in childhood, but to the end of the pathway. It declares that:—

> Satan finds some mischief still
> For idle hands to do.

If I ought to be at Rabbah with the army, and am tarrying at home in ease, then almost certainly some Bathsheba will present herself, by whom I may be utterly undone. And that is not to blame Bathsheba. She also sinned, and shared the wrong of David; but neither would have been involved had he been in his true place on the field of battle.

Satan stood up against Israel, and moved David to number Israel.—1 Chron. 21. 1.

This statement, that Satan moved David to number Israel, at once reveals his motive in doing so, and explains why the action was wrong. The one sin of Satan, originally and persistently, is that of pride and ambition. This was David's sin on this occasion. His victories had resulted in the lifting up of his spirit, and in arrogance he would know the number of his people, that he might make his boast therein. Numbering of the hosts of Jehovah is not essentially or necessarily wrong; everything depends upon the motive. There were occasions when the people of God were numbered by the command of God, and there was always a reason for such commands. It is, however, an action

that we do well to safeguard with the greatest care. When it is born of pride, it is the subtlest of perils, inclining us to trust in the multitude of an host, and thus to cease to depend upon God. Never was there a more untrue thing said than that God is on the side of the big battalions. He may be, but it is by no means always so. It depends upon the character of the men who make up the battalions. Sometimes our numbering is the expression of our despair. A decrease in membership is not always a calamity. God can do more with 300 men of a certain quality than with 32,000 of a mixed mob of fearful and self-centred souls. When we are moved to number the people, we may rest assured that the impulse is Divine or Satanic, and we may determine which by the motive. If the motive is service, it is God. If the motive is pride, it is Satanic.

This is the house of the Lord God, and this is the altar of burnt-offering for Israel.—1 Chron. 22. 1.

Thus the site of the Temple was determined. It was subsequently erected over the threshing-floor of Ornan the Jebusite. The rest of this chapter is occupied with the final things David did in preparation for the building; and with the charge he delivered to Solomon concerning his responsibilities in the matter. For the special value of this verse we need to look back at the previous chapter. These words continue and complete the statement found in the twenty-eighth verse of that chapter: "When David saw that Jehovah had answered him in the threshing-floor of Ornan the Jebusite, then he sacrificed there." The sins of David were the lapses and accidents of his life. This is not to condone them; it is, however, to emphasize the fact that the habitual set of his life was not what these things suggest. The deepest truth concerning him is revealed, not by these failures, but by his action afterwards. In connection with the sin of numbering the people, he chose to fall into the hand of Jehovah for chastisement. In response to his cry of penitence and confession, Jehovah answered him by fire on the altar he had erected in the threshing-floor of Ornan, and there the judgment was stayed. "Then David said, This is the house of Jehovah God." Thus the site of the Temple was the place where the mercy of God operated in staying the plague resulting from the sin of David.

David divided them into courses.— 1 Chron. 23. 6.

David's interest in the building of the Temple, and its establishment as the centre of worship and of the national life, is manifest, not only in the material preparation he made, in the amassing of treasure and in the preliminary work of getting the stones ready, but in other ways.

He practically abdicated the throne, that he might supervise the setting in order of the worship. It was he who "divided them into courses." The specific work of the Levite, as thus arranged, is beautifully described by the chronicler in the closing verses of this chapter. They were the servants of the priests and the House, doing all the things which were necessary in order that the priests might fulfil their specific function, and that the orderliness of the services might be maintained. They were also singers, and were to stand at morning and at evening to praise the Lord. This was a high and holy calling. First, the morning hour of praise, expressive of confidence in God, and of gratitude to His name for all His grace and goodness. Then, the busy hours of service, all in the power of that early praise. Finally, the hymn of adoration for the goodness and guidance of the day, as the shadows of the evening fell. It was a high national ideal, and the measure in which any nation approximates to it, is the measure of that nation's greatness. Israel sadly failed, but the conception was most noble. Never was the true kingliness of David more manifest, than when he sought to make these arrangements for the consolidation around the Throne of God of that kingdom which he was so soon to leave.

Princes of the sanctuary, and princes of God.—1 Chron. 24. 5.

With great care, and perfect wisdom of choice, the courses of the priests were set in order. There was a tactful admixture of the older and the younger men, so that in this highest and holiest national service, the experience of age and the enthusiasm of youth were merged. The former guided the latter, and the latter inspired the former. This description of these men— "princes of the sanctuary, and princes of God"—occurring in the course of this chapter, is full of light. In neither half of the description is there any thought of the exercise of rule on their part. They had no authority over the sanctuary, and certainly none over God. Nevertheless they were princes, and called upon to exercise authority. This description indicates the source of their authority, rather than its sphere of operation. Their government consisted in their obedience, within the sanctuary, to the will of God. This was always the one and only authority of the priests. They, by obedience to all the service of God in the holy places, were to make possible approach to God of the people in order that they (the people) might by direct contact render obedience to His sovereign rule. Today, the true exercise of New Testament priesthood on the part of the Church among men consists of the same thing. In proportion as we of the kingdom of priests exercise our holy service in perfect submission to the will of God in daily life, do we exercise the true authority among men of that mediation which attracts them to God, and makes possible their immediate dealing with Him. To serve is to mediate and reign.

Who should prophesy with harps.— 1 Chron. 25. 1.

That is a very arresting statement. This whole chapter has to do with the sacred service of praise in the House of God. It is easy to imagine with what delight the poet-king would arrange the song-service of the Temple. Music played a very important part in his career. His skill therein had been his first introduction to Saul. Those Psalms distinctly attributed to him in our collection, breathe out all the spirit of the varied experiences through which he passed; the days of his simple life as a shepherd; the period of his exile and suffering; the hours of battle and weariness; the triumph of his crowning; the agony of his sin; the joy of his pardon —these, and many other experiences, are reflected in the great collection. This man, of poetic nature, would necessarily find great joy in making such arrangements that the House of God, which he described as "magnifical," should have proper and skilful attention, as to its service of praise. This brings us to our statement. This work of praise is here, and twice again (verses 2 and 3), described by this word *prophesy*. The use of the word in this connection is a revelation of the value and method of the service of music in the sanctuary of God. There is no doubt that it is used in its full sense of *forthtelling*, rather than in its more restricted one of *foretelling*. Music is at once the medium for expressing the praise of the soul to God, and for the telling forth of that praise in the hearing of men and for their instruction and blessing.

As well the small as the great.— 1 Chron. 26. 13.

David seems to have neglected nothing in his arrangements concerning the Temple. Not only Levites, priests, and singers, but porters also, and such as had charge of all the stores, were set apart for the work. Nothing connected with the House of God was considered in any way as unimportant. Everything was most sacred. Those who were appointed to these offices were chosen from the sons of the highest in the national life, as well as from the sons of those less known. In the casting of lots, a principle was observed full of revealing light. The names were selected, not with reference to any privilege of position, due to wealth or official standing. "They cast lots as well the small as the great." Whatever grading of society into "small and great," "high or low," may be inevitable in the arrangement of affairs on the human level, it ceases to operate when the service of the House of God in any department is in question. In that service there must be equality and opportunity for all. The decision in this case was made by lot, these men believing, as Solomon expressed it in one of his proverbs, that "the lot is cast into the lap, but the whole disposing thereof is of Jehovah." That principle abides. Our method is not that of casting lots, but of seeking the direct guidance of the Spirit. But we need to remember that in our choice of men for office in the work of the Church of God, the things of privilege, which too often count in human affairs, must have no weight with us.

The captains of thousands and of hundreds, and their officers that served the king.—1 Chron. 27. 1.

These words have reference to courses of service, and appointed officers, which are not mentioned elsewhere. They would seem to have been toilers who wrought in some specific work, probably that of the actual labour necessary to the building of the Temple. This further emphasizes what we have previously noted, namely, that David neglected nothing, and that everything connected with the Temple was treated as sacred, and therefore as demanding thought and preparation. It is not too much to say that in all the final acts of his life David was preparing for that Temple. All the ordering of the internal things of the kingdom was in that high interest. The greatness of David as a king was manifested in the acts of peaceful administration, as surely as in his victories on the fields of battle. The tilling of the ground, and its careful cultivation; the rearing of cattle; and all the things pertaining to the welfare of his people; were arranged for, under duly qualified and appointed oversight. Thus the whole nation was enabled to devote itself to that central work of building the House of God. There is no room for doubt that under the reign of David, the Hebrew people reached their greatest strength, even if they did not reach the height of their magnificence till later; and at no period were they stronger than while thus their thought was centred in the Temple. All this work kept the king and people in constant remembrance of the deepest truth concerning the national life, that it was centred in the Divine sovereignty and administration.

Know thou the God of thy father, and serve Him with a perfect heart and with a willing mind.—1 Chron. 28. 9.

These words occur in the final charge of David, the greatest of the Hebrew kings, to his son Solomon. In that charge he first made an impressive declaration of his recognition of the government of God in his own appointment as king, and in that of his son. This, however, was but the background against which he made the declaration which was nearest his heart, that concerning the House of his God. The fact which gave him unqualified satisfaction was that it was to be built. His rejection as builder, and Solomon's appointment, were matters of minor importance. The chief thing to him was that the work was to be done. Therein is revealed the deepest stratum in his make-up—his devotion to, and passion for, the recognition of the Theocracy. Out of that conviction came his charge to his son as to the principles which were to govern him in his rule of the people in the future. In these words the true attitudes toward God are revealed, and the conditions of soul which make those attitudes possible. The duty toward God is twofold—know Him and serve Him. The condition of soul making this possible is also twofold—a perfect heart and a willing mind. To know God is to serve Him. All failure in service is the result of loss of vision of God, misapprehension of Him, due to some distance from Him. The conditions for knowing God are ever that of a perfect heart, that is, an undivided heart; and a mind willing to obey. To these attitudes it is possible for God to reveal Himself. Moreover, He cannnot be deceived, for He "searcheth all hearts, and understandeth all the imaginations of the thoughts."

He died in a good old age, full of days, riches, and honour.—1 Chron. 29. 28.

With these words the chronicler ends the story of David. His had indeed been a great reign, and he was a great man. In the deepest facts of his life he was a man of God; he was also a poet, a warrior, and an administrator. With his passing the day of Hebrew greatness passed its meridian. Through varied experiences David passed, and to employ the words of Paul, "after he had in his own generation served the counsel of God, fell on sleep." Full of beauty and revelation of all that was best in him is the psalm in which he blessed Jehovah before all the people. In doing this, he was exercising a priestly function, and that of the highest, in that he was offering praise. By this act, moreover, his last among his people, he was finally directing their attention from himself to their one and only King, Who would remain with them. This Psalm first ascribed them all when he had passed away from excellencies to Jehovah, and recognized His Throne and Kingship. Then it confessed that all the riches and honour which men possess are derived from Him. These thoughts were then illustrated in a confession of personal poverty and unworthiness, together with an outpouring of gladness, because out of the

Divine gifts, the people had given gifts to God. Praise then merged into prayer that the state of mind in which they had given might be maintained; and for Solomon, that he might be kept with perfect heart to complete the work of Temple building. It was a fitting and glorious ending to a great reign.

SECOND CHRONICLES

There was the tent of meeting of God.—2 Chron. 1. 3.

We now come to the chronicler's account of how Solomon entered into full possession of his kingdom, and took up the great work entrusted to him. He commenced by gathering his people to a sacred act of worship. Although the ark was in a temporary tent in Jerusalem which David had prepared for it, the Tent or Tabernacle, and the brazen altar, were still at Gibeon. Thither, therefore, the king and his people resorted. The description of the Tabernacle in these words is arresting, and helps us to see the value of the change the revisers made when they rendered "Tent of Meeting," instead of "Tabernacle of Congregation." "There was the Tabernacle of the Congregation of God," as the Authorized Version has, it conveys an inadequate impression, as it suggests that it was a place where the people assembled. It was that, but it was much more. It was "the Tent of Meeting of God"; that is, it was the place where the people met with God. That is always the idea; not the meeting of the people with each other, but their meeting with God. This gathering of the people around that Tent was according to Divine order, and it is interesting to note that notwithstanding the fact that the ark was not there, God met with Solomon and communed with him. Thus we have a revelation of the value of observing a true Divine order, and at the same time an illustration of the fact that where obedience is sincere, God is not bound by any strict letter, even of His own law.

Who is able to build Him a house?—2 Chron. 2. 6.

These words occur in the record of the appeal which Solomon sent to Hiram the King of Tyre for a skilled worker, and for timber. They afford evidence of the greatness and truth of Solomon's conception of God, as the words immediately following show; "seeing heaven and the heaven of heavens cannot contain Him." Yet he was about to build a house for God. He declared its value as he understood it, "only to burn incense before Him." Solomon was under no delusion about God, and therefore made no mistake about the Temple. He never conceived of it as a place to which God would be confined. He did expect, and he received, manifestations of the Presence of God in that house. Its chief value was that it afforded man a place in which he should offer incense; that is, the symbol of adoration, praise, worship, to God. This was always so. When Jesus said to the woman of Samaria: "The hour cometh, when neither in this mountain nor in Jerusalem, shall ye worship the Father," He referred to a false centre, Mount Gerizim, and a true one, Jerusalem, and declared that neither was necessary for worship. In saying this, He was not referring merely to the new privileges to be created by His work. This is seen in what He added: "The hour cometh, *and now is*, when the true worshippers shall worship the Father in spirit and truth." Temples, buildings, set apart, have always had, and still have, their place and value; but they never were, nor are they yet, the only places where God may be worshipped.

Then Solomon began to build the House of the Lord at Jerusalem in Mount Moriah, where the Lord appeared unto David his father.—2 Chron. 3. 1.

In this, Solomon was carrying out the instructions and intention of his father. The site chosen, as we observed in a previous note, was full of suggestiveness. In the place where judgment was merged in mercy, the House of God was to stand. In this chapter and the next, we have the account of the building and furnishing of the Temple. In all fundamental essentials, it was on the pattern of the Tabernacle which Moses had made according to the pattern given him by God. Its proportions and relations were identical, but it was larger. Its symbolism was exactly the same, though its material magnificence was far greater. Nothing of ornamentation was admitted which would have interfered with the express command that no attempt was to be made to make anything as a likeness of God. Its structure was representative of the way of man's approach to God, rather than revelative of His nature. That was a mystery beyond the comprehension of the finite mind, and it was a distinguishing element in the Hebrew religion that it made no attempt to explain. "When the fulness of the time came, God sent forth His Son, born of a woman." Then, He explained Himself, for this Son was "the effulgence of His glory, and the very image of His substance." In Him judgment merged in mercy. Thus He became all the Temple symbolized, and infinitely more than it was ever permitted to suggest. He is the way of approach to God, and the revelation of God.

As for the entry of the house, the inner doors thereof for the Most Holy Place, and the doors of the house, to wit, of the Temple, were of gold.— 2 Chron. 4. 22.

These doors were additions to the Tabernacle plan. Therein, the entrances were veils, both to the Holy Place, and to the Most Holy. These veils were still present in the Temple, or at least "the Veil" between the Holy and the Holy of Holies remained, for it was rent in twain when our Lord was crucified. The doors which Solomon· put in the Temple were extra protections for the Temple building, and for the inner shrine which was the very Sanctuary. The statement that they were "of gold" must be interpreted by that in Kings, where we are told that the doors were of olive-wood and overlaid with gold (1 Kings 6. 31, 32); and that the hinges were of gold (1 Kings 7. 50). We can never rightly apprehend the suggestiveness of these stories, if we fail to bear in mind the uniformity of the methods of Biblical symbolism. Gold was ever the emblem of Divine glory and perfection. Thus it will be recognized that when Solomon added to the veils these doors all golden, he intended to symbolize the Divine glory. Those approaching the sacred enclosures were thus reminded of that glory. It was in perfect harmony with all the spiritual significance of this Temple that its doors should be of gold. Our Lord said of Himself: "I am the Door"; and we know that—

Would we view God's brightest glory,
We must look in Jesus' face.

Solomon brought in the things that David his father had dedicated.—2 Chron. 5. 1.

The work being completed, with filial and godly care Solomon carried into the sacred enclosure all that his father had dedicated to the House of God. It was a rich and varied store. If we glance back for a moment to 1 Chron. 29. 2, 3, we find David's own account of his gathering of these treasures. He first said: "I have prepared with all my might . . . gold . . . silver . . . brass . . . iron . . . wood . . . stones." He then said: "I have set my affection on the House of my God . . . I have a treasure of mine own . . . I give it . . . over and above all that I have prepared." This was complete devotion and dedication. There was first the systematic gathering of treasure of all sorts from all sources, and this was done with all his might. Then, when that was completed, he withheld nothing of his own, but impoverished himself by pouring all his possessions into the same treasury. This is the kind of giving which results from a great passion. It is easy to realize with what reverence Solomon would gather up and convey to the House of God all that wealth, doubly sacred because it was the expression of the devotion of his father's heart to that great work which had now been carried to successful completion. Let us note for ourselves the two elements in David's giving: "I have prepared with all my might; I have set my affection." The inspiration of love, and the activity of strength, will ever make our dedications complete, and our offerings worthy.

That Thine eyes may be open toward this house day and night.—2 Chron. 6. 20.

Again, Solomon in this great prayer of dedication, revealed his true understanding of the greatness of God, as he said: "Will God in very deed dwell with men on the earth? Behold, heaven and the heaven of heavens cannot contain Thee, how much less this house which I have builded?" Realizing the inadequacy of any houses built by man to contain God, he uttered this suggestive and beautiful petition, that the watching eyes of God might ever rest upon the house he had built. It was the place where God had said He would put His name. It was the place to which the people would repair to offer their petitions, in the regular exercises of worship, in special seasons of need through sin, in battle, in drought, in famine. The vision of the king created his prayer. He saw the Temple perpetually watched by the eyes of God, so that whatever worshippers approached they were seen by·the God Whose help they sought. That this might be so, he prayed. It was a figure of speech, but one full of suggestive beauty. For us, the great ideal has found perfect fulfilment through "Jesus the Son of God," Who has "passed through the heavens"; "now to appear before the face of God for us." We "draw near with boldness unto the throne of grace," and we do so in Him, the Beloved. The eyes of God are ever upon Him in satisfaction and delight; and so in our approach we are ever seen, but we are seen in Him, and so accepted.

He sent the people away unto their tents, joyful and glad of heart for the goodness that the Lord had shewed unto David, and to Solomon, and to Israel His people.—2 Chron. 7. 10.

These words give an account of how the wonderful ceremonies of the dedication of the Temple ended. The ceremonies had created a profound consciousness of the goodness of God, and this filled the people with joy and gladness of heart. So they went back to their tents, filled with a sense, a true sense, of the greatness of their national life. It consisted wholly in the governance of God. Had the future of king and people only been true to the high altitude on which they stood that day, their history would have been a very different one. In this whole story there is a revelation of the true value of public recognition of God in national life. It serves to keep alive the consciousness of the matters of supreme importance in that life, which are always those of the government of God, and so of His goodness to His people. The method of such recognition may be in some senses difficult today, through the unhappy loss of the sense of the unity of the Spirit, which makes for schism, and therefore for ineffectiveness in the witness of the Church. Nevertheless it is the duty of the Church, the whole Church, to watch for and to seize every opportunity for public testimony to the goodness of God as manifested in His overruling of the affairs of the nation. As in the case of Solomon, such ceremonial occasions should open and close with sacrificial remembrance of the One Sacrifice, and have at their centre the holy exercises of praise and prayer. The methods may have changed, but the spiritual obligation abides.

My wife shall not dwell in the house of David, king of Israel, because the places are holy, whereunto the ark of the Lord hath come.—2 Chron. 8. 11.

These were the words of compromise. Solomon's marriage with the daughter of the king of Egypt was a purely political act, arising out of the fact that he had made affinity with her father (1 Kings 3. 1). There can be no question that such affinity was wrong. God had delivered His people from Egypt; and there was never the slightest need, either military or economic, for such affinity. It was a political seduction which persistently threatened the nation, and which more than once cost them dear. Having made the blunder, and become affianced to this woman, Solomon sought to safeguard against the possible religious danger, by building her house away from the city of David. This compromise was a failure, as compromise invariably is. Let a paragraph in 1 Kings be read (chapter 11, the first eight verses), and it will be seen that presently he built places of idol worship in Jerusalem for "all his foreign wives." Compromise is a pathetic thing, in that it always is a witness to a conviction of what is the high and the true, and an attempt to ensure its realization, while yielding to the low and the false. It is an evil thing, for its invariable issue is that the low and the false ultimately gain the ascendance, and the high and the true

are abandoned. It is when the eye is single that the whole body is full of light. The way of uncompromising devotion to the right is the way, and the only way, of ultimate deliverance from evil. To tolerate wrong in any degree is ultimately to become its slave. To build a house for Pharaoh's daughter outside the Holy City is to open the gates of that city sooner or later to Pharaoh's gods.

Solomon reigned in Jerusalem over all Israel forty years.—2 Chron. 9. 30.

The story of Solomon is one of the most tragic in Biblical history. He was the third, and the last, of the kings of Israel as one nation. He came to the throne with everything in his favour. The kingdom had been brought into unity and remarkable strength under the reign of his father. Wonderful preparations had been made for the doing of the great work of Temple building. In himself he was richly endowed with conspicuous natural ability. Special wisdom was bestowed upon him by God, in answer to his own high choice. His opportunity and equipment were remarkable. In spite of everything he failed miserably as a king. Yielding to certain lower things of his nature, he became a slave to them, and dragged his nation down with him. So long as he remained on the throne, the people were solaced and drugged by material magnificence; but underneath, the spirit of rebellion and revolt was at work, ready to break out into open manifestation directly he was removed. The story is perhaps one of the most striking illustrations of the fact that opportunity and privilege, even God-bestowed, are not enough in themselves to assure full realization. They involve personal responsibilities, of watchfulness and constant devotion; and if these are not fulfilled, the most ghastly failure will inevitably result. Everything "under the sun" is of Divine origin; but if a man forget the things beyond the sun, fail to recognize that the fear of Jehovah continues to be the chief thing—is wisdom —he will be overcome by folly, and his life-story will be one of failure, at least so far as his work is concerned.

He forsook the counsel of the old men which they had given him, and took counsel with the young men that were grown up with him.—2 Chron. 10. 8.

The old men had counselled Rehoboam to conciliate the people by yielding to their appeal for relief from burdens imposed upon them by Solomon. His folly was manifested in his allowing himself to be influenced by the advice of the hot-headed youth of his court, who counselled him to rule autocratically, and to impose still heavier burdens on the people. The advice of the elders was inspired by desire for true national well-being. The advice of the young men was inspired by selfish passion for place and power. The whole situation was a difficult one. There is no doubt that Solomon had been an autocrat, and had ruled with a hand of iron under the velvet. Some of the worst tyrants the world has ever had have robbed the people of their rights, and kept them passive by the drug of gorgeous display. So did Lorenzo de' Medici in Florence, and so did Charles I. With the death of Solomon men breathed anew, and discovered their chains. Now was the time for a bid for freedom. Jeroboam returned from Egypt to be the spokesman of this movement. Here was Rehoboam's chance, and he missed it by taking wrongly-motived advice. The result was immediate. Ten tribes revolted. The nation was rent in twain, and, judging by human calculation, Judah was on the verge of a war which would have ended in her defeat and subjugation. Then God interfered. No human folly has ever been permitted to continue long enough to thwart His purposes. Shemaiah, a prophet of God, declared to Rehoboam that the revolt was in the Divine plan. He immediately submitted; and the period of the two kingdoms commenced.

Out of all the tribes of Israel, such as set their hearts to seek the Lord, the God of Israel, came to Jerusalem to sacrifice unto the Lord, the God of their fathers. So they strengthened the kingdom of Judah.—2 Chron. 11. 16, 17.

Whatever there may have been of right in the revolt of the ten tribes from the despotism of Rehoboam, that movement was misdirected from the first. Jeroboam was a strong man, but actuated by policy on the low level of human cleverness, rather than by faith. He commenced his reign over the Northern Kingdom by setting up a new centre of worship and a new order of priests. He attempted to adapt religion in the interest of the State, and thus destroyed both. One of his acts was that of casting the Levites out of the land. They passed down into Judah. Then the thing happened recorded in these words. In all those northern tribes there were those to whom the deepest things of the national life, those, namely, of its relation to Jehovah, were of most importance. This remnant of loyal souls, gathered out of all the tribes, left their own country and went to Judah. Thus the Southern Kingdom was strengthened in the best way by the accession of faithful souls. These are the people who, in every age, have been the real strength of human history, and through whom God has continued His onward march toward the realization of His purposes; the people who count their relation to Him, and

loyalty to His will, more than kith or kin or country. Exodus and emigration have very often been the ways of God's advance in the course of time. Such movements have always been sacrificial, but they have been deliverances.

When the kingdom of Rehoboam was established, and he was strong . . . he forsook the law of the Lord. —2 Chron. 12. 1.

What tragic words are these; and how perpetually the fact they record has been repeated in human experience! The influx of godly souls from the Northern Kingdom had made Rehoboam and his kingdom strong; and for three years they had gone in the way of David and Solomon (see chapter 11. 17). Then in his strength, "he forsook the law of Jehovah." Man's real strength is ever that of complete dependence upon God. That is to say, it is derived strength. Directly it becomes independent, self-contained, it leads him astray. There is the profoundest truth in the Apostle's words: "When I am weak, then am I strong" (2 Cor. 12. 10). The sequel to this declaration of Rehoboam's deflection is found in the rest of the chapter. God never abandons His purposes or His servants. When those who serve Him depart from the straight way of obedience to His law, He adopts the methods of chastisement. The scourge came now in the person of Israel's ancient foe, the king of Egypt. But the patience of God is ever manifest in His dealing with His people. The repentance of Rehoboam produced the staying and limitation of judgment. The kingdom of Judah passed for the time under the yoke of Egypt. It was saved, however, from complete destruction, not principally for the sake of the king, but because, "in Judah there were good things found" (verse 12). God's judgments are always characterized by fine discrimination.

The children of Judah prevailed, because they relied upon the Lord, the God of their fathers.—2 Chron. 13. 18.

This is really a most interesting chapter, and this account of the victory of Judah is a striking revelation of the readiness with which God ever responds to a genuine cry to Him for help, even on the part of those who are far from worthy. This king Abijah "walked in all the sins of his father" (1 Kings 15. 3). Here, however, in his address, in which he attempted to persuade Israel to submission, he was speaking and acting for his nation. This address in itself was a strange mixture of misrepresentation and religion. The misrepresentation is found in his statement of the reason of the revolt of Israel, which culminated in the crowning of Jeroboam. He attributed the whole thing to the influence of evil men, whereas it arose out of the despotism of Rehoboam, and was misdirected by evil influences. His attempt to prevent conflict by this address was clever, but utterly futile. Deliverance and victory came to Judah, not through this action on the part of the king, but because, when Judah found themselves caught between two armies, "they cried unto Jehovah." It was a poor business, in that it was a last resort, but it was sincere; and the answer of God was immediate, and complete victory resulted. The whole story is another illustration of that truth, to which the Scriptures and human experience bear persistent testimony, of the unfailing grace of God, and of His willingness to forgive and deliver those who call upon Him in sincerity, notwithstanding all their unworthiness. Honestly to rely upon God is ever to prevail over opposing foes.

So the Lord smote the Ethiopians before Asa.—2 Chron. 14. 12.

In the story of the reign of Asa, we find a break in the continuity of naughtiness which so persistently characterized the succession of kings. His was a long reign, and though the reforms he instituted were not as thorough as some which were carried out by subsequent kings, he yet gave the nation some glimpses of a better order. He commenced by breaking down false worship so far as he was able, and by insisting on the observance of the Divine law. As a result, the land had "quiet before him." He took advantage of the peaceful years to build and wall the cities. Then suddenly came the Ethiopian invasion in great strength, threatening the prosperity, and indeed the very life, of the nation. The prayer of Asa, as recorded in this chapter, is a model of simple directness. Its strength lay in the loyalty of this man to his God, and in his perfect confidence in Him. The answer was immediate. Through the hosts of Judah, God operated for the discomfiture and defeat of the invaders. How unfailingly the patience of God is manifested in these records! The repetition of this fact in notes of exposition, becomes almost monotonous. Yet it is glorious monotony, like to that of the perfect music of such as with veiled faces ceaselessly chant the story of His holiness and His love. The condition of the people of Judah at this time was a very sad one. Yet immediately man or nation turned to God with repentance, and in need, He responded with pardon and deliverance.

The Lord is with you, while ye be with Him; and if ye seek Him, He will be found of you; but if ye forsake Him, He will forsake you.—2 Chron. 15. 2.

This chapter chronicles with greater detail the occasion and value of the reforms wrought in Judah during the reign of Asa. It is, however, chiefly remarkable for this word of prophetic interpretation. Azariah, who uttered it, only appears here. He is mentioned nowhere else. Yet, in an introductory word so brief that it only occupies half a verse in our Bibles, he revealed an inclusive philosophy of life under the control of God. Suddenly anointed by the Spirit of God, this man appeared to the king, and in this message gave direction to all his life and reign. If the message was brief, it was indeed weighty. The rest of the address consisted of illustration of the application of the principle it declared to the then existing conditions; and of a direct appeal to the king. The principle declared is of perpetual application. Let it be well considered. It represents God as unchanging. All apparent changes on His part are really changes in the attitude of men toward Him. Man with God, finds God with him. Man, forsaking God, finds that he is forsaken of God. These are the extremes of the truth. Between them—not contradicting them, but complementing them and completing them—is the declaration that if a man seek God, He will be found of that man. A recognition of these things must at once give direction to life, and inspire the heart with courage. It certainly did so in the case of Asa.

Because thou hast relied on the king of Syria, and hast not relied on the Lord thy God, therefore is the host of the king of Syria escaped out of thine hand.—2 Chron. 16. 7.

This is a very sad chapter, telling as it does the story of the lapse and failure of a man who for six-and-thirty years had —considering the conditions under which he lived—been remarkably true to God. When Baasha, king of Israel, commenced to build Ramah with the express purpose of troubling Judah, Asa, who had so often been led and delivered by God, turned to Benhadad, the king of Syria, for help. It seemed, moreover, to have been a successful policy, for Benhadad spoiled the cities of Israel, and Baasha was compelled to leave off his building of Ramah. Yet such seeming was false. It was the result of shortsightedness, failure to see the long issues. Things which appear successful may, in the life of faith, prove to be most disastrous. It was so in this case. The Syrians were, as a matter of fact, far more dangerous foes of Judah than was Israel. As Hanani, the seer, told the king, by this act they had escaped out of his hand. How perpetually men defeat their own ends when, either through lack of faith, or overconfidence in their own cleverness—which are practically the same thing—they attempt to do by policy what God is prepared to do for them in answer to their obedient faith. The story is the more sad in that there seems to have been no repentance on the part of the king. He persecuted the prophet, flinging him into prison. Surely none is ever safe from falling, however long loyalty has lasted. To the end there is need of watchfulness.

They went about throughout all the cities of Judah, and taught among the people.—2 Chron. 17. 9.

With the accession of Jehoshaphat to the throne of Judah, a period of very definite reformation commenced within the kingdom. In this chapter we have, first, the account of his own relationship to God, and the resulting blessing that came to him. Then follows this most interesting account of how he made known the law of Jehovah anew throughout the land. The method adopted was what in these modern times we might describe as the holding of Special Missions throughout the cities of Judah, for the specific purpose of proclaiming and interpreting "the book of the law of Jehovah." Those who went forth to this work were priests, Levites, and representatives of the princes. Thus Jehoshaphat put into practice himself, and, by these special methods, provoked his people to put into practice, the principle which Azariah had declared to his father. Coincident with this activity within the kingdom, a remarkable fear of Jehovah fell upon their enemies round about, so that they ceased to make war upon Jehoshaphat. Thus God was with the man who was with Him. The result was that there was opportunity for strengthening the kingdom within, by the building of castles and cities, by commerce, and by the carrying out of many works. This story has a present value. No better service can be rendered to the nation than that of proclaiming the Word of Jehovah to the people, in cities, towns, villages, and hamlets. By such proclamation the heart of the people may be turned to Jehovah, and so He be enabled to do for them all that is in His heart.

A certain man drew his bow at a venture.—2 Chron. 18. 33.

This is a most suggestive and significant statement, revealing great facts of life which are too often unrecognized by men. Ahab had done everything he could think of, to secure his own safety in the day of battle. In arrant cowardice he had caused Jehoshaphat to enter the field in his kingly robes, thus rendering him conspicuous, while he had disguised himself. The ruse was completely successful as far as Syria was concerned. The captains of the king of Syria were deceived. Ahab was safe, if there were no eyes other than those of men watching him. He was not hidden from the eyes of God. One nameless man "drew his bow at a venture," that is, as the margin reads, "in his simplicity." It was not even a venture in the sense of an attempt, or a gambling against odds, in the hope of killing the king of Israel. It was done "in his simplicity," that is, artlessly, without any special intention other than that of "carrying on" in the ordinary sense of that word. Probably this man had already during the day shot many arrows, and he went on in his simplicity, little knowing that this particular one was to be guided through all the confusion straight to its mark, by the unerring knowledge and power of God. Yet so it was. Thus it is seen how the refuge of lies never hides from the eyes of God. Men may secrete themselves so that other men may never find them; but when the hour of their judgment has come, God takes hold upon some ordinary event, and makes it the highway upon which He comes to carry out the sentence of His purpose. "It just happened," says the man of the world. "God did it," says the man of faith.

Consider what ye do; for ye judge not for man, but for the Lord.—2 Chron. 19. 6.

The story of the affinity which Jehoshaphat made with Ahab is that of a sad lapse in his history. Ahab was perhaps the most evil king who ever occupied the throne of Israel. It was indeed strange company for a man like Jehoshaphat, who was unquestionably a man of God. It imperilled his life, so that he was only delivered from death by the direct intervention of his God. On his return to Jerusalem he was rebuked by Jehu, the son of Hanani, in words full of solemnity, which it would be well for all of us perpetually to bear in mind: "Shouldst thou help the wicked, and love them that hate Jehovah?" Evidently Jehoshaphat realized his wrong, and his repentance was manifest in this new mission which he undertook, to bring his people back to Jehovah, and to establish the internal administration of the kingdom in righteousness. These words addressed to the judges are full of value, and of perpetual application. Those who are called upon at any time, and in any way, to administer justice are acting for God, and not for man. They are not seeking to serve men, but to maintain the strict cause of justice, which is to be measured only by Divine standards. With God there is no iniquity, no respect of persons, no taking of bribes. So must it be with those who act as judges. Thus, and thus only, are the true interests of men served. To seek to please men is to be unjust to men. To seek to please God is to be just to men.

And all Judah stood before the Lord, with their little ones, their wives, and their children.—2 Chron. 20. 13.

This chapter gives us a story which reveals most graphically the simplicity, and therefore the perfection, at this point, of the faith of Jehoshaphat. His kingdom was threatened with powerful and terrible invasion. In his extremity he gathered his people about him, and prayed. It is indeed a great and arresting picture this, of the king surrounded by the whole nation; fathers and mothers with their little ones—that is, the very little ones, the babies; and their children—that is, the elder sons and daughters. It was a genuine national act of simple and direct acknowledgment of God. In the hour of national danger, the nation sought the help of the one true King—Jehovah. The prayer of Jehoshaphat was a powerful outpouring of the soul in the consciousness of need. He pleaded the past evidences of the faithfulness of Jehovah, confessed his sense of his own inability to cope with the danger, and definitely sought the help of God. The answer was not delayed. The Spirit of God came upon Jahaziel, and in the Name of Jehovah he uttered a promise, and made the announcement that all Judah had to do, was to stand still and see the salvation of Jehovah. Then followed the united worship of the people and the solemn chanting of the praise of God. Discomfiture fell upon the foe. It was a moment bright with light amid the darkness. This is ancient history, but we have seen in our days events which can have no other explanation. When after stress and strain our own nation did definitely cry unto God, He heard and wrought deliverance, and that with a suddenness and completeness which amazed us.

He departed without being desired. —2 Chron. 21. 20.

Strange indeed is the human heart. It turns to evil, and pursues it persistently; and yet it never really loves those who lead it in the way of evil. This fact is remarkably exemplified in the story of the reign of Jehoram, as told in this chapter. With the passing of Jehoshaphat, another period of darkness and degeneracy set in for the kingdom of Judah. Jehoram was of an utterly evil nature. He attempted to make his throne secure by the murder of his brothers. He was strengthened in wickednsss by marriage with the daughter of Ahab. This the chronicler makes clear in the declaration: "He walked in the way of the kings of Israel, as did the house of Ahab; for he had the daughter of Ahab to wife." Nevertheless the people followed him, going a-whoring at the high places, and wandering from the ways of Jehovah. In the midst of this wickedness a message was brought to him from Elijah, the prophet of fire, who had exercised so powerful an influence against Ahab in the kingdom of Israel. It contained a terrible message of judgment, which was fully carried out. "He departed without being desired." Love is only inspired by goodness. Men will follow those who lead them in the ways of corruption, but such following is always inspired by evil selfishness, and never by admiration or love. When the evil leader falls, there is no pity for him; he departs without being desired. Thus, even in the midst of the uttermost corruption, God preserves a consciousness of the value of goodness, and a witness to the beneficence of His government.

The house of Ahaziah had no power to hold the kingdom.—2 Chron. 22. 9.

Ahaziah was the youngest son of Jehoram. Immediately succeeding his father, he reigned for the brief space of one year, during which he was completely under the evil influence of his mother, Athaliah, the daughter of Ahab. In these words of the chronicler we are reminded of a truth of invariable application, that, namely, of the powerlessness of evil. There are hours in human history when it seems as though evil were almost all-powerful. It entrenches itself in great strength; it builds up great ramparts; it inaugurates policies characterized by the utmost craft and cleverness. It seems to be able to bind together a kingdom which is invincible. All this is false seeming. There is no finality, no security, in the apparent might of iniquity. Sooner or later, irrevocably, inevitably, the trenches are broken through, the ramparts are flung down, the policies fail, and the kingdom which seemed so secure is dashed in pieces like a potter's vessel, by the strength of God, which is ever the strength of righteousness and goodness. Neither powerful autocrat, nor mighty confederacy of statesmen, can establish a kingdom or an empire by fraud, by violence, by corruption. Nothing will hold a kingdom or an empire or a commonwealth together in strength other than truth and justice and purity, the things of goodness, which are the things of God. Once again we have to say this is ancient history, but it is as modern as the break-up and disintegration of those great powers which in our day we have seen crumble to dust.

She looked, and, behold, the king stood by his pillar at the entrance.— 2 Chron. 23. 13.

There is tremendous dramatic power in that sentence. It is a further proof of the truth emphasized in the words of our previous note, that of the powerlessness of evil. Athaliah had done everything within her power to secure her own position, and to gain her own ends. With vindictive cruelty she had, as she thought, destroyed all the seed-royal of the house of Judah. She was wrong. No evil passions, however thorough their methods, are able to frustrate Divine purposes. Against the wickedness of one woman, God had set in motion the compassion of another.

Jehoshabeath had rescued Joash, and for six years with patient persistence had cared for him under the shelter of the Temple. Now at last the day had come when the well-kept secret should be divulged. The boy was brought out, anointed, and crowned amid the plaudits of the people. Athaliah, hearing the shoutings, came to the Temple, and: "She looked, and behold, the king stood by his pillar at the entrance." Then she knew the powerlessness of evil. In vain she cried: "Treason! Treason!" Her own treason against the true and abiding King of the nation was defeated. Thus, sooner or later, and in ways equally dramatic, the moment arrives when those who plot and plan against Heaven and righteousness, find themselves looking at the evidences of the triumph of God and of goodness over all their wickedness.

The king hearkened unto them.— 2 Chron. 24. 17.

These are very simple words, but they are inexpressibly sad, and full of arresting power and suggestion. Under the reign of Joash real reformation was achieved in Judah, but it was wholly due to the influence of Jehoiada the priest. This is clearly indicated in the statement of the chronicler that: "Joash did that which was right in the eyes of Jehovah all the days of Jehoiada the priest." Nevertheless, during this period it is evident that Joash was honestly zealous in his endeavour to re-establish the true worship of God. The reform circumferenced the Temple: "They set up the house of God in its state, and strengthened it." The worship was maintained while Jehoiada lived. After his death, the princes of Judah, evidently corrupt men, came to the king, and he "hearkened unto them." The house of God was forsaken, and idolatry was again established in the land. Joash, who had been zealous in reform, now became determined in wickedness. The study of the story of Joash offers a striking illustration of how a weak man is easily influenced. It emphasizes the need of strong individual character, which can only be created by direct dealing with God. However valuable the influence of a good man may be, it remains true that if a man have nothing more to lean on than that, if it should fail, collapse is almost inevitable. All foundations fail, save one. When the will of man is yielded wholly to the will of God, and no other authority is sought or permitted, that man is safe. Where this is lacking, every changing tide of circumstances will change the currents of life.

He did that which was right in the eyes of the Lord, but not with a perfect heart.—2 Chron. 25. 2.

These words give us the key to all that follows in the story of Amaziah. The general aim of the man was right, but execution was spoiled by imperfection. Nothing is wholly satisfactory to God save the perfect heart, because nothing else can possibly produce the best in man. His punishment of his father's murderers was tempered with justice. The imperfection of his heart was manifested in his alliance with Israel; and then again his right desire, in the readiness with which he obeyed the voice of the prophet, and broke off that alliance, even at cost to himself. Returning from his conquest over the Edomites, he brought back with him the gods of his defeated foes. Again the prophet visited him, and the unutterable folly of such action is revealed in the question asked: "Why hast thou sought after the gods of the people, which have not delivered their own people out of thy hand?" Punishment for this followed in the defeat of Judah by Israel. What, then, we may ask, as we consider this story of Amaziah, is a perfect heart? The root idea of the Hebrew word rendered "perfect" is that of being whole or complete. An imperfect heart is a divided heart. Imperfection of heart consists in incomplete surrender. Some chamber of the temple is closed against the true Indweller. It is retained for self. What it was in the case of Amaziah we are not told, but the fact is patent, that notwithstanding the general rightness of the direction of his life, either through personal indulgence, or ambition, or carelessness, his whole heart was not set upon doing the will of God. Within the fortress, one apartment possessed by the foe is ever the gravest peril. Sooner or later, the dweller in that chamber opens the door for foes without.

He was marvellously helped, till he was strong. But when he was strong, his heart was lifted up.—2 Chron. 26. 15, 16.

Uzziah was one of the most remarkable of the kings of Judah. He was a man of strong character, and the early period of his reign was characterized by true prosperity. He was victorious in his campaigns against the enemies of his people, and eminently successful in his development of the internal resources of the nation. At once a man of war and a lover of husbandry, he was an ideal ruler for those troublous times. During the first years of his reign he went quietly forward in dependence upon God. Then there came a change over the man, and the story of it is told by the chronicler in these words. How significant they are! The history of men affords persistent witness to the subtle perils which are created by prosperity. More men are blasted by it than by adversity. Man, dependent upon God, is independent of all else. In the moment when the heart begins to feel independent of God, because of personal strength, that very strength becomes weakness; and unless there be repentance and return, ruin is inevitable. Prosperity always puts the soul in danger of pride, of the heart lifted up; and pride ever goeth before destruction, and a haughty spirit before a fall. The pride of Uzziah led him to an act of sacrilege. He entered into the sacred courts, and violated the ordinances of God concerning the offering of sacrifices. He was smitten with leprosy, and the last years of his life were spent as a prisoner, isolated from his fellowmen.

Jotham became mighty, because he ordered his ways before the Lord his God.—2 Chron. 27. 6.

We have very few details of the reign of Jotham. In all probability the sixteen years referred to by the chronicler cover a period in which he was exercising authority, while his father Uzziah was still alive, though excluded from the kingly office on account of his leprosy. He continued the work of his father in the strengthening of the internal conditions of the kingdom by building; and he was successful in a campaign against the Ammonites. While there was no definite national reform during his reign, he seems to have gone quietly forward along true lines, and his strength is attributed to the fact that he ordered his ways before Jehovah his God. Perhaps three things helped this man. First, he reigned during the early period in which Isaiah was exercising his prophetic ministry. Second, his mother was almost certainly the daughter of Zadok the priest. Third, he profited by his father's example—both good and bad, following the good and shunning the evil. All good influences are to be valued, but the ultimate note is always personal. "He ordered his ways." If a man will do this, then he will ever profit by all the influences brought to bear on him, distinguishing between good and evil, and choosing according to the will of God.

In the time of his distress did he trespass yet more against the Lord, this same king Ahaz.—2 Chron. 28. 22.

The reign of Ahaz was a period of terrible and rapid degeneracy in Judah. With appalling fearlessness the king restored all the evils of idolatry, even including the ghastly offering of children as sacrifices to Moloch. In all probability his own son was a victim. As difficulties gathered around him, he turned to the king of Assyria for aid, attempting to procure help from him by giving him treasure out of the house of God. The utter evil of the man is seen in the fact that calamities did not produce the effect in him which they had so often done in the case of his predecessors, that of bringing him to the abandonment of his sin. He was a man evil by deliberate choice, persistent in evil in spite of calamity, blasphemously rebellious notwithstanding the direct warnings of Isaiah. Moreover, as we know from the Book of Isaiah, he openly and deliberately rejected any sign from God. It is certainly a solemn and searching story, revealing, as it does, how possible it is to yield the life so completely to evil, that prosperity only ministers to its degeneration, and adversity only hardens the will in wickedness.

Now ye have consecrated yourselves unto the Lord, come near and bring sacrifices and thankofferings into the house of the Lord.—2 Chron. 29. 31.

With the accession of Hezekiah a great change came over the life of Judah. For a period there was a definite arrest in the process of degeneration. The reformation which he carried out began in his deep consciousness of the wretched condition of the people, and the reason thereof. This is most graphically set forth in the words he addressed to the priests and Levites when he called them together. There was no suggestion on his part that the calamities which had fallen upon them were in any way unjust. On the other hand he traced the story of their sin, and declared that the result of that sin was that the wrath of God had expressed itself righteously in their disasters. He then commenced the work of restoring the true order of worship, and the first business was that of cleansing the actual Temple. Some idea of the calamitous condition of the national life may be gained from the fact that the Levites were occupied sixteen days in cleansing the accumulation of filth from the sacred precincts. When this was done, there followed the ceremony of re-dedication; and in these words we discover Hezekiah's sense of the true order of procedure. Sacrifices and offerings are only acceptable when those offering them are themselves consecrated to Jehovah. The same principle is found in Paul's words in the Corinthian letter: "First they gave their own selves to the Lord, and to us through the will of God." Contributions to the work of God are only valuable as they are the gifts of those who are themselves yielded to God.

So the posts passed from city to city through the country of Ephraim and Manasseh, even unto Zebulun; but they laughed them to scorn, and mocked them.—2 Chron. 30. 10.

This chapter gives us a side-light on the character of Hezekiah which shows how great a man he was. For a long time the ordained feasts of Jehovah had been neglected, both in the northern kingdom of Israel and in his own kingdom of Judah. When he set himself to arrange for the keeping of the Passover, it is very beautiful to see how his heart went out to the whole nation as within the Divine purpose. He sent messengers throughout Israel as well as Judah, inviting them to come to Jerusalem and take part therein. The hopeless corruption of Israel as a whole is manifest in the statement that the people laughed the messengers to scorn and mocked at them. The action of the king was justified and rewarded in the fact that a remnant responded, and gathered to Judah in order to take part in the sacred and solemn observance. It was a motley crowd which assembled, and multitudes of the people were utterly ignorant of the Divine arrangements for preparation. Hezekiah's tenderness was manifested in the pity he felt for these people, and in the prayer he offered on their behalf. His prayer was answered, and the imperfect method was not punished in the case of such as set their whole heart to seek Jehovah. This largeness of heart is always characteristic of men who are really in fellowship with God, for it is in harmony with the heart of God. Such action may be misunderstood by the majority of those on whose behalf it is inspired, but it always produces some results in the opportunity it gives to loyal souls to avail themselves of it.

In every work that he began in the service of the house of God, and in the law, and in the commandments, to seek his God, he did it with all his heart, and prospered.—2 *Chron*. 31. 21.

This chapter gives in general terms the account of the work which followed worship; the reconstruction in the national life which eventuated from the national return to God which had been expressed in the great celebration of the Passover feast. It is very significant that the remnant gathered from Israel became the pioneers in the work of destroying all that remained of idolatry throughout the cities of Judah, and also in Ephraim and Manasseh. The king set in order the courses of priests and Levites; re-arranged the offerings according to the Law; and called for the payment of the tithe. The response was general and generous. The special value of the work was the thoroughness with which Hezekiah carried it out, and this is declared in this final verse. These words reveal his purpose, his method, and the result; and form a revelation of abiding value to all who are called upon to perform Divine service in any form. His purpose was "to seek his God"; and the expression is exactly equivalent to that with which we are familiar: "Seek ye first His Kingdom." His method was that of complete devotion, "with all his heart." The result was that of prosperity, that is, of success in the very work which was attempted. A right purpose and a true method always produce the highest results.

After these things, and this faithfulness, Sennacherib king of Assyria came.—2 *Chron*. 32. 1.

One is almost inevitably halted by these words. It would seem to be a strange answer of God to the faithfulness of His servant, that a strong foe should at this moment invade the kingdom. The story needs more details than are found in this record. They may be found in 2 Kings 18. 7–16. From that passage we find that Hezekiah had flung off the yoke of the king of Assyria which his father Ahaz had consented to wear. Then Sennacherib had invaded Judah; and in a moment of weakness Hezekiah had paid him a heavy tribute, and again yielded to his rule in order to buy him off. The result was not what he desired, for Sennacherib now demanded an unconditional surrender. In this hour of crisis, resulting from his own vacillation, his faith and courage were renewed. He took immediate action to embarrass the foe, by stopping the supply of water, by strengthening the fortifications, by mobilizing his army, and finally by assuring the people: "There is a Greater with us than with him." Then, in answer to further threatenings, he took refuge in prayer, in fellowship with Isaiah. The answer was quick and final, and consisted of the rout of the enemy and the salvation of the people. The lessons of the story are patent. If amid general faithfulness, there is any measure of unfaithfulness, the results are inevitably those of difficulty; but a return to complete fidelity is always answered by deliverance. God ever demands from His servants complete loyalty; and when that is yielded, He never fails to be to them all they need.

Then Manasseh knew that the Lord He was God.—2 *Chron*. 33. 13.

This is a wonderful chapter, giving us the account of two men. Manasseh and Amon, father and son. Both followed the way of wickedness; but one under discipline repented, and was forgiven; while the other "humbled not himself," and was cut off without remedy. The repentance of Manasseh was evidently the chief subject in the mind of the chronicler, and that because the action of God afforded an unveiling of the Divine character. This is evident from these particular words: "Then Manasseh knew that Jehovah He was God." The "then" refers to the account of the Divine forgiveness and restoration, in response to the human repentance and prayer. It is a picture full of light and beauty in the midst of prevailing darkness, this of the readiness of God to pardon. The sins of Manasseh are faithfully described, and revealed in all their hideousness; but this is background, flinging up into clearer relief the ready and gracious attitude of God toward a truly penitent soul. It is always so, if men will have it so. God never willeth the death even of Manasseh, but rather that he should return to Him and live. Nevertheless, if Amon will not humble himself before his God, there is no escape from retribution for his sins. The rule of God is fixed in righteousness. Manasseh and Amon were both in His power. The one found healing by yielding; the other found destruction by rebelling. By His readiness to forgive, God is known in all the fulness of His power. But if men will not learn thus, then it must be that they learn by His just judgments in wrath.

Then the king sent and gathered together all the elders of Judah and Jerusalem.—2 Chron. 34. 29.

The underlining in that sentence, as printed, is mine. By its use I desire to draw attention to the fact that Josiah went on with the work of reformation, even when he knew that nationally it was foredoomed to failure. The story of his life and reign is full of brightness. The conditions of the national life were indeed terrible, but in this boy-king, as he developed to manhood, testimony was borne to the government of God, which was unmistakable. Ascending the throne when only eight years of age, at the age of sixteen he began to seek after God. Four years later, at the age of twenty, he set himself to the actual work of reformation. Then at the age of twenty-six he turned to the work of repairing the house of God, and it was in connection with this that the Book of the Law was discovered. Filled with consternation at what it revealed of the will of God, and so of the appalling degradation of the people, he consulted Huldah the prophetess. She distinctly told him that there would be no true repentance on the part of the people, and therefore that judgment was inevitable. It was *then* that the heroic strength of Josiah manifested itself, in that he went on with his work, fulfilling his obligations as he saw them. Jeremiah began his ministry when Josiah was twenty-one years old (Jer. 1. 2), and this fact may help to account for the action of the king. No pathway of service is more difficult than that of bearing witness to God, in word and in work, in the midst of conditions which are unresponsive.

The words of Neco, from the mouth of God.—2 Chron. 35. 22.

This is one of those arresting illustrations which we find in the Old Testament Scriptures, of the fact that the nations and kings outside the people of the Theocracy were under the government of God, and in some sense at times conscious of the fact. These words of the chronicler constitute a simple statement, which admits the accuracy of what Neco had himself

claimed in the message he sent to Josiah by ambassadors, when he said: "God hath commanded me to make haste; forbear then from meddling with God, Who is with me, that He destroy thee not." The fact that Josiah did not hearken to this message, cost him his life. Such a story must, to say the least, give us pause, and make us enquire as to how far we are ever justified in refusing to consider a word which is claimed as a Divine message, even when it comes from sources from which we should least expect to receive it. It may with reason be asked: How are we to know whether that which claims Divine authority has any right to make the claim? So far as this story is concerned, the answer is plain. Josiah had no right of any sort to be helping the king of Assyria. The only reason for doing so must have been some supposed political advantage. Against that kind of action the prophets were constantly warning the kings. A word claiming to be from God, forbidding what was already forbidden, had a weight of moral appeal almost amounting to certainty. Thus may we, too, test such messages. If they contradict Divine revelation, we may rest assured the claim is false. If they agree, we do well to heed to them, for God may speak in many and unexpected ways.

To fulfil the word of the Lord by the mouth of Jeremiah.—2 Chron. 36. 21.

Jeremiah conducted a prophetic ministry in Judah for forty years, and—so far as producing any result in the directing of the people back to God—without success. Through stress and strain, and as against the keenest hatred and hostility, he continued to declare the word of Jehovah to a rebellious and stiff-necked people. As we said in speaking of King Josiah, in whose reign Jeremiah began his work, such service is the most heroic. In these words the chronicler reminds us that he was vindicated in the march of events. All the things he had foretold, the foretelling of which had stirred the anger of the people, were literally fulfilled. The writings of this great prophet, preserved for us, show that he had no joy in the sorrows that befell his people through their sins, but rather the acutest suffering. Nevertheless he must have had great satisfaction at last in the fact that he had been true to the word of Jehovah delivered to him. The word of Jehovah is always fulfilled, by whosesoever mouth it is proclaimed. Happy indeed, in all the deepest senses of that word, is that man who never fails nor falters in the delivery of that word. It is not so much the selfish joy of seeing things turn out as he predicted; but rather the high joy of realizing that he has been honoured in being the messenger appointed to deliver the Word which cannot fail.

EZRA

The Lord stirred up the spirit of Cyrus.—*Ezra* 1. 1.

To human observation the purposes of God often seem to tarry. The one thing of which we may remain assured is that they are never abandoned. Indeed, there is a very true sense in which they never for a moment tarry. In the Books we have been reading, we have had the story of the complete failure and break-up of the chosen nation. That nation had become "a people scattered and peeled," having lost national position and power; and, to a very large extent, national consciousness also. Nevertheless, God still moved on toward the fulfilment of His ultimate purpose of redemption, not of His people only, but of the race, through them. Through the seventy years of captivity, by the very processes of suffering, He prepared a remnant to return, to rebuild, and so to hold the fort, until He, the true Seed and Servant, should come. The history of this return sets forth clearly the truth concerning this direct overruling of God. He compelled the most unlikely instruments to contribute to the accomplishment of His will. Babylon had carried away His people into captivity, and by so doing had fulfilled His purpose. They, however, treated the conquered nation with undue severity. In process of time, and in fulfilment of the distinct foretelling of Jeremiah, Cyrus the Persian broke the power of Babylon. This Cyrus was now chosen and commissioned as the very instrument for restoring God's remnant to their own land. His proclamation made that return possible. It was the result of Divine dealing, and, moreover, he was conscious that this was so. How constantly in human history God has compelled kings and rulers to carry out His sovereign will!

So the priests, and the Levites, and some of the people, and the singers, and the porters, and the Nethinim, dwelt in their cities, and all Israel in their cities.—*Ezra* 2. 70.

These words summarize the chapter which they close. It contains the register of those who, taking advantage of the decree of Cyrus, turned their faces toward their land, and settled in its cities. The list proceeds in a definite order from the leaders downwards. First the names are given of those immediately associated with Zerubbabel, verses 1, 2. Then follow the names and numbers of families, verses 3–35; the names of members of the priesthood, verses 36–39; the list and numbers of the Levites, verses 40–42; after these the Nethinim, verses 43–54; next the children of Solomon's servants, verses 55–58; then

a number who had lost their genealogical relationship, verses 59–63; and finally the totals of the people, and the lists of the cattle. It is an interesting record, showing the mixed and representative nature of the returning remnant. There are one or two matters of special note. First, the people thus returning are distinctly spoken of as "the men of the people of Israel," verse 2. The reference is patently not to the northern kingdom only, for it was the southern kingdom that Nebuchadnezzar had carried away. It does, however, undoubtedly mean that representatives of those tribes which composed the northern kingdom, also returned. Again, it is noticeable that few comparatively of the Levites are named; ten times as many priests as Levites returned. Another point of interest is the Nethinim. Their origin it is almost impossible to determine. In all probability they were of foreign extraction, and had been admitted to some of the minor forms of service connected with Levitical work. The name signified "giver." Jewish tradition identified them with the Gibeonites (Joshua 9. 3–17).

The old men that had seen the first house, when the foundation of this house was laid before their eyes, wept with a loud voice; and many shouted aloud for joy.—*Ezra* 3. 12.

The leaders in this great movement of return were conscious of the matters of real importance in the life of the people. This is evident from the fact that directly they were settled in their cities, the altar of God was established in Jerusalem. They also observed the Feast of Tabernacles, the most joyful of all the feasts of Jehovah, established all the feasts, and so far as was possible restored the Divinely appointed order of worship. The reason for this activity is expressed in the words, "For fear was upon them because of the people of the countries." Different interpretations have been given of the meaning of this statement, but that which seems to suit the situation best is that they were conscious how, in the neglect of the altar of God in the past, they had become contaminated by the idolatrous practices of surrounding peoples, and in order to prevent a repetition of such failure, they immediately set up the true altar. It is at least significant that they never returned to idolatry. The next step was that of the rebuilding of the Temple. The foundations were laid, and in the second year of the return, with fitting ceremonies, they rejoiced. Then it was that the lamentations of the old men broke out. This can well be understood when the comparative poverty and insignificance of the people and building are remembered. Yet it was an element of weakness. The backward look which discounts present activity in true directions, is always a peril. Regrets over the past which paralyse work in the present are always wrong. Moreover all such regrets, as in this case, are in danger of blinding the eyes to the true value and significance of the present. The Temple these men were building was destined to have more honour and glory than the old one.

Ye have nothing to do with us to build an house unto our God.—*Ezra 4. 3.*

This chapter gives us the account of the opposition of the Samaritans to the work of Temple building, an opposition which proved successful for a time. The first method of opposition was that of an offer of co-operation. Zerubbabel was asked to admit into partnership such as were really enemies of the work. It was a very subtle peril. Human reasoning, acting on the level of policy merely, might be inclined to think that there could be no harm, but only advantage in gaining help from any source. Men of faith have often fallen into this blunder, and have associated with themselves those not sharing their faith, and therefore in the deepest sense opposed to their enterprises. These leaders were not deceived. They detected the peril. Their reasoning was complete, in that it was illuminated by their faith, and took in all the quantities in coming to a decision. This is seen in the answer of Zerubbabel: "Ye have nothing to do with us to build an house unto our God." The words reveal a principle of perpetual application, and persistent urgency. God must be our God, before we can build a House for Him. Men who are not submitted to Him, can have no part in doing His work. That is a false breadth which proposes to seek the aid of those in rebellion against God, in the doing of the work which is in the interest of His Kingdom. Such inclusion of the unyielded is, moreover, a wrong done to them, as it gives them a false sense of security. To have done many works for the King is of no value, so long as He has to say "I never knew you."

With them were the prophets of God, helping them.—*Ezra 5. 2.*

This page of Old Testament history is interesting in itself, and valuable in the light it sheds on the true relationship between prophetic ministry and national life. A study of the prophecies of Haggai and Zechariah make it perfectly clear that the cessation of the work of building was unworthy of the men who had commenced that work. Judged by human standards, they could fairly urge the difficulties of the situation, and the necessity for obedience to the edict of the reigning king. Judged by the Divine standard, which was the true gauge of national prosperity, there was no reason for cessation, and they had no right to cease. It was to this end—the discovery of the true standard—that the burning words of these prophets were addressed. This is ever the contribution which the prophets of God are called upon to make to national life. They introduce into human thinking the quantities which are all too easily forgotten: those of the Divine government, and of the fact that national strength consists in recognition of that government, and right relation thereto. Statecraft which forgets God is powerless to realize the highest conditions for any people. When all the other quantities are considered in the light of His will and wisdom, they assume their proper proportions. Under the inspiration of the prophetic teaching, Zerubbabel, Jeshua, and the people, commenced their work again, and carried it through to completion. Opposition did not cease, but under the influence of the prophets their consciousness of relation to God had been renewed, and they went forward in spite of the challenge of their foes. The moral of national life is ever lifted to the highest degree of strength when there is a sense of right relationship with God.

According to the commandment of the God of Israel, and according to the decree of Cyrus, and Darius, and Artaxerxes king of Persia.—*Ezra 6. 14.*

The right of these men to build had been created by the decree of Cyrus. Tattenai, who was now opposing them as they resumed the work, either did not believe that such a decree had ever been promulgated, or considered that it could not be found. The elders of the Jews, the eye of their God being upon them, persisted in the work, and Tattenai appealed to Darius, that search should be made. That he should accede to such a request rather than exercise his immediate authority one way or the other, was in itself somewhat remarkable. He was as certainly the instrument of God as Cyrus had been in issuing the decree originally. That the search was a thorough one is indicated in the statement as to where the roll was found. The search naturally commenced in the house of the archives at Babylon, but it was not there. It was found at Achmetha in the royal palace. It is easy to realize how easily this might not have been found. If such a document was not in the proper libraries, what more natural than to abandon the search? But under Divine compulsion that search was prosecuted until the decree was found, and the elders were vindicated. Later, another royal decree, that of Artaxerxes, made possible the coming of Ezra, and the beginning of a new spiritual movement.

A ready scribe.—*Ezra* 7. 6.

This phrase, descriptive of Ezra, is full of interest, as it is connected with the emergence of a new order in the life of the nation, that, namely, of the Scribes, which continued through four centuries, and was found in strength numerically, but in degeneracy spiritually, in the times of our Lord's earthly ministry. It is a good thing to study it at the fountain-head. During the time of the monarchy of the united Kingdom, a scribe was a royal secretary. During the later period of the disrupted kingdom, the scribes had become men whose business it was to copy and to study the laws of the nation. With Ezra a new order began. The scribes now became men whose chief business was to interpret the Law, and to apply it to all the changing conditions of life, and the new circumstances constantly arising. As messengers of the will of God, they took the place of the prophets, with this difference: instead of receiving new revelations, they explained and applied the old. Of this new order, Ezra was at once the founder and type. The word "ready" does not apply to his pen, but to his mind. He was expert in exposition and application of the Law. The qualifications for such work are very clearly set out in the statement made concerning him in the tenth verse of this chapter. He "set his heart to seek . . . to do . . . to teach."

I was ashamed to ask of the king.— *Ezra* 8. 22.

These words constitute a fine revelation of the quiet strength and true greatness of this man, Ezra. The journey before him and those who were about to accompany him was full of peril. He was keenly conscious of these perils, and yet would not ask help of an earthly king, however well-disposed that king might be. He said he was ashamed to do so, because he had boasted to that king of the strength of his God That boast was by no means an empty one; and to this man, the matter of supreme importance was the honour of the name of his God in the mind of the king. The voluntary gifts of the king were welcome. They were expressions of the king's sense of the greatness of his God. These Ezra accepted with gratitude. It would have been quite another matter if he had asked the king to help him to do what he had declared God was able to do for him. To ask for soldiers would have been to make a tacit confession of some doubt in his own heart as to the ability or willingness of God to protect his enterprise. He had no such doubt, and therefore he made no such request. This is a fine illustration of the dependence and independence of those who put their confidence in God. God never fails those who act in full dependence on Himself, and so in complete independence of all others.

I sat astonied until the oblation.—*Ezra* 9. 4.

On Ezra's arrival in Jerusalem princes acquainted him with the ....ure and sin of the people. During the sixty years which had elapsed since the Return under Zerubbabel, there had been no return to idols, but there had been the wilful breaking of the law of God against inter-mixture with the peoples of the land, and the chief offenders had been the princes and the rulers. This picture of Ezra in presence of this confession is full of light. It is that of a man tempest-tossed with righteous indignation, and profound grief. As the storm of his passion subsided, in which he had rent his garments, and plucked off his beard, he sank into silent astonishment until the evening oblation. Then he fell upon his knees before God, and poured out his soul in prayer. The prayer is recorded. Beginning with his confession of personal shame, he gathered into his cry the whole of the people, identifying himself with them as he spoke of "our iniquities . . . our guiltiness." He went back over all the history in contemplation as he knelt before God, and saw clearly that it had been one long story of failure and of consequent disaster. He then remembered and spoke of the grace of God as it had been manifested in the making possible of the return of the remnant through the favour of the kings of Persia. Then the surging sorrow of his heart concerning the new future found expression in free and full confession, until at last, without any petition for deliverance, he cast the people upon God, recognizing His righteousness and their inability to stand before Him. This is a revelation of the only attitude in which a man may become a mediator. He must first have a sense of sin. This is the outcome of the deeper sense of the righteousness and grace of God. It finds expression in a confession of sin in which he identifies himself with the sinners.

Be of good courage and do it.— *Ezra* 10. 4.

The sincerity and passion of Ezra's vicarious repentance produced immediate results. The people had gathered about him during the long hours of the day, and it would seem that they were brought to a keen consciousness of the enormity of their sin as they saw how this man was affected thereby. At last one of their number, Shecaniah, spoke to him, acknowledging the sin and suggesting the remedy. In these words he urged Ezra to courageous action. It was true advice, and that for which Ezra had been waiting. He immediately responded, first calling them into sacred covenant, that they would put away the evil thing from among them; and then proceeding to lead them in the carrying out of that covenant along the line of strict and impartial justice and severity. All the marriages contracted with the women of the land were disannulled. By these drastic measures the people were brought back into the place of separation. How widespread the evil was, may be gathered from the list of the names with which the record closes. Priests, Levites, princes, rulers, and people had been guilty.

None was exempt from the reformation, which was carried out with complete thoroughness. Such action is ever the true outcome, and only satisfactory expression, of sorrow over sin. The man who sets himself "to seek, to do, to teach" the law of God invariably brings himself into places where sorrow will be his portion, and intrepid courage necessary.

NEHEMIAH

I asked them concerning the Jews.— Neh. 1. 2.

An interval of about twelve years occurred between the reformation under Ezra, and the coming of Nehemiah The story this book tells is that of the continuation of the work commenced by Zerubbabel in the matter of the rebuilding of the wall. It is intensely interesting, because in large measure it is autobiographical. Nehemiah tells his own story, with a freshness, and a vigour and transparent honesty which are full of charm. In these words we have a revelation of his patriotism. He held the position of cup-bearer to the king, which was one of honour, admitting him, not only into the presence of the king, but into relationships of familiarity. He had no inclination to forget or to ignore his relationship with his own people, for he spoke of those of them who found their way to the court as "my brethren." Moreover, his interest in them was sympathetic and vital. He made inquiry of them concerning Jerusalem. The news they brought was full of sadness, and his devotion was manifested in his grief. He carried his burden to his God in prayer. That prayer opened with confession. Without reserve, he acknowledged the sin of the people, and identified himself therewith. He then pleaded the promises of God, and asked that God would give him favour in the eyes of his master, the king. There was in his heart a resolve to do more than pity, if the door of opportunity opened. All this is patriotism on the highest level. It was based upon a recognition of the nation's relationship to God, and expressed itself in identification with her sorrows and her sins, and in a desire and determination to help her in ways according with Divine purpose and law.

So I prayed to the God of heaven. And I said unto the king.—Neh. 2. 4. 5.

This was practical, and that in both facts. Prayer is always practical, for it reaches and apprehends the actual and final forces. Prayer ever demands action

which is in harmony with its desires. Having sought the help of God, he spoke to the king with perfect honesty when the opportunity came. In the presence of the king, the sadness of Nehemiah's heart could not be wholly hidden. He had not been naturally or habitually a sad man, as he himself declares, but his sorrow for his nation was so real that it was manifest to the king. It has been suggested that this was part of his method, but such an interpretation strains the narrative, for he confessed that when the king detected the evidences of his sorrow, he was filled with fear. Yet, having had audience of God, courage splendidly overcame fear, and he told the king the cause of his grief and boldly asked to be allowed to go up and help his brethren. His request was granted, for his prayer was answered, and he took his departure for Jerusalem. All this is very illuminative. In all our endeavours, prayer is our first and principal line of activity. But more is necessary. God expects our co-operation. He will touch the heart of the king, but Nehemiah must make his venture. There is a profound truth in the commonplace and hackneyed statement that God helps those who help themselves. It is along the line of the use of our reason or common sense, that God works for us, and with us, for the accomplishment of all that we ask of Him.

Next unto him.—Neh. 3. 2.

This is the first occurrence in this chapter of this phrase. It, or its equivalent, "next unto them," runs on through the first half of it, occurring no fewer than fifteen times. Then another pair of phrases "after him" and "after them" emerges, and one or the other continues to the end, occurring sixteen times. These phrases mark the unity of the work. By this linking up of groups of workers the whole wall was built. The description is in itself orderly, and proceeds round the entire enclosure of the city, including all the gates, and the connecting parts of the wall. Beginning at the sheep-gate, which was near the Temple, and through which the sacrifices passed, we pass the fish-gate in the merchant quarter, on by the old gate in the ancient part of the city, and then successively come to the valley-gate, the dung-gate, the gate of the fountain, the water-gate, the horse-gate, the east-gate, the gate Miphkad, until we arrive again at the sheep-gate, when the chapter ends. All this is supremely interesting in its revelation of method. The unifying fact was the wall. All were inspired by the one desire and intention to see it completed. In order to realization, the work was systematically divided. Each group was united, as to its own workers, in the effort to do the particular portion allotted to them. All the groups were united to each other in the effort to complete the wall. It is a striking picture of the unity of diversity, and has its lessons for us. There was no sense of separation. Each worked "next to," or "after" some other; and so the complete union of workers and work was realized.

We made our prayer unto our God, and set a watch.—*Neh.* 4. 9.

That is ever the true attitude of those who are called upon to work for God in face of danger. As the work proceeded, the opposition of the enemies of the people, which first expressed itself in derision, passed to anger mingled with contempt. Nehemiah was conscious of the menace of this attitude to the work he had in hand, and lifted his heart in prayer to his God. An illuminative sentence in the narrative at this point shows how completely Nehemiah had captured and inspired the people. It declares that "The people had a mind to work." Thus the work went forward, until the wall was raised to half its height. At this point the opposition became more fierce, and a determined attempt was made by conspiracy to stay its progress. With immediateness, and a keen sense of the necessity created by this fact, Nehemiah says, "We made our prayer unto our God and set a watch." In this method there was neither foolish independence of God, nor foolhardy neglect of human responsibility and precaution. Everything was done to insure that two-fold attitude of complete faith in God, and determined dependence upon personal effort, which always makes for success. How often God's workers fail for lack of one or the other of these important elements!

I consulted with myself, and contended with the nobles.—*Neh.* 5. 7.

A new difficulty, constituting a yet more dangerous element, now presented itself. It arose within the borders of the workers, among the people themselves. The rich men among them exacted usury from their poorer brethren to such an extent as to oppress and impoverish them. Perhaps nowhere in the story does the nobility of Nehemiah's character shine out more clearly than in this connection. There is a fine touch in this declaration, "I consulted with myself, and contended with the nobles." His consultation with himself resulted in his determination to set an example of self-denial, in that he took no usury, nor even the things which were his right as the appointed governor of the people. This high and disinterested example produced immediate results, in that all the nobles did the same. Thus the people were relieved, and filled with joy, and consequently went forward with the work with new enthusiasm, ultimately completing it. It is from the vantage ground of personal rectitude that a man is really strong to deal effectively with wrong in others. Contention with nobles who are violating principles of justice, which is not preceded by consultation with self, is of no avail. When the life is free from all complicity with evil, it is strong to smite and overcome it in others. It is equally true that consultation with self which produces right personal action, is not enough. No man has any right to be satisfied with his own rectitude. In the interest of those who are being wronged, he must be prepared to contend with the nobles, or with any that are inflicting wrong.

So the wall was finished.—*Neh.* 6. 15.

The significant word in the statement is the word "so," as it calls us to reconsideration of how the dangerous and difficult work was accomplished. Inclusively and exhaustively, we may at once say, the work was of God. That wall was the outward and visible symbol of the inclusion and guarding of the Remnant, until the Messiah should come, and the Faith should appear. From now until then, this remnant was to be kept in ward. The Law was the custodian to bring them to Christ. The wall was the material expression of that isolation and security. When we turn from that consideration of the building of the wall by the will and through the overruling of God, to the human agencies, we find that the wall was built through the patriotism and high devotion of one man; and through the fact that he was able, by his influence and leadership, to weld the people into a unity of heart and purpose and endeavour which carried the sacred work to completion. The efforts of this man and the people were characterized by caution and courage, and passionate persistence against all opposing forces. Perhaps this latter quality is the most outstanding. By all means the enemies of the work sought to prevent its carrying out. Having begun in contempt, and proceeded through conspiracy, they turned to subtlety. Against every method, Nehemiah and his helpers were proof. Nothing turned them aside until the wall was finished. This strength against opposition was the outcome of a clear sense of the greatness of their task. Thus God's walls are ever built, God's work is always done. He leads and guides and compels circumstances to aid His workers; and they respond in agreement with His purpose, and in resolute refusal to allow anything from without or within to hinder them.

For he was a faithful man, and feared God above many.—Neh. 7. 2.

This is a description of the man whom Nehemiah placed in authority over the city of Jerusalem, after the wall was completed. The whole of the arrangements for the safety of the city, as here recorded, were characterized by statesmanlike caution. Through all the country round about there were enemies, and the position of the partially restored city therefore was one of perpetual peril. Nehemiah was conscious of this, and made the most careful provision as to the hour for the opening and closing of the city gates, and as to the arrangements for the watchers. No greater mistake can ever be made in connection with work for God in difficult places, than that of lack of caution. Carelessness is never the sign of courage. True bravery prepares for the possibility of attack. The man who had built, sword in hand, to completion, did not imagine that with the swinging of the gates on their hinges, the time for anything like relaxation in watchfulness had come. His choice of the governor was characteristic. He was chosen for two reasons; his fidelity to duty, and his fear of God. If we speak of these as two, they yet are but the two sides of one fact. Fidelity to duty is the outcome of the fear of God. The fear of God always produces fidelity. There is no sanction sufficiently strong to produce true fidelity other than that of this holy and loving fear. If a man is unfaithful to his appointed task, while yet declaring his loyalty to God, he lies, and the truth is not in him. The secret of the courage that is cautious, of the caution that is courageous, is ever that of a complete fear of God.

The joy of the Lord is your strength. —Neh. 8. 10.

The material side of Nehemiah's work being completed, the spiritual and moral work of bringing the people back more intelligently under the influence of the Law, went forward. Ezra now appeared upon the scene, and we have the account of a most interesting and remarkable religious Convention. The first day witnessed the assembling of the people. The phrase "gathered as one man" indicates their unity of purpose. They had assembled to hear the reading of the Law. This was not merely the reading aloud of passages from the Law, or even the reading of the Law. It was reading, accompanied by exposition, which was undertaken by men specially appointed. It would seem as though there were, first, a public reading, and then a breaking up into groups under the direction of selected Levites. Their work was that of translation and interpretation. The Law was written in Hebrew, and the people spoke in Aramaic. Hence the need for translation. It was a day of conviction, resulting in great sadness, as the people discovered how serious their failure had been, and how severe were the terms of the Law of their God. It was to this state of mind that these words were addressed, and they constitute an interpretation of the real nature and value of the Law. The joy of Jehovah is that which gives Him satisfaction, and that was expressed in His Law. Thus the Law was their strength. Only as they obeyed it could they be strong. This surely was the thought of the Psalmist when he sang: "Thy statutes have been my songs" (119. 54). Because the Law of Jehovah is the method by which He makes known to men the way of strength to them, it is the joy of Jehovah. When we discover that, the statutes which fill us with fear, become our delight, our song. They are indeed our strength.

Stand up and bless the Lord your God from everlasting to everlasting; and blessed be Thy glorious name, which is exalted above all blessing and praise.—Neh. 9. 5.

The wall being completed, the Law expounded, the Feast of Tabernacles was observed. Then, after a brief interval, came a great Day of Humiliation. The people separated themselves entirely from all those who were not actually within the Covenant, and then gave themselves to humbling and confession before God. In all this they were led by the Levites, and this chapter is largely occupied with the great prayer they offered upon this occasion. It may have been a prayer specially prepared for them; or perhaps, in the form in which we have it, it is a condensed account of the line along which they proceeded in their approach to God. The remarkable thing about it is that a prayer of humbling and confession is largely an utterance of praise. Observe its movement. The first section was wholly of praise (5–15). It praised God; for what He is in Himself, in majesty (5–6); for His founding of the Nation through Abraham (7–8); for His deliverance of the people from Egyptian bondage (9–11); for His constant guidance (12–15). The second section sets forth His grace as in constant contrast with the repeated failure of His people (16–31). This section is a frank, full, and humble confession of repeated sin, and yet the burden of it is that of the readiness of God to pardon. The final movement was that of definite seeking for the continuance of His goodness and help, in the form of a new covenant

(32-38). All this is most suggestive, as it gives us a true model of the way of approach to God in confession. The heart is strengthened in the contemplation of His essential glory, and His constant grace. To see God in glory and in grace, is to know our sin, and to be driven to confession and repentance.

We will not forsake the house of our God.—*Neh.* 10. 39.

In this chapter we have some further particulars of the Covenant which the people made with Jehovah, following upon the great Day of Humiliation. This Covenant was sealed representatively by the priests (verses 3-8); by the Levites (9-13); by the rulers (14-27); and to its terms all the people agreed (28). These terms are set forth in general phrases and in some particular applications. Generally, the people promised "to walk in God's law . . . to observe and do all His commandments." Particularly, the ˙ Covenant referred to matters in which the people had already failed—those, namely, of inter-marriage with the surrounding idolatrous peoples, of neglect of the Sabbath, of Temple maintenance and arrangement, and of the offering of first-fruits and tithes. It would seem as though Nehemiah laid special emphasis on these later things, and these concluding words give the reason for this stress. He knew the supreme importance of the house of God to the national life, and therefore he said: "We will not forsake the house of our God." The maintenance in strength of the worship of God is of supreme importance, principally for the sake of the worshippers. There is a very true sense in which it may be affirmed that our worship cannot enrich God. But there is yet another sense in which He is robbed if we cease to worship, for whenever we do, we suffer impoverishment in our deepest life, and that results in moral breakdown. Therefore let us also ever say, "We will not forsake the house of our God."

The people blessed all the men that willingly offered themselves to dwell in Jerusalem.—*Neh.* 11. 2.

In this, and the next two chapters, the arrangements made for the settlement of the cities are set forth. These are the last pages of history in the Old Testament. Some revelations of later conditions are found in the writings of the prophets, but nothing more is distinctly historic until, after a lapse of four centuries, we have the events recorded in the New Testament. The first section of the chapter is devoted to the account of the settlement of Jerusalem particularly. It should be remembered that perhaps not more than fifty thousand, all told, had returned from captivity, and by no means all of these had come to Jerusalem itself. Many of them had taken up their abode in the surrounding cities. Jerusalem was particularly difficult of settlement, seeing that it was the centre of danger, and peculiarly liable to attack. It was, therefore, arranged that the princes should dwell in the city, and that 10 per cent. of the people, selected by lot, must take up their abode there. In addition to these there were some who voluntarily came forward to dwell in the place of danger, and these were specially honoured by the people. The statement is one which gives occasion for some heart-searching. It really is an easy thing, for those who do not volunteer for places of danger, to applaud those who do, but it does seem to be a somewhat unworthy proceeding. Applause of heroism is neither costly nor valuable. It is a good thing that great enterprises are not dependent upon such people. The heroes are always to be found. Their reward is in their deed, rather than in the approbation of those who admire, but who do not help.

The joy of Jerusalem was heard even afar off.—*Neh.* 12. 43.

In this chapter we have an account of the commencement of the solemn dedication of the wall. It would seem as though it had been postponed for some considerable time. Differences of opinion exist as to the length of time. Some place this dedication ceremony in immediate relation to that which is recorded in the following chapter, which would place it twelve years after the first coming of Nehemiah. Others say that the account given here has reference to what took place within a few months of the actual completion of the work. It is difficult to decide, and really the matter is of no vital importance. The ceremony, whenever it took place, proceeded in three stages. First, there were two great processionals, in which the appointed singers chanted the praises of God. This was followed by the reading of the Law, and the consequent separation of the mixed multitude from the people of God (chapter 13). The present chapter is principally occupied with the rejoicing, and in this connection the statement is made that "The joy of Jerusalem was heard even afar off." It was a great day, greater even than these people knew. The reformers had sought to bring the remnant, weak and small though it was numerically, back to a recognition of the deepest truth concerning the national life that, namely, of its relation to God. Their joy that day was the joy of the Lord, and that was indeed their strength. All the pomp and pageantry and material splendour of the days of the monarchy had passed; but in that devotion to the Law, and to the purposes of God as manifested in the building of the wall, there was more of moral power than the old days had ever known, since the time when in their folly, the people had clamoured for a "king like the nations."

I came to Jerusalem, and understood.—*Neh.* 13. 7.

This chapter records Nehemiah's last visit to Jerusalem. After the building of the wall, he had evidently gone back to the court of the king. Twelve years later, seeking permission, he returned, and his last deeds reveal the continued strength and loyalty of the man. Coming to the city, he understood. His viewpoint was still that of the Divine purpose, and therefore he was not deceived—he understood! There were four abuses which he discovered, and without the slightest hesitation or any sign of weakness, but with characteristic energy, he set himself to correct them. Eliashib, the priest, had given a place within the very Temple of God to the man Tobiah, who had done so much to hinder the work of building the wall. Nehemiah flung out the occupant and his furniture, and restored the chamber to its proper use. He found, in the second place, that the Levites, instead of being able to devote their whole time to the service of the Temple, had to earn their living, because the tithes were not being paid. He contended with the nobles and corrected this abuse. He found, moreover, that the Sabbath was violated, and restored the Divine order in this matter. Finally, he found that the people had again been making mixed marriages, and with unsparing force he dealt with the evil. The man who looks at conditions from the standpoint of agreement with the Divine intention, is ever the man who truly understands. Such a man is not careful to seek soft and easy methods in dealing with abuses. To be quick of understanding in the fear of Jehovah, is ever to be merciless to all that is contrary to the will of God.

ESTHER

Vashti refused to come.—Esther 1. 12.

This is the one gleam of light in the picture of the conditions obtaining at the court of Ahasuerus. The feast in the palace of the king was characterized by all the gorgeousness peculiar to the East. It resolved itself into a debauch of drunken revelry. In the midst of this, the king commanded Vashti, his queen, to his presence, and to that of his drunken nobles. She refused to come. She paid the price of her loyalty to her womanhood in being deposed. Incidentally, the story reveals the place which woman occupied outside the Covenant of the chosen people; it was that of being the plaything and the slave of man. It also reminds us that, in the midst of the grossest darkness, the human soul is not without some consciousness of higher things; and that among the least favoured we may at times discover things of real value and beauty. Let the name of Vashti be held in everlasting honour for her refusal. The events recorded in this Book took place between the completion of the Temple and the mission of Ezra. The book in itself would seem to be a fragment of Persian history, captured and incorporated for sacred purposes. It shows us God overruling the affairs of His own people in a foreign land. The feast of Purim, observed to this day, is the living link with the events recorded, and sets the seal of historic accuracy upon the story. That feast celebrates, not the defeat of Haman, nor the advancement of Mordecai, but the deliverance of the people.

The king loved Esther . . . and . . . he set the royal crown upon her head, and made her queen instead of Vashti.—*Esther* 2. 17.

This chapter reveals customs obtaining in the household of Ahasuerus, which show us how far in advance of the pagan world the Hebrew people were, in spite of all their failures. Moreover, we can only read them in thankfulness that, wherever the purifying forces of revealed religion have operated, such things have become impossible. In the midst of the story, Mordecai appears upon the scene. Living with him was his cousin, whom he had adopted as his daughter. In the carrying out of a decree of the king, she was taken to the royal palace in the company of the maidens. Mordecai's action in this matter is certainly open to question. His love for Esther is evident, and the picture of him walking before the court of the house of the women indicates his continued interest in her. One can only hope that her presence there was not due to his scheming for place and power. It looks suspiciously as though it was so, and in any case his advice that she should not betray her nationality was questionable, as her position at the court of the king was one of grave peril for a daughter of the Covenant. We must remember, however, that this story is not preserved for us in order to glorify Mordecai, but rather to show how God overrules all the cleverness and folly of men, in order to carry out His own purposes. The beauty of Esther captured the heart of the king, and she was made queen in place of Vashti. God overruled her presence in the palace, in such wise as to make her the instrument for frustrating the foe, and preserving His people from massacre.

The king and Haman sat down to drink.—*Esther* 3. 15.

And so far as Haman was concerned, he did so with complete satisfaction, because he had now perfected his arrangements for the extirpation of the Jews. There was, however, a quantity with which he had not reckoned, and that was that these people were the people of God. It is questionable whether he had any idea of such a fact; or, if he knew that these people claimed some special relationship with a God, he knew nothing of that God; nor thought it worth while to take such a matter into consideration. And thus he omitted the only factor of real importance. He had power and cleverness on his side. He was in complete favour with the king. Himself, he was haughty, imperious, astute. He had used his power, laid his plans; everything was done. Therefore he sat down to drink with the king. And all the while Mordecai, the Jews, and Haman, were in the hands of God. In the doings of evil men, their cleverness is constantly seen breaking down, in that they do strange and inexplicably foolish things from the standpoint of their own purpose. In the case of Haman, we ask: Why did he delay for months the carrying out of his intention? The answer probably is that he thought by such delay to make the extermination of these people more complete. We see now how that delay gave the necessary time for all the events which ended in the deliverance of the people of God. If men fear God and follow Him, they can always reckon on Him. If they ignore Him in their reckoning, they always find Him sooner or later, to their own undoing.

Who knoweth whether thou art not come to the kingdom for such a time as this?—*Esther* 4. 14.

The action of Haman produced consternation among the Jews, as indeed it well might. The whole diabolical plan had been cleverly conceived, and the arrangements for carrying out the dire purpose had been skilfully made. On the level of human observation, it seemed that there could be no escape from a terrible massacre. Mordecai was overcome with grief, but in these words we discover the one gleam of hope that shone for him amid the prevailing darkness. It was not an affirmation, it was a question; not the expression of confident faith, but the inquiry of a wistful hope. Yet the true answer to that inquiry was an affirmative one. Esther became a direct link between the king and her people. The custom and law of the court forbade her approach to her lord, save at his command. Nevertheless, the urgency of the case inspired her to the heroism of making the great venture. Conscious of her need of moral and spiritual strength, she asked that her people might fast with her. The note of sacrifice on the highest level is discoverable in her word: "If I perish, I perish." This portrait of Esther is a singularly fine one. A beautiful woman, occupying a grave place of peril at the court of this Eastern despot, and that by no choice of her own, she made a great venture on behalf of her people in their hour of peril. She did it in the spirit of conscious dependence upon God, and in that of complete readiness to sacrifice her life. She had certainly come to the kingdom for that time; and she was exactly the woman whom God could use to be the instrument for carrying out His deliverance of His people.

All this availeth me nothing, so long as I see Mordecai the Jew sitting at the king's gate.—*Esther* 5. 13.

What an unveiling of the essentially evil heart we have in these words of Haman! At the back of selfish ambition, some cankering pain for ever torments. In this case, it was that of Mordecai refusing to render homage to him and to his friends. Haman frankly admitted that nothing satisfied him while this condition of things continued. I repeat, what an unveiling this is! Here we see the true reason of all the appalling suffering that this man was proposing to cause to a whole people. It was that of petty pique and pride. If it were not for the awful things which can result from such an attitude of mind, it would seem to be sufficient to hold it in contempt, to laugh at it. But that is the whole mischief. That apparently trivial thing is fundamentally wrong; and that is really so terrible, that when it completely expresses itself it does so in terms of cruelty, rapine, murder, and every evil thing. And all the while the evil root is a torment to the man in whose bosom it dwells. Haman said: "All this availeth me nothing . . . so long . . .!" The only cure for this malady would be the death of Mordecai, and that God would prevent. The gallows for Mordecai was intended to be Haman's comfort during the process of the feast. But in the counsels of God that gallows was not for Mordecai. The more carefully one considers the moral world under the government of God, as to its laws, its methods, its torments, and its triumphs, the more one is constrained to worship in the presence of the infinite wisdom and unvarying justice and mercy of our God. In the meanwhile Esther had made her venture, and the outstretched sceptre of the king was the sign of the Divine rule exercised in that court of earthly pride and pomp.

On that night could not the king sleep.—*Esther 6. 1.*

In this chapter we have a night interlude between the making of a gallows and the holding of a feast. In the economy of God, vast issues follow trivial things. A sleepless night is a matter transient and almost trivial. Yet it has often been a time of revelation and surprise, affecting the after-years. In the case of Ahasuerus, it was another of the ways along which God moved forward for the deliverance of His people. To while away its hours, the king commanded his readers to read to him from the Records. Again the unseen God, directing the mind of the king! When they obeyed, they found themselves reading an entry about a service Mordecai had rendered to the king. Again the unseen God, choosing the particular roll for their reading! Then swiftly and suddenly things developed. Haman was waiting without, for the opportunity of asking that Mordecai be hanged. He entered, heard, and went forth to confer the highest dignities of the kingdom upon Mordecai! Thus God works out His own high purposes, slowly as it seems oftentimes, but surely, and with unerring wisdom, until all things being done, the end is sudden, dramatic, complete. In two very different poems Russell Lowell gave expression to two truths which we may bring together and keep together in our thinking. In "The Crisis," he wrote:

"Standeth God within the shadows,
Keeping watch above His own."

And in "The Biglow Papers," he wrote:

". . . You'll hev to git up airly
Ef you think to take in Gawd."

They hanged Haman on the gallows that he had prepared for Mordecai.—*Esther 7. 10.*

By the way of the banquet Haman passed to the gallows which he had caused to be erected for Mordecai, and the existence of which he had expected to be his special source of consolation during that time of revelry and feasting. It was a fierce and terrible retribution, but it was characterized by poetic justice. The very core of Haman's hatred for Mordecai was that of his own self-centred and self-consuming pride and ambition. This was of so masterful a nature, that one man refusing to render homage to him inspired him to such hatred that he was determined to encompass, not the death of that man only, but also of all those who bore blood-relation to him. The nets of evil plotting and malicious enterprise, swing far out in the tides of human life, but never far enough to enmesh God. He remains beyond them all, and gathering them in the hands of His power, He makes them include the men who weave them to destroy others. The instrument which Haman's brutality prepared for Mordecai,

God employed for the destruction of Haman. Not always with the same spectacular visibility, nor always with the same dramatic suddenness, but always, inevitably, sooner or later, now or in those longer issues, which only the eyes of God can see as yet—"Jehovah bringeth the counsel of the nations to nought."

The Jews had light and gladness and joy and honour.—*Esther 8. 16.*

The deposition of Haman issued naturally in the promotion of Mordecai. The peril threatening the Jewish people, however, was not yet by any means averted. The royal proclamation had gone forth that on the thirteenth day of the twelfth month the Hebrew people should be massacred. By the constitution no such royal proclamation could be directly reversed. Some other way must be discovered if the people were to be saved. Through the intervention of Esther, the king granted permission to Mordecai to send a proclamation under the royal seal allowing them to arm and defend themselves. Thus, through ordinary channels, God brought about the deliverance of His people through the extraordinary method of sending the king's own messengers with haste through the country, urging the people to be ready against what would have been the fateful day of their own slaughter by previous royal proclamation. We can understand what a day of "light and gladness" it was for these people. A very significant fact is recorded, namely, that many from among the peoples of the land "became Jews." Thus, the deliverance was evidently recognized as wrought for these people by supernatural means: and upon the other people the fear of the Jews fell, for the complete reversal of their position was conspicuous. In a distant land, and on a dark day, God thus gave His people a sign of His watchful care over them, and filled their hearts with joy. The whole value of the story is that it reveals anew the greatness of the love of God.

Esther confirmed these matters of Purim.—*Esther 9. 32.*

In this chapter we have a full account of the arrival of the fateful thirteenth day of the twelfth month, and of all that happened thereupon. It was the day on which the changed conditions in the cases of Haman and Mordecai were revealed throughout the whole of the provinces. Men who had persecuted the Jews, and were looking for the opportunity of wreaking their vengeance by royal decree, found themselves filling the places which they had intended their foes to occupy. It was in remembrance of this great deliverance that the feast of Purim was established. The thirteenth day was the day when the lot, according to Haman's devices, was to fall out to the destruction of the Jews. God overruled the lot, and they were delivered. Therefore the fourteenth and fifteenth days were henceforth to be observed as Purim, or lots, a time of festal celebration. This decision was confirmed by the royal consent through Esther. According to a Jewish tradition, "all the feasts shall cease in the days of Messiah, except the feast of Purim." It is a remarkable fact that while there have been breaks in the observance of the other great feasts, and some of them have been practically discontinued, this has been maintained. Whatever view men may hold of the value of this Book of Esther, it is certain that Jewish leaders have ever treated it as an exposition of the method by which God wrought deliverance for His people in a time of peril, even while they were in exile, and so of His unceasing care for them. It has been the inspiration of hope for them in many dark and desolate days.

Mordecai the Jew was next unto king Ahasuerus.—*Esther* 10. 3.

This tiny chapter is interesting as it give us the last picture of this man Mordecai. It is a singularly fine one. Whatever there may have been questionable in some of the methods he adopted with regard to Esther—and here we are not able to be dogmatic—it is evident that he was of fine character. Probably all the experiences of the goodness of God had brought him to finer life. Evidently he retained the favour of Ahasuerus, for his position was next to the king. This did not alienate him from his own people. He continued to seek their good, and to speak peace to them: and therefore was held in highest honour among them, as well as trusted in the realm in which he exercised authority. Perhaps there is no severer test of greatness of soul than that of advancement in the favour of kings. Too often such advancement has meant the undoing of men who, in poverty, or under disfavour in high places, have been true men. The man who can pass to wealth and to position among the great ones of the earth, and still maintain his integrity and his loyalty to his own kith and kin, is ever a great man: and the secrets of such greatness invariably are that his roots are in God.

JOB

Job . . . was perfect and upright, and one that feared God, and eschewed evil.—*Job* 1. 1.

That is the description of the man whose tremendous experiences are recorded in this most wonderful Book. In the next five verses we have an account of his circumstances before the days of these experiences commenced. They constituted the accidentals. In these words we have the essentials. These are the things of the man himself, the things of his character. It is difficult to imagine any higher praise. Two words tell the result, while two phrases reveal the secret. He was "perfect and upright": and that because he "feared God and turned away from evil." To recognize this at the outset, and never to forget it throughout the following consideration, is of vital importance. It will save us from the mistake of thinking at any point of those experiences as having their explanation in the man himself. Not for himself did he suffer. His pains were not penalties for wrongdoing: they were not even chastisements for correction. The soul of this perfect and upright man was a battleground between heaven and hell. A subtle and sinister lie of evil was met and silenced through his experiences. For a long period neither he nor his friends understood the deepest meaning of it all. We, however, are immediately admitted to the secret by the story of these first two chapters, with their account of the questions of Satan and the answers of God. We see Job in these chapters bereft of all the things Satan said were necessary to his loyalty. We shall see him passing through great mental strain in the darkness. We shall see him emerge vindicating faith, and giving the lie to Satan. Thus we are taught that experiences through which loyal souls pass may have their explanation in some far-reaching purpose of God: and that suffering may be an honour conferred. In God's great tomorrow we shall have strange and glad surprises.

None spake a word unto him; for they saw that his grief was very great. —*Job* 2. 13.

This statement gives the true sanction for the use of the word *friends*, to describe these men. By this time in the narrative we have seen this man Job stripped of all the things of privilege on the level of earthly possession. His property, his children, his health, and the comradeship of his wife in his faith were gone. He sat in appalling loneliness and desolation, and there was no gleam of interpreting light. He did not know of any reason for his sufferings. In that dark hour, all the acquaintances who had sunned themselves in his prosperity were conspicuous by their absence. But no, there were three men,

Eliphaz, Bildad, and Zophar, and later a fourth, Elihu, who, hearing of his evil case, came to see him. They consulted together, and they came. His condition touched them to the depths. They desired to comfort him. When they saw him, so changed was he that they knew him not. Then their grief found expression in tears. And then came the supreme evidence of friendship. For seven days they sat with him in silence. That is of the very essence of friendship. Let it be remembered to their credit through all the study. They never spoke until he did. All they said was in answer to his first outpouring of grief, an outpouring made possible by their sublime and sympathetic silence. Their true friendship persisted through all the process. Their mistake was that of trying to find a solution. It was born of their satisfaction with their philosophy, the whole of which was true, but which was not all the truth. Nevertheless, their mistakes were the outcome of their friendship. It is impossible to think this through, without realizing how often the sympathy of a great silence is a far more blessed thing than any speech can be.

After this opened Job his mouth, and cursed his day.—*Job* 3. 1.

This chapter records the first great outpouring of complaint on the part of Job, and, as we have said, the opportunity for it was unquestionably created by the silent sympathy of his friends. That it is a terrible outcry, will not be denied. Taken as a whole, it was a cry for escape, rather than a description of his sorrows. These were patent, self-evident, even to the onlooking friends, although they could not possibly fathom all the terrors through which he had passed, or those in the midst of which he was then living. Escape seemed the only desirable thing. There was no suggestion of seeking escape through death by his own act. But he had come to hate life. Therefore he cursed the day of his birth, and the night of his conception: he lamented that he had been preserved for such days as these: he celebrated the blessing of death through which men escape the sorrows of life. At this point we are tempted to begin our criticism. We say none has any right to curse the day of his birth, or to lament the fact of his life. That is a cold argument —logical, and perhaps even true. But before we say a word, let us honestly place ourselves in similar circumstances. And at once let us say, and remember it throughout, that no word of God rebuked him. Moreover, let us gather the real value of this story, as it reveals to us the fact that there is relief in pouring out all the heart feels in moments of darkness. Such outpouring is a far more healthy thing for the soul than dark and silent brooding. Or to endeavour to remember the whole fact. Here was a man who

through suffering which had no explanation to himself, was co-operating with God. The very agonies here expressed were part of that suffering co-operation. What a revelation this is of the greatness of man.

He putteth no trust in His servants! And His angels He chargeth with folly.—*Job* 4. 18.

These words occur in the course of the first address of Eliphaz. In considering every one of these addresses of the friends of Job, we shall have to distinguish between the truths they uttered, and their failure to bring any help to Job. They were wonderful men, wonderful, that is, in the remarkable light and understanding they possessed. I question whether any exception can be taken to anything they said. But there were so many things they did not know. They did not know the philosophy which would include the experiences of Job. Their persistent mistake was that of attempting to explain everything by their knowledge, which, spacious as it was, was altogether too narrow. Take these particular words. How true they are. So great is God, and so great the universe over which He reigns, that it is impossible for Him finally to trust in any other than Himself. In the ultimate, knowledge, even that of angels, is folly. It is all true, and reveals a very remarkable apprehension of truth on the part of Eliphaz. But what bearing had such a statement on the case of Job? None whatever. Eliphaz thought it had, because his deduction was that such a God punishes evil. He was right so far. But when he concluded that all suffering was punishment, he was wrong. Of suffering as a way of working in the activity of God, and a way of co-operation on the part of man, he never dreamed. Yet that was going on before his eyes. His own statement was a rebuke, had he but known it. Even then God was charging him with folly.

Happy is the man whom God correcteth: Therefore despise not thou the chastening of the Almighty.—*Job* 5. 17.

Eliphaz is still speaking. We first note the inapplicability of these words to Job. God was not correcting him: the experiences through which he was passing were not of the nature of chastening. All his sufferings were produced by Satan, and permitted by God. In this permission God was honouring a man "perfect and upright," and who "feared God and eschewed evil," by admitting him to partnership in operations which at last would give the lie to evil, and indicate the greatness of the human soul. Recognizing that, we may then ponder the splendid truth which Eliphaz uttered in these words. God does correct man for wrong-doing: He does chasten His sons when by any disobedience they cease to be perfect and upright. When those who are His, depart from His fear, and compromise with evil, then by afflictions, pains, sorrows, He corrects, chastens, and so restores them. Happy indeed is the man who is the object of this severe, and yet gracious Divine solicitude and activity. The wisdom of such a man consists ever in submission to the chastisement. At the time it is never joyous but grievous: but afterwards it worketh the peaceable fruits of righteousness. God's eyes in great love are ever set upon that "afterward." What unutterable folly, if in such a case, we despise the chastening: that is, if we fail to yield ourselves to its intentions. To do so, is to prevent the peace toward which it is proceeding. Far better know the troubling that comes from God today, than the disaster of the troubles which come from our own waywardness and wickedness, unchecked by correction and chastisement.

Oh, that I might have my request; And that God would grant me the thing that I long for.—*Job.* 6. 8.

The speech of Eliphaz added immeasurably to the anguish of Job. His friend misunderstood, and read the worst into the situation, attributing his sufferings to some sin in his life. Job knew that the deduction from his friend's philosophy was unjust. Even though he himself did not understand his sufferings, he knew that this solution was false. His anguish became anger, as the whole tone of this reply reveals. And what wonder? Can there be any experience of the soul more trying than that of having sin imputed by friends, when there is an inner consciousness of innocence? Tortured, by the injustice, these burning words escaped him: and those which follow give us the request. He desired that God would crush him—cut him off. We listen to him in profound sympathy, and yet, having all the story, we know how dire a disaster it would have been for him if that request had been granted. The disaster would not have consisted so much in the fact of his cutting off, as that thereby he would have been removed from the high privilege of co-operation with God. What wonderful light there is in all this for us! There is nothing wrong in giving expression even to such a desire as this, when in the fierceness of some fiery furnace of suffering we honestly feel it. But when the answer does not come, when instead of the release of cutting off, we have the continuity of pain, and a great silence, then let us remember this story: and remain confident that there is some explanation, and that when it comes, we shall thank God that He did not give us our request.

If I have sinned, what do I unto Thee, O Thou Watcher of men?—*Job.* 7. 20.

After the more direct and angry reply to Eliphaz, the speech of Job continued in a bitter complaint against the stress and misery of life generally. The toil of life is strenuous indeed. It is a warfare. Man is a hireling, a servant whose labour issues in nothing, and whose rest is disturbed in tossing. Nothing is satisfying, for nothing is lasting. Job piled figure on figure to emphasize this: a weaver's shuttle, the wind, the glance of an eye, the vanishing cloud. There is absolutely no ray of hope in this outlook on life. Because of it, he uttered his complaint, not only concerning life, but directly against God. It was a definite and determined complaint: "I will not refrain ... I will speak ... I will complain." But most carefully note it took the interrogatory form from beginning to end. These questions clearly show us how Job saw God in those days, and we know that it was a blurred vision which he beheld. But this very method of asking questions shows also that he was not satisfied with his own vision. If that be God—as though he had said—then why is He such? Every question was a great question, as any careful consideration of them will show. Moreover, there was, and is, a great answer to everyone; and had it been possible to have given those answers to Job, they would have amazed him, as they amaze us with the amazement that leads to worship. Take this particular one. Its simple meaning was that God is so great that even if a man did sin, it cannot affect Him. The answer is that this was an altogether too small a thought of God: the truth being that God is so great that He is affected, wounded, robbed by human sin. Job was, like his friends, hindered by a philosophy too narrow.

The hope of the godless man shall perish.—*Job* 8. 13.

Bildad was a man of different mould to Eliphaz. His speech was characterized by greater directness. By comparison it lacked in courtesy, but it gained in force, and perhaps in clarity. In his address we discover the same philosophy as in that of Eliphaz. God is just, and prospers the righteous, and punishes the evil. No direct charge was made against Job, but the deduction was inevitable. Again we have to say Bildad was quite right in his statements of truth, and quite wrong in his intended deductions so far as Job was concerned. Recognizing this failure, we may consider the truth thus stated: "The hope of the godless man shall perish." Is there anything more perpetually demonstrated in human experience? Hope, as expectation with desire, plays a tremendous part in human life. It is the continuous inspiration of activity, whether good or evil. The output of life's energy is almost invariably the answer to desire coupled with expectation. Nevertheless, it is a patent fact that human life and experience are full of instances of perished hopes. The expected does not happen, the desire is not satisfied. It is true indeed that men are saved by hope: but it is equally true that men are lost by hope. How are we to account for this? Everything depends upon the nature of the hope. The sentence preceding this in the speech of Bildad explains this one: "So are the paths of all that forget God." It is the hope of the godless which perishes, and by it men are lost. Hope set on God is always realized, and by it men are saved.

There is no daysman betwixt us, That might lay his hand upon us both. —*Job.* 9. 33.

Two chapters are now occupied with Job's reply to Bildad. Carefully notice the opening of it. He first admitted the truth of the general proposition—"Of a truth I know that it is so": and then propounded the great question, which he proceeded to discuss—"How can man be just with God?" We must clearly understand that this question, as Job asked it, was not an expression of guilt, but of littleness and ignorance. He did not mean, "How can a man be made just before God," but rather, "How can a man prove that he is just before God." In a passage of great power he described the greatness of God. He is infinite, invisible, invincible. Therefore it is useless for a man to attempt to be just with Him. Therefore his position is hopeless. His days sweep by him devoid of good. Then there broke from this man this deep cry, giving expression to the profoundest need of the human soul: "There is no umpire betwixt us, that might lay his hand upon us both." That is what man needs in a profounder sense than Job intended, that, namely, of a justification which includes pardon and cleansing. That is what man needs also in Job's sense, that, namely, of a way of access to God by man, and of access to man by God, so that there may be consciousness and intelligent fellowship. Necessarily our thoughts travel in adoring worship to Him Who is the Umpire: the One Who lays His hand upon us and upon God: Who intercedes with God for us, and with us for God. Through Him we have access into the grace wherein we stand: for we are justified by faith in Him.

Let me alone, that I may take comfort a little.—*Job* 10. 20.

Notwithstanding the fact that Job felt that it was impossible for a man to argue with God, yet, because there was no umpire, he made his appeal to God. Turning from his answer to Bildad, he poured out his agony in the presence of the Most High. The appeal was by no means a hopeful one, but it was an appeal made directly to God. After complaining of his sufferings, attributing them all to the action of God, and asking if God really delighted in what He was doing, or if His vision was faulty, Job bluntly asked God to let him alone, that he might have a respite from suffering before he died. It is a terrible revelation of suffering, and of the tempest-tossed condition of soul into which such suffering brought this man. As we read it we feel that the suggestions which Job made about God were entirely wrong: but we remember that they were not wicked, because they were honest. Again also we remind ourselves that throughout the Book there is not a hint of Divine displeasure with Job. Job did not, could not, understand: and all his anguish was part of the co-operation with God, to which he was called. We know the whole story, and therefore it is for us to learn the deepest lessons, and so again we remind ourselves that such prayers as these—perfectly honest, and not rebuked —are nevertheless answered in the highest sense, by not being granted. In that fair morn of morns that is to break, in which we shall have explanation of life's experiences, our profoundest gratitude to our Father will find expression in the thanks we give Him for His refusal to grant some of our sincerest requests. If respite means cessation of co-operation with God, better never find it.

Canst thou by searching find out God? Canst thou find out the Almighty unto perfection?—*Job* 11. 7.

The method of Zophar was blunter than that of Eliphaz or Bildad. His words were fewer, and there was a roughness and directness about him that they lacked. His philosophy was the same. He argued from the suffering of Job that he must be guilty of sin. The special burden of his message was due to the fact that he felt that Job had affirmed the wisdom of God, and yet had called it in question: and in a passage of really great beauty he re-affirmed it, and insisted upon it that this God of infinite wisdom knew man perfectly. The thing he argued was indeed true, and because it was true, his deductions were false. God knew His servant Job, and all the meaning of his pain, as neither Job nor his friends knew it. We may turn then from Zophar's false deduction to his true statement. No man can by searching find out God: no man can find out the Almighty unto perfection— not even Zophar, nor Job. The application is twofold, first to those who are in such case as that of Job, and secondly to those who stand and watch as did Zophar. Let those who suffer remember that God may have reasons, which for today are not discoverable to them, for permitting their continued pain. That is the last refuge of the afflicted, but it is a safe and quiet place. Let those who watch, cease attempting to explain, lest they be found to misrepresent God in their attempted vindications of Him, even more than does the sufferer in all his outpourings of inquiring agony.

In Whose hand is the soul of every living thing, and the breath of all mankind.—*Job* 12. 10.

Job's last reply in this first cycle of discussion was not only an answer to Zophar—it was his refusal to admit the accuracy of the general argument found in all the three addresses of his friends. From beginning to end it thrilled with sarcasm, while it maintained his denial of personal guilt. This chapter is occupied with his more direct dealing with these men. In its first movement we discover Job's sarcastic contempt for their wisdom: and in the second we find his declaration of his clear understanding of all they had said about God, and more. The particular words which we have emphasized show us something of his underlying faith and conviction about God. He recognized that all life is sustained by God—that of the living creatures beneath man in the scale of being, as well as that of man. This is a tremendous conception. It means that nothing ever escapes from the rule of God. In itself, it fills the soul with a sense of awe, and in some senses with helplessness. There is no comfort in it, until we learn the character of God. Job knew this only in part: and therefore, while he recognized the fact, it brought him no consolation. The truth thus emphasized needs to be perpetually remembered. Such recognition will save us from active rebellion. To realize the power of God must be to realize that our wisdom is found in His fear. When we know—as it is given us in the Son of God to know—the facts as to His character, the truth becomes our one consolation in all circumstances of difficulty. The most important question we can ask about God is not "What can He do?", but "Who is He?" That is answered only in Christ.

Will ye respect his person? Will ye contend for God?—*Job* 13. 8.

The emphasis in these questions of Job must be laid upon the character of his friends as he understood it. He was about (as he declared, verse 3), to make his appeal to God directly. Before doing so, he addressed himself to them again in terms of anger. His contempt for them knew no bounds. He described them as "forgers of lies," "physicians of no value"; and proceeded to turn their judgment back upon themselves. They had been speaking unrighteously for God. There is great force in the conception contained in this protest. Whether it was a perfectly fair view of what these friends of his had been doing may be open to question. Personally I think it was. The idea is that men may argue in defence of God upon false lines, through limited knowledge. That is exactly what these men had been doing. The result was that they were unjust to Job. They did not know it: they did not intend that it should be so. But it was so, and that proves their inability to defend God: for He is never vindicated by any argument which involves injustice to any human being. The more carefully we ponder this story, the more does the conviction possess the mind that silence is more befitting in the presence of many problems which are presented to us by the experiences of others. To sit in silent sympathy by the side of those who suffer is always helpful. To affirm to them the fact that God is wise and can make no mistake is always safe. To attempt to explain the suffering, and that by our philosophy of God, may be to lead us into injustice to the sufferer, and to misrepresentation of God. While Job's knowledge of God was imperfect, it was profounder than that of his friends.

If a man die, shall he live again?—*Job* 14. 14.

Let these words be carefully considered in their setting. The end of this reply of Job to the first cycle in the discussions with his friends consisted of a direct appeal to God. In the course of that appeal he dwelt on the fact that man's life is transitory and full of trouble. Moreover, it ended in the darkness and mystery of death? "Man giveth up the ghost, and where is he?" There is hope for a tree that it will bud again, but there is none for a man. This dark assertion seems to have awakened in the mind of Job a wondering hope, and this found expression in these words: "If a man die, shall he live again?" That the question had in it the element of hope is proved by the declaration which Job made directly he had asked it, as he said that if that were so, he could endure all the days of the conflict. It was only a gleam: and was almost immediately overwhelmed in the darkness of his despair, as the next sentences show. But it was a gleam, shining up out of the deepest things in a human soul. Here we touch one of the supreme values of this wonderful Book. As we observe all the experiences through which this man passed, we discover that the human spirit is of such a nature that ever and anon, even in the midst of the most appalling darkness, it expresses its highest capacities by the questions which it asks. It was a tremendous question: but let us remind ourselves that there is no answer to it, save that which came to men through Jesus Christ and His Gospel. As Paul said, it is He 'Who brought life and immortality to light through the Gospel" (2 Timothy 1.

10). The question of Job was answered by Jesus, and that so completely as to leave no room for doubt.

They conceive mischief, and bring forth iniquity, and their belly prepareth deceit.—*Job* 15. 35.

With this chapter we begin the second cycle of discussion between Job and his friends. It is to be noted that the philosophy of these men was the same as in the first, but the method was changed. In the first cycle that philosophy was stated in general terms, and declared that God punishes the wicked and rewards the good, the inevitable deduction being that Job's suffering was the outcome of his wickedness. Eliphaz in this address emphasized one part of that philosophy, that, namely, which declared that God punishes the wicked. It was all true, but it was not all the truth: and so it was not applicable to Job. Apart from its unsuitability to his case, this address of Eliphaz constitutes a magnificent description of the unutterable folly of the man who sins against God. These words consist of a figurative summary of the discourse. The word "iniquity" in the Revised, reads "vanity" in the King James Version. My own view is that both have missed the idea. The Hebrew word *'Aven*, strictly means "nothingness," which would be expressed by vanity; but it was constantly employed to express the idea of affliction. So indeed is it rendered by the Revisers and King James' translators in chapter 5. 6. This is the thought in its aplication to Job by Eliphaz. All his affliction was the result of his evil or mischievous thinking. Of Job it was not true. The truth yet abides, that to conceive mischief is always to bring forth affliction.

Even now, behold, my witness is in heaven, and He that voucheth for me is on high.—*Job* 16. 19.

Job's answer to the speech of Eliphaz practically ignored its argument. He first manifested his impatience with these men. Their philosophy was not new. They were "miserable comforters." He was annoyed at their pertinacity. What moved Eliphaz to answer?—he enquired. While the darkness was still about him, and in some senses the agony of his soul was deepening, yet it is impossible to read this address without realizing that through the terrible stress he was at least groping after light. In the midst of his complaining he said: "Mine adversary sharpeneth his eyes upon me"; and again: "God delivereth me to the ungodly." That leads on to the words we have emphasized. In view of the revelation given to us in the opening chapters of the book, these things might suggest that Job was coming to a measure of understanding of the process through which he was passing, if he did not know

the reason of it. The word "adversary" is not the same as that rendered "Satan," but it indicates an enemy. The statement that God delivered him to the ungodly is suggestive. Be that as it may, in the midst of all this travail of soul, his faith triumphed over his doubt. He believed that God knew the truth about him, and would be his witness. Upon that affirmation of faith he prayed that God would maintain his right with God, and with his neighbour. This is another instance of the light breaking forth, if only for a moment, from his deepest life. If the gleam were but momentary, it yet demonstrates the fact that the light had not been utterly put out. We may employ these words with greater confidence, for the Umpire has come to us, and has now gone to appear in the presence of God for us.

Where then is my hope? And as for my hope, who shall see it?—*Job* 17. 15.

The light faded immediately, and Job passed again into thick darkness. He was in the midst of difficulties. Mockers were about him: none understood him. There was no "wise man." Yet he struggled through the darkness towards God's vindication. Again he thinks of death, but in it sees no brightness. That is the meaning of these questions. They must be read in close connection with the thrice-repeated "If" of verses 13 and 14. If he has been looking for release in death, that means also the abandonment of hope. This is a great unveiling of a mental mood. The idea that a man can live again if he die, was here for the moment forgotten or refused. Yet the spirit of the man was in rebellion against so hopeless an outlook. I repeat that in the movement of this great answer, it does seem as though some outlines of the truth were breaking upon him. He was conscious of the action of God in his sorrows; of an adversary who followed him relentlessly, and tore him pitilessly. Somehow that adversary was at one with God, and yet he knew that God was his witness. At least we see light in these complainings, and we can well imagine how in the after-days he would come to recognize how these strivings of the soul, these passionate desires and outcries for Divine defence, were gleams in the darkness. It is not to be wondered at that this great Book, although it gives no solution of the problem of pain, has ministered comfort and strength to countless distressed souls, as it mirrors their own experiences, and moves on to an end in which the troubled soul is led to rest, even without explanation.

Surely such are the dwellings of the unrighteous, and this is the place of him that knoweth not God.—*Job* 18. 21.

Bildad now resumed the discussion, and as in the case of Eliphaz it is evident from his opening rebuke that he spoke under the sense of annoyance. He was wounded at what he conceived to be the wrong Job had done him and his friends, in that he had treated them as "beasts," and as "unclean." He was angry, moreover, because he considered that Job's attitude threatened the moral order with violence. Turning from the mistaken application of his view to Job, to the things he said, they constitute a powerful statement of the issues of wickedness. These words formed the closing summary, and for interpretation we need the whole of his speech on the subject. He had first declared the preliminary experience of the wicked. His light is "put out." It is a graphic portrayal. In the case of the wicked his own spirit, "the spark of his fire," does not shine and the light without is extinguished. Therefore, his steps are straitened, and "his own counsel" destroys him. His pathway without light to death is described. Lacking the light, he falls into all sorts of snares and traps. Following his death he becomes extinct, so far as earth is concerned; "his remembrance perishes"; he is "chased out of the world"; he leaves behind him no children who enter into his inheritance. This is a tremendously powerful delineation of the way of wickedness. Again we have to say—all true, and therefore to be taken to heart; but not all the truth, and therefore of no meaning in the case of Job.

Know now that God hath subverted me in my cause, and hath compassed me with His net.—*Job* 19. 6.

The answer of Job to Bildad by comparison with his previous answers, is brief, but it touches the deepest note in despair so far, and presently for a moment gives utterance to the most splendid note of hope. What Bildad had said of the wicked was true of him. He was indeed abandoned by men, his kinsfolk, familiar friends, his maids, his servants, his wife, even young children. In his case this was not due to wickedness, but to some unexplained action of God. It is very questionable whether the word "subverted" in this verse is an improvement on the "overthrown" of the King James Version. The Hebrew word *ávath* is a primitive root meaning "to wrest." It is not necessary to believe that Job was charging God with injustice. He was attributing all his affliction to His action, and that gave him his greatest pain, because no explanation of the reason of the Divine action was forthcoming. It was out of this deep darkness that words passed his lips most full of light. He affirmed his conviction that his Vindicator lived, and that at last he would see Him, and that as standing on his side—for that is the meaning of the words: "Whom I shall see on my side." The full value of what he said was not known to Job; but again we have a revelation of the greatness of the human spirit, which out of circumstances of deepest darkness catches some gleam of the essential light. This is poetry. That does not mean that it is untrue, a baseless dream; but rather that it is an apprehension of a truth, which at the moment defies any attempt at demonstration or detailed definition.

This is the portion of a wicked man from God, and the heritage appointed unto him by God.—*Job* 20. 29.

Zophar replied in evident haste, and his speech was introduced with an apology for that haste, and a confession that he was angry. These closing words were in the nature of a summary of all he had been saying. The sufferings he had described were such as fell to the wicked, and that by Divine appointment. All this was true. But other things were true, of which he seemed to have no knowledge. It was true that the same sufferings came at times to men who were not wicked, and that they were not by Divine appointment, but by Divine permission. That was the story of Job. The narrowness of Zophar's philosophy made him unjust to Job. Leaving, then, the false application, and considering only the truth in itself, we have in this address a wonderful description of the nemesis of wickedness. In a passage thrilling with passion Zophar described the instability of evil gains. There is a triumph, but it is short. There is a mounting up, but it is followed by swift vanishing. There is a sense of youth, but it bends to dust. There is a sweetness, but it becomes remorse; a swallowing down, which issues in vomiting; a getting, without rejoicing. The final nemesis of the wicked is that God turns upon him, and pursues him with instruments of judgment. Darkness enwraps him. His sin is set in the light of the heavens, and earth turns against him. Let the history of wickedness be considered, whether in the individual or in nations, and it will be seen how true all this is. Godlessness is folly, for it never brings man what he seeks.

How then comfort ye me in vain, seeing in your answers there remaineth only falsehood?—*Job* 21. 34.

At the close of the second cycle of discussion, as at the close of the first, Job answered, not merely the last speaker, Zophar, but the argument of the three friends. These closing words sum up his arguments as to the breakdown of these men. They had tried to comfort him, but in vain, and that because when applied to him, their truth had nothing in it but falsehood. All they had said was true, but it was not all the truth, even concerning the wicked, for in many cases, for the time being at any rate, the wicked continue in prosperity. It is impossible to read this answer of Job without realizing that, like his friends, he was limited in his outlook, and so failed to interpret accurately the facts of life. All he said was true, but it was not all the truth. If in his friends' arguments there was no comfort for him, it is equally true that in his answers he brought no conviction to them. All this is strangely suggestive. Men discussing human life are almost certain to blunder when they attempt to explain it. There are things of which the mind of man is not cognizant, qualities which elude him, facts and forces of which he is ignorant and, therefore, however sincere and truthful he may be, he cannot find the solution of many actual experiences. Two follies are revealed. The first is that of indulging in the condemnation of any soul on the ground of what we know, for there may be many things we do not know. The other is that of attempting to answer false condemnations by our own philosophies, for they may be as those of our fallible judges. There are hours in which we should be silent, in assurance that what we do not understand, is known to God. In such silence we may wait for Him.

Acquaint now thyself with Him, and be at peace; thereby good shall come unto thee.—*Job* 22. 21.

With this chapter the third cycle in the controversy between Job and his friends begins, and Eliphaz is again the first speaker. In his address there are two movements. In the first he made a definite charge against Job, as he declared the sins which, according to his philosophy, would naturally account for the sufferings which he was enduring. They were the most dastardly sins possible to a man of wealth and position: those of the spoliation of the poor, the neglect of the starving, the oppression of the helpless. In this charge Eliphaz made his supreme mistake. The second movement of his address consisted of his appeal to Job. Realizing its inapplicability to Job, by reason of the falseness of the charges made, when we consider it in itself it is full of strength and beauty. What man needs in order to be blessed himself, and to be a blessing to others, is knowledge of God. The whole matter is first stated in these opening words. Continuing, Eliphaz set forth the conditions of such acquaintance with God. The law is to be received from God. There is to be return by the putting away of unrighteousness. Human treasure is to be abandoned as worthless. Then the way of the Divine answer is described. Instead of the lost treasure, shall be the possession of the Almighty. In Him there shall be delight: with Him communion: and through Him triumph. Moreover the result shall be ability to deliver others. Great and wonderful words are these. Had Eliphaz applied them to himself he would have found that his own imperfect acquaintance

with God was the reason why he was not able to bring any real comfort to his suffering friend.

But He knoweth the way that I take; When He hath tried me, I shall come forth as gold.—*Job* 23. 10.

In replying to Eliphaz directly Job ignored the charges preferred against him. To them he returned in a later speech. He discussed Eliphaz's criticism of his view of God as absent from the affairs of men, and boldly affirmed his consciousness of the great problem. In answer to the advice to acquaint himself with God, he exclaimed, "Oh that I knew where I might find Him!" .He sighed after God, and principally for His judgment seat. He desired to stand before Him, to plead his cause, but he could not find Him, though he went forward or backward. He was conscious of His presence, but he could not see Him on the right hand, nor on the left. Then it was, that suddenly, in the midst of this bitter complaining, there flamed out a most remarkable evidence of the tenacity of his faith. He declared his conviction that God knew the way he was taking. He even affirmed his confidence that it was God Who was trying him, and that presently he would come forth from the process as gold. Again he insisted upon it that he had been loyal to God. Then immediately this faith merged into words of trembling and fear. Whatever God was doing, he could not persuade Him to desist! He knew His presence, but it troubled him. He was afraid of Him, because He had not appeared to deliver him. Notwithstanding these words of fear, the confession of faith was great, greater in its apprehension of truth than even Job understood. God did know; and through all the processes was moving toward the vindication of the true gold in this man. This is the persistent power of faith. It reaches out towards, and grasps great truths, which reason unaided never discovers.

Why are times not laid up by the Almighty? and why do not they that know Him see His days?—*Job* 24. 1.

In the first part of his reply Job had spoken of his consciousness of the problem of God's apparent withdrawal from human affairs as it applied to himself. Now he proceeded to speak of it in its wider application to the world at large. He asked the reason of God's non-interference in these words; and then went on to describe the evidences of it. Men still existed whose whole activity was that of oppression. In other words Job declared that the things with which Eliphaz had charged him were present in the world; and he described them far more graphically than Eliphaz had done, ending with the declaration: "Yet God regardeth not the folly." Continuing, he said that the murderer, the adulterer, the robber, all continued their evil courses with impunity. He admitted that it was true that they pass and die, but for the moment they were in security. He ended all by challenging anyone to deny the truth of what he had said as to God's absence, or at least of His non-interference with the ways of wickedness. Here again we see Job breaking down, not in integrity or sincerity or honesty, but in his attempt to formulate a philosophy on the basis of the appearances of the hour. The truth is that times are laid up by the Almighty; that He does impute wickedness to men for folly. God is neither absent from human affairs, nor does He fail to interfere. There are often hours in which it seems as though God were doing nothing. Such seeming is ever false. Faith holds to that certainty, and waits the issue with confidence.

Dominion and fear are with Him; He maketh peace in His high places.—*Job* 25. 2.

The brevity of this speech of Bildad is in itself suggestive, as it shows that even though Job has not convinced these friends of his that their philosophy does not include his case, he has succeeded in silencing them. Bildad showed that he was not prepared to discuss the general truth which Job had enunciated, but he had no sympathy with the personal application which Job had made of that truth. The same thing was true of Job. He did not quarrel with the general statements of his friends, but protested vehemently against their deductions as to himself. The whole discussion is a revealing one. Men are heard arguing within the limits of imperfect knowledge, and so never arriving at true conclusions. Once more we have to say that, so far as it went in positive statement, this last address of the three friends of Job has nothing in it to which exception can be taken. How true are these opening words, affirming the absolute sovereignty of God, and declaring the effect of the exercise thereof to be peace! This conviction is the very foundation of strength and confidence in human life. To act upon it, as well as to accept it theoretically, is to be silent in the presence of many things which we cannot explain. These men had a correct theory of God in so far as it went, but they did not act in complete harmony with it, or they would not have said much which they did say about His servant Job.

Lo, these are but the outskirts of His ways: and how small a whisper do we hear of Him! But the thunder of His power who can understand?—*Job* 26. 14.

In this chapter we have Job's answer to Bildad. It is characterized from first to last by scorn for the man who had no more to say. In a series of fierce exclamations he revealed the importance of all his friend had said to help him in any way. Then, in order to show the poverty of Bildad's argument, he spoke of the power of God in such way as to prove that he knew that power even more perfectly than his friends. God's power is exercised in the underworld. They that are deceased tremble. Sheol "is naked," Abaddon has "no covering." The whole material fabric is upheld by His power. The mysteries of controlled waters, and light, and darkness are within the sphere of His government. The sweeping of the storm, and its disappearance, are both the result of His power and His spirit. Having thus in remarkable poetic beauty revealed his consciousness of the greatness and government of God, he ended with these words, declaring that all these things "are but the outskirts of His ways," only "a whisper," of Him, and asked: "The thunder of His power who can understand?" In all this we have a further evidence of the greatness of this man's faith, in its revelation of the remarkable apprehension of the greatness of God. The outskirts of God's ways are so wonderful, that the central facts must indeed be beyond our grasp; the whisper of God is so marvellous, that the full thunder of His speech must be beyond our comprehension. And so we are constrained to worship.

As God liveth, Who hath taken away my right; and the Almighty, Who hath vexed my soul.—*Job* 27. 2.

Our reading now brings us to a new stage. Five chapters contain nothing but the words of Job. They fall into two great speeches. Each is introduced by the words: "And Job again took up his parable" (27. 1 and 29. 1). In them he poured out all that was in his heart with complete abandon. After his answer to Bildad he seems to have paused, waiting for the speech of Zophar. The last of the three was silent. Then Job took the whole matter up and made general replies. He began with a protestation of innocence, and thus answered directly the charge which had been brought against him, that his own sin was the cause of all his suffering. In the course of that protestation of innocence he made use of these words, and in them we have a revelation of his state of soul at this time. His faith abides. God liveth, and He is Almighty. Moreover He is governing. It is God Who has taken away his right; it is the Almighty Who has vexed his soul. All this is the language of unshaken faith. But it is the language of perplexity and of pain. His very faith created his suffering. His right was taken away, his soul was vexed, and that not because he was a sinning man. He strengthened all the arguments of his friends as to the punishment of the wicked. It was true—all of it. But—and here was his problem and his pain—it did not account for his sufferings. There must be some other way to account for this. His friends had not found it, and he did not know it.

God understandeth.—Job 28. 23.

These are the strong and central words of this wonderful chapter. After his protestation of innocence, and passionate revelation of the need of some solution of his sufferings other than that which his friends had suggested, Job discussed the question of wisdom. He first described man's ability to obtain possession of the precious things of the earth. Silver, gold, and iron are mined, and the description of how man does the work is full of beauty. Having thus described man's ability, he asked: "But where shall wisdom be found?" The answer is in these words: "God understandeth." The evidences of the truth of this are to be found in the impossible things which God does. He "looketh to the ends of the earth." He makes "a weight for the wind." He "meteth out the waters by measure." He makes "a decree for the rain." Therefore Job arrives at his conclusion that for man, "The fear of the Lord—that is wisdom; and to depart from evil is understanding." This is, indeed, at once our confidence and our comfort—"God understandeth." The things that perplex us, do not perplex Him; the mysteries by which we are surrounded, are no mysteries to Him. And there is more in the truth than that. "God understandeth" us also; He knoweth our frame, He remembereth that we are dust. When our best friends misinterpret our experiences, and therefore misunderstand our complainings, God understandeth. That is the secret of our comfort, the very rock foundation of our confidence. In the midst of all the perplexities and problems and pains of life these words are a song— "God understandeth."

Oh, that I were as in the months of old, as in the days when God watched over me.—Job 29. 2.

Probably, after a pause, Job resumed his speech. This second address was not so much an answer to his friends as a statement of his whole case as he saw it. He was still without a solution of the mystery of his sufferings. That of his friends he utterly repudiated. Everything in his address led up to the utterance of a solemn oath of innocence. These words introduce his description of the old days. Those days he described as to his relation with God: they were days of fellowship in which he was conscious of the Divine watchfulness and guidance. Then in one sentence which has in it a sob of a great agony, he referred to his home-life: "My

children were about me." Then he described the abounding prosperity of those days. He called to remembrance also the esteem in which he was held by all classes of men, even the highest. The secret of that esteem had been that of his attitude toward men. He had been the friend of all such as were in need. Clothed with righteousness, and crowned with justice, he had administered the affairs of men so as to punish the oppressor and relieve the oppressed. In those days his consciousness had been that of safety and of strength. Those days he described in this opening declaration as days in which God watched over him. In that form of introduction his keenest sorrow is discovered. It was that of the feeling that, in some way, and for some reason, God no longer watched over him. He knew that God still saw him, as his previous words have proved, but there was a difference in the watching. Because we know the whole truth, which Job did not know, we recognize that the watchful care of God had never ceased through all the troublous times.

But now.—Job 30. 1.

This phrase introduced Job's description of the circumstances in which he found himself. It is a graphic and terrible portrayal, and is the more startling, standing as it does in contrast with what he had said concerning the old days. He first described what he evidently felt most acutely, how the base held him in contempt. In the midst of this reviling of the crowd, he was suffering actual physical pain, and this he graphically described. The supreme sorrow was that when he cried to God, there was no answer. He claimed that in such suffering as he endured, there was ample justification for all his complaining. It is impossible to read this section without feeling that protest was approaching revolt in the soul of this man. He did definitely charge God with cruelty (see verse 21), and in his questions, "Did not I weep for him that was in trouble? Was not my soul grieved for the needy?" (verse 25), he was contrasting God's attitude toward him with his own attitude toward suffering men in the days of his prosperity and strength. How often when "But now," is the starting-point of our thinking, and we contemplate only the things seen and near, we are driven to exactly the same agonized outcries. Then for our comfort let us remember that God still watched over His servant, uttered no word of rebuke, but sustained him even when he was unconscious that He was doing so.

Lo, here is my signature; let the Almighty answer me.—Job 31. 35.

This whole chapter is occupied with Job's solemn oath of innocence. It was his final and explicit answer to the line of argument adopted by his three friends.

In every cycle they had insisted upon one conclusion, that his affliction must be the outcome of his sin. In a systematic and carefully prepared statement he now affirmed his innocence: personally (1–12): in his dealings with men (13–23): in his attitude toward God (24–34): ending thus with his signature, and demand for definite indictment. The chapter closes with the words: "The words of Job are ended," and these are generally attributed to the author of the book, or to some subsequent editor or copyist. Personally, I believe they constitute Job's last sentence. He had nothing more to say. The mystery was unsolved, and he relapsed into silence. There is an interval filled with the discoursing of Elihu. At chapter 38, we shall come to the words: "Then Jehovah answered Job." No other words of argument on the part of Job shall we find in the book. He only spoke twice again (see 40. 3–5 and 42. 1–6) and in very different tones. At this point, then, we have reached the end of Job's expressions of pain. The end is silence. That is God's opportunity for speech. He often waits until we have said everything: and then, in the silence prepared for such speech, He answers. His answers then are not always what we have demanded: but they bring rest and satisfaction, as we shall see in the sequel.

There is a spirit in man, and the breath of the Almighty giveth them understanding.—*Job* 32. 8.

The last voice in the earthly controversy was that of Elihu. Job never had opportunity to answer him. God took no notice of him except to interrupt him. In the epilogue Elihu has no place. Nevertheless, the thought in the long speech, or group of speeches, of this man, is full of interest, and moves on a higher plane than that of the men who had already spoken. With these words Elihu introduced his argument, by declaring what he conceived to be his right to speak at all. He was not trusting to age or wisdom, but to revelation. Whether he was justified in believing that what he was about to say resulted from such revelation, may be open to question; but this statement is full of interest in that it does reveal the method by which God makes Himself and His thoughts known to man. The first sentence, "There is a spirit in man," reveals man's capacity for receiving communications from God. The second sentence, "The breath of the Almighty giveth them understanding," shows how God makes use of that capacity. In man's essential nature there is spirit, and that is a Divine creation, and of the Divine nature. That makes it possible for man to have direct and intelligent dealing with God. The breath of God reaches that spirit-life of man, and gives understanding; that is, communicates to man the thoughts of God. That God should speak to man is not supernatural, but natural. The deepest truth about man is that he was created with the capacity for fellowship with God. This capacity is destroyed by sin, but it is restored by Grace.

Lo, all these things doth God work, twice, yea thrice, with a man, to bring back his soul from the pit, that he may be enlightened with the light of the living.—*Job* 33. 29, 30.

These words constitute a summary of Elihu's arguments up to this point, as to the methods and purpose of God in His dealings with men. He declared that God is greater than man, and that man has no right to ask explanations. This, however, is not all the truth. God does answer. He speaks "once, yea, twice," that is, in one way, yea in two. (See verse 14.) The two ways are those of the dream or vision of the night, and the operations which produce suffering. It is to this latter that the words we have emphasized refer. This suffering is the work of God. "Twice, yea, thrice," is a figure of speech indicating the persistence and completeness of the method. The purpose is that of bringing back the soul of man from the pit, the enlightenment of life. Elihu's philosophy was that suffering is educational; that through it, God is leading men to some higher plane of life. His philosophy was a wider one than that of his friends, who saw nothing in suffering other than punishment for sin. Elihu saw that it might be a process through which the individual soul gained clearer light, and so fuller life. Undoubtedly he was right. But here again we at once see that the truth did not explain the suffering of Job. Elihu, in company with his three friends, had no conception that men may endure suffering for the sake of others, and so, in suffering be co-operating with God. Evidently satisfied with his own view, he challenged Job to answer him if he had anything to say and if not, to be silent while he continued.

Yea, of a surety, God will not do wickedly, neither will the Almighty pervert judgment.—*Job* 34. 12.

Job gave no answer to the challenge of Elihu, and so he proceeded. His second address occupied this and the following chapter. It may be well to note the whole movement first. Elihu opened with an appeal to the wise men, asking that they listen, in order to try his words. The address then consists of his answers to two quotations from what Job has said (see 34. 5, 6, 9, and 35. 3). Neither of these quotations was literal; each was Elihu's summary of what he had understood Job to mean. The first may be summarized as a contention that he had been afflicted by God notwithstanding his integrity.

The second suggested that Job had argued that nothing was gained by loyalty to God. This chapter deals with the first. Elihu answered this, first by declaring that Job had been keeping. company with wicked men. He then proceeded to argue for the justice of God. This is centrally expressed in the words we have selected. It was a great truth, and his arguments in support of it are incontrovertible. The authority of God is beyond all appeal. He cannot be influenced by any low motive. Therefore, whatever He does is right. Proceeding, Elihu declared that the government of God is based upon perfect knowledge. He sees all men's goings. There is no need for Him to institute special trial. His judgments are the outcome of His understanding. Therefore it is the wisdom of men to submit. How true it all is, and how important, that we should lay it all to heart! But how completely it failed to explain the problem of Job's sufferings. Once more we have to say it was all true, even about Job, but it was not all the truth.

If thou hast sinned, what dost thou against Him? And if thy transgressions be multiplied, what doest thou unto Him? If thou be righteous, what givest thou Him? Or what receiveth He of thine hand?—Job 35. 6, 7.

Elihu used these words in the course of his answer to the second of his quotations from Job. He declared, first, that when Job questioned the advantage of serving God, he was guilty of setting up his own righteousness as being more than God's. In these questions he attempted to lay bare the very foundations of truth concerning the sovereignty of God. He declared in effect that there is a sense in which God is unaffected by man: his sin does nothing to God: and his righteousness adds nothing to Him. This view had been already advanced in the course of the controversy. Undoubtedly there is an element of truth in it: and yet what an illustration it affords of the fact that a partial truth may become an almost deadly error; The complete revelation of God shows that, whereas according to the terms and requirements of infinite righteousness, God is independent of man, nevertheless, according to the nature of His heart of love—which these men did not know—He is not independent of man. The whole Biblical revelation, centred and consummated in Christ, shows that human sin inflicts wounds upon God, and causes sorrow to the Holy One: and that man, living in righteousness, does give glory to God, and cause joy to His heart. Elihu answered Job's declaration that there was no advantage in serving God, by saying in effect that there certainly was no advantage to God in such service, and no disadvantage if it were not rendered. Both Job and Elihu were wrong.

I have yet somewhat to say on God's behalf.—Job 36. 2.

After Elihu had answered the arguments of Job, as expressed in the quotations made, there would seen to have been a pause. Then he commenced his third and last address, which, as we shall see, was never finished. This address falls into two parts, and our chapter-divisions at this point confuse us, rather than help us. The first part is contained in the first twenty-five verses of this chapter, and consists of argument. The second part begins at verse 26, and runs through the next chapter. The first things he had now to say on God's behalf were those of a clear statement of his own explanation of Job's suffering. He was absolutely sure of his ground, and at once plunged into his theme. This opened and closed with statements of the greatness of God. Between these he uttered his words of explanation. It is not true that God "preserveth . . . the life of the wicked." It is true that "He giveth to the afflicted their right." Such as are right with Him are not immune from suffering. Thus Elihu's view clearly was that God has something to teach man which man can only learn by processes of pain. This was a great advance on the solutions suggested by his three friends, but it did not so much as touch the case of Job. In his suffering, God was not attempting to teach His servant anything. He was rather using him in order to answer an essential misinterpretation of the relation between God and man, and thus was conferring high honour upon him. Yet again we feel that the great message of the story to us is that of the wisdom of silence in the presence of suffering.

Touching the Almighty, we cannot find Him out; He is excellent in power; and in judgment and plenteous justice He will not afflict.—Job 37. 23.

As we indicated in our previous note, the second part of this address of Elihu commenced at the twenty-sixth verse of the previous chapter. Now, rising above mere argument, he proceeded to speak of the greatness of God, first as to its manifestation, and then in application to Job. It has been suggested that this last part of Elihu's speech was a description of what was happening at the time. When presently God spoke, He did so out of a whirlwind, and the idea is that it was this very storm, in its approach, which Elihu described. First, there was the drawing up of the water into the clouds, their spreading over the sky, and the strange mutterings of the thunder. Then came the flash of the lightning, followed by darkness; and again the lightning striking the mark, and the cattle were seen taking refuge from the storm. Gradually the violence of the storm increased, the thunder was louder, the lightning more vivid. In a strange mixture, the south wind and the north were in conflict, and ice was intermixed with rain. The purpose of the storm may have been for correction, for the land, or for mercy. That which Elihu desired to impress upon Job is revealed in these concluding words. He was endeavouring to bring him to realize the impossibility of knowing God perfectly, and the consequent folly of his complainings. The truth so expressed is a great one, and had application to Elihu also. He could not find God out, and he did not understand the mystery of Job's sufferings.

Gird up now thy loins like a man; for I will demand of thee, and declare thou unto Me.—*Job* 38. 3.

With this chapter we come to the third and final movement in the great drama, that in which Jehovah and Job are alone. Out of the midst of the whirlwind the Divine voice spoke, for which Job had long been waiting. Its first word was a challenge. This has been variously interpreted as applying to Job, or to Elihu. Personally, I believe the reference was to Elihu. Carefully note that the word of Jehovah did not charge Elihu with false interpretation, but with darkening counsel by the use of words which he himself did not perfectly understand. The theme which he had been attempting to discuss was too great for him, and God took it from him, and dealt with it Himself. In these words He called Job away from discussion with man, and away from lonely brooding. He was to gird up his loins like a man, and hold converse with God. This was a great call, revealing at once the Divine estimate of human dignity, and the conditions upon which God can deal with man. When a man acts like a man, God can speak to him, and he to God. That is a declaration of dignity, and a revelation of a law of life. When God thus spoke to Job, He gave him no explanation of the mystery of his suffering. The method of God was that of unveiling His glory before the mind of His servant, thus leading him to more perfect confidence in Him with regard to experiences which were not yet explained. The first movement in this unveiling had to do with the simplest facts of the material universe, which are sublime beyond the comprehension of man. Through all, God was suggesting His own knowledge, and the stupendous ease of His activity. Job was being led to forgetfulness of himself in a contemplation of God.

Knowest thou?—*Job* 39. 1.

Still the great unveiling proceeded, and by these words the mind of Job was directed to recognition of its own limitation. The voice of God spoke of the mystery of the begetting and birth of the animals, with the sorrows of travail and the finding of strength; of the freedom and wildness and splendid untameableness of the wild ass; of the uncontrolled strength of the wild ox. Did Job know these things? They were all known to God, and were under His government, and within the range of His power. Yet again, the differing manifestations of foolishness, of power, of wisdom, as evidenced among birds and beasts, were dealt with. The ostrich rejoicing in the power of her pinions, and in her folly abandoning her eggs and her young, was described; and her very foolishness was accounted for as resulting from the act of God. No reason was given for this depriving of the ostrich of wisdom, but the fact was affirmed that God had done it. All the strength of the war-horse was declared to be Divinely bestowed. The hawk, with wisdom directing her to the south land; the eagle, placing her nest on high—were revealed as Divinely guided. Thus, everywhere God was revealed, guiding, governing. The reasons of what He did were not disclosed. Job was again reminded of the fact. Thus he was being led to lean not to his own understanding, which was baffled everywhere in the presence of the most common things in the midst of which he lived; and to recognize anew the wisdom and power of God.

Behold, I am of small account.—*Job* 40. 4.

There was a pause in the great unveiling as Jehovah spoke directly to His servant and asked for an answer to the things He had said. The answer of Job was full of suggestiveness. The man who in mighty speech and strong defiance, had been of unbroken spirit in reply to all the arguments of his friends, now cried out: "Behold, I am of small account." The method of God was producing its effects. Job was brought to the consciousness of his comparative insignificance in the midst of a universe so wondrously governed. This very sense of insignificance was also one of comfort, for it came connected with the recognition of the fact of the interest of God in the smallest things, and so spoke of the understanding of God, concerning himself and all his circumstances. This was but the first part of the things he was yet to know; he had yet to be taught that he was of much account to God. For the moment it was important that he should realize the greatness of God. This was breaking in upon his mind with new force. He said: "What shall I answer Thee?" There was nothing he could say. He would lay his hand upon his mouth, and so cause his speech to cease. Silence was at once his opportunity of wisdom and his manifestation thereof. Then Jehovah continued. And again He charged Job to "gird up" his "loins like a man," thus recalling him to a sense of his own dignity. Among all the things over which God ruled, man alone was able to commune intelligently with God. In the midst of his suffering Job had complained of the method of God. Jehovah now called upon Job to endeavour to occupy His place. Let him assume the reins of government in the moral realm in which he had been critical of God. There was a tender and healing satire in the suggestion, as it helped Job to a sense of his own limitation, and of the all sufficiency of God.

Canst thou?—*Job* 41. 1.

The address of Jehovah to Job ended with the suggestion that Job should make two experiments to govern, not in the moral realm, but among the great beasts. It has been objected by some that the descriptions of behemoth and leviathan are interpolations, as they do not seem to fit with the argument. This surely is to miss the meaning. The material always yields itself to man's government more readily than the moral. If then Job cannot assume the moral government of the universe, let him try in the realm of the non-moral. Again, there was the playfulness of a great tenderness in the suggestions Jehovah made to Job about these fierce creatures. Shining through all this, and perhaps perceptible to Job, there may have been suggestions concerning those spiritual beings of wickedness against which the man of faith ever has to contend. Satan may be typified here by behemoth and leviathan. Be that as it may, the question left with Job was this: "Canst thou?" Thus he was called to the recognition of his own impotence in many directions, and at the same time to a remembrance of the power of God. Thus the method of God with this man was not that of explanation of the meaning of his sufferings, but that rather of the unveiling of His own glory.

I had heard of Thee by the hearing of the ear, but now mine eye seeth Thee; wherefore I abhor myself, and repent in dust and ashes.—
Job 42. 5, 6.

This is Job's answer to the words of Jehovah. It is characterized by the stateliness of a great submission. In his words of surrender, the ultimate greatness of the man is revealed. He had been brought to a new sense of God. In the power of it he knew that much of his past speech had been that of ignorance, and he confessed that it was so. In this new attitude of Job, there is revealed a glory of God, not manifest in any other part of the universe. This utterance of surrender is ever the vindication of God. There was no explanation of pain, but pain was forgotten. A man had found himself in relationship with God, and in so doing had found rest.

The epilogue is full of beauty. Jehovah turned to the friends of Job. His wrath was kindled against them, but it was mingled with mercy. Their intention had been good, but their words had been wrong. To them God vindicated His servant in that He called him, "My servant," as He had done at the beginning. They had attempted to restore Job by philosophy. They had failed. He was now to restore them by prayer. The bands of his own captivity were broken, moreover, in his activity of prayer on behalf of others. Having passed through the fiery furnace, the last days of Job were more blessed than his earlier ones. In this great Book there is no solution of problems. There is a great revelation. It is that God may call men into fellowship with Himself through suffering; and that the strength of the human soul is ever that of the knowledge of God.

PSALMS

Blessed.—*Psa.* 1. 1.

That is the first note in the music, not of this Psalm only, but of the whole collection. The Hebrew word is an interjection, and might fittingly be rendered, "How happy!" It is derived from a primitive word meaning literally, "to be straight," which is used in the widest sense. Its real thought is that of prosperity, resulting from straightness. Thus the very word suggests a moral value, and relates happiness thereto. Its most common use is that suggested by our word, "happy." This opening word indicates at once what man supremely desires for himself, and

what God desires for him. The variety of the tones of the music in this collection of songs is one of its great wonders. The strains are major and minor. Here are glad and exultant pæans of praise; and here are also sad and despondent dirges. Throughout, the particular note results from this desire for happiness or blessedness. When it is possessed, the songs are jubilant. When it is absent, they are despondent. The moral value suggested in the word itself is emphasized in this first song. The central light thereof is found in a phrase: "The Law of Jehovah." The man delighting in that law, meditating on it, conforming to its requirements, is the man who is prosperous—he is the happy man. The positive teaching is strengthened by the negative—"The wicked are not so." In their counsel, their way, their seat, there is no permanence, and therefore no true prosperity, and so no real blessedness. The purpose of the Law of Jehovah is ever that of ensuring the prosperity, the happiness of man. It is framed in infinite wisdom, and inspired by perfect love. To rebel against it, therefore, is the uttermost folly, and the most definite wickedness. To obey it, is the true wisdom, and the one and only goodness. Misery is the offspring of wickedness; happiness is the offspring of goodness. The Law of Jehovah discovers to man the way of goodness, and so teaches him the way of happiness.

He that sitteth in the heavens shall laugh.—*Psa. 2. 4.*

This is an arresting statement. Thrice only in the Bible is laughter predicated of God;—here, and in two other Psalms, viz. 37. 13 and 59. 8. In each case it is the laughter of derision, of contempt; and in each case it is the expression of contempt for those who in foolish pride of heart oppose themselves to Him, and to the purposes of His love for men. He laughs at the kings and rulers who oppose themselves to the King Whom He has appointed to bring blessedness to the sons of men. He laughs at the wicked who plotteth against the just. He laughs at bloodthirsty men. This derisive laughter of God is the comfort of all those who love righteousness. It is the laughter of the might of holiness; it is the laughter of the strength of love. God does not exult over the sufferings of sinning men. He does hold in derision all the proud boastings and violence of such as seek to prevent His will for the blessing of humanity, through the establishment of righteousness. There is no note in the music of this glorious song of the coronation of the Son of God more full of comfort than this which tells of the contempt of God for those who covenant together to revolt against His government. His laughter is reinforced by the speaking of His wrath, and the vexing of His displeasure. Yet this Hebrew singer knew the deepest things of his God, for the last of the song is an appeal to kings and judges to yield themselves to the ordained authority, and so to find the blessedness of those who put their trust in the anointed Son.

Arise, O Lord; save me, O my God: for Thou hast smitten all mine enemies upon the cheek-bone.—*Psa. 3. 7.*

There is no reason to question the accuracy of the heading of this Psalm, which attributes it to David, in the time when he fled from Absalom. It was certainly composed under circumstances of trial and of deliverance. The words in verse five warrant us in thinking of it as written in the morning; as verse eight of the next suggests that it was written in the evening. Accepting that view, we see the movement of thought. The fugitive king awoke to a sense of the adversaries (verses 1, 2). He also awoke to a sense of his God (verses 3, 4). He awoke to a consciousness of the restfulness of his sleep, and so to a complete courage (verses 5, 6) Then what? A great personal cry, in view of a relative deliverance. That is the meaning of this verse. Notice the request—"Save me"; and the affirmation—"Thou hast smitten all mine enemies." It would seem as though in the clear light of the morning—it is wonderful how often we see clearly in the sunrise—and in the consciousness of how God had delivered him from his outward enemies, there came to David a sense of his own unworthiness and, therefore, this prayer escaped him as a cry out of the depths of his soul. It is even possible that he recognized that the very rebellion of his son Absalom was due to his own failure. How often we have to cry similarly to God. He delivers us from circumstances of trouble, and the very fact of such deliverance brings home to us the sense of personal unworthiness. We can always add to the prayer the next words of the psalmist, "Salvation belongeth unto Jehovah."

Thou, Lord, alone makest me dwell in safety.—*Psa. 4. 8.*

This was a song at eventide, a meditation at the close of a day which had been by no means free from trouble. It has been very generally associated with the previous Psalm as having been written during the period of Absalom's rebellion. This suggestion is entirely speculative, and certainly not proven. The value of it remains, whatever the local circumstances which gave rise to it. It is the song of a soul, keenly conscious of the difficulties of life, and of hostile forces; but completely confident in God. The meditation closes with words expressing the singer's determination to lie down and sleep; and giving the reason for this determination. This reason is declared in these last words of the Psalm. We are in danger of missing something of their beauty by treating the word "*alone*" as though it meant *only*, and relating it to Jehovah, as though it meant that only Jehovah could do this. While that is true, it is not what the singer meant. The thought of the word *alone* is "*in loneliness*," or as Rotherham renders it "*in seclusion*"; and the word refers to the one who is going to sleep. This is a glorious conception of sleep. Jehovah gathers the trusting soul into a place of safety by taking it away from all the things which trouble or harass. The difficulties and dangers, the mocking foes and opposing forces, are all excluded by Jehovah; and the tried and tired child of

His love is pavilioned in His peace. The soul trusting completely in God, may ever lie down under the wing of the night singing.

Upon God's Will I lay me down
  As child upon its mother's breast;
No silken couch, nor softest bed,
  Could ever give me such deep rest.

O Lord, in the morning shalt Thou hear my voice; in the morning will I order . . . unto Thee, and will keep watch.—*Psa.* 5. 3.

I have omitted the words *"my prayer"* from this verse, as being unnecessary, and indeed as interfering with the true sequence of ideas. The Psalm is a song for the beginning of a day beset with danger. The singer was going forth to face foes who were treacherous and relentless. These words tell of the method of his preparation for such a day. There is a three-fold activity. First, Jehovah shall hear his voice. That is the activity of worship, in which praise and prayer mingle. This is seen in the rest of the Psalm. Following upon that activity, is that of "ordering." The meaning of the word is "to arrange." Ordering the days is making plans for the day. This is very important, but secondary. Too often we plan, and then pray. The true sequence is that of the Psalmist. Having worshipped, and arranged, the next and persistent activity is that of watching. The old rendering—"and will look up"—entirely misses the mark. The thought is not that of watching for Divine guidance or action. It is rather that of watching one's own action and way, that these may be kept in harmony with the initial act of worship, and the planning resulting from that act. That this was the meaning of the singer, is evident from words immediately following (verses 4–6). We face no day which is not filled with danger. Here is the true method of the morning—Worship—Arrange; and here is the method of the day—Watch. Days so begun and so continued may be days of rejoicing and triumph, whatever the dangers, and however many the foes.

The Lord hath heard . . . the Lord hath heard . . . the Lord will receive. —*Psa.* 6. 8, 9.

This is the first of the seven Psalms which are described as Penitential. (The others are 32, 38, 51, 102, 130, 143.) Various suggestions have been made as to the occasion of the writing of this one. None is conclusive. That it was a cry of profound penitence is patent. The first seven verses contain the cry of a soul in anguish. There was great physical suffering; but the deeper pain was that of the sense that God was absent from his consciousness, and that his sufferings were rebukes and chastenings from God. The dread of death was upon the singer, and was accentuated by the fact that in his then condition of mind there was no light in the region that lay beyond. The sudden change at verse eight is dramatic. His human enemies, who had been taking advantage of his physical sufferings to wrong him, are bidden to depart, and their downfall is predicted. The secret of this change is revealed in the words we have emphasized. We have no clue in the Psalm as to how the conviction came, but it came. It was the conviction that Jehovah heard, and that his prayer was received. Perhaps the most arresting fact in this Psalm is that there was no confession of sin. It was simply a wail of agony, and a cry for release. But it was a cry to God; and in the very admission that his sufferings were chastisements, there was at least a tacit acknowledgment of guilt. This reveals all the more radiantly the readiness of God to pardon. When His vexing in sore displeasure has driven the soul back to Him, His answer of love and of healing is immediate.

Judge me, O Lord, according to my righteousness.—*Psa.* 7. 8.

This petition must be interpreted in the light of the whole Psalm. The inscription helps us. We have no information in the history of David concerning the incident referred to. From the fact that this man Cush is named as "the Benjamite," we may infer that he was a partisan of the house of Saul, and an enemy of David. From the Psalm we learn the nature of the charges which he made against David. They were: that he had appropriated spoils which rightly belonged to the king; that he had returned evil for good; and that he had taken toll for some generosity. The charges were false, and that is what these particular words meant. The appeal to God to defend him, and to secure justice for him, was based upon his innocence, and reinforced by the fact that in the presence of these calamities he had a perfectly clear conscience. It is a great thing to be able to stand before the judgment bar of God with a conscience void of offence. It is indeed true that: "Thrice armed is he that hath his quarrel just." Such reflections bring comfort so long as we have nothing to fear, and therefore they constitute an appeal to the soul to be ever on the alert, that nothing in our dealings with our fellow-men be permitted, which under any circumstances may rob us of that sense of integrity. This is more than ever so in the matter of our relationships with those who are our enemies, not so much on the ground of personal hostility, but because they are opposed to the cause we serve, the Kingdom which we represent. Happy and secure are we if we give the enemy no cause to blaspheme.

. . . Man . . . Thou art mindful of him . . . The son of man . . Thou visitest him.—*Psa.* 8. 4.

I have resolutely taken the affirmations out of the interrogations of this verse, because they reveal the facts which created the wonder of the singer. The method of the song is that of contrast. First, the contrast between the glory of Jehovah, set upon the heavens, and the prattle, or possibly the singing, of little children. Second, the contrast between the stately splendour of the moon and the stars, and man—*Enosh*—frail man—and the son of man *Ben-Adam*—of apparently earthly origin. The contrasts are graphic. The fact of difference creates no wonder. That is caused by the attitude of God toward the apparently small and trivial. God builds His stronghold against His foes in the prattle or singing of children. He visits, that is, specially cares for, the son of Adam; He is mindful of frail man. This is the cause of the wonder. But what a revelation it is of the true glory and dignity of man. Because of this, man is in dominion over all the creation, and by reason of this, God is able to find a stronghold against His adversaries in the language of childhood. We have still to say with the writer of the letter to the Hebrews: "We see not yet all things subjected to him." We do see the greatness of man as we see the interest of God in him; but we have never yet seen man realize his greatness. But, with the same writer, we may say that we have seen Jesus. In Him we have had the full revelation of the greatness of man. But we have seen more than that. We have seen Him "crowned with glory and honour, that by the grace of God He should taste death for every man." That vision creates our confidence that man will at last realize the Divine purpose.

Let the nations know themselves to be but men.—*Psa.* 9. 20.

This whole Psalm is a mingling of praise and prayer. The singer celebrates the righteousness of God's government of the nations, and prays for its continuance. This closing petition is a great one. The word for men emphasizes the fact of the inherent weakness and frailty of human nature. The previous Psalm was occupied with the dignity and greatness of man, but that dignity was seen to consist in his capacity for relationship with God. Apart from the realization of that relationship, man is weak and frail indeed. Power belongeth unto God. The nations are always in danger of imagining that it is resident in themselves. To do that is to forget God, and as the singer has declared: "The wicked shall be turned back unto Sheol, even all the nations that forget God." All human history, the most modern as well as the most ancient, witnesses to the truth of this declaration. What prayer, then, can we pray which is of more vital importance than that the nations may know themselves to be but men? Such knowledge must drive them to dependence upon God, and such dependence is the secret of national strength, and of national prosperity and permanence. When men discover that they are but men, it is always the result of the revelation of God, and that always means the discovery of God's thought of man, of His purpose for him, and of His care for him. In right relationship with these facts, nations march invincibly to the realization of all their highest possibilities. These are the lessons which God, in His government of the world, is ever seeking to teach man. In proportion as they are learned, humanity's problems will be solved, its wounds healed, and its prosperity secured.

Why standest Thou afar off, O Lord? —*Psa.* 10. 1.

How often the men of faith have asked that question! Let us at once say that the supposition is inaccurate. God never stands far off. This fact was rediscovered to the singer in the course of his song. Its final movements celebrate the knowledge and the persistent government of God in righteousness. The question arises when for the moment the eyes are fixed upon circumstances. It was so in this case. As the singer contemplated the conditions in the midst of which he was living, he saw everywhere might triumphing over right, he watched the cruelty of evil men against the poor and the needy. It did seem as though God had withdrawn Himself, was standing afar off. We have all lived in hours when, if we saw nothing but the conditions, we were constrained to the same question. The value of a Psalm like this is that it records that mood of the soul, only to lead us on to witness this man's recovery of faith and confidence. It was impossible that God did not know and see; and that conviction became the guarantee of the soul's confidence that He not only saw, but would act. Hence the assurance that there must come full and final victory over all the forces of unrighteousness, with the ending of all oppression, and cruelty, and wrong. Under the rule of God, the day must come when, "That man who is of the earth may be terrible no more." These were the concluding words of the song, and they constitute a fitting answer to its opening enquiry.

If the foundations be destroyed, what can the righteous do?—*Psa.* 11. 3.

That is the final appeal of the man who lives by sight to the man who lives by faith. It has the ring of reasonableness, but it is utterly wrong. The idea is not open to question. If the foundations be destroyed, the righteous are helpless. But the question which the supposition makes imperative is: Are the foundations destroyed? The Psalm is the song of a man who was apparently in grave danger. His friends saw the danger, and urged him to flee. His enemies were all around him, and they were not giving him a fair chance. Their methods were those of subtlety and treachery. To these men of sight, the foundations were destroyed. The whole song is a protest against that misconception. The singer had another vision. To him the surrounding circumstances were not foundations. He saw God, enthroned, watching, acting. To him this was the one foundation. This foundation could not be destroyed. Therefore there was no need for flight. How constantly that which boasts itself as reason, is most unreasonable. True reason takes all quantities into account before it makes its calculations. To reckon with circumstances and to leave God out of count, is to omit the principal factor in any and every situation. What unutterable folly to confuse scaffolding with foundations! And yet that is exactly what men do when they imagine that because circumstances do not seem to be propitious, therefore flight is necessary. To see God is to know that the plastic dance of circumstance is as surely under His control as is the clay. That is the secret of courage.

The words of Jehovah are pure words; as silver tried in a furnace on the earth, purified seven times.—*Psa.* 12. 6.

The Psalm is burdened with the singer's sense of the darkness of the circumstances in the midst of which he found himself. On every hand he was conscious of dishonesty, deceit, and the power of evil. The song opens and closes on this note. But its heart consists of an affirmation of faith in God. This faith fastens upon what God has said; and upon the fact that the words of God are pure words. That is to say, that God is a God of Truth. The affirmation is intended to put the words of God into complete contrast to those of the men who "speak falsehood," who speak "with flattering lip and a double heart." The figure employed is of the strongest. Silver purified seven times has in it no trace of alloy. So are the words of God. This is ever the sure resting-place of those who know God. Over and over again, hours have come which have seemed to be characterized by the ceasing of godly men, by the failure of the faithful from among the children of men. In all such hours the soul may rest assured as to the issue; for the Word of God has clearly declared the will and purpose of God to be that of the triumph of good over evil, of truth over falsehood, of righteousness over every form of wickedness. The Word of the Lord is the Word of Eternal Truth; it abideth for ever. In it there is nothing of dissimulation, duplicity, deceit. It is never void. It must accomplish that which He pleases. Here, then, is our place of quietness and confidence, whatever the appearances of the hour may be. The Word of Jehovah is not to be tested by them; but they are to be tried by the Word of Jehovah.

I will sing unto the Lord because He hath dealt bountifully with me.—*Psa.* 13. 6.

This is the final note in this Psalm. What a contrast it is to the opening note: "How long, O Jehovah? Wilt Thou forget me for ever?" The song is a most glorious one, in its revelation of the progress of a soul from overwhelming despair to highest exultation. Examine that progress. In the Hebrew arrangement there are three strophes, and these reveal the stages of experience. In the first (verses 1 and 2), the sorrow of the singer is evident; God is apparently idle and indifferent; no help is found within; the enemy is triumphant. In the second (verses 3 and 4), the singer is in prayer, and the prayer is characterized by complete honesty and daring urgency. In the third (verses 5 and 6), sorrow is submerged in singing, prayer gives place to praise. What a wonderful revelation of God all this affords! The only explanation of this complete change of tone in the song is the fact of God, in Whose presence the man poured out his heart. Let us observe what the song thus reveals of God. First, His tender and understanding patience is seen, as He listens to the complaining of His servant. Then His power is manifested, as He attends to the prayer of the troubled one, and evidently answers it in a spiritual revelation—for this must be the explanation of the sudden ascent of the singer to the mountains of praise. Thus finally He is revealed as glorified in the confidence in Himself; which in honesty complains, in earnestness prays, and at last in a great assurance praises. Let the whole Psalm teach us that the place to discuss our sorrows is in the presence of the King; and that there we may be honest. He will transmute the dirge into a pæan.

The fool hath said in his heart, There is no God.—*Psa.* 14. 1.

In this declaration, which is cause, and which is effect? Does atheism result from folly, or folly from atheism? It would be perfectly correct to say that each is cause and each is effect. The words describe a vicious circle. Folly denies God, and the denial leads back to folly. When we remember, however, that the Hebrew word here rendered "fool" has a moral note and refers to wickedness rather than weakness of intellect, we are constrained to the view that the meaning of the singer was that immorality is the outcome of atheism. When, for whatever reason or by whatever method, a man says in his heart that there is no God, he becomes a fool, that is a vile person. This is ever so. All wickedness is the result of the denial of God. The denial of God which produces wickedness is the denial of the heart. Honest intellectual agnosticism does not necessarily produce immorality: dishonest emotional atheism always does. The heart is the realm of desire. When a man desires to be rid of God, of His government and interference, and out of that desire formulates a denial of God, the process is in itself immoral, and the issues are bound to be immoral. There is no realm of personality which needs more vigilant guarding than that of desire. Its power over the intellect and the will is amazing. It is capable of completely clouding the intelligence, and capturing the volition. It is possible for a man to yield himself so completely to desire, as to be able to persuade himself that he really does believe what he wants to believe, and thus to set his will free for all evil choices. Thus again the vicious circle is revealed, of an atheism springing out of immoral desires, and proceeding to immoral activity.

He that doeth these things shall never be moved.—*Psa.* 15. 5.

The Psalm opens with an inquiry addressed to Jehovah, as to who are worthy to be His guests, and to dwell in the place consecrated by His presence. It closes with this enlarged and emphatic statement that, given the fulfilment of conditions, a man may be not only a guest of Jehovah, but in such continued fellowship as to be in continued prosperity. Rotherham very literally and very beautifully renders this line. "He that doeth these things shall not be shaken to the ages." The conditions are carefully set out between the opening inquiry and the closing affirmation. The first is that of personal character in harmony with the character of God, righteousness in work, and truth in word. The second covers the ground of relative life. The man who is the guest of God must maintain right relationships with his neighbour. These are important considerations. While, through Christ, our right of access to God, and of maintained fellowship with Him, is created by grace, and founded upon justification by faith, apart from any works of ours, it must ever be remembered that justification is unto righteousness, and grace is the inspiration of truth. Any thought of justification which approaches the idea that it means excuse of sin, or hiding of uncleanness, is utterly unwarranted and wholly pernicious. Through justification God has put righteousness at our disposal. We must not continue in sin, that grace may abound. Grace is entirely holy. It demands holiness. Our comfort is that it does more: it makes

holy. That creates our responsibility. To continue in sin is to frustrate the very purpose of God in grace. To do that is to be excluded from His tent, to be shut out from the holy mountain.

I have no good beyond Thee.—*Psa.* 16. 2.

This is the first Psalm headed "Michtam." There are five others (56–60). The meaning is obscure. Thirtle says: "The term, Michtam, seems best explained by a *personal* or *private* prayer or meditation." This one is attributed to David, but nothing can be said decisively as to the time of its writing. As a whole it is a song of exultant confidence. In its · opening petition the consciousness of danger is revealed, but this is the occasion for a glad confession of assurance in the deliverance of God. Whoever wrote it, and under whatever circumstances, its final value is that it is distinctly Messianic. Peter (Acts 2. 25–31) and Paul (Acts 13. 34–37) not only quote it in reference to our Lord, but argue its Messianic intention. The words we have emphasized reveal the deep secret of this holy confidence. The singer declared that he knew no well-being apart from God-Jehovah, as his sovereign Lord. Only of our Lord Jesus Christ, as an expression of unvarying experience, was this ever true. The will of God was His delight, His meat, His one and only passion: and that as surely in His death as in His life. Therefore, to quote Peter: "It was not possible that He should be holden of it" (that is, death). The measure in which, through His infinite grace, we are enabled to say in very truth, "We have no good beyond Thee," is the measure in which—whatever the perils opposing us, or the apparent calamities overtaking us—we may also be confident in the deliverance of God. In life, and all its experiences, through death itself, we shall be delivered and brought to His presence, in which is fulness of joy, and to His right hand, where are pleasures for evermore.

As for me, I shall behold Thy face in righteousness; I shall be satisfied, when I awake, with Thy likeness.—*Psa.* 17. 15.

These words have been constantly employed as referring to an experience beyond the present life, to the awakening beyond death. There is certainly nothing wrong in such an application of them, but it is equally certain that the Psalmist had no such thought in his mind when he wrote them. The whole song is a contrast between two. ways of living in this world: that, on the one hand, of those who are godless: and that, on the other hand, of those who fear God and seek His ways. In these closing words the singer gave expression to the deepest things in his life. His supreme desire was to behold the face of Jehovah in righteousness, and to be conformed to the Divine likeness. Is not that still the supreme passion of all believing souls? And this the more so, seeing that God has lifted His face upon us in the Person of His Son. Our only satisfaction is that of being conformed to the image of His Son. It is granted that such satisfaction will only be complete in that glorious morning when He "shall fashion anew the body of our humiliation, that it may be conformed to the body of His glory"; but we greatly miss the mark when we persistently postpone experiences which may be ours in a measure even to-day. "Blessed are the pure in heart, for they shall see God," not tomorrow and in heaven only, but now, and all along the dusty and difficult highways of this world.

With the merciful Thou wilt shew Thyself merciful.—*Psa.* 18. 25.

This is the first of four statements, all of which reveal the same principle, viz. that the attitude of God towards men is created by their attitude towards Him. The man who, responding to the Divine compassion, is himself compassionate, finds God ever compassionate toward him. The man who is perfect—that is, completely devoted—will find God faithful to him. The man who purifies himself will discover the purity of God. The man who is perverse—that is, the man who crosses the purposes of God—will find God at cross-purposes with him. Let it be well noted that neither of these men escapes from God. That is an eventuality which the Bible never concedes as being possible. Every man lives and moves and has his being in God. In the hand of God, every man's breath is—even that of Belshazzar, foul with drink and obscenity. That which is possible to man is, that he can and does create his experience of God. The perfect man finds God faithful to His covenant: the perverse man finds Him froward. It is at least suggestive that this particular statement of principle occurs in the Psalm which celebrates God's deliverance of David out of the hand of Saul. The story of these two men forms a remarkable illustrative commentary on the declarations. In all the deepest things of his life David had been merciful, perfect, and pure. Saul from the beginning had been perverse. David had been delivered in the mercy and perfection and purity of God. Saul had been rejected and cast out by the frowardness of God. In God's dealings with men, the balance of justice is perfectly maintained, both in His mercy and in His wrath.

O Lord, my Rock and my Redeemer. —*Psa.* 19. 14.

The last verse of this Psalm is dedicatory. It may have applied, and probably did to the song itself, but also without any doubt to the whole life of the singer, in view of the facts celebrated in the song. This final description of God is in harmony with the facts celebrated in the Psalm. The first movement had to do with the glory of God, as revealed in the order of nature. The second was concerned with the grace of Jehovah as expressed in His revelation of Himself in His Law. In the first, God is seen as *El*—the mighty One. In the second, He is seen as Jehovah—the One becoming to man what he needs for recovery and renewal. In the first, His essential Deity is recognized. He is the Rock. In the second, His attitude and activity in Love is discovered—He is the Redeemer. The singer realized the merging of these two facts in the One Whom he worshipped. The mighty One Whose glories are seen in the day and in the night is the One full of grace. Therefore the glories of His power comfort the soul. The God of grace, full of compassion, is this very Mighty One. Therefore the trusting soul is full of courage. If our Rock were not our Redeemer, we should be without hope. If our Redeemer were not our Rock, still might we be afraid. It is good that we never forget the mutual interpretation of these two revelations of God. We live amid the things which talk to us day and night of the might of God. Let us ever remember that this is the God Who towards us is full of gentleness and most tender compassion. We live in the unveiling of that compassion in redemption. Let us never forget that this redemption has in it all the strength, the ability of the Mighty One. He is our Rock, and our Redeemer.

They are bowed down and fallen: but we are risen, and stand upright.— *Psa.* 20. 8.

This is the language of faith, not after the battle, but before it. The whole Psalm consists of a prayer for the king as he goes out to meet his enemies in conflict. In the first five verses the voice of the people is heard, praying for their king. In one verse (6), the voice of the king is heard, affirming his confidence that the prayers of his people will be heard. Then again the voice of the people is a song surveying the field, and exulting in the coming victory (verses 7 and 8). Once again the song becomes a prayer (verse 9). The secret of this confidence is discovered in the contrast presented in the preceding verse. On the one hand are seen those who depend upon chariots, upon horses—that is, upon material strength. On the other are seen those who find inspiration in the Name of Jehovah their God—that is, who depend upon spiritual forces. To such a conflict there can be but one issue. Already the men of faith see that issue, and celebrate it thus: "*They* are bowed down and fallen: But *we* are risen and stand upright." Faith is rational confidence. That is to say, that when the true balance and proportion of things is apprehended, the reasonableness of the conviction is self-evident, that God in goodness and purity and beneficence must triumph over material forces ranged on the side of evil, impurity, malevolence. But faith is rational in another sense. It is not only so in its intellectual apprehension, but also in its volitional surrender. Faith has only one anxiety and that is to be found ranged on the side of God. When that is so, it can know no fear.

Be thou exalted, O Lord, in Thy strength; so will we sing and praise Thy power.—*Psa.* **21. 13.**

By common consent this Psalm is the companion to the preceding one. It is its sequel. There, the people prayed for the king as he was about to go forth to battle, and affirmed their faith in the coming victory. Here, they celebrate the victory won, and offer their praises to Jehovah. In this closing stanza, two things are set in relation to each other, those namely of the exultation of Jehovah in His strength, and of the songs of His people. The strength of man is ever found in the joy of Jehovah, that is, in the ways of life which are pleasing to Him. It follows that the songs of men which come out of pure joy are ever created by the victories of the strength of God. Test the songs of men by this standard. Songs have been written in celebration of unworthy and even of positively evil things. They all fail in the ultimate quality of pure joy and perfect poetry, however finished their art may appear to be. The songs which celebrate the victories of the pure, peaceable, pitiful strength of God, are the true poetry, even when their art is crude, for they give expression to the real and final joy of life. The strength of God is ever active towards the realization of all the best and most beautiful in life. It is for ever opposed to the things which blast, and produce ugliness. Therefore it creates the true joy of life, which must ever be the inspiration of poetry, the source of true songs.

"Then let our songs abound,
    And every tear be dry;
We're marching through Immanuel's
    ground,
To fairer worlds on high."

I will declare Thy name unto my brethren: in the midst of the congregation will I praise Thee.—*Psa.* **22. 22.**

It has become utterly impossible for the Christian believer to read this Psalm in any other connection than that of Messianic values. For such, there can be no question that, whatever may have been the personal experiences calling it forth, the singer was singing better than he knew. While giving utterance to actual experiences, he was voicing deep and profound matters, the fulness of which came in the experiences of the Saviour of the world. This is demonstrated by the fact that in the supreme hour of His passion, our Lord actually quoted the opening cry of this great song of anguish. If, then, we have here, in the interpretation of the Holy Spirit, some insight into the things of that full and redeeming sorrow of the Son of God, let us carefully note whereunto that sorrow moved. With the words we have quoted, the song merged into the strains of triumph, and these run on to the end. Thus we discover the real value of that very sorrow. Through it, and only through it, could the Name of God be declared, and His praise be made known. Through those sorrows alone, could righteousness be established, and man be brought to the realization of all the loving purpose of God for him. As this song came out of human experience, so it may be appropriated by men. We recognize, as we have said, that its full value is only found in the experience of the Lord of life and glory. Yet in fellowship with Him, we may take our comfort from its revelation, that travail ever leads to triumph. The measure in which it is given to us to have fellowship in His suffering, is the measure in which we may rest assured of fellowship in His victory.

The Lord is my Shepherd.—*Psa.* **23. 1.**

That is not only the first statement of this song, it is its inclusive statement. Everything that follows interprets the glory and sufficiency of the fact thus declared. When this is said, all is said. Whatever may be added, is only to help us to understand the fulness of this great truth. An adequate interpretation of this affirmation demands a recognition of the fact that in all Eastern thought, and very definitely in Biblical literature, a king is a shepherd. This is the supreme song in the Psalter concerning the Kingship of God in its application to the individual soul. Other songs set forth the wonders of His Kingship of the nation, and over all peoples. There are only two persons in this Psalm, Jehovah and the singer—save where enemies are referred to. The personal note is immediately struck—"Jehovah is MY Shepherd!" This eternal King, ruling over all the universe, is also the direct, personal, immediate King of every individual soul. When this is recognized, the glory of the song is discovered. It is a revelation of the nature and method of the Divine government of the individual life. Pondered in this way, the Psalm becomes a beautiful interpretation of that wonderful phrase of Paul—"The good and acceptable and perfect will of God." Under His sway there is no lack. Our peaceful days He creates. If we wander, we are not abandoned. In the darkest hours He is still with us. He upholds us and delivers us in conflict. He entertains us on the pilgrimage, and receives us into His house for ever. All the uttermost of value in this song has been interpreted to us through Him Who said of Himself, "I am the good Shepherd."

The earth is the Lord's, and the fulness thereof.—*Psa.* 24. I.

That is the fundamental note in the music of this song. Everything which follows must be interpreted by its message. If this Psalm was written—as it most probably was—for the occasion when the ark of God was taken into the city of the great king, and placed in the tent which David had prepared for it, the singer saw in that ceremony the symbol of greater things. These first words affirm the sovereignty of Jehovah over the whole earth. Everything is His by creative right. Then, some moral deflection, some necessity for the exercise of executive power, is recognized by the questions as to who shall ascend into the hill of Jehovah. The answer to the question constituted a revelation of the fact that the government of the earth must be established on a moral foundation. The One Who is described, is set forth wholly in the matter of character. Let this be carefully considered. The passage of the description from the use of the singular pronoun to that of the plural, merely sets forth the fact that the generation to be associated with the One must conform to that character. The song immediately returns to the contemplation of the One, Who is now designated the King of Glory. His glory is that of those moral excellencies already described. In these He is "strong and mighty in battle." By this strength He passes to the place of power: in this might He overthrows all His foes: and gains, or regains, His true and rightful place of rule over the earth, and the fulness thereof. The holiness of the King is at once the secret of His strength in government, and the principle of His might in redemption.

Yea, none that wait on Thee shall be ashamed.—*Psa.* 25. 3.

This is not a petition, as the King James' version rendered it, but an affirmation of confidence. It is the first of a series running through the song, and for that reason I have emphasized it. The whole song is the prayer of a soul burdened with a sense of need, and pouring out the tale of that need before God. Its atmosphere, however, is that of complete confidence and of assured faith. This affirmation, and those like it which follow, reveal this fact. The movement of the Psalm is that of alternation between petitions and expressions of complete certainty about God. Thus it becomes a pattern prayer for the children of God in all circumstances of need, whether that need is created by the opposition of foes, or by personal wrongdoing. In such case the soul may come to God, and in His presence speak of the burden which rests upon it. It may do so, however, with every assurance, on the basis of the faith which, after all, is the deepest thing in its experience. This exercise of the affirmation of faith is of the greatest value. How often, under stress of difficult circumstances, we are liable to superficial thoughts about God, and about ourselves, which tend to produce despair. In such hours it is good resolutely and persistently to turn in upon one's own deepest convictions about God, and positively to avow them. Such exercise will open the door of release from the gloom which ever comes from the contemplation of circumstances and from introspection; and lead us out into the light and hope which are always to be found in the presence of God, and remembrance of the truth about Him.

Thy lovingkindness is before mine eyes.—*Psa.* 26. 3.

This Psalm has a note all its own. It is a prayer for justice, on the part of a soul happily conscious of its integrity and uprightness. It is impossible to fix the circumstances under which it was written. Evidently they were characterized by general deflection from the ways of God. The singer was living among evil-doers, and the judgments of God in punishment were abroad. In these circumstances the soul of the righteous appealed to the justice of God for deliverance from being involved in these calamities. The words we have emphasized are those in which we discover the ground of the appeal. He knew and pleaded the lovingkindness of Jehovah. The closing stanza shows that the answer came to him in his faith: "My foot standeth in an even place; in the congregations will I bless Jehovah." The experience is not an uncommon one in the life of faith. There are hours in which the wrong of evil men seems to threaten the safety of those who are endeavouring to walk before God, and who are doing so in the measure of their understanding of His will. In such hours, we may with confidence make our appeal to God for vindication and deliverance, and we may do so with complete assurance, in the light of His lovingkindness. To retain our attitude of loyalty to God under circumstances of difficulty created by the evil ways of godless men, is to enable us to claim His vindication and protection, on the ground of His unalterable lovingkindness. Prayer on these grounds will ever guard the heart against panic.

Lead me in a plain path.—*Psa.* 27. 11.

This Psalm is the song of a soul in danger. In its first movement that danger is recognized, but the singer is confident in God. He celebrates in language of great beauty the certainty of his triumph. It is not prayer, but praise. Then there is a sudden change. The confidence is not abandoned, but the consciousness of the danger becomes more acute, and the supposition arises that the face of God might be hidden. Under stress created by this thought, prayer takes the place of praise, and the singer pours out his petitions. Among them this one occurs, that he may be led in a plain path. The simplest meaning of the word rendered *plain*, is level, or even. The words immediately following, "because of mine enemies," help us to catch the real thought of the petition. The word *enemies* is rendered by Thirtle "watchful foes," and that exactly conveys the idea. It is that of enemies lying in ambush, waiting to catch him unawares, to attack him treacherously. The plain path for which he asks is one, travelling along which there shall be no pitfalls or lurking places for these foes. This is a prayer we may all pray. It is not a request for an easy path, a smooth highway. That would be a selfish and unworthy prayer. It is rather a prayer that the way may be such that we may discover with clearness, and in which we may not be surprised by those who are set upon our destruction. The song ends with the singer's counsel to his own soul, and it is characterized by the highest wisdom. To wait for Jehovah is ever to find the plain path, however rough that path may be.

My Rock.—*Psa.* 28. 1.

Here, these words, "My Rock," are directly synonymous with the title Jehovah, and they constitute a proper name. The figurative idea has emerged before in these songs (see 18. 2 and 31). In this case the figure is positively employed as a designation for God. This, then, may be an excellent place at which to pause and consider the suggestiveness of the title. It is the one figure which in the realm of Nature suggests abiding strength and immutability. The story of the rocks, as we are able to read it, is the story of the complete victory of principle over passion. At last the fixed is reached, the unchangeable, and so the ultimate in strength. It is a remarkable fact that in all the Old Testament literature, "rock" is reserved as a figure of Deity. It is used for false gods as well as for God, but never for man. The only apparent exception is that in Isaiah, when the prophet declared that a man shall be as a shadow of a rock in a weary land. But when the Messianic value of that passage is recognized, this is proved to be no exception, but rather a prediction incidentally of the deepest fact concerning the Person of the Messiah. All this should be in mind when we consider the words of our Lord, in which He declared that He would build His Church on Rock. To return to the Psalm. Observe how this conception of the character of God as the immutable One, gave this singer perfect confidence in the midst of grave perils, and inspired his prayer for his people.

In His temple everything saith, Glory.—*Psa.* 29. 9.

This is in very deed a glorious Psalm It is an interpretation of a storm in application to life. We must carefully note its structure. Verses 3–9 describe the storm. The first two verses constitute a call to the Elim, the sons of the mighty—whether angels or men—to render praise to God. The last two verses give the reason for this call to praise. Jehovah has been seen sitting as King above the storm, and so revealing the fact of His Kingship over all the storms and upheavals of life. If verses 3–9 be read with the eye upon the map of Palestine, it will be seen that the storm gathered over the Great Sea, and burst upon the land in the north, striking Lebanon in its fury. Then it swept southward, shaking the wilderness of Kadesh. From beginning to end the noise of the storm is the Voice of the Lord, and the activity thereof the putting forth of His might. These particular words end the picture of the storm, and declare the conception of the tempest obtaining in the temple. There, "everything saith, Glory!" That song of the temple produces the triumph-song of those who dwell upon the earth where the tempests sweep. Their fury is not uncontrolled: "Jehovah sat as King at the Flood," and "Jehovah sitteth as King for ever." In this confidence we know that He will give us strength—that is, to endure the storm; and that He will bless us with peace—that is, following the storm, and as the outcome of it. How much this Psalm has to say to us about the tempest-tossed years through which we have lived! Let us "ascribe unto Jehovah the glory due unto His Name." Let us "worship Jehovah in holy array."

I said in my prosperity, I shall never be moved.—*Psa.* 30. 6.

This is a common blunder made even by men of faith in hours when circumstances are those of ease and comfort. All is as we desire it to be. We have found a place of pleasant situation in which to live, and work of delight which to perform. And, indeed, all this under direct Divine guidance. Herein is a peril. We are tempted to confide in circumstances rather than in God. Then comes the rough awakening. In the case of the singer it came through sickness which led him to the very gates of death. It may come to us thus, or in many ways. The pleasant place has to be left. The work in which we delighted is taken from us. All our plans based upon our prosperity, are shattered. Is there then anything that is not moved? Yes—read the next verse: "Thou Jehovah, of Thy favour hadst made my mountain to stand strong." The mountain is the stronghold of the dwelling-place of God. That, is never moved. In that we may dwell securely, when all our temporary dwelling-places are taken from us. In abiding fellowship with God, kept in His will, and keeping there, we shall be delivered, not from disturbance and upheaval, but through these very things, from more disastrous perils—the real perils of those deflections from loyalty, which destroy the soul. Confessedly the lesson is not an easy one to learn, but it is of vital importance. There is only one sure resting place, and perfect security for the soul of man, and that is found in the heart of God. To dwell there is to cease to trust in circumstances and to be delivered from depending upon them in any way.

For Thy Name's sake, lead me and guide me.—*Psa.* 31. 3.

Rotherham has suggestively said: "This Psalm might very well be described as a mosaic of misery and mercy." It opens with an affirmation of confidence, and closes with praise and exhortation to the love of Jehovah. In its process, we find ourselves in the presence of varied and multiplied afflictions. Throughout, the sufferer is confident in God, and pours out his soul before Him in appeal for succour and deliverance. In these words we have the statement of the soul's argument with God, the revelation of the ground upon which the appeal is made. The activity of God is sought for the sake of His Name. It is a plea that God will be true to the revelation which He has made of Himself, in the Name by which He has made Himself known. Every name of God was suggestive, and spoke of His greatness in might and majesty and mercy. For the honour of that revelation the singer sought the help of this God. The words strike the very deepest notes in the secret of true life. It is that of desire for the honour of the Name, and that is desire for the glory of God. The appeal is constantly discovered in the Bible. It was for the honour of the Name of God that Moses was concerned in the memorable hour in which he prayed for mercy upon a people who had grievously sinned. Our Lord, in His intercessory prayer, spoke of the manifestation of the Name of His Father as the great work which He had accomplished in the case of the men whom He had gathered about Him. We are ever warranted in urging this plea in our praying; but in doing so we must remember that the revelation of God by His Name, and that superlatively when the Name is JESUS, is

such as to make claims upon us. Those being recognized and yielded to, this plea is always the one which prevails.

I said, I will confess my transgressions unto the Lord; and Thou forgavest the iniquity of my sin.—*Psa.* 32. 5.

This is the second of the seven Psalms which are usually called Penitential. (The others are 6, 38, 51, 102, 130, 143.) It is one of the greatest songs in the Psalter. In it, human experience is vividly revealed. Sin, sorrow, and ignorance are all expressed; and their inter-relationship is recognized. It is a Psalm of penitence, but it is also the song of a ransomed soul rejoicing in the wonders of the grace of God. Sin is dealt with; sorrow is comforted; ignorance is instructed. The fundamental matter is that of sin, and the power of the song is created by the contrast it makes between the soul hiding sin, refusing to acknowledge it, and that same soul confessing it. While there was continuance of silence on the part of the sinner, the hand of God was heavy upon him, and his life was withered. When the confession was made, that sinner found the heart of God, and life was healed, and songs took the place of sighing. These words which are emphasized reveal the Divine heart in the most wonderful way. In them God is set forth radiantly as "a God ready to pardon." Note carefully that when this man *said* he would confess, God forgave. So ready is He to pardon, that He does not wait for the actual and formulated expression. The yielding of the will, the decision of the soul, this is what He seeks. Directly He finds it, His forgiveness is granted, and the soul is restored to the consciousness of communion. This is finally illustrated in the teaching of Jesus. The father's kisses were upon his returning boy, before any word of confession was uttered. It was upon the bosom of his father that he gave expression to the confession already made in his will. Such is our God.

For the word of the Lord is right; and all His work is done in faithfulness. —*Psa.* 33. 4.

This Psalm is patently a sequel to the preceding one. It is a response to the call to praise with which that closes. It starts exactly upon the same note, and continues to the end upon the same strain. In these words the reason for praise is inclusively declared, and everything which follows is in illustration of the truth so declared. The reason, then, for praise is that of the perfection of God in word and in work. His word is right: and His work is ever in faithfulness—that is, it is consonant with His word. That idea persists throughout the song. The illustrations cover a wide area. First, there is reference to the principles of His government (verse 5). Then to the might and majesty revealed in creation (verses 6–9). Then to His active overruling in national affairs (verses 10, 11). Then to His special government of His own people (verses 12–22). In all this we find the true secret of our confidence, and so of our joy. The word and the work of God are ever one. His word never returns to Him empty—it accomplishes that which He pleases; it prospers in the thing whereto He sends it. How significant it is that amid the sacred mysteries connected with the Incarnation, the Angel said to Mary concerning the birth of Jesus and of John: "No word from God shall be void of power!" God has given us His word. Let us never forget that His work will be according to that word. To rest in that assurance is to be perpetually inspired to praise.

I will bless the Lord at all times.— Psa. 34. 1.

It is impossible to escape from the feeling of surprise when this Psalm is studied, if first the title has been read. The title is as follows: "A Psalm of David; when he changed his behaviour before Abimelech, who drove him away, and he departed." The record of that event is found in 1 Sam. 21. There does seem to be incongruity between David feigning madness to save his life, and this exalted outpouring of praise to God as the Great Deliverer. As a result of this apparent incongruity, most modern commentators dismiss the title as spurious. But is that action warranted? Is it not rather a perfect revelation of the state of soul into which a man would be brought, when he found himself delivered, not only from the foes he feared, but also from his fears (see verse 4), and so from the necessity for the supremely unworthy expedient to which he had resorted in the case referred to? After David left the court of Achish, he went to Adullam. For a time he was there alone, at least until his brethren and his father's house went down to him. It is easy to understand how, in the quietness and solemnity of that cave of refuge, he recovered, and that with new power, his sense of the Divine care and wisdom and might and sufficiency. So he sang, and his song commenced: "I will bless Jehovah *at all times*." In itself it was a resolve to remember and rejoice in his God continually. Such remembrance and such rejoicing must ever make impossible the necessity for the resort to the methods of unworthiness. So the song is not only a glorious expression of praise, which is available to us. It is that, but it is also a corrective, reminding us ever that our gladness in our God should save us from the expedients which are unworthy of Him, and so of those who are His.

Say unto my soul, I am thy salvation.—Psa. 35. 3.

This Psalm in its entirety is an appeal for help in the midst of circumstances of cruel and unjust persecution. The sense of wrong is most keen from beginning to end. Those who were causing his sufferings had not only no cause to do so, their action was that of base ingratitude. The Psalmist's sense of wrong found expression in the prayer to God to visit the evil-doers with summary and complete vengeance. These particular words, found early in the song, constitute a clear revelation of the state of mind of the singer. So trying were the circumstances, so poignant the pain, that he was at least in danger of losing his assurance in God. Hence the plea that God would give him the inward sense of certainty: "Say unto my soul— I am thy salvation." It was a request for a renewing or strengthening of the inner communion with God, which is ever the secret of strength in days of turmoil and of sorrow. How constantly we are driven to cry out thus to God! It is the reasonable cry of faith, and it is safe to say that is always answered. When the pressure of circumstances is such as to create the sense of weakness to such an extent that we feel in danger of collapse, then we need some reinforcement within, stronger than the pressure from without. This is ever to be found in communion. The human side of communion is that of this very prayer for the speech of God, direct, immediate, and reassuring. The Divine side is that of the answer. Whenever in extremity the child of God thus cries out to the Father, that answer is given. Sometimes the very voice is heard, sometimes a light suddenly shines, sometimes a great silence which is of the essence of strength enwraps the soul. Whatever the method, it is God, reassuring, comforting; and in the strength of it, the soul stands up bravely against all the outside pressure, and at last is more than conqueror.

O continue Thy lovingkindness unto them that knew Thee.—Psa. 36. 10.

Thus opens the prayer with which the Psalm closes, and it is the natural and restful conclusion to the contrast preceding it. That is a contrast between the man who lives without the fear of God, and the God in Whom the righteous man is trusting. The description of the evil man is graphic. He has by some means persuaded himself that God does not interfere with men. Consequently he has no fear of God, enthrones himself at the centre of his own being, and goes in the way of wickedness in thought and in action. The contrast is not between that man and the man who fears God, but rather, as we have said, between that manner of life and the conception of God which inspires the contrary way of life. God is set forth in His lovingkindness, in His righteousness, in His faithfulness, in all His goodness to men. The prayer is for the continued manifestation of that lovingkindness to those who know this God. Thus the contrast becomes personal. On the one hand are the men who have no fear of God. On the other are those who know Him. The difference is radical, and all the life is affected. To lose the fear of God is to go in every way of wickedness, and ultimately to inevitable destruction (see last verse). To know God is to worship Him, and in His ways to find refuge, satisfaction, life, and light. In the ultimate words of Jesus: "This is life eternal, that they should know Thee 'the only true God, and Him Whom Thou didst send, Jesus Christ."

Fret not.—*Psa.* 37. 1.

This sharp and definite command is a fitting introduction to the whole Psalm. The problem with which it deals is that of the apparent prosperity of the wicked. It is an ancient and also a modern cause of much disquietness. The ways and works of wickedness do seem to be prosperous, and those who are pursuing the ways of rectitude are often perturbed by this fact. In this Psalm the singer calls upon all such to think again, and to set all the appearances of the hour in the light of the truth about God, and in the light of Time. God is governing, and that in the interest of those who are walking in the ways of righteousness. Those who trust in Him, delight in Him, commit their way to Him, and rest in Him, are always vindicated and delivered. The test is found in Time. All the apparent prosperity of the wicked is transient; it passes and perishes, as do the wicked themselves. The reward of those who know and obey Jehovah is sure and permanent. Retribution and recompense are under the Divine control. There can be no escape from the one, in the case of the wicked; and no failure of the other, in that of the good. Therefore, there is no need to fret—to worry—to be incensed and perturbed when the way of wickedness seems to be the way of prosperity. Presently the singer repeats the charge, and adds the significant statement that such fretting tends to evildoing (verse 8). There is nothing more pernicious than the sense of irritation caused by narrow outlooks upon life. The prevention and the cure of such irritation is ever that of a true knowledge of God, and the consequent calm and confident appeal to Time. In its march, God and righteousness and the trusting soul are always vindicated.

O Lord . . . O my God . . . O Lord.—*Psa.* 38. 21, 22.

This is the third of the Penitential Psalms (the others are 6, 32, 51, 102, 130, 143). I have stressed these words in the concluding portions because they reveal the deepest value of this song. It is the cry of a soul in bodily agony and mental anguish, which he recognizes as the result of his own transgression, and therefore does not rebel against. It is, however, the cry of such a soul to God, and its movement shows his knowledge of God, and how in his dire need he is casting himself upon that God in all the fulness of the knowledge which he possesses. The first movement speaks of his personal sufferings both bodily and mental; and is addressed to Jehovah (see verse 1). The second movement describes the attitude of friends and foes; and this is addressed to the Sovereign Lord (Adonai, see verse 9). The last movement is that of the prayer for deliverance, and is addressed to both Jehovah and Adonai as God-Elohim (see verse 15). In this final appeal the three names are found again. Here is a wonderful unveiling of the refuge and hope of the penitent soul. It may expect succour in personal suffering from God, for He is Jehovah, the One full of grace. He may expect justice in regard to men, for God is the Sovereign Lord. He may look for complete deliverance, for Jehovah, the Sovereign Lord, is the Mighty One. If Jehovah forsaketh not; if the Mighty One remains nigh at hand; if the Sovereign Lord makes haste to help—then is there salvation for the penitent soul. And all this is what has been made for ever certain to sinning men in Christ Jesus the Lord.

Lord, make me to know mine end, and the measure of my days, what it is; let me know how frail I am.— *Psa.* 39. 4.

This was not a prayer inspired by a desire to know when life would end; it was not a request to be told the date of death. It was a prayer for an accurate apprehension of the fact that life quantitatively—that is, as to the number of its days—is as nothing. This is clearly seen in the sentences of meditation which follow (verses 5, 6). Then, however, a new note was introduced into the song: "And now, Lord, what wait I for? My hope is in Thee." Here is a revelation of the quality of life, as opposed to mere quantity. The attitude described is the one of ultimate strength and realization. It is that of hope in God. That is life, in which desire and expectation are centred in God. Such life is of an entirely different quality from that in which desire and expectation are centred in self, in circumstances, or in men. Such life is characterized by the approximation of effort, and so of character, to the things of God: holiness and righteousness; justice and truth; compassion and grace. If a man live in this qualitative consciousness, quantitative considerations as to life are conditioned thereby. They are entirely unimportant as a measure of life. The time element is cancelled very largely. But they are of great importance as preparatory to the stages which are yet to come. Every day lived in hope centred in God is rich and full. Every such day is contributing something to all the days yet to come.

He hath put a new song in my mouth.—*Psa.* 40. 3.

This is what God is always doing for those who can say with the singer of this song: "I waited patiently for Jehovah." In this case the reason of the song in all probability was that of the deliverance of David from all the long experience of outlawry and suffering; and the fact that he had been brought to his coronation. The whole song reveals at once the sense of the cruel things through which he had passed, and the fact of the Divine thought of him and care for him. Through these experiences, moreover, he had learned the true secrets of life, and of kingship. He had suffered at the hands of Saul, who had failed in life and kingship. That David had understood that failure, is revealed in a comparison of the word of Samuel to Saul (1 Sam. 15. 22), and verses 6, 7, 8 in this Psalm. The quotation of these words as finding their fulfilment in God's anointed King-Priest (see Heb. 10, 5. 6), emphasizes the fact that David had learned the secret of true authority. Thus the inspiration of the new song was gained in the experiences of suffering. It is always so. The suffering servant of God always becomes the singing one. For, as the secret of song is ever that of waiting for God, doing the will of God, in and through suffering, the result is always deliverance, and the issue a song. We need to guard against the tendency to despair and murmuring in days of trial and darkness.

Blessed be the Lord, the God of Israel, From everlasting and to everlasting. Amen, and Amen.—*Psa.* 41. 13.

The English reader has gained much in the study of the Psalms from the fact that the Revisers have restored the Hebrew divisions of the selection into five Books. There is no doubt that the editing, by whomsoever done, was carefully done, and that in each of the five books there is a dominant idea. In each case this idea is revealed in the Doxology with which the Book ends. The editor—possibly and even probably Hezekiah—may have written this Doxology himself. The verse we have taken is the Doxology with which the first Book ends. Kirkpatrick is certainly right when he says: "This doxology is, of course, no part of the Psalm, but stands here to mark the close of Book I."

The prevailing Name of God found in this collection is Jehovah. The songs have set forth in varied ways all that this Name meant to the men of faith. Thus the Doxology utters the praise of Jehovah, Who is the God of Israel. It recognizes the all-encompassing sweep of the Divine government and grace in the words: "From everlasting to everlasting." It declares the assent of man to this fact, in the concluding double: "Amen, and Amen." The word *everlasting* in the Hebrew means the vanishing point. The idea is that the God of Israel is Jehovah from the past which is beyond human knowledge, to the future which is equally so. Rotherham's rendering is very fine: "Blessed be Jehovah, God of Israel. From antiquity unto antiquity. Amen, and Amen." To us the great truth is made more clear in the words of Jesus: "I am the Alpha and the Omega." In that sense of the eternity of our God, and of the eternity of the things concerning Him unveiled in His Son, is the secret of our songs.

My soul thirsteth for God, for the living God.—*Psa.* 42. 2.

This whole Psalm is the song of a soul in trouble; but in the midst of the trouble the singer is speaking to himself in strains of determined hope. In these particular words we have at once a revelation of the uttermost experience of sorrow, and a revelation of the inspiration of hope. Sorrow is always a sense of lack. The sorrow of bereavement is the sense of the loss of the loved one. The sorrow of sickness is the lack of health. The ultimate sorrow is the sense of the lack of God. This was the supreme sorrow of this singer. All his personal suffering was accentuated by his inability to find his way into conscious fellowship with God. The thirst for God is the most terrible thirst. Nothing can assuage it. Thus the cry of anguish is the expression of hope. That is the one and only hope in the hour of this suffering. To find a way back to God, to come and appear before Him is the only cure for the intolerable thirst. Let it, then, be clearly recognized that the chief value of this song is its revelation of God Himself. Even though this troubled soul had lost his sense at the moment of fellowship, he knew God, and, in the midst of the anguish, believed that God would appear for his deliverance. Apart from this knowledge there would have been desire, but no hope. It was his knowledge of God which touched desire with expectation, and so created hope.

Let them bring me . . . Then will I go.—*Psa.* 43. 3, 4.

That Psalms 42 and 43 are intimately related, is conceded, and is perfectly patent. Indeed, there are those who treat them as one song. A comparison of verses 5 and 11 in the first, with verse 5 in the second, reveals the thrice-repeated refrain in which the singer challenges his soul as to its sorrow, and affirms his confidence in God. Yet there is a distinction. The first reveals a need and a confidence. The second reveals the supply, and shows the way to its appropriation. The way to the realization of hope is, first, that of the leading of light and truth shining forth by the action of God; and second, that of the going of the soul in such light and truth. The going of the soul in light and truth is described as a going first to the altar, and ultimately to God its exceeding joy. The way to God is ever the way of the altar. The way to the altar is opened by the sending out of light and truth from God. The spiritual illumination of this singer of the olden times fills us with wonder. For us, all has its interpretation in the One Who of Himself said: "I came forth from God," "I am the Light," "I am the Truth." This cry of humanity in its sorrow, voiced by the Hebrew Psalmist, God answered when He sent out Light and Truth in His Son. He erected for us the altar by which we find God, and so find exceeding joy.

All this is come upon us; yet have we not forgotten Thee.—*Psa.* **44. 17.**

These words introduce us to the very core of this song. It is a prayer for Divine deliverance from disaster and suffering, which are not caused by the sins of those who are involved therein. The hosts of the people of God had been defeated in battle, and had become the objects of scorn and contempt of their enemies, notwithstanding the fact that they had been loyal to God. Opinions vary as to the historic event to which reference is made, and we need take no time discussing that matter. The arresting fact is, that here is a song revealing an experience of defeat and humiliation, and consequently of suffering, for which no cause is to be found in the conduct of the sufferers. Other songs there are in which we discover the recognition of the reason of suffering to be that of the sins of the people. They are penitential, and contain confession. In this, the claim to have been true is central. It is, therefore, a song inspired by experiences which have been known to the people of God in all ages. Paul quoted from this very Psalm when he was thinking of the forces which assault the soul, and declaring that none of them is able to separate us from the love of God (Rom. 8. 35). Thus we are reminded of the fact that those who are the people of God are called upon to endure suffering for which there is no explanation at the time, and certainly none in their own disloyalty. Such sufferings are part of the high and holy privilege of fellowship with God.

Things . . . touching the king.—*Psa.* **45. 1.**

The beauty of this Psalm is universally recognized. It is always treated as celebrating a royal wedding. The title refers to it as "A Song of Loves"; Rotherham gives "A royal marriage," as descriptive title: and Kirkpatrick calls it "A nuptial ode." All these descriptions are justified by the context. Nevertheless, its supreme note is given in the words we have emphasized. The first verse consists of the writer's introduction to his song, and in these particular words he gives us the subject on which he wrote. He was speaking of "Things . . . touching the king"; and there is more in the Psalm than the wedding. Here again opinions differ as to the particular king to whom reference was made. From the earliest times it has been considered as definitely Messianic; and that by Jewish, as well as Christian expositors. In that way we may study it most profitably. What, then, are the things touching the king which it celebrates? We will endeavour to tabulate them: (1) His beauty and grace of character (verse 2). (2) His equipment and purpose in conflict (verses 3, 4). (3) His power in conflict (verse 5). (4) His victory, and consequent enthronement and glory (verses 6-8). (5) His consort, her devotion, her beauty, her companions (verses 9-15). (6) His seed-royal, reigning in the earth (verse 16). (7) His complete triumph (verse 17). Perhaps nowhere in Old Testament writings do we find a nearer approach to the disclosure of the secret of the Church than in this Psalm. It remained, however, a secret (see Eph. 3. 4, 5; Col. 1. 26, 27). For us, in the light of the complete unveiling of God's plans and purposes through Christ, this song is full of beauty and value.

God is our refuge.—*Psa.* **46. 1.**

This is the first of three Psalms which are intimately related to each other. They all refer to the Divine relation to the Holy City, and set forth the consequent security of its citizens. The three phases celebrated may thus be stated: Psa. 46, God as a Refuge; Psa. 47, God as Ruler; Psa. 48, God as Resource. As to the first, its wonderful power is revealed in the constancy of its use by the people of God. In our own days of strain and calamity, perhaps no other song has been more constantly employed than this. Its note is that of complete and daring courage, resulting from the assurance of what God is in Himself, and the consequent sense of the security of those for whom He cares. It opens with figurative language, as it describes convulsions of the most terrible known in Nature, those of the earthquake and tempest, and declares that these cannot produce fear in the hearts of those who know God. Suddenly it introduces the picture of the City of God, gladdened by the river proceeding from the dwelling-place of God. Then outside, the nations are pictured in tumultuous upheaval. Over all God is reigning, commanding the tumult to cease, and declaring His determination to be exalted. The whole song is the result of the vision of God. That is the vision which gives the heart steadiness and strength at all times. To lose that vision is only, sooner or later, to have nothing left to look upon but storm and tempest, wreck and ruin, the anger and the brutality of the massed forces of iniquity. To retain it, is still to see these things; but it is to see them all under His government, and to discover that they also are compelled to serve His purpose.

God is the King of all the earth.— Psa. 47. 7.

That tremendous truth is the burden of this song. Whereas, in the previous Psalm, the central thought was that of God as a refuge for His own people; here, the Word of God recorded in the tenth verse of Psalm 46 is seen as triumphant, and the outlook is wider. The whole earth is in view. The song opens with a call to all the nations to recognize God as King. His own people are still in view as those through whom His power is to be demonstrated, but He is seen as reigning over all the nations. The princes of the nations are referred to as "the shields of the earth," and they are declared to belong unto God. All this is a subject for our most careful thought. There are times when we are at least in danger of interpreting the reign of God as wholly in the future. There is a sense in which that view is warranted. We have been taught to pray for the coming of the Kingdom. But there is a sense in which God is now King of all the earth. He reigns in absolute sovereignty and power. Neither nation nor individual escapes from that sovereignty, or from the compelling pressure of that power. But this fact does not satisfy the heart of God, and it ought not to satisfy us. He desires to reign by the consent of the governed. He would establish His authority upon the understanding of the peoples. Observe the appeal of the words: "Sing ye praises with understanding."

This God is our God for ever and ever.—Psa. 48. 14.

In Psa. 46 the singer rejoiced in God as a Refuge, and celebrated His presence in the City as the sure guarantee of her security. In this he dwells upon the beauty and security of that City, which is thus protected by the abiding presence of God. After exulting over a deliverance wrought in the hour of dire peril, the song proceeds to dwell upon the exceeding wealth of the resources which a people so delivered have

in such a God. In a pregnant sentence this is stated: "Thy right hand is full of righteousness." This is the secret of the sufficiency of His people, whatever calamities threaten them, or whatever leagues of kings and armies are formed against them. The right hand of God is the emblem of His power. That right hand is full of righteousness. That is to say, that God is a God able to secure to those whom He governs all things that are right and good. There can be no breakdown in His ability, and there can be nothing unworthy in His rule. Therefore those who trust in Him find complete resource in Him. At last, at the close, not of this Psalm only, but of all the three, the note of complete joy and satisfaction, of rest and of realization, finds expression in these words: "This God is our God for ever and ever." That is perfect praise, for it passes far beyond the realms of theory, as it tells of experience.

For the redemption of their soul is costly, and must be let alone for ever. —Psa. 49. 8.

These words constitute a parenthesis. The singer breaks in on a statement with this exclamatory declaration. It reveals the working of his mind. The interrupted statement is contained in verses 7 and 9. If these be read in connection, it will be seen that the statement is that no wealth is sufficient to secure exemption from death. The parenthesis emphasizes this in a yet profounder statement as it recognizes that life itself needs redemption quite apart from the question of materials or bodily death. This is why no man can prevent himself, or his brother, from physical dissolution. The life is already forfeited, and its redemption is costly, so costly that there is no hope of any being able to pay the price—it "faileth for ever." All this leads on in the song to the great affirmation of faith: "But God will redeem my soul from the power of Sheol; for He will receive me." In spiritual apprehension this is a most wonderful Psalm. It is quite possible that this old Hebrew singer sang better than he knew; but it is certain that gleams of the final light were breaking through on him. Moreover, it is evident that he was conscious of the greatness of the thing he sang, in that he commenced by calling all people, of all classes, to listen.

God even God hath spoken.—Psa. 50. 1.

This Psalm is highly dramatic. The first six verses constitute a prologue descriptive of the coming of God to judge His people. Of that prologue this is the introductory sentence, and it is the key to the Psalm. The main movement is that of the record of two speeches of God.

The first (verses 7-15) is in condemnation of formalism. The second (verses 16-21) is in condemnation of hypocrisy. All ends with an epilogue (verses 22, 23), emphasizing the teaching of the Psalm. The first sentence has certainly lost something of its force by translation. We are helped if we transliterate rather than translate. Then the sentence reads: "El, Elohim, Jehovah hath spoken." Thus three names are employed. El stands for the might of God simply and absolutely. Elohim, the plural form, intensifies that idea; and in use always connotes the wisdom of God as well as His might. Jehovah is the title by which He is ever revealed in His grace. This, then, is the God Who speaks, and the things said have ultimate authority, and irresistible appeal, when this is remembered. This is the meaning of the words in the epilogue: "Now consider this, ye that forget God." Let us then lay to heart the things that God says in this Psalm. He condemns the formalities of religion, when men neglect to offer the sacrifices of praise, and cease to pray. He condemns the hypocrisy of those who repeat the words of His law, and violate its teaching in their dealing with their fellow-men. Formalism is a sin against God. Hypocrisy is its outcome, a sin against man, and so still against God.

Have mercy upon me, O God.— Psa. 51. 1.

This, is the fourth of the Penitential Psalms. (The others are 6, 32, 38, 102, 130, 143.) Of the seven it is central, and it is the greatest in spiritual power. The heading gives us the occasion of its writing, and thus we are enabled the more accurately to follow the working of the mind of the sinner. The whole song is a clear revelation of his consciousness that sin can only be dealt with by God. No plan is urged. From beginning to end the song is prayer, petition following petition. It is the cry of a soul who can have no hope except in the mercy of God. In it, too, the truth about sin is revealed. The three words are used: transgression, iniquity, and sin. The first recognizes sin as definite rebellion against God, and so involving guilt. The second reckons that sin is perversion, and so involving pollution. The third realizes that sin is failure and so involving ruin. The standard by which sin is known is that of the soul's relation to God, and therefore in the last analysis this penitent uttered a tremendous truth when he said: "Against Thee, Thee only, have I sinned." Yet again the consciousness of the sinning soul as to its own need is clearly manifested. The penitent asks that sin may be blotted out; that he may be washed, cleansed, made pure, purged with hyssop. The need is for infinitely more than forgiveness, as we are able to extend it to our fellow-men. It is for complete deliverance from the pollution of sin. This great song, pulsating with the agony of a sin-stricken soul, helps us to understand the stupendous wonder of the everlasting mercy of our God. Calvary is God's answer; and it is enough.

Why boastest thou thyself in mischief, O mighty man? The mercy of God endureth continually.—Psa. 52. 1.

In that opening question, and the immediately following assertion, we have the key to the whole of this song. The first part of it describes the mighty man and his action (verses 2-5); while the second part describes the security of the man whose trust is in God (verses 6-9). On the one hand a man is seen who by reason of his wealth and material power is vaunting his ability to encompass his own malicious purposes against a good man. Miles Coverdale rendered this phrase, "O mighty man," as "Thou tyrant," and thus gave an accurate interpretation of the kind of man this Edomite, Doeg, really was. The singer sees the folly and futility of his boasting, because he has clear vision of one great fact, that, namely, of the enduring mercy of God. This is the one and all-sufficient answer to all fear which may be caused by such evil men, when they seem entrenched in certain material strength. Over against that strength of wickedness the mercy of God is eternally operative. The rest of the song shows how much more there is than pity in the mercy of God. It is fierce and forceful: "God will likewise destroy thee for ever; He will take thee up and pluck thee out of thy tent, and root thee out of the land of the living." That is the activity of mercy. Mark the contrast in the case of the man trusting in the Lord. He says of himself: "I am like a green olive tree in the House of God."

There were they in great fear, where no fear was.—Psa. 53. 5.

We have found this song already in Book I (Psa. 14). Its repetition here is of great interest in the light it throws upon the editing of the collection. A comparison of the two will show how in this case Elohim has been substituted for Jehovah in harmony with the general usage in this second Book. The main theme of the songs is identical. Some slight alterations show how a great song may be adapted to meet the need of some special application of its truth. The words we have emphasized give us an illustration of this. In Psa. 14, the words are: "There were they in great fear." Here the addition of the words, "where no fear was," is explained at once if we see in this form of the song an application to the departure of Sennacherib's army (Isa. 37. 7) and its ultimate annihilation (Isa. 37. 26). There indeed were men filled with fear, where there was no natural cause for fear. The words are very suggestive. The fear of God is often thrust upon men suddenly and terrifically, when they have no apparent cause for fear. Such fear is nemesis, and is destructive. There is only one way in which man can be delivered from this fear. It is that of beginning with the fear of Jehovah, and ordering all conduct in the guidance thereof. The fear of God is either an impelling motive, leading in the ways of life; or it becomes a compelling terror, issuing in destruction. To fear God, is to be rightly related to the ultimate fact of the universe. To say in the heart, "There is no God," is to neglect that fact, and sooner or later to discover it in a destructive fear.

The Lord is of them that uphold my soul.—Psa. 54. 4.

The title of this Psalm relates it to the days when David was being persecuted by Saul, and the Ziphites basely betrayed him by discovering his hiding place to his enemy. It is a real song of faith in that it first appeals for the help of God; and then confidently affirms that such help will be forthcoming. The words which we have chosen for emphasis are arresting. Expositors seem anxious to modify them. One says, for instance, that this does not mean that God was "as one upholder among many, but Chief Mover and Upholder of them all"; and another suggests that we render: "The Lord is the Upholder of my soul." Now both these things are true, but there is no need to try and escape the plain meaning of the statement, which is accurately conveyed by this translation, and perhaps even more forcefully rendered by Rotherham thus: "My Sovereign Lord is among the upholders of my soul." The title used of God was Adonai, with the distinct meaning thus expressed by Rotherham—"my Sovereign Lord." The statement recognizes the help of human friends, but accounts for it by the presence among them of God, Who as Sovereign Lord guides and commands them. A reference to the story itself (1 Sam. 23) tells how Jonathan went to David "in the wood and strengthened his hand in God," even before the treachery of the Ziphites. Here, perhaps, is the secret of this song of faith. Through Jonathan, David was strengthened in God. In his song he recognized the overruling of God in the action of his friend. It was a true recognition. God acts through our friends.

Cast thy burden upon the Lord, and He shall sustain thee.—Psa. 55. 22.

These are wonderful words, and their constant use by the people of God shows how great their value, and how profound a philosophy of life they contain. This becomes the more remarkable a word when the burden of the singer is borne in mind. Kirkpatrick has truthfully said: "Despair, sorrow, indignation, faith find expression by turns in this pathetic record of persecution embittered by the treachery of an intimate friend." A mere selection of some of the words used to describe the consciousness of the singer will help us to discover the weight of the burden—terrors, fearfulness, trembling, horror—these are not soft words. Or again, gather out some of the words describing the conditions giving rise to these things—violence, strife, iniquity, mischief, wickedness, oppression, guile—these are terrible words. Then at the heart of the song occurs one of the most pathetic passages in literature, as descriptive of the most poignant agony. The inspirer and instigator of the trouble was a man, the singer's equal, his companion, his familiar friend. This was the burden. With the weight of it upon him, he yet uttered these great words, and who shall doubt that they were expressive of his experience? To cast the burden upon Jehovah is not to be rid of it, but it is to find One Who carries, sustains the burden-bearer, and so the burden also, in a fellowship of love and might. It always seems to me that a wonderful commentary on this word of the Old Testament is found in Paul's description of his experiences (2 Cor. 4. 7-9 and 16-18). The experience of suffering was not taken away from the servant of God, but he was sustained, and so made strong enough to resist its pressure, and through it to make his service more perfect. This is how God ever sustains us in the bearing of burdens.

What time I am afraid . . . I will not be afraid.—Psa. 56. 3, 4.

The title of this Psalm describes it as having been written by David when the Philistines took him in Gath. It is a revelation of his experiences under these circumstances. He was keenly conscious of the malignant hatred of his foes. They were subjecting him to every form of indignity and cruelty. They were seeking every method to bring about his discomfiture. Indeed, they were set upon securing his destruction. He was equally conscious of God. His wanderings were known to Him. His tears were written in His book. He was naturally fearful for his safety in the midst of such enemies; yet his faith refused to be overcome. The song is a record of the fight between fear and faith, and ultimately of the victory of faith. The two things find expression in these two brief sentences. The fear was there, for he said: "What time I am afraid." Faith was also there, for he was able to say: "I will not be afraid." The second word was the result of the action of faith in the midst of fear. It was an act of the will, based upon the activity of reason. The "I will trust" in the hour of fear led on to the "I will not be afraid." This is a song full of comfort in its recognition of the possibility of fear, and of the way of complete triumph over it. The heart of man is frail at its strongest, and there are hours in which the forces against us inevitably suggest that sense of weakness, and thus create fear. In such hours let us exercise our reasoning powers to the full, for that is the true activity of faith.

My heart is fixed, O God, my heart is fixed: I will sing, yea, I will sing praises.—*Psa.* 57. 7.

Fixity of heart is the secret of songs. The idea of this word, *fixed*, is that of being erect; that is, of being stable. It is well to remember that the thought is not that of someone clinging in desperation to someone else who is stronger. There are times when that is exactly what we do. Here, however, the conception is that of a soul strong and courageously facing all the calamities of life because related to the ultimate things of life. The whole Psalm falls distinctly into two parts. In the first, the soul is seen as to its hiding-place in the day of calamity. In the second, the exulting song resulting from its position is heard. Observe the two environments of the singer as they are revealed in the first part of the song. The first is described in the first verse: "My soul taketh refuge in Thee; yea, in the shadow of Thy wings will I take refuge." The second is described in verse four: "My soul is among lions; I lie among them that are set on fire." Under the shadow of the wings of God the heart is fixed, erect, stable, notwithstanding the fiery fierceness of the foes who are exerting all their strength to bring about the destruction of the soul. In such fixity is the inspiration of glad and exulting praise. Here the deepest ·thing in the life of fellowship with God is manifested.

Verily, there is a God that judgeth in the earth.—*Psa.* 58. 11.

The theme of this Psalm is that of judgment, not as punishment merely, but in the broadest and truest sense of true government. Its first movement is that of an invective condemnation of those who are governing wrongly, whose methods are those of wickedness and violence, and who are deaf to the appeal for justice. The second movement is a passionate appeal to God, the final Judge, to sweep away these false judges, so that they may no more misgovern men. The last movement is a confident affirmation that this is the very thing which God will do, and a statement of the result, that by such action men will be brought to know that there is a God that judgeth the earth. The sorrows of humanity multiply under false systems of government, whether they are autocratic or democratic. There is only one hope for man, namely, that they are brought to the hour when they

shall say: "Verily, there is a God that judgeth in the earth." How slow men are to discover this fact and to yield themselves to it! And how persistently God moves towards the compelling of that conviction! How have we seen Him breaking the teeth of the oppressor, and weakening all the strength of the evil governors! Nevertheless, man sees slowly, and even yet is in dire peril of setting up other false methods of government. Every method is false which fails to reckon with God. Our confidence is in Him, and in the assurance that He will never abandon man to his folly, but will bring him at last to right relationship with Himself.

O my strength, I will wait upon Thee: for God is my high Tower.—*Psa.* 59. 9.

This is the refrain with which the first part of the Psalm closes. The second part closes with the same refrain, with slight variations. It runs thus:

Unto Thee, O my Strength, will I sing praises:
For God is my high Tower, the God of my mercy.

In each case the thought of God in the mind of the singer is that of His strength, and of the fact that He is a high tower or place of refuge and retreat to the soul in trouble and danger. In the first refrain, the singer declares his determination, in view of these facts, to give heed to God. In the second, in view of the same facts, he offers the sacrifice of praise, because this God of strength is the God of mercy. Our reading of the whole Psalm reveals the mercy of God which caused the praise of this soul. It was that of His destruction of workers of iniquity, bloodthirsty men. The circumstances of the singer, as suggested by the title, are revealed in 1 Sam. 19. It was a day when Saul was determined to destroy David. His intentions and his methods were of the basest. The men who were his agents were utterly unscrupulous. Their evil character is carefully described in this song. While such men are at large and unrestrained, there can be no security for godly men. The character of God demands that such should be severely judged, and indeed destroyed. In such retributive government the mercy of God is seen.

Thou hast given a banner to them that fear Thee, that it may be displayed because of the truth.—*Psa.* 60. 4.

This is the central light of a great song, revealing the singer's understanding of the true function of the nation. When Amalek fought against Israel in Rephidim, victory came to the people of God as Moses, supported by Aaron and Hur, prayed on the mount and Joshua went forth to battle. After the victory Moses built an altar, and called the name of it "Jehovah Nissi," that is, Jehovah our Banner. That was indeed the Banner of Israel. The nation existed to display the glory of Jehovah before the nations. When, in her appointed warfare against the forces of evil, she was victorious, that Banner was honoured. When she was defeated, it was disgraced. This song was written in a day when the hosts of Jehovah had been defeated. The conception of the meaning of the national life of Israel, revealed in these words, accounts for the anguish of the singer as he contemplated the discomfiture and defeat of the people of God. There was no self-centred pride in the song. The sorrow of the singer was caused by the disgrace to the Banner, by the dishonour done to the name of Jehovah. This conception accounts also for the change in the Psalm to the note of confidence as to the ultimate victory. This sense of responsibility for the truth about God, for the honour of the Holy Name, is the surest guarantee of victory. When the people of God are overcome by the enemies of God, the ultimate tragedy is not that they are disgraced, but that all they stand for is dishonoured. It is because we so often forget this, that we know defeat, and so wrong God. The Church of God is the pillar and ground of the Truth. When she fails, the Truth suffers.

Lead me to the rock that is higher than I.—*Psa. 61. 2.*

This is the song of one who was away from the City and Temple of God. It is conjectured that David wrote it when he was an exile for a time, as the result of the rebellion of Absalom. From that distance, which seemed to him to be the end of the earth, he called upon God when his heart was overwhelmed, and this was the very heart of his prayer. Once more we have the employment of Rock, as symbolic of God, the reference here being to its strength and to its height, as constituting a place of refuge and security. The illuminative phase of this petition is that it puts God as a Rock into contrast with self. These were the words of a man who was supremely conscious of his own insufficiency. From the perils and the sorrows in the midst of which he was living, he found neither help nor hiding place in his own wisdom or strength. Indeed, it may be that he was realizing that bitterest of all experiences, that he had been his own worst enemy, and that the foes he had chiefly to fear were resident within his own personality. Thus his prayer was for elevation above self in God. It was a great cry; and it is one we constantly need to pray. It is only when we find refuge in the Rock that is higher than ourselves, that we are safe from the enemies without or the foes within. There is no such thing as self-sufficiency. Our sufficiency is ever of God.

My soul waiteth only upon God.—*Psa. 62. 1.*

The emphatic word is *only*. Note its repetition: "He only is my Rock" (verse 2); "for God only" (verse 5); "He only is my Rock" (verse 6). Whatever the occasion of its writing, its editorial placing after the one recording the prayer, "Lead me to the Rock that is higher than I," is very significant. That was a cry resulting from a consciousnes of the insufficiency of self, and a confidence in the sufficiency of God as the Rock of refuge. In this the burden is, that the soul finds what it needs in none other than God, and it seems to follow the figure of the Rock in interpretation of the sufficiency which is found in Him. Glance through the Psalm, and the values of God as Rock will be seen radiantly set forth. "My Rock ... my salvation ... my high tower" (verse 2); these same words are repeated (verse 6); "The Rock ... my strength ... my refuge" (verse 7). In view of this, the singer calls upon his soul to be silent only for God, and at last declares the double truth he has learned concerning God. The words, "God hath spoken once, twice have I heard this," might fittingly be rendered, "God hath spoken one thing; two things have I heard." These two things are immediately stated: "That power belongeth unto God; also unto thee, O Lord, belongeth lovingkindness." These are the two things concerning God which had been revealed to his waiting soul, those, namely, of His power and His lovingkindness. Because of these the trusting soul is safe, both with regard to opposing foes and to weakness and failure personally. The power of God is more than the strength of the adversaries; the mercy of God is equal to dealing with all the need of the failing soul. Because God *only* is our Rock, let us ever be silent *only* for God.

My soul followeth hard after Thee; Thy right hand upholdeth me.—*Psa. 63. 8.*

Once more we have a song of the wilderness. The title declares that, and we feel the atmosphere of loneliness and of abounding peril as we read. In these words we have a very striking description of the experience of the man of faith in such an hour. There is first the volitional activity, and then the deep sense of security. The activity of the will is expressed in the words: "My soul followeth hard after Thee." The word "hard" here means close. The thought might be expressed thus: "My soul cleaveth close to Thee." There is the sense of strain, of difficulty; but it is a declaration of resolute action. It is not easy to realize the nearness or presence of God, but there must be no giving up, no relaxing. This is the hour in which to bring all the powers of the being to bear on the one activity of keeping close to God. Then immediately we have a revelation of the sense of the soul in such resolute action. It is that God is near; His right hand is upholding. Indeed, it is by the upholding of that right hand that the soul is enabled to cleave close to God. This is a very valuable word, as it helps us to realize the interaction between the soul's courage and confidence. If the determined maintenance of the attitude of relationship should be relaxed, the sense of that right hand would be weakened. It is equally true that if that right hand did not uphold, there could be no strength for cleaving. The one thing which is certain is that the right hand of God will never fail us. Let us see to it that our cleaving never weakens.

Preserve my life from fear of the enemy.—*Psa.* 64. 1.

The thought of that petition had remarkable illustration in the experiences of our men and boys during the Great War. It is a most arresting and suggestive fact that over and over again, in talking with them of their experiences, they have told us that the one thing they supremely feared was that they should be filled with fear. Generalizations may be somewhat dangerous, but it is almost certain that the fear of fear has delivered these boys almost invariably from fear. And yet is this strange? Surely the fear of cowardice is the very inspiration of courage. This singer was certainly afraid lest 'he should be afraid. And there were causes enough for fear. These first six verses reveal that most clearly. Every sentence reveals the relentless fury and remorseless subtlety and cruelty of the foes by whom he was surrounded. Conscious of all this he had one fear, and that was that he should be afraid of them. The cure of such fear was that of communion with God, and consideration of Him. To remember God, is to see One Who is mightier than all the foes, and moreover, One Who is active against those foes on behalf of His own. This is a prayer we need ever to pray. To fear the foe, is inevitably to be beaten by that foe. To fear to be afraid, is ever to be driven to seek the help of the God Who fighteth on behalf of the trusting soul; and in such seeking is the secret of courage, and the assurance of victory.

Praise waiteth for Thee, O God, in Zion.—*Psa.* 65. 1.

The song was evidently composed to be sung in connection with some gathering of the people in the Temple, and its special notes suggest that the occasion was that of thanksgiving for the co-operation of God with man in the production of the harvest. In any case, it was a song for a festival of praise. These introductory words have caused some difficulty to expositors. Briggs rendered the sentence: "To Thee is recited a song of praise;" and Rotherham adopted this rendering. Kirkpatrick renders it: "Praise becometh Thee," and says that "though prayer may be silent, praise calls for vocal expression." I suggest that here translation is better than either of these attempted interpretations. The word translated "waiteth" comes from a root meaning to be dumb. The idea quite simply is exactly what Kirkpatrick declares to be impossible, viz. that praise is silent before God. This does not mean that there is no praise, but on the contrary that praise is so complete that at first it can find no utterance. Presently it becomes gloriously vocal, but even then fails to express the fulness which compelled the silence. I emphasize this because I am growingly convinced of the tremendous value of silence in the activity of public worship, whether in praise or prayer. In the assemblies of the saints, the sound of a human voice must in some degree tend to deflect attention from God. There must be speech, in prayer, in praise, in prophesying; but its ultimate value is that of preparation for those great silences where the soul is alone with God. The word of Habakkuk is of profound significance: "Let all the earth hush before Him." It was out of his own silence that at last there came the great song of praise.

I will pay Thee my vows.—*Psa.* 66. 13.

This is another song of praise, in two movements. The first is national (1–12), and celebrates a Divine deliverance from trouble, while recognizing that the trouble itself was a part of the Divine method, a chastisement through which the nation was brought into a wealthy place. The second is personal (13–20), and perhaps in it the king, who in the earlier part had spoken of and for his people, spoke of and for himself. The singer had been heard; God had attended to the voice of the prayers he had uttered in the day of his distress. In that day of distress he had made vows to the Lord, and now in the day of prosperity he remembers them and comes into the House of his God with burnt-offerings to fulfil his vows. There is an important principle in these words. The soul of man in hours of distress constantly makes promises to God as to what it will do if He will deliver out of that distress. Such vows are entirely voluntary, and they are not necessary. They do not affect the action of God in the least. Prayer does that, but not vows. But when the voluntary vow is made, it becomes an obligation from which the one making it must not attempt to escape. This was explicitly enacted in the Law. The provision will be found in Leviticus 27. There it is clearly laid down that vows in respect of persons, beasts, houses, fields, are entirely optional; but when made, are compulsory. The life of fellowship with God into which we are admitted through Christ, makes vows more than ever unnecessary. They, however, are not forbidden. Only let us never forget that when made, they must be fulfilled. The reason is not in God, but in us. To fail to keep faith with God is to suffer deterioration of character.

Thy saving health.—*Psa. 67. 2.*

This phrase constitutes a poetic interpretation of the thought of the one word of which it is a translation. The Hebrew word is one, and signifies quite literally, salvation. It is salvation in the sense of deliverance, aid, and so nationally of victory. The conception in its national significance is very beautifully expressed in the phrase, "saving health," of the Authorized Version. The Psalm is a very brief one, but it breathes the very spirit of a clear understanding of the real meaning of the Hebrew nation, according to Divine purpose. Its opening prayer is that God will bless and cause His face to shine upon His own people, in order that His "salvation may be known among all nations." Its closing affirmation is that God will bless His own people, and that as a result, "all the ends of the earth shall fear Him." This is the true interpretation of privilege. The people of God exist for the sake of all the nations. They constitute the illustration of His saving health. Their prosperity is due to His aid, His deliverance, His salvation. The nations, seeing that prosperity, are taught the advantage of His rule. That rule, discovered and obeyed, always produces national health, in all the spacious values of that great word. Health is wholeness, completeness, full realization of possibility, as it is freedom from all diseases, materially, mentally, morally. God alone is able to rule men so as to insure this state of health. His people, then, are called upon to reveal this fact to men, by the health in which they live. What disaster, if by disobedience to the will of God they reveal to men anything less than health! Thus the name of God is blasphemed among the heathen. The privilege is great; the responsibility is grave; the resources in God are sufficient.

He hath scattered the peoples that delight in war.—*Psa. 68. 30.*

The historic relations of this Psalm are obscure, and definite. They are obscure as to the actual time of the composition, and as to the particular events in history which are celebrated. They are definite as to the use which has been made of it by men of faith in the process of the centuries. Kirkpatrick finely says of it: "To the Crusaders, setting out for the recovery of the Holy Land; to Savonarola and His monks, as they marched to the 'Trial of Fire' in the Piazza at Florence; to the Huguenots, who called it 'The song of battles'; to Cromwell, at Dunbar, as the sun rose on the mists of the morning and he charged Leslie's army—it has supplied words for the expression of their heartfelt convictions." To all of this we may add that, during the years of the Great War, perhaps no Psalm, with the single exception of the forty-sixth, was more constantly used. It is pre-eminently the Psalm which celebrates the march of God with His people, against their foes and His, to assured and complete victory. The words we have stressed describe that victory in one application, and in a very remarkable way. The whole song is of war: one is conscious all through of the clash of conflict. Yet it is not a song in glorification of war. God is manifested as the God of battles, but His victory is that He scatters the people that delight in war. He does not delight in it: His purpose is to end it. Here is the true test of the relation of men of faith to war. If the heart delight in war, God will make war the instrument for the discomfiture and defeat of that unholy passion. If the heart hate war, then He will give victory in war to those who thus fight. Whether that end has been reached, it is not for us to say. Certainly the principle had remarkable illustration in 1914–1919.

Let not them that wait on Thee be ashamed through me, O Lord God of Hosts. Let not those that seek Thee be brought to dishonour through me, O God of Israel.—*Psa. 69. 6.*

Here is a Psalm pulsating with pain. The singer cries to God for deliverance from the cruel and evil foes who are persecuting him. He also calls for revenge, in maledictions which to some Christian people seem terrible. In these particular words we discover the deepest note in his suffering, and the reason of his maledictions. His concern was not personal, but relative. He feared lest other believing and loyal souls should be deflected from faith, and dishonoured because of what they saw of his sufferings. Thus his chief concern was for the honour of his God. Let these maledictions be carefully considered in the light of this fact, and it will be seen that their inspiration was that of a consuming passion for the vindication of the righteousness of God, as victorious over all those who rebelled against His government and so insulted His holiness. Nothing in the New Testament revelation proves that this passion was wrong. When it is said that Christ prayed that His murderers might be forgiven, let it be borne in mind that the terms of His wonderful prayer were most explicit. He said: "Father, forgive them, for they know not what they do." That was a prayer inspired by His freedom from all personal vindictiveness. Neither in that prayer, nor in any of His teachings, can we find a word of tolerance for those who do evil, knowing that it is evil. Moreover, as these particular words of the Psalmist are considered, let those immediately preceding them be remembered. In them he referred to his own sin, proving that he realized the relation between his sufferings and that sin. His prayer for deliverance from suffering was, in its deepest value, a prayer for deliverance from sin. His desire for purity was the inspiration of his cry for help and the reason of his appeal for the destruction of evil men.

Make haste.—*Psa.* 70. 1.

These words reveal the mental mood of the singer of this Psalm. They have been supplied by the translators as an introduction, and these must be omitted. They occur, however, immediately; and are repeated in our last verse, and there reinforced by the words, "Make no tarrying." The circumstances were those of suffering, and of that made more poignant by the gloating gladness of enemies, as revealed in their exclamations, "Aha, Aha." The troubled soul knew that help was only to be found in God. His difficulty was that God did not seem to be acting with sufficient speed. He was at least leisurely, when the need seemed pressing; He was not hastening, in spite of the urgency. So it appeared to this troubled heart, and so it has constantly appeared to those who have suffered. One of the supreme glories of the Psalter is that it gives us a song like this, expressing a common human experience, even though it reveals a mistaken conception of God. God never needs to be called upon to hasten. He is never tarrying uselessly or carelessly. Indeed, we may say that often: "Through the thick darkness He is hastening," that is, through the very darkness which makes us imagine He is inactive, or unduly delaying His help. Nevertheless, He understands our cry. We may use any terms in our prayers, if they are directed to Him, knowing that He will understand, and in His understanding, interpret our faulty terms by His own perfect knowledge, and give us His best answers to our deepest need.

When I am old and grey-headed, O God, forsake me not, until I have declared Thy strength unto the next generation.—*Psa.* 71. 18.

This is pre-eminently the song of an old man, and moreover he was still in circumstances of trouble when he wrote it. It is a plea at first for deliverance, and in the course of it the same appeal is made to God to "Make haste." Its dominant note, however, is that of the triumph of faith. He looks back over life, and recognizes the care of God from his birth and through all the vicissitudes of life. That recognition is the inspiration of the prayer for help; and the secret of the note of confidence with which the song closes. The particular words which we have emphasized reveal the true desire of old age. It is that of being allowed to minister to youth. The man who, through long years, has proved God, has a message for those who are facing life. They see but half—as Browning says. It is a glorious half, but it needs the illumination of the whole, lest it should fail. Moreover, there is nothing more calculated to keep the heart of age young, than to stand by the young, sympathizing with their ambitions, heartening their endeavours, and stiffening their courage, by recounting the stories of the strength of God, the experiences of His might. When one is old and grey-headed, there is inevitably a tendency to seek release and rest. Let that last phase of selfishness be guarded against, by the cultivation of comradeship with the young; and then the higher desire will be created, that, namely, of this singer, for continued fellowship with God, in order that service may be rendered to them. There is nothing more pitiful, or else more beautiful than old age. It is pitiful when its pessimism cools the ardours of youth. It is beautiful when its witness stimulated the visions and inspires the heroisms of the young.

Blessed be the Lord God, the God of Israel, Who only doeth wondrous things. And blessed be His glorious Name for ever: and let the whole earth be filled with His glory; Amen, and Amen.—*Psa.* 72. 18, 19.

These two verses stand in separation from the Psalm, and constitute the Doxology with which the second book closes. The dominant name of God in this collection has been Elohim, the name which in itself represents the absolute might of God, and, in its use, associates the activity of that might with His absolute wisdom. It is noticeable that in this Doxology that name is introduced by the great title, Jehovah, thus showing that while the songs set forth principally the wonders of God, they were sung by men who knew something of His grace as that was ever suggested by the title, Jehovah. To that God, this Doxology attributes the doing of wondrous things, and to Him alone; and it resolves itself into an act of worship, expressing the desire that the whole earth should be filled with His glory. Whereas, as we have said, the Doxology must be taken as standing alone, it is fitting that the last song in the collection, the one immediately preceding, sets forth the glory of the government of the world, by this God of wonders, through His own anointed King. Whereas these songs have all been inspired by a consciousness of the might and wisdom of God, they have repeatedly revealed the circumstances of tyranny and oppression under which the people of God have often lived. The last song celebrates the day when under the true Theocratic King, all such as are oppressed, shall be set free, as every form of tyranny is broken.

Until I went into the sanctuary of God, and considered their latter end.— *Psa. 73. 17.*

That is palpably an incomplete quotation, but the method draws attention to the central value of the song. Its first movement is a confession on the part of the singer of how the prosperity of the wicked created a temptation to doubt the goodness of God in government, and consequently, to question the utility of goodness in men. Its second movement sets forth the perfection of the Divine government, re-affirms the faith of the singer, confesses the folly of his suggested breakdown in faith, and declares his determination still to make the Lord Jehovah his refuge. The change in his outlook was created by his going into the sanctuary of God. There, retired from the confusion of circumstances, he was given a corrected view of everything. The one note which these words reveal is; that from the Temple of God, long views of life are obtained. Looking at circumstances only, man necessarily has limited views, he sees only the near. In the Temple, man gains God's view, it is the complete outlook. From thence, he sees the latter end of those who, to-day, are seen as prosperous in wickedness. Their latter end is not one of prosperity, but one of adversity. To be far from God is ultimately to perish: to depart from Him is to be destroyed. For us, necessarily, all this is made superlative through Christ. In Him we have access to the Holiest of All, the inner sanctuary of the holiness and mystery of the ways of God. To enter therein is to be delivered from the folly of interpreting any day by its hours, or any age by itself. There, all is seen in the light of the consummations, and these must harmonize with the character of God.

Yet God is my King of old, working salvation in the midst of the earth.— *Psa. 74. 12.*

"Yet" is sometimes a vital word. It is so here, introducing us to a new realm of facts. In the early part of the song, we have a graphic description of the uttermost desolation. The conditions were actual. All that the singer had said constitutes a statement of facts which were patent. But there was more to be said, and the Psalmist introduced the more by this significant word "Yet". The great declaration is, that in spite of all appearances, God is King, and God is at work in order to salvation. The patent facts were indeed terrible. The Holy Country had been devastated by relentless foes; the Sacred Temple had been desecrated by fire; the City of the King had been reduced to ruins; many of the people had been slain; the Nation had become the scorn of her enemies; all the signs of Divine relationship were obliterated. Things could hardly be worse to the eyes of sight. Then came the declaration of what the eyes of faith beheld. In spite of all these apparent contradictions, God was seen as King, working for salvation. This is ever the victory of faith, and it is the victory of the highest reason. In considering any situation, it is unreasonable to leave out any fact, and it is sheer madness to forget the greatest fact of all. The man of faith is never blind to the desolation. He sees clearly all the terrible facts. But he sees more. He sees God. Therefore, his last word is never desolation: it is rather salvation. The remainder of the Psalm reveals two arguments for the faith of the singer. The one is that of the witness of history to the fact of God's mighty workings; the other is that of the testimony of Nature. To these we may ever add the final argument, that of the revelation of God in Christ.

When I shall find the set time, I will judge uprightly. The earth and all the inhabitants thereof are dissolved. I have set up the pillars of it.— *Psa. 75. 2, 3.*

This is a Psalm of high exaltation, celebrating some victory of God over a proud enemy. The editor of the collection has beautifully placed it next to the one in which the central note was that of the affirmation that in spite of all appearances God is King and at work for salvation. This Psalm celebrates some event wherein that faith was vindicated. Its form is dramatic, and in these two verses the singer gives expression to the truths which had been illustrated by the victory, and he does so in the speech of God Himself. The first statement, "When I shall find the set time, I will judge uprightly," reveals the time and method of the Divine activity. His time is "the set time." That is, He acts, never too soon and never too late. It is a great word. To believe it is to be patient. His method is one of uprightness. In this statement the pronoun "I" is emphatic. Whatever others may do or think, God's judgment is ever upright. The second declaration, "The earth and all the inhabitants thereof are dissolved, I have set up the pillars of it," brings into relationship the same two sets of facts to which we referred in the last note. First, the fact of the upheaval and break-up of all earthly order: and second, the fact of the maintenance of the fundamental things of earthly order by the act of God. There may be apparent and indeed very real dissolution of all human organization and order; but the true pillars of the earth are God-established; and cannot be broken down. This conviction is the citadel of the soul.

Surely the wrath of man shall praise Thee; the residue of wrath shalt Thou gird upon Thee.—*Psa. 76. 10.*

The theme of this Psalm is the same as that of the previous one. It celebrates a victory which God had won on behalf of His people. The singer's chief joy in this victory was caused by the fact that therein God had been made known, and the greatness of His Name proclaimed. This is made clear in the opening stanzas, and it runs through the whole song as the mastertone of the music. In these particular words we have a poetical statement of a great principle. It is a wonderful revelation of God's overruling of evil. The phrase, "The wrath of man," here stands for all that is evil. It refers to the fierce passion of revolt, expressing itself in definite rebellion. Its appalling power has been seen in all the dire conflicts, inspired by evil desire, and unrighteous lust. This singer of the olden time had seen the wrath of man working havoc in human affairs, as we also have seen it. But he had watched closely, and he had seen God, surrounding all its activity by His Own presence and holding it within His Own grasp, and so compelling it at last to work out His Own purpose, and thus to work towards His praise. Then he had seen God, when the limit was reached, restrain this wrath, in the pictorial language of the singer, girding it upon Himself, and so preventing its further action under the will of man. The declaration of this Hebrew singer, from what he saw in his own day, may be applied to all human history. Thus God has ever compelled the wrath of man to praise Him; and this will He do, until He finally gird it upon Himself, a trophy of His victory, a sure sign at once of His power and His love.

And I said, This is my infirmity: but I will remember the years of the right hand of the Most High.—*Psa. 77. 10.*

This verse cuts this Psalm clean in two, and changes its note from the minor to the major. Its first part, "And I said this is my infirmity," summarized all that the singer had said of his own suffering. This suffering had been so intense that he had come to feel that God had forsaken him. The agonized questions of verses 7, 8 and 9 show this. Then suddenly the whole note changes, and the change is brought about by the apprehension of truth revealed in the second part of this verse. It should be observed that the words in italics, "*But I will remember,*" are not in the text; they were supplied by the translators in a desire to make sense. In my judgment it is better to omit them. If we do so, there remains what is virtually an exclamation: "The years of the right hand of the Most High!" That was the truth, the apprehension of which turned the song from a dirge to a psalm of praise. It did not come to the singer as the result of his own volition, but as a sudden illumination. He saw the years, all of them, those of his suffering also, as in the right hand of God. Then he began to make mention, to meditate, to muse, on the deeds, the work, the doings of God. To do that, was to find answers to his questions. The Lord had not cast off; He had not ceased to be favourable; His mercy was not gone; His promise could not fail; He had not forgotten to be gracious; He had not shut up His tender mercies. If the use of the phrase, "The right hand of God" in these Hebrew Scriptures, be considered, the reason of the change in the song will be discovered. If our years are years of His right hand, then all is well, even our sufferings.

That they might set their hope in God, and not forget the works of God, but keep His commandments.—*Psa. 78. 7.*

This Psalm may be described as a poem of history. From verse 9, the singer reviews the history of the people of God, dwelling upon their persistent disloyalties, and the unfailing goodness of God to them both in chastisement and deliverance. All this is a poetical illustration of the principle laid down in the first eight verses. In that first movement, the singer declares that it is the will of God that the story of His dealings with the nation should be taught systematically to the children of each succeeding generation. In these words the reason of this is set forth, as they reveal the effects which such teaching, adequately given, is bound to produce. Under its influence they will set their hope in God, will remember His works, and will keep His commandments. Observe the idea carefully. The immediate is stated last. It is that of obedience to the law of God. In order to that obedience, two inspiring activities are referred to: First, Hope, which has to do with the future; and second, Memory, which has to do with the past. By such teaching of history as sets it in relation to God, hope for the days to come will be centred in Him, and memory will be instructed by His works. This is a wonderful revelation of our duty concerning the young. It is also a key to the true writing of history. History, written as it should be, will always show that all true prosperity comes from God, and that man has no hope save that which is centred in Him. History should ever be the record of the works of God. That is to emphasize the important factor. History thus written, and thus taught, will so affect hope and memory in youth, as to constrain it to obedience to the God revealed; and this is the way of life for man and nation.

Wherefore should the heathen say, Where is their God?—*Psa.* 79. 10.

The circumstances calling forth this song are practically identical with those which produced the seventy-fourth. Enemies had invaded the land, the Temple was desecrated, the city was in ruins, the people were slain, and the nation was the scorn of its foes. In considering that Psalm, we noted the viewpoint of faith. In spite of all the desolation, God was seen as King, working salvation. That declaration of faith is absent from this Psalm, but it is implicated in this word of appeal. The singer sees God reigning and working salvation, but the nations cannot see this. Their only proof of God is that of the prosperity of His people. In the hour of their adversity the nations will say, Where is their God? Here once more, as so perpetually in these holy writings, we see that the supreme anxiety of true souls is for the honour of the Divine Name. The cry of this Psalm is for deliverance from the enemies who are oppressing them and causing them suffering, but its deepest reason is that God should be honoured and vindicated. This is the true note. It is not easy to rise to its level. Selfishness strangely persists in our desiring and our praying. The measure in which it is consumed in a burning passion for the glory of God, is the measure both of our own strength of soul and our ability to co-operate with God in His work.

Turn us again, O God, and cause Thy face to shine, and we shall be saved.— *Psa.* 80. 3.

It is impossible for any student of the New Testament to read this Psalm without consciousness of its spiritual relation to the allegory of the Vine in the Paschal discourse of our Lord. It is not within the province of a note such as this is, to deal with that subject. Suffice it to say that here we have a song written by some singer amid the twilight, which shows how acutely some of these great souls of the past understood the thought and purpose of God in the national life of the Hebrew people; how keenly they realized the failure of that people to understand, or to realize that purpose; and how clearly they saw the only way of realization. All that is a subject for careful study The words we emphasize are those of the refrain. With but slight variation they occur three times in the Psalm: here, and again in verse 7, and in verse 19. First, there must be their turning back, their restoration to God; and that must be by the act of God. Then there must be the

lighting up of the face of God. That is, there must be given to them the clear showing of His reconciled favour. Thus, and thus only, can the failing people be saved. This is true of God's ancient people. It is equally true of the Church, in so far as she has failed to fulfil her calling. Both for Israel and the Church this prayer has been answered in Christ. In Him we may be restored to God. In Him, the face of God is shining upon us in grace.

So I let them go after the stubbornness of their heart.—*Psa.* 81. 12.

This Psalm constituted an introduction to a joyful feast, most probably the Feast of Tabernacles. It opens on the note of joy, and merges into messages of warning. Those later messages interpret the heart of God, as He is revealed as pleading with His people, and sighing over them with longing for their loyalty, for their own sakes. In referring to their disloyalties, to the fact that they had not hearkened to His voice, this word was spoken: "So I let them go after the stubbornness of their heart." It reveals a constant method of God with His disloyal and disobedient children. When they will not go His way, He lets them go their way. But this does not mean that He abandons them. It is rather that He permits them to learn by the bitter results of their own folly what He would have had them know by communion with Himself. How constantly the people of God have gone after the stubbornness of their own hearts only to find sorrow and . anguish; and yet how constantly through that experience they have learned the perfection of the Divine way! This is so, because He is the God of all grace. Nevertheless, His choice for us is that we should hearken to Him, and so be saved, not merely *through* the bitterness of failure, but *from* it.

Arise, O God, judge the earth: for Thou shalt inherit all the nations. —*Psa.* 82. 8.

Such is the prayer with which this song closes. To gather its force we need the whole Psalm. It is a brief but mighty poem concerning justice, the righteous administration of human affairs. Observe its structure. First a brief but luminous description of the ideal (verse 1). Then a protest against the maladministration of the judges with a sentence pronounced upon them (verses 2–7). Finally this prayer. In reading the first verse, we may be helped if we retain the Hebrew words so far as we may, thus: "Elohim, standeth in the congregation of El; He judgeth among the elohim." Here we have the word *elohim* twice, but with differing values. The first is that of the intensive use of the plural, and the word is the name of God. The second is the simple use of the plural, and the word is used of those constituting the assembly of El—that is, of God. It is a singularly radiant picture, this of the final court of appeal. Central to it is God Himself, the One Who judges. Gathered around Him is an assembly of judges who are called elohim, because they are His delegates; they administer His will; they are His executive agents. That is a perfect setting forth of the true way of justice for the world. Read the protest against the judges, who have failed, and thereby know how God judges, and how we may test all human authority. To do so, is to join the singer in this final prayer. When we do so, let us remember that the prayer is already heard, and is being answered; for "He hath appointed a day in which He will judge the world in righteousness by the Man Whom He hath ordained" (Acts 17. 31).

O God, keep not Thou silence. . . . For lo, Thine enemies make a tumult. —Psa. 83. 1, 2.

There is a touch of human nature about this petition which arrests us. The song was written by a man who was very conscious of the isolation of the people of God. He saw them surrounded on every side by implacable foes. Moreover, these foes were united by a common hatred of the people of God, which was a hatred of God Himself. This singer heard the tumult, that is, the uproar of these antagonistic multitudes. He therefore called upon God to answer their noise with His voice. Was he right in this prayer? Yes, I think he was. At least it is so, that there are times when God utters His voice in answer to the raging of the nations; times when He no longer holds His peace, but roars from Zion. There is, however, a difference. The noises of God are never those of tumult, of uproar, of ineffective shoutings. As this singer knew, they are the noises of the fire and the flame, of the tempest and the storm; the noises of effective forces, which destroy and purify, which break down and cleanse. When the silences of God are broken by His noises, men learn that the God of Grace is the Most High over all the earth. We also have heard the tumult of the enemies of God and His people, and we have prayed that God would break His silence. We also have heard the roaring out of Zion, the noises of God asserting Himself in human affairs.

I had rather be a doorkeeper in the House of my God, than to dwell in the tents of wickedness.—Psa. 84. 10.

But of course! We sometimes read this as though there were something heroic about the choice, some touch of sacrifice in the decision. There is nothing of the kind. The singer was a man of profound commonsense. He was choosing the highest, the best. The tents of wickedness have nothing to offer to the man who has a place of any kind in the House of God, certainly nothing to the man who was privileged to have such definite relationship of responsibility as that of a doorkeeper in that House. Let us not forget that this was the song of a Levite. Mark the inscription, "A Psalm of the sons of Korah." The Levites were those who had no possession in the land, because they had special possessions in the service of Jehovah. The writer of this Psalm had peculiar familiarity with the Temple. He had watched it with loving eyes, and seen the birds finding rest and refuge there. He had known the blessedness of dwelling within its precincts. He had also known the bitterness of absence from it. He had experienced the longing for it, the almost fainting for its courts. Restored to it after a long journey through difficult paths, he broke out into this great song in celebration of the glory of that House. In the period of his absence, he had probably been a dweller in the tents of wickedness. There he had found poverty, restlessness, pain. Now, restored to his high and holy service of keeping the door, rendering his service as of the Kohathites in regard to the veils, he affirmed his wealth, his rest, his joy, as he said: "I had rather be a doorkeeper in the House of my God than dwell in the tents of wickedness." The true wealth and rest and joy of life are found in the service of God.

Thou hast turned Thyself from the fierceness of Thine anger. Turn us, O God of our salvation.—Psa. 85. 3, 4.

Rotherham has given a suggestive descriptive title to this Psalm; he says: "Praise, prayer, and prophecy lead up to the reconciliation of earth and heaven." In these words, praise merges into prayer. The note of praise ends with the declaration that God has turned from His anger. The note of prayer begins with the petition that God will turn us, in order that His indignation may cease. This is very suggestive. So far as the will and work of God are concerned, He in grace has turned from His anger, because He has forgiven iniquity and covered sin. But in order to the full appropriation of this activity of Grace, there must be turning on our part, and this first petition in the prayer grows out of the praise inspired by His grace. The truth is further illuminated in the prophetic section of the song. When the Psalmist listens to what God Jehovah has to say, he declares that "He will speak peace unto His people and to His saints; but let them not turn again to folly." In grace God has turned from His anger. That we may appropriate His grace, we must be turned to Him: and then must not turn again to folly. This is the way into peace, into the dwelling of glory in the land, into the harmony of mercy and truth, of righteousness and peace, into the coming of the Kingdom of God.

Unite my heart to fear Thy Name.—Psa. 86. 11.

This Psalm is peculiar in that it is made up almost entirely of quotations from other Psalms. It is singularly individualistic. There are at least thirty occurrences of the personal pronoun in the first person singular. It is a very interesting exercise to read the Psalm rapidly, putting special emphasis upon these pronouns. To do that will reveal the fact that the song alternates between series of petitions and affirmations about God. Let us set this out—First series of petitions, verses 1-4; first affirmation, verse 5; second series of petitions, verses 6, 7; second affirmation, verses 8-10; third series of petitions, verses 11-14; third affirmation, verse 15; final series of petitions, verses 16, 17. The occurrences of the personal pronouns in the first person are all in the petitions. Thus the process of the song is revealed. It is that of a soul in prayer seeking to be brought into personal relation with the great truths about God which have general application. The complete quest of the singer is revealed in the great sentence at the heart of the song: "Unite my heart to fear Thy Name." Here was one who had intellectual apprehension of the truth about God, but who knew that something more was necessary, namely, that the whole personality should be unified in devotion. The method of this song is one which we do well to employ in those hours in which, all other persons being excluded, we wait upon God for the cultivation and culture of our personal life. We may be sincerely orthodox in all our beliefs about God, and yet fail completely to appropriate the resources of His grace and strength. This is only done as the heart is united to fear His Name, and so the whole personality is brought under His sway.

They that sing as well as they that dance shall say: All my fountains are in Thee.—Psa. 87. 7.

In the whole Psalter there is no song more perfect than this in its celebration of the ultimate establishment of the Kingdom of God on earth. The City of God is seen as the metropolis of that kingdom. It is the City of the King and so the City of Law, the City of the Foundation; that is, of *Righteousness*. It is the City in whose citizenship at last shall be enrolled even those who have been the enemies of the people and purpose of God; that is the City of *Peace*. Therefore it is the City which inspires all song and dancing, the expressions of happiness; that is the City of *Joy*. These are the things of the Kingdom of God—Righteousness, Peace, Joy. We have emphasized the climactic word, but let us remember that the fountains of joy spring in the holy mountains, wherein is the foundation of life. In our hymns and in our thinking we have spiritualized this song and made it apply to Jerusalem above, the Mother of us all, and there is a sense in which we are warranted in so doing; but let us not forget that the first application of the Psalm is definitely earthly, and the City it celebrates is a city of men, which yet will be the tabernacle of God, and there is no room for doubt that this City will be the actual Jerusalem of the Holy Land. Wherever men may place the home of the Council of a League of Nations, God has placed it there. There the dream of men will be realized, and that under the rule of our Lord Jesus Christ, God's anointed King.

But unto Thee, O Lord, have I cried; and in the morning shall my prayer come before Thee.—Psa. 88. 13.

That is the secret of the attitude of soul revealed in this song. It is a very remarkable Psalm, and its chief value for us is its tone, its temper. Kirkpatrick says it is "the saddest Psalm in the whole Psalter"; and Rotherham, that it is the "gloomiest and the most touching." Certainly the circumstances of the singer as described are those of the most acute and appalling suffering; and these he sets forth with the vividness only possible to poignant experience. Yet from beginning to end there is no trace of bitterness, no desire for revenge on enemies, no angry reflections on the goodness of God. Rather, the references to God reveal a remarkable sense of His grace and goodness. He is addressed as the God of "salvation"; references are made to His "lovingkindness," His "faithfulness," His "wonders," His "righteousness." While the singer cannot understand the Divine method, and asks his troubled questions, "Why castest Thou off my soul?" "Why hidest Thou Thy face from me?" he nevertheless remains sure of God, and of His grace and justice. The secret of it is that with determination he keeps himself in touch with God, crying to Him, and going out to meet Him at the break of each new day. We thank God there is one such song as this, with its revelation of what results in the character when a soul, in the midst of the most appalling suffering, still maintains the activity of practised relationship with God. We also have met such souls, and their witness to the power of the Divine grace is more potent than any theoretical expositions.

Blessed be the Lord for evermore. Amen, and Amen.—Psa. 89. 52.

This is the Doxology with which the third Book of Psalms ends. In this Book the dominant names of God have been Elohim and Jehovah, the latter predominating. They have all set Him forth as the Mighty-Helper. This final note of praise emphasizes the fact of His grace as helping the needy. In this last Psalm the whole idea of the Book emerges in one great statement: "I have laid help upon one that is mighty" (verse 19); and the whole movement of the song makes the Doxology the more significant. The keynotes of the Psalm are the "faithfulness" and "kindness" of God. Round these all its movements gather, of praise, of prayer, and of lamentation. The first part celebrates the glory of the covenant which God made with His King. The second mourns the failure to realize the benefits of that covenant in the midst of which the singer lived. In this latter movement there is urgency in the prayer that the reproach may be removed, but there is no questioning of the faithfulness of God, nor of His kindness. Thus the soul who has come to a knowledge of God as the Mighty-Helper will worship Him in a perpetual Doxology on the darkest day, remembering His covenant, and being assured that whatever may be the experiences of the moment, in the long issue He will be vindicated. Thus the men of faith render Him ceaseless worship.

Lord, Thou hast been our dwelling-place in all generations.—*Psa.* 90. 1.

This great song, so familiar to us all, is a protest against the dominion of death. As it proceeds it becomes dolorous in its contemplation of the transitoriness of human life. But those who find in it only the dolorous note have surely missed its true thought. The protest against the dominion of death is well founded, in that it begins with this great affirmation concerning the relation of man to God. Addressing Him, not as Elohim the Mighty One, nor as Jehovah, the Helper, but as Adonai, the Sovereign Lord, the singer declares that He has been the dwelling-place, the habitation, the home of man in all generations. He then proceeded to celebrate the timelessness of God. From everlasting to everlasting He is God. A thousand years in His sight are but as yesterday. When the soul has that consciousness of God, and of Him as the home of man, it may contemplate the brevity and trouble of human years with complacency. It will do so in expectation of the morning when His mercy will satisfy, when the work of the hands, even in the troubled years, will be established, as the beauty of the Lord rests upon the workers. When all the lodging-places which man builds for himself are destroyed by the sweeping of the storms; when in themselves the years of life are few and evil—if the soul dwell in God, it has a home of strength, of beauty, of satisfaction.

Therein dwelling, it triumphs over all the things which otherwise would bring despair; and moves on, in conscious power, to face the ages.

He that dwelleth in the secret place of the Most High shall abide under the shadow of the Almighty.—*Psa.* 91. 1.

This Psalm has neither title nor inscription. There have not been wanting those who have held that it also was written by Moses, as was the previous one. Whereas this is mere supposition, it is impossible to escape the sense of relationship between them. It is most likely that some later singer wrote it as a personal testimony to the truth of the former song. *That*, was human and generic; its personal pronouns were plural. *This*, is personal and individual; its personal pronouns are singular. It celebrates the security and satisfaction of the soul homed in God. Moses spoke of God as the dwelling-place, the habitation, the home of man. This singer seems to accept that great idea, and then to speak of the most central chamber of the dwelling-place, referring to it as the Secret Place, and describing its complete security by employing the figure of the mother-bird as he refers to "The Shadow of the Almighty." Moreover, it should be remembered that the true interpretation of this song must be sought in spiritual rather than material experience. Children of God are not always immune from physical plague and pestilence; but they are ever guarded from destructive spiritual forces as they dwell in the secret place of the Most High. As we read this wonderful song of the olden time, we remember how through Christ we are admitted to the closest fellowship with God. In Him, our Redeemer and Lord, we may dwell indeed in the secret place of the Most High.

It is a good thing to give thanks unto the Lord.—*Psa.* 92. 1.

So opens a Psalm which has for its heading the words: "A Psalm, a Song for the Sabbath Day." This one is followed by five others without heading, and it is more than probable that this description applies to the six. Then follows a Psalm headed simply, "A Psalm," and then again one with no heading. It would be wrong to make any dogmatic assertion on the subject, but I suggest that these eight Psalms constitute an octave of perfect praise suitable to the Sabbath Day. In that way I like to read them. Their one theme is that of the Kingship of Jehovah. This first one celebrates the fact that Jehovah is set on high for evermore, and rejoices in the righteousness of His government of the world. I have stressed those opening words, constituting, as they do, an introduction to the Sabbath

Song, whether the one Psalm or the eight. The statement seems an obvious one; no one will be inclined to contradict it. Yet how little we know of this highest function of worship, that of offering the pure sacrifices of praise. Go carefully and thoroughly through the ordinary services of our churches, whether the form be liturgical or what we designate free, or extempore, and note how small a part of them is devoted to the giving of thanks. We speak of our hymn-singing as a service of praise, when the great majority of our hymns merge into prayers or devout meditations. Even the Lord's Supper is often not what it should always be, namely, the Eucharist; that is, simply the Giving of Thanks. I believe that "it is a good thing to give thanks unto Jehovah," and that in its neglect we suffer serious loss.

The Lord reigneth.—*Psa.* 93. 1.

In this brief but glorious song the one truth celebrated in the previous one, is uttered in the finest poetic language. Here is cause for praise, and here is praise which is worthy. Interpretation is almost an impertinence. Let it be done reverently. Observe, then, the facts resulting from the fact, the reign of such a One. The first two facts are those of His majesty and His strength. Therefore the world is safe; whatever disturbances there may be on it, it cannot be moved. Again, His rule is not based upon the changing conditions of a passing hour. His throne and Himself are of all ages, coming up from everlasting, that is out of that which lies concealed from the view of man. Disturbances, did we say? Yea verily, floods have lifted up their voices, and waves; but their liftings up have never reached higher than His throne, or submerged Him, for above them Jehovah is still on high, and He is mighty. His reign, as its way is revealed in His testimonies—that is, His law, His word to men, is sure. Finally, all His reign is in order to Holiness, that true health of life which is the condition for prosperity. Is all this so? Does Jehovah reign? Then let us offer the sacrifices of praise and thanksgiving. He is worthy to receive; and in our giving, there is also the receiving of the benefits of His reign which enrich and glorify our lives.

The Lord knoweth the thoughts of man, that they are vanity.—*Psa.* 94. 11.

This Psalm also is one of praise, but its note is entirely different to the previous two. In Psa. 93 the singer is looking above and beyond the conditions of the hour, and offers praise because Jehovah reigneth. In this he is looking at these conditions and they are such as to seem to contradict the declaration that Jehovah reigneth. The people are oppressed by tyrants who declare that God is not concerned with the affairs of man. He does not see, nor consider. The singer knows the falseness of these declarations, and his song is the argument for his conviction that God does hear, and see, and correct. He summarizes all in this statement, that "Jehovah knoweth the thoughts of man, that they are vanity." In this song we see how the very things which assault faith, and threaten to produce despair, may be made the opportunity for praise, in the place and act of worship. In the long history of the travail and conflict of faith, how constantly have faithful souls been strengthened to bear and endure, by this very exercise of praise! In catacombs, in dungeons, in places of the uttermost desolation—when it has seemed to sense that the way of God was blocked, that His rule was overcome, that all evil things had gained the victory—these songs have arisen, proclaiming Him King, mocking all the vain and foolish thoughts of man, and declaring His ultimate victory. Thus God has been to such souls a high tower, their rock of refuge, and they have found the strength and courage which have enabled them to endure, in this activity of worship by faith.

O come, let us worship and bow down; let us kneel before the Lord, our Maker.—*Psa.* 95. 6.

In this song, praise merges into admonition. The theme is the same: "Jehovah is a great God; and a great King above all gods." His greatness is illustrated in two ways. First, its manifestation is seen in the natural order; the earth and the sea are witnesses. It is manifested also in His creation of the nation, and the relation He bears to it. In these particular words a necessary attitude of the soul in the worship of such a God is declared. It is that of the utmost humility. In His presence, man must bow down before Him, man must kneel in the attitude of complete submission and obeisance. This is a truth of which we need to remind ourselves. We have the right to come before God with great gladness, but never without a sense of His majesty, and what is due to it. When the sense of that greatness is lost, and the worshipper fails to bow down, to kneel, to take the place of the uttermost lowliness before God, something is lacking in worship, which is of its very essence. God crowns us with life and with authority, and therein we may, too, rejoice; but in His presence those very crowns are to be cast before Him. Among really excellent people one sometimes hears flippant and irreverent references to God, and observes a lack of reverent demeanour. This is wrong, and tends to rob worship of its value to the soul, as it dishonours the awful majesty of the Eternal. Before God we must ever bow down and kneel in lowly reverence.

**He cometh to judge the earth.—
Psa. 96. 13.**

In these words another great song of
praise rises to its climax. This is the
reason for the exultant joy which thrills
through every line of it. Let this be
pondered. There are ways in which it is
right to think of the coming of God in
judgment with awe and trembling; but we
have been prone to associate the terrors
of the Divine judgment in some of its
methods so closely with the fact of that
judgment, as to be at least in danger of
forgetting other of its methods, and its
intention. In this song we are reminded of
the glory and greatness, of the honour
and majesty, of the strength and beauty
of God, and of the fact that such a God
judges in equity. The result of the judging
of the earth by this God will be that the
heavens rejoice, and the earth is glad.
God governs the earth with righteousness,
and the people with His truth. This must
inevitably mean that He proceeds against
all unrighteousness and unrighteous men
with wrath; and that all that is false,
and all liars, He smites with destruction.
But the fierceness of His wrath, the weight
of His stroke, are inspired by His love of
man, and His determination to establish
that order of life in which strength and
beauty shall abound, and all weakness
and ugliness be for ever banished. In our
worship we must ever praise Him for His
mercy, and principally because in its
exercise there is no violation of justice;
and we must praise Him for all the terrors
of His anger, for they are inspired by His
love.

**Clouds and darkness are round about
Him; righteousness and judgement are
the foundation of His throne.—Psa.
97. 2.**

Again the keynote of the praise is struck
in the opening declaration of this song:
"Jehovah reigneth." Than this fact, there
is none other to bring real joy to men.
But in the assurance that this is so, there
is rest and hope, and therefore song. In
the course of this series of songs for
worship, perhaps there are no words more
full of comfort than those which I have
emphasized. This is so because they
recognize the mystery of which we are so
often conscious, and at the same time
declare the truths which enable us to
endure. Clouds and darkness are round
about Him. His way is constantly hidden
from us. The mystery of His thought, and
of His method, is often beyond our
apprehension. The darkness of which we
are conscious is often due to excess of
light; and the clouds are often the beneficent instrument which guard that light
so that it does not harm us. Yet we are
perplexed and fearful, until we remember
that "Righteousness and justice are the
foundation of His throne." However deep

the darkness, however thick and threatening the clouds, which hide from us, for the
moment, the method and the meaning of
God, we know that in His government
there can be no departure from righteousness, no deflection of justice. This is the
secret of our confidence, and should be the
inspiration of perpetual songs, of ceaseless
worship.

**His right hand, and His holy arm,
hath wrought salvation for Him. The
Lord hath made known His salvation.
—Psa. 98. 1, 2.**

Still the theme is the same, that of the
reign of Jehovah. This song opens and
closes in almost the same words as in Psa.
96. Here the central matter for which
praise is offered is the salvation which
results from the reign of this God. It
moves in three measures: first, the salvation of God's people Israel, and that in
righteousness; second, the consequent discovery of His Kingship by all the earth;
and third, the gladness of Nature as it
expresses the greatness of God. In these
words at the beginning of the song two
great truths concerning human salvation
emerge. The first statement is that salvation is God's work; His right hand, and
His holy arm, hath wrought "salvation for
Him." The idea is that salvation was in
His purpose; He desired it; He willed it.
That being so, it was imperative that He
should provide. Whatever needed to be
done, He must do. The singer rejoiced
that Jehovah had provided what He
desired. Here the heart of truth concerning salvation, in all the Gospel fulness
of the term, is revealed. God desired the
salvation of men. Men could not provide
salvation. Then He wrought in a mystery
of love and holiness and power; and so
salvation is made possible. The second
statement is that He has made known His
salvation. He has revealed it to men, and
in its victories He makes it known more
and more perfectly. Thus this Hebrew
singer celebrated a truth the full value of
which he hardly recognized. Here we have
in the first statement, a declaration concerning those profound activities within
the Deity, out of which human salvation
is possible; and in the second, a declaration
which covers the ground of the life and
death and resurrection of Jesus. In
Philippians 2. 5-11, we find the New
Testament light on this passage.

**Holy is He . . . Holy is He, . . .
the Lord our God is holy . . .—Psa.
99. 3, 5, 9.**

This song completes the suggested
octave which commenced with Psa. 92.
It is the final note in the Sabbath praise
of Jehovah as the exalted and reigning
King. The words we quote constitute the
thrice-repeated refrain, and the light of
them flashes forth upon all the considera-

tions of these songs of worship. Jehovah is enthroned in Zion over all the peoples, and He is holy. His activities in the government which He exercises are those of righteousness, because of His character, for He is holy. Through all the history of His people He has been faithful, both in forgiveness and in vengeance, and that because He is holy. Therein is the reason for worship. Herein also is the reason for trembling. This song in its entirety helps us to realize the meaning of Holiness as it was revealed to the people of God. While the word itself signifies simply separateness, and was used with reference to other gods by other peoples, it acquired a new significance in this Divine revelation. To others the idea was that of aloofness, of distance, and had no necessary moral value. To these people it came to have that value only. God was revealed as separated from everything unjust, untrue, evil, in His character, and therefore in all His dealings with men, whether in the giving of law, or in the activities of the government. This is the supreme reason for confidence in Him, and so the supreme inspiration of worship. Thus fittingly, then, do we reach the climax of the Song of the Sabbath, the ultimate in its sacrifices of praise.

Make a joyful noise unto the Lord, all ye lands.—*Psa.* 100. 1.

This is the wonderful song which, in metrical version, composed by William Kethe in days of Marian persecution, is known as the Old Hundredth. It is jubilant with confidence for the whole earth, as it contemplates the glory of that earth, when all its people are submitted to the reign of Jehovah. What a pity, by the way, that so many of our hymn-books render the phrase, "Him serve with mirth," as "Him serve with fear," and thus rob the song of one of its chief notes! The relation of this song to the eight preceding ones is unmistakable, and whenever it was composed, its placing here by the guided editor was surely intentional. The eight Psalms have been those of the City of God, of the Sanctuary within that City, of the people who are its citizens, and worshippers. Their worship is concluded, and now their witness begins. It is as though the gates of the City, the courts of the Sanctuary, were suddenly thrown open, and all lands are called to *serve* Jehovah, to *know* that He is God, to *enter* into relationship with Him. Observe that I have italicized the words which mark the movement of this world-wide appeal, *serve*, *know*, *enter*. The relation between these things is very suggestive. Worship is for God. Witness is for men. The strength of witness is created in worship. It is those who know communion in the Sanctuary who are able to call men to God prevailingly. It is equally true that the ultimate value of worship is

witness. To praise God for all the wonders of His reign, and to fail to proclaim those wonders to such as dwell in darkness, is almost to blaspheme. The songs of the Sabbath sung with face lifted toward the throne, and catching the light therefrom, must be sung on all the other days in the highways and byways of human life, with faces irradiated, and so shining upon men.

I will.—*Psa.* 101. 1.

The song is attributed to David, and there is no valid reason for questioning that suggestion as to authorship. It is evidently the song of a Ruler, a Prince, a King. In its first movement (verses 1–4), it records the ruler's decisions concerning himself; in its second (verses 5–8), it declares his decisions concerning the administration of his Kingdom. It is a Psalm of Volition. That is why we have emphasized its first two words. They run through all its stanzas. Trace them. Here is no appeal to others. All the way the singer is exercising his will. His decisions prove that he is doing so under the inspiration of true intellectual apprehension, and pure emotional impulse. The important thing is that he is responding. This is always the matter of principal importance. Moreover, the nature of his decisions, and the order of them, are instructive. This king is evidently seeking to act in every way in harmony with the character and purpose of the One and only King. He begins with himself. He will bring his own character and conduct into conformity with the way and will of Jehovah to Whom he offers his praise. Then he will govern according to the same standards. The persons and things which are unlike God he will not tolerate within his realm. Those persons and things which are in accordance with the will of God, he will cultivate and preserve. This is the true way of authority.

But Thou, O Lord, shalt abide for ever.—*Psa.* 102. 12.

These are the words which to me blaze out from this Psalm as revealing its true value. It is one of the seven which we designate Penitential Psalms. (The others are 6, 32, 38, 51, 130, and 143.) The title is peculiar. It is the song of one pouring out his complaint, but doing so before Jehovah. Now glance at its structure. It falls into three strophes: (*a*) verses 1–11; (*b*) verses 12–22; (*c*) verses 23–28. I draw attention to this carefully in order to make clear a distinction and a difference. The first and the last are pulsating with personal consciousness. Mark well the reiteration of the pronoun in the first person singular, "I," "my," "me." They speak of trouble, of suffering, of sorrow. They are full of the sense of limitation, "my days," "my days." Now I look at the central portion. All that is missing. There is not a single personal reference. It opens with these words which affirm the eternity of God, and proceeds to speak of Zion, the nations, the kings of the earth, the peoples. But now look again at the first and the last strophes. In the first the singer is overwhelmed with his own sorrowful experiences. In the second he has discovered a secret, and is confident of a result. What is the secret? It emerges in the first sentence: "He weakened my strength in the way." What is the conclusion? It is stated at the close: "The children of thy servants shall continue; and their seed shall be established before Thee." This, then, is the light which banishes darkness—the sense of the eternity of God. Then all life is seen as being under His control, and therefore conditioned in the wisdom and intention which include far more than the passing moment, taking into account all the ages. Once more we remember the words of our Lord—"This is life eternal, that they should know Thee, the only true God."

Bless the Lord, O my soul; and all that is within me, bless His holy Name.—*Psa.* 103. 1.

This great Psalm of perfect praise is one of the most familiar in the Psalter. It is a glad outpouring of gratitude to Jehovah; for His ways with men; for what He is in Himself; for His great mercy; for His faithfulness therein; for the order and perfection of His government. For our present help we stress these introductory words, revealing as they do the responsibility of the soul in the matter of rendering praise to such a God. The singer addresses himself. He realizes that he has power over himself, that he is able to give or to withhold that which is due to God. He realizes also the complexity of personality. In order to perfect praise, all its powers need to be arrested, summoned to action, united in order to completeness. Whether intentionally or no, is there not here a recognition of the spiritual nature as supreme, and all mental powers as possessions thereof? The method harmonizes with that of Paul in Rom. 12. 1, where he called upon believers to present their bodies, to seek the renewing of their mind, and thus to render reasonable (or, more accurately, spiritual) service. The one value of these opening words is that they show us that worship is not involuntary, automatic. It calls for the co-ordination of all our powers, if it is to be perfect. This truth should arrest us whenever we enter the place of worship. The sanctuary is not a lounge, a place of relaxation. We should enter it with all the powers of personality arrested, arranged, dedicated. Then we may render a service of praise that is worthy and acceptable.

Let the Lord rejoice in His works.— *Psa.* 104. 31.

This is perhaps the highest and most daring note in all this wonderful song of praise. So impressed with the glory and wonder and beauty of creation was the singer, that he positively called upon God to rejoice in what He had wrought. There is nothing irreverent in this. It is rather an expression of the soul's profound understanding of what God actually feels in view of His own mighty and marvellous works. This song may be read anywhere, and on its poetic pinions of interpretation it will carry us out from the littleness of trivial things, and the pollutions resulting from human sin, to the vastness of Nature, and its essential purity. Perhaps the best conditions under which to read it are found away from human habitations, either among the mountains from which the valleys, with the rivers, can be seen; or out on the splendid solitudes of the sea. Such surroundings interpret the Psalm, and the Psalm interprets them. All these things of beauty and order are seen as proceeding from God; and He is seen, moreover, as present among them, and revealed in all the majesty of His wisdom, glory, and power. This singer saw and understood, and was so overwhelmed with the joy of creation, that in exultant ecstasy he called upon Jehovah to rejoice. And may we not say that the joy of soul which prompted the prayer was also the answer to the cry? The joy of the singer was the joy of God. Through every soul who finds God in His works and rejoices therein, God, in a mystery of communion, is indeed rejoicing; and that means that our joy in creation is fellowship with God in His joy.

He hath remembered His covenant for ever.—*Psa.* 105. 8.

This song has close connection with the next, with which the fourth Book closes. In this, the theme is that of God's faithfulness; in the next, it is that of Israel's infidelity. The burden of this song is expressed in these words. This is the fact which inspired the praise. Whatever the story of His people may be, God has never forgotten His covenant; and with God, to remember is to act. The song is an illustration of this fact by selections from the history of the people, which prove it. The covenant was made with Abraham, ratified by oath to Isaac, and confirmed to Jacob, and so to Israel. He remembered it, and preserved them while they wandered among the nations, possessing no land, in the earlier days of their history. He remembered it in the days of famine, and prepared for their security through Joseph. He remembered it when they came to be oppressed in Egypt, and sent Moses to deliver them. He remembered it when they found themselves free, but in a wilderness, and guided them by cloud and fire, supplying all their wants. He remembered it amid the discipline of the years of wilderness wandering, and at last brought them out therefrom, and into the land promised. A review of history, personal or national, always becomes a revelation of the persistent faithfulness of God to His covenants with man.

Blessed be the Lord, the God of Israel, from everlasting even to everlasting. And let all the people say, Amen. Praise ye the Lord.—Psa. 106. 48.

This is the Doxology with which Book 4 closes. The central theme of this collection has been that of Jehovah as the King of His people. The dominant title has been Jehovah. The worship, in all the songs, has been submissive, that of souls yielded to this authority of grace and power. Observe how in this Doxology, for the first time, adoration is followed by admonition. At the close of the second Book—the burden of which was the wonder-working God—the desire was expressed in the Doxology that the whole earth might be filled with His glory. Here the appeal is to the people. "Let all the people say, Amen!" Throughout this collection, the failure of the people to respond has been recognized. It forms the subject of the last song. Listen to some of its phrases, or sentences of confession: "Our fathers . . . remembered not"; "they soon forgat"; "they forgat God their Saviour." These stand in sharp contrast to the statement which was the theme of the previous Psalm: "He hath remembered His covenant for ever." Thus, at the close of the Book, there finds its way into the Doxology this haunting memory of failure, producing the appeal to the people to respond, to say Amen. There is no need to argue that a merely intellectual Amen—that is, the consent of the reason to truth about the kingship of God—is of no value. The Amen for which He seeks is that of the agreement of the will, and of the acquiescence of conduct. Adoration, to be acceptable to God, must have in it the element of response to the glory which calls it forth. Approbation is futile, admiration is impertinent, unless they produce obedience.

Whoso is wise shall give heed to these things, and they shall consider the mercies of the Lord.—Psa. 107. 43.

Thus a song of rare beauty and great power ends with words intended to arrest attention anew to what has been said. Such a statement compels us to read again, and to do so giving heed, considering. What, then, are the things to which we are to give heed? The question is answered immediately; we are to consider the lovingkindnesses of Jehovah. That is the theme of the song. So it was announced at the beginning, as the reason for thanksgiving was declared in the words, "For He is good; for His lovingkindness endureth for ever." The main body of the song consists of varied and vivid illustrations of the activity of this goodness, the continuity of this mercy. Let us simply group them. Wanderers in the wilderness cry to God, and are led to a city of habitation. Prisoners, in deep affliction, cry to God, and are delivered from bondage, and brought to liberty. Sinners, afflicted for their sins, cry to God, and are saved and healed and delivered from destruction. Storm-tossed mariners cry to God, and He calms the raging waters, and brings them to the haven of their desire. The wilderness, rendered desolate by sin, He renews, and makes habitable for men. The inhabitants, suffering oppression, trouble, and sorrow, He governs, so that men, mighty in evil, are abased, and those who are needy are exalted. It is a great song of the mercy of God. Let its message be heeded, then shall we cry unto God in our distresses, and finding deliverance through His goodness, we shall give Him thanks and praise Him.

Through God we shall do valiantly. —Psa. 108. 13.

This is not a new song, save in its arrangement. It is composed of two quotations. The first (verses 1–5) is from Psa. 57. 7–11. The second (verses 5–13) is from Psa. 60. 5–12. The relation of the quotations shows the different conditions leading to their combination in one song. The first part (verses 1–5) is a song of praise. In the earlier Psalm, this section follows a prayer for help on the part of one in personal peril. The second part is a prayer for national deliverance in an hour of Edomite hostility. In the earlier Psalm this section followed a description of disaster already experienced. Thus our song consists of a praise and a prayer quoted from other songs, but now employed in the circumstances we have described. These final words of the Psalm express the confidence of faith. Observe the line of thought which they consummate. There was first the inquiry: "Who will bring me into the fenced city?" Then the declaration: "Vain is the help of man." Then this affirmation: "Through God we shall do valiantly." What, then, is the meaning of this word? That God will overcome Edom? By no means. Rather that the people who are of fixed heart in God will themselves do the valiant deed, but that they will do it through Him. This is ever the way of victory. The soldiers of faith cannot of themselves take the fenced cities. But they can take them, when they are in such relationship with God, that He can act through them.

The mouth of the wicked and the mouth of deceit have they opened against me.—*Psa.* 109. 2.

Among all the Psalms which have been described as imprecatory, this is the one which has caused the greatest difficulty, for it is, without exception, the most terrible. Such cursing as that found in the paragraph beginning with verse 6, and continuing to verse 19, is found in no other Psalm. In the awfulness of its on-rush, it includes not alone the one principally cursed, but all his kith and kin. It must be admitted that the spirit revealed in this paragraph is not only not Christian, it is entirely alien to the spirit revealed in the Hebrew religion itself. Moreover, the Psalm is attributed to David, and there is no reason to question the suggested authorship. If this be so, then this spirit of cruel and relentless vindictiveness, is utterly unlike David as revealed in his history, or in other of his writings. I entirely agree with those expositors who treat this passage as the singer's quotation of the language of his enemies against him. The words I have emphasized, occurring at the opening of the Psalm, give the reason of this man's appeal to God. In this paragraph we have the words coming out of the mouth of the wicked, proceeding from the mouth of deceit. Rotherham takes this view, and among other reasons for doing so, draws attention to the "Sudden and sustained change from the plural of verses 1–5 (They) to the singular of verses 6–19 (he, his, him)." If this be granted, the spirit of the singer is really revealed in the first part (verses 1–5), and the last part (verses 20–31). It is the spirit of humble committal of his case to Jehovah.

The Lord saith unto my Lord.—*Psa.* 110. 1.

The full Messianic intention of this Psalm is completely settled by our Lord's use of it, and by the New Testament references to it. Moreover, by His use of it, the Lord inferentially claimed Messiahship, and so its fulfilment in Himself. In these six opening words we have the key to the Psalm. Everything which follows constitutes a disclosure made by Jehovah to another whom the singer speaks of as "my Lord." Observe carefully the three persons appearing here. First, Jehovah, the speaker; secondly, the recorder of the speech, King David (according to the title and the words of Jesus), who emerges in the pronoun "My"; finally One of Whom the singer speaks as "My Sovereign Lord," the One to whom Jehovah speaks. I like to connnect this Psalm with the second. There we have Jehovah's decree concerning His Anointed Who is spoken of as His Son. Here we have the disclosure made to His Anointed One, concerning His Mission. Here He is not called the Son of God, but David's reference to Him as "My Sovereign Lord," involved it, as the question of Jesus proves, when He said: "Whose Son is He?" In this song David had reached the highest point of his outlook. Let us content ourselves by noting simply the disclosure of Jehovah to the Sovereign Lord. First, that there would be a time of waiting for the subjugation of His foes, and that during that time He would occupy the place of supreme authority, sitting at the right hand of Jehovah. Secondly, that in due season, Jehovah would establish Him in Zion, and that, on that day of His power, His people would offer themselves willingly, an army, like the dew born in the morning out of the womb of the night. Thirdly, that in His reign He should be a priest like Melchizedek. Then finally, slightly changing the method, while still following a sequence, the Psalm no longer speaks of what Jehovah will do, but of what this Sovereign Lord at His right hand will do. He will completely overcome all His foes. All this is Messianic in the fullest sense.

Praise ye the Lord.—*Psa.* 111. 1.

This opening exclamation, the translation of Hallelujah, is by no means new in this song, nor is it peculiar to it, for a number of others begin in this selfsame way. Nevertheless, this is in a very definite sense the key to the Psalm. This one, and the next, form an intended couplet. This sets forth the excellence of Jehovah, while the next describes the blessedness of the man who trusts in Him. The praise of Jehovah is simple, but inclusive. He is great, in His works, that is, in His deeds— the things already accomplished; in His work, that is, that which He is now doing, there is honour and majesty. His righteousness and faithfulness, His graciousness and compassion, His truth and justice, and His promise of redemption for the people, are all celebrated. The Psalm closes with words which prepare for the next, as they declare that the fear of Jehovah is the beginning of wisdom, and that such as act according to that fear have good understanding. The ethical element in worship is here again revealed. The only praise of God which is acceptable to Him, is that in which approbation of all His glory is so sincere and deep as to inspire the soul with desire and determination to walk in the light, to be conformed to the likeness, to reproduce so far as that is possible the glory admired. When the light of the life harmonizes with the language of the lips, then God is worthily praised.

Praise ye the Lord. Blessed is the man that feareth the Lord.—*Psa.* 112. 1.

As we have said, this Psalm is very clearly the sequel to the previous one,

That closes with the declaration that "The fear of Jehovah is the beginning of wisdom;" this opens with the affirmation, "Blessed is the man that feareth Jehovah." It is occupied with a description of that man. We may cover the ground by saying that this man is—(a) a God-fearing man. That is fundamental. It affects all his outlooks, his relationships, his actions. He is (b) a home-making man. His seed is mighty, his generation blessed; his house is the place of wealth and riches, which are not material terms. He is (c) a helping man. He is light to others who sit in darkness. He is gracious and full of compassion. He is (d) a strong man. He knows nothing of panic in hours of evil tidings. Finally, he is (e) a hated man by the wicked. That is the supreme proof of his goodness. Thus the song depicts this man. Let it now be read again in close connection with the preceding one, and it will be seen that the supreme fact about this man is that he has indeed become like the God Whom he fears and obeys. The very things celebrated in the praise of Jehovah are those which constitute the excellencies of this man who fears Him. Righteousness, fidelity, graciousness, compassion: these are the fundamental things in the glories of the God Whom this man fears. They are reproduced in him. Therefore the approbation of such a man becomes necessarily a song of praise to God, and so opens with the same exclamation, "Hallelujah." It is a great thing so to live, that life is ever saying "Hallelujah."

He maketh the barren woman to keep house, . . . a joyful mother of children.—Psa. 113. 9.

This is the first of six Psalms (113–118) constituting the Hallel, or the Great Hallel. This song was sung at Passover, Pentecost and Tabernacles. It is impossible for me to read it without remembering that it was almost certainly the song which Jesus sang with His disciples in the upper room ere He passed out to Gethsemane and Calvary. The first two (113 and 114) were sung before the meal; and the last four (115–118) at the close. This first song is one in praise of Jehovah for the condescending grace which characterizes Him. Here, as so constantly, poetry, in its daring, utters a truth which prose would fear to speak. The singer says that the Seat of God is so high that in order to behold the things in heaven and on the earth He has to humble Himself; that is to stoop. Then the purpose of that stooping is revealed; it is that He may raise the poor, and lift the needy. The final note is this we have emphasized, in which God acts so as to crown womanhood with motherhood. Rotherham says: "Only to think it possible that a King wrote this Psalm while waiting in patience for the birth of his first-born, is to catch a glimpse of Sacred Romance." That is true; but

when we think of it as sung by the First-born under the Shadow of the Cross, we find ourselves in the full glory of that Romance. In Him the God Who dwells in the heights, above the heavens, had stooped through Motherhood, He being "God-only-born" (John 1. 18), in order that He might lift the needy. As He approached the ultimate depths in this stooping, He sang the song which offers praise to God for this condescending grace, which through motherhood reached men, that they might be reborn and thus raised to sit amid the royalties.

Tremble, thou earth, at the presence of the Lord, at the presence of the God of Jacob.—Psa. 114. 7.

Thus, after the song celebrating the condescension of Jehovah, in order to the lifting up of the needy, the theme is that of the Exodus, for ever associated with the Passover. It is noticeable that the Exodus is thought of in its completeness; not only escape from Egypt, but entrance to the land, for both Sea and Jordan are seen as passed. In the former song, God is praised as Jehovah, the condescending One full of Grace. Here the same Jehovah is seen as Adôn, the Sovereign Lord, and as Eloah, the Mighty One. In order to the accomplishment of His delivering purpose, He is revealed as producing convulsions in Nature, making the sea to flee, Jordan to turn backward, and the mountains and hills to quake. This convulsive action is interpreted in these particular words, and specially in the word "tremble," when rightly apprehended. Our translations, Authorized and Revised, miss the point. Here again Rotherham, with his customary accuracy and daring, helps us, as he renders, "Be in birth-throes, O Earth." When Jehovah, acting as Sovereign Lord, and in His might thus convulsed Nature, it was that a nation might be born. Out of the strain and stress and agony, produced by such action on the part of God, new life emerges, a new order is introduced. In the Upper Room, in connection with the celebration of the Passover, our Lord used the same figure of speech in connection with the sorrows which would come to His disciples as the result of their association with Him (see John 16. 20–22). Not without strain, convulsion, agony, can new life be born out of conditions of bondage and evil; but for the accomplishment of His high purpose, God will Himself enter into those experiences. He did so in Christ, and Christ sang the song that praised Him for so doing.

Not unto us, O Lord, not unto us, but unto Thy Name give glory, for Thy mercy, and for Thy truth's sake.—Psa. 115. 1.

"And when they had sung a hymn, they went out into the Mount of Olives"

(Matt. 26. 30). That was after the Passover Feast, in connection with which our Lord had instituted the New Feast of Remembrance and Proclamation, thus grafting the new upon the old, for the ending of the old and the establishing of the new. There is no doubt that the hymn was this second part of the Hallel. This song was at once an offering of praise and a prayer. Its note is that of triumphant confidence in God, because of what He is, in comparison with all false gods, which are no gods; and so of certitude that He will be mindful of His people, and deliver them from their enemies. No soul—neither that of the composer of the song, nor that of anyone who employs it—ever entered so completely into all its deep spiritual significance, as did the soul of Jesus, as, before passing out to Olivet, to Gethsemane, to Calvary, He sang it with that little group of men. He associated them with Himself in the singing, because they were the first of that Sacramental Host, and representative of all the rest, who, first sharing in the freedom created by His suffering, should also share in that suffering. The glory of the Exodus is due to the Name of God and never to us, and that of the Name, which is supremely illustrated in the release and redemption provided, is revealed in the two words *lovingkindness* and *truth*. These are the two elements supremely revealed in Christ, as John said when he spoke of the Glory of the Father unveiled in the Son, as being "full of grace and truth."

I will take the cup of salvation, and call upon the Name of the Lord.— *Psa.* 116. 13.

This song stands distinguished from the previous one by the persistent personal note which runs through it. It is a song of praise for deliverance from great and almost overwhelming griefs. Thus, in the series constituting the Hallel, it is the song of the delivered rather than that in any sense of the Deliverer. In other words, it can hardly be called Messianic, save as it expresses the praise of one emancipated by Messiah's work. Delivered from death, from tears, from weakness, the soul asks: "What shall I render unto Jehovah, for all His benefits toward me?" Here is the answer. The cup of salvation is the cup of blessing, which is given to the soul. Let the soul take it and drink it, but let him remember that the very partaking is in itself of the nature of a pledge of loyalty; it is the oath of allegiance in which he calls upon the Name of Jehovah. When the disciples joined in this song, their Lord had already taken a cup from the Passover Board, and given it to them to drink, declaring it to be "My blood of the Covenant, which is poured out for many unto remission of sins." If He joined them in that song, and it is most probable that He would do so, He sang as the One

Who, by entering into all the experience of their desolation, Himself being sinless, was able to fill the cup with blessing for them. Within a very little while after this singing, He, in Gethsemane, spoke of a cup, and, in complete surrender to His Father's will, consented to drink it. That was the cup of sorrows, of bitterness, of cursing. Having emptied it, He filled it with joy, with sweetness, with blessing. When we take that cup let us never forget the cost at which He so filled it for us.

. . . His mercy is great toward us; and the truth of the Lord endureth for ever.—*Psa.* 117. 2.

This is the shortest song in the whole collection, but there is none greater or grander in its expression of praise. Its note is universal, in that it appeals to all nations and all peoples to praise Jehovah. The reasons for the appeal, and consequently the inspiration of the praise of Jehovah, are set forth in this central statement. That which filled the heart of the singer was the sense of the greatness of the lovingkindness of God, and the sense that in the exercise of lovingkindness by Him there is no violation of righteousness: "The truth of Jehovah endureth for ever." Here we have the same matter, emphasized in a previous song (Psa. 115), brought before us again, the two elements which are eternally associated in the redeeming activity of God, those, namely, of grace and truth. In all the Biblical revelation, we are never allowed to forget this wondrous fact. What strength and comfort for men and for nations are found therein! If God stood for truth, alone, there would be no hope for us. On the other hand, if the grace of God could act apart from truth, we should equally be without hope; for truth is the only health and strength of life, individually or socially. Once again we can imagine with what perfect joy our Lord sang this song, as He moved to the uttermost in His sorrows; for He did so in full and perfect apprehension of the union of lovingkindness and truth in God; and in fellowship with Him, in those deep and mysterious activities which secured to men His lovingkindness, while establishing them and all their ways in His truth. Truly we may offer to our God the sacrifice of praise for a holy redemption.

Bind the sacrifice with cords, even unto the horns of the altar.—*Psa.* 118. 27.

This is the last of the songs composing the Hallel, the last stage in the hymn which Jesus sang with His disciples before He moved out to Olivet. In it, as Kirkpatrick says, "the spirit of jubilant thanksgiving finds fullest utterance." It is a call to praise for one reason, and that is that "His lovingkindness endureth forever." It tells of deliverance from bondage, from peril, from calamity. It celebrates the entrance of the delivered to the Temple, the House of God. It may be, and it certainly is the Song of the Redeemed, and they recognize how mysteriously and yet how mightily God has wrought on their behalf. It is equally the Song of the One Who has accomplished this deliverance, the Stone rejected of the builders, Who becomes the Head of the Corner. In such a song, how significant that before the final note of praise these words should occur! We recognize that expositors agree as to the difficulty of dogmatic statement as to their true significance. Yet does it not seem fitting that here words should occur which reveal the fundamental need of sacrifice in order to redemption? The sacrificial lamb was at the heart of the Passover feast. The binding with cords to that end was necessary. The principal difficulty is created by the exact meaning of "even unto the horns of the altar." Without dogmatizing, may we suggest that here the idea prevalent elsewhere obtains, that of sanctuary or safety formed by taking hold upon the horns of the altar? Reverently at least apply the idea to the mind of Jesus as He sang. All that was coming was necessary. He was bound to suffer and to die; but He was in the one place of sanctuary, of safety. In His co-operation with God on the sacrificial pathway, He was assured of perfect victory. He was accomplishing the Exodus.

Blessed are they that are perfect in the way, who walk in the Law of the Lord.—Psa. 119. 1.

This opening stanza of a most wonderful song strikes the key-note of its music, and gives us a summary of its spiritual teaching. Notice the broad outline of suggestion. The way of life is recognized, the way along which all men must walk. Men are seen walking along that way who are perfect—that is, upright. Such are declared to be blessed—that is, happy. The first line, then, declares that on the way of life, uprightness is the secret of happiness. The second line tells the secret of that integrity, and so of happiness also. The men who on the way of life are upright and happy, are men who walk in the Law of Jehovah. That is the motif of the music. It runs through the two and twenty strophes, and the one hundred and seventy-six stanzas, with constantly changing expression, but with unvarying persistence. Here the great word *Torah* is used, the word which to the Hebrew stood for the Law, being the word employed to describe the first division of the Bible, that which we call the Pentateuch. In other verses other words are employed, and the word *Torah* needs the others to complete the idea. Let them be considered, and it will be seen that the conception is that of the Will of God made known to men. Thus the Psalm is a glorious setting forth: (1) Of the glory and perfection of the Will of God; (2) of the integrity and safety in every regard, of the man who walks according to that Will; (3) of that Will, therefore, as the secret of true blessedness, the very well-spring of joy. Apparently unconsciously, that is without intention, the song reveals the fact that a man who obeys the will of God as revealed, comes to a personal fellowship with God. From beginning to end, the singer sang as one who had personal knowledge of God and direct dealing with Him.

In my distress I cried unto the Lord, and He answered me.—Psa. 120. 1.

This is the first of a series of fifteen songs each having the Title, "A Song of Ascents." It is not possible to offer any final explanation of the meaning of this title. Some have attributed it to some form in the literary structure; others suggest that they were the songs sung by the exiles returning from Babylon; others that they were the songs sung by pilgrims going up to the feasts; and yet others that they were sung upon the fifteen steps leading from the court of the women, to that of the men. In either case the repetition of the title unifies them in some way, and their perusal shows that their thoughts all circle round the City of God and the Temple as its true centre. This we may profitably bear in mind as we read. This first is patently the song of a soul at a distance from that City, and that Temple. In a foreign land, he was among those who were antagonistic to him, whose methods were those of deceit, and whose passion was for war. His dwelling was the place of distress; and from that place, he cried unto Jehovah, and was answered. Subsequent songs reveal the way and experience of deliverance. In this the principal revelation is that of the sorrows which created the cry: and that of the cry, and the assurance of deliverance. Dwelling in the cities of men, and realizing the hostilities of them, let the soul cry unto God; and in the cry the assurance will be given, the answer of God will surely come. Such distress is in itself a sure sign of better citizenship. Contentment in the place where deceit is practised, and strife is loved, is base contentment. Men of faith must there find the distress which inspires the cry to God.

I will lift up mine eyes unto the mountains; from whence shall my help come? My help cometh from the Lord, Which made heaven and earth.—Psa. 121. 1, 2.

Let the reader carefully note the change the Revisers have made in this first verse. In the King James' Version it read: "I will lift up mine eyes unto the hills, from whence cometh my help." This was misleading, as it suggested that the thought of the singer was that his help was coming from the hills. The Psalm is the second of these Songs of Ascent, and is most closely related to the first. The singer is still absent from Zion and the Temple. In the previous song he had cried out of distress, and had heard the Divine answer. Now, from the distance, he lifted his eyes to the mountains, those upon which Zion was built. Doing so, he asked a question: "From whence shall my help come?" The answer was immediate. Not from those distant and longed-for mountains, but from Jehovah, Who made heaven and earth, and Who therefore, while in some senses dwelling in Zion, is not confined there. He is also near to the soul in the places distant from Zion, and the help the singer needed must come from Him. Observe how the rest of the Psalm interprets this. Though this man is in a place of distance from the City, Jehovah will not suffer his foot to be moved; Jehovah's vigilance never ceases; He does not slumber nor sleep; the goings-out and comings-in of this man are kept by Jehovah. The City of God, and the Temple, are to be desired and delighted in; the mountains upon which they rest are to be remembered. But not from them does help come to distressed souls; it comes from Jehovah, Who makes the City strong, the Temple glorious, the mountains beautiful; yet He is not confined to them, but is present in every place, and watching over His own, as surely in the foreign land and among foes, as in the City of His glory.

I was glad when they said unto me, Let us go unto the House of the Lord. —Psa. 122. 1.

This is the song of the singer, no longer distanced from the City, and Temple, but having arrived therein. It is the song of first impressions. These were concerned with the City as the place of the Temple. Observe that in this opening stanza, and also in the last, the reference is to the House of Jehovah. First there is the record of the gladness which came when the invitation, and so the opportunity, came to go to the House of Jehovah. Finally there is the expression of determination to seek the good of the City for the sake of this House. Approaching the House, the singer was impressed with the City; in its compactness, as the centre for the gathering of the tribes, and as the seat of the Government. He then prayed for, and spoke of, the peace and prosperity of the City. The song reveals the singer's understanding of the true facts of national life. That City was to him the centre of that life. The House of God was the centre of that City. That House was supreme in importance because it was the House of Jehovah. Jehovah, the God of Grace, is the One around Whom the people gather.

The Temple is the means of grace, the Tent of meeting between man and God. The City is the embodiment of the ideals of God for His people, the realization on their part of the order of peace and prosperity which is His Will for them. Whenever the song was written, it was idealistic, for never yet in its history has the City of God realized this conception. But that is the glory of the life of faith. Spiritually it enters into the experience of the high purposes of God, even when actual conditions fall far short of those purposes. Moreover, it is by such high confidence that men move forward towards realization actually and materially of what they already apprehend spiritually.

Unto Thee do I lift up mine eyes, O Thou that sittest in the heavens.— Psa. 123. 1.

When at a distance from the City and Temple, the Singer had declared: "My help cometh from Jehovah, Who made heaven and earth" (Psa. 121. 2). Now, within the City and the Temple, the eyes are lifted to Him. The atmosphere of this song is that of those who were in circumstances very far from the ideal celebrated in the previous Psalm. Their experience was not that of peace and prosperity, but that of turmoil and adversity. Nevertheless, because of their spiritual apprehension of the ideal, they were able thus to lift up their eyes to God, and wait His deliverance. The nature of that waiting is beautifully set forth in the figure employed, that of servants and handmaidens. These look to the hands of their master and mistress, and that statement has a three-fold suggestiveness. The first is that of dependence. The hands of master and mistress provide all that is needed for the sustenance of their servants. The second is that of submission. The hands of master and mistress direct the service of servants. The third is that of discipline. The hands of master and mistress correct the servants of the household. Here, then, is the true way of looking for help from Jehovah. It is that of dependence, obedience, and response to correction. When the eyes lifted to Him are those of such as fulfil these conditions, the help sought is ever found, the mercy of Jehovah is ever active towards them.

Our help is in the Name of the Lord, Who made heaven and earth.—Psa. 124. 8.

In these closing words of this song, the truth affirmed in the previous one is expressed as proven; and the anticipation of the soul, when at a distance from the City and House of God, is confessed and realized (Psa. 121. 2). The singer, looking back, contemplates a great deliverance from a grave peril, and declares his conviction that the deliverance was the work of Jehovah. Had He not helped, there would have been discomfiture and defeat. There had been no such experience. On the contrary, there had been complete escape from the snare. To those who know what it is truly to wait upon God with dependence, obedience, and response, there are constant occasions for the use of such a song as this. To look back over life's way is to realize how constantly we have been brought into circumstances which must have engulfed and destroyed us, had it not been that Jehovah was on our side. Seeing that He has been on our side, the story of life has been one continuous story of His deliverances and of our escapes from perilous positions. Indeed, these words tell all the truth about our deliverances and escapes. We have often involved ourselves in entanglements, through our own disobedience; but we have never been able to extricate ourselves from them. Escape has always come by His action. "Our help is in the Name of Jehovah," and in none other. Let us never fail to remember this; and to give unto Jehovah the glory due unto His Name, in our praises.

They that trust in the Lord are as Mount Zion, which cannot be moved, but abideth for ever. As the mountains are round about Jerusalem, so the Lord is round about His people, from this time forth and for evermore.— Psa. 125. 1, 2.

These two verses must never be separated. They constitute a perfect poetic declaration of confidence, and an illustration of its reason. To understand the figure we must make ourselves familiar with the geography which was in the knowledge of the singer. First, Mount Zion is seen, the very stronghold of the City of the great King. Then the surrounding mountains come into view. Robinson has said: "All around Jerusalem are higher hills; on the east, the Mount of Olives; on the south, the Hill of Evil Counsel, so-called, rising directly from the Vale of Hinnom; on the west, the ground rises gently . . . while on the north a bend of the ridge connected with the Mount of Olives bounds the prospect at the distance of more than a mile." Thus those mountains encircling the Mount constitute its fortifications and defence. That outlook gave this singer his figure. He saw the people of God—those who put their trust in Jehovah—as Mount Zion, immovable, abiding for ever, because he saw Jehovah as those distant mountains, constituting the fortifications and defence of this people. Let us never forget the first phrase: "They that trust in Jehovah." That is the abiding condition of safety. In days when these people failed in faith, the surrounding mountains failed to secure safety to Zion. It was overcome and

trodden down. God is a defence only so long as we trust in Him. To fail to do so, and to turn aside from His law and His grace, is inevitably to know discomfiture and desolation.

Turn again our captivity, O Lord, as the streams in the South.—Psa. 126. 4.

This song would seem to be still that of those restored to the City and Temple. The words we have emphasized strike a sad note. The Psalm opens with memories of the wonderful way in which Jehovah had restored them from captivity and distance. The restoration had been so wonderful as to appear incredible; but it was so real that they had been filled with laughter and singing, and even the nations had seen how great things God had done for them. Then this note, admitting the imperfection of their condition. Doubtless it was the sense of imperfect appropriation on the part of the people of God, of the wonder of His restoration. So the song is a cry for more complete restoration. The figure made use of was a striking one: "As streams in the South." To the south of favoured Judaea stretched the dry and barren district, where in summer-time all the streams ceased to flow. That, to the singer, was the condition of the people. But in the autumn, the rains fill up the stony channels, a very river of life. For a visitation similar to that, the prayer asked. The Psalm ends on the note of confidence; and let it be observed that the confidence is that the very experiences of sorrow though which the people are called to pass will prove the means by which the longed-for blessings will come. How often, after God has wrought great deliverances for His children, they fail to appropriate all the wealth of them, and need to pray for a yet fuller restoration to Himself! Of one thing we may rest assured, that it is good under such circumstances thus to pray. However arid the land, He can send the revivifying streams.

Except the Lord build the house, they labour in vain that build it. Except the Lord keep the city the watchman waketh but in vain.—Psa. 127. 1.

To this Singer, house was home; and the City the place of such homes. One can discover his ideal through his song. It is that of a prosperous city, its enemies kept outside its gates; and that of the secret of its prosperity as being the house well-built, in the spiritual and moral sense, and the families dwelling within such houses as able to deal with its enemies in the gate. Whereas the picture has all the colouring of the East, and conditions which in their detail are not those of our clime or time are described, yet the principles of civic well-being are the same. That city is truly strong which is a city of well-built homes, well-built in every sense, spiritually, morally, and materially. All that has to do with the general conceptions which the song assumes. Its message is contained in these opening words. No house-building is successful which leaves God out of account. How have we seen men build them houses, with care and at great cost, only to see them crumble to pieces because God was forgotten! There is no safety for a city save in the keeping of God. How often have men attempted to gain security for their cities by guarding them against enemies outside, and then the dwellers within, children reared in houses in the building of which God was forgotten, have brought about their destruction! These would be splendid words to cut into granite over the entrance to all our homes, and to emblazon in gold in all the meeting places of those in civic authority. But better still let them be written in the heart of those who make homes, and guard and govern cities.

Blessed is everyone that feareth the Lord, that walketh in His ways.— Psa. 128. 1.

The relation of this Psalm to the preceding one is patent, and is universally acknowledged. The difference is that the former one dealt largely in generalities concerning the home, while this has to do with the man who is a home builder. In these opening words the general principle is stated, and the secret revealed of successful home-making. The man equal to the task is described with reference to his inward life and his outward activity; with regard to the inspiration of his conduct, and its resulting expression. The deepest and central truth concerning him is that he fears Jehovah. The reality of that fear is seen in that he walks in the ways of Jehovah. Such a man is indeed blessed, that is, happy, in the true sense of that word. The song then proceeds to describe the conditions which result from such fear and from such obedience. Personally, he will be prosperous. His home shall be rich indeed in his wife and in his children. Moreover, he shall see the good of the city, and that in the sense of having contributed to its strength and beauty by the home he has created. Let every man who loves his city with the love that desires to make it in some measure the City of God, keep these words ever before him, in the place and hour in which he thinks and plans for the ordering of his life, the building up of his house, the betterment of his city. They will at once warn him, and inspire him. To fear Jehovah is to fear nothing else; to walk in His ways is to be delivered from all those ways which lead to the break-up of home, and the destruction of the City.

Let them be ashamed and turned backward, all they that hate Zion.— Psa. 129. 5.

This is the song of the nation personified, and of the nation as centralized and symbolized in the City of Zion. This is its central cry. It is the cry of a true patriotism, as it seeks for the discomfiture of all those that hate Zion. These troublers of the nation, these haters of the City, have been ever in active opposition; but they have not prevailed, because Jehovah has been righteous and has guarded the City and the nation. The prayer is that this may continue, and be even more perfectly realized. Whereas expositors agree, and accurately, in treating this as a reference to the enemies of the city and the nation who have opposed from without; if we may interpret by the two previous Psalms, those within are also in view. Moreover, it is certain that in the case of Israel and Zion, the troublers within had been more destructive than those without. Indeed, no foe from outside ever triumphed over the people of God, or harmed His City, until their victory had been made possible by internal deflection from His fear, and disobedience to His laws. It is terribly possible to live in Zion, while yet hating it. Concerning those that do so, we may ever pray that they may be ashamed and turned backward. This is not malice toward them, but rather passionate love of the ways of God. That is a false toleration which condones evil, or fails to burn with anger against all men and methods which are out of harmony with the Divine ideal. At the heart of high and holy patriotism there must ever burn a divine anger with all that is opposed to the purpose and plan of God. To hate Zion is to hate God. To tolerate those who do so, is to be confederate with their wickedness.

There is forgiveness with Thee, that Thou mayest be feared.—Psa. 130. 4.

This is one of the seven Psalms which we call Penitential. (The others are 6, 32, 38, 51, 102, and 143.) That is its true note. Whereas in the previous Psalm Israel was personified, in this it is the voice of one individual. Nevertheless it is the song of an individual, speaking out of the consciousness of national sin, and assuming relationship therewith, and consequently accepting responsibility. While it is penitential in the truest sense of the word, it breathes the spirit of complete confidence in the lovingkindness of God, and ends with an appeal to the nation to hope in that lovingkindness, and in the assurance that He will redeem Israel from all their iniquities. In the words of this fourth stanza there is wonderful light. Perhaps the best comment I may make on it is that of telling a story. In the midst of the Welsh Revival, I heard a Welshman praying in English. Evidently he was thinking in his mother-tongue, and translating as he went. He started to quote these words, but stumbled at the second line, seeming unable to express the idea. After one or two attempts he thus rendered it: "O Lord, we thank Thee that, 'There is forgiveness with Thee, enough to frighten us.'" To me it came as a flash of light and revelation. God's lovingkindness is so great and so wonderful, that the apprehension of it fills the soul with such a sense of His love that it is frightened. Frightened, that is, not at God, but at sin. This is the new quality of fear which lovingkindness provides. The heart of man in his sin fears that God will punish, and that is a wholesome fear. But the heart of man, realizing the lovingkindness of God, is filled with fear lest by sin he should wound God. Perfect love casts out the old slavish fear, but it begets a new fear which is holy, cleansing fear.

Like a weaned child with his mother, my soul is with me like a weaned child. —*Psa.* 131. 2.

This short song is a very beautiful one, as setting forth a much-to-be-desired state of mind. We have no means of knowing whether it was written by the same person who wrote the previous one, but it most fittingly follows it, and in all probability was placed here quite intentionally by the editor of the collection. In that, the penitent soul found rest in the plenteous mercy of God. In this, we have a description of the mental experience of that rest. All the light of the song is remarkably focussed in this figure of a weaned child with its mother. The thought is not that of weakness or helplessness in any sense. Indeed, the weaned child is gaining strength. The more simply we interpret the figure, the more accurately we apprehend the truth suggested. The weaned child with its mother is the child who has learned to be independent of that which seemed indispensable, and indeed was so at one time. It is now at rest with its mother, whereas at one time it only found rest in what it derived directly from its mother. This was the experience of this singer with regard to Jehovah. At one time he found satisfaction in the Divine gifts, and looked upon them as indispensable. Now he had stilled all those ambitions which arose out of his own interpretation of the Divine gifts. He was content with God, rested in His Motherhood. Perhaps he had learned what is surely implicated in the figure, that the process of weaning, that is the withdrawal of things which at one time were indispensable, was the process of advancement, of growth. This is certainly so, and it is good to realize it, and to rest in God.

Lord, remember for David all his affliction.—*Psa.* 132. 1.

To understand that opening cry we must attend to the whole Psalm. In it the House of God and the City of God are still in mind. Its first part has to do with the House; its second, with the City as the place of the Throne, the centre of established order. The first part has to do with what David sware to Jehovah; the second, with what Jehovah sware to David (compare verses 2 and 11). The whole has to do with this Covenant. David sware to build a House for Jehovah: Jehovah sware to establish the Throne of David in Zion. The relation is fundamental. Jehovah's promise to establish a dynasty in Zion was made to the man who undertook to provide a Tabernacle for God in the midst of the City. The song dramatically falls into two parts. First, a prayer, based upon the loyalty of David; second, an affirmation of confidence, based upon the faithfulness of Jehovah. Now we may turn back to that opening cry. What was the affliction of David which Jehovah was asked to remember for him? The reference was not to any personal sorrow that he endured; neither was it to chastisements which he endured. The affliction is immediately described, being introduced by the word "how." It was that of his concern for the House of Jehovah, his determined restlessness until Jehovah found His resting-place, his search in Ephrathah and the fields of the wood, until it was found. Here we have at once a revelation of the consuming zeal of David for the highest things in the national life, and an indication of the only kind of affliction of ours which can make any true claim on God. In other words, we have a right to ask God to fulfil His promises, when our concern for His glory becomes affliction in its activity.

Behold, how good and how pleasant it is for brethren to dwell together in unity.—*Psa.* 133. 1.

In this singularly fine song, in briefest sentences, and by the use of two figures, the glory of the true social order is set forth. In that order brethren will dwell together in unity. Having drawn attention to the goodness and pleasantness of that order, the singer describes it by two similitudes. Observe the use of the word "like" twice over: "It is like" (verse 2); "Like" (verse 3). The first figure takes us at once to the House of God, the Temple, as it refers to the anointing of Aaron, the priest. The second figure takes us to the City of God, Zion, as it refers to the dew which falls from Hermon upon the holy mountains, bringing life. In these figures, thus applied, the qualities which characterize, and indeed create, the good and pleasant social order are revealed. That anointing oil, poured upon Aaron, was the oil of consecration, and symbolized his separation from all evil; it was the oil of holiness. The dew was ever the agent of renewal, of refreshment, of fertilizing force: that out of which life was maintained in strength. These are the secrets of the true social order—holiness and fulness of life. The forces which destroy, prevent or postpone, are those of sin and lack of life. Here in each case. is a sequel. Lack of life is due to sin. Life for evermore is due to holiness. Right relationship with the House of God issues in full realization of the benefits of the City of God. Brethren able to dwell together in unity are those who live the holy life of the Temple, and therefore the abounding life of the City of God.

Behold, bless ye the Lord . . .—Psa. 134. 1.

This is the last of the Songs of Ascents. It is a song of the night, and falls into two parts. In the first, the people of the City call to those who keep vigil in the Temple to bless Jehovah. In the second, those Temple ministers respond by pronouncing blessing upon the people, the blessing of Jehovah Himself. This little Psalm is principally valuable as a picture. In it we see the true activity of those set apart to the ministry of holy things. It is first that of representing the people who cannot themselves be present in the Temple Courts, by reason of the duties of the day, or as here, because it is night, and in rest they prepare for work in offering praise to God. It is, second, that of speaking for God to those people in pronouncing His blessing upon them. I have never been able to join with those who speak slightingly of a service in some parish church conducted by the clergy, when hardly any congregation is present; or of an exceedingly small company of believers assembled for praise and prayer in some of our village, or for that matter, city chapels. Those who are there are representatives of multitudes detained by duty. If in each case, there is on the part of those who minister in the sanctuary, a due sense of this representative character of their ministry, they are serving in the highest way to the glory of God, and the well-being of men.

They that make them shall be like unto them; yea, every one that trusteth in them.—Psa. 135. 18.

This is a song of the Temple. It opens with a call to worship, and then becomes an act of worship. Its burden is that of praising Jehovah by contrasting Him with all false gods. He is set forth as manifested great in creation, in government, and in perpetual faithfulness to the covenants of His grace. Idols are described in their futility, in their utter nothingness; they are devoid of breath. In connection with this contrast, this arresting and illuminative word occurs. The makers of idols become like that which they make; and so does everyone who trusts in them. It is for ever true that a man becomes

like his god, approximates in character and conduct to that to which he yields his homage. The fundamental difference between true and false religion is that, in the former, worship and service are rendered to the One Who has created us, and Who is for ever greater than ourselves; while, in the latter, they are rendered to what we have created, and which is therefore less than ourselves. To worship God is to become like Him; that is, to rise to the highest. To worship our own creations, is to become like them; that is, to degenerate inevitably. The principle applies even though materially men make no idols of silver or gold. To put anything of our own creation, whether wealth, or fame, or power, in the place of God, is to begin a process of degradation, the end of which is destructive of everything of high possibility in life.

His mercy endureth for ever.—Psa. 136. 1.

Another great Temple song, of which this phrase is the burden. It is introduced every time with a call to praise. All the rest of the song consists of illustrations of the truth which are reasons for praise. The opening stanzas refer to the One to Whom reference is made throughout, by the three great names by which He was known: *Jehovah*, the title of grace (verse 1); *Elohim*, the name of might (verse 2); and *Adonai*, the title of sovereignty (verse 3). The fact concerning this supreme One which called forth the song, was that of His continued lovingkindness. Were I a musician I would set this song to music for antiphonal singing by quartette and chorus. There are six-and-twenty stanzas which fall into eight groups; six of three verses each, and two of four. The first four groups should be sung, as to the introductory words, by the four soloists in turn; the second two groups by duet—the first, contralto and soprano; the second, tenor and bass; the last two groups by the four voices. Throughout the great refrain, "For His lovingkindness endureth for ever," should be sung by the full chorus. This is the suggestion of an amateur. Let the professionals correct and amend the proposal. Let the ordinary reader forgive the method of the note. It is caused by the writer's sense of the greatness and glory of the one theme of the lovingkindness of God, which persists unto the ages; and by his conviction that it needs the consecration of music to give it adequate interpretation. It is so vast, so true, so glorious a fact, that prose cannot utter it, and even poetry clamours for the lifting wings of harmonic sweetness and strength, to give it adequate expression.

How shall we sing the Lord's song in a strange land?—Psa. 137. 4.

This song is reminiscent of sad days, days of exile from Zion, when the people of God sat sorrowful and oppressed by the waters of Babylon. This question must be interpreted by the preceding verse; from which we learn that in that place of exile their captors had asked them to sing, for their amusement, some of the songs of Zion. That was impossible. They hanged their harps upon the willows, and sat in silence. How could they sing Jehovah's song in a strange land? And yet, there was a song in the silence, not heard of the cruel oppressors, but heard of Jehovah Himself. It was the song of the heart, remembering Jerusalem, counting it the chief joy of life. Such a song necessarily was touched with flame, and cried for strict retributive justice against those nations which had caused the desolation of the City of God. These great songs of the heart, finding no utterance for the ears of men, but expressing some of the deepest things of faith and life, constitute the inspirations which cleanse the soul, and generate the forces which at last break the bonds of captivity, and restore the people of God to the City of their love. Let all tyrants know that if their victims are silent in their presence, singing no song, their memory of the ideals which seem lost constitutes within them the secret of a force mightier than all the strength which attempts to crush them. And let the silent souls cherish that undersong of devotion to the City of God, the realization of His purposes. He, the God of their hope, hears that unuttered song, and will in His own time and way respond to it, and execute judgment upon the oppressors and set the captives free.

The Lord will perfect that which concerneth me.—*Psa.* 138. 8.

That is the language of the utmost confidence. The hope is that of the complete realization of personality, both as to its being, and its purpose. The hope is based, not upon the determination or effort of the singer, but upon Jehovah. It is so unequivocal, and withal so daring, that we ask as to its reason. How was it that this man was so sure about the matter? The Psalm is attributed to David. We are familiar at once with his excellencies, and his persistent defects. In the deepest of his being, the realm of desire, he was surely a man after God's own heart. But how gravely, yea even grossly, he failed. In spite of all this failure, in this song he declared thus his complete confidence that Jehovah would perfect that which concerned him. Again we ask what made him sure? The answer is found in the whole song. Therein are celebrated those facts in God which inspired this confidence. Let us briefly note them. He is a God of lovingkindness and of truth. He is a God of great glory. He is a God Who has respect unto the lowly. These things demand a response on the part of man. He must worship this

God. He must call upon Him. God being what He is, when the soul of man, in its feebleness, and notwithstanding its ofttimes failure, worships Him, and calls upon Him, there can be no question as to the issue. He will perfect that which concerneth that soul. Here is the only place where man can be sure about himself. But here he may be absolutely sure. However dark the day and way; yes, and however great the failure; let the heart be loyal; then, at last, even though it be through the discipline of tears and of suffering, God will perfect the life.

Such knowledge is too wonderful for me; it is high, I cannot attain unto it. —*Psa.* 139. 6.

In its essential burden, this is the greatest song in literature. What that burden is, is at once revealed if the opening declaration and the closing prayer be brought together: "O Jehovah, Thou hast searched me and known me"; "Search me, O God, and know my heart." Here was a singer who had been brought to a consciousness of God's absolutely perfect and final knowledge of his life; and who found such satisfaction in the tremendous discovery, that after setting it forth in a song of rare beauty, he could only end by praying for the continuation of that searching of his life by God. I have emphasized these words because they are central as a revelation of the discovery which the revelation of God's knowledge of him had brought to this man. When he said, "Such knowledge is too wonderful for me; it is high, I cannot attain unto it," he was not referring to the omniscience of God in the abstract, but rather to God's knowledge of himself. It is the supreme discovery, through which man escapes from himself to God. The ultimate word of Greek philosophy, "Man, know thyself," was really valuable because it brought man face to face with the impossible. This is what the Hebrew singer had discovered. He did not know himself, nor could he. But God knew him, with complete finality. To realize that, is to be driven to yield self up to the Divine investigation, in order to be set in the way everlasting. That is a great hour, when the soul realizes its ignorance of itself, in the light of the Divine knowledge. It is the hour when the way of life is found to be that of Divine leading.

I know that the Lord will maintain the cause of the afflicted, And the right of the needy.—*Psa.* 140. 12.

This is a song of trouble; but in these words we find the note of confidence which made trouble the occasion of a song. The trouble was very real, and of that peculiar nature which it is always difficult to endure. The singer was being slandered by evil and violent men, who were prepared if occasion offered to add actual violence to their lying speech. Of all this he was keenly conscious, as all the early part of the song shows. But he set these facts in the light of the greater fact of the care of God, as the latter stanzas reveal. In these particular words the secret is declared, and the inspiration of song is revealed. If sorrow is a certainty, so also is the action of Jehovah. Here again we have an interpretation of the meaning of the words, "He giveth songs in the night." Sorrow and darkness come to all men, but only those who know God and are sure of Him, make suffering, and the night, occasions of triumphant psalmody. Men without God may write poetry in circumstances of desolation, but their poems are dirges, outpourings of pessimistic agony. Those who know Him reach the heights of poetic utterance; their songs are psalms, outpourings of optimistic assurance. Here, for instance, is one radical difference between two of our more modern poets, Swinburne and Browning.

Incline not my heart to any evil thing.—*Psa.* 141. 4.

In this song the circumstances revealed are very much like those of the previous one. The singer is still surrounded by men who work iniquity, but his trouble is different. He has become afraid of himself. It would seem as though his enemies had changed their method. Instead of slander and violence, they are seeking to seduce him from his loyalty to truth and uprightness. The reference to "their dainties" would seem to suggest that they were endeavouring to show him the advantages which he would enjoy if he would throw in his lot with theirs. It was this sense of peril to his own soul which was the inspiration of the song. He realized the force of the temptation, and sought refuge in his God, realizing his own weakness. The peril revealed is a very subtle one. Direct hostility is never so great a menace to the soul, as the suggestion that by compromise with evil and evil men, ease may be found, or that advantage may accrue from complicity in deeds of wickedness. Men of faith fail far more often by so far lowering the standard as to have fellowship with evil men, than by the suffering which results from their slander and violent hostility. This song reminds us that our only safety in such hours of peril is to be found in seeking the Divine strength in the realm of desire, that we may not incline toward any evil thing. The heart garrisoned by Jehovah is impregnable; but there is no other power equal to its perfect keeping.

The righteous shall compass me about; For Thou shalt deal bountifully with me.—*Psa.* 142. 7.

Still the circumstances of this song are similar to those of the previous two. Here the title says that this was a prayer when David was in the Cave. In all probability this introduces us to the period in the life of David when all this group of songs was composed. For this one at least, the fact is of importance as it takes us back to the story of those days when this man, conscious that he was anointed by God to kingship, was nevertheless a fugitive, and the object of the most bitter hatred and persecution, so much so that he had been compelled to take refuge in Adullam. The song was written in an hour of great dejection. He said: "My spirit was overwhelmed within me"; "Refuge hath failed me, no man careth for my soul; I am brought very low." But the song is one of triumph, for every reference to those experiences of dejection is set against other facts. If his spirit was overwhelmed, he said: "Thou knewest my path." If refuge had failed, and no man cared for his soul, he said: "Thou are my refuge." If he was brought very low, he said to God, "Deliver me." Therefore the song ends with this confident note. In spite of all the opposition of men he realized that his God would deal bountifully with him, therefore instead of his foes, he would find himself surrounded by the righteous. Perhaps when he wrote the song he already began to realize that the crowd of men in debt, in danger, and discontented, who were coming to him, would become the mighty men, who would presently bring him into his kingdom. It is a great thing in darkest hours, to set over against the darkness, all the facts about God. To do so is to triumph even in sorrow.

Teach me to do Thy will.—*Psa.* 143. 10.

This is the last of the seven Psalms described as Penitential. (The others are 6, 32, 38, 51, 102, and 130.) It is one of the group we have been reading which were composed by David in circumstances of trial. There are no evidences in it of any experience of alleviation. The singer was still dwelling "in dark places." There is a note here, however, which differentiates between this Psalm and those of the group already considered. Here it is evident that the sense of sin was with him, as he said: "Enter not into judgment with Thy servant; for in Thy sight no man living is righteous." With that sense present he thought upon God, remembering, meditating, musing, until with great longing he stretched forth his hands to God. Having done so, his song became a prayer, packed with petitions, brief, urgent poignant. Among all of them we have emphasized this one, because it is the supreme prayer of the human soul. Those for deliverance from circumstances of suffering are only of real value as the reason of them is that the soul so delivered may be able to do the will of God. The petition suggests two things to which we do well to take heed. The first is, as we have already hinted, that the one and only way of life that is satisfactory is that of doing the will of God. This needs no argument, but it does need application. We ought perpetually to declare it to ourselves, never allowing life, in its desires, apprehensions, volitions, to get beyond the boundaries of that will. The second is that we need to be taught to do that will, which is much more than being taught to know it. For us this prayer finds answer in the fact that "The grace of God hath appeared . . . teaching . . ."

Happy is the people whose God is the Lord.—*Psa.* 144. 15.

This is the song of a king. The title attributes it to David. Almost all expositors agree in treating it as a composite song, containing some quotations from other Psalms, and introducing new elements. This the singer himself seems to have indicated when, after quotations, he broke out in the words: "I will sing a new song." Be all that as it may, it is still the song of a king who understood the true secret of national prosperity, and this found expression in this closing exclamation. In the presence of the stern and awful necessity for war, it is Jehovah Who teaches the hands and the fingers. It is He Who giveth victory to kings. As the result of victory which comes from Him, kings and people are rescued from evil politicians—men whose mouths speak vanity; and from evildoers—men whose right hand is guided by falsehood. Such deliverance issues in a prosperity which is graphically and poetically described in these closing stanzas. Verily then, "happy is the people whose God is Jehovah." All Christian souls believe this to be true. How solemn, then, the obligation which rests upon them to use all their influence in the life of the nation to which they belong, to bring it under the rule of this God! The patriotism of the Christian is such love of country that it seeks at all times and under all circumstances to bring the policies and activities of that country into agreement with the will and way of God.

Thy Kingdom is an everlasting Kingdom, and Thy dominion endureth throughout all generations.—*Psa.* 145. 13.

In these words the exalted music of this wonderful hymn of praise reaches its fullest and richest expression. The whole Psalm is one of praise to God as Jehovah; that is, to the Mighty One, in the condescending grace of His dealings with men. In the opening sentences He is addressed as "My Elohim, O King," and afterwards always as Jehovah (nine times). As the song is read, the facts of human need are seen in the background—the need for compassion and mercy, the failings, and the stoopings, the prayers of those in darkness, and the persistence of wickedness; but its theme is that of God's ways with men, and these are set forth as the ways of "greatness," "honour," "righteousness," "compassion," "goodness"—to group some of the singer's great words. As we have said, this singer reached his highest note in these words, showing, as they do, his grasp upon the fact of the persistence of the Divine Sovereignty. Rotherham has rendered the couplet with more complete literalness thus: "Thy Kingdom is a Kingdom of all ages, and Thy dominion is over all succeeding generations." This is a truth of fundamental and final importance. Too often even the children of God forget it. The fact remains that God never has been, is not, nor ever will be, any other than King. Neither men nor nations can escape His government. They may change their experience of it. By yielding to it, they find it a blessing; by rebelling against it, they find it a blasting. In this truth we find our confidence for the world, and for the ages and the generations. In certainty that this is so, we can go forward with courage and with songs.

Praise ye the Lord . . . O my soul.—*Psa.* 146. 1.

The Psalter closes with five Psalms, each one beginning and ending with the phrase: "Praise ye the Lord," or "Hallelujah!" Dr. Ginsburg treated this as "the Public Reader's invitation to praise" at the commencement of each Psalm. The repetition at the close would then naturally constitute the refrain of the singers, their ultimate expression of worship, in view of all set forth in the song itself. This first of the five strikes the personal note. It is the song of a soul who has found everything in Jehovah, and who has learned the futility of trusting man, even though he have attained to high degree. All the reasons for praise are found in what Jehovah is in Himself, and this is revealed in His activities. These activities are celebrated in this song, beginning at the sixth verse. They may thus be tabulated: His activities are those of Creation, Government, Providence, Restoration, Punishment, Sovereignty, Continuity. The soul that has this view of God, and is conscious of the fact that he lives in the midst of an order over which such a God is ruling, and that he himself is thought of, cared for, governed, by this God, can surely do none other than offer praise to Him. Worship, as glad and exultant adoration, is the natural, and indeed inevitable, outcome of a true knowledge of God. However humbling the thought may be, and to whatever searching of heart it may drive us, it is certain that if, and when "Hosannas languish on our tongues, and our devotion dies," the reason is that we have lost our clear vision of God, our keen consciousness of what He is. To know Him is to praise Him, and that without ceasing.

Praise the Lord, O Jerusalem.— Psa. 147. 12.

Here is the central note of this song, and reveals its burden. It follows the previous song in a natural sequence; in that the note was personal, but it ended with the vision of the God of Zion reigning for ever. This song is characterized by the civic note. The singer is meditating upon the things resulting in the life of the City, when it is under the government of God. After the introductory sentences, the first reason for praise is given in the words: "Jehovah doth build up Jerusalem." Our minds go back to "The Songs of Ascents," in which the thoughts circled round the City of God and the Temple (Psa. 120–134). In one of them the words occur: "Except Jehovah build the house, they labour in vain that build it; except Jehovah keep the City, the watchman waketh but in vain." Now we have a song of praise for the City built up by Jehovah, and the results of that building up are set forth. It is a City of peace and of prosperity, a social order, created by the redeeming and restoring activity of God, in which, not wickedness nor material strength, but meekness, fear of Jehovah, and all spiritual forces are triumphant. All this the song sets forth pictorially, with fine poetic illustrations. Moreover, the true function of such a City in the interest of the world is described. From such a City, "He sendeth out His commandment upon earth; His word runneth very swiftly." The more this song of praise concerning an ideal city is pondered, the more remarkable is it found to be in its spiritual apprehension. It is interesting to note that in this portrayal of the City builded up by Jehovah, there is no reference to the House of God, the Temple, which was so constantly in mind in "The Songs of Ascents." Let this omission be compared with the last picture in the Bible of the City of God, and especially with the statement, "I saw no Temple therein" (Rev. 21. 22).

Praise ye the Lord from the heavens . . . from the earth.—Psa. 148. 1, 7.

In this song the outlook is yet wider. The appeal is universal, from the viewpoint of one who sings the praise of God on this earth. The heavens and the earth are included, and appealed to, to offer Him worship. The reason for praise in each case is clearly revealed. With regard to the heavens, the reason is that of the power and stability of the Divine Law: "He commanded, and they were created; He hath also established them for ever and ever; He hath made a decree which shall not pass away." This is the secret of the order and beauty of angels, and constellations, and the whole super-earthly realm; and in their being, they set forth the glory of the God from Whom they came. With regard to the earth, the reason is that of the order and beauty resulting from that nearness to Him which is realized in obedience to His law and submission to His authority. This is true of all Nature, and of men, whether kings or peoples, young or old. What a wonderful song this is! Look over it again, and note the fact that there is no reference in it, from first to last, to the mercy, or pity, or compassion of God. But that is because there is no reference to evil in any form. The Biblical revelation begins with the august, stupendous, inclusive statement: "In the beginning God created the heavens and the earth." In the Book of Job (38. 7) we are told that when He did so, "The morning stars sang together, and all the sons of God shouted for joy." We can imagine that they might have done so in the words of this song, as they saw the glory and perfection of the Divine purpose in Creation. But this is a song written by a sinning man, in a sin-stricken world. Therefore it sets forth the glory of that redeeming grace, through which, at last, God will realize His own original intention.

Praise ye the Lord. . . . In the assembly of the saints.—Psa. 149. 1.

In considering this song, we are again compelled to notice the relation to the preceding one. The closing thought of that was concerned with "His saints . . . the children of Israel . . . a people near unto Him." This calls for praise in "the assembly of the saints." Thus the final note of the one merges into and becomes the theme of the music of the other. Here the praise called for, and indeed offered, is that of the people through whom the word is proclaimed, the order revealed, and the work finally accomplished, of good earthly government. The history of this song is one of great sadness, due to grave misinterpretation, and grievous misapplication. Delitzsch has said: "By means of this Psalm, Caspar Scioppius, in his *Classicum belli sacri*, . . . inflamed the Roman Catholic princes to the Thirty Years' Religious War And, within the Protestant Church, Thomas Münzer, by means of this Psalm, stirred up the War of the Peasants." That, perhaps, is one of the most superlative illustrations of what may result, in interpretation, from confusing things which differ. There is no reference in this Psalm to the Church of God. As it specifically indicates, it has to do with "Israel," with "the children of Zion." They were, in the beginning of their national history, and they will be yet again, the instrument of the hand of God "to execute vengeance upon the nations;

and punishments (i.e. corrections) upon the peoples." And this is indeed honour, as the singer finally declares. If in the former song, praise was offered for the realization of the Divine ideal, in this it is offered for the process of realization, through the chosen people, by means of vengeance upon evil. It were blasphemy to say that the end justifies the means, if by that the idea is intended that by evil methods, good may be brought about. But of the Divine government of the world, we may say that the end necessitates the means, however much suffering may be involved. But the means are never evil. In them there is nothing of iniquity or injustice.

Praise ye the Lord.—*Psa.* 150. 1.

In reading these Psalms, we have stressed, in each case, the Doxology at the close of the Books. (See 41. 13; 72. 18, 19; 89. 52; 106. 48.) This fifth Book ends with the Doxology of this whole Psalm, of which we have emphasized the opening phrase. Whereas it is true that this Psalm of Doxology concludes this fifth Book, it is also true that it forms the fitting conclusion of the complete collection of the five Books. Kirkpatrick describes this Psalm as: "This full-toned call to universal praise, with every accompaniment of jubilant rejoicing," and that is exactly what it is. The place of praise is: "His sanctuary ... the firmament of His power"; its reason, "His mighty acts ... His excellent greatness"; the instruments of expression are nine in number; the one qualification is breath, which here unquestionably is a figurative description of spirit, as that in which man has relationship with God. This final song is indeed, as Rotherham says, "the magnified appeal of Hebrew praise." In reading the first Psalm we stressed the first word "Blessed" as giving the first note in the music. Fittingly we close our readings by stressing this final, and all-inclusive, note, Hallelujah! Whatever of blessedness, of happiness, of prosperity, man knows, results from the activities of the government and grace of Jehovah. To this fact all the songs in this wonderful collection bear witness, whether the prevailing tone be major or minor, whether the song be a dirge of sadness, or a paean of gladness. So let us ever praise Jehovah; for His thoughts for us are thoughts of good and not of evil, and His methods with us, whether gentle or severe, are the methods which lead us to blessedness.

PROVERBS

The fear of the Lord is the beginning of knowledge.—*Prov.* 1. 7.

In these words we have a declaration of the fundamental principle of Hebrew wisdom, that is philosophy. This book is one of the three Wisdom books in the Old Testament. The others are Job and Ecclesiastes. The first six verses of this chapter reveal the purpose of the book. It was written to teach wisdom, and that rather in its application to life, than in theory. It consists of—(1) A series of addresses on wisdom delivered by a father to his son; (2) Two collections of Proverbs; and (3) Two discourses in the realm of Wisdom, one by Agur, the other by Lemuel. Throughout, the purpose is practical, rather than theoretical. Here, after the introduction or preface, and before the series of addresses, the theory is stated in one inclusive definition. It is of importance to any study of this book that this fundamental and inclusive definition should be rightly apprehended; and in order to that, we halt with the word rendered *beginning*. In the King James Version we find a marginal alternative suggested, viz. "the principal part," and the English and American revisers marginally suggest "the chief part." Why this reading was relegated to the margin remains a mystery, for there is no doubt that this is the real meaning of the Hebrew word. The other truth emerges later (9. 10). The fundamental fact, then, is that in all knowledge, all understanding of life, all interpretation thereof, the fear of Jehovah is the principal thing, the chief part, the central light, apart from which the mind of man gropes in darkness, and misses the way. Whether in prosperity or adversity, in light or in darkness, in life or in death, in order to intelligent apprehension, and true conduct, there must be the fear of Jehovah. That is the sum total of wisdom.

Then shalt thou understand the fear of the Lord, and find the knowledge of God.—*Prov.* 2. 5.

Let us glance back at Chapter 1. In his addresses to his son, this Hebrew father first applied the way of wisdom to home (verses 8 and 9), then to companionships (verses 10–19), and then began a series of addresses intended to help as the boy passed out into the wider world. These addresses, commencing at verse 20 of the first chapter, run on through chapter 9. The first (1. 20–33) recorded the message of wisdom amid the highways of human life, in general terms. In this chapter the value of wisdom in life is dealt with, and the first matter is that of the conditions upon which a man may have wisdom. If the chief thing in wisdom is the fear of Jehovah, the natural question arises as to how a man is to understand that fear, and to find the knowledge of God. This verse is of value, as by its opening word it compels us to return to things already said: "*Then* shalt thou understand." When? The answer is found by relating the statement of result to that of causes, introduced by the word "If." "*If* thou wilt receive ... *if* thou cry after ... *if* thou seek ... *then*." Observe carefully the action and reaction suggested. The fear of Jehovah is the inspiration of the search for wisdom. The search for wisdom, rightly undertaken, becomes the interpretation of the fear of Jehovah, and the way for the discovery of God. But this search must be serious, strenuous. The way of wisdom is never revealed to triflers. It is when the quest for it becomes the master passion of the life, controlling and conditioning all other interests, that it is found, and the soul is brought to understanding, and that final knowledge of God, which indeed is life.

Trust in the Lord with all thine heart, and lean not upon thine own understanding. In all thy ways acknowledge Him, and He shall direct thy paths.— *Prov. 3. 5, 6.*

Continuing his instructions on the value of wisdom in the ordering of life, in these words the father enunciated for his son the complete law of life according to wisdom. So simple and so clear is the statement, that interpretation is unnecessary. The reader, then, will be patient if for this once the writer becomes reminiscent, and so a witness rather than an advocate. I distinctly remember the day when I left home to face life, amid its crowded ways, for myself. My father, whose philosophy was certainly that of the Hebrew Wisdom, gave me these verses as providing a complete guide to life. Looking back over the intervening years I know he was right. In them there has been much of failure, many turnings aside from the straight highway, many devious and sorrowful wanderings from the true paths of life. All such failure, such turnings aside, such wanderings, have resulted from leaning to one's own understanding. The measure in which I have trusted Jehovah, and acknowledged Him, has been the measure of walking in the paths of real life. Doubt of God, pride of intellect, and independence in volition, these are the things which blight and blast. Paths chosen for us by God all lead onward and upward, even when they seem to us to turn about in inextricable confusion, and to move downward to the valleys of humiliation and suffering. He is the All-Wise, and to Him, Wisdom is the way by which Love gains His victory.

For I was a son unto my father, tender and only beloved in the sight of my mother.—Prov. 4. 3.

This chapter opens with a personal testimony, whereby the father endeavours more completely to appeal to his son to walk in the ways of wisdom. He says that he also had received instruction from his father, and verses 4–9 contain his summary of that instruction. If indeed this book was the work of Solomon, this reference to David becomes full of suggestiveness. The life of Solomon was characterized by persistent departure from the ways of wisdom, constant wanderings in the bypaths of folly. The experiences of such wanderings we shall find recorded in Ecclesiastes. In spite of all these sad facts, this man never escaped from the power of these early instructions; and there is no doubt that at last he found restoration to the highest things in personal life, even though he finally failed in his official function as king. Those who receive from their parents direction in the fear of Jehovah, have that for which to be perpetually thankful. They can never escape its power. It may be that they will ultimately reject its appeal, but the fact that they have received it will create for them a way of escape from evil through all life's pilgrimage. Again I say they may never obey it, but I believe it is the hardest thing possible for any son, rightly instructed of his father, finally to resist the appeal of that instruction. The subject must be left an open one as to final issues, but let us not underestimate the value and importance of having received true instruction; and therefore, the obligation resting upon us who have children, to give them such instruction also.

He shall die for lack of instruction; and in the greatness of his folly he shall go astray.—Prov. 5. 23.

This is a tremendous chapter, dealing with a delicate subject daringly, and with great directness. In it, the subject of the way of wisdom is illustrated superlatively, by contrasting the false and the true, in the exercise of the highest functions of physical being, those namely of procreation. Those functions are exercised under the mastery of lust, or of love. Lust is only material; love is ever spiritual. Lust is animal desire; love is spiritual approbation. Lust is lawless in its attempt to satisfy itself; love is law-abiding in its expression. The contrast between the two ways in this chapter is graphic, and proven true in all human experience. Exposition is not necessary. No page in Holy Writ is more explicit. Let every young man, conscious of the strength and glory of his own powers in this marvellous realm, ponder this page with earnest attention. We may summarize its teaching by saying that it brings before us with sharp and clear incisiveness the arresting truth, that in the realm of the highest powers and possibilities of human personality, there lurk the gravest perils. The more wonderful the function, the more terrible the result, if it be exercised apart from that fear of Jehovah which is the supreme thing in wisdom. Men die for lack of instruction, which means here more than ignorance, referring rather to conduct which is not according to instruction. Such refusal to obey is, indeed, greatness of folly, and the issue is always that going astray which leads to destruction.

There be six things which the Lord hateth, yea, seven which are an abomination unto Him.—*Prov.* 6. 16.

Still in the realm of exhortation to the life of wisdom, four ways of folly are dealt with in the four addresses found in this chapter. They are those of suretyship, sloth, mischief-making, and impurity. In dealing with the third of these, the way of mischief-making, that is the way of the worthless person, the father makes this declaration, and follows it by naming the six, yea, the seven. This method is poetic and figurative, and intended to emphasize the complete worthlessness of the person who is guilty of mischief-making; and also to dissect or analyse the character of such a person. Perowne points out that in the Hebrew we have the enumeration of the parts of the body—eyes, tongue, hands, heart, and feet; then the person is named, and his action and influence are declared. The six hated things are the prostituted powers, and the pernicious person; and the seventh is that of the poisonous and destructive influence exerted. In his dealing with this, the writer passed from the abstract to the personal. It is not that this evil of mischief-making is contrary to wisdom, merely; it is something which Jehovah hateth; it is a veritable abomination to Him. None love a mischief-maker, and yet we are apt to think of the sin with something less than the Divine intolerance for it. We may take it as an unqualified certainty, that no man in whose heart the fear of Jehovah prevails and rules, can ever sow discord among brethren.

Say unto wisdom, Thou art my sister, and call understanding thy kinswoman.—*Prov.* 7. 4.

The reference to the way of impurity in the previous address (verses 20–35) leads on to this dramatic and powerful message. Here once more, as in Chapter 5, the subject is that of the folly of the prostitution of the highest function of personality. The method is that of a most graphic description of the ways of the evil woman, and the weakness and stupidity of the one who is enticed and victimized by her.

This description is prefaced by words of appeal in which the way of wisdom, which is the way of strength in the presence of such temptation, is revealed. In these particular words wisdom is personified as a woman, the necessary implicate being that she is a woman of strength and of purity. Let the man who has to meet this kind of temptation, make wisdom his sister, and understanding his kinswoman, that is, his close personal friend. It is when the figure is allowed its full force that its value is discovered. Thousands of men are kept from evil courses by the love and friendship of sisters, and women friends. Recognizing this, the father counsels his son to find strength against the seductions of evil, by cultivating that kind of defensive and defending familiarity with wisdom, which is typified by this love of a sister and of pure women.

Doth not wisdom cry, and understanding put forth her voice?—*Prov.* 8. 1.

These great messages are correlated, and one emerges from the other in a beautiful sequence. In the previous address wisdom was personified as a woman, a sister, a kinswoman; and the son addressed was counselled to treat her as such. Here the figure is taken up and elaborated. Wisdom is allowed to speak for itself, and does so as a woman; and it is impossible to escape the sense of designed contrast to the figure so graphically portrayed in the last address. Than this chapter, there is nothing greater or grander in all the Biblical literature, as setting forth the beauty and grace of that wisdom which has the fear of Jehovah as its chief part. Wisdom cries, and understanding puts forth her voice; and in this inspired self-delineation we have a truly wonderful unveiling. Our summary of content may be helpful even though it is necessarily rough. Let this movement be noticed. The openness of her appeal (verses 1–3); the simplicity thereof (4, 5); its inherent rightness (6–9); its values (10, 11); its sphere (12–21); its eternity (22–31); its urgency (32–36). So great is this passage, that it refuses to be exhausted in its setting, and rises to a height from which we are constrained to some clearer apprehension of the glory of that wholeness of Truth, which is in God, and in none other. I think I may say with perfect accuracy, that I never read this chapter without wanting to turn again to the prologue to the Gospel according to John, as it deals with the Logos, the Word of God, full of Truth and Grace; and with that as resident in, and expressed through, the Son, Who is in the bosom of the Father, in that profound mystery and manifestation of His becoming flesh. Christ is made unto us "wisdom of God, and righteousness and sanctification, and redemption."

The fear of the Lord is the beginning of wisdom.—*Prov. 9. 10.*

This is the last of the addresses of this father to his son. Once more he employs the method of contrast. In the first part Wisdom is personified; in the second, Folly, in the guise of an evil woman. They are both revealed as appealing to men. The contrast is vivid and full of literary balance, as an examination will show. The words we have emphasized occur in the course of the call of Wisdom. We referred to them in our first note (see 1. 7). In this case the Hebrew word is accurately represented by the word "beginning." Whereas at first the declaration was wider (namely, that the chief part, the principal element in wisdom, is the fear of Jehovah), here the whole subject is brought down to the starting-point, as it declares that the first matter, in reference to time and order, in wisdom, is the fear of Jehovah. To remember this, and to act in accordance with it, is to be enabled to live in right relationship with that fear perpetually. We are ever beginning; every morning we start afresh; every task we take up is a new start; every venture in joy or in effort, must have its commencement. Then let every beginning be in the fear of Jehovah. That is Wisdom, and it leads in the way of Wisdom. There is an old saying which runs, "Well begun is half done." This is true indeed when the beginning is inspired and conditioned by the fear of Jehovah. That is to walk in the Light; that is to abound in Life; that is to be upheld by Love.

A wise son maketh a glad father: but a foolish son is the heaviness of his mother.—*Prov. 10. 1.*

With this chapter we begin the second division of this book, which division ends with chapter 24. The first section, ending with verse 16 of chapter 22, is a collection of Proverbs simply; the second section (22. 17–29) consists of a series of proverbial discourses. While we are dealing with the chapters containing these Proverbs, we can do no more than fasten upon some one of them, the light from which has specially searched our own soul. They are not connected as a sequence in any sense. They flash in every direction and upon all sorts of circumstances and conditions. Indeed, they are all searchlights; and they are unified by the conception of Wisdom set forth in the earlier discourses. They are the result of looking out upon life in the fear of Jehovah. It is fitting that the first Proverb should crystallize the teaching of the previous discourses in a conclusive application. A great Proverb this, as a statement of truth, and as an inspiration to youth. True parenthood knows no gladness so great as that of seeing children walking in the fear of Jehovah.. Better that, by infinite measure, than to see them successful, materially, intellectually, socially, if they lack the highest things. It is equally true that there can be no sorrow greater than that of seeing children of our love departing from the highways of the Divine Wisdom. How often the consciousness of this fact has proved the inspiration of wisdom in the life of children! Countless numbers have been delivered in hours of subtle temptation by the fact that they have said: "No, I cannot do this; it would break mother's heart; it would bring down the grey hairs of my father with sorrow to the grave." The light of this word searches the soul of all those of us who are parents, as it leads us to inquire whether by our teaching and life we are making that attitude a necessity for our children.

As a jewel of gold in a swine's snout, so is a fair woman which is without discretion.—*Prov. 11. 22.*

A first reading of this Proverb would seem to suggest that the figure of speech is almost brutal. A closer consideration will show that it is really characterized by a fine delicacy. Let us be careful to keep our terms in right relationship. There are two couplets. The first is that of "a ring of gold" and "a fair woman." There is nothing incongruous in that juxtaposition. The second is that of "a swine's snout," and the condition described as "without discretion." Does that seem violent? Let us look at it. There is no question that the expression "a swine's snout" represents the uttermost of contempt and disgust when employed by a Hebrew. What, then, is this condition of being "without discretion"? Perowne says that the Hebrew word literally means *taste*. It stands, therefore, for that mystic intuitive quality in woman which is the result of her purity and love, and which makes her understanding, discreet; and capable of influencing others to finest issues, in a way which is rarely if ever possible to a man. Now consider the statement of the Proverb. A ring of gold is a beautiful and a valuable thing; but in the snout of a swine it is out of place, and therefore degraded and vulgarized. A fair woman is a precious and glorious creation of God; but if her life is set in a character which lacks that mystic quality of intuitive understanding and influence, it also is out of place, vulgarized and degraded. Beauty which is physical is a gift of God, but if a woman possessing it lack those spiritual qualities which are of her highest glory, that beauty is a peril, to herself and to all others.

The lip of truth shall be established for ever: but a lying tongue is but for a moment.—*Prov. 12. 19.*

That is a pre-eminently superlative way of stating a fact, and there are some facts which can only be adequately stated so. They do not admit of the comparative. They are positive, but in a superlative sense. Taking the second part first—"A lying tongue is but for a moment"—we are inclined to question its accuracy. A lie lives longer than that. Some have seemed to persist for centuries and millenniums. The Hebrew here literally is: "A lying tongue is but while I wink." How is it possible to believe that? The solution of the apparent problem is found in a consideration of the earlier phrase referring to duration—"for ever." That is a phrase of which we often make use, but how seldom do we consider it? We employ it in the sense of time. As a matter of fact it is timeless, because it includes all time. In its presence all mathematical measurements break down. The lying tongue may continue to utter its falsehood for long years by the calendars of men, but when you place those years by the side of the ages of God, they are as a moment, as the winking of the eye, as nothing. Here, then, is comfort. It is truth which abides. A lie must perish. In a world still largely mastered by lies, it is difficult at times to believe this. Yet to review the history of the race is to have evidence of it. Lies are always perishing. Through the ages we see them shrivel and die, however strong their power seemed to be. Truth, oft-time insulted, battered, wronged, never perishes. It has age-abiding life, for it is of God. Let individuals and statesmen observe this, and they will discover the secrets of strength and permanence.

There is that maketh himself rich, yet hath nothing: there is that maketh himself poor, yet hath great wealth.— Prov. 13. 7.

How self-evident a truth this is on the most ordinary level of experience and observation; and yet how slow men are to act upon it! Our own age abounds with men who have made themselves rich, and yet have nothing. They have amassed great wealth, and yet it has no purchasing power in the true things of life. It cannot insure health, it brings no happiness, it often destroys peace. On the other hand, there are those who have impoverished themselves, and have by so doing become wealthy in all the highest senses of the word. How is this to be explained? Is not the solution found by laying the emphasis in each of the contrastive declarations, upon the word *self?* To make *self* rich, is to destroy the capacity for life. To make *self* poor, by enriching others, is to live. It is impossible to consider this saying of Hebrew wisdom, without thinking of the One Who was incarnate Wisdom. He for our sakes became poor, and thereby He gains the ultimate wealth, more dear to His heart and the heart of God than all beside, that of redeemed humanity. Thus the ancient word becomes for us living,

powerful, prevailing in and through Him. To follow Him is to empty self, to make ourselves poor by the outpouring of all for the sake of others; and that is to have great wealth. Let this word be kept in the realm of the material, and then its final interpretation or appeal is contained in the words of Jesus: "Make to yourselves friends by means of the mammon of unrighteousness, that when it shall fail, they may receive you into the eternal tabernacles."

The backslider in heart shall be filled with his own ways: and a good man shall be satisfied from himself.— Prov. 14. 14.

Which simply means that whatever may be within a man, in the deepest region of his personality, will sooner or later be wrought out into actual experience and visibility. The backslider in heart is the man who, knowing the way of wisdom, does not desire to conform to it, but rather desires the ways of folly. The good man is the man who, whatever his consciousness of weakness may be, does in the deepest of him desire the ways of wisdom. In either case, that underlying desire is the most potent factor, and sooner or later will gain its victory, and produce its result in the life. It is possible for a man for a long time to conform to the rules and regulations of wisdom and the fear of Jehovah, while yet in secret he is desiring the forbidden things. Such a man is backsliding in heart, and at last that backsliding will become patent. It is equally true that a man may falter and blunder, and fail, again and again, while all the time he hates his own shortcomings, and earnestly aspires after the highest things. Such a man is a good man, and ultimately that quest after the highest will be successful; he will be satisfied from himself. The revelation of Scripture, both in the Old and New Testaments, is constantly urging this truth. We do well to take heed to it. To do so is to be brought to a realization of our personal helplessness, and our need of a Saviour. We may say with a great deal of reason that we cannot control our desires. Hence the need for the surrender of ourselves to Him Who can create the clean heart, and renew the right spirit within us.

The eyes of the Lord are in every place, keeping watch upon the evil and the good.—Prov. 15. 3.

Let us never forget this, or fail to derive from the fact its comfort and its saving strength. The word employed describes a very active and purposeful seeing. The statement is far more than that God sees; it is that He is investigating, observing, or, in the most satisfactory rendering of the Revised, "keeping watch." He is keeping watch upon the evil. It is never out of His sight. It loves the darkness rather than the light, but He sees as well in the darkness as in the light. The endeavour of evil is to accomplish its purpose secretly, before it can be discovered at its work. It is often successful, so far as men are concerned. It is never so, so far as God is concerned. He keepeth watch, knows the hour, the place, the method, the intention. He is keeping watch upon the good. He never fails to see it. Men often do. It struggles behind appearances, and often behind actions which are denials of itself. Human eyes fail to detect it. Not so the eyes of Jehovah. They discern it, approve it, and reckon with it. The comfort of this truth is created by the character of God. He is the God of unsullied purity; His watching of evil is ever with the intention of limiting it, and ultimately destroying it. He is the God of unfathomable grace; His watching of good is in order to develop it, and make it finally victorious. To remember this truth is to be halted whenever we are tempted to evil. It is to find new courage in all our efforts after the high and noble. He is never deceived as to our badness or our goodness. Therefore to live in His fear is wisdom.

A man's heart deviseth his way; but the Lord directeth his steps.—*Prov.* 16. 9.

This is a very profound word. The more carefully it is considered, the more challenging does it become. It recognizes the freedom of the human will; and then sharply defines the limitations of that freedom. "A man's heart deviseth his way." That is a recognition of the truth of which we are constantly reminded in these sacred writings, namely that the heart, the realm of desire, is the most potent factor in personality. It is also a clear declaration that conduct is directed by the heart, by desire. That is the measure of human freedom. A man can and does devise his own way under the direction of his heart. If desire be evil, the way devised is evil. If desire be good, the way devised is good. But that is not all the truth about life. This also is true: "Jehovah directeth his steps." Every action of a man, whether in answer to the inward desire of good or evil, is an action in a realm of law from which there is no escape. The steps of evil and the steps of good are directed by Jehovah. That is to say that no man can step outside the government of God, no man can devise a way that enables him to escape from God. The warmth of the fire which blesses, is God's action. The heat of the fire which blasts, is God's action. I can devise my way with regard to the fire, but the steps I take are directed, governed, by God. I can, if I will, answer the lusts of the flesh, devising my way accordingly; but God will direct my steps, and the destruction

which comes is the result. I can, if I will, yield myself to the lure of the spirit, devising my way accordingly; but still God directs my steps, and the realization of life which follows is the effect of that directing.

A friend loveth at all times, and a brother is born for adversity.—*Prov.* 17. 17.

This is the one full and final definition of friendship. Personally, I have not the slightest doubt that the marginal reading here should be adopted: "A friend loveth at all times, and is born as a brother for adversity." There is no attempt here to define a brother. The statement, "a brother is born for adversity," would be inadequate and indeed inaccurate, as a definition of a brother; but the statement that "a friend . . . is born as a brother for adversity" is a graphic illustration and application of the inclusive truth: "A friend loveth at all times." This statement is easily read, and is accepted theoretically, quite generally. Let it be applied. Then two startling questions will arise. First, a question as to whether I am really a friend to anyone; and second, a question as to how many real friends I have. As to the second, yes, I have a few. Their love never falters, never wavers, in spite of my meanness, my stupidity, my sin. For them, with tears and laughter, I thank God. As to the first, I can only say, God help me to be a friend in that full way to those about me. All consideration of this great definition leads us at last to one place, to One Person. He is the Friend of sinners. There comment ceases. Let the heart wonder and worship.

He also that is slack in his work is brother to him that is a destroyer.—*Prov.* 18. 9.

In this Proverb a principle is involved which has more superlative statement in other well-known words of Holy Writ. It was in the mind of Deborah when she cursed Meroz for not coming to the help of Jehovah against the mighty. It found explicit statement when our Lord said: "He that gathereth not with Me scattereth." James recognized it when he wrote: "To him that knoweth to do good and doeth it not, to him it is sin." It means that in life there can be no neutrality. Every man lives in the midst of a conflict between good and evil. He must and does take part therein. If he is not helping Jehovah against the mighty, he is helping the mighty against Jehovah. His abstention is a gain to the foe. Every man lives in a world where two forces are at work; one is gathering, the other is scattering. If he is not with the One Whose work it is to gather, he is exerting an influence which scatters. Every man is confronted with the possibility of doing good, or of doing evil. If he does not do the good when he knows it, he is strengthening the cause of evil against which all goodness is ever working. This proverb applies this principle to work. Constructive work is the law of human life and progress. There is an active principle of destruction operating in the history of man; and he who is a slacker at his work, who does not put into it all his strength, is a brother to the man who in wickedness sets himself to the activity of destruction. No living being can be merely a spectator. Each works or wastes. Not to work well, is to aid the process of waste.

Cease, my son, to hear instruction, only to err from the words of knowledge.—Prov. 19. 27.

This is a proverbial appeal. The voice is that of a father deliberately counselling his son not to listen to instruction unless he intends to obey. The truth involved is, that it is better not to know, than, knowing, to fail to do. This cuts at the root of that most pernicious heresy, which yet is so largely held, that knowledge is in itself power. It is not so in any realm of life—scientific, economic, artistic, or moral. Knowledge is only powerful when it is the inspiration of activity in harmony with itself. The application of the truth in this proverb is in the realm of wisdom, and so of things moral and spiritual. The advice is good, because it is not only true that to know is of no avail apart from the doing which it demands—it is also true that unless knowledge is obeyed, in process of time it ceases to appeal. This means that a knowledge of the way of right, which is merely intellectual, exerts a hardening effect upon the finer things of the soul. In that sense familiarity breeds contempt, or indifference, which is, after all, the subtlest form of contempt. There is an old phrase, which some of us heard our fathers use. They spoke of some people as being "Gospel-hardened." A human being may become so accustomed to the Gospel message, that it ceases to make any appeal to mind or heart or will. It is this grave peril which gives warrant to this appeal. If we are purposed to err from the words of knowledge, it is better to cease to hear instruction.

The spirit of man is the lamp of the Lord, searching all his innermost parts. —Prov. 20. 27.

In this great word of Hebrew Wisdom, we have incidentally what we may reverently describe as a revelation of Biblical psychology. The Hebrew word, here rendered *spirit*, is the word rendered *breath* in the passage in Genesis, which says that "God . . . breathed into his nostrils the *breath* of life." The rendering *spirit*, therefore, is unquestionably accurate, and refers to that in man which constitutes him man, and differentiates between him and all animals. By that *breath* or *Spirit* he is separated from the animal world, as surely as the sentient life of the animal is separated from the vegetable life beneath it—and to greater distance. Man is not an animal. That breath or spirit—says this word of Wisdom—is the lamp of Jehovah, searching all the deepest things in the personality of man. Here is the Biblical conception of conscience. Within the mystery of the spirit-nature of every man there is light. It is the instrument of God. It illuminates life. It is that by which man is constantly kept face to face with truth. Let us make no mistake about it: the most evil men know that their works are evil. No specious arguments can prove to the spirit-life of a man that wrong is right, that impurity is pure. The day may come when a man becomes content with wrong, satisfied with impurity. Perhaps the day comes to some when they are unable to make the distinction. I doubt it. But if so, then it is because that lamp of Jehovah is put out, that deep essential spirit-life is atrophied—perished. But that is not the end. That spirit-life cannot cease to be. There is a resurrection to condemnation. There will be a new lighting of that lamp, and therein is the awful mystery of retribution. "In Hades, he lifted up his eyes, being in torments."

There is no wisdom nor understanding nor counsel against the Lord. —Prov. 21. 30.

This is the teaching of Wisdom. Persistently in human history hours come in which all appearances seem to contradict it. There is a wisdom which is "earthly, sensual, devilish," and it is active against Jehovah. There is an understanding which is acquaintance with the methods of iniquity, and it operates against Jehovah. There is a taking of counsel among men full of this wisdom and understanding, and it plots against Jehovah. Oftentimes as we have watched, we have trembled; so subtle, so clever, so cunning are the ways of this underworld of antagonism to Jehovah. Yet look again. Just as persistently in human history, the futility, the feebleness, the failure of this antagonism has been manifested. The evil wisdom is proved folly; the dark understanding is found to be ignorance; the malicious counsel is demonstrated futile. The warrant for the superlativeness of this proverb is found in the fact that all these very thoughts and devices and plots against Jehovah are compelled at last in their outworking to contribute to the purposes of His holy and gracious Will. He makes the wrath of man to praise Him. He makes the buffeting messenger of Satan the means of grace to His troubled, but trusting servant. Therefore it is true, full and finally, that "There is no wisdom nor understanding nor counsel against

Jehovah." And thus it becomes true that, "To them that love God all things work together for good." Here, then, is the place of our rest; here the secret of our confidence; here the inspiration of songs in the darkest night.

Train up a child in the way he should go, and even when he is old he will not depart from it.—*Prov.* 22. 6.

Perhaps there is no Proverb in all the collection which has been more frequently quoted than this; and perhaps also none has been more persistently misunderstood and misrepresented. It is a brief and complete revelation of the true method with a child. In order to a correct apprehension, everything depends upon the real meaning of the words *"in the way he should go."* That is by no means an inaccurate rendering, but the question arising is: What is the way in which a child should go? A more literal rendering of the Hebrew at once answers this question. Such translation would be: "Train up a child *according to his way.*" In every child there are special and peculiar powers. The true business of training a child, therefore, is that of discovering what those powers are, and developing them. It is a disaster to prepare a programme for a child without consulting the particular and peculiar life of that child, and then to endeavour to compel the child to conform to that ideal, to live by that programme. In all training of children the first business of those responsible must be that of considering the children themselves. Herein is revealed the need for individual work. No two children are alike. They cannot be trained in groups, in standards, in grades, in classes. They may thus be dealt with for the impartation of general information, but when the real work of training them according to their ways is undertaken, they must be taken one by one. This is one reason why the school which approximates to the family ideal is most successful. Our methods of training children have hardly begun to reach the Divine ideal.

When thou sittest to eat with a ruler, consider diligently him that is before thee.—*Prov.* 23. 1.

The first collection of Proverbs ended with the sixteenth verse of the previous chapter. Beginning with the seventeenth verse of that chapter, and running through chapter 24, we have a brief series of proverbial discourses. The division of this section into chapters has ignored this fact. The first of these discourses, commencing at chapter 22, verse 17, ends at the fourteenth verse of this chapter. It consists of a social admonition, and reveals the way of wisdom in certain human interrelationships. These particular words commence instruction as to how the man, walking in the ways of wisdom, that is in the fear of Jehovah, is to deport himself when he is the guest of a ruler. In such case the wise man will consider his host, rather than his hospitality. He is to keep his eye on the ruler. The reasons for such watching are revealed in all that follows. The things to be guarded against are: The desire for wealth; and any methods which are unjust to others. All this is suggestive. Think in the realm of this Old Testament word in another way. How many a young man has been robbed of the finest things of his manhood, those of truth, justice, honour, because he has been bribed by the hospitality of men of influence whose lives were impure, and who in their hospitality had ulterior motives of the basest. There is an old adage which says, "Never look a gift horse in the mouth." That may be used, and acted upon, in a disastrous fashion. Let every young man desirous of walking in the ways of wisdom, keep his eye, illuminated by the fear of Jehovah, upon all who put before him their material dainties, lest they rob him of his spiritual excellencies.

For a righteous man falleth seven times, and riseth up again; but the wicked are overthrown by calamity.—*Prov.* 24. 16.

This statement occurs in the second of these proverbial discourses, which commences in chapter 23 at verse 15, and ends at the twenty-second verse of this chapter. The section ends with a third discourse (verses 23 to 34), again concerned with the practice of wisdom in social relationships. This particular discourse consists of parental counsels. It first speaks again of a father's joy in the wisdom of his son; then urges the pursuit of wisdom; then warns against the sins of lust and strong drink. Finally, it sets forth the truth that the way of wisdom is the way of strength in the days of adversity and of calamity. That is the meaning of these particular words. The word "falleth" here has no reference to sin, but to trouble. This is a matter proven true in all human experience. Wisdom, the fear of Jehovah, the way of truth and honour, give a man that quality of strength which enables him to stand up against adversity until he overcome it. We may go further and say that adversity never overcomes the man who is righteous. It is not only true that ultimately he will overcome. It is also true that in the midst of it he will bear himself with invincible fortitude, and out of it will extract something of good, something which will make for his deeper enrichment. The good man is not callous. He suffers, but suffering does not embitter him. On the contrary it sweetens and beautifies his spirit. The real power to stand up against life, to profit by its buffetings, to make capital out of its disadvantages, to collect tribute from its tribulations, is that of the righteousness of conduct which results from walking in the ways of wisdom, by yielding to the inspiration and authority of the fear of Jehovah.

It is the glory of God to conceal a thing; but the glory of kings is to search out a matter.—Prov. 25. 2.

This is the first Proverb of a new collection. Here begins the third section of the book. It ends with chapter 29. It is a collection of the Proverbs of Solomon made in the days of Hezekiah. It is suggestive that those scribes put this Proverb first. It is at least probable that the times in which they lived had given them an interpretation of its meaning. They were wonderful times in their revelation of the wisdom of the Divine government. Out of strange perplexities and trials, the God Whose glory was that He had concealed things and yet had Himself been the All-Wise, had led them into better ways of life. Yet had not all this resulted from the fact that they had been under the rule of a king whose supreme glory had been that of searching out the secrets of wisdom, in the fear of Jehovah? The words, however, have the widest application. They cover all life. When Solomon wrote this Proverb, it is possible that he was remembering a great word of Moses (Deut. 29. 29). The philosophy is the same. The idea here is not that God maintains His glory by hiding things from man. It is rather that all the things so hidden, the things concealed, the secret things, are known to Him. He is the Ultimate in wisdom. That is His glory. That being so, man's true kingliness consists in his ability to search out these hidden things. That is the principle of all the triumphs of scientific investigations; and it is the deepest secret of all advance in spiritual strength. If a man would reign in life, he must begin with the fear of Jehovah which recognizes the glory of His knowledge of hidden things; and he must continue in that fear which maintains the attitude of such right relationship with God as will make it possible for Him to reveal to him His secrets. "The friendship of Jehovah is with them that fear Him."

Seest thou a man wise in his own conceit? There is more hope of a fool than of him.—Prov. 26. 12.

A man, wise in his own conceit, is a man who is perfectly satisfied with his own judgment, his own opinion. He seeks no light or counsel from without. He holds the views of other men in contempt. No one can teach him anything. In this Proverb, which is one of wisdom as defined, the thought is principally that of a man who does not fear God, who does not seek to be guided by the Divine Will. A fool here is simply an ignorant person

who knows his own ignorance. Such a one may be helped. However naturally dull of apprehension, he is willing to be taught. His natural folly makes it difficult to instruct him, but it is not impossible. This other man, starting with the conviction of his own wisdom, makes it impossible to help him, because he will have no help. The Proverb is not one that needs to be defended when we are looking at others. We see it exemplified so constantly, and however mistaken we know this man to be, we leave him to himself, for we know the hopelessness of trying to show him his ignorance. But the Proverb is one which we may safely use as a searchlight for ourselves. The peril is a very subtle one. We are prone to be wise in our own conceits, without knowing that we are so. A simple test may be employed. When we fail to seek Divine guidance in any undertaking, it is because we do not feel our need of it. In other words, we are wise in our own conceit. There is no safer condition of soul, than that self-distrust, that knowledge of ignorance, which drives us persistently to seek for the wisdom which cometh from above.

Better is open rebuke, than love that is hidden.—Prov. 27. 5.

This is a Proverb which gives us pause, as it produces conflicting emotions. We do not really like rebuke. We are inherently inclined to resent it. The fact that we really deserve it, or need it, does not make it pleasant. On the other hand, we do desire to be loved, even though love does not express itself. Moreover, our dislike of rebuke leads us to think that those who love us serve us well when they are silent in the presence of our shortcomings. The word of true wisdom cuts clean across all such wrong and foolish thinking. Begin with the second part. Love that is hidden is not perfect love in either sense. The highest love must and does express itself. It does so in praise of the loved one. An approbation of a person which finds no expression to that person is selfish, and therefore much less than love at its highest. But it is equally true that the highest love will express itself in rebuke, when the object upon which it is set is acting unworthily. The motive of love's rebuke is always that of the highest good of the loved one. Love is never blind, in spite of the foolish adage which declares that it is. It has clearest vision, and sees soonest the thing which threatens to mar the beauty of the loved one. Then love is never dumb; it speaks truthfully and plainly; it rebukes openly. Such open rebuke is proof of love at its highest. Love that hides itself, professes not to see, perhaps does not see, and so remains silent, is love on a very low level. It lacks the elements which inspire the loved one to strive for highest excellence.

Happy is the man that feareth alway; but he that hardeneth his heart shall fall into mischief.—*Prov.* 28. 14.

There is a caution which is of the soul of courage. There is a courage which is of the essence of foolhardiness. The man who is always mastered by wholesome fear, moves not slowly, but with persistent caution. Such a man is delivered from many calamities, and does not involve his friends in trouble. The man who lacks caution may have all the appearance of courage, his refusal to consider may appear heroic; but he inevitably falls into mischief, and brings other people into calamity. Necessarily, fear must be of the right nature. This, as we have to keep on reminding ourselves, is the literature of that Wisdom which is conditioned in the fear of Jehovah, and finally that is what the proverb means. The fear of Jehovah is the true caution. When it perpetually and persistently masters the life, that life is ever watchful of ways and means, as well as of issues. That fear, moreover, cancels all other fear. To fear God is to cease to fear for myself; it is no longer to bargain with consequences; it is never to act without His command; it is to act at all costs when His Will is revealed. When that fear is absent, courage is mere hardening of the heart, recklessness, foolhardiness. The man who shuts his eyes to God, gathers himself up, and desperately plunges forward, is no hero; he is a fool, and without exception sooner or later lands himself in circumstances which break him; and brings those about him into suffering and catastrophe. Safety first is the devil's own suggestion to the soul, if it means take care of yourself. It is the highest principle of life, if it takes in the larger facts of life, and is conditioned in the fear of God.

Where there is no vision, the people cast off restraint; but he that keepeth the law, happy is he.—*Prov.* 29. 18.

The Revisers have helped us by changing the word "perish" to "cast off restraint." Quite literally the Hebrew word means to "break loose." The condition is that of anarchy. Anarchy is lawlessness, not being without law, but refusing to be bound by law. That is the one fundamental trouble with man. John declared that, when he wrote: "Sin is lawlessness." We have been living in days when lawlessness has been rampant. Men have been breaking through covenants, regulations, agreements; refusing to abide by any decisions, even those of their appointed leaders, or those to which they themselves have agreed. In this word of wisdom the reason for this casting off of restraint is given. It is that of lack of vision. That is true, on lowest levels of consideration. Men who so act have no true vision of what they are actually doing, no true vision of the conse-

quences of their action. They have no true vision of society as a whole, and of the necessary obligations of all those individuals who constitute society. They do not see that lawlessness in personal life destroys the possibility of true social conditions; and that false social conditions in turn destroy the individual. But the deeper note is that the lack of the vision of God issues in lack of vision in all these regards. To see God, is, as in the case of Jacob, to bring healing to the individual; and that is to create a healthy community. To lose that vision, is to have no vision which is adequate to meet the needs of man; to have no authority to which man can be submitted. The vision of God is given to man in the law of God, and to-day in that law as it has been interpreted in Christ and made possible of realization through Him. "He that keepeth *that* law, happy is he."

Every word of God is tried; He is a shield unto them that trust in Him. Add thou not unto His words, lest He reprove thee, and thou be found a liar.—*Prov.* 30. 5, 6.

The last division of this book of Proverbs is of the nature of an appendix, and consists of (1) "The Words of Agur;" and (2) "The Words of King Lemuel." These are unknown men. Their utterances are characterized by the true note of Wisdom which has been maintained throughout. Whoever Agur was, he had the true outlook on life. His message opens with a confession of his own ignorance. He then declares that, while compelled to recognize the Holy One by what he sees in Nature, he has not there been brought to a knowledge of Him. This double confession leads up to these words, which thus consist of a declaration that God can only be known through direct revelation, through His Word. This conviction leads to the note of faith, and of warning: "Every word of God is tried," and "Add thou not unto His words." We live in clearer light, and have fuller understanding. For us, the Word of God has been made flesh; and thus the Father has been declared to us. This only emphasizes the truth of this word of Wisdom uttered long ago by this unknown philosopher. The Word of God is indeed tried—that is, purified, which means demonstrated as pure. It is the one final law of life, interpreting, guiding, perfecting. Let us, then, heed the warning, and be careful that we do not in any fancied wisdom of our own, add anything to His words. To do so is to be found liars, those in whom the truth is not.

Her children rise up, and call her blessed; her husband also, and he praiseth her.—*Prov.* 31. 28.

There are those who distinguish between the two parts of this chapter by treating the first nine verses as "The Words of King Lemuel"; and the rest as being quite separate. Personally, I believe the whole are "The Words of King Lemuel"; in the first part he records the words of counsel his mother addressed to him; and in the second he gives us the picture of that mother. This picture of a virtuous woman is full of Eastern colouring, but it is also full of beauty, and, in its deeper notes, is of universal application. It is important that we recognize the true connotations of the word here rendered worthy. The thought is really that of strength. The woman celebrated is the one who realizes in all fulness and richness the capacities and glories of her womanhood, as wife and mother in the home.

The description of her reaches its climax in these words. This is the chaplet of rarest beauty upon the head of womanhood, that her children rise up and call her blessed, and her husband thinks and speaks of her as excelling all others. The secret of this blessedness is revealed later in the words: "A woman that feareth Jehovah, she shall be praised." Wisdom blossoms into beauty in that woman who by love and diligence, by knowledge and devotion, so trains her children that when they pass out from her roof into life, and through all the coming days, bless her and her memory with glad and grateful hearts. There are those of us who will do that through all our days and for ever.

ECCLESIASTES

Vanity of vanities, saith the Preacher; vanity of vanities, all is vanity.—*Eccles* 1. 2.

The sub-title of this book found in our translations, "or the Preacher," we owe to Luther, and it is misleading. As Dr. Plumptre has argued at length, and proved conclusively, the more correct rendering of the Hebrew word Koheleth would be "The Debater." This is important, for it at once reminds us that here we have Discussion, rather than Teaching. In these words we have the general proposition of the Debater. Everything he says from here on to the eighth verse of chapter eleven is in defence of this statement. Then in a paragraph, brief but pregnant (11. 9–12), he gives an entirely different view of life, which is a corrective of this. Let us, then, at once face this opening declaration. It is an absolutely accurate statement of life when it is lived under certain conditions; but it is not true as a statement of what life must necessarily be. There are thousands of men and women to-day who cannot, and do not, accept this to be true of life as they find it; it is not vanity, vapour, emptiness, nothingness. To them life in every way is real, rich, full, glorious. It is well, then, that at the beginning we should understand the viewpoint of the Debater. His declaration is that things in themselves bring no satisfaction to the soul of man. To live on earth without recognition of the supreme wisdom which begins and continues in the fear of Jehovah, to deal only with that hemisphere which is "under the sun," is indeed to find things of exceeding wonder and beauty and power; but it is to find nothing that satisfies, and to be left at last without any reality, to find only vanity, vapour, emptiness.

This also is vanity and a striving after wind.—*Eccles. 2. 26.*

These words occur at the close of a section of the debate, and are a refrain already oft repeated. In the first movement, after stating in general terms his conclusion, the Debater elaborated his statement by describing vividly his consciousness of the grind of the material universe (1. 4–11). Then he began to mass his evidence in support of his contention that all is vanity. He first gave his own experience in personal life. He tried knowledge, giving himself up to a study of "all that is done under heaven." The result was that he "perceived that this also was a striving after wind" (1. 12–18). He gave himself up to pleasure, to mirth, and found "this also was vanity" (2. 1–3). He devoted himself to the amassing of wealth, and this with conspicuous success, only to look on everything and to discover that "all was vanity and a striving after wind" (2. 4–11). He then contemplated life in the light of these disappointments, and came to the material conclusion that "there is nothing better for a man than that he should eat and drink"; and yet he was forced to admit that "This also is vanity, and a striving after wind." This is indeed graphic literature. It shows us a man, richly endowed in himself, living in the midst of marvellous things, of knowledge, of mirth, of wealth, of life; giving himself to these things with all the powers of his being—and yet finding nothing in them. He is starved, homeless, despairing. There is a side to life which he is not counting on, or considering. It is the side which is spiritual, the completion of the sphere over the sun, above the material. Forgetting that, everything is vanity. This is as modern as the ennui of every human soul which seeks knowledge, mirth, wealth, life—and forgets God.

Wherefore I saw that there is nothing better, than that a man should rejoice in his works; for that is his portion; for who shall bring him back to see what shall be after him?— Eccles. 3. 22.

With this chapter the Debater begins to advance evidence of the vanity of all things, from a wider outlook than that of the purely personal. In six chapters (3–8) we find him dealing with relative considerations. First he returned to the mechanism of the Universe, already touched upon (1. 4–11). He sees a recurrence of opposite circumstances continuously manifest, and concludes that man's wisest course is to adapt himself to these. It is to be observed throughout that this man was by no means an atheist. He believed in God, and in His government of all things. But his conception of man was that he is a being living in the midst of this government without any personal fellowship with the God Who is governing. Man is an animal only; he is like the beasts—at least this man was not sure that there is any difference. He was an agnostic. He inquired: "Who knoweth the spirit of man whether it goeth upward, and the spirit of the beast whether it goeth downward to the earth?" Therefore his outlook upon life lacked illumination, and his conclusion was that there is nothing better than that a man should make the best he could out of the things of the earth, that he should rejoice in his own works. This is perfectly natural and inevitable. To attempt to interpret God by circumstances, as they appear to man's partial vision, is to become pessimistic. It is only when the soul looks out upon circumstances from the standpoint of fellowship with God, and knowledge of Him, that it can be optimistic.

Better than them both did I esteem him which hath not yet been, who hath not seen the evil work that is done under the sun.—Eccles. 4. 3.

In this chapter the Debater describes sociological conditions, as he observed them; and this is his terrible finding. The dead are better than the living; but better than either, is not to have been born at all! It is a terrible conclusion; yet it is a perfectly natural and justifiable one to any who looks only upon conditions of life, and has no interpretation gained in fellowship with God. Glance over life with the Debater. The oppressed are seen, and no one to comfort them. Dexterity in toil is seen, producing envy in the hearts of others. Men are seen gathering wealth and passing into loneliness. Age is seen with its folly and weakness, in spite of position, even that of kingship. The outlook is indeed dark and terrible. Life is not worth while. Death is preferable. Yet better than that, is not to have been. Granted that the things described are not all of life as it may be seen; they are yet so prevalent and so poignant as to make the observer unconscious of brighter facts. The existence of such things at all cancels all other considerations. And the conclusion is warranted. Blot out the things above the sun; deny, or be ignorant of the God Who reigns on high—and life as it is seen is a nightmare and a horror. Every joy becomes a mockery: every pleasure a delusion; every hope a mirage. It is only when we know God, and live in His fear, that we come to understand that all these discords will at last be resolved into perfect harmony. It is only as life is conditioned by spiritual facts and forces that it is delivered from despair.

. . . But fear thou God.—Eccles. 5. 7.

The relative considerations continue, as the Debater turns to the subject of religion and of political conditions. These words conclude the paragraph dealing with religion, and express the finding of one who is living "under the sun." As we have pointed out before, this man is a believer in God, but he has no knowledge of God. These words seem to harmonize with the central principle of true wisdom, which is that its beginning and maintenance depend upon "the fear of Jehovah"; but a careful consideration of the whole paragraph will show how utterly different is the conception. Fear, in the sense in which it is used here, is the fear of the slave rather than that of the son; it lacks the notes of confidence, of trust, and of love. All the advice given is good, in so far as it goes; but every word of it is born of the dread of doing anything which will offend a God Who is sovereign, but Whose ways are unknown. This conception of religion is that it consists of securing personal safety, by not doing things which are likely to offend God. I repeat, all is good so far as it goes; but it lacks the positive note, the glad note, the triumphant note; which notes are always present when life begins with the knowledge of the true God. Such knowledge issues in no irreverent familiarity; but it produces a reverent familiarity; it gives the soul freedom of utterance and of action in the presence of God. Men whose belief in God is merely intellectual, never rise above this level. Their religion, if they have any, is always characterized by this kind of fear, and becomes a burden, an oppression, something which robs life of joy.

Whatsoever hath been, the name thereof was given long ago, and it is known that it is man; neither can he contend with Him that is mightier than he.—*Eccles.* 6. 10.

After the paragraph on religion in the previous chapter, the Debater went on to look out upon political matters, those of poverty resulting from the maladministration of justice, and of the uselessness and futility of wealth, and even of knowledge, in the midst of such conditions. In these words we have the expression of fatalism. A man finds himself in the midst of these things, and is himself the creature of a destiny from which he cannot escape. He has no freedom in life, and no certainty of what may lie hidden in the great beyond. This is a hard and crushing view of God, and of the order of life; but it is logical. To this view men invariably come whose outlook is only that of the earth and of circumstances. It is only when man begins with a knowledge of God, coming by revelation rather than investigation, that he escapes from this crushing sense of a destiny which leaves him no room for action. It is impossible to read all this without realizing how great is the contrast between this outlook upon life, and that which inspired the poetry and prophesying of those men of the same nation who were familiar with the revelation of God as Jehovah; and yet how much greater is the contrast between it, and the outlook on life which is found in the New Testament as the result of the revelation of God in Christ! The value of these inspired confessions of one who lived under the sun is that they reveal this contrast.

. . . God hath even made the one side by side with the other, to the end that man should not find out anything that shall be after him.—*Eccles.* 7. 14.

"The one" and "the other" refer to "the day of prosperity," and "the day of adversity" (see earlier part of the verse). These words occur in the midst of a sustained argument, occupying the whole of this chapter and the next, in which, upon the basis of all the foregoing reflections, the Debater declares that the only way to live is to be indifferent to all the facts of life, or to manipulate them so as to make the best of things. Wisdom has its advantages, but it breaks down. Righteousness is good; but don't press it too far, it may destroy you. So also don't go too far in wickedness; it shortens life! Life is necessarily made up, by the ordering of God, of changing and varying experiences of prosperity and of adversity, of wickedness and righteousness; it runs on as a whole along the line of a sort of balanced average. God has so ordered it, that no man can discover the issue of any experience through which he passes. Therefore be sensible; don't worry;

take things as they come; make the best of them! How futile and mistaken the whole conception is, we know; but let us not forget that it is really most reasonable, if a man have no light to guide him other than that which he finds within himself, or that which is discoverable in this material outlook. It is rational, all of it, if a man decline to seek the reason of life and all its experiences in the truth about God, which He gives to those who make His fear the first thing in life; and therefore is unable to see the whole of things.

Then I commended mirth.—*Eccles.* 8. 15.

When? When he had been convinced of the "vanity which is done upon the earth," in that "there are righteous men, unto whom it happeneth according to the work of the wicked"; again, "there are wicked men, to whom it happeneth according to the work of the righteous." Because of these inequalities, these injustices, let a man give himself to mirth, let him eat and drink and be merry! Again, as we read, we realize the folly of all this. But wherein lies the folly? Certainly not in the conclusion resulting from the premises as advanced. If this be so, that a righteous man reaps the reward of wickedness, and a wicked man that of righteousness, then let us ignore both righteousness and wickedness, and give ourselves up to our appetites. This is exactly what thousands of men are doing. The folly lies in the limitation of outlook. Watching life "under the sun," these things often seem to be so. Observing it as "a whole"—that is, taking in the larger view, seeing the things above the sun, beyond the material—it is at once evident that the righteous man reaps the reward of righteousness, and the wicked man that of wickedness. To take one illustration only from the New Testament. Our Lord, in that very solemn and revealing story of the rich man and Lazarus, shows that the final meaning of life is never found on this side of death. Death is but the separation of the essential man from the temporary tabernacle of the body. The issues of deeds done in the body are reached beyond that separation. Herein we discover the folly of all such indifference as is counselled by this man, attempting to interpret life by things seen, which are temporal, and ignoring things unseen, which are eternal.

Whatsoever thy hand findeth to do, do it with thy might; for there is no work, nor device, nor knowledge, nor wisdom, in the grave whither thou goest.—*Eccles.* 9. 10.

With this chapter a new division of this book commences. It closes at the eighth verse of chapter eleven. As we saw, the book opened with the affirmation of the vanity of all things. This affirmation was followed by the massing of evidence in support of this view of life. The proofs given were those of the Debater's own experiences of life, and those derived from his general observation. Throughout, the outlook has been that of a man living "under the sun," and that in the fullest sense possible—that is, having all advantages, and so enabled to test life on this level thoroughly, and so to speak with authority. The result is the conviction that all is vanity. In the section now beginning, this man extols the kind of worldly wisdom at which he has already hinted; and then proceeds to exemplify it. The words I have stressed give a fair example of this worldly wisdom. The advice given is excellent, but the reason is utterly bad; and where it is the inspiration of earnestness and thoroughness, they in themselves become pernicious. Of course, it is good to do whatever we have to do with our might. But if the reason is that this life is all, that the inactive and dark region which this kind of wisdom supposes exists beyond, is to mean cessation, then the earnestness will inevitably be misdirected. James, the Wisdom-writer of the New Testament, speaks of a wisdom which is "earthly, sensual, devilish"; and this is it. Nevertheless, this is the rational decision of all who live "under the sun."

Curse not the king, no, not with thy thought; and curse not the rich in thy bed-chamber; for a bird of the air shall carry the voice, and that which hath wings shall tell the matter.—*Eccles.* 10. 20.

This is an excellent example of worldly wisdom. Having extolled it, this man of material outlook proceeds to give advice as to how to live according to it. From the seventeenth verse of the preceding chapter up to and including this verse, the burden has been that of the necessity for discretion (in the sense of cunning), that is, cautiousness which is bad in motive, and often dishonest in practice. Take this verse and look at it carefully. What does it amount to? This simply: Don't be found out! The fear which is manifested in such advice is not the fear of doing what is dishonourable; it is the fear rather that the dishonourable thing should be discovered. No man whose life is governed by the fear of Jehovah, in the true sense of that word, can ever be influenced by such advice as this. Such a man knows that the dishonourable deed is to be avoided because it is dishonourable. In the last analysis, fear of being found out is fear of punishment; while fear of Jehovah is fear of sin in itself. Herein is revealed the difference between the wisdom which is "earthly, sensual, devilish"; and "the wisdom that is from above," which

"is first pure." It is true that "honesty is the best policy," but the man who is only honest because it is good policy is a rogue at heart. Thus all maxims which have a sound of wisdom need to be tested by the motive which inspires them.

Yea, if a man live many years, let him rejoice in them all; but let him remember the days of darkness, for they shall be many. All that cometh is vanity.—*Eccles.* 11. 8.

These are the final words in the revelation of what life is when it is lived "under the sun," that is, on the material plane, in a hemisphere with no vital relationships with the spiritual world beyond an intellectual assent to its existence. The mind travels on to that which lies beyond this life, and discovers only darkness. That outlook leads to the statement: "All that cometh is vanity." This carries his opening affirmation, "All is vanity," out beyond the present. The man who sees nothing but vanity in the things of to-day sees nothing but vanity in that which lies beyond his ken. There is only darkness, no light, no knowledge, vanity. Therefore let a man take hold of the present, and get out of it all that he can; let him rejoice in the years, because they are the only things of which he can be sure! This is exactly the attitude of thousands toward life. Indeed, it is the only attitude possible to those who have no direct dealing with the spiritual world. This is all they can do, and it is a pre-eminently sensible thing to do. Yet what a vicious circle is that which the mind, so circumscribed, makes in its thinking! Everything here is vanity—that is, void, not worth while; yet because there is nothing beyond, but once again vanity, let a man take hold of and enjoy the present vanity! Can anything be more fatuous? Thus the Debater proves what the book is intended to prove, the utter folly of life "under the sun," that is, life endeavouring to realize itself, while shutting out of its reckoning those larger facts, above the sun, beyond the material.

This is the end of the matter; all hath been heard; fear God, and keep His commandments; for this is the whole duty of man.—*Eccles.* 12. 13.

With verse 9 of the previous chapter the final division of this book begins. It stands in direct and intended contrast to all that has preceded it. That contrast is immediately seen when verses eight and nine in chapter 11 are compared. Both call upon man to rejoice, but the motive is entirely different. The voice of worldly wisdom says: rejoice because all the future is dark and vanity. Now the higher wisdom speaks, and it says: rejoice, by remembering that God brings men into judgment as to the exercise of all their natural powers. Let it be remembered that judgment does not mean punishment, unless and until men abuse those natural powers. Wisdom says: life is to be full of joy, and the way to find joy is to order it under the judgment, that is under the government of God. This is urged in all that follows, until in these words everything is summarized. I cannot refrain from saying that this statement has suffered incalculably from the introduction by translators of the word *duty*. The word does not occur in the Hebrew text. Leave it out, and the statement is: "This is the whole of man." This at once emphasizes the outlook of all that has gone before The outlook of the Debater has not been the whole of man. Life in its wholeness takes in the things above the sun, the spiritual facts and forces; it begins with the fear of God, and brings that fear to bear upon all the lower facts and forces, by walking in His commandments. No man who lives a whole life, ever says that "all is vanity." He, first finding God, finds also the joy and fulness of life in every aspect. To him life becomes a song and a gladness; it is full and glorious.

SONG OF SONGS

They made me keeper of the vineyards, But mine own vineyard have I not kept.—*Song of Songs* 1. 6.

There are those who treat this Book as a song of human love. There are those who consider its only value is that of its mystical suggestiveness. Personally, I believe that both values are here. If it has no mystical intention, it is invaluable as a song of love between man and woman. If it has mystical intentions, they are conveyed by the highest figurative vehicle, that of this very love. This is the language of the Bride to the attendant virgins. It is not that of apology in the sense of confessing failure. It is that of apology in the sense of defence. Note the whole movement. She is black, but comely. She is swarthy, the sun has scorched her; but that, while keeping the vineyards of others. The blackness, the swarthiness, are due to service; the personal vineyard unkept is of the nature of sacrifice in the interest of that service. The watching virgins might wonder at the love of the Bridegroom for this Bride, bearing certain marks of limitation or lack of what they conceived as personal beauty. The Bride declares that these marks are the evidences of that in her which her Bridegroom values. They become the symbols of the truest beauty. On the level of human love how suggestive this is. To a true man, the chief things of beauty in a woman are those which testify to her greatness of soul; oftentimes the apparent disfigurement of the superficial and external is evidence of greatness of character. In the realm of mystic interpretation, we here touch a profound truth. The Bride of Christ is beautiful in His eyes in proportion as she bears the marks of real fellowship with His sacrificial service. He Who emptied Himself, rejoices in those who, in their devotion to the vineyards of others, rise to the height of neglecting their own.

As a lily among thorns, so is my love among the daughters.—*Song of Songs* 2. 2.

This is the language of the Bridegroom. In it, he adopts the description which the Bride has given of herself in the words immediately preceding, "I am a rose of Sharon; a lily of the valleys"; but adds to its impressiveness and beauty by the words "among thorns." The lily referred to was certainly a scarlet flower, and a not uncommon one; just as the rose of Sharon was the violet and white crocus which abounded. Thus the Bride's description of herself was really self-depreciatory, rather than otherwise. It was as if she saw that there was nothing in her beauty extraordinary or out of the common. Here the Revised helps us as it renders "*a* rose of Sharon," rather than "*the* rose of Sharon"; and "*a* lily of the valleys," rather than "*the* lily of valleys." To this the Bridegroom replies by accepting her description of herself as "a lily," but not as one among many, but as one in comparison with whom all others in his eyes are as thorns. This is the true outlook of love. To the man, the wonder in his beloved is ever that she is full of beauty, when others growing in the selfsame soil are devoid of it. When we interpret the words as those of Christ, they are the more arresting, because the description is literally true. Those beloved of Him, flourish and become truly beautiful, in soil which produces thorns. The graces and beauties of the Lord's beloved ones are not those of plants nourished in hothouses; they are those which are developed in places of storm and frost and unpromising soils. Here, necessarily, the mystic interpretation carries us into a realm higher and more wonderful than nature can interpret.

When I found him whom my soul loveth; I held him, and would not let him go.—*Song of Songs 3. 4.*

This is the language of the Bride. It is part of her account of her memories of those days in which her lover was wooing her; and in particular it is the record of a dream. After the beloved had come (2. 8–14); and passed (2. 15–17); the night came; and, in her dreams, she thought she had lost him. Still in dreams, she rose and searched the city for him, inquiring from the watchmen. At last she found him; and then she held him and would not let him go. On the human level, as a story of love, this is very natural and very beautiful. Love creates a perpetual dread lest the loved one should be lost; and this dread, often only subconscious in the day-time, takes the form of actual experience in the dreaming of the night. Then follows the search, and the new grip upon the loved one when he is found. All of this is a poetic and true interpretation of the power of love when it masters a life. When we make the story figurative and interpretative of those highest relationships of the soul with God through Christ, it becomes a wonderful revelation of the sensitiveness of the life which is really in love with Christ, and so with God. We are only safe so long as the dread of the loss of our Beloved keeps us ever sensitive and watchful. When, either in a dream, or in reality we lose our sense of His presence, let us search for Him; and then in the finding, with new devotion, let us hold Him, and refuse to let Him go.

Awake, O north wind; and come, thou south;
Blow upon my garden, that the spices thereof may flow out.
Let my beloved come into his garden,
And eat his precious fruits.
Song of Songs 4. 16.

In the section beginning at 3. 6 we have the story of the betrothal; and in these words the response of the Bride to the proposal of the Bridegroom is recorded. It is the language of her yielding to him, of her acceptance of his call. It is highly pictorial, and poetic with the fine spirit of the East. In the first part of it, she thinks of herself, of her personality, that which is *her* garden. In the second part she thinks of herself as belonging to him, she is now *his* garden. Her desire for herself is that the fragrance of her personality may flow forth for his sake. Therefore she calls for the double ministry of the north and south winds; of that which is cold and health-giving, the spirit of principle; of that which is warm and comforting, the spirit of passion. Under this double ministry, all the beauty of personality is perfected, as principle is suffused with passion, and passion governed by principle. Then, to the garden, so prepared and perfected, let the beloved come, and eat his precious fruits. The dominant desire of the speaker is that of the satisfaction of the Beloved. This consideration rises without strain to the higher realms. The one overwhelming passion of the loved of the Lord, is to give His heart satisfaction, to provide for Him the precious fruits for which He in love is seeking. That we may do that, we call for the north wind and for the south; for adversity and prosperity; for winter and summer; in order that by their varied ministries, we may become to Him a garden of delights.

This is my beloved, and this is my friend, O daughters of Jerusalem.—*Song of Songs 5. 16.*

This is the language of the Bride, and it is the climax of her reply to the question of the daughters of Jerusalem. They had said: "What is thy beloved more than beloved?" I have omitted the word *another*, because while it does express the sense of the question, it is not in the Hebrew text, and to me the inquiry is more forceful without it. They said: "What is there in thy beloved, more than what any other woman sees in her own beloved?" It was a perfectly natural question. And yet there is more, for that woman. The Bride replies by describing him in all the wealth of oriental imagery. Yet any other woman might have used every figure in describing her beloved. But, at last, and as I think, half unconsciously, the truth is out as she said: "This is *my* beloved, and this is *my* friend." That is the truth, and no description of the beloved is satisfactory except to the one employing it, who all the while sees more than words are conveying to others. The application of this in the highest realms transcends the human level. No believer can describe the Lord, for every description breaks down. That is why, for instance, no artist has ever satisfied any other than himself, in portraying Jesus, and it is questionable whether he has done that. The supernal wonder of our Lord is that He is the altogether Lovely One to His Bride, and so to all the multitudes of souls which constitute that Bride. Every one of them can say: "This is *my* Beloved, and this is *my* Friend"; and if each could portray to others what that means, the wonder of the revelation would be that of the many-coloured grace and glory of the Lord. And that is what they will do in the ages to come, when to principalities and powers they reveal the wisdom and love of God, and Christ comes to be admired in His saints.

Who is she that looketh forth as the morning, fair as the moon, clear as the sun, terrible as an army with banners?
—*Song of Songs 6. 10.*

These words are by some attributed to the women referred to in the previous verse. That is not my understanding of the movement. From the fourth verse of this chapter up to and including the ninth of the next one, we have the Bridegroom's musings upon the grace and beauty of his Bride. Having in those musings referred to the praising of the women, he breaks out into this ecstatic utterance. It is the highest note reached in all the descriptions, and can only be interpreted as referring to beauties of character, even on the level of earthly love. The terms are purely poetic. The word for moon means whiteness; and that for sun means heat. They are only used in poetry. Follow the stages of description. The picture is of the dawn moving to noon. First the freshness and beauty of the morning hour just as the night is passing; then the whiteness of the moon, the fairness of purity; then the clarity, and freedom from alloy resulting from the action of fire; and finally the irresistible majesty of an army marching under its banners. These are the ultimate things of beauty in the Bride, the things which capture and hold the love of the Bridegroom. This verse has been a great stronghold for those who have employed the mystic method of interpretation of this song, and justifiably so. Thus Christ sees His Bride, as she will be in that fair morn of morns when the triumph of His redeeming grace is complete in her. Let every member of that Bride ponder the vision, and by ever increasing submission to His grace, press toward the mark of His high calling.

I am my beloved's, and his desire is toward me.—Song of Songs 7. 10.

That is the voice of the Bride, following the musing of the Bridegroom. It is the full, final, ultimate word of love. It expresses complete satisfaction, absolute rest, the uttermost of contentment and peace. There are two elements in it. The first is that of complete abandonment; "I am my beloved's." The second is that of the realization that the beloved is satisfied; "His desire is toward me." There are no words in literature so completely, and perfectly, and yet simply, setting forth the highest experience of human love; and therefore they are words which justify the mystical interpretation of this Song to the full. This is the language of the soul when it has found its final rest and satisfaction in the love of God—both His love for the soul, and the soul's love for Him. This, of course, for us finds its fulfilment in and through Christ. To be able to use these words as defining the relationship between the soul and Him is to have found the highest joy, the profoundest peace, the complete experience of love. The contemplation of the ideal becomes an investigation. We can say without doubt, wonderful as the fact is, that "His desire is toward us." Can we say—each personally —"I am my Beloved's?" It is only as we can, that we begin to know the depth and richness of His love. His desire toward us found demonstration in His Cross. Our appreciation of that desire is in the measure of our abandonment of ourselves to His love.

I adjure you, O daughters of Jerusalem, that ye stir not up, nor awaken love, until it please.—Song of Songs 8. 4.

Let us go back and read 2. 7 and 3. 5. The similarity to this verse is at once recognized. In each case I omit in reading the "my" which is suggested by translators, and adopt the marginal reading "it," instead of "he." In each case there is identity in the call; the only difference is that in this last occurrence the illustrative words "By the roes, and by the hinds of the field" are omitted. When this great Song is carefully set out, it is found to consist in the main of words of the Bride and Bridegroom. To these are added certain words of the virgins addressed to Bride or Bridegroom. But on these three occasions it is yet another voice. This is the voice of Wisdom, uttering a warning, which is needed, and which is made powerful by the matchless love-story. What is this warning? That love is so sacred a thing that it must not be trifled with. It is not to be sought. It stirs and awakens of itself. To trifle with the capacity for it, is to destroy that very capacity. This is the evil of all philandering. Would that these words could be sung into the deepest soul of all youths and maidens. The tragedies of disobedience to the warnings are everywhere. Is there any application of these words possible in that higher realm which we have had in mind throughout our reading? I think there is. They warn us against the peril of endeavouring to force an experience of love to Christ and God in others. Our privilege is to introduce our loved ones, our children, our friends, everybody, to Christ; but they must fall in love with Him for themselves. Was not this in His mind, when He told His disciples to tell no man that He was the Christ? As He had said to Peter, that revelation comes, not of flesh and blood, but of the Father. We wrong the souls of the young, and indeed of any, when we endeavour to force an experience. Let us lead them to Him. He will awaken love.

ISAIAH

I am full of the burnt offerings of rams . . .—*Isa. 1. 11.*

The first verse of this chapter constitutes the Title Page of the book, and gives us with perfect clearness the dates of Isaiah's prophesying. Chapter 6 speaks of Uzziah's death. In chapters 1 to 5 we have the notes of the prophet's messages during the reign of Uzziah. This first chapter Ewald called "the great Arraignment"; and that most accurately describes it. Throughout, the nation is seen from the Divine viewpoint, and its terrible condition is vividly set forth. From the material standpoint, the reign of Uzziah was characterized by great prosperity. Moreover, the Temple service was maintained. At the heart of the chapter these words occur, and they are startlingly revealing of the Divine attitude toward the sacrifices which are being offered. The words, "I have had enough of," are expressive of loathing, produced by satiety. The whole force of this is derived from the fact that all these offerings were Divinely appointed. What an interpretation we have here of the attitude of God toward all religious observances. When the highest and best of these, those of His own ordination, cease to be the expressions of a true spiritual and moral condition, He loathes them. The reason is clearly revealed in a subsequent sentence: "I cannot away with iniquity and the solemn meeting." In all our exercises in worship we need to remember this. The singing of hymns, the offering of prayers, the giving of money, the study of the Word, all may become hateful to God, and do, when the spiritual and moral condition of the worshippers is not in harmony with what these things stand for.

O house of Jacob, come ye, and let us walk in the light of the Lord.—Isa. 2. 5.

After the indictment of the nation contained in the first chapter, there follows a prediction of the ideal conditions which will obtain "in the latter days," that is, in the established Messianic Kingdom. "The light of Jehovah" referred to in this appeal is the glory of that vision of the latter days. It is to be noted that immediately after this appeal, the prophecy returns to the sad conditions then existing, to a denunciation of them, and to a declaration that in order to end them, and bring in the true order, "there shall be a day of Jehovah," and that a day of "the terror of Jehovah." The arresting and instructive fact is that in the midst of the darkness and degeneration, this prophet of God had a clear vision of the ultimate glory, an unwavering faith that it would be realized; and that he described it, and made his appeal to the nation to walk in the light of it. An examination of all the prophetic writings of the Old Testament, and the Apostolic writings of the New, will show that this has always been true of the God-inspired messengers. No men saw so clearly, or denounced so consistently and vehemently, the godless and calamitous ways of wickedness; but they never lost sight of the final triumph of righteousness, and they constantly bade men "rejoice in the hope of the glory of God," and called them to walk in the light thereof. This is a matter which we do well to ponder. In days of darkness, and widespread corruption, we are in danger of becoming so conscious of these conditions, as to forget, or even to doubt, the ultimate issue of the triumph of God. This never happens to those who live in close fellowship with God. They see through all the mysterious present, to the determined end, and in the light of that glory, order all their steps.

. . . The daughters of Zion are haughty . . . —Isa. 3. 16.

These words constitute the central charge made against the women at the court, in this message of the prophet. The whole oracle is a brilliant and satirical exposure of the vanity and futility of their mode of life. This mode of life to the prophet was not vain and futile only; it was positively wicked in view of the fact that the luxury in which they lived was made possible by the crushing of the people, and the grinding of the face of the poor. Yet there is a deeper note here than that. It is not possible to imagine that a prophet like Isaiah would have wasted his time denouncing these women, if he had not recognized how they were involved in the guilt of the rulers, and the degeneracy of the nation. At a later period in this prophetic work he again denounced them (see chapter 32). Amos at the court of Samaria was fierce in his invective against the women. All this is very suggestive. The influence of women is most powerful for good or for ill. I once heard one of the keenest of observers say that no great movement for the uplifting of humanity had been generated in human history but that woman's influence had much to do with it. Whether so superlative a statement is capable of substantiation I do not know; but I believe there is a great element of truth in it. It is equally true that the part that women have taken in corrupting the race has been terrible. When the womanhood of a nation is noble, the national life is held in strength. When it is corrupt, the nation is doomed. Woman is the last stronghold of good or of evil. Compassion and cruelty are superlative in her.

. . . By the spirit of judgement, and by the spirit of burning.—*Isa.* 4. 4.

In the oracle concerning the women, the prophet had foretold the destruction of the city by reason of the corruption in which these women were involved, both as to cause and course. As ever, this messenger of God saw that the retribution resulting from Divine judgment would issue in restoration; and in the brief but beautiful utterances contained in verses 2 to 6 of this chapter he described the new order. In the process of that judgment, evil will be eliminated, and those left in Jerusalm will be holy; the daughters of Jerusalem will be washed from their filth and the city cleansed of its blood. The words we have stressed are those in which the prophet described the agency by which this process of cleansing will be carried out. It is a remarkable description: "The spirit of justice and the spirit of burning." Justice is government in action, and in strict and impartial justice, it is discriminative and irresistible. Burning is a process which exterminates the things that are base and unworthy, and purifies to freedom from all alloy the things which are noble and worthy. This conception of God as a Spirit of justice and of fire, recurs again and again in these Old Testament writings, and passes over into the New Testament with its interpretation of the age of the Spirit. While there are senses in which the Spirit as fire is now available and at work in special ways, as the result of the perfected work of the Son of God, there are senses in which all human history has known the presence and power of "the spirit of justice," and "the spirit of burning." That spirit ever blasts the evil, and establishes the good.

. . . He looked for judgement, but behold oppression; for righteousness, but behold a cry.—*Isa.* 5. 7.

These words are of supreme importance in that they constitute the prophet's interpretation of his own song of the vineyard. In that song he had likened Judah to a plant of Jehovah's planting, from which he expected grapes, but which had brought forth wild grapes. Now the figure is explained. The fruit which Jehovah expected from the nation is described by the two words "justice" and "righteousness." In order to the bringing forth in the midst of the nations of "justice," that is true government; resulting from "righteousness," that is right relationship with God, He had created the nation. Instead of this fruit, it had produced oppression—literally bloodshed—and the cry of the oppressed. Therein lay its failure. Thus, in this remarkable song, did the prophet teach his contemporaries, and all those who study his song, that the Divine government of a nation requires that it should realize a true order within itself, in the interest of other nations; and where it fails to do so, and permits conditions which are those of oppression, He proceeds against it in destruction. We trace this figure of the vine through the Scriptures until we find its final occurrence in the allegory of Jesus. Finding it there, it is good that we should apply its principles to the Church as to her responsibilities for the world. So far as this age and this earth are concerned, she exists to bring forth the same fruits of justice and righteousness. If within her borders, oppression obtains, and the resultant cry, she also is failing.

Holy, holy, holy, is the Lord of Hosts; the whole earth is full of His glory.—*Isa.* 6. 3.

We have all felt the wonder and the glory of this chapter. It records the vision which came to the prophet when Uzziah died. For the first time in Isaiah's life the throne of Judah was vacant. The man who had symbolized national order and authority had passed away. Then he saw the Throne which is never vacant, and the King, the Lord, Who never dies. He saw Him, moreover, surrounded by spirits of fire, serving Him, in worship, or—as in the case of the one who came to the prophet with the cleansing coal—in service. This vision gave him a new conception of Jehovah, and created a crisis in his work. The words we have emphasized constituted the song of the worshipping seraphim. In our thinking of this song we are too apt to think only of the first half, that in which they celebrated the holiness of Jehovah. Certain it is, that this was, and is, the first note. It must never be omitted or placed second. It gives interpretation to that which follows. But let us go on. They in their worship also celebrated the fact that "the whole earth is full of His glory." Thus, here in the Old Testament is emphasized the truth which contradicts the false idea that anything in the earth itself is inherently evil. The earth is full of His glory, which glory is manifested in its form, its colour, its resources for human well-being. Evil is there, but it is a poison introduced from without. Against it, the holiness of Jehovah is for ever at work; and at last, through redeeming activity, its victory will be won. Then, the whole creation, set free from the bondage of evil, will utter forth His praise. These are the fundamental convictions which make great ministries.

But Ahaz said, I will not ask, neither will I tempt the Lord.—*Isa.* 7. 12.

The title page of this book (see 1. 1) refers to "The vision of Isaiah . . . in the days of Uzziah, Jotham, Ahaz, and Hezekiah." In chapter six we have an account of the death of Uzziah, and the vision which then came to the prophet. In chapter 7 we find ourselves in the reign of Ahaz. That means that at least sixteen years had elapsed, for Jotham reigned for that period. He seems to have followed generally in the steps of his father Uzziah, and we have no record of any prophesying by Isaiah. With the coming to the throne of Ahaz the nation was plunged into more definite courses of evil. With his accession also the national life was threatened by a confederacy against it, of Israel and Syria. The king was filled with alarm. Then Isaiah interfered. He knew that Ahaz was likely to seek the aid of Assyria. This the prophet knew would be fatal. Therefore he appealed to him to rely only on God, and offered him a sign. It was to this offer that he replied in these words. Mark them well. They have all the sound of religion and reverence. He would not seek to prove Jehovah! And yet his refusal of the sign offered was irreligious and irreverent, for it was born of the fact that he did not wish to follow the policy which the prophet argued. It was born also of fear. He knew that the sign would be given, and he did not desire it. There is the most solemn suggestiveness in this. How easy it is to deceive ourselves! Let us ever watch lest, under cover of some high-sounding phrases which seem to be those of religious conviction, we refuse the way and the will of God. It is one thing to tempt Jehovah in unbelief; but it is of the nature of the deepest unbelief to refuse a sign which He offers.

And when they shall say unto you, Seek unto them that have familiar spirits and unto the wizards, that chirp and that mutter, should not a people seek unto their God? On behalf of the living should they seek unto the dead? —Isa. 8. 19.

These words are of tremendous import in our day. Mark well the situation. The King had refused the Divine sign. The nation had rejected the Divine policy. The prophet was commanded to seal up the testimony, that is to cease his public ministry. He was to devote himself to his spiritual children, the elect remnant loyal to Jehovah. This he did; and we have no further record of public utterance until we reach chapter 28. All now was instruction to this inner circle. In this ministry the very first word was this of solemn warning against necromancy, against spiritism, or as we now designate it spiritualism. When the voices of Divine prophecy are silent, men are ever prone to resort to this traffic with the spirit-world. Let those loyal to Jehovah beware.

In a brief note we can do no more than indicate the general conception of this most exhaustive passage. There are "familiar spirits." There are mediums, those who have them, that is who communicate with them. They are wizards, and their speech is that of peeping or chirping, and muttering. That is, nothing is clear either in matter or in manner. When men are asked to "seek unto them," the answer should ever be that such seeking is, to say the least, stupid, because men may seek unto God. Why should the living turn from the living God, to seek guidance from dead spirits? Mark carefully this alternative. It is between God the living One, and spirits who are dead. Their death is spiritual; they are evil in that they are cut off from God. This is the Biblical and Christian answer to Spiritism. Those who seek after familiar spirits are those who do not seek after God.

The zeal of the Lord of hosts shall perform this.—Isa. 9. 7.

If the first note of the prophet's teaching of his spiritual children was one of warning against necromancy; the seeking after dead spirits, that is, those cut off from God; the second, immediately following, was one which described a great and glorious deliverance. These words end that description: "The zeal of Jehovah of hosts will perform this!" They are arresting words. Isaiah employed them again (see 37. 32). The same idea is found in Joel (2. 18): "Then was Jehovah jealous for His land, and had pity on His people"; and in Zechariah (1. 14): "Thus saith Jehovah of hosts, I am jealous for Jerusalem and for Zion with a great jealousy"; and (8. 2): "Thus saith Jehovah of hosts, I am jealous for Zion with great jealousy, and I am jealous for her with great wrath." The words zeal and jealousy are identical in the Hebrew. It is a word which stands for passion, and is used in many different ways. When predicated of Jehovah it invariably refers to His anger against that which destroys those whom He loves. It is therefore an anger, love-inspired. This is the force which brings deliverance. The prophet in this message foretold the overthrow of the enemies of the people of God, the destruction of all the implements of war, and declared that this final deliverance would come through "a child born . . . a son given." He would establish the true Kingdom. Then he told the way of this mighty deliverance. It would come to pass by the zeal of Jehovah. We live after the advent of this Child, this Son; and we are living while He reigns; "for He must reign till He hath put all His enemies under His feet." Let us rest assured of His victory, because "The zeal of Jehovah of hosts will perform this."

Shall the axe boast itself against him that heweth therewith? Shall the saw magnify itself against him that shaketh it? As if a rod should shake them that lift it up, or as if a staff should lift up him that is not wood.—*Isa.* 10. 15.

In these words we have the language of one who sees the whole world under the Divine government. They must be interpreted in the light of the opening words of this particular message (see verse 5). "Ho, Assyrian, the rod of Mine anger; the staff in whose hand is Mine indignation." Call to mind the political situation. The Nation, under the influence of Ahaz, was looking toward Assyria for help. The prophet, instructing his spiritual children, declared that Assyria would be an instrument in the hand of God to scourge His people. This he declared in this oracle, and then proceeded to describe dramatically the arrogance of Assyria, who does not recognize the Divine purpose, but has it in his heart to destroy (verse 7). Over against that intention of Assyria, is the intention of Jehovah, Who, when His work is accomplished on Zion and Jerusalem, will punish Assyria for its arrogance. Thus the prophet saw all these nations in the hands of God. For the punishment of His own guilty people, Assyria is His rod and staff; but Assyria can go no further than the fulfilment of the Divine purpose. The light of this teaching falls upon modern conditions as clearly as upon this ancient history. God is still the God of all the nations, even when they fail to recognize Him, or even boast themselves against Him. He will use their power to accomplish His purpose, and then destroy it. The axe is ever in His hand; the saw is doing His work. What folly for either, to boast against Him.

He shall not judge after the sight of His eyes, neither reprove after the hearing of His ears.—*Isa.* 11. 3.

After the oracle foretelling the destruction of Assyria, and, by implication, of all the enemies of the Nation, the prophet uttered to that inner circle of faithful souls this matchless prediction of the Messianic Kingdom. He described the character of Messiah, revealed the methods of His government, gave a glowing description of the results of His reign, and told of how the scattered people would be gathered from the four corners of the earth. These words occur in the midst of the revelation of the methods of government, and they are certainly among the most marvellously arresting things ever said about that great Kingdom of heaven which is yet to be. Their arresting nature is realized when the conception of government and decision is compared with the highest and best methods existing among men. All human laws are made and administered as the result of what men see

with their eyes and hear with their ears; and that because man in his dealing with other men has no other means of knowledge. These laws break down, and justice goes astray, because what the eyes see often misleads, and what the ears hear is not true, or is not all the truth. But in the kingdom of God, government is based upon absolute knowledge, and decisions are the result of perfect understanding. Not alone the deed evident to sight, or the word caught by hearing, but the motive of the deed, the intention of the word, will be known by Him, God's anointed and appointed King, Himself being human, a Child born to us; and Divine, a Son given. Nothing more than this one sentence need be uttered to prove the glory of that reign, or to possess us with a burning passion to hasten its coming.

Cry aloud and shout, thou inhabitant of Zion; for great is the Holy One of Israel in the midst of thee.—*Isa.* 12. 6.

The connection of this song of chapter twelve with the Messianic foretellings in chapter eleven is indicated by the introductory words: "And in that day thou shalt say." The song itself is in two movements. In the first (verses 1 and 2) the singer is the personified nation praising the God through Whom her salvation has been wrought. In the second (verses 3–6) the prophet in glad exultation addresses the nation thus delivered. These words constitute the final note in this movement, and set forth the chief reason for the strength of the city, and the joy of the people. It is that the One Who is great in the midst of her is holy. That is the fundamental note in the Kingdom and City of God, and thus it stands in contrast with all the false ideas of greatness which have blighted and blasted the kingdoms of men. In the midst of human kingdoms which for a time have seemed to be strong, but which have perished, have been those counted great because of military prowess, of diplomatic acumen, of economic shrewdness. None of these is sufficient to create stability or insure permanence. In the midst of the City of God, the Kingdom of Heaven, the Great One is the Holy One. That separation from evil will insure the victory of His warfare, the triumph of His diplomacy, the perfection of His economy. Therefore His City and Kingdom will be stable, and permanent, having no end. That, therefore, is the supreme note in the song that celebrates His reign, and His people's salvation.

The Lord of hosts mustereth the host for the battle.—*Isa.* 13. 4.

With this chapter we begin a section of the prophecy which includes and ends with chapter twenty-three. It consists of ten burdens concerning the nations, and one concerning Jerusalem. These are all to be conceived of as having been delivered to that inner circle of faithful souls, among whom in this period the prophet was exercising his ministry. The value of them as a whole lay in the ˙prophet's presentation of God as governing all the nations. Amos, prophesying in Samaria, was influenced by the same outlook. An understanding of this would reveal most clearly the folly of looking for national safety in alliances with any of these, while neglecting the government of God, and refusing to ask or to act upon His signs. The first of these oracles (13–14. 27) unquestionably had to do with Assyria, the people toward whom Ahaz was looking for help. This is clear from internal evidence notwithstanding the inscription "The burden of Babylon," due probably to the mistake of a copyist, or more likely to some subsequent adaptation of the message to Babylon (see 14. 4). The message in its entirety is a description of the overthrow of this cruel and proud and relentless power, by the might of Jehovah. Hosts are seen to gather against this grim nation which has held the world in thrall, and the words we have emphasized give the word of prophetic interpretation of that gathering: "Jehovah of hosts is mustering the host for the battle." This is the authentic note of the prophet. While men discuss war in the terms of human diplomacies, he passes beyond secondary causes, as he sees the Throne never vacant. To him it is Jehovah Who musters the host for battle. Our watching eyes have looked upon modern events in which the same fact has been patent.

The Lord hath founded Zion.—*Isa.* 14. 32.

These words occur in the Burden concerning Philistia, which is of interest because of its historical allusions. The Burden was uttered in the year Ahaz died (see verse 28). Messengers from Philistia were in the city (see verse 32). From the history found in Kings and Chronicles we know that Ahaz had carried out his policy of seeking help from Assyria, robbing the House of the Lord to send a present to its king. We know also that the Philistines had carried out depredations in the South of Judah (2 Chron. 28. 18). Now Ahaz was dead, and envoys from Philistia were in the city. Probably they were there offering to make terms with Judah, possibly to offer to form an alliance. This called forth the Burden of the prophet. It foretold the discomfiture and doom of Philistia, and gave the true answer to the messengers. It was just this: "Jehovah hath founded Zion"; which was a refusal to seek any safety from alliances with the nations which were corrupt; and a declaration that the safety of Zion lay in the fact that it was founded by God, this necessarily involving the necessity for Zion's maintenance of true relationship with her Founder. Here is a principle of true statecraft. When a nation, which God has created and blessed, consents in the interests of her own safety to alliance with nations which in their deepest life are pagan, such a nation acts for her own undoing. She is safe always, and safe only as she maintains right relationship with God, and finds her confidence in His power to defend her against her foes.

My heart crieth out for Moab.— *Isa.* 15. 5.

The Burden of Moab occupies this and the next chapter. There have been very different interpretations of this oracle. Glance ahead for a moment to verses 3 to 5 in chapter 16. The older expositors treat these as constituting the prophet's message to Moab as to the way by which she may be delivered, and his prediction of the benefits which will come to her under the Messianic reign. On the other hand, many modern writers interpret these verses as containing Moab's appeal to Judah for protection. I refer to this because the interpretation of the burden is dependent upon which view is taken. Without any misgiving, I adhere to the older view. This, then, is one of those instances in which the outlook of prophecy was enlarged so as to take in the wider purposes of God for the ultimate deliverance of all nations. In this chapter the theme is that of disaster for Moab, "In a night," that is with abrupt and startling suddenness two of her principal cities are laid waste, and she is reduced to impotent desolation. The vengeance is just, a righteous retribution for her pride and wickedness. Nevertheless her suffering touches the heart of the prophet of Jehovah; hence the exclamation, "My heart crieth out for Moab." This is the true evidence of sympathy and co-operation with God. Wickedness must be punished, but in the heart of God there is no joy in the suffering of the wicked. The "My heart crieth out for Moab" of Isaiah, is in perfect harmony with the lamentation of Jesus over Jerusalem doomed. The man who talks of the punishment, of the wicked without a sob in his heart, is not in close fellowship with God.

And a throne shall be established in mercy; and One shall sit thereon in truth, in the tent of David; judging, and seeking judgement, and swift to do righteousness.—*Isa.* 16. 5.

These words—as we have said in the previous note—constitute part of the prophet's indication to Moab of the way of deliverance. They may have been intended to represent the language of Moab in its plea for the help of Judah. It is, however, more than difficult, it is impossible for me to believe that words so full of light as to the principles of the Messianic Kingdom should have been suggested by Isaiah as coming from Moab. In either case, however, their value abides as a revelation of the only way of deliverance for Moab, or for any nation, from disaster which must follow the ways of pride and of evil. Such deliverance must result from a Throne, a centre of authority and administration; and from the fact that such a Throne is occupied by One Who is Himself seated on Truth, and Who in the administration of His Kingdom seeks justice, and is swift in the deed of righteousness. We need rightly to apprehend the statement that: "a Throne shall be established in lovingkindness." We are apt to think of it as meaning that a Throne is to be established for the display of leniency, as though· the claims of righteousness may thereby be waived. Nothing is further from the truth. The Throne will insist upon righteousness and justice. Its Occupant is to be seated on truth. The crowning lovingkindness of God to the world is that such a Throne is to be established. The most merciful method of government is that of strict justice. When we see in the midst of the Throne the Lamb as it had been slain, we know by that wondrous token that justice is vindicated, and so the Throne is for ever the Throne of lovingkindness.

In that day shall a man look unto his Maker, and his eyes shall have respect to the Holy One of Israel. And he shall not look to the altars, the work of his hands, neither shall he have respect to that which his fingers have made.—_Isa._ 17. 7, 8.

These words occur in the Burden of Damascus which is principally concerned with the overthrow of the Northern Kingdom of Israel. At the time, Israel was in league with Damascus in order to protect herself from Assyria; while, as we have seen, the policy of the Kingdom of Judah, against which Isaiah protested, was that of seeking the aid of Assyria against the peril threatening her from this coalition between Israel and Syria. In this Burden the prophet foretold the destruction of Damascus, and the breaking down thus of that to which Israel was trusting. The result would be that Israel or Ephraim, would be reduced to a mere remnant. In these verses he declared what the result would be of this Divine judgment. Men would return to God, instead of trusting to their own policies. Isaiah does not state the alternative to confidence in God, as that of trusting in policy, but rather as that of trusting in false altars and false gods. This is a profound word; recognizing as it does, that what man puts his trust in is his god. These politicians of the Northern Kingdom in all probability would not have admitted that in making

alliance with Damascus they were guilty of idolatry. Yet that was the prophet's view of their action. Their refusal to trust in Jehovah, and their seeking of safety in the help of Damascus, was equal to seeking the help of the altars and gods of Syria.

For thus hath the Lord said unto me, I will be still, and I will behold in My dwelling-place; like clear heat in sunshine, like a cloud of dew in the heat of harvest.—_Isa._ 18. 4.

These words occur in an oracle which begins in chapter seventeen at verse twelve, and runs through this chapter. It has two movements, each beginning with the exclamation "Ah!" (17. 12 and 18. 1). There are those who treat this as the burden of Assyria. I understand it rather as a prophetic soliloquy in the midst of the burdens of the nations; and one which is the result of the coming of ambassadors from Ethiopia to the court of Judah. Their coming caused the prophet first of all to utter his consciousness of the tumult caused everywhere by the rushing of the nations. In the first movement he spoke of Jehovah's rebuking of them under the figure of a storm. In the second movement, in the words we have emphasized, he gave another picture of Jehovah. It is that of His stillness. That stillness is that of the heat and the dew, which ripen the grain and produce the harvest. The context here shows that the harvest contemplated was that of His vengeance and punishment of guilty nations; and God is seen by His very stillness and apparent inactivity as preparing for, and compelling that harvest, as the clear heat of sunshine, and the dews prepare for and compel the harvests of Nature. The same conception of God is revealed under different figures in these prophetic writings. It is one which is full of comfort when the heart is assaulted by all the commotions of godlessness, in the presence of which God seems to be inactive. He is never so. When He is still, He is beholding; and His beholding is that of compelling the ultimate purposes of His will.

In that day shall Israel be the third with Egypt and with Assyria, a blessing in the midst of the earth.—_Isa._ 19. 24.

These words occur at the close of "the Burden of Egypt." They constitute perhaps the high-water mark in that element of prophetic utterance which, looking beyond the immediate, and the processes, foresaw a triumph of God wherein the opposition of the nations would be overcome, and they would be included in His realized Kingdom on earth. The first part of this burden had to do with the overthrow of Egypt by a Divine visitation in judgment. The second foretold the ultimate effect of the dealing with God with

Egypt. She is seen as turning to Jehovah; His worship is established within her borders; a Saviour from Him brings her deliverance. Jehovah will deal with Egypt —smiting and healing. Then the prophet saw a still more glorious result. The ancient enemies of Israel, Assyria in the east, and Egypt to the west, are seen united by Israel, her territory becoming the highway over which they pass to and fro in their friendly communication with each other. The three states form a triple alliance, united in the worship of Jehovah and His perfect reign over them. It is a glorious vision. It has never been realized. It will be. Study the map and the newspaper to-day. There is the land of Israel to which Israel is surely returning. Egypt is still there, and through turmoil it is approaching order. Away to the west is the great and fascinating area, and the peoples to whom the power of Assyria will pass. Presently, when the true King comes, the alliance will be consummated. Let us realize the principle involved in its yet wider reaches. Presently under the rule of God, through His anointed King, all those nations, to-day at enmity against each other, will be unified. That will be the lasting and glorious leaguing of the nations, and there is no other way.

And the inhabitant of this coast-land shall say in that day, Behold, such is our expectation, whither we fled for help to be delivered from the King of Assyria; and we, how shall we escape? —Isa. 20. 6.

This is a most interesting chapter, because of its historic nature. First the expedition referred to in the first verse, is now definitely placed by Sargon's inscriptions as having taken place in 711 B.C. Then this reference to an activity of Isaiah is arresting. For three years he went in and out among the people of Jerusalem, in tatters and shoeless, as a mendicant. Here, in close connection with his Burden of Egypt, he gives an account of the reason for this strange action, and the signification of it. We may think of him as doing this during that period in which the testimony to the nation was still sealed, and he was teaching the elect remnant of loyal souls. His wretched appearance was the symbol of what would happen to Egypt as the result of the triumph of Assyria over her. Behind all this we discover the proposed policy of the rulers of Jerusalem. By this time they had learned the futility of looking to Assyria for aid, and were proposing to turn to Egypt for help against Assyria. This was futile, for Assyria would conquer Egypt. The closing words of this chapter enforce the teaching. The inhabitants of this coastland, that is of Palestine in its entirety—will see the folly of their expectation, and cry "And we, how shall we

escape?" It is most probable that Hezekiah the king was at this time among those being instructed by the prophet. Again it is for us to recognize the principle involved. There is no place of security for the people of God, other than that to be found in the rule of God. All expectation not centred in God, is doomed to disappointment and discomfiture. The policies which exclude Him, all, invariably, inevitably, break down.

. . . The morning cometh, and also the night.—Isa. 21. 12.

In this chapter we have three Burdens, those concerning Babylon, Edom, and Arabia. They are characterized by a mystic and visionary note. The first, concerning Babylon, is perfectly clear as to its vital message. It foretold the fall of Babylon. The last, concerning Arabia, that is, concerning the wandering tribes occupying that region, is obscure as to the particular events calling it forth, but it was a definite prediction that within a year the tribe of Kedar should be destroyed. The central Burden, that concerning Dumah, which is Edom, is indefinite as to a message, and that very indefiniteness is the message. The prophet interpreted the mental attitude of Edom as that of inquiry as to whether the night of her desolation was passing. That is the significance of the voice calling out of Seir—"Watchman, what of the night?" To such an inquiry the reply of the prophet was intentionally indefinite. There was no answer, except that there were signs of morning and of night. It has been suggested that the prophet meant that he had no clear vision of Edom's destiny; or that he foretold some relief to be followed by more terrible suffering; or that some would find release, and some destruction; or that there was morning for Israel and night for Dumah. To me none of these is satisfactory. It would rather seem as though the prophet declared an alternative of morning or of night, and by his final words suggested an attitude. If the spirit of inquiry was aroused, let it be maintained; and let them turn and come again. To all the restless crying of men in the midst of trouble as to the passing of the night, the answer of revelation is that there is morning coming, and night also. Men by their own attitudes and choices decide whether they will come to the morning or pass to the night.

And in that day did the Lord, the Lord of hosts call to weeping . . . and behold, joy and gladness . . .—Isa. 22. 12, 13.

That statement gives the key to the situation calling forth this Burden of the valley of vision. In it the prophet turned from his messages concerning the surrounding nations, to give attention to Jerusalem. While many separate between the first part of this chapter (verses 1–14 and the last part (verses 15–25), I cannot do so. In the second part we have again an historical incident. Shebna is seen, holding high office. Nothing is definitely said about his wrongdoing, but it is almost certain that he was the leader of the political party which was looking toward Egypt. The message of the prophet was that he was to be removed from office, and Eliakim appointed. That this was done, we gather from the fact that in the day when Assyria came to the gates, Eliakim held the office, and Shebna only a second place. The city, under the rule of Shebna, was given over to every kind of material festivity. It was against this that the prophet declaimed. There was the gravest danger in the hour; it was a time when the only hope of the nation lay in its tears of penitence and repentance. For these the Lord was calling, and the nation was responding with drunken revelry. To the prophet the sin of Jerusalem in this matter was past forgiveness. Hence his agony and his anger. The words give us solemn pause. How often in our own national history, when we have been indulging in riotous rejoicing, we should have been in sackcloth and ashes! Yet there was a man who refused to be comforted (see verse 4); and around him were gathered a group of loyal souls. By these the nation was better served than by the wild and shouting crowds. It is true national service, to bear national sins upon the heart and conscience, and by our tears to witness to our God, in all such hours.

And her merchandise and her hire shall be holiness to the Lord; it shall not be treasured nor laid up; for her merchandise shall be for them that dwell before the Lord, to eat sufficiently, and for durable clothing.—*Isa*. 23. 18.

In the Burden of Tyre there is no gleam of hope for her ultimate inclusion in the Kingdom of God, as in the case of Egypt and Assyria; but throughout, there is the declaration that she is within that Kingdom as to the fact of the Divine government. In the much fuller and more elaborate article of Ezekiel concerning Tyre, there is the same note of hopelessness. Moreover in Ezekiel the reasons for that hopelessness are very fully revealed. Isaiah foretold the catastrophe that would overtake Tyre, bringing a seventy years' desolation. Then he declared that she would be restored, because Jehovah would visit her. But she would remain a harlot, trafficking as before, with all the kingdoms of the world. It is in that connection that these words were uttered. They do not mean that Tyre will conduct her commerce on holy principles; but that, under

the pressure of the Divine government, her gains will not be stored for her own enrichment, but employed on behalf of the people of God. This prophetic word has an application much wider than to Tyre. The earth is Jehovah's and the fulness thereof, and in the day of His perfected Kingdom on earth, all its resources, which man has exploited for selfish purposes, will be recovered and employed for the people within that Kingdom. The ultimate destiny of wealth is not that of establishing tyrannies, but that of providing sufficiency for the people constituting the commonwealth of God. To this end Jehovah reigneth. Happy are those who dedicate whatever they have or earth's resources to this high and holy purpose.

The earth also is polluted under the inhabitants thereof; because they have transgressed the laws, changed the ordinance, broken the everlasting covenant.—*Isa*. 24. 5.

This and the following three chapters constitute one prophetic utterance. It is a vision of the Day of Jehovah. In the series of the Burdens of the nations the prophet had taken a wider outlook than that of his own people, but always with the nation of God at the centre. Here his outlook is still further enlarged as it takes in the whole earth; but here also God's people are in mind from beginning to end, viewed in their relation to the earth. The vision is in two movements; the first describes the desolation of the earth (24. 1–20); the second describes the restoration which comes by the Day of Jehovah (24. 21–27). The desolation is first declared to be the result of Divine action. It is "Jehovah maketh the earth empty, and maketh it waste, and turneth it upside down, and scattereth abroad the inhabitants thereof." Then—in these particular words—the reason of this desolate activity of God is revealed. It is that the earth is polluted under its inhabitants. The act of God is the operation of the laws by which the Divine creation is governed. Man has transgressed the laws, violated the statutes, and broken the covenant. For an interpretation of these words of Isaiah read Paul—Rom. 1. 18–32. In these words we find a recognition of a true order. In it, man, keeping covenant, observing the ordinance, obeying law, reigns over the earth, and leads it out into all beauty and fruitfulness. When man breaks down in his relationship with God, His laws, His ordinances, His covenant—then he becomes polluted, and he communicates his pollution to the earth. This is the interpretation of all disease, all insanity, all the things of waste, of disorder, of strife, of misery in human history and human experience. A polluted race pollutes the earth, and chaos is the result.

And it shall be said in that day, Lo, this is our God; we have waited for Him, and He will save us; this is the Lord; we have waited for Him, we will be glad and rejoice in His salvation.— *Isa. 25. 9.*

"In that day," is the phrase which unifies the section of this vision of restoration. Note its occurrences, 24. 21, 25. 9, 26. 1, 27. 1, 2, 12, 13. Each time a new line of consideration is introduced, which it is not within our province to deal with now, but which the student will do well to observe. The Day, throughout, is the Day of Jehovah. The words we are emphasizing declare the sense which will result from the activity of Jehovah. In that activity He will subdue all false authority, both spiritual and human. See chapter 24 verse 21, where "the host of the high ones on high," refers to the spiritual forces of evil, and stands in contrast to "the kings of the earth upon earth." The activity of Jehovah in His Day will be that of such retributive justice as will deliver the poor and needy. But let the whole of the chapter be pondered, then this great exclamation will be understood. The truth of it is the song which inspires the hope, the courage, the service, the sacrifice of His people in all the days of travail. The only way of deliverance for the earth from the desolation resulting from its pollution by men who have turned their back upon God, is that God does not forsake the earth or them. He acts in holy wrath, inspired by eternal love, against all the forces of evil. And in His great Day men will discover Him, and know that through Him alone salvation is possible. The discovery of God through His judgments will be the way of the restoration of the earth, since it has rejected His disclosure of Himself in grace through His Son. Yet that discovery will be a discovery of His grace, for He has appointed that the Man of His right hand shall administer the activity of His judgment.

Thy dead shall live; my dead bodies shall arise. Awake and sing, ye that dwell in the dust; for thy dew is as the dew of herbs, and the earth shall cast forth the dead.—*Isa. 26. 19.*

In all this Oracle of the Day of Jehovah as the day of restoration, there is no more wonderful word than this. It is a singularly clear and definite foretelling of resurrection. The truth of immortality had already been declared in the word of the previous chapter, "He hath swallowed up death for ever" (see verse 8). But here the prophetic word goes further. Immortality does not necessarily involve a resurrection of the body. It does mean the persistence of conscious personality beyond that dissolution of spirit and body which we call

death. But here the fact of the resurrection is foretold so clearly that there can be no mistaking of the meaning of the prophet. Let it be granted that we need, and that we have, the full Divine revelation of this fact in the New Testament; it is none the less remarkable that we find it so clearly stated in this wonderful message of Isaiah. Very beautiful is the prophet's poetic figure of the dew. Dr. Skinner says that a better rendering would be, "A dew of lights is Thy dew;" and that "it is a heavenly, supernatural dew that is meant; as soon as this falls on the dead they awake to life." These great facts of immortality and resurrection completely transfigure our conceptions of life, and we respond to the cry of the singer which calls us to awake and sing, even though we dwell in the dust. The dust is not the last word; the narrow confines of the here and the now, are not the boundaries of our being. Beyond, life brings its explanations, its fulfilments. What we know not now, we shall know hereafter. All that we have not attained, we may attain when He shall fashion anew the bodies of our humiliation, that they may be conformed to the body of His glory.

In days to come shall Jacob take root; Israel shall blossom and bud; and they shall fill the face of the world with fruit.—*Isa. 27. 6.*

Those "days to come" are within "that day." Here the fact which had been in the mind of the prophet throughout his vision of restoration for the earth comes out into clear declaration. It will be through God's own nation that the nations of the earth will be restored. The figure of the vineyard, of the plant of Jehovah, of the fruit which it is to bear, is employed. Let the mind go back to the earlier song of the vineyard which the prophet had sung (chapter 5). There the vine was seen, failing, bringing forth wild grapes, and given over to processes of judgment. Here, again, we have a song of the vineyard, but now it is a song of fruitfulness. Through the judgments, the glorious results have been realized. The fruit is unquestionably the same—that, namely, of justice and righteousness; and it is seen as filling the face of the world. Thus we have reached the climax in this great prophecy of restoration, and let us make no mistake about it; it will be literally fulfilled. God hath not cast off His ancient people for ever. He is watching over them, and through the long and fiery discipline of these days, He is preparing them for that day when they, cleansed from their pollutions, and restored to His government, shall be the people through which all the blessedness of His reign shall be extended to all the peoples. Jerusalem has long been trodden down of the Gentiles, but the times of the Gentiles are being fulfilled. Then under the sway of their long rejected Messiah, God's ancient people will fill the face of the world with fruit.

For the bed is shorter than that a man can stretch himself on it; and the covering narrower than that he can wrap himself in it.—Isa. 28. 20.

These words are vibrant with holy sarcasm. Let us carefully note their setting. With this chapter we find the prophet once more exercising a public ministry. In the section beginning here and ending with chapter 33, we have six addresses, each beginning with the word "Woe!" The first five were concerned with the chosen people, and the last with Assyria the threatening foe. The whole section pulsates with the prophet's anger at the false policy which had sought help from Egypt. The outlook of faith as revealed in these discourses was twofold. He saw the real danger in Assyria's advance, and knew that Egypt could not help to avert it. But he also saw Jehovah; and knew that He would deal with Assyria. These two notes alternate in these messages. This chapter is full of dramatic power. Suddenly the prophet broke his long silence and appeared among these politicians, drunk with their own conceits (verses 1-8). They railed on him (verses 9, 10). He replied by employing the language of their tauntings (verses 11-13). Then he dealt with the false security in which they were acting. Interpreting their policy as that of a covenant made with death, and an agreement with Sheol, he declared that all such covenants and agreements the Lord Jehovah would disannul. Then he employed these words. They meant that their godless policies were insufficient to give them rest. We may ever employ the suggestive words of nations or of individuals, when attempts are made to find rest and security apart from God. Life cannot stretch itself out in perfect ease upon any other bed than that of the Divine government; life cannot find warmth in any other covering than that of the righteousness of God.

Their fear of Me is a commandment of men which hath been taught them. —Isa. 29. 13.

In this chapter we have the second and third of the "Woe" messages of the prophet. The first was a condemnation of the city of Jerusalem, addressed as Ariel, for its frivolity and debauchery; but also a declaration that Jehovah would proceed against the foes of His people. The second was a condemnation of the politicians who imagined they could work in the dark, without God knowing; and a foretelling concerning a day in which Jehovah would demonstrate His power gloriously. The words we have stressed occur in the first of these, and are part of a searching criticism of the religious condition of the people. They were maintaining the outward forms of religion, but there was alienation from God, in all the deepest things of their lives. These particular words show that it is possible to have a fear of God, which results from receiving "a commandment of men." This fear is valueless, because even though the commandment so taught may in itself harmonize with the law of God, it is of no value save as it is a direct Word of God to the one upon whom it is laid. Thus a principle emerges which is of perpetual force in vital religion. It is that man must have direct dealing with God. None of us can possibly know the authority of the Bible if he merely receive and respect it, because it is given to him by his father. To accept a rule of life, because it is given by a man, however true the rule, however good the man, is to be without the element of real value in the acceptance. It is by the Word of God that man lives; and that word must be a direct word. Let those who are called upon to teach that Word recognize the necessity for withdrawing themselves from between those whom they teach and the word which they proclaim.

But ye said, No, for we will flee upon horses; therefore shall ye flee: and, We will ride upon the swift; therefore shall they that pursue you be swift.—Isa. 30. 16.

This is the fourth "Woe" message, and it was specifically concerned with the treaty actually made with Egypt, and in the making of which the nation was definitely and distinctly rebellious against Jehovah. In their turning to Egypt, there was evidence of their lack of trust in God; but in their persistence in this course, and the consummation of the policy in the actual treaty—in spite of the prophetic warnings—there was more than lack of confidence, there was positive rebellion. Very well, said the prophet, so be it, for so it must be. The Lord Jehovah, the Holy One of Israel, had declared the way of deliverance and safety; "In returning and rest shall ye be saved; in quietness and confidence shall be your strength." But they had said "No!" They had elected to flee, that is at the enemy, on horses, the horses obtained from Egypt. Very well, said the prophet, you shall have your own way—you shall flee—only it shall not be at the enemy, but from the enemy. They had said: "We will ride upon the swift." Very well, said the prophet, then ride—only those who pursue will also be swift. Thus it ever is. If we will not have God's way, He compels us to take our own; and by the experience resulting, we learn our folly. Thus—as the next verse shows—Jehovah has to wait to be gracious. If in our folly we refuse His way, then He compels us to take our own, and He waits until the disaster of our choice has taught us the folly of that choice. In this connection, observe the last words of the prophet, "Blessed are all they that wait for Him;" that is, those who do not make Him wait for them.

When the Lord shall stretch out His hand, both he that helpeth shall stumble, and he that is holpen shall fall, and they all shall fall together.— Isa. 31. 3.

In the fifth "Woe" message, the prophetic word insists upon the government of God; and alternates between words which show the punitive, and the restoring elements in the activity of that government. Here the treaty with Egypt was consummated, and the politicians were confident in the multitude of the chariots and the strength of the horsemen. The prophet revealed the folly of the confidence, as he said that the Egyptians were men, and not God; and their horses flesh, and not spirit. In this word he recognized the fact that man's true resources are not found in man, but in God; that the strength which accomplishes is not carnal, but spiritual. Then in these words he asserted the fact which he saw clearly. All the cleverness of human arrangements was of no avail. Egypt was to help; Judah was to be helped. Everything was arranged. But those making the arrangement had, in their calculations, left out the one supreme quantity. Jehovah would stretch out His hand. Then Egypt, the helper, would stumble; and Judah, the helped, would fall; and they would all fall together. Thus, with almost monotonous reiteration, the same fact of the Divine sovereignty, and of its activity in all human affairs is insisted on. And this is the one truth which humanity needs to learn, and learning which, it finds the only wisdom, for the ordering of its affairs. The whole of human history testifies to the stupidity of man when he trusts to his diplomacies, and fails to reckon with God. This is no old-story merely. It is as modern as 1914–1919. We then saw the hand of Jehovah stretched out, and the helper and the helped go down in confusion.

And the work of righteousness shall be peace; and the effect of righteousness quietness and confidence for ever. —Isa. 32. 17.

In this chapter we have the second part of the fifth "Woe" message concerning the chosen. It is principally concerned with the conditions which will obtain when the reign of righteousness is established. In the midst of this graphic description the prophet made another appeal to the women. In the earlier days of his ministry he had addressed them with grave solemnity, recognizing their influences for evil in the counsels of the rulers (see 3. 16, 26).

Now, he called upon them to lament at the desolations threatening the city and the nation. The burden of the prophet here, however, was as we have said, that of the glory of the Messianic reign. The words we have emphasized should be read in close connection with the opening declaration of this part of the message: "Behold a King shall reign in righteousness." The processes of righteousness, in the midst of lawlessness, are necessarily those of wrath and a curse, of the storm and the tempest; but the work of righteousness, that is its ultimate result, is peace, and its effect is quietness and confidence. These are the conditions of true joy, and lasting happiness. Peace is impossible so long as righteousness is disregarded; quietness and confidence can never be produced by unrighteous motives and methods. Such a conviction involves another. Righteousness will never be the principle of human life, unless and until that life is submitted to the King Who reigns in righteousness; and there is no king who perfectly reigns in righteousness other than the Man Whom God hath appointed to judge the world in righteousness. He is the Man Who will be as the shade of a great rock in a weary land.

Who among us shall dwell with the devouring fire? Who among us shall dwell with everlasting burnings?—Isa. 33. 14.

This sixth and last of the "Woe" messages in this series has to do with Assyria. It is a singularly exalted prophecy. The cruelty and strength of the foe is recognized and graphically described. In presence of such a foe the nation of Judah is hopeless and helpless in its own strength. Then the word of Jehovah is heard: "Now will I arise . . . now will I lift up Myself; now will I be exalted." Then the outlook changes. All the force of the foe is as nothing in the presence of the fire of the Divine wrath. It is this vision which gives rise to these questions. Note, they are asked by dwellers in Zion, who are sinners. They fear and tremble for themselves. The whole conception is a revelation of the prophet's outlook upon the world. He saw everything in the fire of the Divine holiness. In that fire only things of essential purity and strength could live. Let it be noted that these questions are immediately answered. Those who can dwell in that fire, and not be consumed, are described in the next verse. Those who are righteous, alone can dwell with the everlasting burnings. This is a true vision of the world. It is wrapt in the fire of the presence of God. That fire is surely, if with apparent slowness, destroying everything which is out of harmony with eternal purity. In Nature there is such a slow burning fire. Scientists call it eremacausis. It is seen in the tints of autumn, and in the rust. Its function is that of destroying effete things. What that fire is to Nature, God is to human history and life.

For it is the day of the Lord's vengeance, the year of recompense in the controversy of Zion.—*Isa.* 34. 8.

In these last two chapters of the first part of this book of Isaiah, the prophet again takes the widest outlook. As, at the close of the section containing the Burdens of the nations, he uttered prophecies concerning the whole world (see chapters 24–27), so does he here. Here again his outlook is first upon desolation, and then upon restoration. The indignation of Jehovah is seen proceeding against all nations because of their iniquities. Edom is made the centre and symbol of the antagonism to Zion. Edom is of Esau, as Zion is of Israel. All that the ideal nation stood for, had been opposed persistently by Edom. Now, upon that whole attitude the vengeance of God is seen to fall. In connection with this, let the prophecy of Obadiah be read. There, the antagonism is very clearly brought out. The issue of that spirit of animalism is that of complete annihilation. The vengeance of Jehovah is irrevocable and irresistible. It is at least a most suggestive fact that when our Lord, the one perfect flower and fruit of Israel's race, was here exercising His earthly ministry, an Idumean, that is an Edomite, in the person of Herod, was reigning over the people; and it is more than suggestive in that relation, that he is the one human being to whom Christ had nothing to say. Once He sent him a message full of contempt. When at last He was in his presence, He spoke no word to him. God makes no terms with that for which Edom stood. Its portion is destruction.

They shall see the glory of the Lord, the excellency of our God.—*Isa.* 35. 2.

In this brief but beautiful chapter we have the concluding note of the first part of this great book of Isaiah. It is a perfect song of restoration. It begins with a recognition of the wilderness, the dry land, and the desert (verse 1). It ends with Zion, the city of God, the realization of the Divine order (verse 10). This is the note found in all these Hebrew prophets. No men saw the corruption of life more clearly, or denounced sin more vehemently. At times their messages were dirges, almost, but never quite reaching the level of despair. Never quite, for they saw Jehovah, and that vision made despair impossible. Through all the clouds and darkness, the travail and terror, they saw the day of God coming; and His day was a day of restoration as to its ultimate, although a day of wrath and consuming fire in its processes. The words we have emphasized are the most revealing, in their portrayal of the final world order. The word "They," in the Hebrew "These," refers to the wilderness, the dry land, the desert. "*They* shall see the glory of Jehovah, the excellency of our God." That glory is the glory of Lebanon, the mountain of cedars; that excellency is the excellency of Carmel and Sharon, the places of fruitfulness. This is the final victory of God in the earth. It is the victory, not of creation, but of ransom, redemption, regeneration, renewal. Not that Lebanon should flourish and Sharon and Carmel rejoice; but that the wilderness and the desert places rendered desolate by human pollution, should come to see the glory of Jehovah. When Isaiah heard the seraphim sing, he heard them declare that the whole earth is full of the glory of Jehovah. Here he declares that this glory shall be manifested in spite of desolations widespread and long-continued.

And Rabshakeh said unto them, Say ye now to Hezekiah, Thus saith the great king, the king of Assyria, What confidence is this wherein thou trustest? *Isa.* 36. 4.

This is the first of four chapters of history, inserted between the first and second parts of this book. They record incidents during the reign of King Hezekiah in which Isaiah exercised his influence. The first (in this chapter and the next), is that of the Assyrian threat to the city of God. This came as Isaiah had foretold, and it was defeated by God, as he had predicted. In this chapter we have the account of the coming of Sennacherib, and the speech of the Rabshakeh. That speech was intended to reduce the morale of the nation. With singular astuteness this man asked them to consider their confidence. He seems to have been familiar with the policies of Judah, evidently knowing that there were two parties, the one seeking aid from Egypt, the other—the king most probably being among them —looking only to Jehovah (see verses 6 and 7). With scorn and remarkable accuracy, he described Egypt as a "bruised reed." As to Jehovah, he first suggested that the action of Hezekiah in taking away high places had been a refusal of Jehovah. This was either deliberate misrepresentation, or ignorance, for what Hezekiah had done was to remove the high places of false gods. Later he defied Jehovah, as he declared that no gods had been strong enough to resist the king of Assyria. All this is very illuminating as revealing the weakness of earthly power. Diplomatists, who represent brute force, may gauge Egypt accurately, for their power is as their own; but when they try to explain God, they are ever dealing with that of which they are ignorant. In this God the unknown quantity among such men, is the strength of His people.

Whom hast thou reproached and blasphemed? And against Whom hast thou exalted thy voice, and lifted up thine eyes on high? Even against the Holy One of Israel.—Isa. 37. 23.

When the tauntings of the Rabshakeh were completed, and replied to in silence (see 36. 21), Hezekiah sent to Isaiah. The treaty with Egypt was of no avail. This was patent. Hezekiah, who had been largely in the hands of the politicians, while all the time most probably in sympathy with Isaiah, now, as king, assumed the garb of penitence for the false way. The answer of Isaiah was instant and assuring. Jehovah would intervene, and the King of Assyria would return to his own land and perish there by the sword. The Rabshakeh, returning to his master, found him at war against Libnah; he also heard that Ethiopia was in arms against Assyria. Then he made another attempt to intimidate Hezekiah by a letter, openly defying Jehovah. This the king spread before Jehovah. Isaiah declared the Divine answer to that prayer in the message he delivered. These words are those in which the prophet laid bare the deepest fact in the sin of Assyria. It is good here to turn back to an earlier word of the prophet concerning Assyria (chapter 10. 5–33). In that he had described Assyria as the rod and staff in the hand of God for the chastisement of His people; and had foretold Assyria's pride as boasting itself against the hand that held it. Here, in history, this foretelling was fulfilled; and the prophet denounced Assyria for this sin; and, in language full of force, foretold the doom thereof. The Divine intervention on behalf of Jerusalem came mysteriously, but with complete victory, as the angel of Jehovah smote the hosts and left them dead on the plain. Thus the deeds of God demonstrate the folly of policies which neglect Him, and justify faith in Himself alone.

Thou hast in love to my soul delivered it from the pit of corruption.—Isa. 38. 17.

These words occur in the song of a man who, in mortal sickness, had been to the gates of death, but who had been restored to life by the mercy of God. The first half of it (verses 10–14) is a record of his experiences when, in his sickness, death seemed inevitable. It is full of sadness and darkness. To him there came no ray of light, illuminating that darkness. References to that experience in the after part of the song compel the conclusion that this sickness was of the nature of chastisement. It was for his peace, he admitted, that he had had great bitterness. That will explain his outlook upon death, and the absence of any hope in that outlook. The second half of the song (verses 15-20)

contains his expressions of gladness in his deliverance from death by the mercy and power of God. This song is full of the sense of the deeper spiritual values of the suffering and deliverance. "By these things men live," he said, as he looked back; and significantly added, "wholly therein is the life of my spirit." In the words we have emphasized we have the deepest note of the song, for in it there is a recognition of the whole purpose and method of God in the discipline, and in the deliverance. As our translators have rendered the words, they are full of beauty; but a more literal translation of the Hebrew is yet more arresting. It runs: "And Thou has loved my soul out of the pit of corruption." How wonderfully that tells the story of the Divine activity. He loves our souls out of the pit of corruption, at cost to us of suffering, but at infinitely greater cost to Himself. The full and final interpretation of this old word is found in the marvel and mystery of the Cross; wherein He did Himself fathom the depths of the pit of corruption; and whereby, in love, He lifts us out therefrom.

Then said Isaiah to Hezekiah, Hear the word of the Lord of hosts.—Isa. 39. 5.

This brief chapter is full of dramatic force, and is principally interesting in its revelation of the relation existing between the King and the prophet. It is the record of a deflection on the part of Hezekiah, due largely to his vanity, and to his failure to realize the full meaning of what he was doing. It was the kind of mistake which good men make when they fail, in every detail of life, to seek for the light and guidance of the Will of God. The wrong having been done, Isaiah sought out the king, and the conversation between them is revealing. In it we see who, in those days, was really the representative of the Divine authority. The prophet instituted inquisition, and the king responded without questioning. In that, the better side of Hezekiah was manifested; and also, in his acceptance of the finding of the prophet as he said: "Good is the word of Jehovah which thou hast spoken." This abides the true function of the prophet. He asks no favour of kings, and accepts no patronage from them. He is the messenger of God, and it is his work to break in upon all the doings of men, whether kings, or lords, or commoners, with this self-same formula: "Hear the word of Jehovah of hosts!" He is not responsible to men, but to God. Moreover, he is not responsible for the response of men to his message; but only for its delivery. If men hear and obey, they walk in the way of wisdom. If, hearing, they rebel, even though they slay the prophet, his word will be fulfilled in their ultimate undoing.

Prepare ye in the wilderness the way of the Lord, make straight in the desert a highway for our God.—*Isa.* 40. 3.

With this chapter begins the second part of this book. The theme of this part is that of peace. In its first section (40–48) the Purpose of Peace is discussed. In the second section (49–57) the Prince of Peace is described. In the third section (58–65) the Programme of Peace is declared. The words we have stressed occur in the Prologue of the whole movement. They catch up the ultimate thought of the first part of the book. Glance back at chapter 35. There we had the prophetic outlook upon the restoration of a lost order for the world, following upon the description of the desolation produced in the day of Jehovah's vengeance, contained in chapter 34. This restoration would be that of bringing the wilderness and the desert to fruitfulness (35. 1). Now God is to be revealed in the procedure which brings this result; and in these words the people of God are called upon to co-operate with Him by preparing His way in the wilderness, by making straight His highway in the desert. The keynote of the prologue is the keynote of this second half of the prophecy. It is found in the words, "Comfort ye, comfort ye my people." After the prologue follows a glorious description of the majesty of Jehovah; in the course of which, He is seen in His creative might and wisdom; idols are placed in contrast with Him; and His power and readiness to enable men is declared. In these facts of the majesty of Jehovah the first inspiration of true comfort is found for the sons of men. All this makes the appeal of this verse the more arresting and suggestive. This glorious God, majestic beyond compare, in might and in wisdom, yet calls the faithful among men to prepare His way, to make straight His highway. Let it at once be said that they do this when they yield to Him their complete loyalty, and confide in Him alone.

Keep silence before Me.—*Isa.* 41. 1.

With these challenging words, the prophet introduces a message, which may be described as the manifesto of Jehovah. It occupies this and the following chapters. In the next chapter (42) we shall find its central proclamation. This is introductory and preparatory. In it there are four movements. The first (1–7) constitutes the challenge of Jehovah to the nations concerning the advance of a foe from the east, in which He claims that this powerful one is under the government of His will, and satirizes the attempts of men to secure safety by making new gods. The second (8–20) has to do with Israel, and declares the presence and protection of Jehovah. The third (21–24) challenges false gods to

prove their divinity by prediction. The last (25–29) again affirms that the coming of the foe is by the will and act of God; and claims that the failure of others, whether gods or men, to foretell is proof of their vanity. The words with which all this begins might be rendered, "In silence listen to Me," and this is ever the word of God to men. The persistent clamour of many voices in the world drowns too constantly the voice of God. We are anxious to see the newspapers in order to learn what kings, statesmen, labour leaders, and even preachers, are saying, and the babel of their confused speech prevents our listening in silence for God. The emphasis on the value of prediction as evidence of Deity should not be overlooked. It is the key to all that follows. To make the prophetic messages which follow mere interpretations of contemporary events is to devitalize them. Here the prophet was patently conscious of these events, but was seeing through and beyond them, to greater things. Moreover, this element obtains still. Some of the things, then future, have now become history. Some of them are not yet fulfilled. Let us then keep silence, that we may hear these words of Jehovah.

Behold My Servant.—*Isa.* 42. 1.

That is the proclamation. All that follows is in interpretation of that call to behold. The more complete unveiling of this Servant of Jehovah is reserved for the next division (chapters 49–57). Here we have: (*a*) a wonderful portrait of this coming One (verses 1–9); (*b*) a great song in celebration of the triumph of Jehovah through Him (verses 10–17); and (*c*) an appeal to Israel based upon the facts revealed (verses 18–25). It is good at this point to stay to face the old and debated question as to Who this Servant of Jehovah is. That the reference was to Cyrus is so palpably absurd a suggestion that we need not stay to argue it. That it referred to Israel as she then was, is equally impossible to believe. That it referred to a spiritual element within Israel then existing is a suggestion which breaks down, in that such an elect remnant, which undoubtedly did exist, did not accomplish what is attributed to this Servant of Jehovah. To say that it is ideal Israel, is to say that no part of the forthtellings has yet been fulfilled, for the simple reason that such an ideal Israel is still nonexistent. There can be only one interpretation which satisfies the reason, to say nothing of the heart; and that is that Matthew was right when he deliberately declared that this foretelling found its fulfilment in JESUS (see Matthew 12. 15–21). As against that, it has been argued: "The Servant is invariably spoken of as having a present existence." And why not? It is certain that our Lord and Master, the Son of God, Who became His Servant for redemptive purposes, had then a present existence. To suggest that this prophet could have had no appreciation of the fact is to lower the conception of the Divine nature of the prophetic word. When Jehovah calls men to keep silence before Him, it is always in order that He may say to them, "Behold My Servant"; and there is only One Who can be so described.

But now . . .—*Isa.* 43. 1.

I have stressed these two words because they constitute a distinct and intended link between the Manifesto of Jehovah, of which the central proclamation is "Behold, My Servant," and a series of messages dependent upon that proclamation. These messages are found in this and the next two chapters, each one beginning with the formula, "Thus saith Jehovah." They constitute one great whole of interpretation of matters resulting from the fact that Jehovah has chosen, and anointed His Servant. In this chapter there are four such messages. Their content may thus be summarized. The first one (verses 1–9) affirms God's relation to Israel as Creator and Redeemer, and declares that He will yet gather them to Himself. The second (verses 10–13) declares that they will fulfil their function of being His witnesses, because of what He is, and what He will accomplish. The third (verses 14, 15) promises the destruction of Babylon, the opposing force, because He is Redeemer, Creator, King. The fourth (verses 16–28), referring to the past deliverances wrought, promises a new thing; and appeals to Israel, as unfaithful, promises pardon, and declares the method of punishment as necessary. All this is linked up with the revelation of the Servant by these words, "But now." Not yet in the prophecy is that Servant revealed, either in Himself, His method, or His victory. That will come presently. But the fact of His choice and appointment by God is declared; and these are some of the results. If we are true to the simplest intention of this great Hebrew writing we must interpret these predictions as having to do with Israel. In that case we realize that none of them is literally fulfilled as yet. Babylon as she then existed has been broken; but Babylon as the spiritual force antagonistic to Israel, is yet in power. But every prediction will be fulfilled to the letter. For us, the word of prophecy has been made more sure, because we have seen this Servant of Jehovah.

. . . O Jacob, My servant; and Israel, whom I have chosen.—*Isa.* 44. 1.

In this chapter we have three of these messages of Jehovah. They also are linked with the proclamation concerning the Servant in chapter 42 by the opening words of chapter 43—"But now." Let this be kept in mind as we read. The first message here, called the nation not to fear, in view of Jehovah's redeeming purpose to pour His Spirit upon its seed (verses 1–5). The second is perhaps the finest satire in all the prophecy against false gods, in which the method of their making is mocked at; their futility is declared; and the people of God are called upon to remember these things (verses 6–23). In the last the greatness of Jehovah is celebrated in creation and in government; and His appointment of Cyrus as the instrument to accomplish His pleasure is announced (verses 24–27). We have emphasized these opening words to fasten attention upon the fact that throughout these messages, which interpret the purpose of Jehovah in the appointment of His Servant, the thoughts of Creation and Redemption persist, the ultimate emphasis being upon Redemption; and that therefore the nation is seen and referred to, as failing and yet as fulfilling the true ideal. It is Jacob; but it is Israel. It is Jacob; but it is Jeshurun. Thus we see the outlook of God, and understand His method. He sees Jacob, knows all about the persistent failure; therefore the dispensations of punishment; Jacob must pass through travail. But all the while He sees Israel, as set upon realization; therefore Israel must come to triumph. Once more let us remind ourselves that this redeeming realization of creative purpose will be brought about through the Servant of Jehovah.

I will gird thee, though thou hast not known Me.—*Isa.* 45. 5.

In this chapter we have four messages of Jehovah, closely related to each other in that they take up and elaborate the fact announced in the previous message, that Jehovah had appointed Cyrus to perform His pleasure. The first of them is addressed to Cyrus, and indicates the fact of his government by God, ending with a Woe against him that rebels against that government (verses 1–10). The second re-emphasizes this fact that Cyrus will act under the direction of God (verses 11–13). The third foretells some of the victories which will come to Israel, when she is saved by Jehovah with everlasting salvation (verses 14–18). The last takes in the widest world outlook, and calls upon all the nations to look unto Jehovah in order to be saved (verses 18–25). Cyrus was raised up and used by God, and then set aside. Thus, there was a partial fulfilment of these predictions. But their ultimate fulfilment is not yet. Kings will yet be the instruments of God, under the authority of His Servant, for the accomplishment of His pleasure; and every glorious foretelling will have perfect fulfilment. The words we have emphasized occur in the message directly to Cyrus, and they reveal a principle of perpetual application. Connect it with the sentence found in the first verse, "I will loose the loins of kings," and its significance becomes more clear. The kings and rulers of the earth are all in the grasp of the might of God. Their loins are unloosed, or they are girded, by that power, in order to the ultimate carrying out of His pleasure. There may be in human affairs revolt and rebellion against God, working ruin to the rebels; but, so far as the ultimate accomplishment of His purpose is concerned, men can do nothing against Him.

I have made, and I will bear.—*Isa.* 46. 4.

The prophecy now celebrates the might of Jehovah as manifested in the destruction of Babylon. This has two movements, contained in this and the next chapter. Here the theme is that of the contrast between the gods of Babylon—Bel and Nebo—and Jehovah. Perhaps there is nothing even in the Biblical literature more powerful than this chapter in its unveiling of the essential difference between false gods and the true God. With the finest poetic imagery and passion, the prophet pictured the gods of Babylon, and so all false gods, as being made by men, carried by the men who made them, set in their place by these men, unable to move from the place where they are so placed, and incapable of answering those that worship them in days of distress. Over against that, the truth about the living God is graphically and briefly expressed in these words which we have stressed. He makes, and He carries. Briefer sentences will help us to realize the contrast more perfectly. An idol is a thing which a man makes, and has to carry. The true God makes the man, and carries him. This has application far beyond the bounds of what we designate as heathendom. When a man turns from the living God, he always makes a. god for himself, and that god becomes an encumbrance; he has to carry it, and the burden is too heavy—he is *heavy laden*. When a man worships the true God, he worships his Maker, and he is carried, and so he finds *rest*. "Little children, guard yourselves from idols!"

Thus shall the things be unto thee wherein thou hast laboured.—*Isa.* 47. 15.

These words occur in the second part of the prophetic message celebrating the Might of Jehovah, as manifested in the destruction of Babylon. Having—in the first part of the message (chapter 46), contrasted the gods of Babylon with Jehovah, the prophet uttered this "taunt-song," in which he foretold the doom of Babylon by likening the city to a woman, who having lived in luxury, is cast out to penury and to shame. In the course of this song, the prophet referred to those enchantments and sorceries in which he said Babylon had laboured from her youth (see verse 12). He tauntingly called upon her to test the false teachers to whom she had listened by seeking their aid against the determined doom; and declared the uselessness of such appeal because of the fierceness of the flame of the Divine wrath. This is the meaning of these words. Babylon had laboured from her youth in her traffic with the underworld of evil. That reference to "her youth" carried the mind back to the beginnings of Babylon, which were at Babel, where men attempted to frustrate a Divine purpose, by federating against God. This action was the result of traffic with evil conceptions, and evil spiritual forces. The process had run on through all the history. Babylon as a spiritual apostasy, persists unto this time. Its final testing will come in the flame of the anger of God. In that testing the futility of these dark forces of the under-world will be clearly manifested. "They shall be as stubble; the fire shall burn them; they shall not deliver themselves from the power of the flame." Men who have trusted in them will be left desolate, for "Thus shall the things be unto thee, wherein thou hast laboured."

There is no peace, saith the Lord, unto the wicked.—*Isa.* 48. 22.

These words really stand separate from the chapter, and constitute a conclusion to the first section. We shall find them again at the conclusion of the second section (see 57. 21). In this chapter the prophetic word celebrates in a very remarkable way the mercy of that God Whose majesty and might had already been described, and Whose manifesto and messages had been given. This message of Mercy emphasizes the failure and unworthiness of the people of God, who are the house of Jacob, even though called by the name of Israel; who do swear by the name of Jehovah, and talk about the God of Israel; but not in truth or in righteousness. Their obstinacy is declared to be the reason of the predictive element in prophetic teaching (see verses 3–8). Nevertheless, in spite of all this, for His own sake, Jehovah spares His people. He laments over their disobedience, and their consequent lack of prosperity; but He is their Reedemer, and will deliver them. All this having been said, there breaks in this great prophetic announcement: "There is no peace, saith Jehovah, to the wicked." Mark its relation to the whole movement of this section. From first to last the motive has been that of revealing the Purpose of God to bring Peace to His troubled people, and to the world. To this end He moves in His majesty, His might, and His mercy. This is the revelation of the manifesto and the messages. Nevertheless the people receiving this prophetic ministry, and all readers of it, are suddenly and sharply recalled to holiness and righteousness by this solemn word: "There is no peace, saith Jehovah, to the wicked." When we rejoice in the redeeming activity of God, which we have a perfect right to do, let us never forget this truth. It has two values. First: it accounts for the absence of peace to-day. Secondly: it reveals the only way by which peace can come to-morrow.

And He said unto me: Thou art My Servant; Israel, in Whom I will be glorified.—*Isa.* 49. 3.

We now come to the central section of this prophecy; and any stressing of particular sayings, which failed to see them in relation to the whole, would be disastrous. Having revealed the Purpose of God to bring Peace through His Servant, the prophecy now presents the Servant of God, Who is the Prince of Peace. The section presents Him, first as sustained through Travail (49–53); and then as singing in Triumph (54–57). The first part is made up of words of the Servant, and oracles concerning Him. This chapter opens with the voice of the Servant Himself telling of His call. These are the first words of Jehovah in that call. They are inclusive. To this foreordained One, Jehovah says: "Thou art My Servant;" and the value of that is interpreted in the words: "Israel, in Whom I will be glorified." Another man had borne that name, meaning Ruled-by-God; but he had failed to fulfil the ideal. The nation had borne that name; but in its history God had not been glorified. Now to another Man the suggestive name is given, and in Him the purpose will be accomplished. God will be glorified; and through Him eventually the failing nation will realize its high destiny—through it God will be glorified. The Servant is conscious of the difficulty of the service to be rendered, and speaks of the apparent vanity of His spending of strength; and records the word of Jehovah which sustained Him, declaring that the realization of Israel's destiny is too light a thing for Him; He shall be also a light to the Gentiles, God's salvation to the end of the earth. Let the rest of the chapter—its words to the Servant spoken by Jehovah, and its declarations to Zion—be considered in the light of this record of the call of Jehovah.

The Lord God hath opened Mine ear; and I was not rebellious, neither turned away backward.—*Isa.* 50. 5.

Here again we hear the voice of the Servant of Jehovah; and in these words we have His response to the call of Jehovah. As we saw in the previous chapter, He is represented from the beginning as conscious of the fact that His service means suffering. This consciousness is yet more definitely marked in this record of His response. It grows in intensity until it culminates in the fifty-third chapter. Here, it is a consciousness of the sufferings which His enemies, these being the enemies of Jehovah, will inflict upon Him. The physical figures are arresting—the smiting, the plucking off of the hair, the shame, and the spitting. The call of Jehovah to His Servant was a call to these experiences; and in regard to this fact he said, "The Lord Jehovah hath opened Mine ear, and I was not rebellious, neither turned away backward." This statement, "The Lord Jehovah hath opened Mine ear," is very significant. We must not confuse it with another great Messianic word, "Mine ears hast Thou opened" (see Psa. 40. 6), where the reference is to the willing surrender of the Servant to His Master's service. Here the thought is that of the communication of the secret of the Master to His Servant. To His Servant, Jehovah had made known His secrets; He had revealed to Him, not only the experiences awaiting Him, but the meaning and purpose of them. Thus the following statement, "I was not rebellious, neither turned away backward," means that between Jehovah and His Servant there was no conflict, but perfect agreement. Therefore this response to the call of Jehovah, involving consent to suffering, was vibrant with confidence in the help of Jehovah.

Hearken to Me, ye that follow after righteousness, ye that seek the Lord.—*Isa.* 51. 1.

These words introduce us to what has been aptly described as "a series of short impassioned oracles, mostly of a lyrical character." They continue to the twelfth verse of the next chapter, and are full of abounding joy and confidence, resulting from the vision of the Servant of Jehovah in perfect fellowship with Jehovah for the accomplishment of His redeeming purpose. First, there are three messages to the elect remnant of souls, who amid abounding apostasy are loyal to the Throne, and love righteousness. These begin, "Hearken to Me" (verse 1); "Attend unto Me" (verse 4); "Hearken unto Me" (verse 7); and call such souls to look to the Rock; to attend to the Law which is salvation; and to know no fear. Then follow three messages, each beginning, "Awake, awake." In the first case it is the cry of the nation for Divine interference; and it is answered; "I, even I, am He that comforteth you" (verses 9–16). Then it is the call of Jehovah to His people, recognizing the sufferings resulting from sin, but promising deliverance (verses 17–23). Finally it is the call of Jehovah, specifically answering the call of His people. They had said "Awake, awake, put on strength, O arm of Jehovah"; He replied, "Awake,

awake, put on thy strength, O Zion"; and again promised redemption (52. 1-10). All this is concluded by a poetical description of the return of Jehovah to Zion, full of beauty and power. Thus we have summarized the chapter, necessarily running over into the next, in order that the general impression may be gained of what the prophet saw; all of which would result from the suffering service of the Servant of Jehovah.

Behold, My Servant shall deal wisely, He shall be exalted and lifted up, and shall be very high.—Isa. 52. 13.

With these words we are introduced to the last movement in the presentation of the suffering Servant of Jehovah, a movement, in which the sense of triumph is present through all the amazing unveilings of travail. The short paragraph with which this chapter closes introduces and belongs to the next chapter. It constitutes a pregnant summary of what here is given in detail. Moreover it is a Divine summary of what there, is human observation. These are the words of Jehovah concerning His Servant. While we have stressed only the opening words, a consideration of them involves the whole paragraph. Observe carefully then, that taken as a whole, it is a declaration of the victory and exaltation of His Servant. So it begins; so it ends. At the heart of it all, the fact of suffering is recognized. That recognition is contained in these words: ". . . many were astonished at Thee." That is a graphic and awe-inspiring reference to the impression made upon men by the appalling spectacle of Him in the hours of His suffering. It is further emphasized by the words in parenthesis: "His visage was so marred more than any man, and His form more than the sons of men." But now most carefully observe the full statement. That reference to suffering is introduced by the words "Like as," and these are completed in the "So," which leads on to "shall He sprinkle many nations; kings shall shut their mouths at Him." Thus then, we behold the Servant of Jehovah from the standpoint of Jehovah. His sufferings are seen. They are beyond compare. But the issue and result of them is commensurately incomparable. "Like as . . . So." To apprehend the glory is to fathom the sufferings. To fathom the sufferings is to apprehend the glory. We are not equal, with our finite intelligence, to do the one or the other, for the sufferings and the glory are infinite. But we can trust, and worship.

He shall see of the travail of His soul, and shall be satisfied.—Isa. 53. 11.

Is there any single statement in all the Oracles of God which brings to the heart of the child of God quite so profound a sense of perfect joy as this? I think not. We have joy in our forgiveness, and in all the riches of our inheritance in our Lord; we have even greater joy in all the victories of our Lord, in the glories which are His, resulting from His passion. But the joy of knowing that He will be satisfied is still greater. In this great chapter we are introduced to the mystery of the suffering of the Servant of God, in a way which can only make the lips dumb, and bow the soul to the most complete prostration of wonder and amazement. So great is the revelation that pity is impertinent; and sympathy is irreverent. We can only watch, and wonder, and adore, as we see Him; of men, despised and rejected; of God, bruised, and put to grief; in Himself, a Man of sorrows, and acquainted with grief; at last, cut off out of the world of the living, His grave with the wicked. And all this because, "All we like sheep have gone astray . . . and Jehovah hath laid on Him the iniquity of us all." With necessary self-abnegation and complete abasement and shame, I am constrained to say: Was it worth while? That is, was man worth it? Am I worth it? The answer is in these words: "He . . . shall be satisfied!" Then I have but one thing to say, and it is this:

Love so amazing, so Divine,
Demands my life, my soul, my all.

Sing.—Isa. 54. 1.

That is the word which arrests us. It is the only fitting word, if indeed "He shall see of the travail of His soul, and shall be satisfied." It introduces the second movement in the section presenting the Servant of Jehovah as the Prince of Peace. That movement ends with chapter 57. In it we have first, this song of assurance (chapter 54); then the great prophetic appeal resulting from this vision of the Servant of Jehovah (chapter 55); and finally a message dealing with the administration of this Divine triumph (56 and 57). This song naturally and necessarily celebrates the triumph of the Servant of Jehovah in its bearing on the nation of Israel, personified as a city under the figure of a woman. As we watched the sufferings of that wondrous One, we inevitably thought of wider applications, those which include the Church and humanity; and we have been justified in doing so. But in doing so, let us not fail to appreciate the application to Israel. It is in her redemption and restoration to fellowship with God, as that of a wife to her husband, that "the whole earth" is to be reached. The glowing and glorious description of the City of God, with its foundations, its pinnacles, its gates, all full of beauty, is a description of Jerusalem, as it will be in the Kingdom of Heaven. God has not cast off His earthly people for ever. They will yet see Him Whom they pierced, and mourn because of Him. Out of that mourning, their joys will spring. Through the One Servant of Jehovah, and by His travail and His triumph, shall they become the servants of the Lord, thus fulfilling the Divine purpose. To them the final words of this song belong: "This is the heritage of the servants of Jehovah, and their righteousness which is of Me, saith Jehovah."

Behold, I have given Him for a Witness to the peoples, a Leader and Commander to the peoples.—Isa. 55. 4.

After the song celebrating the triumph of the Servant of Jehovah resulting from His travail, comes this perfect oracle of appeal. So perfect is it that every evangelist has felt its power, and used it in his sacred work. Opening with a description of life, as thirsty, hungry, unsatisfied, and so not life in the true sense at all; it closes with a picture of life in the midst of the garden of rest and fruitfulness. At its centre are the words which reveal the way from the one condition of life to the other. Man is to seek Jehovah; to forsake his way, and his thought, and to return to Jehovah, Whose thoughts are not man's thoughts, nor His ways man's ways; for the Divine ways and thoughts for man are high as the heavens, while man's ways and thoughts for himself are earthbound. If man will so return, Jehovah will have mercy and will abundantly pardon. But upon what grounds is such a declaration made? The answer is in these words. To Whom is reference made in the proclamation? "Behold I have given Him for a witness?" Certainly not to David. Here we see the continuity of thought running through the section. The reference is to the One Whom we have seen as the Servant of Jehovah proceeding through Travail to Triumph. By the way of that travail in which "the chastisement of our peace was upon Him," it is possible for Jehovah to have mercy and to abundantly pardon. He then is the one and only Leader and Commander to the peoples; and He is that by virtue of His Cross.

Thus saith the Lord: Keep ye judgement, and do righteousness; for My salvation is near to come, and My righteousness to be revealed.—Isa. 56. 1.

This and the following chapter constitute one message, with which the section presenting the Servant of Jehovah as the Prince of Peace closes. These words give us the key to the message. It is the word of Jehovah to men in view of the salvation and the righteousness which result from the work of the Servant of Jehovah. The salvation of Jehovah is always in order to righteousness; and His righteousness can only be revealed through His salvation. To the men for whom this prophecy was spoken or written, the coming of salvation and the revelation of righteousness were associated with the appearing of the Servant of Jehovah. That was always near in the purpose of God, though on account of the persistent failure of His people, centuries elapsed before He came. But He did come, and fulfilled the prophecy as to His travail to the letter. The completion of the work will come when He appears a second time without sin unto salvation. In the purpose of God that salvation is near, and that revelation of righteousness; but it is still postponed through the failure of His people. To them this final message appeals as it alternates between comfort for the loyal-hearted, and denunciation of the false and disloyal. In this chapter there is first comfort for all those who in any measure have suffered loss for love of the name of the Lord; and then stern denunciations of those watchmen who fail to fulfil their true function, and give themselves to the false excitements of strong drink. In such a time the call of Jehovah to those who love His name and wait for His appearing is ever that they keep justice and do righteousness.

There is no peace, saith my God, to the wicked.—Isa. 57. 21.

We stressed words similar to these before. They concluded the first section of this great prophecy, that dealing with the Purpose of Peace. In doing so we pointed out in conclusion that the statement had a double value; first, that it reveals the reason why we lack peace to-day; and secondly, that it suggests the only conditions upon which peace can ever come to men. Now we come to the end of the second section, in the process of which, we have seen the Prince of Peace, the Servant of Jehovah, Who through the Travail passes to the Triumph of establishing peace. This section closes, as we have said, with a message to men in view of the nearness of salvation and righteousness. In the part of that message contained in this chapter we again have the two notes we found in the last. First, fierce denunciation of an apostate community which had given itself to all evil practices in its forgetfulness of God. Then a message of consolation for those of contrite and humble spirit, who are loyal to Him. Then the whole movement ends with this central statement. It is to be observed that there is a difference. In the first occasion the title of God was Jehovah; here it is God, that is, Elohim. To those who observe the use of Divine names and titles this is suggestive. In the section dealing with the purpose of peace the affirmation is made by Jehovah, that is the title of grace. In the section dealing with the Prince of Peace the affirmation is made by Elohim, that is the name of absolute might. God in grace purposes peace. When He makes it possible through His suffering Servant, His Might insists on the terms. If in spite of all the travail of the suffering One, men persist in wickedness, then there is no peace for them, even by the way of that travail.

Cry aloud, spare not, lift up thy voice like a trumpet, and declare unto My people their transgression, and to the house of Jacob their sins.—Isa. 58. 1.

This chapter and the next constitute, if not one message, certainly one movement. With them the last section of this prophetic unveiling begins. In the first, the burden was that of Jehovah's purpose of peace. In the second, the supreme teaching is found, that namely of the presentation of the Servant of Jehovah, the Prince of Peace, through Whom the purpose of Jehovah is to be realized. Now the prophetic word was influenced by prevailing conditions; and it showed what the programme of peace must be, in view of these conditions. In the words of this first verse, this movement opens with the prophet's recitation of the words which had commanded him to say what he was about to say. He was charged to declare to the people of God, their transgressions and their sins. They were sternly rebuked for observing the ritual of religion, while failing entirely to produce its true results. In the name of Jehovah the prophet repudiated the value of an attitude and activity of humility and lowliness before God, when in their dealings with their fellow-men, there was an absence of justice and of compassion. Thus sharply were those people recalled from the consideration of the purpose and grace of Jehovah, to the fact of their immediate unworthiness; and were warned that for them the way, and the only way, into the realization of the blessings which He would provide, was that of turning from their wickedness, and so vitalizing their religious observances. It is a principle we do well to ponder. The operations of the Divine grace are never in conflict with the requirements of the Divine holiness.

Behold, the Lord's hand is not shortened, that it cannot save; neither His ear heavy that it cannot hear.— Isa. 59. 1.

If in this chapter we have a second discourse, the theme is the same as in the previous one, with a different application. There, these people were brought sharply face to face with their sins. Here, the truth involved in that message is stated plainly, namely, that these sins are preventing the fulfilment of the Divine purpose. In these opening words a statement is made which was probably intended to correct a false view of the delay in the realization of the declared purpose. It is conceivable that there were those who were declaring that Jehovah was either powerless to deliver them, or indifferent to their sorrows. The prophet declared that neither thing was true. His hand was not shortened; His ear was not heavy. Observe what immediately follows. "But," said the prophet—and beyond the "but," he uttered words which placed the blame on them. Note the short, sharp sentences, and the personal element—"Your iniquities ... your sins ... your hands ... your fingers ... your lips ... your tongue." To them he said—describing the attitude of the people as he vehemently denounced it—"The way of peace they know not." That is constantly the answer to those who charge God with inability, or indifference. When men say: Why does not God act? the reply is that His inaction is due to man's failure. Nevertheless, the last note is still that of confidence. When things are at their worst, and no man is found, then Jehovah arrays Himself as a warrior, and proceeds to accomplish His purpose.

Arise, shine; for thy light is come, and the glory of the Lord is risen upon thee.—Isa. 60. 1.

This is the first of three chapters which constitute one movement, which thrills and throbs with joy in the certainty of the accomplishment of God's purposes of peace, through the Servant of Jehovah. This chapter is addressed to the nation, as she is revealed in "The City of Jehovah, the Zion of the Holy One of Israel" (see verse 14). This opening call was addressed; not to Jerusalem as she was in the time when the prophecy was uttered; not to Jerusalem as she has ever been in her history even to the present time; but to Jerusalem as she will be, when she is established in righteousness and beauty, through the travail and triumph of the Servant of Jehovah. Then the city will be the centre of the world's light, for then the glory of Jehovah will rest upon her, and will radiate throughout the world. In that day affairs will be as this great message describes them, Nations will come to the light, and kings to the brightness. The children of the city, long scattered, will be gathered. The peoples of the world will come, not grudgingly, but gladly, bringing their gifts with them, and pouring their wealth into this city of God. This is the city which Abraham saw and sought. This is the city concerning which John declared the nations shall walk in the light of it, and shall bring their glory and honour into it. It has never yet been built. All this is either only wild dreaming—and very beautiful at that—or it is Divine prediction, and must yet come to pass. As to which, there can be no question. Every word of it will be fulfilled for the blessing of all the world.

The Spirit of the Lord God is upon Me.—Isa. 61. 1.

In this great chapter we hear again the voice of the Servant of Jehovah. Of that there can be no question in the light of the use made of the words by our Lord Himself. Again the subject is that of the city of God, and the people of God as fulfilling the Divine purpose. It is impossible for us to read these words save in the light of our Lord's employment of them. He closed the Roll, from which He read in the synagogue, at the words, "To proclaim the acceptable year of the Lord." That is, He broke off His reading in the midst of a statement, ending at the point where our punctuators have supplied a comma. The next phrase is, "And the day of vengeance of our God." He did not read that, because He had not then come to proclaim that day of vengeance. In the "acceptable year of the Lord," there have already been nearly two thousand human earthly years. How many more there will be the Lord alone knows. That it will be succeeded by "the day of vengeance" is certain; and that the Servant of Jehovah will also proclaim that day is equally certain. All the rest of this chapter is still prediction. Beyond the day of Jehovah's vengeance, and as the result of it there will come comfort for mourning Zion, and her complete restoration to prosperity, peace and power. For the accomplishment of all these things of the Divine programme, the Servant of Jehovah is anointed with the Spirit of Jehovah. When He came, He came by the overshadowing of the Spirit; in the power of the Spirit, He gave His teaching and did His works; through the Spirit He offered Himself in death. The acceptable year is the period in which the Spirit interprets the Servant of Jehovah. That same Spirit will be the fire of the day of vengeance, and the Comforter of the mourners.

And they shall call them The holy people, The redeemed of the Lord; and thou shalt be called Sought out, A city not forsaken.—*Isa.* 62. 12.

This chapter completes the movement celebrating the result in human affairs of the work of the Servant of Jehovah. Still, the city is in view, and that even more definitely than before. Nevertheless, the existing conditions were clearly in the prophet's mind. First, he declared his determination to continue his ministry towards that consummation; but there was no question as to the issue in his mind (verse 5). Then, the watchers on the walls were charged to take no rest from their holy vocation of prayer, as Jehovah's remembrancers; but again the issue was not in doubt, for Jehovah was committed by oath to accomplish His purpose (verses 6–9). Finally, the call was uttered to prepare the way back for the returning exiles; but that they were coming was certain, for Jehovah's proclamation had gone out to the end of the earth (verses 10–11). Thus the sense of

responsibility, and assurance, ran through the oracle. All closes with these words, descriptive of the nation and the city, when the purpose of Jehovah is fulfilled. The nation shall be known as "The holy people; the redeemed of Jehovah." The issue and victory is the holiness of the people; the way of realization is that of the redeeming activity of Jehovah. The city shall be called "sought out," a name descriptive of her attractiveness. This is an arresting word. It means that there is a beauty in holiness which the nations of the world will recognize. When they at last see a really Holy City, they will name it "Sought out." True beauty is always the outcome of holiness and is always attractive.

Who is this? . . . Wherefore art Thou red in Thine apparel?—*Isa.* 63. 1–2.

The section of the prophecy contained in this and the two following chapters, is a very remarkable one. We need to seek its natural parts and ignore the chapter divisions, if we are to apprehend its significance. In it there are three movements. First, the prophet's vision of a great Warrior returning from conflict (63. 1–6). Then a prayer, offered out of the midst of desolation (63. 7–64). Then the answer of Jehovah to that prayer (65). Here we stress the questions of the prophet, because they fix our attention upon the vision which he saw. It was a vision of One returning from Edom, with garments dyed from Bozrah; of One glorious in apparel, marching in the greatness of His strength. Seeing this One, the prophet asked, "Who is this?" The answer was immediate and clear: "I that speak in righteousness, mighty to save." This gave rise to the second question—Why were the garments red? What was the conflict from which the Warrior was returning? The answer was full and final. This vision has been interpreted as of Jehovah. In certain senses that is true. But it was the vision of the Servant of Jehovah, as the Instrument of Jehovah's act. It was a vision of Him in His first activity beyond that of proclaiming "The year of Jehovah's favour" (see 61. 2). The next phase in His work is that of proclaiming "The day of vengeance of our God" (see again 61. 2). Now, the Warrior is proclaiming that day as accomplished: "The day of vengeance was in My heart" (see verse 4). The prophet sees Him returning from the accomplishment of that purpose. He has trodden the winepress, so compelling the evil fruit of all godlessness to express itself. This is a persistent method of the Divine government of the world; and it will have its final expression and victory in Armageddon—which is not yet.

Oh that Thou wouldest rend the heavens, that Thou wouldest come down, that the mountains might flow down at Thy presence.—*Isa.* 64. 1.

These words occur at the heart of the prayer (63. 7–64. 12), in which the prophet expresses before Jehovah his sense of the desolation of the nation and the city, and cries for a Divine interference. It follows naturally the vision of the Warrior. It is as though the prophet agrees with the necessity for just such action; and prays that it may take place. This cry is the highwater mark of the great utterance. This, as the prophet understood it, was the real prayer of the nation. All that preceded this cry, and all that followed it, gave urgency and interpretation to it. The prayer opened with praise for the past lovingkindnesses of the Lord (63. 7–9). That is always the ground of confidence in an appeal to Jehovah:

"His love in times past, forbids us to
    to think
He'll leave us at last in trouble to
    sink."

Then there followed an acknowledgement of rebellion, and of the discipline following it, and the deliverance. Throughout this confession there ran the notes of assurance that the relationship, if disturbed, was not destroyed (63. 10–19). Then this cry was uttered; and it continues to the end of the third verse. Immediately the prayer became a meditation on the wonder of God's ways; a new confession of unworthiness; and an appeal to the Father-heart of Jehovah, in view of the desolate condition of the city (64. 4–12). How often, in hours of desolation, are men of faith constrained thus to cry out for the intervention of God in might and majesty. Let them ever do so in the spirit of this prayer of the prophet; remembering past mercies; depending upon God's faithfulness; confessing sin; acknowledging the righteousness of discipline; and appealing to the heart of the Father.

I am inquired of by them that asked not for Me; I am found of them that sought Me not.—*Isa.* 65. 1.

In this chapter we have the prophet's interpretation of the Divine answer to the prayer of the people. These sentences are introductory, exclamatory, inclusive. They recognized first the prayer of the people in the words: "I am inquired of . . ." They declared secondly the response of Jehovah in the words: "I am found." In each case attention was called to the failure of the people. They had not asked for Jehovah. Out of trouble they were doing so; but their trouble was due to their failure to ask. They had not sought Jehovah. That is why they had not realized His presence. Directly they sought, He was found of them. Then the whole prophetic interpretation of this answer moved forward on the line of these introductory words. In the first movement (verses 1–7), the resolute refusal of the people to respond to the Divine call was declared; and the relation of that wickedness to their sufferings was made plain. They had not asked for Jehovah; they had not sought Him; He had sought them; but they had refused, and turned to all evil things. Hence their desolation. Then the Divine answer to the prayer became the promise of restoration; and it moved forward to a description of the peace and prosperity yet to come to Jerusalem and the people of God through the accomplishment of His purpose. Throughout the movement the principle of discrimination is evident. Those that still forsake Jehovah are destined to retribution. Even in the established order of peace and prosperity, if there be a sinner, he shall be accursed. Thus in this section, from the vision of the Warrior to that of the established Kingdom, this even justice is manifest. God, determined upon mercy, never sacrifices holiness. So will it be to the end. The final triumph of compassion will be a victory for righteousness.

Thus saith the Lord, The heaven is My Throne, and the earth is My footstool.—*Isa.* 66. 1.

This is the keynote of this last message of this great prophecy. The message is of the nature of an epilogue, in that it catches up, and carries out, the great ideas, or principles, of the government of God, as they apply to all the coming ages. Jehovah is omnipresent; that is the meaning of these first words. There can be no escape from Him. No temple made with hands can contain Him. From that standpoint He judges and discriminates between the false and the true, between the ignoble and the noble, between the corrupt and the pure. Therefore Jerusalem will at last be saved, and will realize its true function for the sake of those of humble and contrite spirit who tremble at the word of Jehovah. Therefore all evil and polluted souls, notwithstanding all their craft and boastings, will be overcome, cast down, and destroyed. The new heavens and the new earth, which Jehovah will make, and which will still be respectively His throne, His footstool, will realize life, around Jehovah, as moon by moon, and Sabbath after Sabbath, they worship before Him. Then the things of evil will only be known, as they are still seen wrapped in the consuming fire, and held in abhorrence by all flesh. Thus the prophecy ends on a note of dread and suggestive solemnity, in which the wrath of Jehovah is seen. Let it be remembered that the fire of this wrath proceeds against those things of evil which have brought all the desolations and sufferings of men. Its fierceness is the fierceness of Love against all that destroys; and it is because love makes no terms with evil that at last there is the restitution of all things.

JEREMIAH

Before I formed thee in the belly I knew thee, and before thou camest forth out of the womb I sanctified thee; I have appointed thee a prophet unto the nations.—*Jer.* 1. 5.

Among all the prophets of the Hebrew people none was more heroic than Jeremiah. So far as moral and spiritual results among the people to whom he delivered his messages are concerned, he was foredoomed to failure. Through forty years at least, his was the task of uttering the word of Jehovah in the midst of a people who were rapidly moving down the steep declivity toward the final catastrophe; and he fulfilled that task with splendid loyalty. It was not easily done; he shrank from his work again and again; he suffered intensely, not merely from the persecution of his foes, but in his own soul, in its fellowship with God and with his nation; he needed very special Divine sustenance, and sought and found it in many an hour of protesting prayer in which Jehovah patiently led and upheld him. There can be no doubt that through all the travail of that long ministry these words of the original call of Jehovah remained with him as the abiding inspiration of his loyalty. The call of Jehovah came to him while he was very young. Its terms were such as to reveal to him the fact of his pre-natal ordination to his work. This ordination was based upon knowledge, such knowledge we must describe as foreknowledge. God knew His man, before the man had existence; and therefore He sanctified him and appointed him. Happy is the prophet of God who has the assurance that his separation and appointment to prophetic work is that of God, based upon His knowledge. In facing prophetic work, and in many an hour of supreme difficulty therein, he may feel that he is unequal to his task. Then he may and must take refuge in the fact that he is other than he thinks he is, and that his call is the result of what he really is, as that is known to God. The true prophet is content with the Divine knowledge of himself, however dissatisfied he may feel with himself.

For My people have committed two evils; they have forsaken Me the fountain of living waters, and hewed them out cisterns, broken cisterns, that can hold no water.—*Jer.* 2. 13.

In twelve chapters of this book (2–13), the prophet is revealed to us exercising a ministry in constant communion with Jehovah, through which his mission is progressively interpreted. The section alternates between messages to be delivered to the people, and records of intimate conversations between Jeremiah and Jehovah. These particular words occur in the midst of the Divine impeachment of the nation, and constitute a summary thereof. The nation was charged with having committed two evils, and these are figuratively described. The first was that they had forsaken Jehovah, the fountain of living waters; the second was that they had hewed them out cisterns—which turned out to be broken cisterns. Let us keep the two separate in our thinking. The first was fundamental; the second was resultant. The first was that they had forsaken the One Who is the fountain of living waters. Carefully observe the phrase "living waters" (compare John 7. 38). What are living waters? Simply waters rising from springs, always fresh, and always flowing. To understand that is to apprehend the second evil. What are cisterns? Tanks for holding water, storing it. Directly water is stored in a cistern, it ceases to be living; it is stagnant, and the process of deterioration begins. Here was the second evil, then. When these people had removed themselves from the living waters by removing themselves from Jehovah, they still felt their need of water, and so hewed them cisterns to store what they no longer had in the abundance of the streams from the fountain. This was the resultant evil. The fact that their cisterns were broken was a further revelation of failure. Suppose they had not been broken, the waters which they would have stored would have ceased to be living by that act of storing. Moreover, man can never hew cisterns which will hold. They are all broken. We must live by the streams, or we perish. The spiritual significance is patent.

Backsliding Israel hath shown herself more righteous than treacherous.—*Jer.* 3. 11.

These words necessarily demand the context in order to interpretation. That context describes the sin of Israel, and the Divine judgment upon that sin. Israel had been unfaithful to God, had broken her relationship with Him. The whole impeachment is illuminated by the figure of the marriage relationship. Israel, loved of Jehovah, married to Him by covenant, had gone after false gods, had been guilty of spiritual adultery and whoredom. Therefore Jehovah had given her a bill of divorcement, had put her away. Could anything be worse than this? Yes, the sin of Judah was worse. Judah had seen all this, knew the history of Israel's sin, and Jehovah's judgment; and yet she feared not, but herself was guilty of the selfsame sins. But there was a yet deeper vein of iniquity in Judah, and it is revealed in the word "treacherous." Here observe carefully that this message of the prophet was delivered in the days of Josiah. In his days there had been great reform outwardly. The king had wrought with a true passion for righteousness, but as Huldah, the prophetess, had told him, the reforms, so far as the people were concerned, were unreal, they did not touch the deepest things in life. In this connection it is interesting to read the prophecy of Zephaniah, which also, though delivered in the times of Josiah, ignored the reformation. Here, then, was the treachery of Judah. She was masquerading in the garments and attitude of reform, while yet continuing in the ways of infidelity to Jehovah. The nation and people which abandon all pretence at goodness in their devotion to evil, are more righteous than those who attempt to hide their evil courses under a mask of reform and simulated righteousness. That is the way of treachery, of hypocrisy, and that in the eyes of the God of truth, is the ultimate evil. The contrast between our Lord's attitude, in the days of His flesh, toward open sinners, and hypocrites, is a striking enforcement of this matter.

Then said I, Ah, Lord God! Surely Thou hast greatly deceived this people and Jerusalem; saying, Ye shall have peace; whereas the sword reacheth unto the soul.—*Jer.* 4. 10.

These words must be treated as a parenthesis. They break in on a message in which the prophet was foretelling the judgment to fall upon Judah for her treacherous sin, and reveal at once the anguish of his heart, and his inability to reconcile the promise of Jehovah with His actions. This parenthesis has caused a good deal of trouble to commentators, and various attempts have been made to explain the words in such a way as to get rid of their first sense, that of charging God with practising deceit. Is there any need for such attempts? I think not. Here we have an outburst, in which the prophet said what he thought. Many men think things like this who never utter them. The Divine ways constantly pass human comprehension. There are hours in which it seems that the Divine promise is not being fulfilled, when instead of peace, God employs the sword. All such seeming is false. It is due to limited vision. We are watching methods, rather than understanding purpose. The value of this verse, and indeed of this whole movement is that it reveals the patience of God with a perfectly honest soul. When the heart is hot and restless, and it seems to us that God is breaking down, we never dishonour Him by crying out to Him in language which reveals our agony. We dishonour Him far more by the treachery which

nurses this conviction of His failure, and attempts to hide it by professions of loyalty. And let a matter be observed which a hasty reading may overlook. The prophet addressed God here by the two titles Adonai and Jehovah, those which speak respectively of His sovereign Lordship and His grace. In this the ultimate attitude of his soul is revealed. Those who maintain this attitude may pour out before Him all their thoughts. He will understand, be patient, and presently explain.

The prophets prophesy falsely, and the priests bear rule by their means; and My people love to have it so; and what will ye do in the end thereof?—*Jer.* 5. 31.

In this summary the prophet revealed the utter degradation of the nation. Life was corrupted at the inspirational sources, and therefore, in all its streams. This bringing together of prophets, priests, and people is significant. If we go back to the book of Exodus we find that the people were called to be "a kingdom of priests, and an holy nation" (chapter 19. 6). Because they were not able to rise to the height of that great ideal, an order of priests was created, whose office it was to mediate between the people and God, in order that the people might realize their relationship and fulfil their function. In process of time the priesthood became corrupt, and then the prophetic order was created to reveal to the people the will of God. The prophets were constantly employed in denouncing the priests, as well as the kings. But now, the prophets also had become false, they were not uttering the word of God, but their own opinions. The priests had entered into agreement with them, and were exercising authority by their false teachings. And the final and fatal thing was that the people loved to have it so. It was a terrible and hopeless condition. Prophets are always false or true; their word is their own, or it is the Word of Jehovah. If it is the Word of Jehovah, their one responsibility is to Him, and their one passion is to please Him. If it is their own, their one desire is to please the people, and this they do by uttering views which harmonize with popular prejudices and desires. Prophets of God are the nation's truest servants and friends. False prophets are the worst enemies of the nation. Their popularity is the last evidence of national decay.

They have healed also the hurt of My people lightly, saying, Peace, peace; when there is no peace.—*Jer.* 6. 14.

These words occur in the midst of an oracle describing the coming of the army which was to be the instrument of Divine judgment upon the guilty and corrupt nation. In all the prophetic messages of judgment, the prophets of God were careful to show that the reason of such punitive activity was the sin of the people. This Jeremiah did at this point. (Read verses 13–15.) The whole nation was given over to covetousness, under the influence of the false prophets and priests. In these words he charged these spiritual rulers with uttering words of comfort, when the people were in the direst danger. That danger arose from the fact that they committed abomination without shame; that they had lost the power to blush! The word of the prophet in the presence of evil must ever be war. His business is to create a sense of shame in the souls of men, so to place their corruption before them as to compel the hot blush to their faces. To fail to do that is to leave the people in a false security, to leave the festering wound healed lightly, eased by opiates, and so not heard at all. It is much easier for prophets to do this than to deliver the Word of Jehovah, which probes the wounds, creates a smart and a shame, compels the blush. They may be saying peace, peace, when there is no peace, in many ways. They may do it, by silence, refusing to refer to evil practices. They may do it by speaking of evil as though it were only the under-side of good, an inevitable thing. They may even do it by denying that there is any such thing as evil. Whatever the method, it is the last apostasy of the prophet, that he should endeavour to create a sense of peace when there should be holy panic, to ease a pain of conscience which should be poignant. That, for the prophet, is indeed the sin that has no pardon.

Trust ye not in lying words, saying, The Temple of the Lord, the Temple of the Lord, the Temple of the Lord, are these.—*Jer.* 7. 4.

Observe carefully where these words were uttered. Commanded by Jehovah, Jeremiah stood in the gate of Jehovah's House. The occasion probably was that of the observance of some feast in the later years of the reign of Josiah. The temple had been cleansed, and its order of worship restored. As we have seen before, the reformation under Josiah, so far as the people were concerned, had been superficial; it had not reached down to the deep things of life. There had been no true repentance or return to God. Nevertheless, the people were laying the flattering unction to their souls that because the temple was there, and its services maintained, all was well with them. Jeremiah stood in the gate as the crowds assembled, and first called the people to a true repentance, as he said: "Amend your ways and your doings, and I will cause you to dwell in this place," declaring that this was the message of "Jehovah of Hosts, the God of Israel." Then he charged them to put no false confidence in the temple. This is a radiant revelation of the true place and value of holy places and things. The temple is the House of Jehovah in which men may dwell in fellowship with Him, and so in strength and rest, if their ways are in harmony with His will. But the temple is not a refuge for men who are living in rebellion against Him. It gives security and rest to obedient souls. It offers no security to men if they are living in sin. We have not done all that is necessary when we have built, or renovated the temple, if our own hearts are unclean; and when that is so, the temple gives us no more protection from judgment than does the place set apart to our idolatries and iniquities. Even a correct and orthodox confession of faith is of no value when evil things are reigning in the life. Let the solemn truth be pondered and applied by each of us, not to other people, but to his or her own heart.

. . . Lo, they have rejected the word of the Lord; and what manner of wisdom is in them?—*Jer.* 8. 9.

Observe the context here carefully. The prophet was dealing with the fact which rendered the situation of Judah so utterly hopeless, that namely, of their fatal and persistent lack of repentance. He showed that this was due to the misinterpretations of the scribes. It is of these scribes that this statement was made, "Lo, they have rejected the word of Jehovah." This is the more arresting in view of the fact that they were saying: "We are wise, and the law of Jehovah is with us" (see verse 8). Here is a situation which startles us into attention. Men had the Law of Jehovah, and it was their one occupation to interpret it, and apply it to the people. Yet they had rejected the word of Jehovah. That is to say, they had rejected the very thing they were possessing and claiming to teach. To borrow a New Testament phrase, they were handling the word of the Lord deceitfully, lowering its standard of requirement to meet the degenerate condition of men, compromising its requirements, devitalizing its message. Than this, there is no more heinous sin. It is the sin of corrupting the streams of life at the sources. The question of the prophet is persistently pertinent. When men reject the word of Jehovah, "What manner of wisdom is in them?" The answer is that the manner of such wisdom is, to quote James, "earthly, sensual, devilish" (3. 15). Humanity has had a tremendous answer to this inquiry of Jeremiah in the past century. Those systems of philosophy which began with a rejection of the Word of Jehovah in the denial of revelation, have progressively wrought themselves out until they eventuated in the welter of wickedness which we call the Great War. Great indeed, in its revelation of the manner of the wisdom which rejects the Word of Jehovah.

. . . Behold I will melt them, and try them, for how else should I do, because of the daughter of my people. —*Jer.* 9. 7.

These words occur in the midst of a great paragraph in which Jeremiah is revealed as in communion with Jehovah (8. 18–19). The prophet was overwhelmed with sorrow in the presence of the afflictions of the people, and he longed for some method of giving adequate expression to that sorrow (9. 1), and for some way of escape (9. 2). He was, however, keenly conscious of their corruption, and described their sin with unsparing faithfulness. To this mood of his soul Jehovah replied; and these were the opening words of that reply. He declared the inevitability of the method of affliction, and revealed its purpose. The words "melt" and "try" are those of the refiner. By these activities gold and silver are set free from dross, and proven pure. This is the meaning of affliction, and God employs it because there is no other way by which the end can be reached. Let us note that there was no rebuke of Jeremiah for his sorrow. Rather, the fact that Jehovah thus declared to His servant that there was no other way, proves that He was in sympathy with that sorrow, that the method of affliction was not one in which He delighted, that He only resorted to it because of the corrupt condition of His people. This story is full of searching light. It reveals God, and a man in perfect fellowship with Him. There can be no toleration of sin. Therefore the method of melting and trying by the fires of affliction must go forward. Nevertheless neither Jehovah nor His servant are callous or indifferent to the sufferings of the sinning people. When to men was given the vision of God incarnate, He was seen as making no terms with sin in Jerusalem, and therefore pronouncing its doom. But He did so with tears and lamentation. This is our God, and if we are in real fellowship with Him, we shall manifest the same spirit.

O Lord, I know that the way of man is not in himself; it is not in man that walketh to direct his steps.—*Jer.* 10. 23.

The oracle of this chapter was concerned with idolatry, its sin and its judgment. The first movement is a striking and balanced contrast between idols and Jehovah, between the men who trust in idols and the men who trust in Jehovah. The contrast is the same as that which Isaiah had emphasized (see Isaiah 46). Men make idols. Jehovah makes men. The idols which men make are always men's attempts to project, from their own inner consciousness, gods to whom they can yield obedience; or in other words, the making of idols is an attempt on the part of man to direct his own steps. It is against that profound mistake that these particular words were directed. "The way of man is not in himself"; man is devoid of the understanding of himself which will enable him "to direct his steps." Here we are brought into the light of the truth which man universally ignores or denies. The whole history of man, apart from his relation to God, willingly recognized and obeyed, is the history of his attempt to understand himself and govern himself. All autocracy is the attempt of men to direct the steps of men. It breaks down because these rulers do not understand men, neither themselves nor their vassals. Democracy removes the governing centre from the few, and attempts to establish it on the basis of common humanity. It says quite clearly, and definitely, the ways of man are in man, man can direct his own steps. And it is wrong, radically wrong. Democracy will produce conditions more tragic than autocracy ever did. There is only one hope for man or for humanity, and that is that he and it be governed by One Who, knowing man perfectly, is able to direct his steps perfectly. That one is God.

Then answered I, and said, Amen, O Lord.—*Jer.* 11. 5.

For Judah the sin of idolatry was the sin of breaking the covenant between Jehovah and His people. The first part of this chapter (verses 1–17) consists of an oracle dealing with this sin, and showing how persistently the nation had been guilty of it. When Jeremiah was commissioned to repeat to Judah the curse pronounced by Moses (see Deuteronomy 27), he replied "Amen, O Jehovah." That was a confession of consent to the righteousness of the Divine government; and a consecration to the service to which he was appointed. Here is a revelation of the secret of this man's splendid and heroic loyalty. His ministry was one long experience of suffering. He suffered persecution at the hands of those whose ways of wickedness were rebuked by his messages. He suffered more, in sympathy with the sorrows of the sinning people. Nevertheless, he bore right onward, never turning aside from his appointed task; and that because in his deepest life he was in agreement with God, and said "Amen" to all His words and ways. There is a vast difference between the liturgical "Amen" which is merely conventional, and which in the saying means nothing, and in life costs nothing; and the Amen which comes out of the deep inner agreement of mind and heart and will with the purposes and methods of God. The former carries us nowhere; it ceases when the days of stress come upon us. The latter holds and sustains us as we tread the path of obedience, when that path is one of suffering and sacrifice. To the will and ways of God, Christ is the One Amen. The proportion in which we are mastered by Him is the proportion of our ability to utter the true Amen, and so the proportion in which we are equipped for all His will appoints of service and of suffering.

If thou hast run with the footmen, and they have wearied thee, then how canst thou contend with horses? And though in a land of peace thou art secure, yet how wilt thou do in the pride of Jordan?—*Jer.* 12. 5.

We have now come to the last stage in the progressive unfolding of his commission to the prophet. Throughout the earlier stages of his ministry, he has been revealed to us as completely loyal, and yet shrinking from the terror of the words he has been called upon to utter. Through the process he has been sustained in a constant communion with God, in which he has honestly poured out his complaint, and Jehovah has answered him in patience and in sympathy. This last stage commenced in chapter 11, at verse 18, and it runs to the end of chapter 13. The plot against him by the men of Anathoth was revealed to him by Jehovah, and in the presence of it he cried out against the persistence and prosperity of the wicked. In view of it he shrinks anew from his task. In these words Jehovah commenced His answer to His servant. Their first meaning was that the sufferings which he had already endured were as nothing to those to which he was coming. He had been contending with footmen; he would have to contend with horsemen; comparatively he had been dwelling in the land of peace; he would pass to the experience of the pride, the turbulence of Jordan. Beyond the questions, Jehovah gave him words full of comfort. The effect of the questions must have been that of emphasizing the prophet's sense of his own weakness, and thus driving him to yet completer dependence upon God. But in the questions is there not another revelation? God never calls us to contend with horsemen, until He has trained us by the lesser strain of contending with footmen. He never allows us to face the pride of Jordan until He has prepared us by service in a land of peace. Through the strain of to-day, He equips for the greater strain of to-morrow, and never allows that greater strain to be put upon us until we are so equipped.

. . . Woe unto thee, O Jerusalem! Thou wilt not be made clean! How long shall it yet be?—*Jer.* 13. 27.

If the story told in this chapter is historic rather than merely symbolic, it covers a considerable period of time, for the distance from Jerusalem to Babylon was two hundred and fifty miles. Personally, I believe that it is history, that Jeremiah actually travelled to Babylon and back twice. That being so, we have here a condensed account of a period in which the prophet was being led to a deeper understanding of the hopeless depravity of the nation, and of the consequent necessity for judgment. That is the burden of the oracle. In these last words we have the whole situation presented in a brief but forceful summary. The doom of the city is certain: "Woe unto thee, O Jerusalem." The reason of it is explicitly stated: "Thou wilt not be made clean." But what is this last question? "How long shall it yet be?" Observe carefully that the prophet reports it as part of the charge of Jehovah to him, which begins at the eighteenth verse. These, then, are the words of Jehovah. In them merge two notes unmistakably. The first is that of sorrow. That is the inspiration of the question. But that question reveals a confidence that there will be an end to this attitude of determined refusal to be made clean. The inquiry involves the hope of ultimate restoration. It is wonderful how constantly in reading Jeremiah we are reminded of our Lord. He it was Who pronounced the doom of Jerusalem finally, and when He did so, His sentence ended on the same note of hope: "Ye shall not see Me henceforth till ye shall say, Blessed is He that cometh in the name of the Lord" (see Matt. 23. 37–39).

And the Lord said unto me, Pray not for this people for their good.—*Jer.* 14. 11.

We now enter upon that section of this Book in which, the prophet's commission having been completed, and interpreted to him, we find him conducting his heroic ministry in the midst of the darkest and most hopeless circumstances. From here to the end of chapter 39, we have messages delivered before the Fall of Jerusalem. The first movement is parabolic. Under the figure of the drought the judgment determined against Judah was foretold. This is immediately followed by the account of controversy in communion between Jehovah and Jeremiah. The prophet urged excuses for the people, and cried for mercy upon them, and that persistently. Again and again Jehovah replied, showing His servant the uselessness of all such praying. In these particular words the prophet recorded the command of Jehovah that he should not pray for the people for their good. In view of this command, and all the context, two matters impress us. The first is that, in spite of it, Jeremiah continued to plead for the people, and that Jehovah permitted him to do so, patiently arguing with him, until at last He brought him to submission when he cried out: "O Jehovah, Thou knowest" (see chapter 15, verse 15). The second is that Jehovah did know; and that it is possible for men to persist in evil so thoroughly and persistently, that God cannot have mercy upon them, and that prayer on their behalf which seeks the exercise of mercy, is unavailing. It is a most solemn consideration, and perhaps the most helpful comment on it is that we need never cease praying until Jehovah Himself forbids us; and then we may find our refuge in the words: "O Jehovah, Thou knowest."

If thou take forth the precious from the vile, thou shalt be as My mouth.— Jer. 15. 19.

These words occur in the last reply of Jehovah to Jeremiah in the controversy, the record of which occupies this and the preceding chapter. As we saw in our previous note, Jehovah commanded Jeremiah not to pray, but when he continued to do so, He patiently bore with him, and argued the case until the prophet was brought to the confession, "O Jehovah Thou knowest." This confession he immediately followed with a prayer for himself, affirming his loyalty to the Word committed to him, but complaining of his pain, and expressing perplexity and doubt. To that prayer Jehovah responded, and in these particular words at once definitely rebuked His servant, and revealed to him a principle of vital importance in prophetic ministry. The figure is that of the process of refining by which true metal is separated from alloy. In Jeremiah's heart there were unworthy thoughts of God, and these had found expression in his utterances. Let him purge his heart of such alloy, and devote himself only to the true gold of truth concerning God. So, and only so, would he be fitted to be as the mouth of God in uttering His messages. A word like this is in itself a searching fire. Those who are called to speak for God are ever in peril of having their message devitalized by conceptions of God which are unworthy. To rebel against the severity of Jehovah's judgments is to question His wisdom; nay, it is to question His righteousness and His love. It is equally true that to rebel against His compassion—as Jonah did—is to raise the same questions. Let us ever, and with complete consecration, in our thinking take forth the precious from the vile. So, and only so, can we be the mouth of God.

O Lord, my strength, and my stronghold, and my refuge in the day of affliction.—Jer. 16. 19.

These are words of response on the part of the prophet to a new charge given him by Jehovah. After the controversy (chapters 14 and 15), Jehovah called His servant to a new and more definite separation from the existing conditions. He was to live the life of personal asceticism, in that he was not to take a wife, nor have sons and daughters. He was to refrain from sympathy with the people in their bereavements, not going to the house of mourning. He was to stand completely aloof from all their festivities, having no part in their mirth. He was about to witness the desolation of the people, and in the midst of it, in answer to their inquiries, he would be called upon to show them the relation of their sorrows to their sin. It was indeed a charge calculated to make the stoutest heart quail. And this was Jeremiah's response. It was an affirmation of complete confidence. He realized what his work would mean. That is revealed in his reference to his affliction. But in the processes of communion he had learned the sufficiency of Jehovah for all his need. His weakness he knew; but Jehovah was his strength. The attacks which would be made upon him he recognized; but Jehovah would be his stronghold. The sorrows coming to him he foresaw; but Jehovah would be his refuge. Moreover, if the rest of this reply of the prophet be read, it will be seen that he was not only confident in Jehovah for himself, but in perfect agreement with the righteousness and sufficiency of the Divine method. Here the precious is set free from the vile, and the prophet is equipped to be the mouth of Jehovah.

A glorious throne, set on high from the beginning is the place of our sanctuary.—Jer. 17. 12.

Thus Jeremiah answered the message in which Jehovah had declared that the man who trusts in man is cursed; and that the man who trusts in Him is blessed. This may be described as one of the greatest words of the Old Testament. It expresses the deepest secret of life; the discovery of which gives the soul perpetual peace and poise and power, whatever may be the circumstances of the passing hour. Two words stand out from the rest—the words *throne* and *sanctuary*. The first stands for authority, executive action, government. The second represents retreat, refuge, security. In this declaration the ideas are brought into relationship. The throne is sanctuary; in the authority, the executive action, the government of that throne, man finds the place of safety and refuge from all the forces which are against him. Let us be careful to get our emphasis accurately. The statement is not that the sanctuary is the throne, as though God was ruling by mercy, and so man might find deliverance from the requirement of His government under the shelter of that mercy. It is rather that the throne is the sanctuary; that is, that God reigns, and always reigns without deviation from the eternal principles, and that man finds security only as he is brought into conformity with those principles. Observe that the prophet emphasized the eternal fact of the Throne as he described it as "on high from the beginning." The word "*set*" in our translations is supplied; it is not in the Hebrew text, and it somewhat robs the idea of its force. The Throne was in no sense "set" on high, if that suggests the time element. It is "on high from the beginning"—that is, eternally. These words are the more forceful as to the relation between government and grace, when we see in the midst of the Throne a Lamb, as it had been slain.

I went down to the potter's house, and behold, he wrought his work on the wheels.—Jer. 18. 3.

Jehovah sent Jeremiah to the potter's house for an interpretation of the activity of that Throne, the eternity of which he had confessed; and in which he knew there was sanctuary for man. Could any illustration be imagined at once so simple and so sublime? There, in that potter's house, everything was reduced to simplicity, almost to poverty. All the accidental trappings usually associated with the conceptions of kingship were conspicuous by their absence. When he looked, he saw a man, a wheel revolving in answer to the movement of the foot of that man, clay kept in motion by that moving wheel, the hands of that man upon that clay moulding it. He saw as he watched, that a thought in the mind of the potter was coming into manifestation in the clay as it yielded to the pressure of the potter's hands, brought persistently round to that pressure by the wheel revolving also by the power of the potter. He saw that the clay was powerless, and yet realized a high destiny, as in plastic yielding it answered the hands of the potter. But he saw more. Something happened as he watched. The clay was suddenly marred, twisted; it failed to express the potter's thought. No explanation of the marring is given; the fact is stated. What then? He saw the potter did not abandon it. "He made it again another vessel." And the re-made vessel was conformed to the thought of the potter, it was "as seemed good to the potter to make it." Thus he discovered that there was more than mechanism in the activity of the Throne. There was a mind, capable of adapting method to meet failure, and in such wise as to realize purpose in spite of failure. Thus in the material poverty of the potter's house, Jeremiah saw the unveiling of the riches of government and grace in the exercise of Divine sovereignty.

Even so will I break this people and this city, as one breaketh a potter's vessel, that cannot be made whole again.—Jer. 19. 11.

It is impossible to escape from the impression of intimate relation between this chapter and the preceding one. There the prophet was sent to the house of the potter to watch him at work on the wheels, and the suggestive picture had been full of illumination. Now he was commanded to "buy a potter's earthen bottle," the finished product of the potter's house, and to enforce a message of judgment on sin, by breaking that vessel in pieces. Here, then, at once is the corrective of any tendency to make improper use of the facts disclosed in the potter's house. There God was revealed as making again a marred vessel. That was the unveiling of sovereignty acting in redemption and restoration. But let no man or nation presume upon that revelation, for here the Potter is disclosed as taking a vessel, formed by His own hands and breaking it so that it "cannot be made whole again." This is the revelation of another activity of sovereignty; and it is as beneficent in the interest of the complete purpose of the Love of God, as is the redeeming activity. If man or nation, in spite of all the patient grace of God, persist in courses of evil and rebellion, then He will break in pieces. To find in the redeeming purpose of Jehovah a tolerance of sin, is of all evils the most terrible. To continue in sin that grace may abound is the sin which puts the soul outside the sphere of grace, and brings it into the realm of the breaking, destructive activity of the eternal throne. And were it otherwise neither earth nor heaven would be safe.

And if I say, I will not make mention of Him, nor speak any more in His name, then there is in my heart as it were a burning fire shut up in my bones, and I am weary with forbearing, and I cannot contain.—Jer. 20. 9.

This chapter opens with a paragraph of history. It recounts how Jeremiah was persecuted because of the messages he had delivered, in which he had foretold the destruction of the city on account of its sin. Pashhur, the chief Temple officer, smote the prophet, and put him in the stocks. The expression "smote Jeremiah" is a technical one, and in all likelihood means that the official scourging of "forty stripes save one" was administered. After that, he was placed in the pillory, an object for the derision of men. Following this story we have the account of the outpouring of the prophet's soul. The dominant note of this outpouring is one of complaint, and yet other notes mingle with that note, those of confidence, of triumph, even of song. It is a remarkable unveiling of his state of heart, of the conflicting emotions which swept him like a storm, making him sing to Jehovah, and curse the day he was born. In these particular words we see the prophet in the deepest things of that consciousness which made him so great. Under the stress and strain of his sufferings, he was tempted to abandon his work, to refuse to speak any more in the name of Jehovah. But when he attempted thus to find release from suffering in silence, it was impossible; for such silence became more intolerable than suffering; the word became a fire in his bones, so that he could not contain himself. This is the burden of the Word of Jehovah. Perhaps only those who have experienced it can understand it. To publish that word at times brings suffering; but to refrain brings far more terrible suffering. Paul understood this when he said, "Woe is unto me if I preach not the Gospel."

Peradventure the Lord will deal with us according to all His wondrous works.—*Jer. 21. 2.*

These were the words of Zedekiah, a man of whom the historic recorder said: "He did that which was evil in the sight of Jehovah" (2 Kings 24. 19). By this time the city was invested by the hosts of Nebuchadnezzar. Thus the prediction of Jeremiah which had stirred the rulers to anger, was approaching fulfilment. The king, and those associated with him politically were in favour of rebellion against the Babylonian yoke. To cast off that yoke, would be to falsify the prediction of Jeremiah. While moving in that direction, the king sent to the prophet, asking that he inquire of Jehovah, and the purpose of the inquiry was the desire thus expressed: "Peradventure Jehovah will deal with us according to all His wondrous works." What a revelation this is of the degraded attitude which is possible to the heart of man toward God. Here was a king, politically planning to take action in order to invalidate the declared purpose of God; yet in his heart there was a conviction of the power of God; and he positively dared to make the attempt to seek for the intervention of that power in some way, so that his own ends might be served. The answer to such "Peradventure" is one of unequivocal certainty. Jehovah will deal with men according to His wondrous works; but that, not in order to deliver rebellious souls from the just punishment of their iniquity, but rather to hand them over to that punishment in spite of all the cleverness of their policies. And yet even in the darkest hour the Divine government offers to the rebellious heart of man a way of escape. Read carefully the prophetic word to "the house of the king," as it is found in the eleventh verse.

Hear the word of the Lord; O king of Judah.—*Jer. 22. 2.*

With this chapter a section begins which continues through chapter 27. It contains, first, a message to Zedekiah directly; and then is made up of messages concerning his three predecessors, Jehoahaz, Jehoiakim, and Jehoiachin; and concerning the false prophets. Jeremiah was commanded to go to the house of the king of Judah, to deliver the word of Jehovah. This he did, delivering these messages, in which he repeated some of those which he had given during the reigns of these predecessors. A glance ahead to 27. 12 will show where these particular messages ended. Observe the opening words of this chapter (22): "Thus said Jehovah." The revised version has restored the past tense here accurately. Therefore, we are to understand that in the arrangement of the Book we are now taken back to a visit which Jeremiah had made to Zedekiah in the earlier days of his reign. All that the prophet said to him then should have saved him from his evil courses, had he been ready to hear and obey the word of Jehovah. The word of Jehovah to kings, as to people, is the word of wisdom. Hearing it, and obeying it, they execute judgment and righteousness, and so establish their kingdoms in strength. To neglect that word, or to rebel against it, in favour of policies resulting from watching events, observing circumstances, and making calculations, is to bring destruction, inevitably and irrevocably. The centuries run their course, kings rise and fall, kingdoms advance and perish, and we watch the process, and see that there is but one hope for kings and kingdoms; and that is that they should hear the Word of Jehovah, and hearing, obey.

Thus saith the Lord of hosts; Hearken not unto the words of the prophets that prophesy unto you; they teach you vanity; they speak a vision of their own heart, and not out of the mouth of the Lord.—*Jer. 23. 16.*

This chapter is occupied with the prophet's denunciation of the false rulers of the nation—kings, prophets, and priests. It is chiefly occupied with the prophets, and is conspicuous as a revelation of the appalling nature of the evil of false-prophesying. There can be no peril graver to humanity than that of men who profess to be dealing with the spiritual, that is with the inspirational things of life, when such men are uttering falsehood. Better, far better, that there should be no prophets, no messengers dealing with these spiritual facts and forces, than that they should be misinterpreted. Man is so constituted that he ever seeks in some form for direction from the spiritual world that lies behind all material manifestations and forms. This quest creates the opportunity of evil men, who having no true light from that world, yet speak as though they had, and so mislead those who hear them. The difference between the false and the true is clearly shown in these words. The false prophet speaks a vision of his own heart; the true utters the message which he has received from the mouth of Jehovah. The false prophet, then, is the man who observes events, compares them, deduces from his observations and comparisons certain conclusions, which he then declares as a message from the spiritual world. The true prophet lives in communion with God, waits for the making known of His will, and then declares that will, showing its bearing upon events. The first is necessarily limited by his own futile mind, and influenced by his own desires. The second is illuminated and inspired by the final Truth. The first teaches vanity. The second teaches wisdom.

. . . Figs; the good figs, very good; and the bad, very bad, that cannot be eaten, they are so bad.—*Jer.* 24. 3.

This is the prophet's description of the vision which was given to him of "two baskets of figs set before the temple of Jehovah." The oracle contained in this chapter records that vision, and gives Jehovah's explanation of it to His servant. Let us remember that we are still considering the messages which Jeremiah delivered on the occasion of his visit under Divine command to the house of Zedekiah. In this message then he contrasted the captives who had been carried away into captivity by Nebuchadnezzar in the reign of Jehoiakim, with those who had remained, and were now still in the city and land under the rule of Zedekiah. It was a startling comparison. It is most natural to suppose that those remaining would lay the flattering unction to their souls that those carried away were ·the more corrupt. This message was in direct contradiction of the false assumption. Those who had gone, were being prepared by the purifying force of their suffering for return. The eyes of Jehovah were upon them for good. Those remaining, had refused to profit by the warning of their brethren's chastisement, and were continuing in the same ways of evil. Thus they were adding to their corruption, and so hastening a judgment upon themselves yet more terrible and more complete. When men refuse to learn the lessons taught by the discipline of others, they add an element of wickedness to their ways, which brings about a more hopeless condition of corruption. When the calamities of Divine judgment overtake men, if we are immune, let us profit by the solemn warning, and cleanse ourselves from the sins which brought them into calamity. To fail to do so is to sin a deeper sin than they, and so to insure a severer judgment.

The word that came to Jeremiah . . . in the fourth year of Jehoiakim. —*Jer.* 25. 1.

There are those who say that the messages of Jeremiah in the house of Zedekiah ended with the previous chapter. Personally, I do not so understand the arrangement. I believe that we are still listening to his message upon that occasion; but he goes back and repeats the message delivered in the reign of Jehoiakim, and that because of its bearing upon the situation under Zedekiah. In doing so, he was very careful to date the original uttering of this message. It was delivered in the fourth year of Jehoiakim, the first year of Nebuchadnezzar, and the twenty-third of his own prophetic ministry. All he then said he now repeated. Some of it was in process of fulfilment, for the hour of the fall of the city was approaching. That being so, it was intended to be an argument with Zedekiah concerning the fulfilment of the rest. The message in its entirety was one of judgment. It described the processes of the Divine procedure in judgment in enlarging circles. First, there would be the judgment of Judah, Babylon being the instrument. Then would follow the judgment of Babylon by many nations. Then the judgment of the nations shall follow. Finally, the whole earth will be involved. In that final judgment those principally named are the Shepherds, the principal of the flock. Thus the judgment of Jehovah is seen as proceeding to bring to naught all false authority and rule and power, in order to the establishment of His own authority and rule and power. This Divine activity is persistent in human history. To our thinking at times, the process is a slow one, but it is sure, and it is wholly beneficent in its intention, and will be vindicated so in its ultimate victory. This is our only hope for humanity, but it is a blessed hope as for us it is made more sure in meaning and in certainty, as the vision is interpreted in Christ.

It may be they will hearken, and turn every man from his evil way; that I may repent Me of the evil which I purpose to do unto them because of the evil of their doings.—*Jer.* 26. 3.

Still speaking in the house of Zedekiah, the prophet went back to a yet earlier period, to the beginning of the reign of Jehoiakim, and that in order to recount the words which Jehovah had then charged him to utter, and to record the incident of how he was threatened with death, but saved by the intervention of the princes of Judah. This was intended to recall Zedekiah to the recognition of the patience of Jehovah. By sending His word, He had created an opportunity for the people to turn from evil, and so escape the purposed punishment. In these particular words this conception of Jehovah as capable of repentance, that is, of change of mind and method, is brought out. It is admittedly a difficult idea, and one which superficial or mechanical thinking about God rejects. Nevertheless, it constantly appears in these Divine oracles, and as a matter of fact emphasizes the unchangeable nature of the purpose of God. It is because He never changes in His love, and His determination to bless, that He changes His method. When man repents of loyalty and turns to rebellion, God changes His method of blessing, and turns to that of punishment. When man repents of his rebellion, and turns back to loyalty, God changes His method of punishment, and turns again to mercy and blessing. Thus the changes of the method of God are ever due to the immutability of His love. The pride of man which says "Because I have said I will do thus and so, I must do it, however much the conditions have changed," cannot be predicated of God. That in Him which changes not is His purpose of love and holiness. All His activities change in consonance with these unchangeable things.

. . . Bring your necks under the yoke of the king of Babylon, and serve him and his people, and live. Why will ye die?—*Jer.* 27. 12, 13.

This was the prophet's appeal to Zedekiah, and to the nation through him, to submit themselves to the discipline which their sins had made inevitable. The situation was acute. Jeremiah was foretelling with determined insistence the fall of the city. The false prophets were declaring that the city was safe, and were counselling resistance to the king of Babylon. All the politicians, and the king, were influenced by these prophets, because their statements harmonized with their own desires. Jeremiah knew that such resistance was not only useless, but was wicked, and would inevitably bring yet worse sufferings upon the people. He plainly declared that Nebuchadnezzar was in this hour the servant and instrument of Jehovah; and, therefore, to rebel against him was to rebel against God, and that was futile and the ultimate in wickedness. When God chastises for sin, the true action is that of yielding to His discipline, by accepting the stroke which He sends. When we do so, we find that the suffering is the way of restoration. To rebel against such suffering, and to oppose our wills and our strength to it, is not to escape it, but to miss its restoring intention, and to involve ourselves in more terrible suffering. It was an understanding of this which made David, when he had sinned in numbering the people from a wrong motive, say: "Let us fall now into the hand of Jehovah; for His mercies are great; and let me not fall into the hand of man."

The Lord hath not sent thee; but thou makest this people to trust in a lie.—*Jer.* 28. 15.

In this chapter we have a page of history graphically illustrating one of the chief difficulties with which Jeremiah had to contend in the exercise of his ministry. It is the story of Hananiah, one of the false prophets, probably the chief of them. His message is recorded, and serves to show how it might easily deceive the people. Its introductory formula was that of the true prophets, "Thus speaketh Jehovah of Hosts, the God of Israel." It was characterized by the element of clear and definite prediction, as it declared that in two years the yoke of the King of Babylon would be broken. That prediction harmonized with the desires of the people, and the findings of the politicians. Of course this was an intended contradiction of Jeremiah's message, which foretold a period of seventy years of captivity. The sin of such prophesying is revealed in these words of Jeremiah to Hananiah, "Thou makest this people to trust in a lie." How much of human prophesying is covered by that word! All those philosophies which attempt to interpret life without the light of revelation—all so-called theologies, which result from speculations which invalidate the revelation; make men trust in lies, and that because they are the utterances of men not sent by Jehovah. We may say dogmatically that no message to men, on any subject, is of any value, save as it is uttered by the messengers of Jehovah, for He alone knows the ultimate truth, and therefore He alone is able to direct the ways of men. Whether in theology, sociology, or economics, the speculations of men are lies, trusting in which men insure their own undoing. We should earnestly heed the words of Jesus, "Beware of false prophets."

Seek the peace of the city whither I have caused you to be carried away captive, and pray unto the Lord for it; for in the peace thereof shall ye have peace.—*Jer.* 29. 7.

This letter of Jeremiah proves that the popular school of prophecy at the time, that is, the school which preached rebellion against Babylon, and denied the messages of Jeremiah, had its messengers, not only in Jerusalem, but in Babylon among the captives there. By their messages a false hope of speedy return was created, threatening to produce unrest amongst them. This was undoubtedly what the false prophets, and the politicians influenced by them, desired. So they hoped to stir up the spirit of rebellion, and insure the fulfilment of their prophesyings, and the successful issue of their policies. Confident in the certainty that the programme of God must be carried out, Jeremiah sent this letter to them, charging them to settle where they were, giving no heed to these lying spirits. Seventy years were before them. Let them act accordingly. In the midst of this counsel, these words occur, and they contain a principle of persistent application. They constitute an appeal for sanity. When in the grip of adverse circumstances which are the result of the Divine will, let men endeavour to secure the best conditions possible, and let them do it by the best means, by prayer. Jeremiah had foretold the ultimate overthrow of Babylon with no uncertain sound. Of that issue there could be no doubt. But so long as it remained, and they were held there as captives by the will of God, let them secure peace for themselves, by seeking the peace of the city, and that by prayer. The advice was that of the highest religious feeling, and it was that of practical common sense. These two things are never divorced.

. . . till He have performed the intents of His heart.—Jer. 30. 24.

This is the first of four most wonderful chapters. They are central to the whole Book, and in spite of all its warnings, tears, solemnities, reveal its deepest note. They record Jeremiah's prophecies of hope. The remarkable thing about them is that they were delivered in the very darkest period, and from the midst of circumstances which were calculated to fill the heart with despair. The city was invested, its fall was imminent, its people were already suffering from pestilence and famine: and the prophet was in prison. Out of that prison, and amid that darkness, these prophecies were uttered. The first message was of the nature of a song. It occupies this and the following chapters. Its theme is that of the restoration of the people of God. This chapter contains the first movement of that song, that which dealt with the process of restoration. It recognized the trouble of the people, their sorrows, their sufferings; but showed that these are the methods which produce the triumph. It most forcefully described the friendlessness of the nation in the hours of its desolation; but saw it brought by the experiences of that friendlessness into the condition of favour with God. All is summarized in the concluding paragraph; in which "the tempest of Jehovah," "His wrath," "the fierce anger of Jehovah," are seen as the ministers of what is in His heart. Thus do these Divine oracles perpetually and persistently unveil the deepest fact about God, as being that of the intent of His heart, the purpose of His love. All the ways of His wrath, made inevitable by human sin, must be interpreted by that intent. When this is done, songs issue out of the darkness, and from the prison.

I will put My law in their inward parts, and in their heart will I write it.—Jer. 31. 33.

In this chapter the great song of restoration is continued and completed. It describes in language full of poetic beauty the restored order. The city is to be rebuilt; to it, scattered Israel is to be regathered; all sorrow and lamentations are to cease; there is to be perfect contentment and satisfaction with the Divine government and administration; and all this is to be established and perpetuated by a new covenant. The nature of that covenant is revealed in the words we have emphasized. The old covenant was based upon a law given to them, set before their eyes, on which they were to look, which they must obey. Their whole history had been, and may it not be said, still is, that of the breaking of this covenant, by the breaking of that law. The new covenant will still provide a law, but no longer as external and objective; it will be internal and subjective. That is necessarily to say that the way of restoration of order will come by a change of heart, and spirit, in which the law of Jehovah is made known in spiritual communion, and obeyed in perfect agreement and in delight. The writer of the letter to the Hebrews quoted these words, as made possible of fulfilment through the One sacrifice of Jesus Christ, and by the witness of the Spirit. Thus we to-day are living under this covenant, and those of the seed of Israel, who believe in Jesus as Messiah, enter also at once into the same covenant relationship with Jehovah. For Israel as a whole the prophecy is not yet fulfilled; but it will be, and there is no word of this glorious song of restoration which will not be fulfilled to the letter.

Then I knew that this was the word of the Lord.—Jer. 32. 8.

In this chapter we have the account of a message of Jeremiah, in which he told the story of a transaction, that of buying a field in his native place of Anathoth, and gave an interpretation of it. The act was remarkable in view of the conditions. The land was about to pass to Babylon, and the prophet was himself in prison. Moreover, when he had completed the purchase he was perplexed, and said so in his communion with God (see verse 25). The explanation of the act given to him, and by him announced, was that this purchase of land was a sign that God would restore the land to the people. It was not a sign of Jeremiah's faith, for he was perplexed, while obedient. The sign was in the command; it was God's sign to His servant. The impressive fact as to Jeremiah is that he was obedient even though perplexed. When we ask for the secret of that obedience, we find it in his assurance that the command was indeed the command of God. Now observe the reason of that certainty. He became certain when Hananiah came and urged him to buy. He had heard the word of Jehovah already, but evidently was not sure that it was His word. When the offer came to him, he was made sure. This is very suggestive. It would seem that the word of Jehovah came to him as an impression, as it so often comes to us. We often have impressions which seem to be from the Lord. Let us rest assured that what He commands He will make possible. When the call is followed by the open door, we need have no hesitation. Until the clear way is marked 'tis often the highest wisdom to wait.

I will cleanse them from all their iniquity, whereby they have sinned against Me; and I will pardon all their iniquities, whereby they have sinned against Me, and whereby they have transgressed against Me.—*Jer.* 33. 8.

This chapter contains the second word of Jehovah to Jeremiah while he was in the prison, and it is a song in celebration of the assured ultimate restoration. That restoration is described first as moral and then as material; the method of its coming through the Branch of righteousness, the King Priest, is declared; and its certainty is affirmed by the signs of day and night. The words we have emphasized are those which reveal the fact that restoration to material conditions of well-being can only come through restoration of a true moral order. The two words of paramount significance in this promise are the words "cleanse" and "pardon." The first indicates a process by which a condition is created. The second describes an act by which a relationship is restored. Cleansing removes guilt, pollution, defilement, morally. Pardon brings the offender back into relationship of favour and fellowship. The order of statement is the order of procedure, and of experience. God never pardons polluted souls; He first cleanses them. Pardon, apart from the communication of purity, would perpetuate pollution, and so violate the moral order beyond remedy. It is to this profound work of cleansing the human soul in order to its pardon, that God in grace committed Himself in all the promises made to His sinning people; and this is what He accomplished in the mystery of that passion which for us had unveiling in the Cross. Let us never insult that Cross by thinking of it as a means by which we obtain forgiveness, save on the basis of complete cleansing.

Ye turned and profaned My name.—*Jer.* 34. 16.

In this chapter we have an arresting story. The city was closely besieged, and the activity of the hosts of Nebuchadnezzar was moving toward its capture. Jeremiah was still insisting upon the inevitability of this consummation, because it was so ordained of God. Right in the midst of these circumstances, and perhaps as the result of the pressure of them, a wrong was committed. In fulfil-ment of the Divine law, the proclamation of liberty to Hebrew man-servants and maid-servants had been made. Then all this was changed, the liberty was withdrawn, and those thus set free were compelled to return to their subjection. As we have said, the action may have been caused by the difficulty of the hour, taking the form of a State conscription of labour. Whatever the reason for the action, this prophetic message shows that it met with the disapproval of God, and called forth His anger. This is arresting, as it reveals to us that no political necessity must be made the reason for breaking a Divine law, and doing wrong to our fellow-man. The deepest note in such sin is made clear in these words—"Ye turned, and profaned My name." The liberty given to these men-servants and maid-servants was by command of God. Those finding it would realize this and in their souls bless the name of Jehovah. Its withdrawal would create in the minds of the sufferers a reaction in their thought of God Himself. That is the ultimate wrong; and those who cause it are to blame. Let us ponder this. All injustice of man to man creates in the mind of those who suffer, questionings about God. Thus His name is profaned; and His anger is ever stirred against those causing the profanation. The wrong of man to man inflicts on God a deeper wrong.

The words of Jonadab . . . are performed; . . . but . . . ye have not hearkened unto Me.—*Jer.* 35. 14.

Thus, from a fuller statement, we select the central words as they reveal the very heart of the lesson which the incident is intended to teach. We notice, first, that the dating of this incident, and that of the next chapter, takes us back at least seventeen years from that of the preceding messages. This either means that these chapters are out of place in the sequence of Jeremiah's ministry; or—and this is our view—that in the days of the siege he recounted these events of an earlier period. The incident itself was that of the offering of wine to the Rechabites, and their refusal to touch it. We of course understand that it was known that they would refuse, and the offer was made in order to elicit that refusal. Here was the whole situation. Men were absolutely loyal to a command laid upon them by their forerunner Jonadab; while the people of God refused His speaking, which was persistent through His messengers. How many such illustrations might be adduced in the history of the people of God. Men are often more loyal to a family tradition than they are to the will of God as it is immediately and continuously made known to them. Let us carefully observe that such loyalty to tradition is not wrong, if that tradition be founded upon right. The Rechabites were not rebuked for their loyalty, but rather commended and rewarded. The teaching is by contrast. Men who are true to a right principle when it is made binding by the will of a dead ancestor, are disloyal to the highest things when they are demanded by the living God. It is indeed a strange mystery; but it is a fact in human experience. Be it ours, while true to all good tradition, to be far more zealous to obey the will of our God!

Take thee again another roll, and write in it.—*Jer.* 36. 28.

This incident has practically the same dating as the former one. But the story of the chapter records, not only the incident of the writing and destruction of the first roll; but that of the writing of the second, and the adding to it of many other like words. Thus, in all probability we have the account of a message in which Jeremiah told the story in the days of Zedekiah and the siege. The story is full of detail and of suggestiveness. At a time when Jeremiah was shut up, and unable to go into the house of the Lord, he was commanded to write. This he did, and Baruch was his scribe. The writing being completed, Baruch was sent to read it. Eventually it came to the King. So hardened were the King and those about him, that before the reading of the roll was completed, "when Jehudi had read three or four leaves," the King cut it up and cast it into the fire, and "they were not afraid, nor rent their garments." Sin may so deaden spiritual and moral faculties, that men will without fear cast the messages of God to the fire, and commit His messengers to death. But such action never destroys the Word of God, nor invalidates its findings. That Word lives, and is preserved, in the mind of God. His servants are still at His disposal. Another roll was written, and all its statements were carried out irrevocably. It is always so. Herod may imprison John; but Jesus moves into his tetrarchy of Galilee and delivers the message which John had delivered. An apostate Church may buy and burn copies of the Scriptures; but their number will multiply until it is impossible to commit them to burning. "All flesh is as grass; but the word of the Lord abideth for ever" (1 Pet. 1. 24, 25).

And the king asked him secretly in his house, and said, Is there any word from the Lord? And Jeremiah said, There is!—*Jer.* 37. 17.

This chapter records a remarkable interlude in the experience of the besieged city. Suddenly, for a brief space, the siege was lifted. The army of Pharaoh had moved out of Egypt, and the Chaldean army, fearing trouble from that quarter, broke the siege in order to deal with this new menace. Directly that Egyptian army moved, Jeremiah warned the people that no hope was to be entertained on that account. Nevertheless it is evident that the people were excited by the movement, and full of expectancy that the fate predicted by the prophet might be averted. It was under these circumstances that the king sent for the prophet, and asked this question, and received this answer: Jeremiah proceeding to declare, that in spite of all appearances, the Divine word would be fulfilled. That the king asked his question secretly, goes to show that it was a question of fear; fear growing out of the fact that, in spite of all this man's weakness and wickedness, he knew the power of God. Under stress of such fear this question is often asked, and there is always the same answer—"There is!" There is always a word from Jehovah; and no change in circumstances causes a change in His Word. His Word is never void of power, and proceeds irresistibly to accomplish that which He pleases. A change of heart in man will produce a change in the attitude and activity of God; but a change in circumstances, never.

And Zedekiah the king said, Behold he is in your hand; for the king is not he that can do anything against you.—*Jer.* 38. 5.

What a revelation we have in these words of the weakness and wickedness of Zedekiah. They were spoken to men who were clamouring for the blood of the prophet. These clamouring princes were unquestionably the politicians who had influenced the king against the word of the prophet; and had advocated resistance to Babylon when Jeremiah had persistently declared its futility, and had urged king and nation to yield to the Divine chastisement. There can be no question that Zedekiah had no desire to see Jeremiah destroyed, but he felt that he was helpless, and in these words confessed his impotence. Thus he sought to fling the blame upon them, and to escape responsibility himself. It was a weak and unwarranted position. If it were true that he had so passed into their hands that he was then helpless, it was also true that his passing into their hands was the result of his original and persistent disobedience to the voice of that great prophet who had exercised his ministry to the people during the whole period of his reign. We have modern examples of this same kind of endeavour to shift a responsibility for wrong done. It cannot be thus shifted. The first sin of yielding to false policies in disobedience to Divine revelation, involves the helplessness which follows, which thus remains personal sin. The truth applies to the individual. That a man was drunk when he murdered his victim does not exonerate him from blame. He had no business to be drunk. That a man is outvoted in the counsel of the ungodly does not excuse him. He has no right to be in association with such counsel.

. . . He went out the way of the Arabah.—*Jer.* 39. 4.

After eighteen months of siege the city fell. The word of Jehovah was verified; the lying of the false prophets was contradicted. The folly and futility of the politicians who had counselled resistance was revealed; the wisdom of the way to which Jeremiah had called was demonstrated. It was now too late to take that moderate course of willing submission to the yoke of Babylon because it was the will of God that they should do so. This, the King, and politicians, and people, urged by false prophets, had refused to do. Now the stroke had fallen; and, because of their persistent opposition to the Chaldeans, which, in view of Jeremiah's ministry, was rebellion against Jehovah, there would be no amelioration of that stroke. When in the gate of the city of God the princes of Babylon were seen sitting, Zedekiah fled, and these words show the direction he took. He set his face toward the wilderness beyond Jordan, the region in which for forty years his nation had been led when they had no king other than God. Whereas it is not suggested that Zedekiah had any reason for this choice of direction other than that of a desire for safety in solitude, it is suggestive that this last of the line of kings "Like the nations" (to quote the words of the clamour which was that of the rejection of Jehovah as King in the long ago), should set his face to that region in the ultimate hour of catastrophe. But he never reached that wilderness. He was captured in the plains of Jericho, before he crossed the Jordan. The God Who had governed and led His people there, excluded this fugitive from the region. There is no escape from God possible. We must have to do with Him. In obedience we may find His Grace. In disobedience we can only know His wrath.

Then went Jeremiah unto Gedaliah, the son of Ahikam, to Mizpah, and dwelt with him among the people that were left in the land.—*Jer.* 40. 6.

We now reach the last phase in the ministry of Jeremiah, that of the period after the fall of the city, and the carrying away of the people into captivity. This section of the book consists of a mixture of history and prophetic utterance, the history in each case giving us the background of the prophetic word, and thus the reason for it. It is quite evident, and remarkable, that the Babylonian authorities were conscious of the government of Jehovah, and that Jeremiah had been His messenger. This knowledge, on their own confession, accounted for the leniency with which he was treated. They left him free to go where he would, offering him protection and provision if he cared to go to Babylon. In these words we discover his choice. There had been left in the land he loved so well, a remnant, poor and weak and small. Jeremiah chose to remain among them. This remnant was placed under the governorship of Gedaliah, and it was increased by the return of Jews who were refugees in Moab, in Ammon, and in Edom. This Gedaliah was a good governor as to his home administration, but too confiding and unsuspicious, as the sequel will show. It is a revealing fact of the character of Jeremiah, that when, undoubtedly, he might have secured safety and even comfort for himself in Babylon, he elected to remain in his own land and among the weak remnant of his own people. He remained to utter the word of Jehovah to them for their good; but as we shall see, so far as producing results among them was concerned, that ministry was a failure to the end. Nevertheless it was successful in the highest sense, because he never failed to speak for God; and that is the only responsibility resting upon a prophet.

Because of the Chaldeans; for they were afraid of them, because Ishmael the son of Nethaniah had slain Gedaliah.—*Jer.* 41. 18.

The incompleteness of this quotation is obvious. The "because" refers to the purpose recorded in the previous verse, and these words give the reason as they summarize the story of the chapter. That story is concerned with the slaying of the governor Gedaliah by Ishmael, who had come out of Ammon. Having accomplished this evil act, this man had carried away into captivity the residue of the people who were in Mizpah. Under the leadership of Johanan, Ishmael was routed, and the captives were brought back. But fear was in their hearts, and not the fear of the Ammonites, but the fear of the Chaldeans. It should be remembered that Gedaliah was one of themselves, and the son of an old-time friend of the prophet. (Compare verse 5 with chapter 26, verse 24.) Johanan did not know who might be appointed as governor in his place, and he feared a new oppression under some Chaldean ruler. The purpose he had was to lead the people into Egypt, in order that they might be safe from the peril, as he saw it. This was a persistence of the policy which for many years Jeremiah had opposed. It was a looking to Egypt for safety, in an apparent forgetfulness of God. It is noticeable that in the words of this Johanan, reported in the previous chapter, and in this one, there was no reference to God. They were all characterized by human insight and foresight, but evidenced no recognition of God. Thus may men hear the word of the Lord, live through experiences in which it is vindicated, and yet ignore it.

Ye have dealt deceitfully against your own souls.—*Jer.* 42. 20.

These words of Jeremiah flash the light into the whole situation described in this chapter. Johanan, having come to a conclusion in the light of his own astuteness, came with all the people and asked Jeremiah to pray for them in view of their weakness, asking that Jehovah would show them the way, promising to obey. Jeremiah responded to their appeal, sought the mind of God, and with great plainness of speech told them that there must be no going to Egypt for safety. If they would abide in that land, God would protect them from all dangers; if they went to Egypt, they would perish. It is evident that Jeremiah knew that their decision was already made, for in the course of this address, making known the mind of Jehovah, he rebuked them for refusing to obey. It was in this rebuke that he used these words. It is possible to deal deceitfully with our own souls. We do so, as these people did, whenever we ask for Divine guidance, having previously decided as to what our course of action is to be. Such praying is only a superstitious activity. It is of the nature of gambling with God. We pray, hoping that His answer will square with our own desires, for if it does, we feel that we shall have some sort of reinforcement. But if His decision be against our desires, then we mean to follow our desires. What a revelation such an attitude is of lack of real confidence in God; and moreover, what a revelation of baseness. Yet this is a peril constantly threatening us, and therefore we need to recognize persistently our need that our prayers should be guided by the Holy Spirit. When prayer is conceived of as a means of getting our own desires fulfilled, it is a superstition.

Then came the word of the Lord unto Jeremiah in Tahpanhes.—*Jer.* 43. 8.

In spite of the prophetic warnings, the "proud men" (see verse 2), had their way, and, lacking the fear of Jehovah, and so mastered by the fear of the Chaldeans, the people went down into Egypt. Tahpanhes was on the Egyptian frontier; and there it was necessary for the people to halt in order to deal with the Egyptian authorities, for in that place Pharaoh had a palace. Jeremiah, who failed to dissuade them from the going, did not abandon them, but accompanied them. The probability is that his going was of compulsion, however. Johanan would fear leaving him or Baruch where they might have communication with the Chaldean ruler. Their suspicion of Baruch was avowed (see verse 3). Thus the false policy prevailed. They ignored the word of Jehovah, and, indeed, openly and wilfully refused it, consoling themselves by denying that it was the word of Jehovah (see verse 2). But they had not escaped from God, nor passed beyond the reach of His word. That word can reach men in Egypt as surely as in Palestine; it can find utterance in Tahpanhes as certainly as in Jerusalem or at Mizpah. And when it is heard, it speaks the same message. These people had not crossed the frontiers of the Divine government, if they had crossed those of their land. The protection of Egypt against Chaldea was futile, when God had ordered the destruction of Egypt by Chaldea. Such was the word of Jehovah in Tahpanhes; and such is the word of Jehovah to-day to men who seek safety for themselves in any way, or by any policies, which involve disobedience to His law.

We will certainly perform every word that is gone forth out of our mouth. . . .—*Jer.* 44. 17.

In this chapter we have the last of the messages of Jeremiah which are dated consecutively. It has the same note of determined loyalty to the word of Jehovah against all the false findings of human rebellion and opinion. The circumstances are startling. These people were openly and defiantly turning from the worship of Jehovah to that of the moon, that is the queen of heaven. These particular words were the words of the women, although the men were with them, and definitely associated themselves with the decision. That this was so, is seen in the concluding words, which claimed that they did nothing, as they said, "without our husbands." Moreover, it was a definite return to practices which had been rebuked long ago (see chapter 7, verses 17, 18). This they affirmed, and declared that when they had worshipped the queen of heaven they had known plenty and prosperity. So do men misread history, when their hearts are set on evil. The last message of Jeremiah corrected that false reading, as it pointed out that the very calamitous situation in which they found themselves, exiled from their own land was due to their apostasy from Jehovah. Finally he gave them the sign of a prediction that the king of Egypt should be delivered into the hands of his enemies, as Zedekiah had been delivered into the hands of Nebuchadnezzar. When men or nations come to definite decision, such as that expressed by these people in these words, the government of God compels them to abide by that decision to its ultimate issue.

Seekest thou great things for thyself? Seek them not.—*Jer.* 45. 5.

This short chapter is very arresting and interesting. It contains a word of Jehovah through Jeremiah to one man. This man was Baruch. He was most evidently in full sympathy with Jeremiah, and had been closely associated with him in his ministry. He it was who had written the prophetic messages in the days of Jehoiakim, and had read them to the princes and the King. He it was who, after the King had mutilated and burnt that first roll, had written another, adding many words to it. It is most probable that he wrote the whole of the book. Observe the care with which the writer draws attention to the fact that the final action (chapter 52) was not the composition of the prophet, by the words with which he closed the previous one: "Thus far are the words of Jeremiah" (51. 64). All of which makes this chapter 45 the more arresting. What lies behind it? Almost certainly a temptation which assaulted Baruch of coming to think of himself as in some way entitled to honour for his part in the work. This attitude of mind was rebuked. He was reminded that the work of building and breaking down, planting and plucking up, was Divine work. That reminder carries us back to the words of the Divine commission to Jeremiah (see chapter 1. 10). For this work Jeremiah was the instrument, as he was chosen to be the mouthpiece of the word of Jehovah. Therefore, let not Baruch invade that office in desire. It is a solemn story, as it sets the prophetic gift and office in its true relation; showing that no man can assume it. It is by the will and act of God alone that a man can utter the word of God. That Baruch profited by the message is at least suggested by the incorporation of this story in the book.

Why are thy strong ones swept away? They stood not, because the Lord did drive them.—Jer. 46. 15.

Here we begin a series of prophetic utterances concerning the surrounding nations. They were delivered at different times during Jeremiah's ministry, but are gathered together here at the close of the book. Some of them are dated; some are not. It is noticeable that in this arrangement, that concerning Egypt is placed first, and that concerning Babylon last. The vision of the prophet was that of the victory of the army of Nebuchadnezzar over Pharoah-necho at Carchemish. Graphically he told the story of the preparation, and advance, and rout of the proud hosts of Pharaoh. Contemplating that rout, the prophet uttered this question and answer. Why were the mighty hosts of Pharaoh so overcome? That was the question. The politicians in Judah had calculated for many years on the strength of Egypt, and believed that it would prove superior to that of Babylon. On the basis of human observation and calculation, they were probably right. Egypt ought to have been victorious by the standards of human preparation and power. But Egypt was defeated Why? "They stood not because Jehovah did drive them!" If we are tempted, as we sometimes are almost unconsciously, to read these records as opinions of men in the twilight, and to imagine that they were mistaken, or that God is not acting to-day, it is well that we think seriously of the years 1914-1918. There we have seen the same thing, and even with more startling clarity. By every law of human calculation, Germany ought to have mastered those opposed to her. She did not. She was broken and routed. Why? There is but one answer, and it is that of Jeremiah. "They stood not because Jehovah did drive them." And so it is, and will be, until the King comes. Over all the policies of men, and the clash of armies, He is reigning, and moving forward in righteousness towards the goal of His intended purpose.

The Lord will spoil the Philistines, the remnant of the isle of Caphtor.— Jer. 47. 4.

The Philistines had long been the implacable foes of the people of God. In this brief oracle the prophet foretold their doom. By a flood out of the north they were to be overcome and driven away, all their cities left bald and desolate. This reference to them as "the remnant of the isle of Caphtor," is doubly suggestive. It first described the weakness of their condition as the result of the long period of their conflicts. But it goes deeper than that. It traces them back to their origin. There can be no certainty as to the geographical situation of Caphtor. There are those who identify it with the island of Crete. While that is open to question, it is certain that these people sprung from Caphtor, wherever it was. Moses referred to the fact in the first of his great farewell discourses (see Deut. 2. 23), where the Philistines are called the Avvim, and the Caphtorim. In his ministry to the northern kingdom, Amos had referred to this relation in a startling way, as he said, uttering the word of Jehovah: "Have not I brought up Israel out of the land of Egypt, and the Philistines from Caphtor, and the Syrians from Kir?" (Amos 9. 7.) To this Divine government of other nations Jeremiah referred as he called the Philistines "the remnant of the isle of Caphtor." It is well for us to keep ourselves reminded that what Paul wrote has the widest application. "Is God the God of Jews only? Is He not the God of Gentiles also? Yea, of Gentiles also" (Rom. 3. 29). It is He Who, again to quote Paul concerning the nations, "determined their appointed seasons, and the bounds of their habitation, that they should seek God." Nations rise, and nations fall; and the reason of their rise and fall is found in their relation to Him, as that is created by their obedience or disobedience to the light given them.

Moab hath been at ease from his youth, and he hath settled on his lees, and hath not been emptied from vessel to vessel, neither hath he gone into captivity; therefore his taste remaineth in him, and his scent is not changed.— Jer. 48. 11.

This burden concerning Moab is a very remarkable one. While it foretold the judgments which would fall upon it for its sin, and that with no uncertain sound, yet the sorrows of Moab called for the lamentations of the prophet, as did those of Israel; and in the end he saw her restoration. In the burden there is perhaps nothing more suggestive than these words which we have emphasized. One secret of the corruption of Moab had been that of its comparative ease. Moab had never been removed from its own land, it had never been carried away captive. In his learned interpretation of the Moabite Stone, Dr. Ginsburg has shown that although the land of Moab was part of the inheritance of Reuben, her people had never been driven forth, but had managed to dwell there with the children of Israel. Jeremiah saw in this very lack of disturbance a secret of corruption. The conception gives us a light upon life of which we do well to take heed, especially in its application to individuals. To dwell at ease, to know nothing of disturbance, to be free from turmoil, may be to miss the very processes which make for salvation and full realization of life's deepest meaning. By upheaval and uprooting, and pouring out as from vessel to vessel, we may be in the way of deliverance from corruption. Everything depends upon our relation to God, and upon our discovery of His will and our response to it.

But afterwards I will bring again the captivity of the children of Ammon saith the Lord.—Jer. 49. 6.

In this chapter we have five of the oracles concerning the nations. We stress these words at the close of the first. They are found also at the close of the burden of Moab (see 48. 47); and again in that concerning Elam (see 49. 39). Moreover, the same note of hope is found in the first concerning Egypt (see 46. 26). The presence of these statements in prophecies concerned with the doom of these nations for their sins and corruption, is a revelation of how this prophet of God understood the principles of the Divine government. Jeremiah saw God governing. That fact was, of course, the rock foundation of his faith. He saw, moreover, that all His wrath was moved against sin; His stroke

in judgment was upon those who were corrupt by reason of their disobedience to light. But he saw also that the ultimate purpose of the activity of wrath is that of restoration, not in the case of Israel only, but also in that of all the nations. The fact that for some of these nations no such restoration is foretold, reveals the awful possibility of resisting not only the mercy of God, but His judgments also, so completely that there is no possibility of restoration. Other prophets in their messages reveal the same conception of the discriminative justice of God in His government. It is to be observed that there is no gleam of hope for Babylon; that power, for some time material, and persistently spiritual, which was conceived in an attempt to make man great by frustrating Divine purpose. Her doom is irremediable in Old and New Testaments.

Their adversaries said, We offend not, because they have sinned against the Lord, the habitation of justice, even the Lord, the hope of their fathers.—Jer. 50. 7.

This and the following chapter are taken up with the prophetic message concerning Babylon. It constitutes a fitting close to the record of this wonderful and heroic ministry. For long years, in spite of all the opposition of politicians inspired by false prophets, Jeremiah had declared that Jerusalem would fall to Babylon. He had lived, moreover, long enough to see his words vindicated, and the consequent confusion both of politicians and prophets. But he was under no delusion concerning Babylon itself. He knew its wickedness; and he knew that though God so overruled the affairs of men that Babylon was His instrument of chastisement, she herself must be judged of that God. In this great message of doom, the prophet rose to the highest level of sublime utterance. These particular words are very full of revealing light. In them we see what Jeremiah had more than once recognized in his earlier messages, the understanding of the sin of the people of God as being that of turning their back upon God. But here we see also how these nations had trespassed upon that knowledge, and made it the vindication of their cruelties to this people. Therefore, they themselves were to know the terribleness of the Divine wrath. The attitude of mind revealed in these words has been persistent in history. The Jew has been held in contempt as the afflicted of God, and that has been the excuse urged sometimes even by so-called Christian nations for injustice and wrong done to him. Let it never be forgotten that God has not cast off His people, though He chastise them; and whatever nation persecutes them, sooner or later knows the fire of the Divine wrath.

Thus saith the Lord of hosts: The broad walls of Babylon shall be utterly overthrown, and her high gates shall be burned with fire; and the peoples shall labour for vanity, and the nations for the fire; and they shall be weary.— *Jer.* 51. 58.

Such were the concluding words of Jeremiah's burden concerning Babylon. They foretold the complete overthrow of the city itself; and the falling of poetic justice upon the nation, as her people were doomed to pass to the same experiences which they had inflicted upon other nations. So far as the city which then existed, and the nation as then constituted, were concerned, this prophecy was fulfilled to the letter. But Babylon as a spirit was not then destroyed. Like an evil spirit it found other places in which to dwell, and work its designs, and through which to exercise its dark and baleful influence among men. And this because, at the very core of Babylon, is Satan himself. Through all the centuries, that spirit has persisted, and always in conflict with God, and the spirit of faith in God. It is alive to-day, and working with tremendous power in the affairs of men. It is the spirit which excludes God, and attempts to realize human possibilities along the line of human thought and endeavour, whether in policies, or wars, or education, or art, or religion. It is still saying, as at the first: "Let us make us a name." But the word of Jehovah by Jeremiah moves to its complete fulfilment. It may be that Babylon will yet have another materialization, even in the old spot, that plain of Shinar. But the last victory will be with faith, and with God, for the anthem will yet be sung; "Hallelujah; Salvation, and glory, and power, belong to our God; for true and righteous are His judgments; for He

hath judged the great harlot, her that corrupted the earth with her fornication, and He hath avenged the blood of His servants at her hand."

Then a breach was made in the city. —*Jer.* 52. 7.

The last sentence of the preceding chapter: "Thus far are the words of Jeremiah" leads us to the conclusion that this final chapter was written by another, most probably by Baruch. It consists of a page of history recounting the fall of Jerusalem, as found in the book of Kings, and in an earlier part of this book; but giving some extra details, and omitting some other. Its real value at the close of the book would seem to be its reiteration of the fact of the historic fulfilment of the word of Jehovah which Jeremiah had so persistently proclaimed in spite of opposition and. persecution and suffering. At last, in spite of long waiting, in spite of the hopes aroused by long siege, and once by the temporary relief of the siege by the departure of the Chaldean hosts to engage those of Egypt, "a breach was made in the city." That breach in the material structure was made by the material forces of the hosts of Babylon; but no such breach had ever been made, except for the spiritual and moral deflection of the people of God. It was the kings, the politicians, the false prophets, and the people seduced by them, that made the real breach in the city. They broke down its true fortifications, and undermined its real foundations by their infidelities. It is ever so. No hosts encamped against the people of God can gain any advantage over them, so long as they remain loyal in heart and mind and will to their One King. But when they are disloyal, and persist in disloyalty, then no force can save them from the opposing hosts.

LAMENTATIONS

How doth the city sit solitary.— *Lam.* 1. 1.

In this book there are five songs of sorrow. They were doubtless composed by Jeremiah after the fall of Jerusalem. In them the man is wonderfully revealed. That which he had foretold had come to pass. The city of the great King lay in hopeless ruins. The people of God were scattered far and wide. The outlook on circumstances was one of complete desolation. The prophet indulged in no exultation. He was consumed with sorrow for the condition of the city and the sorrows of the people. These five songs constitute the outpouring of his soul. In the first two, he contemplated the situation. In the

third, the central one of the collection, he identified himself completely with the people. The last two were concerned with the desolation, and the consequent appeal to Jehovah. Three of these, the first, the second, and the fourth, that is those of contemplation, begin with the word "How." The word (in the Hebrew, Aichah) gives the title to the book in the Hebrew Bible. This is significant. "How" expresses the whole fact of which the song so begun, attempts a description. It is exclamatory, and suggests the impossibility of description. In this first song there are two movements: The first is the language of an onlooker (verses 1–11); in the second the city personified, speaks herself of her desolation (verses 12–22).

In each, the cause of her sorrow is confessed (compare verses 8 and 18). When the prophet personified the city he began with an appeal: "Is it nothing to you, all ye that pass by?" He saw that the sorrows of the people of God had their message to all other peoples. This is the true meaning of this inquiry. When we use it of Christ, let us not forget this. The appeal is not one for pity, but rather that men should know the issue of sin.

How hath the Lord covered the daughter of Zion with a cloud in His anger.—*Lam. 2. 1.*

Again the song opens with this word "How." The prophet was still contemplating the tragic conditions of his city and his nation; and once again was so deeply impressed with what he saw that he commenced with this exclamatory How! What, then, were the things which he saw? First, that all the desolation upon which he looked was brought about by Jehovah; and secondly that this activity of Jehovah was made inevitable by the sins of His people. The judgment of Adonai, the Sovereign Lord, Who is also named as Jehovah in the course of the description, had fallen upon all material things, and had swept out the sacramental symbols of spiritual relationship. All this because the people had been seduced from their loyalty to Jehovah by the false prophets who had "seen false and foolish visions." At last the song became an appeal to the people in their affliction to come to penitence and contrition, and out of that to make their appeal to Jehovah on behalf of the next generation, that is, "for the life of thy young children." These opening words of the song are poetically suggestive. Neither Jehovah nor the daughter of Zion is conceived of as departed, or destroyed. She is covered in a cloud, and so cut off from the vision of Jehovah, that is, she cannot see Him. Clouds hide God from men; they never hide men from God. Here, then, is the thought. The loss of the vision is the judgment upon those who ceased looking to Jehovah. That condition continues even yet. The daughter of Zion is covered in the cloud. She does not see her God. But her God, watching over her, neither slumbers nor sleeps.

I am the man that hath seen affliction by the rod of His wrath.—*Lam. 3. 1.*

This is the central song of the five; and its dominant note is that of the prophet's complete identification with the people in the experiences of their sorrow; and his complete agreement with, and understanding of the purpose of God in all His dealings with His people. In these first words he strikes the keynote, and reveals this identification with the people in the experience of affliction. Presently he declared the goodness of God as he had seen it, and said that it was of Jehovah's lovingkindness that they had not been consumed. On the basis of this recognition he uttered his appeal to the people, including himself, as he said: "Let us search and try our ways." Finally, he called to mind his own personal experience of how, when he had called to God out of the lowest dungeon, He had heard, responded, delivered; and upon that experience he based his certainty that God would ultimately overthrow those who were the instruments of the suffering of His people. As we have said, that which is most impressive in this song is the identification of the prophet with the people and with God. He recognized the necessity for the suffering, but he suffered with the sufferers. The real emphasis of these opening words would seem to be on the very first word, "*I.*" This is the authentic note of the messenger of Jehovah. He it is who feels most poignantly the pain of those who through their own determined disobedience are punished. If that be so of the messenger of God, it is supremely so of God Himself. In that realm of thought we ultimately and inevitably reach the Cross.

How is the gold become dim!—*Lam. 4. 1.*

Again this fourth song commences with the exclamatory "How!" The prophet had been meditating, considering, pondering. He was about to give expression to the things which had occupied his mind, and the first word of the message of interpretation is one which means that the facts defy expression—"How!" Yet here, in a sentence, the whole result is gathered up and uttered, before the detailed explanation. That one sentence tells the whole story. "The gold is become dim!" Those which follow express the same fact in slightly varying form. "The most pure gold is changed! The stones of the sanctuary are poured out at the top of every street!" Follow the prophet, and the next statement interprets the figure. "The precious sons of Zion, comparable to fine gold. How are they esteemed as earthen-pitchers, the work of the hands of the potter!" That is the appalling spectacle, compelling the introductory "How," and inspiring all that follows. This was the vision of a man who saw the facts in true perspective and proportion. The tragedy of Israel's breakdown and desolation was created by the glory of the Divine purpose for that nation among nations of men. "Gold," "the most pure gold," "fine gold;" these were the words and phrases fittingly expressing the glory of the Divine thought and purpose for that nation among the nations of men. But the gold had become dim; the most pure gold was changed, the fine gold had become common earth. This is the deepest note of calamity whenever the people of God break down in loyalty, and so are broken down in necessary judgment. The failure to fulfil an appointed function in the Divine economy, is a more terrible thing than personal shortcoming, and personal suffering.

Remember, O Lord.—*Lam. 5. 1.*

Thus opens the last of the five songs, the final message of this great heroic messenger of Jehovah. The first movement of the song described anew the sorrows of the suffering people; the actual desolation in the midst of which Jeremiah lived; the afflictions of all classes of the community; the prevailing and abundant grief. His description prepared for, and led up to prayer. In that prayer the eternity of God, and the stability of His Throne were first confessed. Then, notice very carefully, that following what seems to be a protest against the long forsaking of His people by Jehovah, the central concluding petition of the prophet was not that God

should turn unto His people, but rather that He would turn His people unto Him. The notes of this final song are full of value for us In days of darkness and discipline, in which many loyal souls, like Jeremiah himself, may be involved, it is ever given to them to speak of their sorrows before Jehovah; and that speaking may ever take the form of appeal to Jehovah to remember. It is not to be supposed that Jeremiah imagined that Jehovah could forget, but here was his last resort. He himself remembered all the afflictions of the people and of his own soul, in communion with God, and in this call to Jehovah to remember, he was realizing that communion, and finding reinforcement for his own soul in the process of trial. Thus, prayers which break down in intellectual logical consistency are ofttimes those which in experience bring us nearest God; and thus find surest answers in that they make it possible for Him to act with us and for us in ways not possible unless and until we have such communion.

EZEKIEL

I saw visions of God.—*Ezek. 1. 1.*

Ezekiel is pre-eminently the prophet of hope. He was the contemporary of Jeremiah, but a much younger man. Probably Jeremiah was exercising his ministry when Ezekiel was born. His work lay among the exiles in Babylon. In the first three chapters we have the account of his preparation for that work. Then his messages fall into two clearly defined sections; the first dealing with the Reprobation of the nation, and the second foretelling its ultimate Restoration. He saw clearly the righteousness of the reprobation; but he saw with equal clearness that the original purpose of God for His people would be gloriously realized. In the words emphasized we have the secret of this clear outlook in each case. This man's call to prophetic ministry began with visions of God. These preceded the voice which commissioned him. The symbolism of that vision of God is very wonderful, and is to be carefully pondered. That is not possible in a brief note. The arresting fact at the outset of our reading is that to a man in exile, and at a time when the national outlook was of the darkest, God granted these unveilings of Himself in mystic and marvellous imagery. The inspiration of all well-founded hope in days of darkness and desolation, is a clear vision of God. The reading of this chapter may have the effect of making us think, that if such visions were granted to us, we could have such confidence and hope. Let us think again. All that was suggested to Ezekiel

by the fire, the living ones, the wheels, the spirit of life, has been more clearly revealed to us in the Son of His love. To have seen the glory of God in the face of Jesus is to see the righteousness of all His judgments, and to be sure of the final victory of His love. In the Revelation we see again these symbols of Ezekiel gathered round a Throne in the midst of which is the Lamb, as it had been slain.

And He said unto me, Son of man, stand upon thy feet, and I will speak with thee.—*Ezek. 2. 1.*

After the vision come the voice; and the first command of the voice was that the man who, prostrated by the glory of the vision, lay upon his face, should stand upon his feet, and hear the words of Jehovah. Let us consider this carefully. First came the vision, and therefore, whatever was to be said would come to this man with the authority of all that was revealed in that vision. There is no doubt that through all his ministry, whether Ezekiel listened to the voice, or spoke the messages entrusted to him, he did so in the consciousness of the glory of Jehovah as he had seen it in those visions. But when that vision had been seen, and the soul had responded in the act of worship which expressed itself in prostration, there was something more to be done. That prostrate soul was called to a new attitude, for which it had been prepared by a vision and the prostration. It was that of standing erect before God in order that face to face he might receive the word of God. In order to the delivery of His message God requires more than the worship which at its highest consists of the cessation of activity. He needs a man erect, in the attitude of alertness and attention, ready for action. Remember this was not a call to stand erect to utter the word of Jehovah, but to hear it. And yet more carefully observe what follows: "The Spirit entered into me . . . and set me upon my feet." This is the Divine energy, enabling a man to come to the height of his manhood, and so to find readiness to hear the word of Jehovah. Those of us who are called ·to prophetic ministry might with profit have these words engraved before our eyes in the places of preparation for our work. Here are words to hang on study walls.

And He said unto me, Son of man, go, get thee unto the house of Israel, and speak with My words unto them.—Ezek. 3. 4.

This is the last stage in the preparation of the prophet. Mark the sequence—visions of God; prostration in worship; standing erect to hear; going to speak the words of God. The work for Ezekiel was not going to be easy, and this was made clear to him. He was going to a people who would not hearken, as was the case with Jeremiah. But his equipment was sufficient, and his responsibility was not that of producing obedience, but that of uttering the words of Jehovah. But that was, and is ever, a grave responsibility, how grave is revealed in the central paragraph of this chapter (verses 7–21). A phrase which our fathers often used, is not heard to-day frequently, about the work of the prophet. I refer to the phrase "blood-guiltiness." Yet that phrase finds its warrant in this paragraph. There is such a thing. If the wicked die in wickedness for lack of the prophetic word, the prophet is guilty of his blood. If the righteous man fall into sin because the prophet fails to warn him of his peril, the prophet is held responsible for his perishing. If the wicked or the righteous sin and die, in spite of the prophet's warning, then is the prophet not guilty. Verily to a prophet silence may be sin; to withhold the word of Jehovah from fear or for favour, is to be involved in the wickedness of the evil-doers. All this gives the most solemn pause to those responsible for speaking the words of God to men. Nevertheless the whole teaching of this wonderful story of Ezekiel's preparation reveals the perfection of the provision which God ever makes for those whom He sends to the holy service.

Thou also, son of man, take thee a tile . . .—Ezek. 4. 1.

Here we have a clear instance of the mistakes made by those who divided these Holy Writings into chapters. In this chapter three signs are given, whereas in the sequence there were four. The fourth is found in the first four verses of chapter five. We have emphasized these opening words because they show that the prophet was in communion with God, and listening to His word. These signs were given him, and through him to the people, by Divine command. As these signs are pondered, their spiritual and moral significance is patent. The first set forth the actual fact of the siege of Jerusalem. The second emphasized the sin which had brought about this punishment, and the consequent inevitability of that punishment. The third illustrated the methods of punishment, and again laid stress upon the pollution of the people. The fourth illustrated the thoroughness of the retribution overtaking the nation, and at the same time insisted upon the discriminative justice of God in punishment. These were the signs which opened the ministry of Ezekiel, and introduced the first part of his prophetic message, that which was concerned with the reprobation of the people. It may be well to glance at the movement in its entirety. First the prophet dealt with these judgments which were the result of reprobation (chapters 4–14); then he showed the reason of the reprobation (chapters 15–19); and finally argued for the righteousness of it (chapters 20–24). All these lines start from these four signs, which in their unity suggest all these facts. In these prophetic writings we have an arresting revelation of how carefully God interprets Himself, and indicates His ways, for those called to be His messengers.

. . . Because ye are turbulent more than the nations that are round about you . . .—Ezek. 5. 7.

. Terrible indeed are the descriptions which this chapter contains of the judgments to fall upon Jerusalem and the people of God; and here is the reason of those judgments: "Because ye are turbulent more than the nations that are round about you." The force of these words lies in their revelation of the complete subversion of the Divine order and intention. This city was intended to be a city of peace, resulting from righteousness; and the people a people of quiet strength, because of their relationship with God; and all this in the interest of the surrounding nations, that they might have a revelation of the perfection of the ways of God through His people. Instead of that, the city had become more polluted than surrounding cities; and its people more turbulent than those of other nations. Thus the name of God was blasphemed. The history of the Hebrew nation is a witness to great truths, an illustration of abiding principles. Let us be careful, not only to understand these things in their application to Israel, but also to apply them to ourselves. We are called to be salt, to be light. If our light do not shine before men, that they, seeing our good works, glorify our Father, our failure is complete. For salt that has lost its savour, our Lord had only words of uttermost contempt: "It is fit neither for the land nor for the dunghill; men cast it out." Let us not count on the privilege of relationship as a safeguard against reprobation, if we fail to fulfil the responsibilities of that relationship. That is what Israel did, and for the doing of which the judgments of God overtook her.

I have been broken with their whorish heart.—*Ezek.* 6. 9.

The King James version rendered this "I am broken," while the English and American Revisions have translated in the same way "I have been broken." This is a change of tense only, and undoubtedly is justified. But there is no change in the verb. In each case the verb is passive and not active. I emphasize this because some expositors have felt the difficulty, and have changed this to the active form, saying that it should read, "I have broken their whorish heart." Such changes are always unjustifiable and pernicious. In this case, so to change the verb is to miss one of the supreme notes of this word of Jehovah to His people. The paragraph is one dealing with a remnant which through the processes of terrible judgment will be restored. Leaving the verb in its passive form, we have a revelation at once arresting and graphic, of the effect the unfaithfulness of His people has upon Jehovah. The strongest figure possible is used to portray the Divine suffering. God is represented as broken. The suggestion is daring indeed, but the most daring and superlative of human words and figures of speech are needed to convey to the human mind the sufferings of the Eternal Love when those upon whom it is set, turn from Him in lewd or whorish practices. The amazing truth is most vividly brought out in the prophecy of Hosea, a man who was brought into an understanding of the suffering of God, by his own domestic tragedy. That is the force of these words. The same great unveiling of the Divine heart is created by this sentence in the course of Ezekiel's denunciation of sin and description of judgment.

. . . Thus saith the Lord God unto the land of Israel, An end.—*Ezek.* 7. 2.

This chapter consists of a denunciation of the Kingdom of Judah, a prediction of the dissolution of the State. The words here "An end" are exclamatory. That is the message in its entirety—"An end!" The time of patience was over, there was to be no more waiting. This denunciation has two movements; the first in short, sharp sentences, broken with emotion declares the Divine decision; the second in more measured manner describes the break up of the nation. Thus the prophet told the exiles in Babylon, what Jeremiah was telling them in Jerusalem, that the opportunity for recovery was past, that the nation had overstepped the boundaries of the forbearance and waiting of God. The end was come. The consideration is full of solemnities. We are often amazed at the patience of God. Sometimes it makes us impatient. We cry, How long, O Lord, how long? as those who would hasten the action of Divine punishment. We have no need to fret our souls in such wise. There is a limit to the patience of God. It is set at the point where man's rebellion has so calloused him that there is no hope of his repentance. Then there is an end. When it comes, it is thorough, complete, final. Follow the prophetic message through and see how complete the end is when God says "An end!" It falls upon the land; upon the people; upon persons and property. A study of human history will yield many illustrations of this, outside the Hebrew race. God waits long for nations, and gives them opportunities of return to righteousness. If they persist in unrighteousness the hour comes when He says "An end!" And that is the end.

. . . Is it a light thing to the house of Judah, that they commit the abominations which they commit here?—*Ezek.* 8. 17.

In this question, Jehovah appealed to the prophet in such wise as to bring his consciousness, his reason, into agreement with the terrors of the determined end. Elders from Judah had come to see him in his own house, most probably to gain his view of the affairs at Jerusalem. While they were there the hand of the Lord Jehovah fell upon him. That is to say he was, either in a trance, or in open vision, given to see things. His first vision was again a vision of God as fire. Then he was carried in spirit to Jerusalem, and caused to look. In the Temple precincts he saw an image set up, which he called the image of jealousy, because it provoked the Lord to jealousy. Again he looked, and saw the elders practising the rites of abominable idolatries within the court. Again he looked, and saw the women engaged in the evil practices of the women of the surrounding idolatrous peoples. Finally he saw men, between the porch and the altar, and their backs to the altar, worshipping the sun. We are not to suppose that these things were going on in Jerusalem literally. One phrase explains the situation, the one which says: "Every man in his chambers of imagery." This makes the condition all the more terrible. While the external rites of the Temple of Jehovah were being observed, these very observances were made a cloak for the thoughts, desires, activities of the heart. This is the most hopeless stage and state of pollution. Such, indeed, is not a light thing. When men come to this pass, a true and righteous God can do none other than make an end.

Set a mark upon the foreheads of the men that sigh and that cry for all the abominations that be done in the midst thereof.—Ezek. 9. 4.

The hand of Jehovah was still upon the prophet. Having seen the abominations of the people, and having been called into agreement with the righteousness of the fury of Jehovah, he saw the first process of that judgment in the slaughter of the dwellers in the polluted city. But the terror of the vision was further vindicated as righteous, by the discrimination of the activity of wrath. The man with the ink-horn setting a mark upon those who sighed and cried was the instrument of this discrimination. Those so marked were to be spared. In the most corrupt conditions God has never been without a remnant of loyal souls. They dwell among abominations, but have no share in them. They live in perpetual grief, they vex their righteous souls from day to day, they sigh and cry for the abominations. When the whirlwind of the Divine fury sweeps out from the Divine presence to make an end of the appalling corruption, it does not touch them. They are marked by the man with the ink-horn, and are exempt from the blast of the Divine wrath. Thus the question which Abraham asked has persistent answer. God does not destroy the righteous with the wicked. Dr. Davidson has pointed out something in connection with this oracle which for us to-day is full of suggestiveness. He says that the word "mark" (set a mark) is the Hebrew word TAV, which is the last letter of the alphabet, and the old form of it was a cross. Those to-day who sigh and cry amid prevailing abominations are surely those marked with a cross.

Take fire from between the whirling wheels, from between the cherubim.— Ezek. 10. 6.

The prophet was still seeing in vision the judgment determined against the city and the nation, because of the idolatrous abominations of which they were guilty. He had seen those abominations and had observed the discriminative nature of the activity of God in wrath, and he watched the mission of the man with the ink-horn. He now saw the process of the judgment. This chapter gives the account of a preliminary vision. Its bearing on the whole is that of its revelation of the source of destructive fire which was to fall upon the

city. It is largely a symbolical vision of God, of the Throne, of those manifestations of wheels, and faces, and energy, which spoke of the authority, power, and majesty of God. The vision harmonizes with that described as having been granted to him by Chebar. It is highly pictorial and mystical, yet makes upon us the impression which undoubtedly it was intended to make, that namely of the awe-inspiring might, wisdom, and majesty of God. It was the God thus revealed Who had declared that "an end" had come; and the destructive fire was to proceed from Himself. This fact is full of dread solemnity, and at the same time of great comfort. The fire from God is the fire of perfect knowledge, and perfect holiness. No refuge of lies can constitute a hiding-place from its burning; it will make no terms with corruption. Fire that proceeds from Him will be absolutely just in its activity. It will harm nothing save that which is evil. The wrath of God is terrible, but it is never passion overleaping the boundaries of righteous action. It is always restrained by the strictest justice.

. . . Yet will I be to them a sanctuary for a little while in the countries where they are come.—Ezek. 11. 16.

In this chapter we have the account of the last phase of the vision given to Ezekiel while the elders were in his house. Notice the last two verses of this chapter. This phase was a revelation of the mingling of mercy with judgment. The words we have emphasized occur in the midst of the answer of Jehovah to a question of the prophet. That question is found in verse thirteen: "Ah, Lord Jehovah, wilt Thou make a full end of the remnant of Israel?" The question was inspired by the sudden death of Pelatiah, one of the leaders of the evil courses of Jerusalem (see verse 1). This sudden activity of Divine judgment brought home to the prophet most powerfully the terribleness of the Divine wrath, and for the moment it seemed to him as though Israel would be completely destroyed, even the remnant. Hence his question. The answer of Jehovah was immediate, and unequivocal. The fiery judgment upon Jerusalem did not mean the destruction of Israel, nor the abandonment of God's purposes for His people. For the time being, the exiles constituted the nation in the purpose of God; and for the period of their absence from their land and the earthly temple, He would be their Sanctuary. Herein is revealed the grace of God. When His people are passing through discipline and chastisement, for the sake of their correction and purification, as was the case with those exiles, He is the place of their refuge and safety. How constantly the people of God have found it so. Cut off—and that often through their own wrongdoing—from all the means of His grace, He has Himself been to them all they have needed of refuge and strength in their times of trouble.

What is this proverb?—*Ezek.* 12. 22.

This was the question of Jehovah; and it challenged a popular mental attitude, which had expressed itself in a proverb which ran thus, "The days are prolonged, and every vision faileth." The mental attitude was that of disbelief of what the prophet had uttered as to the coming of judgment, and of the conviction that visions were vain, that is empty. God gave His servant another proverb to contradict this one, and it ran, "The days are at hand, and the fulfilment of every vision." They also had another saying which represented another attitude of mind. It ran, "The vision that he seeth is for many days to come, and he prophesieth of times that are far off" (verse 27). This was the view of those who did believe in prophecy, but comforted themselves by the assurance that there would be no immediate fulfilment. That view was contradicted by the declaration that there would be no further postponement. The heart of man, set upon evil courses, constantly adopts one of these two expedients to comfort itself. Either it mocks at the prophetic word, or says that fulfilment is postponed. Concerning how many sayings of men which express their views Jehovah may ask this question, "What is this proverb?" Many such sayings, which appear to be warranted by the outlook in existing circumstances, are entirely false and pernicious.

When one buildeth up a wall, behold, they daub it with untempered mortar. —*Ezek.* 13. 10.

In this oracle the prophet of Jehovah denounced the false prophets and prophetesses who were misleading the people. The words we have quoted constitute a striking figure of speech. The word rendered "wall" is an unusual one. It describes a very weak structure, rather than a strong one. The phrase, "untempered mortar," is the translation of one word, which Dr. Davidson strikingly renders "whitewash." There is no doubt that this brings us nearer to the idea, which is not that of a cement holding together the material of which the wall is built, but rather that of a covering, or veneer with which the structure is hidden. This helps us to see the forcefulness of the figure, "One buildeth up a weak wall." That is a reference to the politicians or others who were devising means of preventing the coming of the Divine judgment. Then the work of the false prophets is described: "They daub it with whitewash," thus at once hiding its weakness, and giving it the appearance of

strength. That is the essence of false prophesying. Men, who have no Divine message, but pose as though they had, seek to find favour with those to whom they speak, and so agree with them in their desires and policies. The unutterable wrong of this is at once patent. It gives a false sense of security to those who are in rebellion against God, in that it assures them that they are acting in accordance with the will of God. When the pernicious effects of such action are considered, it becomes doubtful if any sin of which man is capable, is so reprehensible and deadly as this. It is noticeable how constantly the Biblical revelation deals with this evil in no uncertain way. The Hebrew prophets denounced it in the most definite way; and our Lord with words of superlative significance warned us against it.

Though these three men, Noah, Daniel, and Job, were in it, they should deliver but their own souls by their righteousness, saith the Lord God.— *Ezek.* 14. 14.

These words occur in a message which Ezekiel delivered to a company of elders who came to him. Evidently they came to inquire about the state of affairs in Jerusalem; and the whole message would lead us to suppose that they were suggesting that the predicted doom might be averted by the fact that there were good people in the city. The reply of the prophet, received directly from Jehovah, was twofold. First it dealt with these men and denounced them. They were dishonest. While inquiring of Jehovah, they were secretly disloyal; "they had taken their idols into their hearts." Seeking to know the mind of Jehovah in the case of such men was hypocrisy. Here was, however, a message for them, and it foretold their destruction. Then the prophet answered their suggestion, the whole answer is focussed in these words. Righteous men in an utterly polluted city cannot save the city, they can only save their own souls. The answer finds its superlative note in the mention of Noah, Daniel, and Job. It is very remarkable how evil men believe in goodness, and in hours of danger hope that its influence will protect them. I was once told by a multi-millionaire, who was completely materialized, and had become boastfully cynical concerning Christianity, that perhaps the piety of his wife would secure him entry into heaven. If that remark ·was also cynical, it was by so much the more terrible. In any case, the thought is false; and the hope, if hope it be, is groundless. No man, even by his righteousness, can deliver his fellow-man from the penalty of his wrongdoing. Our Lord does not redeem by His righteousness, but by His death. "Without shedding of blood is no remission."

What is the vine tree more than any tree, the vine branch which is among the trees of the forest?—*Ezek.* 15. 2.

With this chapter the note of the prophet somewhat changes. Not yet had he reached the great theme of restoration. He had much more to say concerning reprobation. So far his messages had been mainly concerned with the results of the Divine Reprobation of the nation in the actual calamities overtaking the city and the people. Now he commenced a series of messages dealing with the reason of that Reprobation, as it was found in the pollution of the people. This first message is most arresting. The prophet employed the familiar figure of the vine as setting forth the Divine ideal for Israel. (Consult Psa. 80, Isa. 5, Isa. 27, Jer. 2, Hosea 10, Matt. 21 and John 15.) He makes no allusion to that which is always the chief idea in the use of that figure, its fruit. He only thinks of it as wood. The reason is self-evident. The nation was barren of fruit, it had utterly and completely failed to bring forth the intended fruit. It was wood only. Then let it be compared to other nations in that way. The comparison is graphic in its revelation. As wood, the vine is useless. No man will employ it in work, not even a pin to hang a vessel on. What solemn pause these words must give to those who are branches in the True Vine. The only value of the Church is that it bears fruit. As wood for making works of other kinds it is useless. There can be no failure in Him Who is the True Vine; but if a branch in Him beareth not fruit, it is taken away, cast forth, and burned in the fire. Such is the teaching of our Lord.

Cause Jerusalem to know her abominations.—*Ezek.* 16. 2.

The message of Ezekiel, recorded in this chapter, was given in obedience to this command. The purpose was still that of setting forth the reason of her Reprobation. The chapter is one of the most powerful. The allegory is that of a child born, but from birth neglected; this child, taken and cared for, and nourished to beautiful womanhood; this woman taken in marriage by the one who had found and reared her; this wife, playing the harlot, and worse, for she did not sell herself for hire, but paid her lovers; this unfaithful wife visited with poetic punishment; and at last this abandoned woman restored. Thus the abominations of Israel are seen, for this was the history of the nation. But the truth brought out is that of the heinousness of the sin, in view of the goodness and grace of Jehovah. As Israel is represented by the foundling, cared for, married, and beloved, Jehovah is represented by the Benefactor, who becomes Lover and Husband. It is a most arresting fact that God, through His

prophets, and through His apostles, employs this figure of marital relationship as setting forth His relation to His people as He desires it, and feels it. In earthly inter-relationships, the marriage relationship is the highest in sanctity, because it is the highest in the experience of Love. By this figure, then, God sets forth for us what His heart feels for us, and what He desires from us in return. His love is of the strongest and tenderest, and He looks for a return of that love in uttermost loyalty. Here, then, was the deepest fact in the pollution of Israel. The prophet, called to make her know her abominations, did so by setting her conduct in the light of His love. While the discourse revealed the reason for Reprobation, it ended with the Divine purpose of Restoration. Such is the unfailing grace of the Divine heart.

Son of man, put forth a riddle.—*Ezek.* 17. 2.

In the allegory of the foundling in the previous chapter Ezekiel was dealing with the spiritual and moral malady of Israel. In this message he was concerned with her political folly and wickedness. The riddle of the two eagles and the vine is explained. The nation had looked to compromise with Babylon, and protection from Egypt, as means of restoring national being and fruitfulness. This had been her political sin. The prophetic message demonstrated the futility of such wickedness. The vine was still Jehovah's, and the eagles were also within His power. The things they did were all within His power, and under His government. Therefore the transplanting of the vine was of no avail. His east wind found it, wherever it was placed, and it withered in spite of all its attempts to maintain its life by these false means. Thus the political iniquity, resulting from the spiritual abomination, was visited with the Divine judgment. The reprobation of God could not be annulled by the policies which forgot Him. Here also the last note is one declaring the coming restoration, but clearly showing that it will be brought about, not by human policy, when the policy is conceived in rebellion, but by the action of His Own power, and in answer to the inspiration of His never failing grace. This chapter is full of light for statesmen and politicians if they will but consider its teaching. The one fact which abides is that of the Divine sovereignty. God is governing, and there is no escape from Him. Eagles, and vines, are under His control. Happy are they who frame their policies by consulting Him, and order their ways in His fear.

Behold, all souls are Mine.—*Ezek.* 18. 4.

This is a tremendous chapter, and is of the utmost value in our modern life. It consists of the prophet's discussion, under Divine command, of a false outlook on life which had found expression in a proverb: "The fathers have eaten sour grapes, and the children's teeth are set on edge." Its present importance is created by the fact that men are still using this proverb, and so using it as to show that they think the saying is true. As a matter of fact, no saying more false was ever coined. It is based upon a one-sided philosophy of heredity. Evil, whether as a moral malady, or personal suffering, is accounted for by the sins of the fathers. The proverb is at once an attempt to escape from responsibility for sin; and a protest against punishment. The false and pernicious conception is inclusively answered in these words of the prophet, which he uttered as the spokesman of God; "All souls are Mine." The rest of the message consists in the illustration and application of this saying. The great truth revealed is that every individual has a relationship with God available, which is mightier than all the facts resulting from physical relationships. It may be true that in my physical being I have inherited tendencies to some forms of evil from my father; but in the fact of my essential relation to God there are forces available to me more and mightier than all these tendencies. Therefore if I die, it is not because of the sin of my father, but because I fail to avail myself of my resources in God; and if I live, it is because I have availed myself of these resources. Neither righteousness nor evil is hereditary. The former results from right relationship with God, and the latter from failure to realize that relationship. All souls are His, and that means that every soul is made for first-hand personal dealing with Him.

This is a lamentation; and shall be for a lamentation.—*Ezek.* 19. 14.

Thus ends Ezekiel's elegy on kingship. Let us very carefully note that this phrase "elegy on kingship" correctly defines the song or message. Expositors agree in the view that the first young lion was Jehoahaz, the second Jehoiakim, and the final reference was to Zedekiah; and there is no doubt that they are right. But observe that the prophet mentioned none of them by name. He was not thinking of them as men, but as princes, or kings. Observe, further, that he did not speak of Judah but of Israel; he was thinking of "the princes—that is the kings—of Israel." Whereas the Northern kingdom of Israel had passed into slavery and only the Southern kingdom of Judah remained, and it was about to pass, that was for the moment the nation of Israel, and its last kings were the last of the long succession resulting from the clamour of Israel for "a king like the nations." In taking these, as illustrations, he referred to those who

passed into the hands of Egypt, and Babylon, omitting Jehoiakim, who died in peace. Just glance at the page and note the nations mentioned: Israel, Egypt, Babylon. Now the song becomes clear. The nation of Israel is the Mother. That in itself implicates the relation of Jehovah as Father. That Mother couches among lions; and brings forth young lions, the kings. With what result? Their stature was exalted, and they were seen; but she was plucked up, cast down, her fruit was dried up, and her strong rods—these same kings —were destroyed. At last she is planted in the wilderness, with no "strong rod to be a sceptre to rule." That is the story of the monarchy in Israel. The nation produced kings, who became conspicuous, but thus she destroyed herself, for they destroyed her.

I wrought for My Name's sake.— *Ezek.* 20. 9.

This and the next four chapters contain the messages constituting the last movement in Ezekiel's dealing with the Reprobation of the nation. In the first of these movements (4–14), he had dealt with the Fact of this Reprobation; in the second 15–19), he had dealt with the Reason of it, as found in the pollution of the people; now he argued for the Righteousness of it. This first message was called for by the coming of certain of the elders of Israel. The word of Jehovah to His servant declared that He would not be inquired of by them; but the prophet was charged to judge them. This judgment is expressed in this message. It has three movements; first, a review of the past (5–26); second, an examination of the present (27–32); and, finally, a foretelling of the future (33–44). The whole argument is a vindication of the righteousness and inevitability of their reprobation, in view of the nature of their sin. The purpose of Jehovah in dealing with them is revealed in the words we have emphasized: "I wrought for My Name's sake." Note the recurrence of the idea (verses 14, 22, 44) as it illumines the message. For His Name's sake He had delivered them from Egypt, had disciplined them in the wilderness, had showed mercy to their children, and was now dealing with them in judgment. The deepest note in their sin was not that of the actual deeds of evil, but that by such deeds they were blaspheming the Name; which they had been created to extol and glorify. This fact was the vindication of the righteousness of Reprobation. To have permitted that people to remain a nation among the nations, would have been to perpetuate a misrepresentation of God among those nations. The principle is of abiding application to all those who receive from God privileges and blessings in order to the revelation of Himself to others.

I will overturn, overturn, overturn
it; this also shall be no more, until He
come Whose right it is; and I will give
it Him.—*Ezek. 21. 27.*

This prophetic message begins in the
previous chapter at verse 45, where in
the Hebrew Bible the chapter begins. Its
whole theme is that of the activity of the
wrath of Him Whose name has been
blasphemed by the sin and failure of the
people. The central movement in the
message is that of the Song of the Sword
(verses 8–17). The first paragraphs led up
to that, and those after depend upon it.
The vision of that glittering, furbished,
active sword is indeed a terrible one. But
it is the Sword of Jehovah. Observe how
that fact is kept in mind. The king of
Babylon is seen halting at the parting of
the ways, endeavouring to decide by
divination whether he shall proceed
against Ammon or Judah. The arrow
directs him to Jerusalem. This was by the
act of God. In the end of the chapter,
Ammon is portrayed as drawing a sword,
but by the will of God she is to put it in
the sheath. The whole message is full of
force as it reveals to us the prophetic
vision of Jehovah enthroned over all the
doings of men. Israel, Babylon, Ammon
are all made to contribute to the accomplishment of His purpose. The method
and meaning of this Divine activity is
revealed in these words we have emphasized. God "overturns, overturns, overturns" nations, and dynasties, and civili-
zations. They appear, they disappear, and
all by His power. And all until He come,
Whose right it is. The reference was
patently Messianic. The prophet saw God
overturning false nations, dynasties, civili-
zations, in order at last to establish His
own Kingdom under His appointed King.
His operation did not cease when He
came in lowliness for human redemption.
It is still proceeding, and will do so until
He appear again, and establish the
kingdom of heaven on earth.

I sought for a man among them,
that should make up the fence, and
stand in the gap before Me for the
land, that I should not destroy it; but
I found none.—*Ezek. 22. 30.*

In this message the prophet set forth
the utter evil of the city, as vindicating
the righteousness of its reprobation. De-
picting the sins of the city, he described
the fiery process of the judgment. The
outlook was, indeed, of the darkest.
Priests, princes, prophets, people, were
involved; all were utterly corrupt. In these
particular words, the utter hopelessness
of the situation, so far as any chance of
recovery as from within the national life,
was revealed. The man needed was one
who would interpose himself against the
prevailing tide of iniquity, and hold it
back. Such men have appeared in dark

hours of human history; they have been
men of clear vision, of pure life, of strong
character; they have been able to halt a
nation in its downward way, and turn it
back into the paths of obedience. But at
this time, God sought for such a man;
but none was to be found. In all the
national life there was not a man, either
priest, or prince, or prophet, or son of the
people, with enough spiritual discernment
or moral passion, to enable him to turn
the thoughts and actions of the nation
back toward God. In such an hour the
methods of patience and mercy are useless;
it is only by the fiery furnace that the
dross can be destroyed, and the corrupted
silver be recovered. Thus the reprobation
of Israel was vindicated, not only on
account of its pollution, but in order to its
ultimate restoration, for there was no
force in her which could lead her back to
the God from Whom she had departed.

And as for their names, Samaria is
Oholah, and Jerusalem Oholibah.—
Ezek. 23. 4.

Thus at the beginning of this message,
the prophet gave the key to its application.
Samaria and Jerusalem were the capitals
respectively of the northern kingdom of
Israel, and the southern kingdom of Judah.
These capital cities were the centres of
government—the places of the politicians.
This particular message was concerned,
not so much with the sins of the people
in their evil practices, as with their
national policies. The whole history was
passed in review. Samaria had sought
alliances with Assyria and Egypt; and
Jerusalem with Assyria, Babylon and
Egypt. These policies had been the direct
result of turning away from God, and
constituted attempts to secure national
safety by intrigues with these nations.
The nature of that sin is set forth in this
graphic chapter. It was a sin of infidelity,
and of harlotry. This was so because of
the peculiar relation of the Israelitish
people to Jehovah. They were His creation;
He had made them in a peculiar way to
be a people for Himself. He had delivered
them from bondage, and given them a
place and a power. They needed no
defence other than Himself, and they owed
everything to Him. Egypt might with
propriety make alliance with Assyria; or
Babylon with either. They were, to use a
very suggestive modern phrase, "world-
powers." But Israel was separated from
the nations by her relationship to God;
and for her to follow policies of alliance
with these powers, was to be guilty of
national harlotry. The principle involved
is of application to the Church as "the
holy nation" to-day. Whenever she seeks
enrichment or strength or stablishing, by
alliance with the world, she is unfaithful
to her God, and is guilty of the sin of
spiritual adultery. Such was the meaning
of James when he wrote: "Ye adulteresses,

know ye not that the friendship of the world is enmity with God."

In the ninth year, in the tenth month, in the tenth day of the month. —*Ezek.* 24. 1.

Some dates fasten themselves upon the mind without any effort. This was such a date. The historic recorder, and the writer of the appendix to Jeremiah's prophecy, give this date with the same accuracy. (See 2 Kings 25. 1 and Jeremiah 52. 4.) It was the day when the armies of Nebuchadnezzar encompassed and invested the city of Jerusalem. It was the beginning of the end. For Ezekiel it was a date doubly significant, for on that very day at eventide, the desire of his eyes, his wife, suddenly died. The high dignity and solemn responsibility of. the prophetic office is seen in his action. In the presence of the national calamity he refrained from all manifestation of private sorrow. Indeed, he went further, and under Divine command, made his abstention a sign to those to whom he ministered. In a graphic figure, that of the caldron, he described the judgment about to fall upon the city: and he commanded the people not to mourn for it. The reason for such a command was the very thing he had been enforcing, that namely of the righteousness of that Divine judgment. They were not to mourn nor weep. This was perhaps the darkest day for Ezekiel in all his ministry, and the most difficult. There is a gleam of light in the word of Jehovah to him, which in commanding him thus to abstain from outward expressions of grief, yet said: "*Sigh, but not aloud.*" In that we see the understanding heart of God. He knew the sorrow of His servant's soul, both personal and public, and did not rebuke it. In days when public testimony demands that we rise superior to private sorrows, it is good to know that He understands the difficulty, and does not forbid the sigh.

Ye shall know that I am Lord.— *Ezek.* 25. 5.

The messages of Ezekiel now turned to the theme of Restoration; and that theme was introduced by prophecies concerning the nations which had been the enemies of Israel. These prophecies occupy chapters 25 to 32. Seven nations are dealt with: Ammon, Moab, Edom, Philistia, Tyre, Zidon, and Egypt. A glance at the map will show that the prophet's outlook passed over the enemies of Israel as they encompassed her. He first dealt with those on the East, passing from North to South—Ammon, Moab, Edom; then with those in the West, passing from South to North—Philistia, Tyre, Zidon, then to the South—Egypt. In order to the restoration of Israel to the Divinely-appointed land, all these must be dealt with and removed. These "burdens" declared that

this was what God would do. Such action was necessary. In this chapter we have the first four of these messages, those concerning Ammon, Moab, Edom, Philistia. The words we have emphasized are arresting in the fact of their repetition through these oracles concerning the nations. They are employed in every one of them. Concerning Ammon, 25. 5 and 7; concerning Moab, 25. 11; concerning Edom, 25. 14; concerning Philistia, 25. 17; concerning Tyre, 26. 6; concerning Zidon, 28. 22, 23 and 24; concerning Israel (parenthetically), 28. 26; concerning Egypt, 29. 6, 9, 16; concerning Israel (parenthetically), 29. 21; concerning Ethiopia (parenthetically), 30. 8; concerning Egypt, 30. 19, 25, 26 and 32. 15. That is a Bible-reading, but it is worth while. Here is the one purpose of Jehovah in His dealings with all nations. Those who fail to find Him in the light of His revelation of Himself by law or in the natural order, He brings to know Him through judgment.

Thus saith the Lord God; Behold, I am against thee, O Tyre.—*Ezek.* 26. 3.

The prophet's message concerning Tyre occupies nearly three chapters in our arrangement, 26–28. 24. This is an arresting fact. Tyre's strength and influence were commercial rather than military, and it is interesting and suggestive that in this connection we find the most graphic and illuminating portrayal of Satan to be found in the whole Bible. To that we come presently (chapter 28). This message of Ezekiel is dated so as to help us to understand the situation. Jerusalem had fallen, and the news had reached the prophet and Tyre. In Tyre that 'news caused great jubilation, and for one reason, which is clearly stated in her own words: "Aha, she is broken; the gate of the peoples; she is turned unto me; I shall be replenished, now that she is laid waste" (verse 2). All this is perfectly plain. The kingdom of Judah lay across the great routes by which the people from Egypt and the South-lands travelled north to Tyre. Undoubtedly this had put some restriction on the commercial enterprise of Tyre. When Jerusalem fell to Babylon, the only thing that interested Tyre was that an obstacle to her commercial activities was removed. What a revelation of the sordid condition of soul which was hers! It was this exultation which called forth the prophetic word containing the declaration of Jehovah: "Behold I am against thee, O Tyre." It is for ever so. God is against any nation whose life has become so materialized by commercial prosperity that she can rejoice over the calamities of other nations, because such calamities increase her opportunities of barter and amassing of wealth. Any nation to-day which gauges her attitude towards other nations by what their rise or fall may contribute to her wealth has God against her.

A lamentation for Tyre.—*Ezek.* 27. 2.

That is the true title of this chapter. The prophecy was a dirge, an elegy. It is a description of the city that said "I am perfect in beauty," in the complete desolation to which she is brought because of her self-centred pride. This is a case where the word "lamentation" does not suggest sorrow, but merely description of tragedy. Merely from the standpoint of literature this chapter is incomparable in its descriptive force, both as to the prosperity of the city, and as to the complete and unregretted catastrophe which overwhelmed her. Because of her position by the sea the prophet employed the figure of a ship as personifying the life of the city. She is first described in the splendour of her outfit (verses 1–11); then in the wonder of her cargoes (verses 12–25); and finally in her wreckage, and the consternation produced thereby among other seafaring men (verses 26–36). The whole theme is that of commercialism, and may thus be set out; her commercial supremacy, 1–7; her commercial enterprises, 8–25; her commercial ruin, 26–36. It is impossible to read this message of the prophet without a twofold consciousness resulting. The first is that of the lure of material advantage which results from successful commercial enterprise. The other is that such lure, yielded to until it destroys all other inspiration of life, leads to the uttermost ruin. The Bible and history make one cause in their revelation of the peril of material prosperity. There is nothing more calculated to destroy a people. And yet how slow man is to learn the lesson.

A lamentation for the king of Tyre. —*Ezek.* 28. 12.

This chapter contains the end of the burden concerning Tyre, and the burden concerning Zidon. The end of the burden of Tyre consists of a message to its prince, and a lamentation for its king. While closely related, these must not be confused. That is too often done. One expositor says: "The prophet appears to use the terms king and prince indifferently." If that be true generally, and I think it is very doubtful, it certainly is not so here; and to fail to discover the difference is to miss the point of this burden. The prince of Tyre was the reigning prince at the time; but the king of Tyre was the awful and sinister power behind the throne, the personality who is ever the inspirer of such pride of heart, and deification of self as that of which the prince was guilty. Ezekiel in clearest vision saw this being, and saw the whole truth concerning him; and as we saw in a

previous note, here we have the most graphic and illuminating portrayal of Satan to be found in the whole Bible. His original power and greatness, wisdom and beauty, and exalted position are all set forth. Then the secret of his fall is declared without explanation: "Unrighteousness was found in thee." No details are given. Perhaps here we have the sentence which takes us further back than any other on the mysterious subject of the genesis of evil in the universe. We must leave it there. Finally, God's dealing with this fallen one is described. He is cast out from his exalted position. Out of the midst of his own being the fire proceeds which ultimately destroys him. So is he cast out and cast down. The revelation of the diabolical inspiration behind all human pride is clear; its wisdom, seductive beauty, and tremendous power are patent. But God is seen as still governing, and casting down this king of evil kings, involving them in the ruin of the one to whom they have yielded themselves.

I am against thee, Pharaoh, king of Egypt, the great dragon that lieth in the midst of his rivers, which hath said, My river is mine own, and I have made it for myself.—*Ezek.* 29. 3.

We now come to the last of Ezekiel's prophecies concerning the nations, and it has to do with Egypt. It occupies four chapters (29–32); and consists of seven oracles, all of them dated but one. The reader must observe these dates, for that enables him to realize the situation. All of them—except one—were uttered in connection with the fall of Jerusalem; four of them in the year preceding it, two of them during the year after it; while the exception to which I have referred, was delivered fifteen years later, though incorporated here. As we have realized in reading this prophecy and that of Jeremiah, the political peril had been that created by the looking of these people toward Egypt. This accounted for the length and definiteness of these messages. In this chapter we have the prophet's message concerning Pharaoh, as representing the power of Egypt (verses 1–16). Here also is inserted the prophecy uttered more than fifteen years later concerning the conquest of Egypt by Babylon. In these words the central sin of Pharaoh and of Egypt is laid bare. The Nile was in every way the secret of the wealth and power of that land and people. Here Pharaoh is represented, not as worshipping the River, but as claiming to possess it, and to have created it. It is a graphic method of again drawing attention to the fact that all forgetfulness of God amounts at last to self-deification. That is the sin of every king and of every people who fail to recognize God, and to deal with Him.

I will hold up the arms of the king of Babylon, and the arms of Pharaoh shall fall down.—Ezek. 30. 25.

In this chapter we have two of the Egypt prophecies. The first (verses 1–19) is undated. It was most probably delivered in close connection with the first (chapter 29. 1–16). It is concerned with the coming judgment of God upon the helpers of Egypt, and upon Egypt itself. The fourth message (20–26) was delivered about four months before the fall of the city. Many were still looking to Egypt in hope of help from her. Indeed, as we saw in reading Jeremiah (chapter 37), Pharaoh had made a movement with his hosts out of Egypt, and this had caused the Chaldeans temporarily to abandon the siege of Jerusalem. That action of Pharaoh had met with defeat. Most probably this was what Ezekiel had in mind when he said that the word of Jehovah to him said: "I have broken the arm of Pharaoh, king of Egypt." He now declared that Jehovah would break both his arms, so that he would be unable to bear the sword. In the words we have emphasized, the whole situation was declared. These apparently mighty monarchs of Egypt and Babylon were both in the hands of Jehovah. Their apparent successes and failures resulted from His action. They were completely in His power. The uplifted arms of the one, were uplifted by God; and the broken, helpless arms of the other were so by the act of God. Ezekiel was a prophet in the truest sense. He interpreted current events in the light of eternal and unchanging facts. The false prophet ever attempts to interpret a situation by considering current events. As we have constantly said, all this is very modern in its values.

To whom art thou thus like in glory and in greatness among the trees of Eden?—Ezek. 31. 18.

This chapter contains the fifth of the oracles concerning Egypt. It was spoken about two months before the fall of Jerusalem, and was the last before that event. It foretold the downfall of Pharaoh and the State of Egypt. The word Assyrian in verse 3 is surely wrong. As Dr. Davidson has pointed out, the word is "Asshur," and is the name of a tree, so that it should read, "Behold a great tree of a cedar." The language is poetic and full of force. Pharaoh and his multitude are portrayed as a tree towering over the tops of the other trees, so that fowls and beasts took refuge in its branches, and beneath its boughs. This tree is brought down, nations depart from under its shadow. The proud king is seen passing to Sheol, the underworld of the dead, and commotion is caused there by his coming, and the other fallen ones find satisfaction in that he too is brought low. This question, asked at the close, can have but one answer. In his greatness Pharaoh was like that awful and mighty one, described as king of Tyre. The question is a flash of light, bringing to mind once more, what had been so forcefully declared in the Burden concerning Tyre, that behind these great and mighty tyrants of earth, there was always the same sinister and awful personality. Their pride of place and power was of his inspiring, and indeed was his method of opposing himself to the will and purpose of God. It was no use; it is no use; it never will be! God has cast Satan out of the mountain; and every successive representative of his revolt will be cast down and cast out. Thus have we seen it in history. Thus shall we see it still, until the last tyrant, the Man of Sin himself, will be destroyed by the brightness of the coming of the Lord.

I will spread out My net over thee with a company of many peoples.—Ezek. 32. 3.

In this chapter we have the sixth and seventh of the Egypt messages. Each is dated. They were delivered about a year and seven months after the fall of the city. In the seventh no month is given, but we may presume that it was the same month as the sixth, and so about two weeks later. The sixth foretold the downfall of Pharaoh; and the seventh that of his people. He and they are seen removed from earthly power and place, to the dark underworld, where they are impotent. The conception of that underworld is suggestive and terrible. The kings and nations are gathered there, but they are represented as at the end of activity. They do not deed. They are broken. They are conscious, for they speak to Pharaoh when he arrives, and they are ashamed, and filled with shame. The great purpose of the message was that of showing how the defeat and discomfiture of mighty people should speak to men so as to amaze them and fill them with fear. The figure of these particular words is a forceful one. The kings of the nations, and the nations, are seen in the turbulent waters, and troubling those waters; but over and around them all, are the meshes of the net of God. At His will they are drawn forth from the waters and cast to die and rot upon the land. Thus the Kingdom of God, that is the rule over human affairs, is a dragnet swaying to the tides. When He will, He is able to draw that net in, and separate between the good and the bad. See Matthew 13. 47–48, where the application is to Kingdom processes in this age, but the principle has ever had application.

I have set thee a watchman unto the house of Israel; therefore hear the word at My mouth, and give them warning from Me.—Ezek. 33. 7.

Having delivered his messages concerning the doom of the nations opposed to Israel, as necessary to her restoration, Ezekiel turned to the nation itself. There is only one date in the series of prophecies on that subject, which begin here and end with chapter 39. That date is found in the twenty-first verse of this chapter, and in all probability the series was given at that time. The date of the arrival of the fugitive was about six weeks before the final messages concerning Egypt's doom (compare 32. 1 and 33. 21). There is some confusion about these dates, which need not concern us, as the progress of the prophecy is natural. The situation was that Israel, both as to the Northern and Southern sections of the one nation, was in captivity. Ezekiel was among the captives in Babylonia. Jeremiah was with the remnant, probably now in Egypt. The desolation was complete. Now Ezekiel came to these messages of hope. This first one was concerned wholly with the function of the prophet, and that function is inclusively defined in these words. He is a watchman, having one function, and a twofold responsibility. First he is to listen; then he is to speak. He must hear the word of Jehovah; and then proclaim it. If he do this, he has no further responsibility. If he fail, he is accountable to God for the calamities overtaking the people he failed to warn. The full message makes very clear the moral intention of prophetic ministry. He is to speak to men in order that the righteous may be prevented from turning away from righteousness; and that the wicked may be persuaded to turn from wickedness, in order, in each case, that they may live. The will of God is life for His people; that is ensured by righteousness; the prophet calls men to that righteousness.

Behold, I Myself, even I, will search for My sheep, and will seek them out. —Ezek. 34. 11.

Having defined the function of the prophet as that of bringing men to rectitude, by uttering the word of Jehovah, Ezekiel turned to the idea of the corporate, or national life of the people. This message was concerned with the royal house, that is, with the kings of the nation, the shepherds of the people. The shepherd is ever the type of the king, rather than of the priest or prophet. The failure of kingship is set forth in the first part of this message (verses 1–10); and as we read it, if we carefully consider all that these kings of Israel did not do, we shall know what they ought to have done, and thus understand the kingly office according to the Divine ideal. The description of failure was the prelude to the prophet's declaration that what their kings had failed to do for the people, Jehovah would Himself do, and that by setting up one Shepherd over them, even David, the name being employed idealistically, and in reference to Messiah. As we read

this chapter, our minds inevitably travel on to the New Testament, and that paragraph at the close of the ninth chapter of Matthew, in which the writer describes for us Christ's vision of the multitudes, the compassion of His heart, and His consequent sending out of the Twelve. In Him we see the fulfilment of this old-time prophecy. In Him, Jehovah, Himself, even He came to search for the sheep, and to establish the true Kingdom. Again we read the first part of the message, and find in it a perfect description of His work. Not yet is it completed; but it will be; for Israel, and for the "other sheep," not of that fold; whom also He will bring, so that there shall be one flock, one Shepherd.

Because thou hast said, These two nations and these two countries shall be mine, and we will possess it, whereas the Lord was there.—Ezek. 35. 10.

Ezekiel now uttered a message descriptive of the new order to be established under the true Shepherd. The first part of this message however was of the nature of a parenthetical turning aside to deal with Edom. Edom is represented as having a perpetual enmity against Israel, as rejoicing in her calamities; and in these words the inspiration of that rejoicing is unveiled. It was that of cupidity, lust for territory. In the troubles of Israel and Judah, Edom had seen the opportunity of enriching herself, by gaining possession of the land. In their calculations the politicians of Edom had made the mistake which politicians have so often made, that of leaving out a supreme quantity. They had looked at the desirable territory, and had seen it held only by a weak and broken people. They had failed to see, or had ignored the fact, or had counted it as of no moment, that "the Lord was there." Yet this was the supreme fact, the only one which mattered. Edom as descended from Esau, as was Israel from Jacob, was not ignorant of the Divine election of Israel. But here the very spirit of Esau was manifested, that of ignoring, or deliberately setting aside, Divine purposes for the sake of material advantage. If Edom forget that the Lord is there, that forgetfulness does not change the fact. That land was, and is, sacred to the carrying out of a Divine purpose, for the world, and through Israel; and God has never abandoned it. He is still there; and whosoever may covet it cannot hold it, for He will dispossess them.

. . . The nations shall know that I am the Lord, saith the Lord God, when I shall be sanctified in you before their eyes.—Ezek. 36. 23.

Having uttered his message concerning Edom, the people coveting the land of Israel, the prophet foretold the restoration of the land, and the people to the fulfilment of the Divine purpose. The first movement of the message was an oracle concerning the land itself, but considered as the dwelling-place of Israel. Then followed a wonderful prediction as to the way of restoration. The land would be restored by the salvation of the people. That salvation would consist in moral and spiritual renewal. First, they would be cleansed from their pollutions; then changed in nature; and then energized by the Spirit of God within them. Very impressive is the prophet's insistence upon the fact that this is to be done, not for the sake of Israel, but for the sake of the Name of God. In such regeneration and restoration Israel would find blessing; but the purpose of blessing is always the honour of the Name of God, and the interpretation of that honour to the nations. Yet what higher honour could any nation have than that intended for Israel, that, namely, of sanctifying God in them, that is, of setting Him apart so that He may be seen and understood? Israel has never yet fulfilled that function. But she will do so; and the geographical base of her national life will be that very land, still kept within the purpose and power of God for her. For the present age the Church—whose ultimate vocation is in the ages to come—is the holy nation, whose office it is to show forth the excellencies of Him Who has called her out of darkness into His marvellous light. Let her also remember that her gifts and calling are not for her sake, but for the honour of the Name; that, being sanctified in her, God may make Himself known to the nations.

Behold, they say, Our bones are dried up, and our hope is lost; we are clean cut off.—*Ezek.* 37. 11.

The whole of this great message of Ezekiel may be said to be the Divine answer to these words, which were the words of Israel. They were the words of despondency, born of the realization of the desolation produced by the Divine Reprobation. It was an accurate description. Considered as a nation, Israel was indeed but a skeleton, and worse—her bones were scattered; there was no hope as within herself: she was clean cut off. To prepare him for his message, Jehovah gave the prophet a vision of a valley filled with dry bones, and asked him the question: "Can these bones live?" The prophet's answer was characteristic of his loyalty and faith: "O Lord Jehovah, Thou knowest!" Then he saw the secret of hope. By prophecy—the Word of God; and the four winds—the Spirit of God; that valley of dead bones became a valley peopled with living men, the hosts of Jehovah. Then another sign was given him, that of the two sticks, showing that God would yet gather together and bind

into one the two nations, which through their own sin existed as two, and establish them as one nation under one Shepherd King. The teaching has wider application than to Israel. It is the story of humanity. Through sin the whole earth has become a valley of dry bones. There is no hope for humanity in man. But these dry bones can live. By the Word, and the Spirit of God, men can be reborn; and at last healed of their separations, and united under one King. The valley is yet the place of dead bones; but the word of Jehovah is being uttered; and the Spirit of God is breathing over the dead; and the processes of Divine recovery and restoration are proceeding. When the King comes, the work will be cut short in righteousness.

Son of man, set thy face toward Gog, of the land of Magog.—*Ezek.* 38. 2.

This and the next chapter contain two messages of Ezekiel, but they are concerned with the same matter. That matter is an arresting one. While his theme now was that of the Restoration of Israel, at this time he was borne along to see visions of events beyond that restoration. Let this be clearly noted. The invasion of Gog and his allies was an invasion not of a land desolated, but of the land in which the people of God were seen dwelling in peace and prosperity. Notice also that none of these enemies are the old ones with which we are familiar as hostile to Israel. It is a new confederacy and antagonism. Here the prophet saw the final manifestation of antagonism to Jehovah and His people. He saw it gathering itself in terrific force, the mightiest alliance that had ever acted against Israel. But still the prophet saw God reigning. It was He Who brought forth Gog with his armies; that is, He compelled the incipient antagonism to express itself. For us there can be no doubt that here Ezekiel had a vision of that which even yet is more than a thousand years ahead. John, in the Apocalypse, refers to it, and definitely places it beyond the period of the thousand years (Rev. 20. 7–8). Whatever men may think as to the speedy elimination of evil from human affairs, the Bible has no such teaching. The process is, by the measurement of human lives and calendars, a long one; but God is never defeated. He watches its working, and curbs and restrains it within limits, and compels it to the fullest expression, in order to its complete and final defeat.

Behold, it cometh, and it shall be done, saith the Lord God; this is the day whereof I have spoken.—*Ezek.* 39. 8.

In this message the prophet took up and completed the subject of this final antagonism to the people and purpose of

God. Its burden is that if there be such antagonism, it is equally true that God is antagonistic to it; and that not passively, but actively. He will compel it to its last and mightiest manifestation in order that it may be completely and for ever destroyed. The words we have stressed emphasize the Divine determination to complete the destruction of evil. Again John in brief sentences makes the same affirmation (Rev. 20. 9, 10). The most arresting thing in this burden of Ezekiel is its account of how, after the defeat of this mighty alliance by the intervention and fire of God, the people of God give themselves to the complete cleansing of their land from the last dead remains of the pollution. With the greatest diligence they bury the dead hosts, persevering until not a bone is left above the ground to pollute it. And not the dead bodies alone, but all the vast quantities of the implements of war are to be for fuel and burning, the final destruction of the things wherein man trusted in his opposition to the will of God. Again we say that, judged by the measurements of human lives and calendars, the process is a long one, but the end is certain: "Behold, it cometh; and it shall be done." Be it ours within the span of our lives to count it the highest of all honours that we by faith and patience are permitted to have some part with God in the work which brings the glorious end. It is a great thing to be a "partaker—in the tribulation, and kingdom, and patience which are in Jesus."

Declare all that thou seest to the house of Israel.—*Ezek.* 40. 4.

We now come to the final section of this book of Ezekiel. These visions were given to the prophet some twelve years after the latest of those already considered, except the brief one concerning the overcoming of Tyre by Nebuchadnezzar (29. 17–20), which was incorporated with the burdens of the nations. These last messages were descriptive, rather than didactic, although their purpose was moral, in that the prophet was commanded to declare them to the house of Israel "that they may be ashamed of their iniquities" (see 43. 10). The prophet, in the visions of God, was brought to the land of Israel, and there he was given a portrayal of the final order, when the people of God are spiritually, morally, and physically restored. In reading these messages, we find ourselves in an entirely new order. Difficulty has been created in the minds of many by the merging of things which are distinctly and definitely material, with those which have all the elements of heavenly conditions and spiritual experiences. Yet this is of the essence of the revelation. The earth separated from heaven, or heaven separated from earth, is not the original order. It resulted from human sin. When that has been dealt with, the inter-relation

between heaven and earth will be that of natural intercommunication, not as now, merely by faith, but actually, positively, definitely, by sight and by sense. The first phase of the vision of the restored order presented the Temple as at the centre of the life of the people. In this chapter we have the description of the courts round about the Temple proper, and of the porch leading to the house itself.

It was made with cherubim and palm trees; and a palm tree was between cherub and cherub, and every cherub had two faces.—*Ezek.* 41. 18.

In this chapter we have the prophet's description of the Temple itself; first its general structure and then its ornamentation. The dimensions as to the actual sanctuary were those of the Tabernacle. Moreover, its general form was the same, as the distinction was maintained between the Holy Place (verses 1 and 2) and the Holy of Holies (verses 3 and 4). The buildings round about constituted an addition. Within, he saw the ornamentation, the symbols of beauty, and of suggestiveness. These were alternating cherubim and palm trees. The cherubim constitute a part of the visions of God, granted to Ezekiel at the beginning of his ministry. Here he saw two of the faces only, those of the man and the lion. The palm trees were the symbol of national or racial life in its full realization and glory. Thus into each palm tree the eyes of a man and the eyes of a lion were ever looking. God in His fullest expression in man, and in His sovereignty, typified by the lion, is watching with complacency and satisfaction the full realization of His purposes as typified by the palm tree. These symbols were seen upon the wall of the Temple, and upon the folding doors admitting thereto. Thus at the centre of the new order of life was the Temple; and in its very heart these symbols of the condition of life as realized in that order. Life in full fruition, watched over by God in love and in authority.

It had a wall round about . . . to make a separation between them which was holy, and that which was common. —*Ezek.* 42. 20.

This chapter is devoted to the description of the buildings surrounding the Temple proper, or the Sanctuary, but all within the sacred precincts. These buildings were for the use of the priests while engaged in the sacred service of the Temple. Finally the measurement of the great wall surrounding the whole Temple area is given; and concerning that wall these words were written. Thus in the vision of the final order, a distinction is maintained between that which is holy and that which is common. Perhaps the word "common" employed by our revisers is better than the "profane" of the King James' Version; but that is because of our more modern use of this word "profane" which associates with it the idea of evil. A similar difficulty however is created by the word "common," which we now use as meaning in some sense inferior, or less worthy. Neither of these ideas is present in the distinction between the holy and the profane, in the text. It is rather a distinction between the exercise of man in relation with God, and his exercises—neither evil nor unworthy—in relation with his fellow man. This is a distinction. It is the difference between worship and social intercourse. The first is the highest activity of which man is capable, and can only be rendered to God; and is at last the only relation which man can bear to God. The second is a blessed and glorious activity, the realization of the joy of the family of the One Father, of the happiness of the subjects of the One King. This sense of distinction is to be maintained in the final order; how carefully therefore we should observe it now. This vision of the final earthly Temple has much to say to us to-day as to the reverence and sanctity of true worship.

Thou, son of man, show the house to the house of Israel, that they may be ashamed of their iniquities.—Ezek. 43. 10.

Having completed the description of the new Temple, the prophet told how he saw Jehovah return to His House. As in the days when Moses completed the Tabernacle, and Solomon the Temple, the glory of Jehovah came and filled the House. It was that manifestation of the Presence, which had constituted the real value of Tabernacle and Temple; and so it will be in the new Temple. All the beauty of the structure in each case was but a symbol and harmonic setting for this essential wonder. Ezekiel had seen this glory depart (10. 19 and 11. 22, 23), and now he saw it return. In these particular words we find the value of the messages which the prophet was now delivering. The vision of the glory of the House was given in order to produce shame in the hearts of the people for those evil ways which had robbed them of their glory. This is a very suggestive word, and it is impossible not to see its application to the Church of God. So far as the fulfilment of her function of revealing the glory of God to the world in her corporate capacity is concerned, few will deny her comparative failure. The recognition of it is the inspiration of many modern movements toward unity. Perhaps nothing would be more valuable than a renewed vision of God's ideal of the Church, as that is revealed in the New Testament. That vision would be of the spiritual unity which has never been destroyed;

nor can be; but which we have largely hidden from the world, and even lost sight of ourselves, through our differences and diversions, in non-essential things.

As for the Prince, He shall sit therein as Prince to eat bread before the Lord. Ezek. 44. 3.

In this chapter and the two following, the Temple is still in view, and all its ordinances are declared. It is noticeable, however, that the Temple is considered as at the centre of the city, and so of the national life. Within its boundary, the Prince of the people is found, surrounded by the priests. This place of the Prince is arresting. Ezekiel had seen the glory of Jehovah entering by the east gate. That gate was now closed, and none was permitted to enter thereby. But within the courts, right in that gateway, the Prince is to find His place; there He is to eat bread before Jehovah. Notice, He is not called the King. In this restored order, there is only One King for this people, the One Whom they had rejected from being King. Through the discipline of reprobation, He restores them to Himself; they constitute a Theocracy. Their visible ruler is a Prince, and He sits in the gate through which Jehovah enters, and there eats bread before Him, in fellowship with Him, and in His rule representing Him. In so far as all this is a vision of the ultimate earthly order, we know who the Prince will be; and in this suggestive portrayal of His place in the Temple, we have one phase of application of that consummation which Paul saw, when he wrote of the time when the Son shall deliver up the kingdom to the Father, that God may be all in all. In so far as the picture represents any stage short of the ultimate order, it reveals the place of the Prince or Ruler, at all times, as that of complete submission to the one authority of Jehovah.

All the people of the land shall give unto this oblation for the Prince in Israel. And it shall be the Prince's part to give the burnt offerings . . .— Ezek. 45. 16, 17.

Here in the setting out of the new order of the land, provision is made first for the area for priests and Levites in close association with the Temple. The territory of the Prince is also appointed. To Him the people are to pay their dues, of their flocks and of the soil; and out of these He is to provide all that is necessary for those ceremonial offerings, which perpetually set forth the truth concerning the relationship of the people to Jehovah as it is based upon redemption. Thus a change is seen from the old order. In that, every person was responsible for bringing offerings to the priests. Now all these are brought to the Prince, and He provides what is necessary. Thus, in some senses the Prince is more than Ruler; He is exercising the supreme function of the Priest in receiving from the people and providing the offerings of atonement. Peter charged the men of Israel with having "killed the Prince of life," and declared that the heaven had received Him "until the times of restoration of all things, whereof God spake by the mouths of His holy prophets" (Acts 3. 15, 21); and on another occasion said: "Him did God exalt with His right hand to be a Prince and a Saviour, to give repentance to Israel, and remission of sins" (Acts 5. 31). To His people Israel, He will indeed be a Prince and a Saviour, ruling over them in fellowship with God, and that on the basis of that perfect redemption which He has provided, through which their restoration must come.

And the Prince . . . shall worship at the threshold of the gate.—*Ezek.* 46. 2.

Still the description of the new order continues, and is now concerned with the arrangements for the observance of the Sabbath, and the offerings of the Sabbath and the new moon. The whole outlook is earthly; that is to say, that the order described is that of life in this world. Men are still employed in their earthly vocations, and so the Sabbath is observed. In this day of restoration, the ceremonial offerings are observed, with this difference, that until Christ came they were prophetic and anticipatory, whereas now they are memorial. That the sacrifices are symbolic rather than actual I think there can be no doubt. That which is most arresting throughout, is the presence of the Prince. Whereas He has His place in the gateway of the Divine return to His people, and eats His bread before Jehovah, He is identified with the people in their worship. In this worship He is first alone, at the threshold of the gate; then He is with the people; whether it be the company of those who pass from the north to the south, or that which passes from south to north. He goes in the midst of all. When we think of all this as finding fulfilment in Christ, we need to remember that it is in representative capacity only, as completely one with His people, that He can be thought of as a worshipper; and that is the ultimate of grace. John in the Apocalypse never refers to Him as worshipping, save only as He, in unity with His people, is identified with the worship of the four living creatures. But these are worshippers of God and the Lamb. Thus, the highest symbolism fails to interpret finally the mysteries of grace. The one truth which is clear is that of the complete identification of the Prince and Saviour with those over whom He rules as Redeemer.

Everything shall live whithersoever the river cometh.—*Ezek.* 47. 9.

The glory and beauty of this great message has been fully recognized by the people of God, and constant and most justifiable use has been made of it in interpretations of the fulness and fertility of life in the Pentecostal baptism and indwelling. It is a message constantly referred to in consideration of the words of Jesus on the last day of the Feast of Tabernacles when He said: "If any man thirst, let him come unto Me, and drink. He that believeth on Me, as the Scripture hath said, from within him shall flow rivers of living water" (John 7. 37, 38). Considering it in its relation to Ezekiel's visions, we observe its place. The new order is established; the Temple is built, and its services are arranged; the city is established around it; the land is apportioned in relation to it; Jehovah has returned to dwell among His people; His will is administered by a Prince upon the basis of redemption. All is completed. Now the river of life flows forth from that House, and so from that Divine Presence; it comes by the way of the altar; it proceeds to the Arabah, the wilderness; it flows into the Dead Sea; and in its progress there is life—"Everything shall live whithersoever the river cometh." That is the life of restoration. For that which is desolate because reprobate, there is no other way of recovery, of restoration. But there is this way, because of the character and nature of God. The end is not yet. The wilderness is still barren; the sea is dead; but the river is flowing out from the Sanctuary by the way of the altar; and the "seasons of refreshing from the presence of the Lord" are assured, because He will "send the Christ—even Jesus"— for the "restoration of all things."

The Lord is there.—*Ezek.* 48. 35.

That is the final word of this great prophet of hope, Jehovah-Shammah. It is one of the great Jehovah titles and interpretations, and here Ezekiel employs it as giving the name of the city of God. There, in exile from Jerusalem, that city dear to his heart, in the possession of aliens, its walls broken down, the Temple destroyed, its glory dead, this man had received visions of God. These visions had interpreted for him the corruption of his people, and the infinite depth of the grace of God. He had seen Jehovah leave His people, and their consequent reprobation and desolation. He had argued for the righteousness of that reprobation. But he had seen more. He had been brought to understand that through reprobation, God was working for restoration. He had seen the processes of that restoration, and the glory of it, in the re-established and ennobled order. In his last message he had described the new division of the land among the tribes of Jehovah, each territory running from east to west; and the whole, including all the land promised to the fathers. At the centre of everything was the Sanctuary, surrounded by the territory of Prince, Priests, Levites, and The City. The City with its twelve gates is the final vision. The prophet beheld it, and its complete glory being seen, he named it "Jehovah is there." The name tells of complete satisfaction; that of God, and that of man. God is seen at rest among His people, His original purpose realized. Man is seen at rest in God, his true destiny reached. To John in Patmos, also came the vision of the city of God, and the final glory of it was the same: "Behold, the tabernacle of God is with men, and He shall dwell with them, and they shall be His peoples; and God Himself shall be with them, and be their God."

DANIEL

Daniel purposed in his heart.—Dan. 1. 8.

In this first chapter we have an introduction to Daniel. The dating shows that he was carried away into captivity before Ezekiel was, having been among those who were taken from Jerusalem in connection with the first invasion of Nebuchadnezzar, during the third year of Jehoiakim's reign. Evidently at the time he was but a youth. He seems never to have returned to Jerusalem. His history is very remarkable, in that, notwithstanding the fact that he was one of the captive people, he came to occupy positions of power in three kingdoms, those namely of Babylon, Media, and Persia, and this without deflection from unswerving loyalty to the God of his fathers. In this regard his very first experience placed him in grave danger. He was among the number selected for the royal service, and thus brought into court relationship from the first. He was to be taught the learning and language of the Chaldeans, in order that he might be attached to the person of the king. Here, indeed, was a peril for the age of youth, so impressionable, and so likely to be influenced by the glitter of material splendour. But Daniel suffered nothing of deterioration of character either then, or subsequently. These words give us the secret of that strength. He "purposed in his heart." That is a fine phrase, revealing a conviction, made dynamic by the reinforcement of the will. Having thus inwardly made his choice, he acted in harmony therewith, as he requested permission to live and act according to his conviction. Then God acted, as He made him "to find kindness in the sight of the prince of the eunuchs" that "he might not defile himself." The first thing in life is that of a purpose definitely recognized and accepted; and then acted upon. If that purpose be true, God is always in co-operation, and He is able to control circumstances in the interest thereof.

Daniel went to his house, and made the thing known to Hananiah, Mishael, and Azariah, his companions.—Dan. 2. 17.

In this chapter we have the account of the first activity of Daniel in fulfilment of his Divinely-appointed work. All that he did in the three world-kingdoms with which he was associated was of secondary importance. He was chosen of God to live among those kingdoms in order to see them in their relation to the Kingdom of God, and to interpret that relation to those to whom he spoke, and to men for all time through the writing of this book. The method of God was that of causing kings to dream dreams, see visions, be arrested by supernatural manifestations, all of which Daniel was to interpret. Nebuchadnezzar saw in his dreams a colossal image, and was troubled. None of his magicians or astrologers could reconstruct the dream, much less interpret it. Daniel was enabled to do both, not, as he said, by his own wisdom, but by the revelation given to him by God. One can imagine the occasion, and the most natural sense of its difficulty in the mind of Daniel. He was utterly unable to do, in his own wisdom, any more than the king's magicians could do. Yet quite evidently he was conscious of a Divine calling and relationship. Very beautiful is the account of his first action. He called together the little group of his friends, like-minded with himself in loyalty to the God of their fathers, and he sought their co-operation in prayer. That prayer was heard, and answered: the secret was revealed to Daniel in a vision of the night. If the first secret of life be that of a purpose of heart, there is no force equal to keeping life not only safe, but serviceable, like that of prayer, and prayer gains in power when it is reinforced by fellowship with those mastered by the same purpose. Let every man called to Divine service, cultivate a comradeship with loyal souls, not so much for discussion, as for prayer,

But if not . . .—Dan. 3. 18.

That is a very incomplete quotation, but it introduces us to faith in its finest expression. The chapter tells the story of Nebuchadnezzar's pride. In the dream which Daniel had interpreted to him he had been described as the head of gold in the colossus of world-power. He now set up an image of gold. We are not told that it was intended to represent a god; and the probability is that it was rather intended to represent his own power. All were commanded to prostrate themselves before it and worship. Daniel does not appear in this story, but his three comrades, with whom he had sought fellowship in prayer, are here. Here was a test for their loyalty to the God of their fathers, and to His law, which strictly forbade the yielding of worship to any image whatsoever. There was no hesitation on their part. They refused, and were brought before the king. To him, in language full of respect for him, but inspired by complete loyalty to God, they declared that there was no need to answer; their position was known. They declared further to the proud monarch that God was able to deliver them, and affirmed their confidence that He would do so. That was a splendid faith. But it went further as they said: *"But if not,* be it known unto thee, O king, that we will not serve thy gods, nor worship the golden image which thou hast set up." That is faith at its highest. Deliverance is to be desired, and expected; but if it come not, still there can be no abandonment of the One true God. Death, as the result of loyalty to Him, is preferable to deliverance, at the price of denying Him. This is the faith which overcometh the world.

. . . His Kingdom is an everlasting Kingdom, and His dominion is from generation to generation.—Dan. 4. 3.

In the first three verses of this chapter we have the proclamation which Nebuchadnezzar made as the result of an experience through which he had passed. The full account of that experience is then given in verses 4 to 36. The last verse is connected with the first three, in that it adds the note of praise to the proclamation. The period of the experience covered at least eight years. First there came to him the vision. This was interpreted to him with great fidelity by Daniel. A year later the madness overtook him. It continued for seven years, during which he lived on the level of the beasts. The sin of the king was that of pride, and the consequent forgetfulness of God. That pride found expression in the words recorded in verse 30. The lesson which he was taught is contained in these words: "His Kingdom is an everlasting Kingdom, and His dominion is from generation to generation." Notice how the idea recurs in the narrative of experience (see verses 17, 25, 32 and 34). This statement of the proclamation is complete. The Kingdom of God is recognized in its duration: "His Kingdom is an everlasting Kingdom;" and in its continuousness, "His dominion is from generation to generation." This is a truth which men of faith sometimes fail to grasp, or feel the force of. God is not dethroned; He never has been; He never will be. He rules to-day, in the kingdom of men; and He gives the kingdom to whomsoever He will. We pray as Jesus taught us for the Kingdom to come; that is that men may volitionally surrender to it, and find its blessings. While we do so, let us never forget that even though men do not yet do so, "Jehovah reigneth." The true strength of all earthly kings and rulers lies in the discovery of this fact, and in yielding to it.

The God in Whose hand thy breath is, and Whose are all thy ways, hast thou not glorified.—Dan. 5. 23.

In these words the sin of Belshazzar was stated in its deepest meaning. The scene represents him in the midst of a thousand of his lords, drinking wine out of vessels taken from the Temple of Jehovah, and offering worship in the act to gods of gold, of silver, of brass, of iron, of wood, and of stone. This man was the son of Nebuchadnezzar. He was familiar with the things that had happened to him. He knew through what experiences his father had been brought to acknowledgment of the Kingdom of the Most High. This, then, in itself, was an occasion and an act of defiant rebellion against that Kingdom. For that final act his doom was sealed. In that night he was slain. Daniel, now an old man, interpreted the mystic writing on the wall, and in these words revealed the true nature of Belshazzar's sin. There is tremendous force in the statement. It recognized the relation of the man to God. His breath—foul then, with obscenity and profanity—was in the hand of God; his ways—crooked and perverse and rebellious—were yet under the Divine control. Yet this man had used his breath for blasphemy rather than for praise; and his ways had been those of self-indulgence, rather than those of fulfilling the will of God. Therefore he lost his pleasure, his power, and his life. With many different manifestations, this is the one sin which brings about human ruin. The breath of every man is in the hands of God, and so also are the ways of each. Let life respond to that fact, rather than rebel against it.

Now his windows were open in his chamber toward Jerusalem.—Dan. 6. 10.

The Revisers have accurately, and helpfully, put these words in parenthesis.

They constitute for us an open window through which we see the secret of Daniel's loyalty. By this time, he was in a position of power under Darius. The other rulers envied him, and laid a cunning plot to bring him into trouble. The temptation created for him by this plot was not to the committal of any positive sin or act of idolatry. It was rather to the neglect of a habit of his religious life. He had only to abstain from prayer for thirty days, and their plot would be frustrated. But this he could not do. Dr. Driver's rendering of this verse is helpful: "Now he had in his roof-chamber open windows fronting Jerusalem." In a flash we see the habitual life of Daniel. There, on the roof of his house was an extra chamber; and it was so built that its open windows fronted Jerusalem. That was his house of prayer. There, three times a day, he worshipped his God, asking what he needed, and giving praise. His eyes were ever toward the city of the great King, while his heart held communion with Him. Around that attitude and activity, all his life was ordered. To neglect that for a single day would have spelt disaster to such a man as this. Therefore he could do none other than he did. When our lives are centred in God, we can ever afford to leave circumstances to the compulsion of the One in Whom we trust. The occasional is always affected by the habitual. Then let the habitual for us be ever that of windows fronting Jerusalem, and the heart in communion with God.

. . . Behold, the four winds of heaven brake forth upon the great sea. Dan. 7. 2.

With this chapter we begin the second section of this book. In the first six chapters we have been made conscious of the historic night in the midst of which Daniel lived; and we have seen something of the influence he exerted upon the great world-powers in the midst of which he held high office. The rest of the book is occupied with the prophetic light given to him, and through him to us. In this chapter we have the account of a vision which came to him in the first year of the reign of Belshazzar. Inclusively, it was a vision of the succession of four great world-powers; and their final overthrow in a Kingdom of the Son of Man and the saints, which is the Kingdom of the Most High. The student will compare this vision with that of Nebuchadnezzar, which Daniel had interpreted (chapter 2); and in doing so will see the same development of world-powers, moving to the same consummation. I have stressed these words because they afford a fundamental revelation. Looking out over the great and troubled sea of human affairs, Daniel saw these great world-powers emerging from that sea; but they were forced to their appearance by "the four winds of heaven,"

which "brake forth upon the great sea." The final authority did not rise out of that sea. But those which did, came forth under the compulsion of those heavenly winds. God has never yielded up human affairs. Men work out that of evil which is in them to complete manifestation; and they do so under Divine compulsion.

He shall also stand up against the Prince of princes; but he shall be broken without hand.—Dan. 8. 25.

The vision of Daniel recorded in this chapter came to him in the third year of Belshazzar. As the explanation of it, given by Gabriel, shows, it was concerned with the overthrow of the Medo-Persian empire, by that of the Greeks. It was a remarkably lucid foretelling of all that came to pass, and especially of the doings of Antiochus Epiphanes. His pride carried him so far that by his actions he openly challenged and defied God, as he violated His sanctuary. The title of "Epiphanes" which he assumed, means "Manifest," and the assumption of that title was in itself a claim of Deity. Thus he stood up against the Prince of princes. This is the logical issue of autocratic ambition. It sets itself against all rule and authority other than its own, and if it be successful over human competitors, it attempts to fling off the final authority, which is that of God; and this it does by claiming Divine power and authority for itself. This has happened again and again in human affairs; and it will happen at least once more, in the Man of Sin, the Antichrist. But when it does this, it comes to its doom, it falls upon Rock, and is broken without hand, that is, not by human intervention, but by the direct act of God. Antiochus died, not in battle, but by the swift stroke of God, taking the form of mental derangement. Whereas this vision of Daniel had to do primarily with Greece, its principles are of perpetual application, and will have their complete fulfilment in the final things of this age.

Seventy weeks are decreed.—Dan. 9. 24.

As the time approached for the ending of the seventy years of Jerusalem's desolation as foretold by Jeremiah, Daniel set himself to seek the Lord in repentance and prayer on behalf of his people. The prayer, as recorded in this chapter, was a great prayer, its urgency and intensity finding expression at last in short sharp sentences, "O Lord hear; O Lord forgive; O Lord hearken, and do; defer not; for Thine own sake, O my God, because Thy city and Thy people are called by Thy name." The answer to that prayer was the coming to Daniel of Gabriel, and the discovery to him of the times and seasons of Israel's trouble and restoration. This unveiling was singularly explicit. A period altogether of 490 years was involved, and this divided into three parts: first, seven weeks, i.e. forty-nine years; secondly, sixty-two weeks, i.e. four hundred and thirty-four years; finally, one week, i.e. seven years. The total is seventy weeks, i.e. four hundred and ninety years. The fulfilment of this prediction was literally accomplished. The sixty-nine weeks commenced with the decree of Cyrus, and ended at the Baptism of Jesus. There the seventieth week commenced. In the midst of it, the Messiah was cut off.

. . . For my comeliness was turned in me into corruption, and I retained no strength.—Dan. 10. 8.

The last three chapters of this book are closely related. They give us the account of the last of the visions of Daniel, and of the secrets revealed to him during the vision. The experience came to him in a time of great grief. We are not told the cause of his sorrow, but there is practically no room for doubt that he was filled with concern for his people and their future. The vision is described in this chapter, and the revelations are contained in the next two. The words which we have emphasized tell us the first effect produced upon Daniel by the glory of the Being upon Whom he looked. It is interesting to observe his references to this Being. He is described as "A man" (verse 5); "One in the likeness of the sons of men" (verse 16); and "One like the appearance of a man" (verse 18). Each time the description is accompanied by a declaration of contact, "A hand touched me" (verse 10); "One . . . touched my lips" (verse 16); and "There touched me again" (verse 18). The similarity of all to the experience of John in Patmos is self-evident (Rev. 1. 9–18). There are those who say John borrowed from Daniel. We do not think so; but, rather, that his own statement is true, and that he recorded what he saw. Then to Daniel the same One appeared, and we have here the most remarkable Christophany of the Old Testament. It is an arresting fact that such was the glory of this vision, that Daniel, a man more than once described as "greatly beloved," at sight of it was overcome with a sense of his utter unworthiness. A vision of Christ always produces this effect; but His touch is ever that of healing and strength.

And now will I shew thee the truth. —Dan. 11. 2.

Thus the revelations, given to Daniel by the glorious Being Whom he saw in vision, are introduced. They occupy the whole of this chapter, and the first few verses in chapter twelve. We should bear in mind that the vision and revelations were given to him in answer to his sadness of heart concerning his own people. The revelations would show him that, however the outlook on circumstances might perplex him, these were all clear to the mind of God, and that all things were moving forward to His predestined purpose. In this chapter we have a singularly full prediction of things which were to happen. To-day we may read it as history. It foretold the events of the Persian period under four kings briefly; and then the doings of Alexander, and the disruption of his empire at his death. It describes the compacts and conflicts between Antioch and Egypt; and then, most in detail, the period of Antiochus Epiphanes. Without a break, the revelation then overleapt centuries and millenniums, and described the final period in which for the children of the people of Daniel there would be "a time of trouble," issuing in deliverance, resurrection, and glory. That "time of trouble" followed swiftly the dark hour of the cutting off of Messiah. The story of the suffering of the Jews during the next generation is one of the most appalling in history. It came to its great climax with the fall of Jerusalem. The deliverance, resurrection, and glory are not yet.

But go thou thy way till the end be; for thou shalt rest, and shalt stand in thy lot, at the end of the days.—Dan. 12. 13.

These were the last words of the glorious Being of the vision to Daniel. At the close of the revelations he heard the clear and emphatic declaration that the period of trouble should last for three and a half years. This exactly coincided with the declaration made in the earlier vision as to the power of the final foe (see 7. 25); and with the reference to half the week of seven years in another vision (see 9. 27). The explicit statement left Daniel perplexed, and he asked: "O my Lord, what shall be the issue of these things?" The answer declared that these things were not for revelation then; and therefore that the attitude of faith and of blessedness was that of waiting. Then came these very last words, and they were full of light and comfort. Daniel would go to the grave; but it would be a going to rest and to waiting, not to the loss of actual realization. At the end of the days, when all the purposes of God should be accomplished, he would stand in his lot, that is, in his appointed place in the triumphant order. So Daniel and the whole host of souls who, of like faith, with him, fulfilled their earthly service, wait in that life where they count not time by years, until the consummation. When it comes, in the time Divinely appointed, all who shared the travail, will share the triumph. In the fullest sense we may use these words of all who, since the cutting off of Messiah, sleep in Jesus. Them, God will bring with Him, when He enters into the final glory of His Kingdom established on earth.

HOSEA

When the Lord spake at the first by Hosea, the Lord Jehovah said unto Hosea . . .—Hosea 1. 2.

These words are important, and must be rightly interpreted if we are to understand their significance. I think we are helped by adopting Ewald's rendering, "At the first, when Jehovah spoke with Hosea." The word *with* is unquestionably preferable to *by*. The reference is not to a message which Jehovah delivered through His servant; but to something which He spoke in communion with him. Again, the phrase *at the first* is important, as showing us that when this was written, the writer was looking back, and interpreting events in the light of the experience which those events produced. In these first three chapters we have an account of the tragedy which came to Hosea in his domestic life; of how through it all he lived in communion with God; and of how through that tragedy and that communion he was brought to a new understanding of the sin of Israel as it was felt by Jehovah Himself. In this chapter the tragedy itself does not appear, save as it is referred to in these opening sentences. Hosea was married to Gomer, and children were born; and as they came, they were named in such wise as to show the prophet's sense of the national outlook. There is no reason to think that Gomer had fallen into sin before marriage, nor in the early days of marriage. Hosea did not know that she was capable of infidelity. But God did, and He permitted His servant to pass through the suffering that he might understand the Divine heart. And the whole story proves how well worth while it was, for at last even Gomer was restored, as we shall see. How constantly the backward look reveals Divine guidance where it seemed most unlikely.

The valley of Achor for a door of hope.—Hosea 2. 15.

What a wonderful phrase that is, and perhaps more so when we translate Achor, and read: "The valley of troubling for a door of hope." We are now introduced to the tragedy in the life of the prophet. Gomer had proved unfaithful, and that in the worst way, being guilty not of adultery only, but of harlotry. But while his own heart was thus stricken, Hosea was still in communion with God about Israel, and preparing for his ministry to the people, perhaps already exercising it. Into that communion his personal sorrow entered, and Jehovah made it the means of making the prophet understand what the infidelity of Israel meant to Him. Thus the prophet's words pass almost at once into the language of Jehovah. The anger of Jehovah is that of wounded love, and His dealings with His people are to be characterized by the severity which grows out of such anger. Through stern discipline, Israel will be restored; that restoration being the purpose of the discipline: "The valley of troubling for a door of hope." It is easy to understand the wonder created in the soul of Hosea by all this. Suffering through the sin of Gomer, he was taught how great the sin of Israel was, as Jehovah interpreted His own suffering by the suffering of His servant. Having dealt with Gomer by cutting her off from himself he agreed with the rightness of the Divine judgment of Israel. But was not this a new revelation to him? Jehovah spoke of such discipline as a "valley of troubling for a door of hope!" How about Gomer? Is that how he had thought of the action which he had rightly taken in regard to her?

Go yet, love a woman beloved of her friend, and an adulteress, even as the Lord loveth the children of Israel. —Hosea 3. 1.

We ended our previous note with questions; and we think we were warranted in doing so. The prophet's experiences had interpreted the sin of Israel had vindicated the justice of her punishment. In communion he had learned the Divine purpose in that punishment; but he had taken no action with regard to Gomer. Now the word of Jehovah came to him as a command in these words. If Hosea learned the nature of Israel's sin from Gomer's, and so, the righteousness of the Divine rejection of Israel, he was now taught the nature of love in this command of Jehovah. The closeness of his fellowship with God is seen in his immediate obedience in regard to Gomer. How low she had sunk is revealed in the price he paid for her; and, indeed, in that he had to buy her. The price in money and kind amounted to about thirty shekels, the price of a slave, which in all probability she had literally become. Observe that the command of Jehovah was not to redeem her, but to love her; but her redemption was the necessary issue. Thus Hosea, through tragic experiences in his own life, was brought into closest fellowship with God, and prepared for his ministry to Israel. All through his messages the great notes are sounding, which tell of his understanding, of the appalling nature of sin; of the righteousness of the

Divine judgment; and supremely, of the unconquerable might of the Divine Love. It is indeed the love of God which "alters not when it alteration finds;" His is the love that "never faileth." All suffering on the part of His messengers is worth while, which brings them to such apprehension of sin, of judgment, of love.

Ephraim is joined to idols; let him alone.—*Hosea* 4. 17.

In the last eleven chapters of this book we have carefully edited notes, rather than verbatim reports of the prophetic utterances. These may be divided into three sections. The first (4. 1–6, 3) describes the pollution of the nation of Israel, and dealt with its cause. The cause was that of the pollution of the priests; which issued in the pollution of the whole nation. In the course of his prophesying to Israel, Hosea's mind turned to Judah, and he interpolated a message to the southern nation to beware of any complicity with Israel. This is the meaning of the words we have stressed. Ephraim was at the time the dominant tribe in Israel, and that accounts for the prophet's constant references to it (thirty-seven times the name occurs). This word has often been interpreted as constituting a sentence on Ephraim, as though Jehovah declared that He abandoned the nation altogether. But that were to contradict all the teaching of the prophet. It was rather a solemn word to Judah, warning her against any political alliance with Israel. The distinction is revealing. God does not abandon His people wholly, even when they are unfaithful to Him, but through discipline and troubling brings them back to Himself. Nevertheless, those who are loyal to Him, must stand aloof from the disloyal; they cannot have fellowship with those who are joined to idols. To the Christian Church the word of the apostle of love involves this, as indeed all his letter shows. We are thinking of that final injunction of this first epistle, "Little children, guard yourselves from idols."

I will go and return to My place, till . . .—*Hosea* 5. 15.

The word *till*, with which we end the quotation, is an arresting and illuminating word. In this chapter we have the prophet's special message to the priests, to the people, and to the king, concerning the national pollution, and the Divine judgments consequent thereupon. These latter are described in their progressive nature. First there was the judgment of the moth and rottenness. This was already upon them; they were sick and feeble, who should have been strong. Then there would be the judgment of calamity from without, suggested under the figure of the lion and the young lion, both hunters

of the prey. The final form was that of the Divine withdrawal. Jehovah declared that He would go and return to His place. This was the direst calamity necessarily which could befall this people. It will be remembered that much later, Ezekiel saw in visions this very thing happen in the case of Judah. It was in connection with his final phase of judgment that the prophet used this word *till*. The Divine withdrawal was not to be final; it was a method intended to produce a result which would make His return possible. "In their affliction they will seek Me earnestly," and when that is so, He returns. The ultimate glory of Ezekiel's vision was that he saw the return of Jehovah to His house and so to His people. That note is ever to be found in the words which speak of the judgments of Jehovah upon His people. When, long after these things, the Messiah had to pronounce a doom upon the city, and prolong the period of the desolation because He was rejected, we still find the word *till*; "Behold, your house is left unto you desolate; for I say unto you, Ye shall not see Me henceforth TILL ye shall say, Blessed is He that cometh in the name of the Lord."

Your goodness is as a morning cloud, and as the dew that goeth early away. —*Hosea* 6. 4.

With this fourth verse of the chapter, the second section of the prophetic messages commences. It runs on to the fifteenth verse of chapter 10, and is principally concerned with the punishment which must fall upon the polluted nation. In the first movement (verses 4–11 of this chapter), the whole case is stated briefly. The Divine desire was that of finding a way to bring the people to a deep repentance, and to the activity of mercy, and the knowledge of God. The human response was that of transgression, treachery, and the consequent ways of wickedness. Both Ephraim and Judah had their moments and moods of goodness, but they were evanescent, they did not last, they produced no permanent results. These manifestations of goodness were like a cloud in the morning, a mist coming up from the sea, too feeble to produce a harvest, being quickly dissipated by the blazing heat of the sun. What an arresting figure of speech this is, and how conscious we are that it accurately describes our goodness. In times of our wandering and disloyalty, we also have moments and moods of goodness. We realize the better way, we return to it, but we fail again and yet again. We need something far more than our own goodness to produce a life fruitful in holiness. Such fruit only comes from "a tree planted by the streams of water." That tree "bringeth forth its fruit in its season," and its "leaf also doth not wither." Human admiration of goodness and aspiration after it, do not result in realization. It is only as our human life is supplied by the Divine streams, that its goodness is abiding.

. . . He knoweth it not . . . He knoweth it not.—Hosea 7. 9.

This chapter contains the prophet's diagnosis of the disease of the nation. He declared that the desire of God to deal was frustrated by the pollution of the nation, and its wilful ignoring of God. In all this description there are no words more pathetic and tragic than these, twice repeated in this verse. The figure employed is that of a man, whose strength is being destroyed by strangers; and whose debility is manifesting itself to others—as witness his grey hairs—but he is ignorant of both things. That, said the prophet, was the condition of the nation of Israel. Its strength was devoured by its alliances; the signs of decadence were patent to the outside observer; but the nation was ignorant of the truth. That made the situation the more difficult. When a nation knows its weakness it is halfway to recovery. That is true also of a man. Can any condition be conceived of more tragic than that of this disease and decay of which the sufferer is all unconscious? Yet how often it has been the condition of nations. They maintain the outward semblance of vigour and freshness, by all sorts of artifices which deceive none except themselves. So also with men. Whether for nations or men, the only hope in such a case is that by some awakening word, or quickening judgment, the true consciousness may be created. The sense of departed strength, the discovery of grey hairs, may be the way of healing and restoration. To bring men and nations to such sense, to such discovery; God is ever acting, by prophetic word, and punitive act.

Set the trumpet to thy mouth.—Hosea 8. 1.

The words constitute an abrupt and startling command, evidently given to the prophet. He was commanded to warn the nation of imminent judgment. This he did in one short, sharp sentence: "As an eagle he cometh against the house of Jehovah." The next word, "Because," introduces the main burden of this message, which is that of the clear statement of the reasons for the calamity. The first is that of transgression and trespass, that is, wilful disobedience to law. The second is that of rebellion, as revealed in the setting up of kings and princes, not of Divine ordination. The third is that of idolatry, the making of false representations of God—the calf of Samaria. The fourth is that of seeking aid in alliances with other nations. The fifth is that of erecting false altars, and desecrating those of Jehovah. Thus, in brief sentences, the prophet recapitulated the statements of the sins of the nation which all the prophets denounced. Finally, he described the whole situation as to national sin and Divine retribution, in the words: "Israel hath forgotten his Maker, and builded palaces; and Judah hath multiplied fortified cities; but I will send a fire upon his cities, and it shall devour the castles thereof." Whenever a nation forsakes God it ensures its ruin. It may, for a time, dwell in luxury, building palaces; and give itself a sense of security, by fortifying its cities; but sooner or later the Divine fire will destroy the cities, and devour the castles. There is no true pleasure, nor any real security, but such as are found in the maintenance of right relationships with God. "Except Jehovah build the house, they labour in vain that build it: Except Jehovah keep the city, the watchman waketh but in vain."

My God will cast them away, because they did not hearken unto Him; and they shall be wanderers among the nations.—Hosea 9. 17.

The prophet in this message described the whirlwind of calamity which would overtake Israel for her pollutions. He forbade all indulgence in false merriment, and declared that all the reasons for joy would be taken away. The people moreover would be carried into exile. The prophetic word would cease. Their fornications would be punished by childlessness. The words we have emphasized constituted the last statement of the prophet concerning the nation. The people were to be castaway of God, and were to be wanderers among the nations. The word wanderers has the sense of fugitives, those who are away from their home, and not able to find a home. They are not refugees among the nations. Refugees are those who are hospitably welcomed. Fugitives are not welcomed. This word of Hosea has had long and wide fulfilment. The people of God are still His people. Their separation from other peoples has never ceased. But they are wanderers, fugitives, homeless ones; and they will never find their home until they find it in right relationship with the God to Whom they would not hearken. Long after Hosea's time, He came to them in the Person of His Son. They cast Him out. Therefore the discipline continues. It is discipline, and not destruction. They will yet be brought home, and that through the One Whom they rejected. And that will be a glorious thing for the world; "For if the casting away of them is the reconciling of the world what shall the receiving of them be, but life from the dead?" (Rom. 11. 15.)

Israel is a luxuriant vine, which putteth forth his fruit . . .—Hosea 10. 1.

With this chapter the second section of the prophecy ends—that in which the theme was that of the punishment of pollution. It consists of one message which is in the nature of recapitulation and appeal. In the two opening verses the whole case is stated, both as to the national failure; and as to the Divine judgment. In these particular words, interpreted by those immediately following, the fact of failure is inclusively declared. The prophet employed the figure of speech so often employed by these servants of God in the old time—and presently by our Lord Himself in His teaching—that of the vine. That they should do so was inevitable, for the vine was the national emblem, the symbol of the purpose of God in the creation of the nation. The whole emphasis in these words of Hosea must be placed upon the pronoun "*his*." The sin of the nation was that it had failed to bear the fruit of Jehovah, and had borne instead its own fruit. "According to the multitude of *his* fruit he hath multiplied *his* altars." Isaiah stressed the same matter when he said that the vine had brought forth wild grapes, instead of grapes; and later, Jeremiah described Judah as "the degenerate plant of a strange vine." Here is a test for the people of God at all times. All their resources are Divinely bestowed; and that with a view to the production of fruit according to the purpose of God. When they prostitute those very resources to the bearing of fruit to suit their own desires and purposes, they are guilty of the basest failure. The figure of fruit-bearing wherever found, suggests the producing of that which is according to the will of God; and that on behalf of others. Fruit is never for self-consumption. To receive gifts from God, and to consume them upon our own lusts, that is, upon our own desires, is the uttermost in sin.

How shall I give thee up, Ephraim? —Hosea 11. 8.

The last four chapters of this book contain the final section of the prophet's messages. Their dominant note is that of the love of Jehovah. To read them intelligently it is necessary to observe the portions which give the words of Jehovah, and those which record those of the prophet. These alternate, and it is worth while setting that out—Jehovah, 11.-12. 1; Hosea, 12. 2–6; Jehovah, 12. 7–11; Hosea, 12. 12–13. 1; Jehovah, 13. 2–14; Hosea, 13. 15–14. 3; Jehovah, 14. 4–8. Throughout the words of Jehovah are words of love; while those of Hosea trace the history of Israel, show the national failure, and thus throw up into clearer relief the wonderful love of Jehovah. In the love messages of Jehovah, the first movement sets forth the past love of Jehovah, "When Israel was a child, then I loved him;" and reveals the continuity of that love. That is the meaning of this question: "How shall I give thee up, Ephraim?" and of these which follow. How radiant is this revelation of the heart of God. It is the cry of a Father concerning His child. The child has forgotten the Father, turned away from Him, rebelled against His authority, despised His love. There is no reason in justice why the child should not be given up, completely cut off. But there is a reason. It is found in love. Love cries out in protest: "How shall I give thee up?" What is the answer? It is that love does not give the loved one up; but rather finds the way by which the uttermost claims of justice may be met, and the glory of holiness maintained, and the loved-one regained, restored, kept by love. That is exactly what grace has done; and that at infinite and unfathomable cost.

He is a trafficker, the balances of deceit are in his hand, he loveth to oppress.—Hosea 12. 7.

These are again the words of Jehovah. They are exclamatory, and vibrant with sarcasm. The words "He is" are supplied by translators, and while giving a smooth and not inaccurate reading, rob the word of some of its force. It would be better rendered as an exclamation, "A trafficker!" As a matter of fact even that is interpretation, rather than translation. The literal rendering would be "Canaan!" Thus Jehovah calls Israel by the name of the peoples which Israel had been called to extirpate by reason of their corruptions. That is satire of the most biting kind. Yet it was true. Read this exclamation in close connection with the immediately preceding word of Jehovah (11. 13–12. 1); and with those directly following (12. 8); and this will be seen, Israel had sought, and apparently found, material wealth, and claimed that she had done so honestly. This Jehovah denied. She had practised deceit and falsehood, and had sunk to the level of Canaan. These words of Jehovah prove the falseness of that specious saying "Love is blind." Love is never blind. It sees most clearly. Jehovah's love for Israel drew forth the great cry "How shall I give thee up?" But Jehovah was not blind, nor could He permit Himself to be. Love never fails to see sin; and love insists on bringing sin into the light. It will not permit it to find a hiding place; it exposes all its subterfuges. Love calls sin by its right name, and portrays it in all its corruption. And all this because it is Love. That which excuses, condones, palliates sin, is not love. It is folly, and at last complicity with sin.

I will ransom them from the power of the grave; I will redeem them from death. O death, where are thy plagues? O grave, where is thy destruction? Repentance shall be hid from Mine eyes.—*Hosea 13. 14.*

These also are the words of Jehovah, and they reach the highest point in the declaration of His love. At first, He declared His past love. "When Israel was a child, then I loved him"; then, He revealed His present love; now, He affirmed the persistent continuity of that love. The outlook embraces the whole of life and beyond, including the grave and death. From these, love will ransom and redeem. Love, in its might, challenges these dark forces: "O death, where are thy plagues? O Sheol, where is thy destruction?" and then declares that, concerning this determination to ransom and redeem, even from the grave and death, there will be no repentance, that is, no change of mind or action. This was a great word, and very remarkable, in those days, when as yet life and immortality had not been clearly brought to light. It shows how wonderfully Hosea had come to an apprehension of the love of Jehovah. He realized that nothing could be powerful enough to hinder the victorious operation of that love. Before that love, death and the grave stood challenged, and defeated. We do not wonder that Paul, writing in the full light and glory of the resurrection of the Lord, and knowing what that resurrection meant to men, should recall these words of Hosea, and adapting them to his argument, make them the prelude to his final note of victory and praise; "Thanks be to God, Who giveth us the victory through our Lord Jesus Christ" (1 Cor. 15. 57).

Ephraim shall say: What have I to do any more with idols? I have answered and will regard Him; I am like a green fir tree; from me is Thy fruit found.—*Hosea 14. 8.*

Once more we have the words of Jehovah. They constitute the Divine prediction of the ultimate victory of the Divine Love. The name Ephraim means fruitfulness, and that thought has been present throughout. When the prophet was dealing with the punishment of pollution, he had declared that Israel was a luxuriant vine, producing its own fruit (see 10. 1 and my note). Now the word of Jehovah stands in direct and intended contrast to that. The day will come when Ephraim will say to Jehovah: "From me is *Thy* fruit found." As in the former passage, we pointed out that the "*his*" was emphatic, so here let us note that the "*Thy*" is emphatic. The day will come when Ephraim, that is, Israel as the vine of God, will bring forth the fruit which He seeks; no longer wild grapes, but the grapes of His culture. And that will be when Ephraim is completely redeemed from idols, and answers and regards Jehovah. Then will be the time of abounding life, out of which the true fruit will come. That will result as the victory of the love of Jehovah. Note the opening words of this final message of Jehovah: "I will heal their backsliding; I will love them freely." Thus, this most wonderful book ends in a song of triumphant love. This is the more arresting from the fact that no prophecy more clearly reveals the appalling character of sin, and the terrible nature of judgment. Yet love is its master note. Indeed, it is this which reveals the sinfulness of sin, and vindicates the righteousness of judgment. That amazing love, which Hosea so radiantly set forth, found its ultimate and complete revelation, in the fulness of time, in the Son of God's love, and in the awe-inspiring mystery of His Cross.

JOEL

Alas for the day! for the day of the Lord is at hand.—Joel 1. 15.

Joel was a prophet to Judah. His message, as found in this book, seems to be one; rather than the notes of a long period of ministry as in the case of Hosea to Israel. The occasion of its delivery was that of the desolation of the land by a locust plague. In the beginning of this chapter, we have his description of that desolation, and from it we learn how terrible it was. It was an hour in which men would be likely to brood upon the calamity, moved very largely by pity for

themselves. Then the prophet spoke, and his word interpreted the situation, and called men to recognize the real meaning of the calamities in the midst of which they were living. This was the Day of Jehovah, which meant that it was the Day of Divine government and activity. The coming of the locusts was no accident. They came in ranks, in order; and they wrought the will of God. Therefore the prophet called the priests and the people to humiliation. Here then is the first note of this prophecy. The burden of Joel from first to last was that of the Day of Jehovah, that is, the fact of the Divine government of human affairs; and his first application of that burden was that of calling the people to a recognition of the fact that the Day of Jehovah was then present, it was at hand: that is, it was near, not in the sense of approaching, but rather in the sense of actual and immediate activity. There is more to say—as we shall see—but let this first fact be carefully noted. The Day of Jehovah is here and now. He is reigning to-day. The calamities through which men pass, are all under His control. Instead of mourning over sorrow, men should mourn over sin, and cry unto Jehovah.

The Day of the Lord cometh; for it is nigh at hand.—Joel 2. 1.

In these words we have the same fundamental idea, but stated with a variation in method. Having interpreted the locust plague, by declaring that the Day of Jehovah was at hand, the prophet now said: "The Day of Jehovah cometh, for it is nigh at hand." In that sentence the word "for" has the force of "because." The truth emphasized now was not so much that of the actuality of the Divine government, as that of its continuity. Joel declared that the Day of Jehovah was not over. There were still other experiences before them of the Divine judgment. Under the figure of the locust plague, he described the imminent invasion of a foe which would bring far more terrible desolations to the people. Therefore again he called the nation to repentance, and declared the way by which they might change the very character of the Divine government into that of mercy, and healing, and restoration. Here again is a matter for our careful attention. The Day of Jehovah is not only present; it is always coming. When some great activity of God has ended, His government has not ceased. He proceeds upon His way without intermission. If by one manifestation of His power and majesty, men do not learn the lessons He would teach, then they have not escaped from Him. By yet other means, more terrible than those

already experienced, He will make Himself known. This is the story of humanity; and so it will continue until "the great and terrible Day of Jehovah come," the day of the final putting forth of His judgment of evil in order to the establishment of His Kingdom upon earth according to the grace of His heart.

The day of the Lord is near in the valley of decision.—Joel 3. 14.

Once again we have the same burden, but in its final application. The prophet having interpreted the locust plague and foretold a further activity of God in government, was lifted up, and borne along far beyond his own immediate times. That movement began in the previous chapter, at verse 28, with the words, "And it shall come to pass afterward." That afterward carried his vision forward to the age of the Spirit which commenced on the day of Pentecost. Two verses only deal with that age (28 and 29). He then told of the signs which would indicate the ending of that age, and the ushering in of another which he described as "the great and terrible day of Jehovah." The final movement in his message has to do with that ultimate Day of Jehovah, the day of decision. In that day, Jehovah will restore Judah and Jerusalem, find His lost people Israel, deal with the nations through the processes of war, make Zion the centre of His earthly Kingdom, and Israel as a complete nation the instrument of His government. Thus to Joel was given the plan of the ages. He saw the near, the imminent, and the ultimate; and he saw that the Day of Jehovah was present, persistent, powerful, to the complete realization of Divine purpose. It was a great vision, and our secret of confidence is found in walking in its light. We live in the unmeasured age of the Spirit. It has lasted over nineteen hundred years. We know not when it will end; but we do know that beyond it is "the great and terrible day of Jehovah"; and therefore we are sure of the ultimate realization of all His purposes for men.

AMOS

Thus saith the Lord; For three transgressions of Damascus, yea, for four.—Amos 1. 3.

Amos was a man of Judah, who was sent by God to prophesy in Israel. In this book we have the notes of his ministry. No prophet, in the technical sense of the word; nor the son of a prophet, that is he had no training in the schools of the prophets, he nevertheless was a veritable prophet of God. His outlook upon the

Divine government was of the widest. He saw God judging, not Judah and Israel only, but all the nations. The first section of the book contains eight oracles concerning the nations, setting forth this fact. Each one of them is introduced by these words, "For three transgressions . . . . yea, for four." The language is patently figurative, rather than mechanical. The truth thus emphasized with reference to all the nations is that of the Divine patience, and justice. Upon all these nations the wrath of God was to fall, but not until their persistence in wickedness was such as to leave no room for any other method of dealing with them. The "three transgressions" represent fulness of iniquity; but when that becomes "four," then the iniquity has passed beyond the bounds of the Divine patience. This is ever the law of God's dealings with nations. The stroke of His judgment never falls until sin has become so complete that there is no room for the exercise of mercy. When that is so, His judgments inevitably come, and that in the interest of humanity as a whole. A careful reading of these declamations will show that the national sins against which God proceeds, are ever those of wrong done to other nations.

Ye gave the Nazirites wine to drink; and commanded the prophets, saying, Prophesy not.—Amos 2. 12.

It is noticeable that Amos included Judah and Israel among the nations. This method in itself must have been an arresting one to the people of that Northern Kingdom. Both Judah and Israel had come to think of themselves as separated in some privileged way from surrounding nations. In some senses they were right, but they had failed to understand that their privileges created yet greater responsibilities. This is what Amos desired to enforce, and he did so first by stressing the fact that God was ruling over all the nations, and doing so upon the same principles. The greater the light, therefore, the graver the responsibility. The last of these oracles concerned Israel, and he was careful to show the nature of her sin. He charged the nation with injustice, avarice, oppression, immorality, profanity, blasphemy, and sacrilege. In the words we have quoted, we have the statement of the uttermost and basest element in their sin. In the preceding sentences the prophet declared that Jehovah had raised up prophets for them, and had given them Nazirites, men who by the purity of their lives testified against their corruption. So determined had they become in their courses of evil that they had seduced the Nazirites from loyalty, and had silenced the voices of their prophets. Beyond this it is impossible to go in evil. When men deliberately set themselves to corrupt the pure, and to silence the prophets, they are indeed beyond the hope of recovery by mercy. Then the pressure of the Divine wrath is inevitable.

You only have I known of all the families of the earth; therefore I will visit upon you all your iniquities.— Amos 3. 2.

Having uttered his oracles concerning God's government of all the nations, and having included Judah and Israel among them, Amos proceeded to deliver his special message to Israel. This he did in three discourses, each beginning with the formula, "Hear this word" (3. 1; 4. 1; 5. 1). The first of these is contained in this chapter, it deals with Jehovah's verdict and sentence. The words I have quoted are the opening words of Jehovah's indictment. They explicitly state the principle to which we referred in our last note, namely, that in the Divine government privilege creates responsibility. The word which must have startled those who heard this message into attention was the word *therefore*. Observe what effect it had upon the whole. The first part was a declaration of privilege superlatively made: "You only have I known of all the families of the earth." That was true. In no other people had God made Himself known in the same way. Of them we may use the words of one of the greatest of their sons, Paul: "Whose is the adoption, and the glory, and the covenants, and the giving of the law, and the service of God, and the promises; whose are the fathers." This being so, said the Lord by His servant, "*Therefore*, I will visit upon you all your iniquities." The false deduction which is too often made is that if we are the privileged people of God, *therefore* we may look for His mercy, He will not punish us. That is not so. The measure of our privilege, in the Divine economy, is the measure of our responsibility. Therefore if we fail to fulfil that responsibility He will not pass over our sins, but rather will visit upon us all our iniquities. It is well that those nations who boast of the Divine favour, should lay this lesson to heart.

Proclaim freewill offerings and publish them.—Amos 4. 5.

This chapter contains the second message introduced by the words "Hear this word." Its burden was that of the summons of Jehovah, found in verse 12: "Prepare to meet thy God O Israel." That was not a call to repentance, and to such attitudes as would prevent punishment, although many preachers have used the text in that way. It was a summons to judgment, and that as punishment, because there had been no repentance. Everything in the message led up to that summons. The words we have emphasized occur in a passage vibrant with sarcasm, in which the prophet mocked at the futility of the religious observances of the polluted people. This was the last phase to which he referred. Freewill offerings were not obligatory; they were spontaneous. Special reference had been made to them by Moses (see Deut. 12). They were supposed to result from the devotion of the heart to Jehovah. This was their distinctive value. Here, then, is seen the sting of Amos' word. These people were making such offerings, but they were publishing them, announcing them, making them known to others. The motive, then, was not the love of Jehovah, but the desire to appear as lovers of Jehovah to other men. Such a motive vitiates the gift. This was the disqualifying element in the religion of the scribes and Pharisees in the days of our Lord (see Matt. 23. 5). The light from such a word is a very searching one. What effect has it, as it shines on our names in modern subscription lists? If our gift was to the Lord, the fact that our names are published does not rob it of value. If we gave to have our names in the list, the Lord rejects the gift.

Woe unto you that desire the Day of the Lord.—*Amos* 5. 18.

The last of the great proclamations of Amos introduced by the formula, "Hear this word," occupies this and the next chapter. It opened with a lamentation followed by an explanation of the reason of the sorrows of the people. This prepared the way for the uttering of two great denunciations, each beginning with the word "Woe." These denunciations reveal two classes of people, both wrong in their attitude. Perhaps this first woe is the more startling. There were people who were evidently in some measure conscious of the evil times in which they were living; they were desirous of the day of Jehovah, because they expected it would bring better times to them; they maintained therefore all the external observances of religion. These were thus denounced. The reason of their desire was wrong, and their interpretation of the Day of Jehovah was false. The prophet warned them that the Day of Jehovah would be a day of darkness and not of light; a day in which they would not be able to escape His wrath. Their hypocrisies were denounced in tremendous words, the words of Jehovah: "I hate . . . I despise . . . I take no delight . . . I will not accept . . . I will not regard . . . I will not hear . . ." Let us lay to heart the teaching. To desire the Day of Jehovah, if the life be out of harmony with its principles of righteousness and judgment is folly, and more, it is wickedness. The one glorious hope of humanity may become a curse and a blight if it is wrongly interpreted, and so fails to produce the character which is in accord with that hope.

Woe to them that are at ease in Zion, and to them that are secure in the mountain of Samaria.—*Amos* 6. 1.

This is the second of the denunciatory "Woes." Here another attitude of mind is revealed. Its secret is declared in the words, "Ye that put far away the evil day." This is entirely different from desiring the Day of Jehovah. These were people who perhaps recognized the fact that the Day of Jehovah would be a day of judgment and of wrath; but they did not believe it was near. They did not expect to be involved in its calamities, so they cared nothing for its principles. Therefore, they gave themselves up to the life of sensuality which the prophet described in graphic fashion. They stretched themselves on divans, gave full satisfaction to their appetites, amused themselves with music, sought exhilaration in drink, and banished all concern as to the true condition of the nation, "the affliction of Joseph." This is the more common attitude of the human heart toward the whole subject of a coming Day of God. When in regard to these things men become "mockers," they are always found "walking after their own ungodly lusts" (Jude 18). It is noticeable that the prophet flung back this word of warning to Judah also, as he spoke of those "at ease in Zion," as well as of those that were "secure in the mountain of Samaria." And verily the principle is of abiding application. To be "at ease in Zion," or "secure in the mountain of Samaria," or content in the things which minister to carnal appetites, while the laws of God are being broken and the ways of life corrupted because the Divine judgment is conceived of as distant, is of the very essence of evil. Against all such attitudes and activities the word of God utters its "Woe!"

And the Lord took me . . . and the Lord said unto me, Go, prophesy.—*Amos* 7. 15.

In the last three chapters we have the third phase in the ministry of Amos. It consisted of five visions of the process of the Divine judgment against Israel. The first four are introduced by words in which the prophet claimed that the visions were given to him by God; the first, the second, and the fourth, "Thus the Lord Jehovah showed me"; and the third, "Thus He shewed me." The fifth was a vision of Jehovah, and opens with the words, "I saw the Lord." The first two, those of the locusts and the fire, revealed judgment threatened and restrained. The third, that of the plumbline, revealed the hopeless failure of the nation, and the consequent inevitability of punishment. When Amos uttered that note, Amaziah interfered. He reported Amos to Jeroboam, and charged the prophet to return to Judah. The words we have selected are those in which Amos declared to Amaziah the authority for his mission. This herdman from Tekoa was what in the speech of to-day would be called an "irregular" because technically an untrained man. This is what he meant when he said, "I was no prophet, neither was I a prophet's son." But he had the only prophetic qualification; he was called and sent by God. When this is so, the technicalities of regularity are of no moment; and when it is not so, they are of no value. Let a man know himself called and sent by God, then there will be no hesitancy or fear in his heart. Only, let him be indeed sure of this, or in spite of all "training" he will lack authority and power.

I will send a famine . . . of hearing the words of the Lord.—*Amos 8. 11.*

After the encounter with Amaziah, Amos proclaimed the fact that judgment was nigh at hand, as he described the vision of "a basket of summer fruit." The figure revealed the ripeness of the hour, as to the fullness of Israel's sin, and as to the harvest of Divine wrath. In an impassioned address he denounced the money-makers for their greed and cruelty; and described the terror of the Divine judgment. Then, in one of the most striking passages in prophetic literature, he described the curse which follows courses of wilful wickedness, such as the nation had been guilty of. They would experience a famine—not, let it be observed, of the words of Jehovah, but "of *hearing* the words of Jehovah." The condition described is that of being deaf to the words of Jehovah, not able to hear them. It is that of the death of spiritual sensibility. It is not a case of God withholding His revelation; but of people being in such a state that they do not see it, do not hear the words. When this is so, the soul does not cease to need what that word only can supply; and so men hunt for it, search for it, but to no avail. The issue is that of the failing of strength, even in the strongest; "the fair virgins and the young men faint for thirst." Here we have an explanation of the feverishness, the restlessness of human life. Men wander and travel, and seek for any and every new sensation to satisfy the craving of their deepest life. But all to no purpose. Only the words of Jehovah can meet the need, and when there is a famine of hearing them, the end is destruction.

. . . Yet shall not the least grain fall upon the earth.—*Amos 9. 9.*

In this chapter we have the last of the prophet's visions of judgment. It is contained in the first ten verses. It is one of the most awe-inspiring visions in the Bible. Jehovah was revealed to Amos, standing by the altar; and the stroke of His judgment was seen to be irresistible. But it was reasonable and discriminative, and the fact is declared with great force in these words. The house of Israel was to be sifted "among all the nations like as grain is sifted in a sieve; *yet shall not the least kernel fall upon the earth.*" This is ever so. The judgments of God never involve the righteous with the wicked in punishment and destruction. In the process of that judgment, the righteous do suffer with and for the guilty; but such suffering is never destructive. It is often healing and constructive, and becomes the way in which the righteous have highest and fullest communion with God Himself. The ultimate purpose of judgment is set forth in the last message of Amos which immediately follows, and with which the book closes. It is a message of restoration. The opening phrase of it, "In that day," connects it with all that has preceded it, and so interprets for us the purpose of God in His activity in wrath. Thus the final word is vibrant with the hope which is born of the certainty of the ultimate triumph of love; and this declaration that "not the least kernel shall fall upon the earth" assures us that in all the terrible and fiery processes made inevitable by human sin, nothing of real worth will be destroyed. When He thoroughly cleanses His threshing floor, "He will gather *His wheat* into the garner;" it is "*the chaff* He will burn up with unquenchable fire."

OBADIAH

The Kingdom shall be the Lord's.— *Obadiah 21.*

That has ever been the ultimate hope of the men of faith. The prophets of God have always insisted upon His present and active sovereignty; but they have also declared with perfect unanimity that the day will come when that sovereignty will have its perfect victory in the subjugation of all things to Himself in the mind and heart and will of man. That victory is not yet. Men are in His Kingdom, but not willingly. Therefore, they know nothing of the peace and joy which are His will for them. They fight against righteousness, and so fail to find peace and joy, because righteousness fights against them. When in the final order, righteousness is the condition of human life, peace and joy will inevitably follow. That is what we pray for when we say, "Thy Kingdom come." Faith is the assurance that this prayer will be answered. These final words of Obadiah's prophecy are the more remarkable, seeing that the burden of his message was that of the doom of Edom, the people who had persistently opposed Israel, and practised cruelty towards her. For this sin God would bring her down from her high and proud place, and utterly despoil her; and Israel should be given possession of her rightful inheritance. Having uttered this message, the prophet rose to a greater height, and saw the outworking of the Divine sovereignty, bringing deliverance even to Edom. Out of Zion saviours would come to judge the Mount of Esau, and then "the Kingdom shall be Jehovah's." That remains the one hope for the world; and it is the one sufficient secret of confidence in all the days of darkness and travail which lead to the victory.

JONAH

. . . But Jonah rose up to flee unto Tarshish from the presence of the Lord. —Jonah 1. 3.

That is to say, in modern speech, that he resigned his office as a prophet of Jehovah. He had exercised that office with good effect in dark and difficult times in the history of Israel (see 2 Kings 14. 25). Now he determined not to continue longer in that office. A command had come to him to go to Nineveh, which lay overland to the north-east. He left his country by water, setting his face west, to a port at the far end of the Great Sea. Why did he do this? The answer is found in his own words later in the story: ". . . I hasted to flee unto Tarshish, for I knew that Thou art a gracious God, and merciful, slow to anger, and abundant in lovingkindness, and repentest Thee of the evil." Let these words be most carefully pondered. Jonah fled because he knew God well. His resignation was not due to ignorance of God, but rather to accurate understanding. He was commissioned to proceed to Nineveh, and cry against it on account of its wickedness. He knew that if he did this, and Nineveh should repent, God would spare it. This was what he did not want God to do. The cruelties of Nineveh had been brutal, and in the heart of Jonah there was no pity for her. He was in complete sympathy with the righteousness of God proceeding to punish the wicked; but he had no sympathy with the Divine compassions. Therefore he fled. This is the story of breakdown on a high level, but it is breakdown. A passion for righteousness, which makes us vindictive and incapable of forgiveness, even in the case of those as cruel as Nineveh, puts us out of fellowship with God. Let us not forget that Jonah had the courage of his convictions, and the decency to pay his fare when he ran away!

Then Jonah prayed unto the Lord his God out of the fish's belly.— Jonah 2. 1.

The "then" reminds us of the events following the flight of the prophet. Jonah was a true prophet, a real servant of Jehovah, and one who knew Him well, as we have said. Jehovah does not allow such a man to escape Him easily. Circumstances were in his favour; he "found a ship going to Tarshish;" he paid his fare and embarked. Then God began to act. He "sent out a great wind upon the sea." Jonah understood the storm. He said to the mariners, "I know that for my sake this great tempest is upon you." At his own request, they cast him into the sea. "And Jehovah prepared a great fish to swallow up Jonah." Out of that grave in the deep the prophet prayed. Let that prayer be considered, and it will be seen how fitting it was. It was made up of quotations from the psalmody of Israel, just such quotations as would occur to one familiar with that literature, in such an hour of mystery and darkness. It referred to circumstances of darkness and affliction, but persistently celebrated the delivering power of God. But carefully observe that there was not a line in it which suggested any yielding on the part of this man to the compassion of God as it might move out towards Nineveh. It was personal from first to last. Twenty-four occurrences of the personal pronoun in the first person singular! The prayer does reveal, however, that the sense of his relation to Jehovah had become more acute. At least he had discovered that he could not easily sever relationship with Him.

And the word of the Lord came unto Jonah the second time.—Jonah 3. 1.

That is a word of pure grace. It is in many ways the central light of this wonderful prophetic story. Judging by human standards, the highest and best of them, we are inclined to say that when a messenger of Jehovah had so broken down as to withdraw from his work and decline to deliver a Divine message because he did not desire results to be produced by it which might conflict with his own conception of what was due to righteousness, by such act he had for ever disqualified himself for service. But it was not so in the thought of God. He did not cast away His servant because of this failure. He gave him his second chance. "The word of Jehovah came unto Jonah the second time." There is nothing to be said except to utter words of wonder and amazement and thanksgiving that it was so, and that it is so yet. How many of us who have been called to deliver the word of Jehovah, would still be doing it, if it were not for this patient and perfecting grace of God? Surely not many! How have we failed Him, and broken down in our ministry; and often not on ground so high as that of Jonah's failure. It is all of His mercy that we have not been completely cast away from our holy work. In hours of our failure and deflection, He has led us through dark and dismal experiences, in which we have found Him anew, and out of the very "belly of Sheol" have cried to Him. Then has He delivered us. That in itself has been a wonder of grace. But to this He has added the yet greater wonder, that He has entrusted us again with His Word, and sent us forth to deliver it. Such grace keeps the soul in the dust of self-distrust; but lifts it to the height of confidence and loyalty.

I do well to be angry even unto death.—*Jonah 4. 9.*

These are the last recorded words of Jonah in this story, and they are positively startling. God gave him his second chance, and he obeyed, going to Nineveh, and delivering the Divine message. The result had been as he himself expected. The city had repented, and her judgment for the time was averted. Jonah was angry. He had made no advance. He was not in sympathy with the compassion of God. It is a remarkable ending. But is that the ending? Hardly. There are two things to be said. The first is that God is revealed as still patient with His servant, talking to him, giving him the chance to utter his anger, and to complain, and in gentlest way arguing with him as to the falseness of his position. The second is that Jonah wrote the story. That in itself is evidence that he was brought at last into sympathy with the heart of God, for the value of this writing for his own people was that it rebuked the spirit of vindictiveness and revealed the Divine grace. The reading of the story carries us on to the days of One Who said of Himself, "A greater than Jonah is here"; One Who was as perfectly in sympathy with the righteousness of God as Jonah, and infinitely more so, but Who had complete fellowship with the compassion of God. He it was Who in order to fulfil righteousness gave Himself to bearing the sin of the world. It is ours to have the mind of Christ. We need, therefore, the warning of this book, and its encouragement also.

MICAH

Hear ye peoples, all of you. . . .— *Micah 1. 2.*

Micah was a prophet to the people of God contemporary with Isaiah and Hosea. His messages were concerned with Samaria and Jerusalem, the capitals respectively of the Northern and Southern kingdoms, as being the centres of national thought and action. Their burden was that of authority. He denounced the false, and announced the true. The book contains three discourses, each commencing with the same formula "Hear" (see 1. 2; 3. 1 and 6. 1). The words we have emphasized constitute the introduction to the first of these. Necessarily the message was for the nation to which he spoke, but he couched it in the form of an address to all nations; and to the whole earth. The burden of the message is that of declaring the coming judgment of God upon the chosen nation on account of its apostasy. The nations are called upon to listen to this message, and to witness the Divine judgment. Micah recognized the Divine purpose of the chosen nation. It was to be the medium through which God bore witness concerning Himself to all the nations of the world. Israel, obedient to the Divine government, realized the blessings of the Divine government, and revealed its beneficence to the world. Israel disobedient to that law must be judged and punished, and thus the righteousness of the Divine government would be manifested to all the nations of the earth. Either in blessing or in blasting, Jehovah reveals Himself to the nations by His dealing with His ancient people. This is still so, if men have minds to apprehend. Let the rulers among the nations consider the history of the Hebrew people; let them ponder the reason of their long-continued suffering and scattered condition. God is speaking yet to the nations through the Jew.

Therefore thus saith the Lord; Behold, against this family do I devise an evil . . .—*Micah 2. 3.*

After a graphic description of the coming judgment (1. 6–16) the prophet declared the nature of the sin of the nation (2. 1). It will be noticed that the sin was peculiarly the sin of the ruling classes. The period was one of material prosperity, but the power of this was in the hands of the rulers. In view of this power, they planned and plotted in the night, and in the day carried out their plans. Their rule was that of oppression. The note in this charge which reveals the deepest wrong, is that in which the prophet declared that the oppression was not an action of sudden passion, or of swift moral collapse. It was premeditated. Observe the force of the word *devise*: "Woe to them that *devise* iniquity." This gives force to the declaration: "Behold against this family do I *devise* an evil." Men deliberately plot and plan in the darkness, *devise* iniquity in the night, when their fellow men cannot see, do not know. But God is not deceived, He knows; and over against the *devising* of wickedness, is set His *devising*. They *devise* iniquity against their fellows; but Jehovah *devises* evil against them. This is ever so, and the evil which God *devises* against the *devising* of iniquity is ever the outworking of that very iniquity in its reaction upon the evil workers. There is no escape from God; and that fact is the reason of confidence, and the secret of peace, in the days most full of the apparent triumph of evil men.

The heads thereof judge for reward, and the priests thereof teach for hire, and the prophets thereof divine for money.—*Micah* 3. 11.

The second of Micah's messages was addressed to the rulers, and was concerned with the coming of God's true Ruler. Its first movement is contained in this chapter. It consisted of a denunciation of those in authority, both princes and priests and prophets, and an exposure of the falseness of their authority. In these words the whole evil is graphically stated, and relentlessly unmasked. The heads, that is the civil rulers or princes, exercised their judicial function for reward. They were open to bribery, their decisions could be bought by those able to reward them. The priests taught for hire, and therefore their teaching was accommodated to the desires of those who paid them. The prophets were seeking for money, and therefore—let this be carefully noticed—they divined. That was not the true method. The prophet speaks what God gives him to speak. But God's word cannot be bought. Therefore the prophets turn to wizardry, to necromancy; they divine. In each case the inspiration of the exercise of authority, whether that of prince, or priest, or prophet, was the desire of self-enrichment. This is the evil principle in false authority. When government is in the interest of the governing classes, instead of the governed, it is evil. Let all human attempts at government, whether autocratic or democratic, be examined in the light of this principle, and an explanation will be found of persistent failure, and also of any measure of real success. By it, Tsarism and the reign of the proletariat stand condemned. Rule, inspired by the self-interest of the rulers, spells ruin.

Out of Zion shall go forth the law, and the word of the Lord from Jerusalem.—*Micah* 4. 2.

Having denounced the false rulers and revealed the evil principle of their exercise of authority, the prophet described the true order in a prediction concerning its establishment. His outlook was that of the true Israelite; he recognized the Divine purpose in the national life of his people. Not for themselves did they exist in an isolation of privilege, but rather as a rallying centre for humanity, an order to which the people would flow, a revelation and realization, attracting the nations and inspiring them to inquire for the ways of Jehovah, the God of Jacob. In these particular words the chief glory of the national life of Israel is revealed. Zion is to be the hill of Jehovah, and out of it the law which men need, shall go forth; Jerusalem will become indeed the city of the Great King, and from it the word of Jehovah will be uttered. That is what the world waits for, and failing to find, or rather refusing to receive, it carries on, under a false interpretation of life, and cursed by the oppressions of false rulers. When life is governed by the law of Jehovah, and sustained by His word, strife will end, war will be no more; then peace and prosperity will be realized. That day has not yet come, but the gleams of its glory are everywhere appearing. Peace is found to-day in men in whom He is well pleased; and prosperity is the portion of the meek, who already inherit the earth, even though they seem to be excluded from its possession. The men in whom He is well pleased are those who live by His law; and the meek are such as are sustained by His word. But the Day is yet to be.

But thou, Beth-lehem Ephrathah, which art little to be among the thousands of Judah, out of thee shall One come forth unto Me, that is to be Ruler in Israel, Whose goings forth are from of old, from everlasting.—*Micah* 5. 2.

And now in the prophet's message the great secret was out. This was the reason of his confidence that the Day of perfect realization would come. Here is the solution of the long problem of authority. The Kingdom will be realized under the King; the true order of life will result from the exercise of the true authority. The wonderful thing, that which sets this prophecy of Micah among the noblest of all, is this detailed and explicit prediction of the birthplace of God's King; and this description of the mystery of His Person. As to human history and human experience, He would come forth from Bethlehem. This was so definite that hundreds of years afterwards, both scholarly opinion (see the view of chief priests and scribes, Matt. 2. 6), and popular belief (see the view of the multitudes, John 7. 42), accepted it as true. But this One would not begin to be, in that coming forth from Bethlehem; His "goings forth are from of old, from everlasting." The men of His day knew that Jesus had come forth from Bethlehem. That His goings forth were "from of old from everlasting" was that which, men believing, found life. That is the key to the Gospel of John (20. 30, 31). Thus God gave the world its King. The world rejected Him. It can find no authority and no peace. But God has not done with the world. That King is reigning now; and will be manifested again to establish the Kingdom. Until He come there will be no final peace, no true prosperity. It is for those who love His appearing to hasten it by loyalty to Him in life and service.

O My people, what have I done unto thee? And wherein have I wearied thee? Testify against Me.—*Micah* 6. 3.

The last message of Micah was addressed to the chosen people, and was concerned with the controversy between them and Jehovah. It is highly dramatic. The prophet summoned Israel to hear, and the mountains also; and then the controversy proceeded. In reading this message it is of the utmost importance to distinguish between the alternating voices of Jehovah, the people, and the prophet. This the reader will do. It opens with a plaintive appeal by Jehovah, of which these are the first words. What a radiant revelation they afford of the love of Jehovah for His people; and the unutterable wrong of their infidelity: They had turned their back on Him, they had grown weary of Him. They had broken His law, neglected His word; and sought to govern themselves, and to find sustenance in debased forms of life. Jehovah appealed to them to declare what He had done to them to cause this infidelity; by what action or attitude of His their weariness of Him had been caused. Necessarily there was no answer to this, except that their deflection was the result of something in themselves, rather than

something in Him. The question is a very arresting one, and a very searching one. It is ever the inquiry of God when His people prove unfaithful; and whenever they will hear it, and face it, there must result the sense of the wrong and shame of their infidelity. His ways have ever been those of love, redeeming from bondage, and defeating the evil consultations of those who would harm us. Thus the heinousness of all our wanderings is revealed.

I will bear the indignation of the Lord, because I have sinned against Him.—*Micah* 7. 9.

These words occur in a section of the controversy in which the nation personified is speaking (7. 1–10). It is the language of the nation realizing the truth concerning itself both as to its experience of suffering, and its purpose in the Divine Economy. It is a speech in which confession of sin and of the justice of punishment merge into hope and confidence in the redemptive victory of God. This is the language of genuine penitence. The indignation of Jehovah is recognized as just, and therefore the soul submits to it. Not only is it recognized as just; it is also confessed as beneficent. Through it the sufferer sees the light breaking, and the righteousness of God becoming manifest. Herein is discovered the difference between remorse and penitence. In remorse a man is sorry for himself; he mourns over his sin because it has brought suffering to him. In penitence he is grieved by the wrong sin has done to God; he yields to his personal suffering in the confidence that by it God is setting him free from his sin. This is a vital distinction. The world-penitence, through which it will be restored to God, and enter into His peace, will be of that nature: "Behold, He cometh with the clouds; and every eye shall see Him, and they that pierced Him; and all the tribes of the earth shall mourn over Him." That is not remorse, the sorrow over personal pain; it is penitence, the sorrow for the wrong which sin has done to Him. When humanity is brought there, it will find release, for "the chastisement of our peace was upon Him."

NAHUM

I will make thy grave; for thou art vile.—*Nahum* 1. 14.

This is the prophecy which sets forth, more clearly than any other, the truth concerning the wrath of God, in its national application. Its burden is that of vengeance. It contains three messages. The first is a statement of the verdict of vengeance (1); the second gives us the

vision of that vengeance (2); the third is an argument in vindication of that vengeance (3). It was concerned with Nineveh, and was delivered almost certainly when she was at the height of her power. One hundred years before, Jonah had preached in her streets, and she had repented, and been spared. In the interval she had repented of her repentance, had continued her oppressions and cruelties. Her spirit had become incarnate in one who defied Jehovah (see verse 11, the reference being to Sennacherib); therefore, the time of the "full end" had come. In these words we have sentence and verdict. The sentence was that this great and arrogant and brutal power should be buried, the verdict against her being that she was vile. Thus the Divine vengeance is revealed as to its principle of action and its completeness of execution. The whole message is remarkable for the care with which the prophet insisted upon the goodness of God, thus emphasizing the righteousness of His vengeance, in that it proceeds only against those who have finally resisted His mercy. But when that is done, then His wrath makes a full end; it is irresistible, complete, final. All this is good tidings. That pride and cruelty and vice are doomed, because God reigns, is certain, and the certainty is comfort indeed.

She is empty and void and waste, and the heart melteth, and the knees smite together, and anguish is in all loins, and the faces of them all are waxed pale.—*Nahum 2. 10.*

These words describe the effect of the Divine vengeance, as manifested in the city and the people. The condition of the former is set forth with graphic force in three words, "empty, void, waste." There is the utmost of finality in this collocation of words. Nothing remains to be said. The proud city, of splendid architecture, of accumulated treasure, of the utmost luxury, is seen as a dreary, degraded desolation. The literal fulfilment of this Divine sentence is a matter of history. The condition of the people as the result of the vengeance is described with equal force. When the Divinely appointed scourge fell in hammer blows upon the vile nation, the heart melted, that is, inward courage failed; therefore, the knees smote together, that is, outward courage failed; anguish was in all loins, that is, the vital forces were filled with agony; and the faces of all waxed pale, that is they paled in death. What a commentary this prediction, and its historic fulfilment,

are on the exclamation of the writer of the letter to the Hebrews, "It is a fearful thing to fall into the hands of the living God." These aspects of the Divine government abide. He is still "slow to anger," but when men or nations persist in wickedness in spite of His patience, then still "with an overrunning flood, He will make a full end." And again we say, this certainly gives the trusting heart comfort and courage. However proudly evil rear its head and vaunt itself, it is doomed.

Whence shall I seek comforters for thee?—*Nahum 3. 7.*

The final message of Nahum was concerned with the righteousness of the wrath of God, and is a vindication of the activity of His vengeance. It alternates between descriptions of Nineveh's vice, and Jehovah's judgment. To study it, is to be convinced that the vice demanded the vengeance. In the presence of corruption so complete, of cruelties so brutal, of depravity so profound, any other method than that of a vengeance so complete as to blot out the plague, would have been injustice. In this question there is revealed a principle often insisted upon by these Hebrew prophets. The idea is that in the overthrow of Nineveh, all nations would agree. None would bemoan her. None would pity her. None would be found to comfort her. The principle is that in the underlying conscience of man the sense of justice is never destroyed; and that means that the beauty of righteousness is recognized, and the repulsiveness of evil is admitted. This is ever so. Men and nations go in evil ways, and persist therein; but they do so, knowing the wrong of it. For some fancied temporary advantage, they sin against this deep conviction; but it is still there, and it surges to the surface when the wrath of God proceeds in vengeance; and it always agrees with the rightness of His action. When the full process of the Divine government has completed its work, the whole universe will agree with its righteousness and its judgment. That which then is doomed, will be so, not by God only, but by the consent of the whole creation.

HABAKKUK

O Lord, how long shall I cry, and Thou wilt not hear?—*Hab. 1. 2.*

This prophecy deals with the problems created by faith; and with the Divine answers to the questions which express those problems. These opening words reveal the first problem. Habakkuk lived in an age when the outlook on circum-

stances seemed to contradict his faith in the righteous government of God. The times were characterized by violence, iniquity, perverseness, spoiling, strife, contention. All the ways of justice were perverted. God was apparently doing nothing; and, in spite of the troubled cry of His servant, remained silent. Let it at once be observed that the value of this book is that it reveals a man who, in the presence of this problem, stated it to God, rather than made it the occasion of unbelief. The problem was created by his faith, and his faith acted in declaring it to God. By such action he made it possible for God, in communion with him, to give him an explanation. That was a great gain. Let it at once be granted that the first answer did not satisfy Habakkuk. Indeed, it created a new problem more bewildering than the first. The Divine declaration was that God was not inactive. He was employing the Chaldeans, the avowed and bitter enemies of His people, to carry out His purposes. This, to the mind of this man of faith, was more bewildering and inexplicable than that God should be inactive and silent. A further unveiling followed, to which we shall come. So far, we see that faith may have its problem; that when it has to face it, it should do so in communion; and that therein it may find that its reading of circumstances is wrong, in that God is indeed acting when He seems to be indifferent. The method of His action may create a new problem, but it is something to be assured of the fact of it.

And the Lord answered me.—*Hab. 2. 2.*

Here we reach the central word of this prophecy, the great revealing word of perpetual and persistent application. When Jehovah revealed to His servant the fact that He was employing the Chaldeans, Habakkuk was filled almost with consternation, as the last part of the preceding chapter reveals (12–17). But faith again triumphed, in that he stated his difficulty, and betook him to his watch tower to wait further Divine communication. To that action Jehovah responded. This is the meaning of this statement "And Jehovah answered me." The answer consisted in the declaration of a principle by which all men and movements in all ages may be tested. It is stated in the form of a double contrast; on the one hand between the proud or puffed up, and the just; and on the other, between the results. The result in the case of the just is that he lives by his faith. The result in the case of the puffed-up is not stated; . but that Habukkuk at once understood, is evident by his following description of the doom of such. The im-

mediate value of the word was that Habakkuk learned that God's employment of the Chaldeans did not mean the permanent power of this evil people. While, for the moment their power would be employed to discipline the people of God for their pride; in the end their own pride would bring about their doom. The government of God is always true to this principle. He overrules the ways of men, compelling them to contribute to His purposes. The wrath of man He ever makes to praise Him, and then He restrains it. Faith is the principle of life, pride the passion which issues in death. To this, there is no exception; from its working there is no escape.

O Lord, revive Thy work in the midst of the years.—*Hab. 3. 2.*

This is the prayer of faith resulting from the experiences of communion. The real idea of it is not that which is generally associated with it. It is not a cry to renew an activity which has ceased, but to maintain an activity which has not ceased. We might render with complete accuracy "O Jehovah, keep alive Thy work in the midst of the years." Observe how this completes the process. Faith, looking out upon circumstances, was perplexed that God was not working; and declared its problem to Him. To this He replied by the affirmation that He was at work; "I am working a work in your days." Then faith could not understand how God could do the work which He said He was doing; and again said so, and waited for a reply. To this Jehovah replied by revealing to His servant the principle of His government. Now faith had only one desire, and that was that God would keep alive His work. But let the change in Habakkuk's desire be observed. When it had seemed to him that God was doing nothing, he had desired an operation of punishment against violence and iniquity. Now that he had seen the wrath of God in its operation, he agreed, and prayed for its continuity; but he prayed also "In wrath remember mercy." And who shall doubt that this desire also was the result of his communion with God? In that communion, the soul of this man had been brought into a very real fellowship with God. The last notes of the book are those of triumphant faith

ZEPHANIAH

I will utterly consume.—*Zeph.* 1. 2.

Zephaniah exercised his ministry in the days of Josiah. This is an interesting fact, because in his days there was a great reformation, and yet the prophet makes no reference to it. An examination of the history of that reform will show that, so far as the nation was concerned, it was superficial. The king was loyal to God, and sincere. He was also popular with the people, and they followed him in his reforming work, as to external things. But there was no true repentance. Therefore Zephaniah did not recognize the reform; and indeed, in all probability the insincerity of it gave greater vehemence to his denunciation of the sin of the people. Taken as a whole this prophecy sets forth the severity and goodness of God with overwhelming force; and shows how these apparently contradictory elements of His government move to the same end. The words we have emphasized give the key note to the prophet's message as to the action of God, consequent upon the sins of the people. This chapter is wholly taken up with the day of Divine wrath. The outlook was wider than Judah. It began with the declaration that the whole creation, so far as it was polluted, should be destroyed. It then dealt with the nation itself, denouncing its sins, and announcing the consuming wrath of God as proceeding against princes, extortioners, the city, the merchantmen, the luxurious. It is a terrible setting forth of the severity of God against apostasy. There was no equivocation, no uncertainty, no hesitancy, in the prophet's words. They abide for all time, a revelation of the fact that God not only will make no terms with sin, but that He will proceed against it in fiery indignation that it may be utterly consumed.

Gather yourselves together.—*Zeph.* 2. 1.

In this chapter we have the prophet's appeal, on the ground of the approaching day of wrath. This opening call might with accuracy be rendered in our colloquialism: "Pull yourselves together." That is the exact idea. All the Nation was spiritually and morally relaxed, and so mentally dulled, and unable to realize the true meaning of its own sin. The prophet stood before the Nation as a physician, and cried to it sharply, urgently: "Pull yourselves together." The sign of moral paralysis was that the Nation had no shame. To a sense of sin, and a consequent sense of shame, the prophet sought to bring them, in view of the decree of the Divine judg-

ment which was determined against them. He commenced by describing the judgments which were to fall on the surrounding nations, Philistia, Moab, Ammon, Ethiopia, and Assyria; and then proceeded to show how this same fiery destructive force would fall on Jerusalem (3. 1-7). In the course of this appeal the prophet specially addressed the remnant of elect souls who were loyal to Jehovah. Two things are impressive in this section of the prophecy. The first is that this is the very call that nations constantly need to hear; and that it is difficult for them to obey. To-day, those nations most highly privileged need to pull themselves together, and to face moral and spiritual facts. The second is that the souls within the national life who are loyal to God are those who constitute the only hope of the nation being able to do this.

Therefore wait ye for Me, saith the Lord.—*Zeph.* 3. 8.

That is the sentence in which the theme of the severity of God merges into that of His goodness. It is most significant, when the force of the "therefore" is considered. Observe the immediately preceding words: "They rose early and corrupted all their doings." "*Therefore*," because there is no hope of recovery in the people themselves, "wait ye for Me saith Jehovah." When the case is most hopeless, as to man's corruption, then Jehovah acts, and He does so in "indignation," in "fierce anger," in "the fire of His jealousy"; but all that in order to the ending of corruption and the restoration of the sinning people. From that point the prophetic message is one of hope; it becomes a song of love, and there is none more full of exquisite beauty in the Bible. It is a celebration of the Motherhood of God, in which the prophet described Him rejoicing over His people, silent in His love, and then breaking the silence with a song of love. That victory is the victory of love. That is to say that it can only issue from the action of the God of love. There is no hope in human effort. The only thing that man can do is to wait for God. But that waiting is a responsibility. To wait for God is to be at the end of self; it is to be submissive to His way of judgment; it is to return to Him with complete surrender, the surrender of utter hopelessness in any other than Himself, the surrender of acknowledged and yielding weakness. Wherever there is such waiting, in love He chastises to purification; and then in love rejoices as His purposes are fulfilled in the restoration of those upon whom His love is set.

HAGGAI

Is it a time for you yourselves to dwell in your cieled houses, while this House lieth waste?—*Hag.* 1. 4.

For the first time (except in the case of Daniel) a prophetic book is dated by Gentile dynasties. Israel's days are counted by reigns outside the Covenant. The remnant was restored to Jerusalem from captivity, but was still subject to Gentile powers. In these two chapters we have four messages, each carefully dated. They were all directed to one end, that namely of bringing these people to build the House of God, which, notwithstanding the fact that they had been restored over fifteen years, yet lay in incompleteness. In his work Haggai was helped by Zechariah; and they were successful, for the House of Jehovah was built. The first of Haggai's addresses is found in this chapter. Its positive note was a call to 'arise and build; its method was that of combating the mental attitude which had prevented the building. These particular words constituted the prophet's answer to that mental mood. The people were waiting for the right time, and saying that the right time was not yet come. The prophet revealed the falsity of the attitude by this question. They were not waiting for some special time, some psychic moment, for the building of their own houses. Into that, they were putting physical energy. The psychic condition needed for the building of the House of God was that of minds determined to employ physical energy enough to do it. How persistent is this folly of waiting for psychic moments to do Divine work, when the one thing needed is immediate action. The truth was, and is, in all such cases, that action is the outcome of desire. To desire the House of Jehovah is to build it. What we need is true apprehension of relative values.

The latter glory of this House shall be greater than the former.—*Hag.* 2. 9.

In this chapter there are three messages, all of which were called forth by moods of the people which threatened to prevent their accomplishment of the great work. The first message aroused them, and under the leadership of Zerubbabel the governor and Joshua the high priest, they started well. After about seven weeks came the feast of Tabernacles with its necessary cessation of work. During that period they were assailed by the lamentations of those who bemoaned the poverty of the House they were building, in comparison with the glorious House which had been destroyed. Such lamentation tended to dishearten them, and to correct this the prophet made this great declaration. Here again is a persistent peril. Men are constantly tempted to think meanly of the work they are doing as they compare it with the glories of past achievements. It is an utterly false and unwarranted thing to do. To that House, lacking in some material splendour which had characterized the former one, there was to come the Desire of all nations, and so a spiritual glory which the former House never knew. Let us lay the lesson to heart. We may be working better and greater things than we know. It is always futile to judge the value of God-appointed tasks by the appearance of the hour in which they are done. If they are indeed appointed by Him, that is enough for us to know; and more, that is the assurance that they are better than the past, for God is ever moving towards the higher, the grander, the nobler; and will do so, until He has wrought out the final perfection of His will.

ZECHARIAH

Be ye not as your fathers . . .—*Zech.* 1. 4.

This book has been aptly described as the Apocalypse of the Old Testament, on account of its visional representation of the history of Israel up to the time when it is completely restored. Zechariah was contemporary with Haggai, and helped him in his particular work. His first message (1. 1–16) was delivered about a month after Haggai's second message; his second, consisting of visions (1. 7–6. 15), two months after Haggai's latest; his third, consisting of voices (7–8), nearly

two years later; whilst his last concerning the king (9–14) was delivered after the temple was completed, at least four years after Haggai. These words are taken from the first message. The people were looking back, and lamenting the past greatness of the glory of the Temple. Haggai had told them that the glory of the latter house should exceed that of the former. Zechariah reinforced the appeal of Haggai from another standpoint. He charged them to learn the true lesson of the backward look, that of how the glory was lost through the disobedience of the fathers to the word of God. That was, and is, a salutary word. It is a persistent habit, this of talking of "the good old days," and so weakening our powers to serve our own age. It is well that we be reminded that in many ways they were bad old days; and that we take warning from the failures of the past, and so make our work of a more abiding nature.

For I, saith the Lord, will be unto her a wall of fire round about, and I will be the glory in the midst of her.— Zech. 2. 5.

At the seventh verse of chapter 1 begins the series of eight visions in which the history of Israel from then to the consummation of the Divine purpose was foretold. The first, that of the myrtle trees (1. 7–17), shows the long period during which the chosen people of God must dwell among the shadows. The second, that of horns and smiths (1. 18–21), recognizes the forces which will be against these people; and the forces which God raises up to destroy those who scatter them. These words occur in the third vision, which occupies the whole of this chapter. It is a radiant setting forth of the restoration and prosperity which will eventually come to Israel as the result of the Divine care. It is a glorious vision of Jerusalem as it will be. A young man was seen going forth to measure the city. He was stopped and told in effect that no measurement of his could encompass the spacious glory of that city of God which would stretch out into the garden lands like villages. Then came this fine and final figure of speech. When that city is established at last, she will need no material walls to render her safe, Jehovah will encompass her as a wall of fire and be in the midst of her as her supreme glory. The city of God has ever been the goal of the men and women of faith in their pilgrimage, their witness, and their warfare, and no suggestion as to its glory and beauty and safety, in all the Biblical literature, is more perfect and wonderful than this.

I will bring forth My Servant, the Branch.—Zech. 3. 8.

This chapter contains the fourth vision. It is that of Joshua, the priest, cleansed, and fitted for the fulfilment of priestly function. Israel was chosen to fulfil that function among the nations, to be a dynasty of priests, in that she had access to God. Through her sin she had failed, but by the way of cleansing from that sin she is yet to fulfil that office. The way of restoration for Israel is to be that of the bringing forth of Jehovah's Servant, the Branch. The meaning of the word is simple, it is that of a shoot, or branch, springing out of the tree itself. The use of it is revealed by the Septuagint translation which rendered the word *anatolé*,

"that which rises or springs up." This is the word rendered *Dayspring* in Luke 1. 78: "The Dayspring from on high shall visit us," in the prophecy of the priest Zacharias, the father of John Baptist. Here then was the hope of Israel's cleansing and restoration to priestly work. She had failed because the Divinely appointed order of priests within her national life had failed. And how persistently they failed! Their final failure was that of their murder of the very One Who fulfilled in His Own Person and office this great prediction. Yet He came; the Servant of God was brought forth; the Branch, the Dayspring visited and redeemed His people. The result must be at last the cleansing of that nation, and her exercise of priestly function among the nations of the world. This is all of grace. Such grace is indeed amazing, but it is almighty.

Not by might, nor by power, but by My Spirit, saith the Lord of Hosts.— Zech. 4. 6.

In this chapter we have the fifth vision. It is that of the golden candlestick. To the devout Hebrew its signification was patent. In the Holy Place, just outside the Holiest of all, there stood the golden lampstand, a perpetual symbol of the function of the nation in the purpose of God; as the table of shewbread was a symbol of its fellowship with Him. The nation was created to be a centre of light to all the nations. In the visions granted to Zechariah, this, then, was a representation of ideal Israel. It fittingly followed that of the priest, cleansed, and so prepared for the fulfilment of the priestly office. The whole vision was intended to show that the nation could only fulfil that function as it was in direct and maintained communion with God. Not by her might or power among the nations could she reveal the truth about God; but only by the life illuminated and energized by His Spirit. Zerubbabel and Joshua stood symbolically for the offices of king and priest, merged in Messiah; through submission to Whose authority, and appropriation of Whose mediatorial work, a perpetual supply of that Spirit can be received. The vision is beautifully pictorial, and full of illumination. The principles apply to the Church equally with Israel. Not by might and power, of money or of organization, can she witness to her Lord; but only by His Spirit. A full supply of that Spirit is ever at her disposal through Him, Who is the one King-Priest.

An house in the land of Shinar.— Zech. 5. 11.

Two visions, the sixth and seventh, are found in this chapter, those namely of the flying roll, and the ephah. They are visions of administration. The idea is that when Israel is restored, and realizes her true function in the Divine economy, she will exercise a true moral influence in the world. The flying roll is the curse of evil; it represents the principle of law, as it will be applied by Israel. Evil-doers will be discovered, and punished. The ephah with the woman seated in it, recognized, what later prophecy clearly revealed, that the principle of wickedness will have its final stronghold in commerce (see Rev. 13. 16 and 17); and read the newspapers). Under the influence of Israel restored, that manifestation is for a period to be restricted. It is to be carried to, and centralized in, the land of Shinar. There the tower of Babel was erected (Gen. 10. 10); and there Babylon was built. In the revealed scheme of prophecy, the reference here must be to the millennial reign; during which the spirit of lawlessness will not be destroyed, but restricted and held in check. Babylon will have fallen as a power in the affairs of men; and, under the compulsion of the true moral principle, will be localized and mastered. Beyond that, Satan will be loosed, for one purpose only; to gather together all in whom that principle of lawlessness still has a place, that they may be destroyed, while he is cast out finally.

The counsel of peace shall be between them both.—*Zech.* 6. 13.

In this chapter we have the eighth and last vision; and the record of a great symbolic and prophetic ceremony actually performed under the direction of Zechariah. The vision was of four chariots driven from between two mountains of brass; and the explanation given was that they represented the spirits of heaven going forth from the presence of the Lord to walk to and fro in the earth. The suggestion is still that of administration; and the revelation is that this is to be accomplished by spiritual forces. The ceremony was that of setting crowns upon the head of the priest. Thus a great revelation was made, that of a priest upon a throne. The prediction was that the fulfilment of the idea suggested should come in the person of the Man Whose name is the Branch (see chapter 3. verse 8). Then these particular words occur: "The counsel of peace shall be between them both." In this statement the words *"them both"* refer, not to two persons, but to two offices, those namely of King and Priest, as they merge in the one Person, Who is that Branch. That is a great, a central, a final word on the subject of peace. In the midst of long continued and growingly disastrous and bloody wars, men have discussed the way of peace, but without producing "the counsel of peace." In the widest sense it is true that "The way of peace have they not known." There is only one way of peace. It is that of the exercise of authority over all human affairs by the One Who is not King only, but Priest also. The One Who is able to loose men from sin, is the only One Who is able to bind them together in peace.

Should I weep in the fifth month, separating myself, as I have done these so many years?—*Zech.* 7. 3.

In this and the next chapters, we have the third section of the prophecy. It consists of three messages of Jehovah to the people. These were delivered about two years later than those giving the visions; and two years before the completion of the Temple. The words which we have emphasized introduce us to the reason of these messages. During the times of trouble certain fasts had been instituted by the people. The four of them are mentioned in 8. 19. The question of the deputation from Bethel was as to whether now that the walls of the city were rebuilt, that fast should still be observed which was instituted in connection with their destruction. The first answer to that inquiry is found in this chapter. Its two movements are important. In the first the prophet reminded them that the institution of the fast was not Divine. Themselves had done it. He did not say it was wrong to have done so; but implicated in his words was the warning not to give Divine sanction to human arrangements. In the second movement the prophet delivered the direct word of Jehovah in which they were reminded of the reason of the calamity which caused them to institute this fast. It was that of their iniquity, consequent upon their disobedience. All this is full of suggestiveness. Human appointments may be justified by circumstances arising out of human attitudes which are not justified. Let them not be thought of as of the same nature as Divine ordinances.

The fast . . . and the fast . . . and the fast . . . and the fast . . . shall be . . . feasts.—*Zech.* 8. 19.

This chapter contains the second and third of the messages of Jehovah in answer to the inquiry of the deputation from Bethel. In the second (verses 1–18), the Divine determination to restore Zion was set forth; and appeal was made to the people to act in accordance with this determination. The movement began with the arresting declarations: "I am jealous"; "I am jealous with great wrath"; "I am returned." The result will be that of the establishment of truth in the city, and holiness in the mountain; and the consequent security of the aged, and the playtime of the children. The third and last message returned directly to the question which had been raised, and taking a wider outlook than that of the particular fast named, included the four which had been instituted by the people in the days of calamity. The feast of the tenth month mourned the besieging of the city; that of the fourth, its taking; that of the fifth, its destruction; and that of the seventh, the murder of Gedaliah. None of these things had been in the purpose of God for His people; they had resulted from their sins. The fasts therefore were the result of their sins. In jealousy and fury, the outcome of love, Jehovah would put away their sins, and so restore them to true prosperity. In that day let them still remember and observe, only let the observance be a feast in celebration of God's grace, instead of a fast in memory of their sin. In all this a principle of Divine action is revealed. The grace of God is ever transforming the fast of penitence into a feast of love. Is not this the deep meaning of the Holy Supper to the saints of God?

How great is His goodness, and how great is His beauty.—Zech. 9. 17.

The last six chapters of Zechariah contain two burdens. They are undated, but we may be certain they were uttered after the completion of the Temple. In the messages already considered, the purpose of the prophet had been that of inspiring the people to complete the work of building that Temple, by showing them the far-reaching effect of their work in its relation to the Coming and Kingdom of Messiah. These final burdens are of the nature of intepretations of some aspects of that Coming and Kingdom. Some of these interpretations were of the nature of predictions of events comparatively nigh at hand; but they were all seen as related to the reign of Messiah; some of them had reference to His first advent and rejection, and these have had literal fulfilment; some of them had reference to the ultimate glory of His reign, and they are still unfulfilled. In this chapter the protection of the city against Alexander was foretold (verses 1–8); and the victory of Judas Maccabaeus over Antiochus Epiphanes predicted (verses 10–16). Between these foretellings the clear announcement of the advent of the Messiah was made. (verse 9). The words we have stressed constitute an exclamation of wonder and adoration resulting from the prophet's vision of the action of Jehovah, and may we not say, as seen in the King? The combination of ideas in the phrases, "His goodness" and "His beauty," is very suggestive. These are things of God, revealed to the pure in heart, in nature, in providence, but with finality and perfection in "the Son of His love."

Ask ye of the Lord rain . . .—Zech. 10. 1.

This chapter should not be a chapter. That is to say, it is most clearly the continuation and completion of the first movement in this burden celebrating the coming of Messiah and the victories He will win. It continues and develops the declarations already made. Perhaps, however, there is this justification for the division, that at this point the prophet made a direct appeal to the people to whom he was speaking. He had referred to the fruitfulness, which would follow the reign of Messiah, in the words, "Grain shall make the young men flourish, and new wine the virgins" (9. 17); and at once he charged the people to seek these things in the rain which comes from God, rather than from the teraphim and diviners who had always led them astray. Here is revealed an element in prophecy of perpetual application. It is that of its immediate intention. The prophet of God in the most exalted moments of prediction, never forgot that the true purpose of his ministry was to produce immediate results, and not to satisfy curiosity, even on the highest level. Let those who look for an ultimate fruitfulness remember that it will come as the result of rains which God sends; and let them remember that such rains are available to them now, if they will ask of Him. Waiting for future blessings may resolve itself into selfishness, and indeed postpone these blessings. Let there be an immediate seeking, not first for the fruitfulness, but rather for the Divine rains by which such fruitfulness will come.

So I fed the flock of slaughter, verily the poor of the flock. And I took unto me two staves; the one I called Beauty, and the other I called Bands; and I fed the flock.—Zech. 11. 7.

In this chapter we have the second movement in the first Burden. It stands in striking contrast to the first movement. That predicted the coming of the true King; this, in figurative language, told of His rejection. The first sentences described the judgment which would result from that rejection. Then the fact of the rejection was foretold. It should be remembered throughout that the Shepherd is always the King, whether false or true. The nation is seen oppressed by false shepherds; then God raised up a good Shepherd, that is, a true King. The method of the prophet here was that of personating this King in his speech. He exercises a double office as the symbols of the staves signify. Beauty speaks of the grace of the King, both in His method and His purpose for His people. Bands tell of His might, also in method and purpose. The hire the people give him is thirty pieces of silver, the price of the slave! Therefore, He breaks His staves, and casts them away. As a result, the people pass under the oppression of another false shepherd. Thus the prophet had vision of the rejection of the Messiah, and of a Roman conquest and oppression, which would result therefrom. The remarkable element in this prophecy is that of its exact foretelling, even in detail, of what would happen to the one true Shepherd,.

They shall look unto Me, Whom they have pierced.—*Zech.* 12. 10.

We come now to the second of the Burdens. This first section of the prophecy has to do with things which are yet unfulfilled. The King Whose rejection was foretold in the previous Burden, in this one is seen coming into His Kingdom. The Burden again has two movements, which are complementary. In the first (12.–13. 6), he shows how the oppressing nations will be dealt with in judgment; and how the people of God will be restored through the acknowledgment of their rejected King, and by their own spiritual cleansing. In the second (13. 7–14), he views the same events from the standpoint of the King, going back first to His rejection, and then describing His coming day, as to its process and administration. How full of suggestiveness are these words: "They shall look unto Me, Whom they have pierced." What a day that will be for God's ancient people when they find that the One Whom they rejected is indeed their Messiah. What sorrow will be theirs; and yet because of His grace, that sorrow will be turned into joy. The national experience had wonderful illustration in the case of Saul of Tarsus. This is exactly what happened to him. When we think of that experience in his case, we may have some idea of what it will mean to the world when it is multiplied to a national dimension. This thought was surely in his mind when he wrote: "What shall the receiving of them be, but life from the dead?" (Rom. 11. 15.)

In that day there shall be a fountain opened to the house of David and to the inhabitants of Jerusalem, for sin and for uncleanness.—*Zech.* 13. 1.

When the people are brought to sorrow by the revelation of their Messiah as the One Whom they had rejected, they will find, in the mystery of the Divine grace, that God wrought, through that very rejection, a way for their cleansing. About this there are two things to be said. First, this is indeed a mystery; that is, something the truth of which is revealed and proven in experience, but which transcends the grasp of the mind of man as to its method. The fact is that of the cleansing of spirit which is provided for men through the Christ, and through Him alone. The second matter is that this is the one and only way by which the Divine purposes for Israel, and for humanity at large, can be realized. Sin and uncleanness must be put away. They cannot be excused, condoned, or compromised with. The foundations of the Throne of God are righteousness and justice; the foundations of human society are those of moral cleanness and spiritual rectitude. These two notes are fundamental in all the messages of the prophets; those of the necessity for cleansing, and of the action of the Divine grace as alone able to provide that cleansing. The Christian Church has taken hold of these words and employed the idea in her hymnology as setting forth a truth concerning humanity and that accurately and appropriately. But let us not forget that their first application is to Israel and to God's way of restoration for her.

And the Lord shall be King over all the earth; in that day shall the Lord be one, and His name one.—*Zech.* 14. 9.

That is the ultimate victory, the far off Divine event to which the whole creation moves the goal of God's activity for humanity, and the realization of humanity's highest experience of life. That hour will come when the feet of the rejected King stand again upon the Mount of Olives, no longer in the pathway of sorrows, but in recognized and acknowledged authority, "feet like unto burnished brass, as if it had been refined in a furnace" (Rev. 1. 15). The earthly centre of His reign will be Jerusalem, that very Jerusalem so long trodden down of the Gentiles, but at last the city of the great King, not only in the intention of God, but in the experience of history. The people through whom the administration of His will will be effective, will be His people Israel, at last cleansed from all sin and uncleanness, and able to fulfil their priestly-kingly function in the world. In Christ Jesus we have had every word of prophecy made more sure; and were there no signs in human affairs which pointed in this direction, we should still be certain of their fulfilment. But to-day signs multiply. The eyes of the world are already centred on Jerusalem; and men who seek no light from revelation are looking to see what will transpire concerning her, expecting, as they say—"interesting developments." We know what they will be presently. The King Himself will be there; and, "Jehovah shall be King over all the earth, in that day shall Jehovah be one, and His Name one."

MALACHI

**I have loved you, saith the Lord.—
Mal. 1. 2.**

That is the key-note of the messages of
the last of the prophets sent to the people
of God until the herald of Messiah immediately preceded Him. The tense is not
past in its intention, but continuous. If
we treat it as past, we must recognize
that it covers the whole of that past.
There had been no falling off or failure
in the Divine Love for His people. The
declaration is all the more arresting when
it is seen that the people had lost their
love for Jehovah to such a degree that
they questioned His love for them. They
said: "Wherein hast Thou loved us?"
Malachi exercised his ministry probably
about a hundred years after Nehemiah's
time. The people were established in the
city, the Temple services were observed,
and they were enjoying a good measure
of material prosperity. But they were
alienated from God in affection; their
religious observances were formal; their
morality was external, and in many ways
was failing even so. This man was raised
up, and sent by God, to recall them to the
deeper things of their life, and all these
were conditioned within the fact of the
Divine Love; and only possible of realization by their consciousness of that Love,
and response to it. The whole prophecy
is true to this key note. The sensitiveness
of the Divine heart is wonderfully revealed
from first to last. Love speaks throughout.
It is severe in its denunciation of sin;
but it never abandons the loved ones. It
argues with them, pleads with them, warns
them, appeals to them; and it is all love,
and always love, and that in spite of
their coldness, pride, and lack of response.
This is the unveiling of God with which
the Old Testament ends.

**Ye have wearied the Lord with
your words.—Mal. 2. 17.**

These words occur at the close of the
prophet's formal accusations of the nation
for its response to the love of Jehovah.
These accusations were against the priests
(1. 6–2. 9); and against the people (2. 10–
16). The priests were corrupt. They had
degraded their office by profanity, sacrilege, greed, and weariness; and so had
misrepresented God to the people. The
people were guilty of profaning their
covenant with Jehovah by two sins; the
first was that of contracting mixed
marriages; and the second was that of
divorcing their true wives. The inter-
relation between a corrupt priesthood and
a corrupt people was inevitable. The
deepest note in their sin was that of their
misinterpretation of God. That is the
meaning of this charge, that they had
wearied Jehovah with their words. They
had a false view of His love; they said
"Everyone that doeth evil is good in the
sight of Jehovah." That was equivalent to
saying, God is so good that He does not
punish wickedness. They had a false view
of His holiness; they said, "Where is the
God of justice?" That was equivalent to
saying, God is indifferent to these things,
He does not govern or interfere. These
are the words which weary God, because
they are words revealing a false view of
Himself, a failure to understand His love
as to its nature and its processes. As we
ponder these words we feel that in much
modern teaching about God, there must be
much that wearies Him. Yet thank God,
His weariness has nothing in it of failure
or fainting. It necessitates discipline, but
such discipline is but a further method of
His unceasing and unchanging love.

**I, the Lord, change not; therefore ye,
O sons of Jacob, are not consumed.—
Mal. 3. 6.**

This chapter contains the prophet's annunciation concerning the coming of the
Lord to His Temple, in the Messenger of
the covenant. It constitutes an answer to
the words which wearied God. They were
saying, "Where is the God of judgment?"
Here was the reply. Jehovah was not only
still with them, watching over them; He
was coming into manifestation; and to
administration. He would purge the priesthood, and judge the people righteously.
In the midst of this great announcement
these words occur. The hope of the sons
of Jacob is in the unchangeable nature of
Jehovah. That also is the only hope of
humanity. If He changed in holiness, then
the uttermost corruption of man would
ensue, and that would mean the complete
destruction of humanity. If He changed
in love, then He might hand man over to
this issue of his own sin. If He changed,
then indeed the sons of Jacob, and the
sons of men, would be consumed. But in
this word we find our assurance. He
changes not. He will make no terms with
sin. He will not abandon man to his sin,
but will provide a redemption for the
sinners. To-day, amid widespread corruption, and false philosophies, words
which weary God, we may rest assured
that He remains unchanged, the God of
unsullied holiness and undeviating righteousness; the God of unfailing love, and
unconquered grace. This is the secret of
our songs, and the inspiration of our
service.

. . . Lest I come and smite the earth with a curse.—*Mal.* 4. 6.

So ends the prohecy of Malachi; and so closes the Old Testament. In reading this prophetic portion the rabbis never end with these words, but go back and repeat the words found in verse 5, ending so. With the same object of ending, not with the word curse, the Septuagint places verse four after verses five and six. This desire to escape the impression of the word curse is understandable, but it is a revelation of a literalism which was wholly false. The last word is curse, but the last thought is not. The emphasis is on the word *Lest*. This suggests a way of escape from the curse. The curse is something to be prevented. It would fall if something were not done. That is the truth revealed in all the Law, the Prophets, the Writings.

How then may it be prevented? The question drives us back to what has preceded the word "Lest." What is it? The promise of an action of Jehovah, by which the hearts of the people shall be changed. If the condition of escape from the curse had depended upon some action of man, we might despair. But it does not, save as the action of God will produce a change in the heart of man. Beyond the Old Testament we have the New; and there we find the fulfilment of the Divine promise, and all that it involved. For beyond the messenger preparing the way (Elijah—that is, John), the Messenger of the Covenant (the Messiah—Jesus) came. True, He was rejected; but His day is coming yet, a day of burning and of sunrise; and yet again before it, Elijah will come to the people of God. God's final word is never curse, but blessing.

LIFE APPLICATIONS FROM
EVERY CHAPTER OF THE BIBLE

MATTHEW

It is He that shall save His people from their sins.—*Matt.* 1. 21.

The whole value of this statement is found by placing the emphasis upon the "HE." The name which the angel commanded Joseph to give to Mary's Child was one that was common at the time. It had a wonderful history. It had been made by Moses for his immediate successor, by the weaving together of his name, Hoshea, which meant Salvation, with some of the letters of the Divine name Jehovah, so that its full significance was "The Salvation of Jehovah." Thus the Name Jesus, is equivalent to the Jehovah of the Old Testament, combined with the revelation of the ultimate meaning of that name, that of Salvation, in all the completeness of the great fact. As Jehovah—or Yahweh—meant, "The Becoming One," or "The One Who becomes"—that is, the God of Grace, Who becomes to His people whatever they need, so, when in the fulness of time, He, in His Son, "*became* flesh," the Name given to Him signified the ultimate in this mighty, but condescending Grace. This is indeed, then, the Name which is above every name. The hope expressed in the Name was about to be fulfilled. Through the One Who was now to bear it, salvation from sin was to be made possible.

This contrastive value abides. Still there is none other name which stands for that possibility. Infinite are the glories of Him Who received that Name anew when He was exalted to the right hand of God, but among them all, for us who are sinning men and women, this is central and supreme. This we should ever remember for our personal comfort, and in all our service. As we are perpetually engaged in the struggle against sin, it is for us to fight in the assurance that He is able to deliver us, not only from the penalties of wrongdoing, but from the power of evil in every form. That also must ever condition our service. However varied the claims of our Lord may be, and however wide the area over which it is our business to insist upon His Lordship, everything begins, continues, and ends, in this glorious fact that He deals with sin, forgiving its penalty, cleansing from its pollution, and destroying its power.

Herod will seek the young Child to destroy Him.—*Matt.* 2. 13.

Like a flash of clear light these words reveal the dark and sinister things of evil. Look at the young Child. He is the Child born to humanity, the Son given by God. Full of all grace and strength, He is the explanation of God's ideal for man, and the unveiling of God's love for man. Look at Herod. He is the very incarnation of pride, of perversity, of pollution. Herod will seek the young Child to destroy Him! He will not succeed. It is Herod that will be destroyed, and that by the young Child. But the way to victory will be the way of wounding, of anguish, of death. It is well that all the significance of these things should ever be before us. Herod is still seeking to destroy, and he and his ways may always be discovered by his hatred of the young Child. Everything that threatens childlife, however gorgeously it may be arrayed, however it may employ the language of a false culture, is inherently evil. Herod is Edom—that is materialism, sensuality, the Esau who sells a birthright for a mess of pottage. When children are looked at from the materialistic standpoint only, whether in palace or tenement house, whether amid the debasing luxuries of wealth, or in the squalid miseries of poverty, they are attacked by their most deadly foe. When God came into human life, to reveal us to ourselves, and to unveil Himself to us, He began as a Babe, a young Child, and so compelled us to guard those first years of human experience. The perils are subtle and the destructive forces mighty. Let us not imagine that things have changed. We must go with the Child all the way of witness, and of suffering, if we are to share in His triumphs. But that inevitably means that we must be at war with Herod; and must not have the slightest complicity with his outlook on life, or with his methods. Love of self always means hatred of the Child, and ruthlessness. Love of the Child always means self-emptying and sacrifice.

The work of the Shepherd for the lamb is often stern work, demanding the long journey over the mountains, and the fierce and bloody conflict with the marauding and destroying wolf. But it is work with

God, and that means that fellowship in His suffering, ever leads to fellowship in His triumph.

Thus it becometh us to fulfil all righteousness.—Matt. 3. 15.

"Thus." How? What is the real significance of this first recorded word of our Lord as He approached His public ministry? The answer is to be found in a consideration of the reason for the protest of John, to which it was a reply. John's baptism was to repentance and remission of sins. As he looked at Jesus, he knew that He had nothing of which to repent; no sins to be remitted. Why then should He submit to this baptism? The answer to that inquiry our Lord gave. The reason for His baptism was that through all which it symbolized He would fulfil righteousness; and only through such action could He do this. In baptism He confessed, as His own, sins which He had not committed, and repented of them before God. He was numbered with transgressors and bore the sins of many. It was at once the prophecy and interpretation of His coming passion-baptism.

The most arresting fact here is that in this word we have the revelation of a new element in the Righteousness of God—new that is, in the sense that it had not hitherto been revealed. Included in the Divine righteousness is the determination to make it possible, by the way of vicarious suffering. Thus love is seen, mastered by righteousness; and suffering, in order to make the unrighteous righteous. Thus righteousness is seen, acting in love, that men may be brought into the place where love can bestow all its gifts. That is the righteousness unveiled in the Gospel. That is the righteousness which exceeds that of the Pharisees. How far have we entered into the personal experience of it?

When He heard that John was delivered up, He withdrew into Galilee.—Matt. 4. 12.

This is a statement revealing our Lord's courage rather than His caution. There are instances on record of how in hours of danger He moved out of the danger-zone. This is not one of them. Here He went into the danger-zone. The word "withdrew" simply means that He went. Galilee was the tetrarchy of Herod, who had imprisoned John. Into that region then, our Lord went to continue the ministry of the man thus silenced, and to begin His own more public propaganda. As another Herod had sought the young Child to destroy Him, so now this one, given over to evil courses, attempted to silence the troublesome voice which had denounced the sin of the court as sternly as the sin of the crowd. When Jesus heard it, He moved into the region of Herod's influence, and took up the message of His herald, and gave it more publicity and more power.

Thus it has ever been, and still is. Evil may silence a voice, but it cannot prevent the proclamation of the Word. If John be imprisoned, Jesus takes up the message; and that means that it will be proclaimed with clarity, directness, and power, more arresting, disturbing, and prevailing. We need have no trembling of heart when evil seems for the moment to have gained an advantage, and to have triumphed over truth. It is Truth which is mighty, and God ever finds some new instrument through which it will proceed to yet greater victories.

First be reconciled to thy brother, and then come and offer thy gift.—Matt. 5. 24.

This is Christ's law of approach to the altar of worship. It is the altar of worship, for the exercise is that of giving—the highest activity of worship. It is an amazing thing, but nevertheless true, that our God seeks and values the gifts which we bring Him, of praise, thanksgiving, service, and material offerings, which are sanctified by sacrifice. In all such giving at the altar, we enter into the highest experiences of our life of fellowship. But, in these words, our King and Priest utters the most solemn warning. The gift is acceptable to God in the measure in which the one who offers is in fellowship with Him in character and conduct; and the test of this is in our relationship with our fellowmen. Wrong done to a brother, which is unconfessed to the brother, cancels the value of the gift; and we are thus strictly charged to postpone the giving to God, until right relationships are established with men. It is a searching word, and should give us constant pause in our most holy exercises. We are reconciled to God through the prevailing mediation of our one and only Priest; but we may not appropriate the privileges of that reconciliation save upon the basis of having sought reconciliation with our fellowmen in any matter in which they have aught against us. May not neglect of this be the explanation of much of the barrenness of our worship, and the futility of our service? The practical application is one which each one of us must make for himself or herself. We can only neglect it at our peril.

Thy Father Which seeth in secret.—Matt. 6. 4.

That is in some sense the central light upon a section of our Lord's ethical teaching. He had warned His disciples against doing righteousness to be seen of men; and He applied that warning in the matters of alms, prayer, and fasting. The one conditioning motive in each case must be that of the Divine approval. This being so, we are to remember that our Father seeth in secret. In this assurance there is great solemnity, and great comfort. The solemnity is created as we remember His holiness. Nothing can be hidden from the eyes of eternal Purity. He knows why we give or pray or fast. We may deceive others, and unless we are ever conscious of the watching eyes of God, we may deceive ourselves. Him we cannot so deceive. All things are naked and open to the eyes of Him with Whom we have to do.

All this is most solemnizing, and yet its chief note is that of comfort. The very sense of fear which the statement creates in the soul is of the nature of health. It makes us afraid of the base, the ignoble, the impure; for He approves the high, the noble, the pure. And more, it is good to know that He sees in secret, and understands when men misunderstand. That great confidence has enabled men and women to endure with courage and cheerfulness in terrible hours of opprobrium and suffering. The certainty that our Father sees in secret, is a sanctuary into which we may retire at all times, for correction, for encouragement, and for comfort. Let that knowledge be at all times, and under all circumstances, the inspiration and strength of our lives.

Founded upon the Rock.—*Matt.* 7. 25.

In the closing sentences of His ethical manifesto, our Lord claimed full and final authority for all He had said; and that superlatively, by thus declaring that to hear and to do, is to build upon a rock foundation, so securely that no storms can destroy the building. This figure of building may be applied in many ways. Indeed, in every way in which men are attempting to do constructive work, in individual character-building, in every phase of social realization, in national affairs, and in all international and racial matters, His words are fundamental and final. They result from His perfect understanding of all the deepest facts concerning humanity. To order one's own life according to His teaching is to realize all its meaning and strength, and so to make it proof against all destructive forces. To obey His law is to realize the true commonwealth of human lives, and so to ensure the order which abides, and in which righteousness issues in peace and in joy. All this, however, is only possible as we are brought into living relationship with Him by the way of the Cross. We may hear His words, and even admire them; but we cannot do them save in the power of the life He bestows when we trust Him first as our Saviour. The Mount of ethical enunciation reveals the need for the Mount of the Cross. Yet once more let it be said that the gift of life received through Grace must be wrought out to its full realization

by obedience to the laws of life given in Truth. We are saved by Grace and Truth. Therefore all our building, if it is to abide, must be sure-founded on the rock of His teaching.

Himself took our infirmities, and bare our diseases.—*Matt.* 8. 17.

This word takes us beyond the teachings of our Lord, to a record of the marvels which He wrought. As we read we are impressed, and rightly so, with the ease with which He dealt with all the need and suffering of men. In these words, quoted from Isaiah, Matthew suddenly reminds us of another side of truth concerning these doings of the Lord. If His word and touch brought instant deliverance to men, it was because in a great mystery of grace He suffered in order to save. Every wonder of healing was made possible by the profounder wonder of atonement. Our infirmities pass from us, and our diseases cease to vex us, because He takes our sins, and bears them. This is a truth that we should ever bear in mind. The giving of God to us is bounteous and super-abounding, but it is never cheap. The blessings we receive from Him are most precious, because most costly. They are hallmarked with Blood. The water from the well of Bethlehem is the red wine that comes from Calvary. It is as we remember that tremendous fact that we are able to render to Him, our adorable Redeemer, the praise and honour due to His Name. When we drink the wine and eat the bread, let us never permit ourselves to forget the wormwood and the gall! When our pains are eased, let us reverently remember the pains which He bore. Thus shall we ever render Him the worship which is His due.

Go ye and learn.—*Matt.* 9. 13.

These words are the more arresting when we remember that they were addressed to the teachers of men. The Pharisees were amazed when they saw the Lord eating with publicans and sinners. Their astonishment was due to their conception of God. They thought of Him as aloof and distant in His holiness from men who neglected the ceremonial observances of religion, and so considered that all teachers of religion should observe the same attitude. The rebuke of Christ showed that they did not know God, and He bade them go and learn the meaning of their own Scriptures.

Herein is revealed a constant peril. It is terribly possible to be zealous for a wrong conception of God, and of Truth, and so to fail to co-operate with Him in the very enterprise which is dearest to His heart. Nothing is more important, especially in the case of those who are in any way called upon to represent God to men, than that we should go and learn for ourselves the truth about Him. For us there need be no difficulty in this matter, for He has revealed Himself completely in the Son of His love. The hard morality of pharisaism is impossible to those who have learned the truth as it is in Jesus. It follows necessarily that there is nothing of greater importance to all who are called to the service of God in the service of men than that they should go and learn. Time and strength of mind and heart and will must be given to the cultivation of that fellowship in which we ever grow to fuller knowledge.

Not one of them shall fall on the ground without your Father.—*Matt.* 10. 29.

Christ was not speaking of seraphim, nor of saints, but of sparrows. Of one of them He said that if perchance with broken wing, or fainting heart, it fall on the ground, it is not alone, for God is with it. Observe carefully that the declaration is not "without your Father's knowledge," but "without your Father." God not only knows, He is with the falling bird. Like a flash of light, these words enable us to see God's world and God, as Jesus saw them. Nothing is outside His knowledge; nothing is beyond the tender strength of His nearness. He is the Comrade of the bird, which man values at half a farthing! This conception of God creates the fear of Him which cancels all other fear. Knowing Him, we fear with the fear which is born of love. Certain of our safety in His knowledge, and nearness, we fear lest we should grieve Him or disappoint Him in any way. When that fear masters the life, we become devoid of all fear as to what man can do to us. He may kill the body, but that is of little moment. Even if he do, as we fall, the God Who is with the falling sparrow will be with us, and that is the life of the soul, to-day and for ever. This superlative application involves all lesser ones. Fear of pain, of poverty, of adverse circumstances, is cancelled as we know this God, and walk the way of life in His company.

Blessed is he, whosoever shall find none occasion of stumbling in Me.— *Matt.* 11. 6.

These are the final words of the message which the Lord sent to John the Baptist, when he inquired as to whether He was indeed the Christ. They constitute a warning which we all need to bear in mind. There can be no question that John was perplexed by the methods which the Lord was adopting, and that perplexity was due to the fact that even he had not fully apprehended the meaning of Messiahship. Had Jesus preached so as to raise a revolution and create an army, John would have been more satisfied.

This is a perpetual peril. It is not easy yet to understand why God does not do something more startling. It is that idea which underlies the question which we sometimes hear as to why God does not do thus or so. It is that idea which inspires all those activities in the Name of Christ which are attempts to improve upon His methods. To all such restless impatience, He utters the same warning. We are called upon to trust Him so completely as to be content to follow Him in those quiet, persistent methods which consist of attending to individuals, and getting things done one by one, simply, quietly, and with persistent patience. There are hours for demonstration, for, under some circumstances, if men do not shout, stones will cry out. For the most part, the way of the Lord's service is the way of plodding perseverance in the doing of apparently small things. The history of the Church shows that this is one of the lessons most difficult to learn. It also proves that the measure in which it is learned and practised is the measure of real co-operation with God.

Behold, My mother and My brethren. —*Matt.* 12. 49.

Jesus said this with His hands outstretched towards His disciples. By the act and the words He most definitely and distinctly put those disciples into contrast with His mother and brethren after the flesh. These latter were at the time seeking Him, perchance with all kindliness of intention, to persuade Him to abandon His work, and to return home with them. Such action showed how far they were away from Him in all the deepest things. He was in the world to do one thing, and one thing only, and that was the will of His Father. Those who were one with Him in that purpose and were content to abide with Him, were nearer to Him in the real things of life than even those who were related to Him after the flesh. His next of kin are always those who are one with Him in spiritual devotion to the will of God. This is an instance of great value in its revelation of our Lord's conception of the essential spiritual nature of man. He never undervalued the body, but He never treated it as secondary and subservient. It also clearly reveals His conception of what constitutes health and strength in spiritual life. It is simply the doing of the will of God. This, however, is what none can do, save as He makes us one with Him, by communicating His very nature to us. This is the deeper note of His exclamation. He did not exclude His mother and brethren after the flesh, from their relationship; but He did clearly indicate that only upon its basis could they be really one with Him.

He did not many mighty works there because of their unbelief.—*Matt.* 13. 58.

The place referred to was "His own country"; the place where He had grown from childhood to manhood, and had advanced in grace, as Luke tells us. There He had so taught that they were astonished at His "wisdom" and "mighty works." Then He withheld His power, and ceased doing these "mighty works." Why? "Because of their unbelief." He arrested their thought by what He did and said. They were compelled to acknowledge the astonishing nature of these things. Then they allowed unworthy prejudice to prevent their complete and reasonable response to the astonishment of their minds. This was their unbelief. Not that they did not believe that He had said and done wonderful things; but that they did not permit that intellectual conviction to lead them to corresponding volitional action. That is the point at which the Lord is always hindered. It is not that He needed their faith to enable Him to do anything. It was rather that the giving of His teaching, and the doing of His wonders, to and for people who do not yield themselves to the claims which such teaching and doing set up, is of no value to them or to God. Is it not perpetually so that Christ is limited in the individual soul, and in the Church, because of that very quality of unbelief? He comes to the soul and to the assembly, and astonishes with His teaching and His power; and that astonishment leading to nothing, or to foolish attempts to account for Him on human levels, He is hindered, and the mighty works cease.

He went up into the mountain apart to pray.—*Matt.* 14. 23.

In nothing is the perfection of the humanity of our Lord more strikingly seen than in His constant resort to the practice of fellowship with His Father in prayer. Essential human nature needs that practice for its sustenance. Apart from it, it must falter and fail. This our Lord knew, and therefore constantly observed it. Thus the practice is the sign, not of the weakness of the human in Him, but of its full and perfect strength. Neglect of prayer is at once a source and sign of weakness. Surely we need to remind ourselves constantly of this fact as demonstrated in the life of our Lord. Having become our Saviour and Lord, He is our pattern. If then He found the necessity for such times of communion with His Father, apart, alone, how can we hope to live our lives, or render our service acceptable to Him, if we neglect them? There can be no question, moreover, that in His case these seasons were not merely occasions when He asked gifts from His Father. In all probability petition occupied a very important place in such seasons, but by no means the principal place. They were times of communion in which He poured out the joy of His Spirit in adoring praise; and in which He remained in silence, and heard the speech of God in His own soul. And so it must ever be with us, if our lives are to be strong in themselves, and victorious in their service.

Every plant which My heavenly Father planted not, shall be rooted up.—*Matt.* 15. 13.

In order to understand this saying of Jesus, we must carefully note its setting. He had been denouncing the Pharisees for making void the Word of God because of their tradition. His disciples observed and reported to Him the fact that the Pharisees were offended. To them He said that every plant, which was not of His Father's planting, should be rooted up. Here, then, we find the test of all human teaching however well-intentioned. If it be not based upon and rooted in the Word of God, or if it depart in any degree from the true intention of that Word, it is without pity to be rooted up. By this test we need ever to try our traditions, customs, habits, rules, regulations. Man is always in danger of destroying the very thing he desires to safeguard, when he adds to the simplest things of the Divine revelation. This was exactly the story of Pharisaism. Starting with a passion for the Law of God, it had attempted to preserve and enforce it by the addition of rules and burdens, which were intolerable, and which, positively in many applications, destroyed the sanction of the original Law. Christianity has often suffered from the same method. We are strangely in danger of being in bondage to human opinion, interpretation, and requirement. From all such it is our duty to break away, when for a moment, or by a hair's breadth, they relegate us to a distance from the will of God.

Flesh and blood hath not revealed it unto thee, but My Father.—*Matt.* 16. 17.

By this statement our Lord claimed that He had accomplished so far, the purpose for which He had been sent into the world. Through Him the Father had revealed the truth to this company of men—for there is no question that here Peter was speaking not for himself alone, but on behalf of that little company of whom Christ had inquired: "But who say ye that I am?" The Father's revealing truth concerning the Son of God had come through the Son of Man. That explains our Lord's subsequent charge to them: "That they should tell no man that He was the Christ." Their telling could bring no conviction. The Father Himself, through the Son, is alone able to do this.

Does not this give us a very clear sense of our limitation in Christian service; and at the same time make perfectly clear what our true work is? We can never convince men that Jesus is the Christ, the Son of God by our arguments, however sincerely they may state our convictions. Our perpetual business is that of leading men to Him, and leaving them with Him. It is in this latter matter that we often fail. We do not seem to be quite sure that they will come to a right view apart from us. The fact is that they will never come to a right view through us. It is when we have retired, and they are with Him alone, that the light breaks upon them.

This is my beloved Son, in Whom I am well pleased; hear ye Him.—Matt. 17. 5.

Thus by a voice out of an overshadowing cloud, God broke in upon and corrected the confused and foolish suggestion of Peter, the dazed disciple. That it was a foolish suggestion might be shown in many ways. We should remember that Mark tells us that Peter said this when he "knew not what to say," and Luke that he spoke "not knowing what he said." We are warranted, however, in carefully noticing the emphasis of the Divine interruption. Peter suggested the retention of the three in association: Moses, the lawgiver; Elijah, the reformer; and Jesus, the Messiah. The voice declared in effect that such an association was impossible. First, because of Who Jesus was—This is My Son. This Peter had confessed at Caesarea Philippi, but evidently he had not realized the full significance of the fact. The Son of God can never be placed on the same level as servants in the House of God, however faithful they may be. And again, because the Son came to deliver the full and final message of God to men. When He has spoken, we have no need of any partial truth revealed through others. Hear ye Him! By that voice on the Holy Mount, Peter and all Christian teachers are forbidden to look upon the Son of God as One among others. In Him God has said everything that man needs to hear.

How think ye?—Matt. 18. 12.

In this question we have an instance of a method which our Lord often adopted in His teachings, which is arresting, and most suggestive. It was that of appealing to men to test Divine actions by their own. In doing this, He was assuming man's capacity for understanding God, and His assumption was based upon His knowledge of human nature. He knew its depravity, and once, in making use of this very method of appeal, He declared it as He said, "If ye then, *being evil*." Nevertheless, He also knew that if man could be brought to true thinking, to reasoning with God,

he could understand God. In some senses this was a superlative instance, for here He was interpreting God's attitude toward the lost; and He appealed to that instinct in man—"any man," as He said—which would send him out to the mountains to seek the one sheep which had gone astray. Is there not something here which we should do well to remember and imitate in our dealing with men, when we desire to explain and justify the ways of God to them? It must be done with carefulness. We cannot argue the ways of God from the ways of men, but we may be perfectly sure that the ways of God may be illustrated to men by what they will understand of themselves, if they will think simply and truly.

He laid His hands on them.—Matt. 19. 15.

This He did after He had rebuked His disciples for attempting to prevent their being brought to Him. The mistake was very natural, for they did not understand the strategic importance of little children in the Kingdom of God. All that, we learn from this chapter. Our Lord enfranchised the children, and this was symbolized in this act, as it was declared in His works. These hands were those of the King, the Priest, the Teacher. By their laying-on, the children were claimed for His rule, His redemption, His guidance. I have often wondered what became of those particular children. A great and reverent story might be written, making some one of them its hero or heroine. And yet everything would depend upon those who had the care of them afterwards. If they, the fathers and mothers, saw the real value of what took place that day, the children would enter into it all as the years went on. That is the real point of the story for us. So far as He is concerned, those strong and tender hands are laid upon the heads of all our children. Do we recognize that? If so, it will have its effect upon all our dealings with them. They are ours, but they are His by deeper, more sacred, more tender ties; and our principal responsibility concerning them is, not that we should have joy of them, but that He should possess them in very deed.

Ye know not what ye ask.—Matt. 20. 22.

How constantly this is true of our praying, even when it is seeking for the highest things! These men, when they preferred this request, were on a higher level of desire than they had ever reached before. Carefully observe the contrast. He had just been telling them of His coming shame and death, and also of His resurrection. It was then that they asked association with Him in His coming power. It was a request born of faith, and characterized by the noblest aspiration. Yet they did not know what they asked. They did not understand the cost. They did not understand the principle of precedence in that Kingdom.

So it is often with us. The desires we express are well-born, and in so far they are worthy. But our very limitation makes it impossible for us to know whether they can be granted. God is always dealing with His own individually, but always also with a view to their place in the much larger whole of His complete and final purpose. It is patent, therefore, that one element which can never be omitted from true prayer is that of submission. We must believe when we pray, not only that God is generous. To believe that only, will make us doubt it, when He denies. We must believe also, in His perfect wisdom and justice. To do so will enable us to praise Him with equal sincerity whether He give or refuse to do so. That is the fulness of faith, and it is only as we so pray that we can find perfect rest and peace.

Now in the morning as He returned to the city, He hungered.—*Matt.* 21. 18.

This ever seems to me to be one of the statements in which we find the merging in our Lord of the physical and the spiritual. There is no doubt that He was conscious of physical hunger, but His action shows that His supreme consciousness was that of His passion for righteousness. Quite apart from the significance of what He did in the sphere of His mission, this is a most arresting revelation of the truth concerning His personality. He was perfectly human and therefore physically hungry, for hunger is a sign of health. But the deeper note is that because He was so perfectly human, the supreme things of life, which are the spiritual, were still dominant, and His action shows how to Him the physical is ever sacramental, and the medium of the spiritual. This is an ideal of life which we do well to consider. We are terribly in danger, in actual life, of separating between the physical and the spiritual. To put it quite bluntly, we too often lose our spiritual sense when we are physically hungry, or forget our physical needs when spiritually hungry. This is all wrong. In proportion as we are truly submitted to the mastery of our Lord there will be no such one-sidedness of experience. To live the Christ-life is in very deed, whether we eat or drink, or whatever we do, to do all to the glory of God. Then every power of the physical becomes an expression of the spiritual.

God is not the God of the dead, but of the living.—*Matt.* 22. 32.

These words were spoken to the Sadducees who denied the resurrection; and they were intended to constitute one argument for resurrection, and that a final and conclusive one. That argument is that Abraham, Isaac, and Jacob are not dead, but alive. The words of God which Jesus quoted were uttered long after the three men named had died (see Exod. 3. 6). To Moses, God made the declaration; and now our Lord declared that though dead in the ordinary sense, that is as to their earthly bodies\ and experience, they were not dead in the sense of having ceased to be.

This was our Lord's consistent interpretation of death. Of Jairus' daughter, and of Lazarus He said that they slept, when as to bodily life they certainly were dead. Thus we must ever remember that the Christian doctrine of death is not that it is in any sense cessation of being. It is rather separation. Physical death is the separation of the spirit from the body. Spiritual death is separation of the spirit from God. The spirits of the just made perfect are more alive than they ever were, because they are more consciously with God. For them, being absent from the body is being at home with the Lord, and that is life indeed. He is indeed the God of our loved ones who as to this earth have fallen on sleep, and that means that they are alive. By-and-by, in resurrection, they will awake, even in bodily form, in His likeness, and that will be their final perfecting. And this is, as we have said, a final and conclusive argument for resurrection. Man is not perfect as a disembodied spirit. He needs a body for perfect expression. Thus the perfecting of the saints will come in the moment of resurrection.

Woe unto you.—*Matt.* 23. 13.

These are strangely solemn words, and the more so when we remember that they were the words of One Whose heart is full of all tenderness, and Whose love for men is unfathomable. Yet here they are, and seven times repeated. In six cases the reason for the woe is revealed by the use of the word "hypocrites," and once by the words "blind guides." No amount of argument can rob these words of their terrible import. They stand upon the page for evermore speaking to us of "the wrath of the Lamb." The full context clearly discloses to us the reason of that wrath. It proceeds against those who are wronging men by misrepresenting God. In their teaching these Scribes and Pharisees had removed the emphasis from all the essential things of the soul, and had placed it upon trivialities. They had made the religious life a burden with no moral or spiritual value, when it should be the strength of all these things. For wrong done to men, and so to God, these men were denounced. Thus the very heat of the anger of the Lord is that of His perfect love. How little men know of the depth of that love who imagine that wrath has no place in the mind or will of God. These woes stand over against the beatitudes at the opening of the Manifesto of the King, which reveal His purpose for man. They declare the result of preventing the realization of that purpose; and they were uttered against men who, by virtue of the office they held, were responsible for interpreting to men the Kingdom of God, and who by their hypocrisy were hiding that Kingdom.

Behold, I have told you beforehand. —Matt. 24. 25.

In these words our Lord revealed to His disciples then, and for all time, the real value of these prophetic utterances at the close of His public ministry. He saw the end from the beginning, and all the processes leading thereto, and was under no delusion as to the strength of the evil forces to be dealt with before the final and perfect establishment of the Day of the Lord. He declared these things beforehand that we also might be free from all such delusion, and that through all the periods and processes of catastrophe and deceit, our hearts should be kept firm and faithful to Him in the assurance of His knowledge. The perspective of prediction is at all times perplexing, and it is certainly so in these foretellings of Jesus. The general principles and facts are perfectly plain, and concerning them we can make no mistake. Wars and distresses, false prophets and false Christs, are to continue and multiply, until the Coming of the Son of Man. If this view of the course of events is not consonant with human ideas of how things ought to happen, it certainly is true to the actual facts of history and experience until now. We may rest assured that He Whose predictions have been verified completely so far, was not mistaken about the consummation. The Son of Man is surely coming, and when He comes there will be no mistaking the fact. Let us not be seduced from our loyalty to Him by any false Christ.

Watch therefore, for ye know not the day nor the hour.—Matt. 25. 13.

This is our Lord's word to His own as to their attitude toward the fact of His Second Coming. That He is coming again He most plainly declared, and all the New Testament writers affirmed the truth. The light and glory of that certainty falls upon all the darkness of the processes through which the victory of the Kingdom of God is to be won. Nothing will be completed until He come; but everything is working under His mediatorial reign to that consummation. Nothing is more explicit in His references to that glorious end, than the declaration that the day and hour are not revealed. The hiding of that time is part of the Divine counsel.

To seek to discover it is to attempt to be wiser than our Lord, in His infinite wisdom, intends that we should be. Our attitude is to be that of those who watch. To know the day or the hour would be to make watching largely unnecessary; and this would rob us of that alertness which is of the very essence of true discipleship both in life and service. Concerning the times and seasons we need have no care. They are within the Father's authority, and there can be no failure with Him. Knowing beforehand both the strangeness of the period of our waiting, and the certainty of His coming, it is ours to have our lamps burning, our loins girt about, and to be so occupied about His business that when He comes we shall be neither surprised nor ashamed. That is patient waiting for Christ, and it is far removed from the fussy impatience that seeks to know what He has chosen to hide, and in such seeking spends time and strength which should be devoted to His service.

When they had sung a hymn, they went out unto the mount of Olives.— Matt. 26. 30.

These words, interpreted by a reverent imagination, present one of the most wonderful pictures. Twelve men are seen singing. The company is composed of One, and eleven. The circumstances, judged by human standards, can only be described as tragic. The eleven are losing the One. He is going out to bruising, to buffeting, to a death of shame. And yet they sing, and it is impossible to doubt that He led the singing. We shall be helped in considering the wonder if we glance at Psalms 113 to 118. These constituted the Great Hallel which was always sung at the Passover. All that had been foreshadowed in that Feast was now approaching completion, and this company of eleven were permitted to join Him, the Paschal Lamb by God appointed, in singing. If we are amazed at a song in so dark an hour, we also see its fitness and its glory. If they thought they were losing Him, it was not so in the counsel of God. He was gaining them, that so they might gain Him, in a sense in which they had never possessed Him. He was going forth to bruise the head of the Serpent, to put to shame all the evil things that had destroyed men. He was passing in travail to the final triumph. No sweeter singing, no mightier music ever sounded amid the darkness of the sad world's night than the singing of Jesus and His first disciples, as He moved out to the Cross of His Passion, and their redemption. They sang the anthem of humanity's emancipation and of God's glory. And so persistently, through all the ages, those who have fellowship with His suffering march along the sorrowful way, singing the song of the final triumph!

Make it as sure as ye can.—*Matt. 27. 65.*

It is almost impossible to read these words of Pilate to the priests and Pharisees without detecting the tones of restless impatience, and of a sarcasm which was born of some great uncertainty in his own heart. He had passed through strange experiences in dealing with Jesus. Under stress of political expediency he had violated his own conscience, and had given Him over to death. But was He dead? Or if He was, what strange things might not be about to happen? Yes, said he, take the guard, make the sepulchre as sure as ye can! Perhaps Pilate really hoped that, if there were anything in the weirdly haunting fears that assaulted him, the guard might prevent their fulfiment; so strangely do men attempt to deal with spiritual forces by material means. In many different ways that is what evil is always saying. The one fact which it is necessary for evil to prevent or deny is that of the actual Resurrection. All the claims of Christianity depend upon that. If Jesus of Nazareth lived and died, and His dust remained in the Syrian tomb, then everything breaks down. Then His teaching was untrue. His avowed intention was frustrated. He was at the best, a deluded man, and we are deceived if we trust Him as Saviour and follow Him as Lord. But mark the limitation of the words, *"as sure as ye can"*; and wait the issue. Man's efforts to prove Him not risen are as futile as those he employed to prevent Him rising. He left the tomb triumphantly, and He emerges in new power and glory from every attempt to declare Him dead.

Risen, even as He said. — *Matt. 28. 6.*

Thus the fact in history vindicated the word He had spoken. It should ever be remembered that our Lord is never recorded as speaking of His coming Cross without at the same time foretelling His resurrection. This is God's eternal answer to all the might of evil. Herod sought the young Child's life to destroy it. At last they put Him to death. His body they placed in a tomb, guarded by soldiers. They made it as sure as they could, remembering that He had "said while He was yet alive, After three days I rise again." And this is the issue: "Risen, even as He said!"

That is the secret of our assurance in the darkest day. The forces of evil are mighty, but God is Almighty. The plotting of evil is full of cleverness, but the wisdom of God holds it all in perfect knowledge, and His plans move ever forward to realization with absolute and splendid certainty. But let us make no mistake about it, we have no certainty of His almightiness, nor of His absolute wisdom, apart from His Resurrection. We have no other sufficient evidence of the one or the other. Herod seeks still to destroy the young Child. Priests and politicians still crucify the Lord, and set guards over His grave, declaring Him to be dead. But by this sign, amid the ages, we know that it is Herod who must and will be destroyed, and that the men who crucify will find salvation by the Cross, or by it will be cast out into the nethermost darkness.

MARK

The . . . Gospel of Jesus Christ, the Son of God.—*Mark 1. 1.*

These words give us Mark's conception of the value of the story he was about to write. It was wholly good tidings, a story to cause gladness, news which would bring hope to those who should need it. That is a truth which should never be forgotten by those who are called to declare the story. Sometimes the dark and awful facts of human life are in danger of giving an almost gloomy note to the preaching of the Gospel. It never should be so. Sin is a terrible fact, and the more we understand our message the more will its terror be felt. But that message is first, and always, the good news of the possibility of complete deliverance therefrom. The preacher of that good news should always be confident, jubilant, a veritable optimist in all the richest senses of that often much-abused word. He is full of hope,

and it is hope well founded. He hopes in God, on behalf of man, and his right to do so is that of the Crucified and Risen Christ.

The secrets of the Gospel are suggested in the remaining words—"of Jesus Christ the Son of God." The good news is simply and wholly the story of that Person. His twofold being and relationship are set forth in the first and last of the words describing Him; and the meaning of His presence in the world—in the central one. He is Jesus, Man of our humanity. He is the Son of God, and of His very essence He is the Anointed King-Priest, reigning over man, as God, and reconciling man to God as Man. This is indeed a glorious Gospel.

I came not to call the righteous, but sinners.—*Mark 2. 17.*

That is, even yet, as surely as when it was first uttered, a startling, solemnizing word. In a general, superficial way, men accept it. All must agree in the more positive aspect of it. He certainly did come to call sinners. It is the negative aspect which startles. He plainly declared that He had no message for the righteous. If any man shall refuse to be reckoned among sinners, then, according to this declaration of the Lord, that man stands outside the circle to which His appeal is made.

The context shows the true value of the saying. The moral teachers were criticising Him for consorting with sinners, and in these words He gave His reason for doing so, and at the same time made it clear that He had no message for any men who refused to take their place with those very sinners.

In such a saying, under such circumstances, there is discoverable a gentle satire, and a great compassion. These self-satisfied men, who will by no means consent to be counted among the sinners, are taken at their own valuation. They are whole, and so have no need of the Physician! They are righteous, and so do not require His call! And yet the deepest note is that of His compassion. He knew their sickness, and so was willing to heal them. He knew they were sinners, and so was calling them also.

When we accept the Divine judgment that "There is none righteous," then we find His call is indeed to us. To resent that finding is to put ourselves outside the number of those to whom the Son of God calls.

He surnamed . . . He surnamed.—
Mark 3. 16, 17.

This is a very suggestive story. To three of His twelve Apostles He gave surnames. Perhaps He did the same for all. We do not know. The action in regard to these three is illustrative. Perhaps He ever does the same for His own. If so, one wonders how He is surnaming us. The idea is purely speculative, but it is speculation on a profitable level, especially in the light of these revelations.

"Simon He surnamed Rock." This Simon was impulsive, restless, inconsistent, lacking cohesion. Yet He surnamed him Rock. The name was an indication of his unrealized natural capacities; and of the Lord's ability to realize them. The sons of Zebedee, James and John, He surnamed Sons of Thunder. They were men of gentle, filial nature, quiet men, content to abide at home in the service of their father. Yet He surnamed them Sons of Thunder; men of authority and power. The principle was the same. In James was the capacity to be so loyal to a Master and a cause as to die for them. In John was the mystic power which would make him a seer, and an interpreter of the great things of life. The Lord was able to bring these things to realization,

and to employ them for His own glory in co-operation with His service.

And so again we wonder what is He naming us? The consideration is for the hour of lonely communion with Him. In such an hour we shall discover that His surnaming is ever based upon two things; first, our capacities as the result of our first birth; and secondly, His power to realize those capacities. We shall find, moreover, that His power becomes operative when we are wholly yielded to Him.

The earth beareth fruit of herself.—
Mark 4. 28.

The statement shows the reign of man's responsibility and impotence. In the matter of harvest man has things he can do, and those he cannot do. He can sow. He can reap. These are necessary. Apart from sowing there is no harvest. Apart from reaping the harvest is wasted. Beyond these his place is that of weakness and of waiting. His waiting is not that of restlessness. He goes quietly on with his life, sleeping and rising. His confidence rests upon two things: first, his having done his appointed task; and secondly, the certainty that work is being done which is outside the realm of his power, for "the earth beareth fruit of herself."

The statement does not exclude God. The earth is full of His glory. All the wonderful processes of death into life which go forward without fail within the embrace of the soil are operations of the power of God. While they are active, man must wait.

And Jesus said: "So is the Kingdom of God." This clearly defines the realm of our responsibility. We must sow. We must reap. There our operations cease. The mightiest work is Divine. The soil in which we sow is the realm in which God alone can work. But it is for us to know that He is working there, even through the long wintry days when the results of our toil are not yet visible. Happy indeed are we if we learn to work in our appointed places, and then to wait in the double assurance of our limitation and of His power.

The child is not dead, but sleepeth.
—Mark 5. 39.

In these words we discover our Lord's outlook upon death. There was no doubt whatever that the maiden was dead as to her bodily being, her earthly consciousness. Christ's outlook on personality was such that He took in the whole fact. Death of the body was not cessation of being. The child was not dead. She was alive. As to her consciousness of earthly things, she was asleep. Perchance her father and mother had often looked upon her in her sleep in days of health. While she was asleep, she was quite unconscious that they were near her, and they could not communicate with her, save by ending the condition of sleep. Jesus told them that this was so now. From ordinary sleep they could have awakened her. From this deeper slumber they could not. But He could; and that is what He presently did. He used the same word to describe actual bodily death in the case of Lazarus, until the dullness of His disciples compelled Him to say plainly, "Lazarus is dead."

This outlook upon death is full of comfort. Our Lord always stands by our dead and says to us: "Not dead, but sleeping." He does not always waken them. Indeed He rarely did so in His earthly ministry. Such waking would mean for them return to all life's fitful feverishness. Still they are not dead, and one glad day He will waken them again to bodily consciousness in a new and better order. Then we shall gain them, and with them be for ever with Him.

They told Him all things, whatsoever they had done, and whatsoever they had taught.—*Mark 6. 30.*

That is an account of how the first Apostolic mission ended. After a period of preparation by being with Him, they had been sent out by two and two to do His work, and thus enlarge the area of His activity. They had been successful in all the work to which He had appointed them. As a result of their mission, "His name had become known" more widely. Then they returned to him and they came back to report. The picture suggested is a very beautiful one. The Lord Who had sent them, and Who had never been separated from them during their absence, is seen listening to them as they told Him the things He knew perfectly. The sequel shows that He understood that such work is costly. They were tired, and He called them to rest awhile.

Are we not a little in danger of missing the real value of this story? We are more apt to report what we have done, for Him to each other, and to the world, than to Him. Such reporting is not necessarily wrong. But for our own souls' good, and for our more perfect equipment for further service, it is better to report to Him. Yet this is a largely neglected activity. It is not prayer. It is not praise. It is telling Him what we have done and taught. Regularly to do this would be to make us more than ever careful in all our doing, and all our teaching.

He could not be hid.—*Mark 7. 24.*

The explanation of this statement is found in the story which follows, of which story it is the introduction. A mother, whose heart was wrung with anguish by reason of the suffering of her child, sought the aid of Jesus, and from such an appeal "He could not be hid." The declaration is made the more arresting by the fact that it follows the statement that He desired privacy: "He entered into a house, and would have no man know it." And yet again it is interesting in view of the method of apparent reluctance which He adopted with her. These very surroundings serve to add new emphasis and value to the declaration. May we not at once say that here incidentally we have an illustration of the very reason of the Incarnation, and all that it accomplished? From human suffering God cannot withdraw Himself. He cannot be hidden. It appeals to Him irresistibly, because of the grace of His nature. When there is no eye to pity, His eye always pities; when there is no arm to save, His arm brings salvation. Herein, and herein alone, is our hope that at last sorrow and sighing shall flee away. And, moreover, in the fact that it is God, Who is thus compelled by His nature to come to the relief of the sorrowing, is our guarantee that there will be no slight healing of our wounds. He does not deal with symptoms merely, but with the dire root of the disease. As He comes forth from His hiding-place, compelled by human agony, He comes to make no terms with that which has caused the pain; but He comes to end the pain by removing the cause.

Do ye not yet understand?—*Mark 8. 21.*

These are the final words in a paragraph recording how our Lord rebuked His disciples. It begins in verse seventeen, and it is impossible to read it without feeling that there was a note of real severity in what He said to them. Notice the rush of His questions. "Why reason ye because ye have no bread? Do ye not yet perceive, neither understand? Have ye your heart hardened? Having eyes, see ye not? And having ears, hear ye not? And do ye not remember?" What, then, was the fault of these men? They were missing the point of His spiritual teaching, because they were anxious about material things. He recalled them to a remembrance of what they had already witnessed of His ability to deal with material need. It is always a strange story, this. It seems inconceivable that these men, really remembering the facts, as their answers show that they did, should yet have failed to apply those past experiences to present needs. Yet is it strange? Is it not a peculiar and persistent failing of the human soul, that in the presence of some immediate danger, it forgets, or fails to apply, the value of past deliverances? Yet it should not be so; and it was this very thing which our Lord rebuked. The true attitude of the soul is that of being without carefulness, in the consciousness of what has been done for us. The superlative statement of this is found in Paul's words: "He that spared not His own Son, but delivered Him up for us all, how shall He not also with Him freely give us all things?"

And Jesus said unto him, If thou canst!—*Mark 9. 23.*

This was the response of our Lord to a man who came to Him haltingly. He was a father, in sore trouble. His boy from childhood had suffered, and nothing could be done for him. The man had heard of the fame of Jesus, and brought the boy to Him, only to find that He was not with His disciples, having gone away to the mountain. In this dilemma he appealed to the disciples, and they were unable to deal with the case. Perhaps it was this inability on their part which made him doubtful as to whether their Master could help. It is probable that men are often hindered from faith in Christ, because of our failure to do things which we could do if our fellowship with Him were more complete. Be that as it may, his cry was that of a great anguish, in which hope and doubt mingled: "If Thou canst do anything, have compassion on us and help us." To this the reply of the Lord was an ejaculatory and rebuking repetition of the man's word, "If thou canst!" He then revealed the secret of His own ability to be that of faith as He said, "All things are possible to him that believeth." He was the file-leader and vindicator of faith. The man immediately understood the principle and applied it to himself as he said: "I believe; help Thou mine unbelief"; and the response of Christ was immediate. It is when our faith is inspired by His that we make contact with His ability to do the things which we cannot do ourselves.

Jesus . . . was moved with indignation.—*Mark 10. 14.*

Mark alone of the Evangelists gives us this revealing touch in connection with this story of the reception and blessing of the children. When we recite His words spoken on that occasion, the tone of a great tenderness almost invariably finds its way into our voices. And that is natural, for the words are full of comfort for all those who love little children. It is nevertheless important, for our warning, that we should never forget that when our Lord uttered the words, He was angry. He was moved with indignation that any of His disciples should so misunderstand Him as to endeavour to prevent the children from getting to Him. There is no doubt whatever that these disciples meant well. They were on their way to Jerusalem, and His converse with them had been concerned with His coming sufferings. They were quite unable to understand Him in all this, but at least they knew that His mind was occupied with tremendous things, and they felt that He ought not to be disturbed by children.

The story reminds us, then, that it is possible to mean well, and to do ill; and it gives us for evermore to understand the place which the children occupy in His heart. In any way to hinder them from getting to Him is to cause Him to be moved with indignation. Conversely—to help them to Him, is to give Him joy. The children are all about us, and so everywhere are opportunities for giving Him this joy.

Whensoever ye stand praying, forgive.—*Mark 11. 25.*

That is a law of prayer. May it not be that much unanswered prayer is the result of forgetting this? Forgetting is the right word. If we remember it, we either cease to pray, or we forgive. It is impossible to pray easily when the heart is hot and angry with someone who has done us wrong. But in the underlying depths of our consciousness there are often feelings toward others which are those of resentment, even though at the moment we are not occupied with them. If it be so, then, according to this word of Jesus we have no right to expect that our Father will forgive us our trespasses. Let us think what it would mean if we always remembered this word. If we did so, our first inquiry whenever we desired to pray would be: Is there any person whom we have not yet forgiven? Of course, the presupposition is that the person has really wronged us in some way. Apart from that there would be nothing to forgive. Is there such a person? Then, before we can pray, we must forgive that person. Then, after we have prayed, we shall have to carry out our act of forgiveness by seeking the forgiven person, and establishing the relationship that results from forgiveness. What gracious results would follow in the communion of the saints if this word of Jesus were remembered and obeyed? Love would win wonderful triumphs, and prayer would become powerful and prevailing.

Have ye not read even this scripture?—*Mark 12. 10.*

A reference to the previous chapter (verse 27) will show that our Lord addressed these words to "the chief priests, and the scribes, and the elders." That is to say, they were spoken to the religious, moral, and civil rulers—that is, to men who were certainly familiar with the Sacred Scriptures. It is impossible to suppose they had not read the words He quoted, many, many times. That it was a familiar passage is suggested by our Lord's use of the word "even" in His asking of the question. And yet, according to His meaning, they had not read this Scripture. Here, then, emerges a matter of supreme importance concerning the reading of Scripture, and that more especially in the case of such as are devoted to the work of teaching and interpretation. A Scripture is not read rightly when its words are known. Nor is it read until God's meaning is discovered. These men were face to face with the events in which the great principle declared in these words was being carried out; and they were blind to the events in their real significance, because they had never truly read the words with unprejudiced minds, and so under the illumination of the Spirit of God. We are constantly in peril of the same superficial and harmful reading of the Sacred Writings. Therefore we should never come to them without a due sense of our own weakness, and in complete dependence upon the Holy Spirit.

Heaven and earth shall pass away, but My words shall not pass away.— Mark 13. 31.

Perhaps this was our Lord's superlative word concerning His teaching. A statement more definite and plain it would be impossible to frame. Whereas the claim had undoubted reference to the whole of His teaching, it is important that we should remember that He uttered it in connection with His apocalyptic prophecies. It has been the fashion of certain thinkers to discredit the validity of these sayings of Jesus. First it was suggested that the records were not authentic. That view has been largely abandoned; and now it is suggested that He was mistaken in accepting the views of His age. Yet, according to this word, it was in connection with these very things that He made this supreme claim.

It is well to remember this to-day. However difficult it may be to come to perfect agreement in the interpretation of these Olivet discourses in detail, it is unquestionable that their general ideas are far more in harmony with the world-conditions in the midst of which we are living, than are the views which have been advanced as to the course of things proceeding gradually, and without upheaval, to the establishment of an order of peace and goodwill among men. This claim is being vindicated in our own times. It is evident that He understood the human heart better than the modern teachers who have thought Him mistaken. We may still rest assured that the march of history will vindicate Him at every point, and in that assurance we shall find our safety and our joy in believing Him and obeying Him.

They all left Him, and fled.—Mark 14. 50.

That was the last stage in a process which had been going on almost from the beginning of our Lord's public ministry. He had irresistibly attracted men by the charm of His personality, and the radiant splendour of His ideals. But men could not reach Him. They came so far, and then halted, and went back. First the rulers; then certain of His earlier followers, who went back and walked no more with Him; then the crowds themselves, as they yielded to the influence of the rulers; and now at last the inner circle of His disciples, as they were perplexed and terrified by the force of circumstances which were closing in around Him. And it is all quite understandable. Man can only come to fellowship with Him in thought and life as he is made nigh by the work of Grace which results from His Cross. These men were presently regathered by the fact of the Resurrection, and ingathered by the baptism of the Holy Spirit. Then they were able to share His Cross. It is always so. Mere admiration of the Person of the Lord, or consent to the perfection of His ideals, will not outlive the experiences through which attempts at following Him will lead men. Men may applaud Him, and be prepared to cast their votes for a Kingdom such as He described; but under the pressure of opposing forces they will only follow Him as they are united to Him in death and resurrection.

He saved others; Himself He cannot save.—Mark 15. 31.

This is one of the instances of which there are a number, when the enemies of our Lord, in hatred or in mockery, said things about Him which were profoundly true. That may be said to be the whole truth concerning His dying. In order to save others He could not save Himself. His inability was not, as His enemies suggested, the inability of weakness. It was the inability of eternal strength. It was not that He was unable to save Himself; but rather that He was able not to save Himself. Therefore He is able to save to the uttermost all who come unto God through Him.

While the great fact is supreme, and in all highest senses lonely in the Person of the Son of God, the principle has perpetual application in the case of those who share His life, and are called into fellowship with Him in the work of saving men. We have no power to save others, save as we have power not to save ourselves. The claims and desires of the self-life are very insistent. They may be perfectly proper within the limits of personality. It is only when we have the ability to deny them, in our determination to serve others, that we are approaching the region of saving strength. This is the real Christian secret. When at Caesarea Philippi, Peter said to his Master, "Spare Thyself," he was uttering the words of worldly wisdom— he was minding the things of men. That was why he was so sternly rebuked by Him Who, minding the things of God, actuated by the heavenly wisdom, could not spare or save Himself, because He desired to save others.

The Lord working with them.— Mark 16. 20.

That is Mark's last word about the Lord. He is co-operating with His messengers in the delivery of their message, and confirming the word by deeds of power which are the signs of His presence. The previous statement reveals Him as sitting at the right-hand of God, having been received up into Heaven. These two pictures should ever be in our mind as we go forth on His business. He is the triumphant One. All He came to do, He did. His return to the Father was that of victorious accomplishment. But it was not the return to inactivity. From that supreme place of authority and power He directs and accompanies all the journeyings and activities of those who are His messengers to men.

Two matters should be carefully noted. First, that He works with the preachers of the Word, in the actual work of preaching. Too often we are in danger of preaching as though in the act we are alone. It is not so. In proportion as we are true to Him, and His message, we may rest assured that He is Himself actually, by the Holy Spirit, working with us, making His own direct appeal to those who are listening to us. The truth is full of comfort. Then, second, we must recognize that it is He Who gives the signs. It is not for us to choose what they shall be. Sometimes they are wholly spiritual; sometimes they are wrought in the mental and physical realms. We have nothing to do with them. Our only responsibility is that of preaching the Word. He will give such signs as He knows to be necessary for the fulfilment of His purpose, and to the glory of His name.

LUKE

Hail, thou that art highly favoured, the Lord is with thee.—Luke 1. 28.

These were the words which Gabriel employed when, sent from God, he came to Nazareth, to tell Mary the awful and tremendous secret of the part she was chosen to take in the Divine activity of human redemption. Thus the angel greeted her in the terms of respect, born of his apprehension of the greatness of the sacred sorrows and joys which were to be her portion. Moreover, his words reveal the fact of her character and fitness for the high honour; she was a woman "endued with grace," and one with whom the Lord was in communion.

The Christian Church generally has, in the process of time, fallen into two attitudes toward the Virgin Mother, one of which is utterly wrong, while the other is mistaken. The first is that of the Roman Church, which has placed her between humanity and the Son of God. This is idolatry, and its effect has been disastrous. The second is that of Protestantism, which in a warranted re-bound from Mariolatry, has forgotten to hold the mother of our Lord in the esteem which is due to her. Mary was a member of the sinning race, and needed and shared in the redemption which was provided by her Son; but the honour conferred on her was of the highest, and our thoughts of her, and our language concerning her, should at least not lack the dignity and respect manifested in the words of Gabriel. Hers was the crown and glory of all Motherhood, and we should ever think and speak of her reverently.

Wist ye not that I must be in the things of My Father?—Luke 2. 49.

These are the first recorded words of our Lord. I resolutely adopt the second marginal reading of the Revised—which is direct translation from the Greek. They were spoken when He was twelve years of age, being then, as Luke so beautifully describes Him, "the boy Jesus." It has often been pointed out that they are very significant as giving the key to the whole of His life and work. The compelling force, the "must" behind all His doing and teaching, was ever the same: the things of His Father. He lived and wrought only to do the will of God.

There is, however, another value in them. Because He was "the boy Jesus," a most real and true Boy, we gather from these words not only the inherent grace and truth of His character, but also how careful had been His training from babyhood. From the annunciation to Mary, and the revelation to Joseph which Matthew records, those two people in a holy fellowship had shared the secret as to that wonderful Child. With what reverent awe and tender solicitude they must have watched His growth and development! And again, because He was a real human Child, they were responsible for all His earliest instruction in "the things of God." The result is seen in this simple, natural, unaffected word, spoken, be it noticed, to both of them: "Knew ye not that I must be in the things of My Father?" The difference between this Boy and our children is admitted; but let us not forget His identity with them. If we remember, we shall ever seek to train them to the same complete conception of life. It is a great thing when as the result of our training and example, our children relate all their lives to God by its "must" of complete surrender.

Jesus . . . the son of Adam, the son of God.—*Luke 3. 23 and 38.*

While there are supposed to be difficulties in reconciling the two genealogical tables of Matthew and Luke, it is patent that Mary and Joseph came of the same stock, and that both were of the house of David, and of the seed of Abraham. As a matter of fact there are no difficulties— or should not be. In Matthew we have the legal birth book of Jesus as the adopted son of Joseph. In Luke we have His actual genealogy through His Mother. The peculiar value of Luke's is that in it he passes back through this house and seed to the human origin in Adam. The last named in his table is Adam, and through the successions Jesus is the Son of Adam. But Adam is here called the son of God, and so in this way also Jesus is the Son of God. This is a matter of supreme importance in the light it throws upon human relationship to God.

Our Lord was The Son of God in a separate and lonely sense, but as the Son of Mary, a child of the human race, He was also a Son of God. That then is the deepest fact of all human life, and it is when the fact is realized that the appalling tragedy of human life is also realized. By sin man is alienated from his birthright, cut off from God, degraded and lost. Jesus of Nazareth, Child of Mary, and ultimately Son of Adam and Son of God, was sinless in His human nature, and so lived in His birthright, in fellowship with God, full of grace and truth. Herein we find the element which made it possible for Him to act with God, for men; as the other, that of His eternal Sonship, enabled Him to act with men for God, and as God.

To-day hath this scripture been fulfilled in your ears.—*Luke 4. 21.*

What a wonderful day that was! The Lord was back in Nazareth, in His boyhood's home, among the people who knew Him best, so far as the incidental things of His earthly life were concerned. Luke says that He went into the synagogue "as His custom was."

What visions that suggests of His regular presence in that gathering-place through the years! How often He had been there mingling with the worshippers, and yet separated from them by the mystery of His being, and by the consciousness of His mission! And now He chose to make that synagogue the place where He claimed the fulfilment in Himself and His work of the wonderful foretelling of the prophet so long before,

Reference to the passage in Isaiah (61. 1, 2) will show that the place where He ceased reading is revealing. In our versions only a comma separates what He read from the words, "and the day of vengeance of our God." For that He was not then anointed. In the time appointed He will carry that out also, with all that follows of restoration. How long the interval represented by that comma, only God knows. The times and seasons are within His authority. So far the interval has lasted nearly 2,000 years. This is still the day of His Gospel, His work that of delivering of captives. It is still the acceptable year of the Lord.

Who can forgive sins, but God alone?—*Luke 5. 21.*

This was a question asked by the enemies of our Lord, and it was asked in connection with their charging Him with blasphemy because He had said to a man: "Thy sins are forgiven thee." It is a startling and suggestive situation. The theology of these men was correct; their application was wrong. It is true that none can forgive sins, save God. There is a sense in which a man can, and indeed ought to forgive sin committed against him by his brother man. But it is a very limited sense, being peculiarly relative and personal. In the deeper nature of sin no man can absolve his brother. The Psalmist in the olden days uttered a profound truth when, in the midst of his penitential outpouring, he said: "Against Thee, Thee only have I sinned." Therefore it is God alone Who can forgive. Thus the word of Jesus to this man was the word of God, and His word of forgiveness is always the word of God. Only as that is so, can the heart of sinning men be satisfied. When my brother forgives me for the wrong I have done him, I am thankful to him, but this forgiveness has not lifted the burden from my conscience, nor cleansed the stain from my soul. When God forgives, He does both. Our rest in the sense of forgiveness is always created by the certainty that it is the gift of the grace of God.

Why call ye Me Lord, Lord, and do not the things which I say?—*Luke 6. 46.*

How familiar these words of our Lord are to all of us! We agree with their intention. It is wrong, it is futile, to call Him Lord, if we are not acting in harmony with the profession which such naming of Him involves. To call Him Lord, is to declare that we are His subjects. To neglect to do what He commands, is to give the lie to our declaration. All *that* we recognize. Now the arresting thing here is that our Lord did not upon this occasion convey the truth in the form of a statement, but in the form of a question.

Therefore the incisive word is the introductory "Why?" What is the answer? If we are disobedient why continue the profession of obedience? To find the answer will be to search the inner life diligently and ruthlessly. The "Why" of Jesus penetrates to the deepest things of the life. It refuses to be put off with any hypocrisy, or superficial excuse. "Why!" Therefore it is a question to which it would be almost dangerous to suggest possible answers. Each soul guilty of the wrong referred to, must face this "Why" alone. All that need be said is, that to do so will inevitably be to discover the unworthiness of the reason, and moreover, that there is no necessity for such hypocrisy. Indeed, the Lord has a better chance to help any man who ceases to call Him Lord, when he ceases to obey His commands. This "Why" of Jesus is like a sharp instrument which cuts into the very core of a malady.

Seest thou this woman?—Luke 7. 44.

When Simon saw the woman of the city who was "a sinner" in contact with Christ, he came to the conclusion that the fact that the Lord permitted her to act as she was doing, was proof of His lack of perception. Evidently, thought Simon, He was unable to detect the truth about her; He was spiritually blind. The recognition of this conception of the Pharisee gives point to the question which the Lord addressed to him: "Seest thou this woman?" Having asked the question, He proceeded to help Simon to see her. The difference between Simon's attitude toward her and that of the Lord is, that while Simon was not looking at her, the Lord was doing so. Simon was judging her by her past. Jesus was judging her by her present.

Are we not all in danger of falling into Simon's mistake? It is not easy for us to blot out a past, and to free ourselves from all prejudice resulting from our knowledge of that past. Yet that is exactly what the Lord does. And He does so, not unrighteously, but righteously. He knows the power of His own grace, and that it completely cancels the past, and gives its own beauty to the soul. When we allow memories of the past to blind us to the transformation wrought by grace, we are proving how meanly we think of grace.

Where is your faith?—Luke 8. 25.

This is an arresting word, taken in relation with the circumstances that called it forth. The story is that of our Lord's putting forth of power to help those who appealed to Him in distress, and then rebuking them for that distress. It is a strange and yet beautiful story, revealing at once the tenderness of His heart, and its highest passion for His own. It is probable that their distress was more than personal. The "we" in their cry "Master, Master, we perish," included Him as well as them. If that boat went down, all went with it—His mission, their hopes, and the great enterprises which He had called them into fellowship with Himself to carry out. To that cry, in tenderness and strength, for their sake, He immediately responded by changing the circumstances from storm to calm, thus proving to them what all the time was true, that

"No water can swallow the ship where lies
The Master of ocean and earth and skies."

Then He asked them, "Where is your faith?" thus rebuking them for their distress, and showing that His desire for them was that they should have such confidence in Him as to be undisturbed amid all disturbances.

How often we are over-anxious about the enterprises of our Lord! In the hour of storm we imagine everything is about to perish. Then He ever says to us: "Where is your faith?"

As He was praying alone, the disciples were with Him.—Luke 9. 18.

The paradox is a revelation. He was not actually alone, for the disciples were with Him. But He was praying apart. A careful study of the Gospel narratives has led to the justifiable conclusion that our Lord never prayed with His disciples. Often He left them when He would pray. When in their company He prayed, it was not in association with them, but in separation. He commanded them to pray. He taught them to pray, He promised them the widest franchise in prayer. But His praying was on a different plane. When referring to His own communion with His Father, He never employed some words which He did employ in speaking of their praying. His approach to God was different from that of sinning humanity. He had claims which men have not; those of identity of Being, and equality of Sovereignty. Thus He ever prayed alone; and thus He ever intercedes alone. His intercession is of a different nature from all others. That is why the idea of the intercession of His Mother and of all the saints, as being of use or of value by comparison with Him, is utterly false. It is right that we should pray for each other. It is conceivable, and most probable, that the glorified saints are still praying for those that are yet in the midst of earth's trials and temptations. But at last there is One only Intercessor within the veil, and He has a right of access and intercession which can never be shared by any of His creation. There is our rest and confidence. We may ever be with Him as He prays, but He prays alone.

He rejoiced in the Holy Spirit.—Luke 10. 21.

Luke has a time note here which is significant. He says: "In that same hour." The seventy had returned, naturally rejoicing at the true success that had followed their mission. In that joy there was a subtle element of peril, against which He had warned them. It was that of the sense of their ability, in His Name, to exorcise evil spirits. In the most holy work there always lurks this danger of the glorification of the self-life.

In contrast, the rejoicing is seen in its inspiration and its reason. Its inspiration was that of His perfect fellowship with His Father in the understanding which came to Him by the Holy Spirit. Its reason was that of the will of His Father to hide the counsels and powers of His grace from merely human cleverness, and to reveal them to the simple-hearted, to babes, to such as these seventy were.

And surely, in this sense also, the ancient word has application and fulfilment: "The joy of Jehovah is your strength." We may test our strength by discovering the reason of our joy. If there enters into our joy the element of self-glorying, in never so small a degree, by that much are we weakened. If our joy is caused by the wisdom and grace of our God, then our service will be of prevailing power.

Look therefore whether the light that is in thee be not darkness.—Luke 11. 35.

Is it possible for light to be darkness? The question may be answered by asking another, growing out of the earlier words of our Lord upon this occasion. Is it possible for a lighted lamp to be darkness? It is. That lighted lamp is darkness when it is put out of sight, in the cellar or under a bushel. That lighted lamp is light when it is placed on a stand, so that they which enter in may see the light. Light, then, is only of value when it is kept shining, and the steps are guided by it. Light hidden is darkness. Truth disobeyed is valueless. Knowledge unyielded to is ignorance.

How often the light within us is darkness! The will of the Lord, clearly revealed to us, is apprehended intellectually, but not carried out in practice; *then* the light is darkness. The Word of the Lord, studied, and interpreted by the Spirit, is retained in the intellect, but not permitted to be the guiding principle of the will; *then* the light is darkness. In such cases the way of life is the way of darkness. For such life there is condemnation far more severe than for the groping of souls to whom the light has never come. Another word of Jesus is full of significance in this connection. It was spoken to Nicodemus in the darkness of a wonderfully illumin-

ated night. It will be found in John 3. 19–21, and may be read with profit.

Man, who made Me a judge or a divider over you?—Luke 12. 14.

When our Lord thus refused to interfere between this man and his brother in the matter of their inheritance, He did not mean to suggest that He had no interest in these things, or that such matters were outside the realm of His authority. The words which follow clearly reveal His meaning. He warned those who listened, against covetousness, declaring that "things" possessed are not the true strength of life, and enforcing His teaching by the parable of the rich fool. Christ and His Church have nothing to do with dividing things up for men. The Christian message is addressed to men, and deals with their inner life. The man desiring that the inheritance should be divided was as covetous as the man refusing to divide. The word of Christ hit both men alike. If each of them learned the real meaning of life, and sought as its chief endeavour to be "rich toward God," the question of possessions would settle itself. The one would be eager to share, while the other would be careless about receiving.

This is Christ's method with all social problems. He never begins with conditions, but with causes. If life is what it ought to be, conduct will be what it should be. To divide property between covetous men is to prepare for future strife. To make men free from covetousness, is to make peace. The word which marks the Christian attitude toward life is not the word divide; it is rather the word share. Christ creates the love which is eager to give, to share; rather than to get, to divide.

I must go on My way to-day, and to-morrow, and the day following.—Luke 13. 33.

These words of our Lord were uttered in an hour when the Pharisees, desiring to get rid of Him, told Him that Herod was seeking His life. They form part of His answer to them and to Herod. They reveal His own undisturbed outlook upon His work, and the quiet intrepidity of His devotion. The "to-day" and the "to-morrow" were days in which He would continue unhindered the exercise of His ministry of beneficial power. The "day following" was "the third day," in which He was to be "perfected." Looking back, as we are able to do, we know that the "third day" was the way of the Cross and all that issued from it. That third day was arranged by the counsel of God, and not by the opposition of men. To Him the whole pathway of power, and the perfecting through suffering, was marked out by God, and no hostility of rulers or malice of kings could deflect Him by a hair's breadth from that pathway. In this consciousness lay the secret of His strength. In proportion as His disciples are in true fellowship with Him they too may take their way without perturbation or hesitancy along the path of life and service. No hostile power is strong enough to prevent them doing whatever work is appointed to them; and if presently the pathway leads through apparent defeat and much suffering, it is still the pathway of power, and thus they come to perfecting. This sense of a "Covenant ordered in all things and sure," is the secret of victorious life. To realize that we are in the will of God, is to be delivered from any care about the secondary things of circumstances. If sometimes we seem to be in their grip, we know all the time that they are in the grip of God.

Jesus answering spake unto the lawyers and Pharisees.—Luke 14. 3.

In reading this statement, the arresting word is the word "answering." These men had said nothing, yet He answered them. In the course of these stories we often find this kind of thing recorded. It is a revelation of His perfect understanding of all those who were round about Him, and of His desire to correct and help them. Take this story as illustrating this. These rulers were hostile to Him, and "they were watching Him," without any doubt watching for something upon which they could fasten as a reason for finding fault with Him. He knew this, and He answered their thoughts and intentions.

Then observe what He did. He made His appeal to their true intelligence, and to the capacity for tenderness and mercy which was latent within them. They knew that the work of healing was most sacred, and that no sanction upon which the Sabbath rested, could for a moment be violated by giving to the man who was suffering from dropsy, the blessing of healing. Indeed, was not the element of pity so strong within them, that if an ass or an ox had fallen into a pit they would not hesitate to draw him up on a Sabbath day? Thus, while our Lord rebuked the wrong attitude and temper of these men, He did so by appealing to the best within them, and calling them to be true to it. His purpose is not that of shaming men, but that of saving them; and the shame He produces in the soul when He answers its inward thoughts, is ever intended to produce the results which will be for its recovery. This method of correcting the evil, by appeal to, and reinforcement of, the good is one full of possibility and power.

Dead, and is alive; and lost, and is found.—Luke 15. 32.

Thus, in this matchless story of the love of the Father's heart, our Lord gives us the Divine estimate of the contrast between the condition of those who are away from God, and those who are restored to Him. The contrast is a double one, dealing with the experience of man, and the experience of God. Given the man away from fellowship with God—he is, in his own experience, dead; in the experience of God, he is lost. Given the man restored to God—he is, in his own experience, alive; in the experience of God he is found. The man away from God is dead. There is a sense in which he still lives; but everything is less than the real, withered at the heart, and unfinished; and he lacks entirely the deepest things of life, which are those of the spiritual and eternal powers and joys. To God that man is lost. In his loss God is defrauded. And we miss the deepest note if we fail to detect the tone of Divine sorrow in the word. The man restored to God is alive. There may be many things which as yet he is excluded from, but everything is touched with life, strong at the centre, and satisfied; and he lives in the profound peace and power of the abiding. To God that man is found. In his restoration God is enriched. And again we miss the deepest note, if we do not catch the glad ring of the rejoicing heart of God. The whole truth about life is here. The man lost to God is dead. The man found of God is alive.

If they hear not Moses and the prophets, neither will they be persuaded, if one rise from the dead.— Luke 16. 31.

This statement runs counter to most popular human conceptions, and yet is vindicated by persistent human experience. We are constantly in danger of thinking that faith can be compelled by what we describe as the supernatural, and therefore we are ever desirous that something spectacular, weird, out of the common, should happen. We argue that if something transpires which men cannot explain, they will be persuaded to believe. This is what our Lord superlatively denies in these words. He declares that the sacred writings are in themselves as powerful as anything like the delivery of their message by one risen from the dead. The only thing that can inspire faith is truth, and truth is not made more powerful when it is proclaimed in some way which is beyond human explanation. From Him men were ever asking signs, which He refused to give, and that for this reason.

Whereas, stated thus, we may be in doubt as to the correctness of the statement, an appeal to human experience vindicates the truth of the declaration. Under stress of fear or of wonder, produced by such mysterious things, men do experience certain emotions and sensations of the soul, which may be mistaken for conviction. But they are transient, and with the passing of the first surprise these things cease and leave no permanent results. It is the Truth which makes free; and the Truth alone is able to inspire living faith.

Where are the nine?—*Luke* 17. 17.

There is a plaintive note in this question of Jesus. On the border line between Samaria and Galilee, ten lepers had appealed to Him for help. He had put their faith to the test as He had commanded them to go and show themselves to the priests. As they made the venture they were all healed. One of them, and he a Samaritan, turned back and rendered his homage and his thanksgiving to the Lord. Then the question was asked, and it at once proves the value He sets upon the service of praise. The glad outpouring of a grateful heart was acceptable to Him, and He missed that of the nine who had faith and were healed, but forgot to return to Him with expressions of their gratitude. One wonders whether it is not so that our Lord has been asking this question very constantly. We are all in danger of failing to give Him the adoration which is ever due to Him. Sometimes we may be restrained by the very natural feeling that our offerings of praise must be, at the best, poor and unworthy. But we have no right, for any such cause, to withhold from Him what He evidently values. Let us neither be forgetful, nor mastered by a modesty which may become pride; but rather let us with the abandon of our utmost love, go to Him constantly, telling Him of our joy and gratitude. All such worship is the very incense which gladdens His heart, however amazing the fact may seem to us.

The things which are impossible with men are possible with God.—*Luke* 18. 27.

These words of our Lord are capable of two interpretations. They may mean that God is able to do what men cannot. Or they may mean that men are able to do, with God, what they cannot do by co-operation with other men. There is really no doubt that the second is the true interpretation of their meaning. The first is true, and so evidently true that the saying of it under circumstances would have solved no difficulty. The second exactly answered the difficulty in the minds of those who were perplexed. If a wealthy man, whose power with his fellowmen is ever great, cannot procure the right of entry into the Kingdom of God, then what chance is there for any man? That was the problem. Our Lord's answer immediately revealed the profound mistake which created the problem. A man does not enter into the Kingdom of God by acting with men. He must act with God. Directly he does so, the impossible becomes possible. And that is not only a profound truth; it is the profoundest

of all truths in this regard. Man is ever attempting personally and socially to enter into the Kingdom of God by endeavours with men, and he never succeeds. With God the thing is possible. If the young ruler had shut out all thought of men and acted alone with God, he would have followed Christ at all costs. All those insuperable difficulties of desire, inclination, and fear, are overcome by God within the soul, when man yields himself completely to God in submission and faith. That which a man cannot do alone or acting with men, he can do when he acts with God.

If thou hadst known!—*Luke* 19. 42.

These words arrest the soul, and fill the heart with wonder. They were spoken by our Lord as, with weeping, He looked at Jerusalem, and knew that its doom was sealed on account of its failure to know the time of its visitation. They reveal the heart of God in a wonderful way. The cry was that of a frustrated desire. He had visited the city, with the desire to deliver it from the things of destruction; and with the offers of the things of peace. The spiritual blindness of the rulers and people was such that they did not discern the meaning of the visitation. The result was inevitable. There could be no escape from the destruction.

Then we see the heart of God. It is greater than the heart of man. It is mastered by holiness and justice, but none the less moved by compassion. There can be no sacrifice of the principles of righteousness, but there is no satisfaction of a selfish nature in the calamities that overtake a sinning city. The judgment must fall in disaster, but its pain is felt in the heart of God. "If thou hadst known," suggests all the blessing for the city which was in His purpose for it, and shows His sorrow over its refusal of such blessing through its blindness. The story should ever remain with us, warning us against anything in the nature of gloating over human suffering, even when it is directly the outcome of human sin. Many years ago Dr. Dale, of Birmingham, said to me that D. L. Moody was one of the few men who, in his judgment, had any right to speak on the subject of the punishment of the wicked, and his right was created by the fact that he never did it without tears in his voice.

David therefore calleth Him Lord, and how is He his Son?—*Luke* 20. 44.

In that question, our Lord fastened the attention of His enemies upon a mystery concerning the Hebrew Messiah as suggested in a psalm of their own king, David. He had sung of the Messiah as his sovereign Lord. How could He be at once his Lord and his Son? Reference to the Psalm (110.) will show that its description of Messiah was that of sovereignty. "Jehovah saith unto my Adonai"—that is, my Lord as sovereign. Now the idea that a son should rule over his father was utterly impossible to the eastern mind. What then did David mean? It is evident that our Lord was attempting to compel these men to face this problem of their sacred writing, in order to help them to understand some things concerning Himself which were perplexing. This central mystery of the Person of Christ still abides, only it is solved when we remember that He was in very deed, and in special sense, the Son of God. As Paul said, He "was born of the seed of David according to the flesh"; but He was also, "the Son of God, according to the spirit of holiness." All attempts to account for him on the level of the human only, leave the mystery of his sovereignty unexplained. While the mystery of His Person for ever transcends human interpretation, the mystery of His sovereignty vanishes when we realize that in very deed He is the Son of God.

When these things begin to come to pass, look up, and lift up your heads.— Luke 21. 28.

What, then, are the things which are to produce in the disciples of the Lord the hopeful look, and the erect and confident bearing? They are the things which make men faint for fear, the things that make for the distress of nations, the things of storm and upheaval, the things which are characterized by the trembling even of the powers of the heavens. The Lord said that all such things are processes in "redemption." When wild confusion is all about us, God is surely at work, and is moving forward by necessary upheaval and turmoil towards the realization of His steadfast purposes of love. This certainty comes only of faith; but the foundations of faith are the Lord Himself, and the vindication of His words already vouchsafed to men in the passing of the centuries.

In view of these facts, we realize how "feeble knees," hands that "hang down," and all depression of spirits, are unworthy of faith, and dishonour our Lord. A true knowledge of God through Christ changes all the outlook, and

"What seemed to us mere wild confusèd Babel
Becomes a fire-tongued Pentecost
Proclaiming, Christ is able!"

In the midst of all turmoil and the disturbance of human affairs, those who trust the Lord will "look up" and walk with heads erect, knowing that "redemption draweth nigh!" This does not mean in any sense that they will be callous. They will enter into all the experience of the pain, feeling it most acutely; but all the while knowing that it moves forward to deliverance and new life.

I am in the midst of you as He that serveth.—Luke 22. 27.

These words constitute our Master's supreme and perpetual rebuke of the spirit which prompts the desire for that greatness which consists of power to compel others to serve our ends. Thus they reveal the true greatness, which consists of the power to yield ourselves up entirely to such activity as shall serve the ends of others. There is no more powerful evidence of how sorely we need His grace, than that of the slowness with which we learn this lesson. The persistence of the desire to be served is appalling. It invades our highest spiritual experiences, save as we pass completely under the dominion of the Spirit of God. Service given, not gained, is the true greatness, for it is the sign of a real fellowship with the Lord Himself. The prophetic prediction concerning Him has indeed been verified. He is great, and His greatness is rooted in that self-emptying wherein and whereby He for ever serves others.

The very greatness of God is finally demonstrated, not in the height and glory of His eternal throne, but in the depth and grace of His amazing stoop to our humanity and to the death of the Cross. In the midst of the throne is "a Lamb as though it had been slain." He reigns and rules in undisputed and unhindered authority because He laid His glory by to serve. Shall we not seek with all earnestness the greatness which comes by the way of service? Our unceasing eagerness should be to find need, and to serve in comradeship with our Lord.

Father, forgive them; for they know not what they do.—Luke 23. 34.

This was the supreme word of the perfect humanity of our Lord, and therefore it was a perfect revelation of the heart of God. And how wonderful it is. The plea was not that wilful sin should be excused. Such a plea our Master never urged. The men who nailed Him to His Cross were ignorant. They had no understanding of what they were doing. Therefore He thus prayed for them. In that plea we see the operation of the Divine justice, which is eternally reasonable. The judgments of God are ever based upon His perfect knowledge, not of actions alone, but of the motives that prompt them. Yet the very motives, while the result of ignorance, may be utterly unworthy, and need the forgiveness of God. For this the crucified Lord has the right to ask, because in the deepest fact of His Cross He was there by that determinate counsel which was set upon the redemption of man at uttermost cost. Thus in the very prayer, as in the fact of the Cross, the elements of justice and mercy are seen acting in perfect harmony. That the prayer was answered there can be no question.

Those men, in ignorance expressing the worst of sin, were forgiven by virtue of the mystery of the pain which He bore, that pain so much deeper than the physical suffering which they inflicted upon Him. All sins of ignorance are forgiven. It is only the sin against light, which has no forgiveness.

While He blessed them, He parted from them.—*Luke 24. 51.*

The last attitude and activity of the risen Lord of which the disciples were conscious as He left them to ascend to His Father, were those of the uplifted hands and the uttering of a beatitude. This is a perpetual sign. Thus He remains until He comes again, His hands uplifted, and His lips pronouncing the blessedness of His own. Behold those hands! In them are the sacred signs of His love and His all-conquering grace. Listen to His blessing! It is more than the expression of a desire on His part for the happiness of His own. It is a declaration of His ability to give them the only true happiness. While we see those uplifted hands, there can be no room for doubt or fear, when other menacing hands are stretched out to harm us or vex us. Whether in life or death, in adversity or prosperity, in sorrow or in joy, we know by that token that we are safe. While we hear His voice pronouncing the blessing, it matters not what voices slander or curse, we know that our peace and joy are assured. What wonder that they return to Jerusalem—as hostile to them as to Him—with great joy! Let us never lose sight of that wonderful vision. The clouds will enwrap Him, and the bodily sight end, but the spirit will know that beyond the clouds, and beyond the physical manifestation, He ever lives, with hands that argue our safety outstretched, and with words that ensure our blessedness upon His lips.

JOHN

Full of grace and truth.—*John 1. 14.*

In that phrase John recorded the full and final impression made upon him and his fellow-disciples by their time of comradeship with Jesus Christ. They were written in all probability long years after that time of comradeship, so far as His bodily presence was concerned, was over. They lived with Him, travelled with Him, listened to His teaching, watched His works, and above all observed Him in all the circumstances of the varied days; and when the whole result needed to be written, John did it by saying, "Full of grace and truth."

The description moreover, is given in a yet briefer way by the use of one word in the preceding parenthetical statement, they beheld His *glory*; and in the whole of that statement the sublimest truth is declared—it was "glory as of the Only begotten from the Father." Here then we find the content of the glory of God. It is the unity of grace and truth. Here then we have the exposition of grace and truth. It is found in Jesus Christ. These two ideas should hold our minds and direct our lives. God is grace, and truth. Not the one without the other; not the other apart from the one. In His government there can be no lowering of the simple and severe standard of Truth; and there is no departure from the purpose and passion of Grace. To say that, is to realize that the Cross was necessitated by the nature of God. Then, when we would know Truth we must know Jesus Christ; and when we would apprehend Grace we must come to Him.

Jesus did not trust Himself unto them.—*John 2. 24.*

Here the verb "trust" is the same as "believed" in the preceding sentence, "many believed on His name." Their belief in Him was not full commitment of themselves. It was really intellectual conviction produced by the signs which He did. Those signs convinced them of His power, and in some sense necessarily of His authority. That was all. Seeing this was so, He did not commit Himself to them fully. He could not. This is a principle of perpetual application. The law of relationship between Christ and men is ever that of all for all. As D. L. Moody once said, "Christ is as great a Saviour as we make Him." When our convictions are yielded to, and we surrender ourselves completely to them, He is able to give Himself to us in all His fulness. Until that is so, He cannot trust us. This withholding of Himself is not capricious. John is careful to point out that it was based upon His knowledge of men, and not upon suspicion. How true it is that we often miss the complete joy and strength of our Christianity, because by withholding ourselves from Christ, we make it impossible for Him to give Himself to us in all the fulness of His grace and truth. Such withholding on our parts creates, and then proves, our unworthiness. It is a solemn thing to say, but it is nevertheless true, that He is true to the command He laid upon His disciples—He never casts His pearls before swine.

This is the judgment, that the light is come into the world, and men loved the darkness rather than the light.— *John* 3. 19.

Here the word judgment has the sense of condemnation, the verdict and sentence against men; and so the principle is revealed upon which men are judged. It is always that of the coming of light, and the opportunity which it creates. The coming of Christ was the coming of light. in Him we know the truth about God, and about ourselves. Thus in Him we know the truth about our relationship to God, and what our life ought to be. The special truth about God revealed in Him, is that of the Divine love, which makes possible, at infinite cost, the healing and restoration of those who have sinned and failed to realize the meaning of their own lives. That is the burden of the context. If men refuse to avail themselves of this Divine grace, they are by that refusal declining to walk in the light, and so are condemned. The reason why men love darkness is that they desire the things which the light condemns. Here is the mystery of lawlessness. It knows that the things of darkness are things of destruction, and yet for the momentary experience it deliberately rejects the things of light which are the things of life. And here each soul stands alone. The light is shining. Shall we come to it and walk in it? Or shall we shun it and walk in darkness? The choice is personal. But the verdict is already found. Upon our answer depends whether we are condemned or justified.

I have meat to eat that ye know not. —*John* 4. 32.

In these words our Lord revealed the secret of His strength, and that of the weakness of His disciples. They had not yet risen to the full understanding of life. They still conceived of it as being sustained by the supply of the physical only. He knew that while physical food is a necessity, there is a deeper need; and moreover, that there may be circumstances in which for a time a man may live, in the fullest sense of the word, even when he lacks the nourishment of the physical. His meat, as He subsequently declared, was to do the will of His Father, and to accomplish His work. And that is life indeed. When that is the master passion of life, a man lives. If the physical for a time lacks its peculiar sustenance, the man is still sustained in all the strength he needs for the accomplishment of life's highest purpose. It is better to die as to the physical, in the will of God, than to live therein, outside that will. That is the deepest truth about life. It may at once be said that physical life is also in the care of God, and He will always maintain it for the accomplishment of all that is for the well-being of man. Man's care, however, is to be active, not first or only in that realm, but first and finally in the matter of the Divine will and work. When that is so, life becomes full, radiant, joyful. When Jesus said this, these men did not know that meat, but He came to give them that knowledge, and subsequently they lived by it.

If ye believed Moses, ye would believe Me; for he wrote of Me.— *John* 5. 46.

This most explicit statement of our Lord has a double value for us. It first sets the seal of His authority upon the Pentateuch. It also gives us the key to the interpretation thereof. When He referred to "Moses" there can be no question that He did so knowing exactly how the reference would be understood of the Jews to whom He was speaking. The name "Moses" was thus constantly employed to describe the first five books of the Canon. Here our Lord not only referred to them thus technically, but He did so in such a way as to show that He thought of them as actually written by Moses. To say He was accommodating His language to ignorance would be to charge Him with perpetuating ignorance.

Of these writings He said that they were concerned with Him. That is the key to their interpretation. In their history we are to discover the first movements towards His advent. In their teachings we are to discover the first unveilings of His ethical standards. In their revelations of God we are to discover the elements which were to have final interpretation in Him. Thus the writings of Moses were prophetic. In them nothing was completed. They pointed on to other things, which came to pass when He came. Thus in this word we find at once the authority and limitation of Moses.

He Himself knew what He would do.—*John* 6. 6.

What a revealing word this is, and how full of comfort for all those who love and follow the Lord. He had suggested a great problem. How were they to procure bread to feed the multitude? The difficulty is revealed in the answers of Philip and Andrew. The first calculated the cost. The second emphasized the inadequacy of their resources. He had asked His question, as John says, to prove them. By a facing of their own poverty they would learn the value of His power. How often He brings us into such places of perplexity. Something is to be done that seems impossible nay, that is impossible if we argue from our own private resources. May we not learn from this incident that in all such cases our wisdom will consist in our confidence that He Himself knows what He will do. Is it not intended that we should better their replies by saying: Lord we do not pretend to know how things are to be done, but we bring whatever resources we have to Thee and are confident that whatever Thou hast in Thy heart to do, Thou art able to do with these poor things of ours! We know not; but Thou knowest; and so we do not ask to know. All we ask is that we may be directed by Thy wisdom, so shall we be enabled by Thy power. If we can only take up that attitude, how strong and quiet life will be.

Judge not according to appearance, but judge righteous judgment.—*John* 7. 24.

And does not that necessarily mean that in some senses we are not to judge at all? After all, what can we know of any man beyond "appearance"? The secret things of the soul are hidden from all save God. In His ethical manifesto our Lord distinctly said, "Judge not, that ye be not judged." All of which means that our judgments of our fellow-men must always be reserved. We should ever bear in mind that "appearance" may be deceitful, and therefore with the love that hopeth all things, we should be ready to give men the benefit of any doubt or uncertainty that is in our minds.

All that being granted, it remains that within limits we are compelled to use the faculty of judgment, and our Lord uttered the positive word, "Judge righteous judgment," as well as the negative. What then is righteous judgment? It is judgment which is free from prejudice, and which, considering things as they are, draws true conclusions. The context is illuminative. Wrath prevented these men from true thinking about the wonder Jesus had wrought in healing the man in Bethesda's porches. How perpetually wrath prevents righteous judgment. To form true conclusions we need a mind free from all bias, and mastered by love. Even then our judgments are only valuable as guides to our personal conduct. We never have any right to make them the basis of decisions concerning our fellow-men.

As He spake these things, many believed on Him.—*John* 8. 30.

When this statement is read in its true connection with the record of the things our Lord has been saying, it is found to be a radiant revelation of the impressiveness of His personality. He had been speaking in an atmosphere of criticism and enmity. Moreover, He had sternly and openly rebuked and denounced the Pharisees. Then He made to those very men, and in that hostile atmosphere, superlative claims for Himself, declaring that He worked and taught in fellowship with God, and that He always did the things that pleased God. It was then, "As He spake these things, many believed on Him." The force of all this may be gathered if we try to imagine any other teacher making such claims. If we heard any man do so, we should at once doubt his sincerity, his truthfulness. Yet when these people heard Jesus make them, "many believed on Him." There can be no explanation other than that of the harmony between the claims He made and the impression of His personality. He was what He claimed to be. Men knew it. There was no escape from the impressiveness of His reality. Truth not only fell from His lips. It emanated from Himself. This quality is still pervasive, even when men find Him in the written words. It is possible to disobey Him, even to deny the practicability of His ideals; but it is not possible to deny the beauty of those ideals, or to disbelieve in the sincerity and glory of the Lord Himself.

Jesus heard that they had cast him out, and finding him . . .—*John* 9. 35.

The casting out of this man meant his excommunication from his religious rights in Temple and synagogue. It was the act of the religious rulers, and was the result of their anger because, in loyalty to his convictions, he had spoken words which charged them with blindness. The Lord found him, and admitted him to Himself as a worshipper. It was a significant action, and led to the wonderful discourse about the Shepherd, the sheep, and the one flock. As one reads it, the sense of how often it has been repeated comes to the mind. Organized religion has often made the mistake of excommunicating those who, in loyalty to conscience, run counter to its prejudices. What a warning the story is of the danger we run of excluding the Lord also, when we act in this way! And how futile such action is. The man cast out by blind religious leaders is received by the living Lord, and finds his way to the one and only Centre of true worship. Thus it is seen that at times a man may excommunicate a community, as surely as be excommunicated thereby. This consciousness of the understanding of the Lord, and of His reception of loyal souls in spite of all human refusal of fellowship with them, is the strength which will ever enable them to be true to Him. If He finds and receives, what does it matter who rejects?

The sheep follow Him; for they know His voice.—*John* 10. 4.

In the case of the eastern shepherd, that is literally true; and as the next words declare, "A stranger will they not follow, for they know not the voice of strangers." The strangeness of other voices is a warning to the sheep; they do not know the voices, and so take no risks. How full of value is the suggestiveness of all this in the case of those who belong to the Lord! There is no doubt that such do know the voice of the Lord. They may not immediately understand what He is saying, but there is no mistaking His voice. It is the voice of understanding, of tenderness, of strength, of authority. There is none other like it. It often corrects us, runs counter to our desires, calls us to service that we dread, and sometimes to suffering which we fain would miss. But we know when He speaks; and then it is ours to follow, knowing that He makes no mistakes, and that every word He utters to us—the sternest as well as the tenderest—is love-inspired. This being so, our wisdom ever consists in refusing to follow any strange voice. We do not, cannot know others as we know Him. Their suggestions may be false even when their intention is good; or their intention may be evil, when their suggestions are pleasant. Let us listen only to the Voice we know, and hearing let us follow.

I am glad for your sakes that I was not there.—*John* 11. 15.

That is a revealing word, and full of strength. The supposition which it makes is that if Jesus had been at Bethany, Lazarus would not have died, for He would have healed him. Because He was not there, he had died, and the Lord said that, for the sake of His disciples, He was glad. The sequel gives the explanation of His gladness. Death was no stronger in His presence than disease, but these men did not realize this. They would think of Death as the unconquerable. It was so to them. With disease men may grapple, and fight, and often overcome. But in the presence of death they are helpless. It is beyond their control. Not so with Him, and He was glad that they should have yet another opportunity to see His power. We say "another," for twice already they had seen Him raise the dead, once in the house of Jairus, and once at the city of Nain. How slow we are to believe! And that makes His gladness all the more beautiful, as it reveals His patience. And so we may learn that He often permits us to pass into profounder darkness, and deeper mysteries of pain, in order that we may prove more perfectly His power. Let the thought abide with us, if our pathway lies in some dark valley where for the moment no light is shining, and no path is known. He knows, and all He permits will only serve to reveal Him more perfectly, and so give us a yet stronger confidence.

This He said, signifying by what manner of death He should die.—*John* 12. 33.

This is the Holy Spirit's interpretation of the words which our Lord had just uttered. They were triumphant words, claiming a coming victory over the prince of the world, and His own lifting up out of the earth to a place of universal power.

This, then, was the manner of His death —that is to say, this was the nature of His death. It was triumphant death. We may miss the whole value of the statement if we think only of the fact of the Cross on the human level. It gives us at once to see that the human murder of Jesus was a secondary thing. His death was not in weakness, but in strength; not the death of defeat, but that of triumph. He died to cast out the authority and power of evil in which the world was enslaved. He died to create a centre, coming to which, men would enter into freedom and life. The manner of His death was in that sense unique. None other had so died. His is the one and only death which is in itself victorious. And now all who are gathered to Him around that Cross, receiving its pardon, receive also its gift of life; and so they also triumph in their dying. To die in Christ is to rise with Him into complete victory over the prince of the world, and to find the fulfilment of life. The first experience is spiritual, and immediate to the trusting soul. The final experience comes when we fall asleep in Him, and find the awakening in His presence to be the triumph.

Jesus, knowing that His hour was come.—*John* 13. 1.

Repeatedly in the Gospel of John reference is found to "the hour" of the Lord. Here the phrase finds explanation. His hour, the supreme hour of His mission, was the hour of His Cross. For *that* He had come into the world. It was the central fact in His mission. Yet here notice how John refers to it. It was the hour in which "He should depart out of this world unto the Father." There can be no question that this was our Lord's conception of that hour. It was the hour of departure from the world, lonely, dark, full of unutterable anguish; but it was the hour of going to the Father. Beyond the loneliness, there was the restoration of fellowship; beyond the darkness, the eternal light; beyond the anguish the fulness of joy. To Him, in contemplation of the hour, there was no misgiving as to the issue. In all the experience of travail He wrought as God with God, and therefore the triumph was certain. Knowing all this, He loved His own to the uttermost. That love was the inspiration of His going by the way of the Cross; and that going was the full and final expression and activity of that love. His going was with perfect knowledge. He was not groping heroically through darkness, uncertain as to His destination. He was walking in the light, even as He passed through the darkness.

If it were not so, I would have told you.—*John* 14. 2.

These words were parenthetical in what the Lord was saying, but they are most suggestive. They mean that there are some things concerning which He would not allow His own to remain in ignorance. What He was saying at the time gives us a perfect illustration. He was going away and they were filled with sorrow. To help them, He told them that in His Father's house there are many abiding-places. That is to say, that absence from this world, which is one of the abiding-places in the Father's house, simply means that the absent one is at home in some other abiding-place in the one great House of God. They were not to think of Him as having ceased to be when they could not see Him. He had only gone to another abiding-place to prepare for their coming; and, moreover, He would come back to receive them when they should come. It was about this that He said that if it were not so, He would have told them. If this world were the only place, and this life were all, He would have said so. From this incidental word, then, we may argue that He has said all that we need to know. He has not left us in doubt on any essential matter. That this is so, the experience of those who have walked according to His teaching proves. They have all had the light of life, and have not walked in darkness.

Even as the Father hath loved Me, I also have loved you.—*John* 15. 9.

This surely is Christ's superlative word concerning His love for His own. It leaves nothing more to be said. What the love of the Father is for the Son, who can tell? The very suggestion fills the soul with the sense of profound depths which cannot be fathomed, of heights that cannot be scaled, of breadths which cannot be encompassed, and of dimensions beyond our knowledge. And that love of God for the Son, is the measure and nature of the love of the Son for His own. And yet, how passing wonderful it is, when we remember that, however vast that love of God for His Son may be, that Son is worthy of it, while we are unworthy of love at all. Yet here is the glory of His love. He loves us in spite of our unworthiness, knowing that He is able to make us worthy. In very deed such love is,

"A deep where all our thoughts are drowned."

Two thoughts are immediately suggested. The first, by what He had said before: "Therefore doth My Father love Me, because I lay down My life that I may take it again"; and the second, by what He added now: "I have kept My Father's commandments, and abide in His love." The perfection in us which He seeks, and which inspires His love, is that of the selflessness which suffers to serve. The law of abiding in love is that of obedience.

Do ye now believe?—*John* 16. 31.

In these words Jesus, very tenderly but very definitely, challenged His disciples in the hour when they declared that their belief in the Divinity of His mission was confirmed. They were perfectly sincere. They felt that they had at last passed beyond the region where it would be possible to doubt. How much better He knew them than they knew themselves! He knew that presently they would find themselves in shattering circumstances, and that they would then doubt everything, and be scattered. Yet observe the reason of His question. He was preparing them for those very experiences, creating a foothold for their faith, even when the floods should sweep around them. The very fact that He had known and had foretold the course of events, would be something to hold on to, and the memory of it would help them back again to faith. Two lessons of great importance may be learned here. The first is that our faith is a poor foundation; indeed that it is *no* foundation. We do verily believe to-day, but to-morrow may bring storms which will for the moment strain faith to the breaking-point, and make it of no value. The other is that He is faithful, and that *is* the foundation. In the fiercest hour of upheaval, He it is Who creates some possibility for our failing faith to gather strength. So, as to our faith also, we ever have to say: "Not unto us, O Jehovah, not unto us, but unto Thy name give glory."

Neither for these only do I pray.—*John* 17. 20.

These are the most comforting words for us in this great prayer of our Lord, because they bring us into its interest and intercession. We are among the number of those who have believed on Him through the apostolic word, and so His requests were all on our behalf also. This outlook of the Master is very suggestive. There He was, after three and a half years of public ministry, approaching an end which seemed to be that of defeat. He was surrounded by a few loving men, who nevertheless would soon all be scattered for very fear. The outlook was very dark to all but the Lord. He also saw the darkness, and understood it better than any other. Yet He saw *through* it, saw the light clearly shining down the coming age; saw these very men, gathered after their scattering, going forth publishing the Word; saw the sacramental hosts of souls believing that Word, and for these He prayed. And His prayer for all of us was as His prayer for those men who were about Him. He knew their weakness, and how they would fail. He knows our weakness, and all about our failures. He prayed for them. He prays for us. He knew His intercession for them would prevail. He knows His intercession for us will prevail. Then let us rest in Him, with the rest of loving obedience and of surest confidence.

The cup which the Father hath given Me, shall I not drink it?—John 18. 11.

These words were spoken to Peter, in the moment when in love for his Master, and in mistaken zeal, he had struck a blow in order to attempt to deliver Him from the hands of His enemies. They are revealing words. They show us how the one dominant passion of all our Lord's life was still triumphant as He passed to death. He had but one passion, and that was to do His Father's will. The other Evangelists tell us how the question of this cup had just been raised in communion with His Father, and always under the constraint of that same master-passion. That hour of inquiry was over. The cup had been given Him to drink. Therefore there was no further question. In the form of the statement we discover His perfect rest; the cup had been given Him by His Father, by the One Who loved Him, by the One Who confided in Him. Therefore there could be no further question. The question raised and settled in communion could not be raised in any other form, or with any other beings. And once more, we see how the highest love, the love of God, must ever qualify, and often cancel, the suggestions made by other loves, however loyal and well-intentioned they may be. The love of God is always wise. The loves of men are often unintelligent. Of course, in our Lord we see all these things superlatively, but there are profound values in them for us, to which we do well to take heed.

It is finished.—John 19. 30.

Luke tells us that, "When Jesus had cried with a loud voice, He said, Father into Thy hands I commend My spirit, and having said this He gave up the ghost" (23. 46). John says that, "He said, It is finished, and He bowed His head and gave up His spirit." There can be no doubt that what He said "with a loud voice" was "It is finished." It was the cry of triumph. The hour was come, and He had accomplished all that was within the determinate counsel and foreknowledge of God. He had entered into, and passed through, the deep mystery of spiritual death. In that experience He had cried, "My God, My God, why hast Thou forsaken Me?" and in that mystic cry revealed all that it is possible for men to know of that experience. All was over, except the physical dissolution which was the sacramental symbol of the spiritual death. To that He passed with calm composure as He said: "Father, into Thy hands I commend My spirit." In that exultant cry of accomplishment the soul of man hears the good news, of emancipation from all the slavery of sin, and of the possibility of realizing all the purposes of God. While there is much for man to do in working out his own salvation with fear and trembling, there is nothing for him to do to make his salvation possible. Everything is done, and now it is possible for God to work in us to will and to work of His good pleasure.

Peace be unto you . . . peace be unto you.—John 20. 19 and 21.

Twice our Lord uttered the words of greeting to His disciples on the evening of that first resurrection day. The words were not new. They were almost commonplace, constituting as they did, the ordinary form with which men greeted each other. Yet how new and wonderful they were as He spoke them! They had behind them the authority of His death and resurrection. He had faced and defeated all the forces which destroy the peace of man. As He said, "Peace be unto you," He was doing infinitely more than expressing a wish. He was making a declaration. He was bestowing a benediction. He was imparting a blessing. The repetition was significant. The first was a greeting addressed to men who were filled with fear on account of the hostility in the midst of which they were living, the self-same hostility which had encompassed His death. He said: "Peace be unto you." The things you fear are powerless to harm you. Death is not the end; beyond it, behold Me alive! Be at peace, for whether in life or death you are safe. The second prefaced a commission. They were to be sent out, as He had been sent out, to accomplish a Divine purpose. Let them be at peace, knowing by the fact of His resurrection they would be victorious, even though they went His way of suffering and death. It is a striking commentary on these words of Jesus, that Christian souls have never had more perfect experience of peace than when they have been called upon to suffer for His Name.

Two other.—John 21. 2.

The suggestiveness of these words is arresting. This was a wonderful occasion on which the Lord was specially manifesting Himself to a group of disciples. Every phase of the doings of that morning is full of light and glory. The risen Redeemer and Ruler was showing men His interest and power in the commonplaces of their lives and in the greatest responsibilities thereof. He touched their daily doings with light and glory, their daily fishing, and preparing breakfast. He gave them the grandest conception of their fellowship with Himself in His work of gathering together in one the sheep that were scattered abroad. Who were the men? They were Simon Peter and Thomas, and Nathaniel, and James and John—all outstanding figures. But there were "two other," and they are unnamed, and I believe purposely unnamed. They represent the anonymous and hidden multitudes of faithful souls, whose names are never published in human documents, and whose deeds are never recorded in human reports. To these He manifested Himself, as surely as to the others. Those "two other" represented the majority of the saints. Let all such remember that of His fulness they also receive. Manifestations are needed for fidelity in obscure places of service, and they are granted. To all His own, He ever comes with unveilings of His glory, with ministrations of His grace and truth.

THE ACTS

Ye shall be My witnesses.—*Acts* 1. 8.

In the matter of the responsibility of the Christian soul, and the Christian Church, these are the arresting words of this first chapter of Luke's second treatise. This book is of priceless value as it gives the story of the first movements in the work of the Church. The incidents selected by Luke cover a period of about a generation and illustrate how varied were the forms of her service; and in them we have a revelation of her one mission, and of the method by which she is to fulfil it. That mission is simply and inclusively that of making Christ known, and the method by which it is to be accomplished is that of the witness of all her members. Because of the infinite fulness of the Lord, and the complex need of man, that mission is infinite. There is no possible experience of humanity, individual or social, to which He does not speak, in His infinite wisdom and in His redeeming power. Therefore the fulness of this witness demands all the natural and spiritual resources of His people. Nevertheless the simplicity of this statement enables us to make the most personal application of the truth. The question by which we may persistently test ourselves is: "How far am I living—thinking, speaking, doing—so that the Lord may be seen and heard and known?" The measure in which every Christian soul is a living witness, is the measure in which the Christian Church is fulfilling her true mission.

They were all filled with the Holy Spirit.—*Acts* 2. 4.

If the words: "Ye shall be My witnesses," reveal the mission of the Church, and the method by which she is to fulfil that mission, these declare the secret of her power. It is a power which is hers by gift, and is not in any sense her own, except as it is thus bestowed. This is a distinction which it is of the utmost importance that we never forget. As the Church has grown she has ever been enriched by the natural abilities of all her members. Those wonderful capacities resident within human lives are all needed and must be dedicated to the work of witnessing. But none of them is of any use whatever apart from the Holy Spirit. The fulness of the Spirit means fulness of the very life of Christ concerning which witness is to be borne. That fulness of life possesses and employs all natural capacities, so that through them the things of the mind of Christ may be made known to men, the things of the heart of Christ may be persuasive among men, and the things of the will of Christ may be prevailing in men. This is the wonder and glory of the Spirit-filled life. All natural gifts, which in themselves are powerless to witness for Christ, are by the Spirit cleansed, energized, and directed, so that they may become the media through which Christ is made known. The story of the Acts, and of the whole Church, in so far as it is the story of the victories of Christ, is the story of the capture and employment of all natural human capacities by Christ through His Holy Spirit.

Silver and gold have I none; but what I have, that give I thee.—*Acts* 3. 6.

These were not the words of apology. By comparison with what Peter had to bestow, silver and gold are the veriest dross. To give silver and gold to a cripple is a good thing indeed, if that is the best you can do for him. But it only maintains him in his disability. To give him strength to walk is to set him free from the need of alms. This is the difference between Christianity and all merely humanitarian efforts for the relief of the incapable. *They* help to make the conditions of continued inability somewhat bearable. *It* cancels the inability, and so ends the conditions, and makes the efforts for relief unnecessary. Therefore Christianity never has any need to apologize for itself. The service it renders to men, individually and socially, is of the highest. It deals not so much with conditions as with causes. By so doing it necessarily deals with conditions also. The principle illustrated in the case of this man is of the widest application. Apart from Christ, humanitarian efforts deal with surroundings, but cannot touch the man. Christianity begins with the man and so makes him the instrument for changing his own surroundings. Humanitarian effort plants a garden round a man and leaves him to spoil the garden. Christianity remakes the man, and he makes the garden.

They took knowledge of them, that they had been with Jesus.—Acts 4. 13.

That is to say that they were witnessing in the true sense of the word. Not only were they talking about Him, they were doing it in such a way as to make those who heard them think of the Lord. That is the whole point of this statement. The rulers and elders and scribes before whom Peter and John were arraigned had known Jesus. Among their number were undoubtedly some who had been amazed as they had listened to Him, their amazement having been caused by the fact that, as they said, He had "the letters, never having learned." In these two men they discovered the same reason for astonishment. They were unlearned and ignorant men, yet they employed "boldness of speech." They were speaking about Him but what they said was characterized by the notes of certainty, authority, and power, just as had been the case with their Lord. It was this very fact which impressed the rulers. We often ask, in a hymn, that we may speak in living echoes of His tone. That is more than to say true things. It is so to say them, that they carry the authority of Christ. That is true witness, and the secret is given in an earlier verse: "Peter, filled with the Holy Spirit" (verse 8). It is only by such filling that our witness gains that authentic note which carries men through us to the Lord.

Rejoicing that they were counted worthy to suffer dishonour for the Name.—Acts 5. 41.

What a radiant unveiling we have in these words, of the new outlook, conception, motive of life, which Christ gives to those who are His witnesses in fellowship with the Holy Spirit! Notice that it is not said that they rejoiced in suffering, but that they rejoiced that they were counted worthy to suffer. Surely there is a very deep note here. Suffering was suffering. The actual pain of the brutal Roman rods was not lessened. The indignity was very real, and yet it was transfigured for them, and they realized that the dishonour was an honour. The secret was that they constantly remembered that He, too, had suffered exactly in the same way, and now they understood some of the profound meanings of His sufferings. It was by His stripes that they had been healed. And now the result of their witness to Him, the witness of their, words, and of their lives, had brought them into actual participation in like sufferings, through which His redeeming power and purpose were served. Herein lay the high honour of this dishonour. Such suffering was the highest seal of the approval of Him Who had crowned their Lord with glory and honour that He might taste death for every man. That they also were so, in measure, crowned was surely justifiable reason for rejoicing. When the Cross is really endured, the shame is despised, and it becomes the reason for joy.

Men of good report, full of the Spirit and of wisdom.—Acts 6. 3.

These were the qualifications for those who were to be set apart to serve tables, to look after the financial and business affairs of the Church. Note carefully the three things deemed essential for such service. First, they were to be "of good report"—that is, quite literally, "of good witness." They must be witnesses who had proved themselves as such, men in and through whom Christ had been made known. Second, it is said they were to be "full of the Spirit." That adds emphasis to the first requirement, for it is only men "full of the spirit" who are "of good witness." It also shows that the same witness to Christ must be borne in the work to which they were appointed. Finally, they were to be "of wisdom." That is the recognition of the necessity for natural ability for business affairs; and, in its relation to the fulness of the Spirit, shows how the natural ability must be under His control. What a condemnation all this is of the way in which the Church has too often appointed men to manage her business affairs! No man should be allowed to share in such work who is not himself a witness by the Spirit. It is equally true that no witness should be appointed to this work if he lack wisdom, for that is essential to all true serving of tables.

Jesus standing on the right hand of God.—Acts 7. 55.

This attitude of the Lord arrests us. The New Testament references to Him as having entered the heavenlies describe Him as having *sat down* on the right hand of the Majesty on high. Here He was seen by Stephen *standing*. The two figures of speech remind us of two aspects of His work on behalf of man. When He had made the one offering which provided perfect and plenteous redemption, He sat down. This is the attitude which speaks of the completion of His redemptive work. But that work is being continued in its administration through all His witnesses who have fellowship with Him in the fulness of the Spirit. They are making up that which is behindhand in His afflictions. His having completed His work does not mean that He is in any sense separated from them, or that they endure the Cross in loneliness. He is with them in sympathy and in service. Thus Stephen, having completed the testimony of life and speech, and being about to consummate and crown that witness in agony and death, saw the Lord standing. It was to him the assurance of his Lord's co-operation and fellowship. The result is seen in that Stephen passed as his Lord had passed, commending his spirit to his Lord, and praying for his murderers. For the assurance of my soul as to its salvation, I see Him seated at the Father's right hand. For the assurance of my soul in its service and suffering, I see Him standing.

They therefore that were scattered abroad went about preaching the Word.—Acts 8. 4.

Again we are reminded of the place and power of suffering in the propaganda of the Word. That Word is always the Word of the Cross. The paragraph preceding these words is a condensed account of real suffering. The violent passions of hostility which had done Stephen to death swept on over all the Church in a blood of bitter persecution. The followers of the Lord, His witnesses, were driven out from home and kindred. They were scattered abroad. It is easy to read the statement, but we should not forget what it meant of anguish and apparent desolation. Those who in their anger brought it about would surely feel that they were at last putting an end to all that they so bitterly hated. They were mistaken. The witnesses can be scattered, but that is only to diffuse their witness over a wider area, and to aid in the propagation of their message. Persecution has never hindered the preaching of the Word. It is only by patronage that the enemies of the Gospel can weaken the witness of those who have believed and have received the fulness of the Spirit. Persecution ever compels the witnesses to completer dependence upon their Lord, and so to fuller realization of His grace and strength. That issues in more perfect conformity to His likeness, and more intense rest in Him. Thus the witness continues in the growing beauty of lives according to the pattern, and in the glad boldness of speech that testifies to the power of His grace.

A chosen vessel unto Me.—Acts 9. 15.

How unexpected, and how surpassingly wise are the elections of God. "Saul breathing threatenings and slaughter against the disciples of the Lord": "A chosen vessel unto Me." Saul was a man of Tarsus, a Hebrew of Hebrews, and withal a free-born citizen of Rome. All his earliest years had been spent in the atmosphere of Tarsus, a city which was Greek in its outlook. He had been educated religiously, in the straitest of sects, that of the Pharisees. Through all his life, whether in Cilicia or Judaea, he had moved in the liberty of Roman citizenship. His youth had been clean: as touching the righteousness which is in the law he was blameless. He was free from all hypocrisy, and intense in his devotion to what he believed. This man was the chosen vessel of the Lord, to bear His name before Gentiles and kings and the children of Israel. This is perhaps the supreme instance in the New Testament of how natural gifts and capacities are possessed by the Spirit, and made the media through which witness is borne to Christ. All those elements which made him the most powerful antagonist of Christianity became the forces which created the power of his protagonism. It was a critical hour for the Church. In the affairs of men critical hours are hours of uncertainty and therefore of peril. In the economy of God they are hours of victory, for He finds the man; and His gifts and callings are without repentance, for His wisdom is final and unclouded.

I perceive that God is no respecter of persons.—Acts 10. 34.

With what perfect precision and poetic beauty the ways of God move forward to the accomplishment of the purposes of His Grace. Saul, the chosen vessel for bearing the Name to the Gentiles, had passed out of sight to Arabia, and back to Tarsus. It would be many years before he was called to the great work for which he was chosen. In this chapter we have the account of how God prepared for that work by bringing Peter to an understanding of the wider meanings of His purpose in Christ. Peter's outlook naturally was narrow. He lacked full understanding of God's love for the Gentile. This he must be brought to see. In these words we have his declaration that the truth had broken in upon him. His words, "I perceive," show that a new light had come. God was seen as He had never been seen before, and therefore the Gentile was seen as never before. It was a day of great enlargement. Lifted to a new height, the horizons were set back, and territory which had been considered outside the range of the Divine Grace was seen bathed in its glory, and transfigured by its power. How powerful was the effect produced upon him is discovered in his subsequent words in Jerusalem: "Who was I that I could withstand God?" Even though there were moments later when Peter faltered in his yielding to this light, there is no doubt that this experience prepared him for fellowship in that work to which Paul was especially called. Thus, as God works with all, are all enabled to work together.

Men of Cyprus and Cyrene.—Acts 11. 20.

Who were they? None can tell. They remain anonymous. And yet it was their action which prepared the way for Paul's missionary journeys. They, coming to Antioch, overstepped the boundary of the Hebrew people, and "spake unto the Greeks also, preaching the Lord Jesus." That action was followed immediately by the most far-reaching effects. That it was unusual, is proved by the action of the

Church at Jerusalem which immediately sent Barnabas down to investigate. That it was of God, is proved by the action of Barnabas, "who, when he was come, and had seen the grace of God, was glad"; and after awhile went away to Tarsus and brought Paul to his work. In the processes of this age of the Church's witness it is in the purpose and plan of God that men shall appear, whose works are manifest, and whose names are widely published abroad. But when the age is consummated many names unknown and unpublished during its processes will be made known. No man called to the places of conspicuous service has any right to attempt to hide, but every such man knows that his work is prepared for, and sustained by those who are anonymous on earth, but whose names are registered in Heaven. This registration, rather than our success in service, should be the cause of our joy, as our Lord distinctly told His disciples in the days of His flesh.

But the Word of God grew and multiplied.—*Acts* 12. 24.

The opening word "but" drives us back to the words immediately preceding, which are these: "And he was eaten of worms, and gave up the ghost." The contrast is graphic. The chapter opens with the words: "Now about that time Herod the king put forth his hands to afflict certain of the Church." Herod's opposition was that of political expediency. He desired to gain favour with the Jews, and this was the cause of his action. Luke mentioned certain other of his political matters, and briefly gave the story of his tragic end. Then he added: "But the Word of God grew and multiplied." It is an instance of that which has persistently taken place. Every force arrayed against Christianity expresses itself for a reason in such fashion as apparently to weaken and hinder them, and then works on its own lines, to its own undoing and destruction. The Word of God, in spite of all such opposition, and indeed oftentimes helped rather than hindered thereby, grows and multiplies. Once really to believe this is to be saved from all panic in days when outward appearances seem to suggest that the Word of God is in danger. It is not so, but all that oppose, however strong, however subtle, pass and perish inevitably in the onward movements of a world that is still in the hands of God.

They sent them away. So they being sent forth by the Holy Spirit.—*Acts* 13. 3 and 4.

Barnabas and Saul were sent away by the church at Antioch, and were sent forth by the Holy Spirit. Luke made the statement quite simply as revealing the natural order of procedure. It is a splendid revela-

tion of the true method of activity in all missionary enterprise, and the whole story is of the utmost value in this regard. The Church is in existence, and it is occupied in the ministry to the Lord. To the Church under such conditions it is possible for the Spirit to make known the will of the Lord; and for the Church to apprehend it. Then the Church is able to act with order, and with full and final authority. The men thus chosen and separated, go out to their work with the consciousness that they are the instruments of the Church and the Spirit. They thus go as in the Name and with the full authority of Christ. What great things He is able to accomplish when such are the conditions, the sequel will show. The story gives us pause, and makes us wonder how much of our failure may not be the result of our departure from these fundamental principles. At least we should remember that no cleverness of our own will ever take the place of close fellowship with Christ by the Holy Spirit.

They returned to Lystra, and to Iconium, and to Antioch.—*Acts* 14. 21.

This is a singularly interesting statement in many ways. First it reminds us that Paul was more than an evangelist. He was a pastor. His missionary work was first that of proclaiming the Gospel and bringing men to decision; but he never rested there. He, of all men, realized the importance of subsequent teaching, in order to confirm the faith of the new disciples; and of setting them in order in Church life. Therefore he returned. Again, this particular story reveals his heroism, as it resulted from his complete devotion to his work. Recall the facts concerning his visits to these places. From the borders of Antioch, in Pisidia Paul and Barnabas had been cast out. From Iconium they had been compelled to flee. At Lystra Paul had been stoned, dragged out of the city, and left for dead. Yet they turned back, to the place of the stones, to the place of intention to stone, to the place that had cast them out. This returning to places of peril was made necessary because in every place they had been led in triumph, so far as their Gospel was concerned, in spite of apparent defeat. In Antioch they had left a company of disciples filled with joy and the Holy Ghost; in Iconium a multitude of Jews and Greeks who had believed; and in Lystra also those who were disciples. Thus the way of the Cross was the way of perpetual triumph and persistent travail.

For it seemed good to the Holy Spirit, and to us.—*Acts* 15. 28.

Here we have another instance of that glorious and remarkable consciousness of co-operation between the Church and the Holy Spirit which characterized these early days. It is not merely the fact of it which is arresting, but the keen sense of it, which these disciples knew. These words occur in the midst of what we may term the official apostolic document sent to the Gentile Christians concerning the trouble which had arisen about circumcision. The decisions embodied in that document were arrived at after much discussion, not, we may gather, without some heat. Yet at last they came to such findings as they did, certain that they had the mind of the Spirit; and they said so, naturally and simply. These words constitute the real seal of authority upon the document. How seldom we find anything akin to this in modern documents of the Church. This may be accounted for by the fact that we have a wholesome dread of anything in the nature of unwarranted dogmatism; but the absence of the note leaves something lacking in our documents. If we are not sure that it is so, it would be nigh unto blasphemy to use the words; but such unsureness should drive us to heart-searching as to the cause of it. It is as possible for us to know the mind of the Spirit as it was for these men. If we do not, why not?

Forbidden of the Holy Spirit . . . The Spirit of Jesus suffered them not.—Acts 16. 6, 7.

Without note or comment Luke wrote these almost startling words. Two men, commended to the grace of God by the Church in order to speak the Word of God, were forbidden by the Holy Spirit to do so; and being sent forth by the Holy Spirit into all the world were not suffered by the Spirit of Jesus to enter into a certain region. Thus they were compelled to journey silently in directions other than they would have chosen. The sequel gives the explanation. The plan of the Spirit was that they should pass over into Macedonia. Thus they were guided by hindrance. Judging by our own experiences, we are compelled to the conclusion that for the moment the experience was a perplexing one. The lesson we are to learn is that of the importance of obedience to the guidance of the Spirit when we cannot understand the reason, and indeed when it seems to us that the way marked out, is preventing us from fulfilling the highest things of our most sacred calling. The experience is not rare. Over and over again in the path of true service we are brought to just such places. A great opportunity is open right before us, and we are not permitted to avail ourselves of it. Or we are in the midst of work which is full of real success, and we are called to abandon it. We should never hesitate. This wonderful page of apostolic history teaches us that God's outlook is greater and grander than our own. We may always leave the issue to Him, and presently we shall learn how wise His way, how strong His will.

Now He commandeth men that they should all everywhere repent.—Acts 17. 30.

The call to repentance is the persistent call of Christianity, but it is always based upon the facts of Christianity. The *now* of these words leads on to the *inasmuch* immediately following them. God has placed the world under the government of the Man Whom He hath ordained, and the proof of it is given to the world in the fact of His Resurrection. In the light of these facts men are called to repentance—that is, to change of mind. The call to repentance is a call to reconsideration, to new thinking, to the testing of all things by these facts. The times in which men were ignorant of the truths made known by this fact of resurrection, God overlooked. But now He commands them to conform their conceptions to the light which is shining. In the Divinely ordained Man, raised from the dead, men have a new revelation of God, of man, of the world, of the life that lies beyond the earthly. Life can only be truly lived here, as the truth is known about these very things. To be ignorant of God, of the real nature of man, of the deep secrets of the world, of the facts of the life beyond, is to be unable to live according to the truths of things as they are. While such ignorance is unavoidable, God does not hold man guilty; He overlooks the failure. But when the light is given, His command that men should repent is reasonable and beneficent. To walk according to ignorance when the light is shining, is to sin.

I have much people in this city.—Acts 18. 10.

This word of the Lord to His servant gave him his warrant for a lengthy stay in the city of Corinth. It was without doubt at the time the principal city of Achaia. If Athens was the centre of learning, Corinth was the centre of politics, of wealth, of corruption. There were resident Romans, Greeks and Hebrews. It is probable that Paul was at this time chiefly drawn to Macedonia, and inclined to return there. It would seem from this very message of the Lord that he had some fear of opposition. The words remind us of that which we are ever in danger of forgetting, that all our work is directed by One Who knows the hearts of all men. Corinth did not seem fruitful soil; it was given over to carnality—that is, to materialism. But the Lord knew all that was going on in the souls of men resident there; the restlessness, the heart-ache, the unsatisfied desires. He knew that there were many there who would respond to the message of His Gospel. He saw them, while as yet they saw not Him, and therefore He charged His servant to remain there, and promised him His comradeship and protection. What a glorious service it is, to proclaim amid the multitudes the message, which, being heard and believed, will bring to Himself in experience and outward confession, those whom the Lord already knows. In whatever city we may be working it is surely true that the Lord has much people there.

I must also see Rome.—Acts 19. 21.

In these words Paul gave expression, not to a desire only, but also to a conviction. That it was in harmony with the will of his Lord, subsequent events proved; but it is probable that at the time he had little consciousness of how long it would be ere he reached Rome, or how difficult would be the pathway thither. These things we shall see as we proceed. Perhaps the chief interest in this conviction of Paul at the moment is that of its revelation once more, of how in the economy of the Holy Spirit the natural things of a man are taken hold of, and pressed into the service of the enterprise of Christ. As we have seen before, Paul was 'a freeborn Roman citizen. He would be very conscious of the power of Rome in all human affairs. He knew how from that City of the Seven Hills the highways radiated to all parts of the world. He knew then the importance of the Christian Church in that great city. It was already in existence, having been planted almost certainly by the "sojourners from Rome" who were in Jerusalem at Pentecost. It was this sense which caused him to write his letter to them, and now made him desire to see the city. Thus the true apostle of Christ Jesus is ever lifting his eyes to larger things than those of his immediate work. He is always planning for advance, rather than contemplating withdrawal.

Not knowing.—Acts 20. 22.

This phrase from the lips of Paul reveals one of the things that, through very varied experience, he had come to know. He knew that there were things in his programme that he did not know. Locally, the phrase was expressive of uncertainty as to the reception he would receive in Jerusalem. But its chief value for us lies in the fact that it is so used as to show that such ignorance did not interfere with the certainties of the future. He had received a ministry from the Lord Jesus, and the one and only thing that concerned him was that he should accomplish that ministry. What lay in the course, of bonds or affliction, or even death, mattered nothing; the doing of the appointed work was supreme. Thus there is the touch of a splendid carelessness in the words "not knowing"; a carelessness as to minor matters, born of a constant carefulness as to the principal matter. Thus the "not knowing" of Paul meant not caring to know, not asking to know; indeed, it meant preferring not to know. That is the true attitude of all who are walking in an appointed course, in the service of the Lord. We know Whose we are and Whom we serve. We know the way of His will for us. As to the rest, we can say "not knowing"; and that is the ignorance of a perfect rest.

I am ready not to be bound only, but also to die at Jerusalem for the name of the Lord Jesus.—Acts 21. 13.

Paul was still journeying toward Rome, though he would not arrive there for years. The immediate goal was Jerusalem, and still he did not know what awaited him there. He had now reached Caesarea, and his friends were attempting to dissuade him from going, for the prophet Agabus had foretold that he would be bound and handed over to the Gentiles. This was Paul's reply to these beseechings of these friends. It was a declaration again of his devotion to the main path of duty, and of his carelessness as to what experiences he might pass through as he trod that path. To follow Paul thus, and to observe his steadfastness, impresses us with the strength of the man; but it impresses us more with the greatness of the work to which he was called. To him nothing could compare for grandeur, and dignity, and spaciousness, with the career of proclaiming the Name. Nothing else counted. The toil, the travail, the perils—these were incidental. He was entirely careless concerning them. And is it not always so, that any slacking in devotion is proof of some failure in conception as to the glory of the service? Any weakening in our sense of the supreme fulness and power of the Name will inevitably result in a growing sense of difficulties; and this will fill us with the fear that paralyses. While the Name is to us what it is to God, the Name above every name, the cost of proclaiming it is never counted.

The Lord said unto me, Arise, and go into Damascus.—Acts 22. 10.

Paul was now in Jerusalem and in the midst of the circumstances which Agabus had foretold. He was a prisoner, and, by that fact, protected from the hostility of the Jewish mob. Having obtained, from the soldiers who had arrested him in order to protect him, permission to speak, he told the story of his apprehension by the Lord in the days long before. In the light of all that had happened to him since, these words are full of interest. In them we have the first command which the Lord had uttered to him after he had made the complete surrender. When, to his amazement, he found that Jesus was alive, without any equivocation or hesitation he yielded to Him his allegiance, and asked, "What shall I do, Lord?" Then he received his first orders, and they were of the simplest. He was told to go to Damascus and to wait. That was the way of the

Lord with His chosen vessel, and it is His way with all whom He commands. He indicates the next step, and commands that we wait for further orders. Whereas He did give him the larger outlook upon his ministry presently, in general outline, the particular method through all the years was that of one step at a time. How gracious and beneficent a method this is! If we could be told ahead all the detailed experiences through which we pass, should we dare face them? However, we need not speculate on that, but rejoice that He leads us one step at a time.

The night following, the Lord stood by him.—*Acts* 23. 11.

The words "the night following" are very suggestive. Paul had passed through two tremendous days. The bitterness of his foes was such that no limit would be set to what they would do to him if they could. The chief captain was afraid that they might tear him to pieces, and so had rescued him by force and secured him in the castle. The "night following" such days would inevitably be a time of reaction. Bold, courageous, fearless during the day, the night of loneliness finds the strength spent, and the enemy is never slow to take advantage of that fact. Oh, the dreads and questionings and shrinkings of the night! Then we must need help. And then it was that "the Lord stood by him." Through all the stress and strain of those terrific days Paul had maintained in speech and demeanour the honour of the Name, and now the One Who bore the Name came to him manifestly, definitely, personally. Very beautiful was the word He spoke to His servant. Paul had long before declared his conviction that he must see Rome. Perhaps the form of despondency threatening him that night was that he might never do so. It would seem so from the very fact that the Lord's message to him was that he should certainly witness at Rome also. The value of all this is patent. Loyalty to the Name will often bring the witnesses into days of strain and so to nights of foreboding. But HE always comes, and even if not manifestly, yet He always stands by.

He reasoned of righteousness, and self-control, and the judgment to come. *Acts* 24. 25.

Felix sent for Paul, and "heard him concerning the faith in Christ Jesus": and this is what he heard, and he "was terrified." The faith in Christ Jesus is infinitely more than a soft love-story. It is always a love-story, but the love in it is the love of God, and that cuts like a sword, burns like a fire, searches like an acid, in the case of some. Paul was a true doctor of divinity. He not only knew the faith, he knew how to preach it so as to meet the need with which he was called upon to deal. His diagnosis and his prognosis were accurate. That is to say that he knew the nature of the spiritual malady of Felix, and also the course that disease would pursue. Therefore he handled this man's soul in the true way. The man was immoral: therefore he reasoned of righteousness. He was swayed by his passions: therefore he reasoned with him of self-control. He was rebellious against authority: therefore he reasoned with him concerning the tribunal before which he must ultimately render his account. But all this by the standards of the faith in Christ Jesus. By that faith Felix might find the power for righteousness, the strength for self-control, and so the readiness to stand uncondemned before the final judgment-bar. Surely it is a terrifying faith, for it rebukes sin, but the terror it awakes is the inspiration of new life. What the issue is, depends upon the response of the soul.

I appeal unto Caesar.—*Acts* 25. 11.

In making this appeal Paul was acting as a citizen of the city of God, and in the interest of that citizenship making use of his earthly citizenship. The processes of earthly justice were threatened by the proposal made, to hand him over to the Jews by sending him for trial to Jerusalem. Against that danger Paul acted by appealing, as he had a right to do, to Caesar directly. In doing this, moreover, he was acting in accordance with his philosophy of human government, as set forth in his letter to the Romans. He believed that the powers were ordained of God to be terrors to the evil. If in the event it should prove that even Caesar's judgment was not according to that standard, the final condemnation would be Caesar's. In the meantime, he availed himself of the right which was his, basing that appeal upon the right vested in Caesar by God. It is a valuable illustration of what earthly citizenship means to those who are burgesses of the City of God. We have every right to avail ourselves of the administration of justice which is vested in earthly governments by the will of God. By doing so we are creating for these governments the opportunity to exercise their functions in a true way, and so the dignity of our citizenship in the City of God is seen. At last Caesar was judged by what he did with the man who appealed to him.

Except these bonds.—*Acts* 26. 29.

In this little phrase we have a revelation of the central victory of grace in Paul. He had been talking to Agrippa and without any question, striving to win him for his Master. When the libertine sneered at him, saying: "With but little persuasion thou wouldst fain make me a Christian," Paul had declared that his one most ardent desire for Agrippa and all who heard him was that they should be as he was, except for his bonds. He would give them his freedom but not his chain; his joy, but not his pain. Contrast that with the man as he was when first we met him. He was then "breathing threatening and slaughter," and all his fierceness then was the outcome of his honest devotion to what he believed to be the truth. Before Agrippa he was none the less honest, intense, devoted; but he was a new man in Christ Jesus, and therefore his desire for those opposing was, not that they should be imprisoned, but that they should be free; not that they should be put to death, but that they should find life. This is always the result of fellowship with Christ. It is the mystery of the Cross, the deep compassion in which the supremacy of holiness is never lost sight of, but which will take responsibility and bear suffering, in order that holiness may be realized in others, and those the most unworthy.

I believe God.—*Acts* 27. 25.

This was an affirmation of faith to pagan men under stress of great and grave difficulty. Luke's story of the stormy voyage and the shipwreck is one of the most graphic things in literature, and for us it is centred in Paul and his quiet courage throughout. So far as he was concerned, he knew that it was impossible that he should perish, for had not the Lord stood by him in the night more than two years ago, and assured him that he should witness in Rome? All through he comforted and strengthened those who sailed with him. When things were at their worst, an angel came to him and told him that he should stand before Caesar, and that none of those sailing with him should be lost. Then it was that he made his affirmation. The effect of that affirmation on those in authority is seen in the way in which they followed his directions subsequently. The value of a definite confession of confidence is very great. It is often that men who do not profess themselves to believe in God do believe in a man who does believe in Him, and are prepared to follow him. How much of influence we lose by slowness to confess the faith that is in us! The man who with definiteness will declare his belief in God, as against all contrary circumstances, is making other men put God to the test, and so is winning victories, for God never fails.

So we came to Rome.—*Acts* 28. 14.

The "so" of that statement refers to much more than the story of the voyage. It goes back at least to the occasion when in Ephesus Paul had said: "I must also see Rome." Since then probably three years had elapsed, and what strange experiences of bonds and afflictions he had passed through! At last he arrived in the imperial city as a prisoner, and Luke wrote: "So we came." The conviction that he would arrive had been challenged again and again by circumstances, and once perhaps when shut up in the castle in Jerusalem that conviction had been shaken. Then the Lord stood by him and assured him, and from that time there is not the slightest evidence of any tremor. Thus the "so" has more in it than the reference to the trying circumstances and the long delay. It referred also and principally to the power of the Lord, against which the hostility of Jerusalem, the vagaries of governors, and the wrath of the elements, were all alike powerless. And so it ever is. A man walking in a Divinely-marked pathway is perfectly safe. If it be the will of God that we should reach a certain place, and do a certain piece of work for Him, nothing can prevent our arriving, nothing can hinder our doing that work, save disobedience. The way of our coming, and the circumstances of our arrival may not be what we had anticipated, but we shall arrive, and God's purpose will be served.

ROMANS

As much as in me is.—*Rom.* 1. 15.

To begin to read this great letter of Paul, is to find ourselves in the very atmosphere of the closing chapters of the book of the Acts. There we found Paul expressing his conviction that he would see Rome; and we followed him through the years of stress that at last brought him there. It was almost certainly during his stay at Corinth, before starting on that long journey, that he wrote this Epistle, which opens with the expression of his desire to come to them. In connection with that expression of desire, he declared that he was ready to preach the Gospel to those in Rome, and then he used this qualifying phrase, "as much as in me is."

The phrase seems to me to be at once a recognition of limitation, and of resource. The sense of limitation was the result of his overwhelming consciousness of the greatness of the Gospel. He knew that no one man was equal to its interpretation. And yet, I think, that quite unconsciously to him perhaps, the phrase was a recognition of resource. More lay within this devoted man than his natural capacities. Christ was formed within him: he was indwelt by the Spirit. Hence his ability to preach the Gospel in all its fulness as he did in this very letter. Is not the deduction patent? The measure in which a man is conscious of limitation, is the measure in which he makes possible the operation of those powers which are his in Christ.

God shall judge the secrets of men, according to my Gospel, by Jesus Christ.—Rom. 2. 16.

In this declaration the phrase "according to my Gospel" is a parenthetical qualification. The statement is that "God shall judge the secrets of men by Jesus Christ." This fact Paul declares to be part of the Gospel. Here we have a wonderful instance of the merging of the elements of the grace and severity of God in the Gospel. The Gospel is the good news that God has made righteousness available to sinful men through Christ. But the Gospel is also the declaration of the fact that men will be judged by the One through Whom that grace has been made available. There we see the finality of the Gospel message. The Saviour is to be the judge. Let us put that in another way. The judge is the Saviour. He Whose eternal right it is to sit as judge of men has in His Son provided perfect redemption for men. By so doing He has not relinquished His right as judge, but has established it. If men refuse His salvation, the justice of His sentence against them cannot be called in question. All men must meet Him as judge, but before they do so He comes to meet them with a righteous and just way of saving them from their sins. If they refuse that salvation, the Gospel declares that by so doing they have not escaped Him as judge. The Gospel never lowers the standards of Divine requirements. It makes them possible of realization. If it be refused, then the Saviour as judge condemns and punishes.

As it is written.—Rom. 3. 4.

This is not the first time we have found this phrase in this letter: (see 1. 17 and 2. 24): neither is it the last occurrence: (see 3. 10–18; 4. 17; 8. 36; 9. 13, 33; 10. 15; 11. 8, 26; 12. 19; 14. 11; 15. 9, 21). In all those cases this formula of reference to the Old Testament is employed. Beyond these, there are many other quotations or allusions thereto. There are at least seventy-three verses in which such direct references are found. This is a most interesting study, as it shows the place which the Old Testament Scriptures occupied in the thinking of Paul, and as it reveals his method with them, and so the real value of them. As to the first, it is to be noticed that he never referred to any Old Testament Scripture in order to deny or correct its teaching. Every reference or allusion is to the Sacred Writings as authoritative. These quotations are from each section of the Hebrew Bible; Moses: Genesis, Exodus, Leviticus, and Deuteronomy; The Prophets: 1 Kings, Isaiah,

Jeremiah, Hosea, Joel, Habakkuk, Malachi; and The Writings: Psalms, Proverbs. As to the method of quotation, Paul quoted generally from the Septuagint, and sometimes from the Hebrew, and he constantly changed the actual wording, but never the essential meaning, thus showing us that the truth embodied is authoritative, rather than the particular words employed to convey it. A careful study of these facts will help us to a right attitude toward the Old Testament.

Who in hope believed against hope. —Rom. 4. 18.

That account of Abraham's mental attitude, as the result of the promise of God to him, is also a description of the experience of all those who live by faith in Him. Hope is always the expectation of good things to come, with a corresponding activity toward the realization of them. There can be no hope where there are no grounds of expectation. To Abraham there were no grounds of expectation in circumstances that he should have an heir. They absolutely denied the possibility. Nevertheless he hoped. Upon what grounds? Those of "the promise of God." To the man who believed in God, they were sufficient; and therefore he hoped, that is, he expected that the thing would happen, and he ordered his life accordingly. That is the very genius of the life of faith. All the great things for which we look are impossible things by the standards of circumstances. If we compute the possibilities of realization upon the basis of things seen, ours is the most hopeless of enterprises. For the bringing to birth of the new order, man is dead, and woman is barren. But if we reckon with God, then we are the most hopeful of all men. He has promised, and no word of His can be void of power. Therefore we hope against hope. When there is no ground for expectation in circumstances, we find it in God; and thus with jubilant songs we cheer the night, and journey toward the Day of God.

. . . Because the love of God hath been shed abroad in our hearts.— Rom. 5. 5.

These words lead us a step further in our understanding of the nature of Christian hope. Not only is it true that it triumphs because it knows and believes God. It is also true that it is not put to shame. That is, it is never overthrown or discredited in any way by the circumstances of tribulation through which we must pass in order to its realization. On the contrary, we rejoice in these very tribulations because we realize that they are parts of the working force which is ever operating toward the realization. The secret of this victorious hope is that the love of God hath been poured out in our hearts. Here the idea is not merely that God loves us, though necessarily that is involved. It is rather that He fills us with His love by the Spirit, so that we love what He loves, and as He loves. That self-emptying sacrificial love becomes the inspiration of all our thinking, of all our doing. And it is more than that. It is the power of all our service. It is not only patient love which endures; it is mighty love which accomplishes. It is the secret of that abounding toil which never tires until its object is achieved. Where there is such love filling and mastering the life, hope is never put to shame in the processes of tribulation, and it will be ultimately saved from shame as all the toils are vindicated in the glory of the results.

Present yourselves unto God, as alive from the dead.—*Rom. 6. 13.*

Christianity is a living religion. The way of entrance is that of death, but it is the way that leadeth into life. This was so in the work of our Lord. In order to save, He died. The salvation into which He brings men through His death is that of life, and that more abundantly. So with all who receive that salvation. The condition upon which they do so is that of death, the self-denial which is the ending of all confidence in self, and all endeavour to win life by effort. When that condition is fulfilled, life is received as a grace-gift of God. Then dedication begins. This is an important distinction. When the soul yields to Christ, it is not giving anything to God. It has nothing to give. It is sinful, unworthy. It yields just as it is, because it cannot make itself worthy, and because in grace He calls for its surrender and trust. When this surrender of a sinful and unworthy being is made, He takes the polluted life, and pardons, cleanses, and renews it. Now the renewed, cleansed, pardoned one is called upon to present himself or herself to God, as alive from the dead. "Just as I am," I cannot dedicate myself to God; but I can yield myself to the Saviour. When I am what the Saviour makes me, I can present myself to God, and I shall be accepted in the Beloved. Such dedication is implicit in my yielding to Christ. It must be explicit in the resulting life.

The law is spiritual; but I am carnal. —*Rom. 7. 14.*

That word of the Apostle reveals at once the supremacy and inadequacy of the law, and helps us to understand the difference between it and grace. The law is spiritual. That means, first, that it is not the result of human contrivance; it has the authority of revelation; it is not something thought out by man. It is the authentic revelation of the will of God. It also means that the law appeals first to the essential in man, which is spiritual; it

can only be obeyed in material activities, as it is accepted and yielded to in spirit. But that is its limit. It is a revelation, not an enablement. It tells man what to do, but it does not help him to do it. And that would be sufficient for man, were he living under the power of his spiritual nature. But he is not. As Paul bluntly states it, every man has to say, "I am carnal." He is living under the power of his flesh, and so, while consenting to the truth and beauty of the ideal revealed in the law, is unable to realize it. Thus the law has no final function other than that of revealing this very incompetence. It is a great function, for to understand my failure and incompetence is at least to leave me without excuse if I refuse the gift of grace. Grace does not lower the standard of law, but it does exactly what the law cannot do, it enables man to live according to that standard.

More than conquerors.—*Rom. 8. 37.*

To conquer is to subdue; that is, to master, to overcome, in the sense of defeating an attack. To conquer tribulation would be to put an end to it; to conquer anguish would be to replace it by joy; to conquer persecution would be to turn it into patronage; to conquer famine would be to provide food; to conquer nakedness would be to provide clothing; to conquer peril would be to secure safety; to conquer the sword would be to destroy the sword. In all these things Paul says we are "more than conquerors." This does not mean that, in the senses referred to, we conquer, and more. On the contrary, it may mean that we do not conquer at all, but that we do more, we wrest from defeat values that could never be gained by conquest. Enduring tribulation, we are thereby brought, through patience and proving, to the hope that is not put to shame. Experiencing anguish, we are having fellowship with the suffering which saves. Bearing persecution, we are demonstrating the meaning of true godliness. Suffering hunger, we are proving that man does not live by bread alone. In nakedness, we reveal the beauty of spiritual adorning. Living amid perils, we are revealing the power of our Lord. Dying by the sword, we are demonstrating the weakness of the sword. This is more-than-conquering, and it is only possible "through Him that loved us."

It is not of him that willeth, nor of him that runneth, but of God that hath mercy.—*Rom. 9. 16.*

This does not mean that we are not to will, that we are not to run. Neither does it mean that we enter into the blessings of salvation apart from willing, apart from running. We must will to do, and we must run well, allowing nothing to hinder. It does most clearly mean that no willing on our part, no running of our own, can procure for us the salvation we need, or enable us to enter into the blessings it provides. It means more than that. Of ourselves we shall have no will for salvation, and shall make no effort toward it. Everything of human salvation begins in God. His will is to have mercy. His work enables Him to do so. It is only as that will is made known to man, that he wills to receive the mercy. It is only as that work operates within man, that he is able to work out his salvation. Our wills must be exercised, our running must be positive; but we enter into salvation, and shall at last reach the crowning at the goal, only because of the everlasting mercy of God. There is neither merit nor cause for glorying in our choice or our effort. If God had not willed our saving, neither should we. If God did not work within us, we should work nothing out. Even if, of our service, we can ever say we laboured abundantly, we shall have to add: Yet not we, but the grace of God which was with us.

How? . . . How? . . . How? . . . How?—Rom. 10. 14, 15.

This sequence of inquiries follows a declaration, which is a quotation from Joel: "Whosoever shall call upon the Name of the Lord shall be saved." Whatever its value in that prophecy, or in Peter's quotation thereof on the day of Pentecost (see Acts 2. 21), Paul here evidently employed it in reference to man's responsibility concerning the salvation provided in Christ Jesus. That whole responsibility is revealed in the one word "call." Salvation comes to a man when he calls on the Name of the Lord. The inquiries reveal the place and nature of the call. The call follows belief. The belief follows hearing. The hearing follows preaching. The preaching follows sending. Thus the Apostle traces the movement back to its origin. Let us state it in the other order that we may apprehend the nature of man's calling on the Name of the Lord. God has a message of salvation, and this He sends preachers to proclaim. The preachers proclaim that message. Men hear the preachers' message, and believe it. Observe that they are not saved by that belief. So far as it is merely intellectual; it is conviction that the message is true. That does not bring men into salvation. They must now "call upon the Name of the Lord." At once we see that the element of volitional surrender to the message believed, is necessary in order to salvation. Everything begins with God, but the final responsibility is with man.

God is able to graft them in again.— Rom. 11. 23.

Paul's great subject in all this section was that of the salvation of the ancient people of God, Israel. He saw "some of the branches . . . broken off," whereas the root-purpose of God through them and for them was not destroyed. The breaking-off was very real, and it resulted from their unbelief. Now the Apostle declared that if they continued not in unbelief, they would be grafted in again, for "God is able to graft them in again." Beyond the immediate application to Israel, these words are full of significance, as they reveal principles of abiding importance. The mind almost inevitably recurs to our Lord's allegory of the vine, in which also we read of fruitless branches being cast out of the vine. In presence of all that is involved of solemnity in that idea, how amazing a revelation is here of the grace and power of God! He is able to graft in again branches that have been broken off. Even though, in the interest of the Vine, and because of our fruitlessness, we have been cast forth, He is able to graft us in again. But while we recognize that, we must not forget the condition. It is that we continue not in the unbelief which was the secret of our fruitlessness. God will never graft in branches broken off, merely out of pity for them. He will do so when, by return to the true principle of life, it becomes possible for them to fulfil their function in the Vine.

Let love be without hypocrisy.— Rom. 12. 9.

This twelfth chapter begins the apostolic application of the doctrines of salvation to the actualities of life. After the statement of the great principles of true Christian life, Paul passed to some general illustrations in a series of injunctions. Of these, this is the first. It is very simple, but very searching. Everything in Christianity proceeds out of the love of God, and its ultimate and glorious fruitage is that of love mastering men. Hence there is always a danger lest love should be professed when it is not possessed; or, on the other hand, that love should be untrue to its central element of holiness. Hence the warning of these words. Love must be without acting, for that is what hypocrisy really is. The language of love, where love is not, is of no avail. Even the activities, which are properly those of love, practised in order to make it seem as though we loved, are of no value. That is what Paul meant when he wrote in another Epistle: "If I bestow all my goods to feed the poor . . . but have not love, it profiteth me nothing." So also, to violate love by failing to abhor evil, even when the violation is that of actions of tenderness, is in itself evil. Love is hypocritical, it is acting, it is untrue to itself, when it condones evil in any form. Love must cleave to good, or be untrue to its very deepest nature.

Love therefore is the fulfilment of the law.—*Rom.* 13. 10.

Here again is a simple statement of a most profound truth, and its apprehension will correct many mistakes. Man is at least inclined to think of law and love as being antagonistic. We have heard John's words, "The law was given through Moses; grace and truth came through Jesus Christ," so recited as to give the impression that there was radical difference between them. Indeed, over and over again a "but" is introduced between the two parts of the one declaration. There is no difference. The only distinction is that law tells us what to do, and grace enables us to do it. Thus not only is there no antagonism between love and law, there is no separation between them. Law is an expression of love. To understand that, is to realize that love is also the fulfilling of law. Paul's method of showing this is most simple and most conclusive. It is impossible to sin against our fellowmen if we love them; or we may say that every sin we commit against them is due to some cooling or failure of love. Love is the most vigilant and severe sentinel of all our actions. It is the only motive strong enough to make us true under all circumstances and at all times. Fear will carry us far, but under stress of fierce temptation it will break down. Love will carry us all the way, and leave us still desiring better things than we have ever attained.

Let each man be fully assured in his own mind.—*Rom.* 14. 5.

This is a far-reaching word. Its application in Paul's argument was to such very disputable matters as the observing of days, and the eating of foods. It is really passing strange how these and similarly unimportant matters have been, and continue to be, reasons for much bitterness between the children of God. Two matters are contained in this instruction—first, that of a man's personal duty; and second, that of his attitude toward all other men. The first is explicit; the second is implicit. The personal duty is that a man be fully assured in his own mind. That means first, that he is to have an opinion. He has no right to be guided in these things by the opinions or habits of others. That way lies the paralysing of the powers of personality, and therefore weakness. It may be that coming to full assurance will demand time and thought, and in the process he may be helped by conferring with others; but at last he must find his own stand. This being so, it follows that he will recognize the right and obligation of every other man to the same process. Therefore no man can have any right whatever to impose upon any other man his own convictions. All this is important and reasonable, because one man may be helped by the observance of a day, while another is not; one may find strength in abstinence from certain forms of food, and another weakness.

The offering up of the Gentiles.—*Rom.* 15. 16.

In this phrase an idea is included which is very beautiful, and which we are in danger of forgetting. It is that of the priestly nature of all ministerial work. Paul was a chosen vessel of God to the Gentiles. He was sent to preach the Gospel to them, and to build them up in their faith. As we saw in the Acts of the Apostles, he was diligent in carrying out both these things. Here he described that whole work by a phrase which shows its deepest value. All those who were won by the preaching of the Gospel, and perfected as he exhorted and admonished, were sacrifices laid upon the Altar, offerings verily made by fire unto the Lord. Thus in the doing of all this work Paul was exercising the priesthood of worship. What a radiant light this sheds upon all our evangelistic and pastoral effort! Every soul won by the preaching of the Gospel is not only brought into a place of safety and blessing; it is an offering to God, a gift which gives Him satisfaction, the very offering He is ever seeking. Every soul carefully and patiently instructed in the things of Christ, and so made conformable to His likeness, is a soul in whom the Father takes pleasure. Thus we labour, not only for the saving of men, but for the satisfying of the heart of God. This is the most powerful motive. There may be times when we are tempted to think of men as not worthy of our sacrifice. We always feel that He is worthy to receive.

Wise unto that which is good, and simple unto that which is evil.—*Rom.* 16. 19.

This is one of Paul's last expressed wishes in this letter for the saints in Rome, that little company of souls delivered from the kingdom of Satan, who yet lived in a city where was his seat of authority. That city, like every great city in human history, was full of the deep things of Satan. Evil lures men by its subtlety, its mystery, its darkling depths. The seduction of it is very powerful—men are desirous of knowing. Thousands of men, of real natural ability, have found destruction because, as they say, they desired to see life. What they saw was not life, but death. For these children of God, Paul desired that in all these things they might remain simple. There are things in the underworld, the very knowledge of which pollutes the soul. It is better not to know. The children of God are admitted to the mystery of good, which is the mystery of godliness, the mystery of light, of purity, of beauty. In this realm he desired that they might be wise. By their relation with God in Christ men are admitted into this wonderful realm. Herein they see life, and share it, the more abundant life, the life eternal. In this world of the upper things the soul is purified, ennobled, glorified. Here it is better to know. Let all such as are in this fellowship follow on to know. Let them come to full knowledge. This is the true wisdom. Let it be sought earnestly and persistently.

FIRST CORINTHIANS

Called into the fellowship of His Son, Jesus Christ our Lord.—I *Cor.* I. 9.

The purpose of saintship is fully described in these words. That is the meaning of the Church in any city. Its members are "called" and "saints," because they "call upon the Name of our Lord Jesus Christ," and so they are "called into the fellowship of His Son." This word fellowship is rich in suggestiveness. We touch its deepest note when we recognize its first meaning. The simple idea is that of having all things in common.. It is the word which marks the most perfect realization of unity in every way: in possessions, in purpose, and in effort. Perhaps the ground may be covered by saying that it means that those who are in fellowship have resources and responsibilities in common. Here, then, is the truth about the relationship existing between all Christian souls and the Lord. All His resources are at their disposal. All their resources are at His disposal. They are committed to His responsibilities. He is committed to their responsibilities. That covers the whole fact of Christian life and service. It is because of that we may truthfully sing—

I nothing lack if I am His,
And He is mine for ever.

The searching thought is that, if there be any failure in this relationship of resource and responsibility, it is in us, and not in Him. Are our resources all at His disposal? Are we availing ourselves of His resources? Are we facing His responsibilities? Are we trusting Him to undertake our responsibilities? Thus may we question our souls when we are alone with the Lord.

We received . . . the Spirit which is of God, that we might know . . .— I *Cor.* 2. 12.

This is really a very wonderful declaration, which we are in danger of failing to apprehend. Let it be noticed that it follows Paul's quotation of a passage from the prophecy of Isaiah; and then let us remember how constantly men quote that passage in order to prove that the things that God has prepared for them that love Him cannot yet be known. This use of the passage, moreover, is almost invariably with reference to the future blessedness of the people of God. Now as a matter of fact this use is entirely unwarranted. Isaiah was referring to God's method of working for those who wait for Him. Paul was referring to all the Divine wisdom, as manifested in redemption. These are the things which cannot be apprehended by the seeing eye and the hearing ear of human intelligence. They need Divine revelation and interpretation; they must be made known by the Spirit of God, Who alone knoweth the deep things of God. Here, then, is the wonder of the statement. We are not to live in ignorance of these things. "We received . . . the Spirit which is of God, that we might know." Does not this fact rebuke an attitude of soul to which we are prone, and which may seem to be that of rest and humility? The child of God who has the Spirit of God has no right to be content not to understand the deep things of God. The Spirit is ours, that we may know. Therefore we should give all diligence to know, in dependence upon the teaching of that Spirit.

Saved; yet so as through fire.— I *Cor.* 3. 15.

These words describe a possible condition of a saint of God in the Day of final testing. The subject is one of service. That of life is not in view, save as in some senses that is always involved in service. As we have seen, the saint of God is in fellowship with the Lord in responsibility. That means work: and Paul here deals with it under the figure of building upon the foundation. All such building is to be tested by fire. That which is true and precious will be made more beautiful by the fire. That which is false and unworthy will be destroyed by the fire. When that is so, the man himself will be "saved, yet so as through fire." His ultimate salvation will be secured by the destruction of his work. Can anything be more calculated to give us pause in our work? What are we building? That is, what sort of material are we laying upon the foundation? The things of gold, silver, costly stones, are the things of eternity. Those of wood, hay, stubble, are those which are only of time. When the saints of God are tempted to forget the spiritual and eternal implication and application of all they do, they are in danger of doing work which must be destroyed in order that they may be saved. We are humbled by the grace which will destroy our unworthy works to save us. We are constrained thereby to take heed how we build.

What hast thou that thou didst not receive?—1 Cor. 4. 7.

This is a truth the recognition of which will keep the children and servants of God from being "puffed up, for the one against the other." The reference of the Apostle was to the foolish pride which some were manifesting in himself, others in Apollos, and so on. He did not deny the importance of that in his ministry, or that in the ministry of Apollos, in which they were boasting. He reminded them that in every case they had received as a gift that which had helped them. And this was as true in the case of one as of the other, in that of Apollos, as of himself. Pride, therefore, was entirely out of place. Instead, there should have been gratitude, and recognition of the value of the gifts bestowed upon others, which probably they had not shared. The application of the principle was to the teachers as well as to the taught. Paul had nothing of his own, neither had Apollos. What they had ministered, they had received. Therefore they were, as he had already said, "ministers of Christ, and stewards of the mysteries of God"; and in their ministry, as administering the estate of the mysteries, there could be no place for pride. All this is of the widest possible application to Christian life and service. The gifts by which we serve, and the gifts which we receive through the service of others, are all gifts of God. We do not create them, we receive them. We may do so thankfully, joyfully, but there is neither place nor time for pride; and when we allow it to gain ascendancy, we are frustrating the grace which bestows, and is bestowed.

Put away the wicked man from among yourselves.—1 Cor. 5. 13.

This was the Apostle's final word in dealing with a specific case in the Corinthian Church. One of the members of that church had been guilty of the most flagrant wrongdoing, and no discipline had been exercised by the Church. Indeed incredible as it seems, it nevertheless appears that in some way they were glorying in the matter. It is incredible that they were glorying in the sin. It is more likely that they were glorying in the lack of discipline, probably thinking of it as toleration. It was against this attitude of the Church that Paul protested. Within its borders, no disintegrating leaven must be permitted to remain. The life of the Church is a perpetual Passover Feast, and it must be maintained in sincerity and truth. This is a subject of supreme importance. The Church of God is always weakened when it lacks the power to maintain its purity. Toleration of evil in any form within the fellowship of those whose one business it is, individually and collectively, to reveal the Lord to men, must be of the nature of treachery. Yet it should be remembered that discipline should ever be exercised in the spirit of love. Its purpose is not only the purity of the Church; it is also the saving of the one disciplined. If in his apostolic authority Paul charged them to exclude the sinning man from fellowship, it was in order that his spirit might be saved in the day of the Lord Jesus. This harmonizes with the teaching of the Lord Himself, Who showed that the purpose of discipline was that of gaining our brother. (See Matthew 18.)

Is it so, that there cannot be found among you one wise man?—1 Cor. 6. 5.

There was in this question a note of definite, if gentle, sarcasm. Some members of the church in Corinth were engaged in litigation, and taking their cases before the courts of the city. This, according to the mind of the Apostle, was wrong. All such disputes among the saints should be settled before a court of saints. Where it was not so, there was cause for shame. "Is it so," said the Apostle, "that there cannot be found among you one wise man?" Much is involved in this question, and the view of the Church which it postulates. It is questionable whether the Church has ever risen to the height of his conception in actual practice. The Church is here viewed as being a society, a household, self-contained; having the power and right to deal with all matters arising within itself; having no need to seek guidance or direction from those beyond its own borders; and consequently lowering the standard of her life, and weakening the power of her testimony, when she allows any interference with the affairs of her own members from those outside her fellowship. In cases in which the principles and practices of righteousness have to be maintained as between members of the Church, and those who are outside its borders, it is right and necessary to appeal to civil courts, as Paul himself did more than once. But the relationship between Christians in Christ is so close, so wide, that there can be no dispute or difficulty that cannot be adjusted by the Church itself in His wisdom and in His grace.

Let each man, wherein he was called, therein abide with God.—1 Cor. 7. 24.

The ultimate value of these words is that they teach us that circumstances are of minor importance in saintship. They neither help nor hinder the believer in realizing all that grace and truth of character, or that purity and strength in service, which are the outcome of saintship. Note the applications of the principle as found in the context. The married or the unmarried; the circumcised or the uncircumcised; the bondservant or the free; in neither case does one condition nor the other affect the fact of saintship, either to help or to hinder. On the contrary, the fact of saintship changes and qualifies all these conditions. Therefore the idea which has been very prevalent, and is still in some forms persistent, that if we can change our circumstances we may develop our saintship, is entirely unwarranted. The experience of the saints has been that the very pressure and friction of conditions which seem to make saintship a difficulty, have contributed to the perfecting of Christian character. The secret of life is that it be lived with God. When that is so, the fellowship transfigures the circumstances, and transmutes the forces which hinder into forces that help. How glorious a conception of life this is, that whatever my calling be, of family relationship, of religious training and habit, or of social position, I can remain therein in the company of God, and so make the circumstances of life the occasion of manifesting His glory.

Knowledge puffeth up, but love edifieth.—1 *Cor.* 8. 1.

Two ways of life are here contrasted—the way of puffing up, and the way of edifying; the way of inflation, and the way of building; the way that tends to swift destruction, and the way of permanence. The contrast is peculiarly Biblical, and goes back to Habakkuk, and the difference between the righteous living by faith, and the puffed-up moving toward destruction. The arresting note is Paul's contrast between knowledge and love, as he distinctly affirms that the former puffs up, while the latter edifies. Is knowledge therefore wrong? By no means. He had just said: "We know that we have all knowledge," in the matter under discussion, that, namely, of things sacrificed to idols; and there was no hint that such knowledge was in itself harmful. The knowledge was conviction of truth that "no idol is anything," and that there is "no God but one." All such knowledge is of supreme value. When, then, does it become dangerous? The answer is self-evident. When we have pride in what we know, and allow that pride to be the inspiration of the use we make of knowledge, we ourselves, becoming puffed up, are unable to act towards others as we should. Love will condition our use of knowledge so that it becomes of service to others, and thus tends also to our own building up. The man who knows, but lacks love, is a dangerous man. The man who knows and loves, is a man who blesses wherever he comes.

I am become all things to all men, that I may by all means save some.—1 *Cor.* 9. 22.

That would seem a superlative application, and it is somewhat startling. Moreover, it is none the less so when interpreted by Paul's illustrations of its working in his own case; to the Jews, under law, he had become as one under law; to the Gentile, without law, he had become as one without law; to the weak he had become weak. The question arises as to how far we may go in this direction. Many applications might be suggested which would seem to us in danger of imperilling our testimony and our usefulness. A second look at the Apostolic word will save us from all doubt in the matter. Paul became all things to all men *that he might save some.* The purpose in view must for ever qualify our accommodations. To go so far with men as to imperil our chances of saving them, is wrong. Thus the idea of these words is, not that the end justifies the means; but rather that the end qualifies the means. In our modern life, it means that I may travel sympathetically with men along the pilgrimage of their doubts, but I must not go so far as to deny my faith. If I do, I cannot help them to faith. Or again, it means that in order to save men I may enter into their social life and share their recreations, but never in such ways as to imperil my power to help them in spiritual matters.

These things were our examples.—1 *Cor.* 10. 6.

Here is our warrant for reading our Old Testament history in order to the strengthening of our life of faith. Paul covers the whole ground first, and then gives some illustrations. All God's ancient people were delivered, all shared the sustenance He provided; but "most of them . . . were overthrown in the wilderness," and so failed to reach God's intended goal, the Land of Promise. The illustrations follow. They lusted after evil things; they became idolaters; they committed fornication; they tempted the Lord; they murmured; and by these things they failed. Every reference is to some incident the history of which is found in the Old Testament. This gives us a key to the true method of studying those stories. The times have changed. All the material and even mental surroundings are entirely different. But the spiritual things abide unchanged. Moreover, all these stories are concerned with people who lived in the comparative twilight of the revelation by law. We live in the full light of the revelation by Grace. Nevertheless, the principles of relationship are the same. Thus we may read with profit these stories of the men of the past, and of God's dealings with them, always remembering with holy fear that we have at our disposal in Christ greater spiritual resources than they had. Such remembrance will not make us careless, but more full of care, lest we fail as they failed. "If they escaped not, when they refused Him that warned them on earth, much more shall not we escape, who turn away from Him that warneth from heaven" (Heb. 12. 25).

Let a man prove himself, and so let him eat of the bread, and drink of the cup.—1 Cor. 11. 28.

These words are blazoned over the portal of every place where the members of the Christian fellowship gather together to observe the Holy Ordinance of the Communion. The places vary as to situation and as to structure, from the stately cathedral to the lowliest cottage. The methods may be as far apart as that of a solemn ritual and that of a simple rite. These after all, are the incidental, indeed, the accidental, things. In themselves they do not matter. They are neither essentially right nor wrong. Finally, the differences matter nothing. Let every man be fully persuaded in his own mind, and let him be true to that persuasion, while he respects the persuasion of others which he does not share. The supreme thing, the essential thing, is the sacred act of communion, the practice of a communion which is constant. It is the act in which the soul is called upon to exercise the highest function of its ransomed nature, that of worship in its purity, and in which it is strengthened for the exercise by the fullest realization of fellowship with the Risen Lord. All that reveals the supreme importance of this injunction. Before the holy hour of fellowship and of worship, there should be solemn self-examination. It should not take place in the service, but before it. The Table of the Lord is not the place for the confession of sin; that must precede it. The absolution of our High Priest is to be sought and found before we enter into the Holy of Holies to offer to Him the sacrifices of our adoration. So, we are to eat the bread and drink the cup, as cleansed worshippers, having no more consciousness of sins. It is at our peril that we neglect such preparation.

God set the members each one of them in the body, even as it pleased Him.—1 Cor. 12. 18.

What a wonderful chapter this is, in its unveiling of the unity of the Church! The figure of the body which the Apostle employs is surely the most perfect. The Psalmist of the olden time was constrained to exclaim, We are "fearfully and wonderfully made"; and the more carefully we consider our bodies the more we realize the truth of the saying. The astonishing unification of the most diverse powers and capacities, all fitting instruments for our life-realization and expression, is indeed most wonderful. Such is the Church of God, the very Body of Christ, the instrument of the Spirit. The particular words upon which we have fastened our attention are words that should bring to every heart the most perfect rest, and the truest comfort. My place in the Body of Christ is not the result of my own choosing; neither is it the result of the appointment of the other members of the Body. I am where I am in the Body, and I am what I am therein, by the good pleasure and placing of God Himself. To realize this for myself, is to be saved from any dissatisfaction. No place is unworthy, if it be a place God has chosen. No service is mean, if it be a service to which He has called us. To realize that this is true of all others, is to be delivered from the possibility of thinking unworthily of their places within the Body. To realize this, is to take seriously and joyfully whatever our appointed work may be, knowing that purpose; knowing also that, as we do so, we are enabling all the other members to do likewise.

Love never faileth.—1 Cor. 13. 8.

That is not only a glorious declaration, it is one of the most searching for the soul. If that be true, how much that we have thought was love, should be called by some other name? Its final proof is in God, and there we are secure. His love never faileth, and the measure and strength of it can only be expressed by the mystic "so" of the declaration that "God so loved the world"; and we only begin to appreciate the real significance of that "so," as we complete the statement: "that He gave His only-begotten Son." That is the love that never faileth. In the presence of it, we are sometimes almost afraid to call anything of ours love at all. There is so much of selfishness lurking in us all. We do so often love them that love us, and that because they love us. Well, such love has its place, but there is neither merit nor praiseworthiness in it. Of such love, Jesus said: "What thank have ye?" True love, the love with which God loves—the love which is shed abroad in our hearts—loves in spite of unworthiness, in spite of failure. That is the love which inspires and indeed compels service, which is sacrificial. All the attitudes and habits and activities of such love are set forth in this wonderful chapter. The more we ponder it, the more we feel how far we come short—nay, that we are helpless—and that we can only love like that, as the very love of God Himself shall possess and master us.

Let all things be done unto edifying. —1 Cor. 14. 26.

That is the test of the exercise of spiritual ministry within the Church, the ministry which in its holy fellowship may be exercised by any of its members as they are led of the Spirit of God. There is to be liberty for such ministry, but only in so far as its exercise tends to edification. And let it be remembered that this idea of edification so often occurring in the apostolic writings, is never that of the deepening of the spiritual life of the individual. It is always that of the erection of the house, the making of the entire building; and so the test of ministry is that of its value in perfecting the Church. This is a simple test, but its effects are far-reaching. No member of the fellowship has any right to exercise a gift, even a gift bestowed by the Spirit, in order to secure glory or popularity. Of course, this needs no argument, but so subtle is the self-life, that it does need to be constantly borne in mind. Moreover, no member of the Church has any right to exercise a gift in the assembly in order to personal advancement in Christian life and character. There is a place for such exercise, but it is in loneliness; it is to be done "to himself and to God." The law of ministry within the Church is that of selflessness. When there is no seeking for glory, and no thought of profit to one's own soul, ministry becomes powerful.

If in this life only we have hoped in Christ, we are of all men most pitiable. —1 Cor. 15. 19.

That is a superlative statement in which Paul clearly revealed how central and fundamental to his Christian experience was the truth of the resurrection of the Lord. To him, that fact opened the gates of the age-abiding life, and guaranteed the franchise of eternity. And yet there is a sense in which we are sometimes inclined to wonder how far it is true. There is such actual joy and present freedom in serving Christ, that we are inclined to think that if the story of Jesus and the resurrection were not true, they have created a delusion so beneficent in its results that it is worth while. And who that has known anything of real Christian life and service will deny it? Yet the Apostle was surely right. We are helped to a truer understanding of what he meant by the word "pitiable" which the Revisers have substituted

for "miserable." It is rather the view of others, than the experience of believers, that was in his thought. We may not be miserable, but our very happiness, if there be no ground for it, proves how pitiable is our plight. The spaciousness of the outlook which belief in our Lord's resurrection creates and the joy of the soul, are so wonderful that surely we are to be pitied if it is all false. Yet is it not so, that the very strength and joy which so invariably result from belief, go far to prove the reality of the thing believed? Is it conceivable that a delusion could so powerfully and persistently create such joy?

Upon the first day of the week let each one of you lay by him in store, as he may prosper.—1 Cor. 16. 2.

That is the true system of Church finance. Whether the money be needed for the succour of the saints who are in need, for the maintenance of the work of God in a given centre, or for the carrying of the Gospel to the uttermost parts of the earth, if this rule were followed by all the members of the Church, there would be no lack, and no languishing exchequers. To read these words carefully, simply, thoughtfully, is to realize how final they are. First, it is an activity for an appointed day, the first day of the week. That is the day of resurrection, the day in which in assembling with the saints, we worship, and prepare for all the coming days. Secondly, it is an individual responsibility. In the transaction no third person can take part. It is something between the soul and the Lord. That will deliver us on the one hand from meanness, and on the other from the dishonesty of giving what we cannot afford, in order to keep up appearances. Thirdly, the giving is to be the laying by in store. That is, the gift is to be separated from all other possessions, devoted to special use, put aside in order that, as occasion demands, it may be available. This is not raising money to pay debts. It is providing so that no debt be incurred. Finally, the measure of giving is, as we prosper. That means continual readjustment. What we put away last week is never to be the measure of what we give this week. Each week the income of the previous week must be considered.

SECOND CORINTHIANS

Ye also helping together on our behalf by your supplication.—2 Cor. 1. 11.

This is pre-eminently the comfort chapter of the New Testament. Writing to his children in Corinth and Achaia, Paul was recalling a dark experience through which he had passed in Asia, when he had in affliction come so near

to death, that he had actually died but for the deliverance of God. In all that time of suffering he had known the comfort of God, and now knew that through such experiences of trial and of comfort, he had been prepared to comfort others. The deliverance of the past filled him with confidence about whatever the future might bring. He was confident that He would still deliver him. It is at this point that the words we have selected flash out upon us. Notice the surprising connection: "He will also still deliver us; ye also helping together ... by your supplication." Our prayers for our loved ones help God to work deliverance for them. That is a deep mystery, but it is a fact of which we do well to take heed. There are things which God can do only when we pray. It was surely that conviction in the olden days which made Samuel say as he retired from his judgeship to make way for Saul, "Far be it from me that I should sin against Jehovah in ceasing to pray for you." Observe carefully that he did not say that by ceasing to pray he would sin against them, but that he would sin against Jehovah. When we cease to pray, we limit God, and wrong our friends. We may not understand this, but we ought to act upon it. By our supplication, we are helping together in the deliverances God works for our loved ones.

Lest by any means such a one should be swallowed up with his overmuch sorrow.—2 Cor. 2. 7.

It is generally agreed that here Paul was referring to the man whom he had charged the Corinthian church in his former letter to exclude from its fellowship, in order that his spirit might be saved. It would seem that they had acted in accordance with his directions, and that the punishment had produced in him a true sense of his sin, and genuine sorrow for the same. In such an hour as this, that man was open to a new and strange device of Satan, that of the suggestion that for such as he there could be no mercy. Therefore the duty of the church was clear. They were to forgive him, and comfort him. If discipline is largely lacking in the Church of to-day, so also is the grace of forgiving and comforting those who, having done wrong, are truly repentant. How often, alas! souls have been indeed swallowed up with overmuch sorrow because of the harshness and suspicion of Christian people toward them in view of some wrong which they have done. It is true that there should be no toleration of evil out of a false charity; but it is equally true that there should be ungrudgingness and delight in forgiveness. Love never slights holiness; but holiness never slays love. Notice, moreover, Paul charged them not to forgive only, but also to comfort. There may be a judicial forgiveness which is hard, and leaves the soul always conscious of the past. Comfort takes the soul to the heart and forgets. That is how God forgives, and so should we who are His children.

This ... veil ... is done away in Christ.—Cor. 3. 14.

This is a superlative statement of the perfection and permanence of the glory of Christ. The illustration is taken from the story of how Moses veiled his face when speaking to the people, after he descended from the Mount. The reason for that veiling was not that they should not see the shining of his face, but that they should not see that it was passing away. They saw the shining and it was so glorious that they were filled with fear, and Moses did not put the veil on until he "had done speaking with them" (Exodus 34. 33). Paul distinctly says that the veil was worn by Moses, "that the children of Israel should not look steadfastly on the end of that which was passing away." They looked on the glory, and then it was veiled, and the sense of the glory remained. Had they seen it pass, that sense would have been lost. This interprets these words: "This . . . veil . . . is done away in Christ." It is done away because His glory has no waning; it does not pass away. The ministration of Moses, that is, of the law, is that of condemnation. The ministration of Christ, that is, of grace, is that of righteousness. The former has a glory, and it is sublime, but there is no hope in it for sinning men; and so it passes, for it leaves them sinners. The latter has a glory, more sublime, for there is hope in it for sinning men; and so it never passes, for it makes them righteous. Because of the finality of the glory of Christ, He lifts an unveiled face upon men.

Our light affliction . . . worketh for us.—2 Cor. 4. 17.

The first impression made upon the mind as these words are read is that almost of amazement that Paul could speak of his afflictions as light. He had described them very clearly, as he spoke of himself and of those associated with him in ministry, as "pressed," "perplexed," "pursued," "smitten down," "always bearing about in the body the dying of Jesus," "always delivered unto death." And these were no mere figures of speech. Very literally these things were true. And yet, summing them all up, he described them as "our light affliction." Moreover, he thought of them all, not as foes but as allies of the soul, for he declared that in their totality as affliction, it "worketh for us." This was the conviction which made him speak of it as light. That to which it tended was glory so wonderful that he could only describe it as "an eternal weight of glory." Still further let it be noted that this reference to glory was not merely to the glory of the life beyond. It was a present experience, and a growing one, for, said he, affliction "worketh for us more and more exceedingly." In the process of affliction glory was present, and it grew. That is the real burden of all this teaching. Over against every description of affliction is one of glory, "not straitened," "not unto despair," "not forsaken," "not destroyed," "the life of Jesus . . . manifested in our body," "the life of

Jesus . . . manifested in our mortal flesh."
These are things of glory, and all the
affliction which accompanies service works
these things. Thus it ever is. Fellowship
with the suffering Saviour is fellowship in
the glory of His triumphs.

As though God were intreating by us; we beseech.—2 Cor. 5. 20.

What urgency breathes through these
words! The subject is that of the reconciliation made possible between man and
God, because "God was in Christ reconciling the world unto Himself." That word of
reconciliation is committed to those
called to serve Christ. They are ambassadors on behalf of Christ. Therefore
the urgency. They must deliver their
message in a way worthy of the One Who
sends them: "As though God were intreat-
ing by us; we beseech." That was Paul's
conception of the way to preach Christ;
and it is manifest in all the records we have
of his journeyings, his spoken messages,
as well as in his letters. The marvel and
the glory of the Divine provision, and the
terror and peril of human need, were such
as to make anything in the nature of
indifference to results or coolness in
presentation impossible. Every call was
a beseeching. Moreover he dared to say
that in this attitude he was representing
God; and every soul who knows anything
of the real meaning of the Cross, knows
that this is a true word. God does not treat
human salvation as a matter about which
He can be indifferent or careless. The
Cross is His passion, His earnestness; may
we not dare to say, that by which He
entreats men to be reconciled. In face of
that, what can be worse than to declare
His message as though it were not a
message vital, tremendous, demanding all
passion and power in its delivery? All this
makes us think! And perhaps the thinking
is better done alone!

In everything commending ourselves, as ministers of God.—2 Cor. 6. 4.

In these words the participle "commending" has close connection with the
participle "working" in the first verse of
the chapter. "Working together with God
. . . in everything commending ourselves
as ministers of God." Here we have the
secret of power, and the burden of responsibility in all Christian service. Whatever
we are called upon to be, or do, or suffer,
we find the necessary resources in our
fellowship with God. Our responsibility is
that we commend ourselves (first to God,
and also to those among whom we serve)
as ministers of God. Some of the things
included in this "everything" follow in the
Apostle's letter. First, things of trial;
patience, afflictions, necessities, distresses;
stripes, imprisonments, tumults, labours,
watchings, fastings. Then things of grace;

pureness, knowledge, longsuffering, kindness, the Holy Spirit, love unfeigned, the
word of truth, the power of God. Then
things of conflict; the armour of righteousness, glory and dishonour, evil report and
good report. Then things of experience, the
double experience of the servants of God,
that of what the world thinks of them,
and that of their secret life with God;
deceivers, yet true; unknown, yet well
known; dying, and living; chastened, not
killed; sorrowful, yet always rejoicing;
poor, yet making rich; having nothing,
yet possessing all things. In all these
things, working with God—that is comfort
and strength. In all these things, commending ourselves as ministers of God—
that is purpose and responsibility.

I overflow with joy in all our affliction.—2 Cor. 7. 4.

What a wonderful and glorious word
this is! Observe the circumstances, and
the experience. The former were those of
affliction. Already in this letter we have
seen much of the sufferings of this man.
Immediately following this declaration he
referred to other phases of them; the flesh
with no relief; fightings without, fears
within. Surely there was nothing in circumstances to cause joy. Yet notice the
experience. It was not that of stoical
indifference. It was more than that of calm
resignation. It was even more than that
of quiet content. "I overflow with joy."
It is the language of a happy, and even
exultant heart. What was the reason of
such joy amid such circumstances? It was
that of the manifestations of true Christian character in the children of God.
Titus had visited him and told him the
effect produced in the Corinthian Christians by the letter which he had sent to
them. That letter had been one of rebuke,
a letter calculated to produce sorrow and
repentance, and all the things of a true
Christian experience had been manifested
in them. This was the reason of his over-
flowing joy. And it is ever so. John, writing
to Gaius the beloved, said: "Greater joy
have I none than this, to hear of my
children walking in the truth." This is the
present reward of all who, "working with
God" . . . commend themselves as His
servants. No circumstances of personal
affliction can dim the gladness of seeing
souls grow in the grace of the Lord Jesus.

We take thought for things honourable . . . in the sight of men.—2 Cor. 8. 21.

This is a principle which should ever be
observed in all the business and financial
matters of the Christian Church. The
subject was that of the collecting of funds.
Titus was appointed to this work, but he
was not to go alone. Paul, in conjunction
with the churches interested, appointed

another to go with him; and the reason was that all the monetary matters of the churches should be dealt with in such a way as to give no ground of suspicion to men of the world. Christian men will act in all these matters in the sight of their Lord, and that to other Christians is sufficient guarantee of their integrity and uprightness. But men of the world do not understand that. They look for the guarantees of the oversight of man by man. They are not prepared to accept the view that a man who trusts in God is to be trusted. Therefore it is the business of the Christian community to do its business in such a way that these men of the world shall have no cause to suspect anything contrary to righteousness in its affairs. This is at once a tribute to the supremacy of righteousness, and an acknowledgment of the fact that men are able to appreciate that which is righteous. Titus and the one appointed to act with him needed no watching in order to make them straightforward; but the fact that they were so, needed to be vindicated to all men. Therefore they were to travel and to act together. This is very practical, and very important. It is the warrant for the careful auditing of all Church accounts.

Thanks be to God for His unspeakable gift.—2 Cor. 9. 15.

Thus Paul ended all he had been writing about giving. It was an exclamation, revealing the inspiration of all he had been saying, and of all these people had been doing, and were now being urged to continue to do. They had given, they were urged to continue to give, in order to meet the need of their fellow-believers who were suffering. Why should they do so? What motive would be sufficiently strong to inspire them to do so? The answer is found in this exclamation. They were children of God, and they were such because He had given His only-begotten Son. It was indeed "His unspeakable gift." It is safe to say that about nothing in human history has so much been spoken as about this gift of God. One moment's thought of all the literature of the Christian Church will prove that this is so. Yet it remains an unspeakable gift; a gift about which, however much may be said, the final thing can never be said. The things spoken concerning it are only of value as they ultimately lead the soul to the speechlessness of adoring awe and wonder, in which it comes nearer to apprehension of the ultimate meaning and value of the gift than in any other way. This gift then is the inspiration and type of true Christian giving. Whenever we are called upon to give, let us first think of the unspeakable gift of God. Then love will be the inspiration of our giving, sacrifice will be its measure, and real blessing to others its result.

Not he that commendeth himself is approved, but whom the Lord commendeth.—2 Cor. 10. 18.

In this chapter we find Paul dealing with subjects which were very immediate. There were those in the Corinthian Church who were discounting his authority, or rather attempting to do so, by declaring that he could write a letter, but that personally he carried no weight. To this charge he replied quite definitely that his letters exactly expressed himself. Then he dealt with the principles upon which men should test themselves, and they may thus be stated. First, the opinion of others concerning a man is no true standard of what a man really is. Again, a man cannot discover the truth about himself by comparing himself with others. Finally, and this is in the words of our verse, a man's commendation of himself is of no value. It is only when the Lord's judgment is sought, and is found to commend, that a man may be sure he is approved. This holds us right up to the highest law of life, as it carries all the other ideas to a true conclusion. I may claim freedom from bondage to the opinion of others, but that is of no value unless I submit to the judgment of the Lord. The measure in which I cease judging myself by comparing myself with others, is the measure in which I need to seek to know the Lord's thought of me. Not what does my neighbour think of me; not how do I compare with others; not what do I think of myself; but what does the Lord think of me, is the thing that matters.

Anxiety for all the churches.—2 Cor. 11. 28.

That was the central anxiety, burden, care, of this great Apostle. As we have seen more than once in reading this letter, he knew much of affliction. There were many causes for anxiety. In this chapter another paragraph occurs in which he referred to perils and travails connected with the work of the ministry. Then he described them as "those things that are without," or as an alternative marginal reading has it, "the things that come out of course." They were incidental things. That which pressed upon him daily, from which he had no escape, which constituted the central anxiety of all his days, was the need of all the churches. What that meant in the case of Paul is understood as we think of the churches he had planted, and of those to whom his letters were written. They were widely scattered, and very diversified in their experiences, attainments, needs; but he carried them all in his heart, and laboured for them in prayer, and in every way possible. That is true Christian ministry. We make a modern application of the principle by saying that while denominational loyalty may be, and within limits certainly is, an excellent thing, it must never be allowed to exclude other churches from our spiritual anxiety. In matters of ecclesiastical government, and of theological opinion, we may be separated from other communions; but in the deepest fact of the unity of the Spirit, we are one with them. Therefore we must pray for all, and so far as is possible, labour for all.

Unspeakable words, which it is not lawful for a man to utter.—2 Cor. 12. 4.

This is the second time that we have come across this word "unspeakable" in our reading of this letter; but the words Paul used were not identical. Where he wrote of God's "unspeakable gift" (9. 15) he employed a word which meant *not expounded in full*, and there he was thinking of the infinite wonder of the gift. Here his word meant *inexpressible*. On the occasion to which he refers, he had heard words which he could not express, some secrets that were not for publication; it was not lawful to utter them, that is, he was not permitted to do so. The idea which this statement of the Apostle conveys to the mind is that in the life of service and fellowship, God may communicate to the soul, in hours of high experience, secrets which will affect all life and service, and yet which are not to be proclaimed in ministry. The value of such revelations is that of the effect which they produce in the life and character of those to whom they are granted. This is a subject which may be very profitably considered. There are some who seem eager to talk of visions and revelations which they have had. The question is as to whether such eagerness is not a proof that the visions and revelations are not "of the Lord." When they are granted (and they certainly are granted to the

servants of God under certain circumstances), they produce a reverent reticence. They are too solemn, too overwhelming, to be lightly described or discussed, but the effect of them will be apparent in all life and service.

For we also are weak in Him.— 2 Cor. 13. 4.

This is a startling statement, taken thus away from that which immediately follows it. Finally to isolate these words would be to wrong the teaching of the Apostle, which is intended to emphasize his power, and that of all those called to the ministry of the Word. Nevertheless it is good to get fast hold of the truth they declare. The sense in which we are weak in Christ is revealed in the statement concerning the Lord with which this verse opens: "He was crucified through weakness." It is with that statement that we are to link these words: "we also are weak in Him." All that the Cross meant of weakness to Christ, we share in fellowship with Him. In what sense was He crucified in weakness? In one sense only—He was unable to deliver Himself from the Cross, if He were to be able to deliver men from sin. He Who could have asked for twelve legions of angels to scatter His foes, could not do so if He were to make possible the saving of those very men. Thus, in that sacred love-compelled inability, He was crucified. This then is our weakness. In proportion as we are identified with Him, we are for ever unable to spare ourselves. What comfort this brings in every hour in which our strength is expended, exhausted in His service! We might conserve it by parting company with Him. When we refuse to do so, and are weakened by the way, "we . . . are weak in Him." That is ever the condition for the operation of the power of God. It was so in Him. It is so in us.

GALATIANS

To reveal His Son in me, that I might preach Him.—Gal. 1. 16.

The experience which the Apostle thus described was at once the inspiration of his preaching, and the secret of that conviction as to the authority of his Gospel which called forth this letter. To him the Gospel was infinitely more than a doctrine, a truth heard from others, and intellectually accepted. It was his very life, and the deepest thing therein. In this first chapter he made three references to his experience, which are revealing. First he wrote of a "revelation of Jesus Christ." Then, in our verse, of a revelation of "His Son in me." And finally he declared that the churches of Judaea glorified God in him. The first of these references was undoubtedly to

that wondrous hour in which Jesus of Nazareth was unveiled before his astonished soul, as risen, and active in the affairs of His people. The experience on the road to Damascus was one of revolution. To this man the whole scheme of things was turned upside down. Then, in the quiet seclusion of those waiting days in Damascus, that which had been an arresting and blinding revelation from without, became a convincing and quickening revelation within his own soul. Christ was unveiled within him. That is the secret of preaching. A consciousness of Christ which is purely objective is fundamental, but it is not enough to equip any man for preaching. There must be this deeper knowledge of Christ, the subjective unveiling of Him within the life. A man who knows much about Christ, may talk about Him, A man who knows Him, can preach Him.

If righteousness is through the law, then Christ died for nought.—*Gal.* 2. 21.

Dr. Rendel Harris has aptly described this letter of the great Apostle to the Gentiles as an "explosive epistle." Its force lies more in the truths it declares than in the way in which they were stated; yet the method of statement is most arresting. Perhaps in the course of the whole argument, nothing is more tremendous in the impact upon the mind than this superlative declaration. If the Law, which does reveal righteousness, is able to produce righteousness, then the death of Christ was a mistake; it was unnecessary; He died to accomplish something which might have been accomplished in some other way. Those then who hold that a man may reach righteousness through the Law are compelled either to get rid of the whole conception of the atoning death of the Lord, or to say that God was mistaken. Moreover, if the Law could not make righteous, and the death of Christ is able to do so, then why superimpose upon faith in that which is able, the rites and ceremonies of that which is without force? That is the whole case of the letter; and it is that truth, so forcefully stated, which has made this letter the high explosive which more than once in the history of the Church has shattered false doctrine as to the way of salvation. It was Martin Luther's weapon. Because the heart of man is ever prone to add something of human device to the Divine provision, it is well to keep this writing at hand, for its power is as great as ever.

Are ye so foolish? Having begun in the Spirit, are ye now perfected in the flesh?—*Gal* 3. 3.

In these questions we have the principle for which the Apostle contended, applied to the processional aspect of Christian experience. If Christ did not die for nought —that is, if we indeed are admitted to the possibility of righteousness through faith in Him, and through that alone—then is it to be supposed that we shall be able to realize in actual experience the things of righteousness by going back to those methods which were unable to create the possibility or to communicate the power of righteousness? The first phase of salvation is justification; that is, the reconciliation of our essential spirit-life to God. There we begin our Christian life. Is it reasonable to suppose, that departing from that central and initial way, we may now hope to make progress in the Christian life and experience by employing the methods of the flesh? Is it so, that any activity of the flesh whatever can strengthen the life of the Spirit? It is inconceivable. And yet here is the place where repeatedly the children of God have been carried away. All sorts of fleshly devices have been resorted to in the vain and foolish hope that activity of the flesh tends to strengthening of the spirit. It is ever so. The process is exactly opposite. The spirit controls the flesh, employs it, commands it, sanctifies it and thus makes it the instrument of service to others. Therefore the process of the soul to perfection is ever by faith, a spiritual activity; and never by works, a fleshly method.

My little children, of whom I am again in travail until Christ be formed in you.—*Gal.* 4. 19.

Here suddenly, amid the anger, the satire, the severity of the letter, the deepest thing in the soul of the Apostle breaks through in a flash of revealing glory. It is that of his tenderness, his compassion, his love. He was angry, but why? Because the danger, threatening them, threatened the highest and best things in their lives. He was satirical, but why? Because by such a method he was likely to arouse them from the false lethargy which resulted from resting in rites and ceremonies, instead of exercising faith in Christ. He was severe, but why? Because the courses they were pursuing under false teachers were subversive of their very life in Christ. All the anger, the satire, the severity of the letter, resulted from his profound love for them. It was all the outcome of the care of the churches which he carried daily. How deep and strong that was, is revealed by the daring of this figure. It is the most sacred figure of motherhood. He was "in travail" for them! How searching is this gleam of light! How it rebukes us and instructs us! As we consider it, we are made ashamed of any bitterness which may at any time have entered into our defence of truth. Anger, satire, severity, yes, these are proper things, providing always that no element of personal bitterness enters our heart. The peril is so subtle that we need ever to watch and pray that we may be delivered from falling in this matter. It is only as our love of our fellow-disciples is kept alive, and our solicitude for their spiritual well-being is the one and only motive of our action, that we have the right or the ability to defend the truth.

For the whole law is fulfilled in one word . . .—*Gal.* 5. 14.

The Law is the revelation of God's way of life for men. In it are many words. Its statutes and judgments and commandments are multiplied. They deal with every phase of human life—personal, social, religious. They condition all its attitudes and activities—of food, of raiment, of dwelling-places, of health, of sanitation. They cover all its relationships

—political, economic, family. They arrange its worship, make its calendar, define its responsibilities. In short, there is nothing in the whole course of life, from cradle to coffin, that is not dealt with in some of its many words. Behind all these words there are ten; the words of the Decalogue, gathering up within themselves the whole of the others, in broad and general statements, so perfectly that if men will live according to their revelation, personally and socially, they will live in the ideal kingdom. All this Paul knew, none better than he. And yet he declared that "the whole law is fulfilled in one word." There is one word, which includes the ten, as the ten include the many. And that word is LOVE! In saying this, Paul was only saying what his Lord had said before him. The only difference is that here he took for granted the first activity of love, which is Godward, and named only the resultant one, which is manward. Who will challenge the truth of this saying? It is impossible that any man who obeys only the law of love in his thought and speech and deed should break either of the ten words, or come short in obedience to the many.

Henceforth let no man trouble me . . .—Gal. 6. 17.

There is a fine touch of independence in these words, a claim that the writer is exempt from interference, that if any shall break in upon his quietness, the intruder is guilty of misdemeanour. After reading the letter, with its clear logic and its splendid passion, we feel that he has won the right to write thus. And yet it is not upon that ground that he bases his claim. His ground is that he bears branded on his body the stigmata of Jesus! There has been much mystical interpretation of these words of Paul, which may be warranted. I believe that the reference was a very simple and very actual one. In his proclamation of the Gospel committed to him, he had given his physical powers without reserve, and in the process had been actually bruised and broken by the brutality of those who had opposed him. He carried the actual scars of this brutality, and knew actual physical weakness as the result of his devotion. These all were to him the true stigmata of Jesus, sweet and terrible companions of the very wounds of his Lord. Let them appeal to men to recognize his right not to be troubled. And so his appeal finally was to the Gospel which was thus evidenced, as to its compelling and sustaining power, by the very sufferings through which he had passed, of which these scars were the sure signs. It is really a very keen word this. Have we any right to claim exemption from the troubling of men, such as Paul had? What stigmata do we carry about with us that speak of suffering or deprivation, or limitation, resulting from our persistent and passionate devotion to the Gospel of the eternal grace?

EPHESIANS

Him Who worketh all things after the counsel of His will.—Eph. 1. 11.

It will readily be conceded that in this letter Paul reached the highest level of his teaching concerning the Church, as he reached that concerning the Christ in the Colossian letter. These particular words occur in the opening movement of the letter, in which he was showing how the Church was the outcome of a purpose and plan of God from before the foundation of the world. God had chosen its members to "be holy and without blemish before Him in love"; and in order that this purpose should be realized, He foreordained them to "adoption as sons through Jesus Christ unto Himself." The whole conception is stupendous, and as we read it in the light of what we know of our own weakness and waywardness of will, we wonder more and more. It is when that wonder threatens us with hopelessness that these words come to reassure us. Our God is a God Who not only wills, He works; and He works according to His will. Notice how the thought moves backward, until it reaches the will of God. That is the ultimate reach. Next in order is His counsel, and that is more than the will of God as desire. The word *counsel* stands for deliberate planning and arranging, in which the ways and means of carrying out the will are considered and provided for. Finally, when the counsel is complete, God works. He does in His own might, all that He has planned to do in order that His purpose may be realized. That is the place of our assurance and confidence.

> He wills that I should holy be;
> What can withstand His will?
> The counsel of His grace in me
> He surely will fulfil.

But God, being rich in mercy.— Eph. 2. 4.

The word "But" here puts two matters into contrast. The first contrast is between man and God; the second is between the state of man and the mercy of God, and this is the main thought in the mind of the writer. The picture of man's state is very dark: "dead through your trespasses and sins"—that is, cut off from all the true things of life; therefore, walking under the dominion of "the spirit that now worketh in the sons of disobedience"; therefore living "in the lusts of the flesh"; therefore "children of wrath." Can any conditions more hopeless be imagined? How can it ever be that those living under such conditions shall become "holy and without blemish?" What wisdom can plan such a deliverance? What power can be equal to carrying out such a purpose? The complete and final answer is given in these words: "But God, being rich in mercy!" In the wealth of His mercy there the wisdom that plans, and the might that accomplishes. Mercy is compassion, and in God that is more than passive, it is active; it is pity, working on behalf of those who are helpless; it is love, doing the things that love desires to be done. When that compassion, pity, love, is predicated of God, the vastness of it is postulated, the sufficiency of it is recognized. This is the very heart of the Gospel. Over against all the appalling facts of our weakness and wickedness, we must place the wealth of the mercy of God, which had its unveiling and found its mode of action in Christ. Presently Paul referred to the "exceeding riches of His grace"; and we feel the power of the expression. It exceeds all our need. It is an ocean in which all our emptiness is filled without loss to its superabundance.

The love of Christ . . . the fulness of God.—*Eph.* 3. 19.

Here are two great phrases. They occur in one of the Apostolic prayers for the saints. In that prayer the ultimate desire is that they should "know the love of Christ," in order that they "may be filled unto all the fulness of God." The idea, then, is that the knowledge of "the love of Christ" brings to the soul the experience of "the fulness of God." To be "filled unto all the fulness of God" is to find the ultimate experience of life. Where this is so, there is no true desire of the soul unsatisfied, no power of the soul undeveloped or idle. The true meaning of life is discovered, and that not as an ideal seen but unrealized, but as an actual experience. It is eternal life; it is perfection; it is satisfaction. How then can it be attained? By the knowledge of the love of Christ, for in that there is the very fulness of God; and so wonderful is it, not only as a vision, but in its power, that to know it is to be transformed by it into the likeness of itself. To the finality of this knowledge and experience we have not yet attained; but if we know anything of the love of Christ, we know something of the filling of this fulness of God. That is the story of the beginning, the process, and the consummation of true Christian experience. The love of Christ captures our hearts, and the life of God produces rest and quietness. The love of Christ is

progressively interpreted to us by the Spirit, and the fulness of God brings us more and more into the joy of life. At last we shall come to full apprehension. Then we shall come to a final perfection in the final fulness of God.

Grieve not the Holy Spirit of God.— *Eph.* 4. 30.

Two ideas are brought prominently before the mind in this injunction, and their interrelationship is very suggestive. The first is that of the character of the Spirit, in that Paul here, with evident intention, employed the full and solemn description, "the Holy Spirit of God," every word of which is full of meaning, while laying the supreme emphasis upon the holiness of the Spirit. The other is that of the deep love-nature of the Spirit, in that Paul speaks of Him as being capable of sorrow, for the simple meaning of the injunction is, "Cause not sorrow to the Holy Spirit of God." The interrelation of the ideas reveals to us the effect which sin produces on the Spirit of God. It causes sorrow. Perhaps no Apostolic injunction, if its force be rightly apprehended, constitutes a more prevailing incentive to a walk which is in holiness and truth. Thus is created that new fear which is of the very essence of safety. The old slavish fear of God, which was fear of His anger, and of suffering which such anger might bring to us, is completely done away by the manifestation of His love in Christ; but now a new fear takes possession of us; and that is a fear lest anything we do or say should cause sorrow to Him. The old fear produces no high spiritual or moral results. This new fear keeps the soul in living touch with the loving Lord, and so ensures its growth in strength and purity and beauty.

Be filled with the Spirit.—*Eph.* 5. 18.

Much has been written about this injunction, and everything has been of value. It certainly is a central word to the saints. To men outside the Christian experience it has no meaning. For them, the first necessity is that they should be born of the Spirit, that they should receive Him. To those that have been so born, and who therefore have become temples of the Holy Spirit, the one and inclusive responsibility is that they should obey this word. The filling of the Spirit is not an event which takes place once; it is rather a continuous experience which has to be maintained. The indwelling Spirit is a spring of living water. As He is yielded to, He fills all the life, and persistently to such an extent that the rivers overflow, and running forth bring life to those beyond. This filling is hindered when any part of the life is shut up against the Spirit. Our constant responsibility is that of yielding ourselves to His inspection, to

His direction, to His effective operation. As we do so, He fills, and that means He cleanses, energizes, and transforms the life; and so passes out through the life in the influences which heal and help others. It is interesting to read the words immediately following, in which the Apostle gives us two results which always follow the filling of the Spirit. The first is that of the exercise of praise, which glorifies God. The second is that of mutual submission, which ministers to the needs of others. Thus the filling of the Spirit means the end of the self-centred life; and the realization of such life as glorifies God and blesses men.

Take . . . the sword of the Spirit, which is the Word of God.—Eph. 6. 17.

The life of the saint, in this world to the end, will be one of conflict; and the conflict will be more keen because it is waged against the dark forces of the underworld, "the spiritual hosts of wickedness." Towards the close of this letter, Paul dealt with this matter, recognizing the inevitability of the conflict, understanding its fierceness, and giving a description of the armour by the use of which the saint is not only to stand, but also to withstand, and having done all, to stand. In this description all the weapons are defensive, save one. The only offensive weapon is "the sword of the Spirit, which is the Word of God." The weapon itself is the Word of God. Here the familiar phrase stands in its lonely splendour, and for us connotes all that it truly stands for. It is first the will of God as it is made known to men. It is therefore centrally and supremely the Son of God, in Whom that will has been completely and finally spoken to men. It is therefore the body of the writings through which, and through which alone, we know anything about Him. Notice carefully that the Apostle here claims that this is the sword of the Spirit. It is the one weapon by which He attacks and puts to flight the hosts of wickedness which fight against God and against man. Let us put perfect confidence in it; and, moreover, let us learn to use it with skill. It is the weapon by which we may attack and defeat all the evil forces which are massed against us in our spiritual conflict.

PHILIPPIANS

To you it hath been granted . . . to suffer.—Phil. 1. 29.

This is Paul's great singing letter. It was at Philippi that he had sung in prison at midnight, in the company of Silas. Now he was again in prison, this time in Rome, and writing to "the saints in Christ Jesus that are at Philippi." This letter thrills to the tireless music of a psalm. It is a glorious revelation of how life in fellowship with Christ triumphs over all adverse circumstances. The triumph, moreover, is not that of stoical indifference. It is rather that of a recognition of the fact that all apparently adverse conditions are made allies of the soul and ministers of victory, under the dominion of the Lord. "The things which happened unto me have fallen out rather unto the progress of the Gospel" exclaimed the Apostle. His very bonds opened the door of opportunity throughout the Praetorian guard. It was this sense of the power of life in Christ which inspired the particular words which arrest us. In them, suffering on the behalf of Christ is referred to as an honour conferred, rather than a burden to be endured. It is something granted to the saint, as a privilege, the very granting of which is a favour, a gift of grace. To this conception all will agree who have ever really known what it is actually to suffer on behalf of Christ. They are not callous; the suffering is very real, very acute; but it brings a sense of joy and gladness which finds no equal in human experience.

Lights in the world, holding forth the word of life.—Phil. 2. 15, 16.

That is a very beautiful figure of the mission in the world of those who are "blameless and harmless, children of God without blemish." The marginal reading substitutes the word "luminaries" for "lights." I do not think this helps us much, save as we remember that the word "luminaries" refers to the heavenly bodies, and mainly to the sun and moon. The idea is not that of the lampstand, but of the light itself. The Greek word only occurs twice in the New Testament, here and in Rev. 21. 11, where, speaking of the holy city, the seer declared: "Her light was like unto a stone most precious." There the reference was not to the light the city diffused, save in a secondary sense. It was to the light she received, which is directly after described in the words: "The lamp thereof is the Lamb, and the nations shall walk amidst the light thereof" (verses 23, 24). What then, the Lamb is to be; in final glory, to the City of God, the children of God are to the world to-day. This function of shedding true light upon the darkness of the world will be fulfilled as the "Word of life" is held forth. To live by the Word, is to shine in such wise that those who are in darkness may have guidance and help. The conception fills us with a sense of our weakness, and that the more, when we ponder the conditions already quoted, viz. that we are to be "blameless and harmless, children of God without blemish." Yet, thank God, these words follow the glorious declaration that it is ours to "work out with fear and trembling" what God works within of His good pleasure.

I counted . . . and I count.—*Phil.* 3. 7, 8.

These words occur in the page of autobiography in which Paul employed his own experience as an argument in appealing to his spiritual children in Philippi. They refer to a mental and spiritual activity. The two exercises were separated by at least thirty years. The first took place when Christ broke through upon him in all the radiant glory and revolutionizing power of His risen life. The second took place as he wrote, in prison, and amid all the difficulties and trials created by his Apostolic ministry. Between the time when he counted his gain loss and abandoned everything, and this hour, what experiences he had passed through! Nothing had occurred which in any way altered his first reckoning and decision; and so, to the "I counted" of the first revelation, he added the "I count" of the present experience. And this should ever be so. We are never more in peril than when we are trusting to a past experience. Yet how often it is done! We remember the day when the light broke upon us. It was a very real thing. It changed all our outlook. It compelled us to reconsideration of all the facts of life. We obeyed. We turned our backs upon all sorts of gains, counting them as merely worthless things. We yielded to the call and glory of the life in Christ. It was all excellent. But what about the present? Is the old attitude

maintained? Are the activities of to-day those of the first days? Or have we gone back to the abandoned things? Do we allow ourselves to seek again the lower things? It is only as we can express the decision of the past in terms of the present, the "I counted," as "I count," that there is any real value in the past.

The peace of God, which passeth all understanding.—*Phil.* 4. 7.

There are three great phrases in which peace and God are brought together. They are "Peace from God," "Peace with God," and "Peace of God." They are all the result of a truth enshrined in another, "the God of peace." The first, Paul constantly employed in the introduction to his letters. It reminds us that our peace comes to us a gift from God The second describes the relationship into which we are brought with God, through Christ Jesus. The third refers to the peace which is the experience of God Himself, because of what He is in Himself, the God of peace. At once it admits us to a realm which this particular passage indicates. The peace of God is beyond "all mind"; that is, beyond our power of thinking. That means two things: first, that the peace of God is so wonderful that we are not able fully to apprehend it; but second, it means that the peace of God, being the result of the wisdom and might of God, is far more wonderful than any cleverness of our own. That is the main value of the whole declaration of which this phrase is a part. It is that peace which will guard, as with a garrison of defence, our hearts and thoughts in Christ Jesus. If we by our own cleverness attempt to guard our hearts and thoughts, we shall fail. The forces opposed are too strong for us. They will break through upon us. They can never do so, as we are guarded in "the peace of God."

COLOSSIANS

The might of His glory.—*Col.* 1. 11.

That is a far more arresting translation than the old one. "His glorious power," and it is more accurate. The latter is a phrase in which the emphasis is laid on a quality of the power—it is glorious. The real thought of the phrase is that it lays an emphasis on a fact concerning His glory, and that is, that it is characterized by might. The Apostle was recording his prayer for the saints, that they might be filled with knowledge in order to walk worthily, bearing fruit. The condition for all this is that they should be strengthened with all power. Of this power he gives a description in this phrase, "The might of His glory." God is essentially the God of

might. The first great name by which the Hebrew people knew Him was Elohim, which speaks of that might in all its greatness. Everything of God has in it this quality of strength. In no application is the fact more unusual than in this of His glory. Glory is splendour, all the qualities of beauty and brilliance, whether material or mental; and one of the most marked qualities of human glory is that of its weakness. *Sic transit gloria mundi*, is a proverb expressing this conviction. Glory fades, passes, and that because of its weakness. The glory of God knows no fading, no passing, no perishing. It abides undimmed because of its strength. When the glory of God is seen, when to realize it becomes the passion of a life, it is found that in the vision there is strength, in the effort there is energy. His glory not only captures the mind: it empowers all upon whom it shines. It not only lures—it lifts.

The mystery of God, even Christ.—Col. 2. 2.

The phrase occurs in the record of another of the Apostle's prayers. His desire for all the saints was that they might know "The mystery of God, even Christ." That he desired this, shows us that in the true Christian sense a mystery is not something which cannot be known. It is something which man is unable to discover or explain; but it is something which may be disclosed to him, and which therefore he may know. And that is perhaps Paul's ultimate word about Christ. The last word has never yet been spoken about Him. There is nothing more wonderful than the persistence and ever-increasing discussion of all sorts and conditions of thinking men concerning the Person of our Lord. The subject is never exhausted; it never becomes out of date. Again and again men feel that they have formulated a Christology, only to find that some others have seen other facts not included in their system. And so He moves on, the Enigma of the ages, the inclusive Word, Whose ultimate secret is not expressed, the very mystery of God. Nevertheless through all the intellectual processes, He finds the heart of man, and gives Himself to it, so that in Him it finds rest, joy, satisfaction. Multitudes of simple souls who are unequal to any explanation, live in daily comradeship with Him. They know Him, and know Him well. They are more intimate with Him than with their dearest earthly friends. They tell Him all their griefs and joys, their doubts and hopes, their successes and failures; and they hear Him speak to them positively, prevailingly. He is indeed the Mystery of God, profound in the wonder of His being, and yet so real that the tiniest child talks of Him with sweet familiarity.

Covetousness, the which is idolatry. —Col. 3. 5.

In the paragraph from which these words are taken, we have a dark list of evil things against which Paul warned the saints. Perhaps the one which would by the ordinary standards of life be considered least harmful, or at least, less repugnant than the rest, is covetousness. Admittedly it is not a pleasant word, and describes something which we all dislike in other people; but the ordinary man would hardly bracket it, for instance, with fornication as equally reprehensible. And yet it is the one evil thing which Paul stops to characterize, and he does so by declaring it to be idolatry, the most

heinous of spiritual sins. It is evident that the Apostle looked upon it as a most deadly form of sin. In his Roman letter he declared that it was the commandment, "Thou shalt not covet," which awoke in him the consciousness of sin. What is there in this sin which is so deadly? First, it is idolatry, in that it only obtains when man thinks of life as consisting in things possessed, rather than in righteous relationship to God. No man covets until he has lost the true outlook on life, and imagines that it can be conditioned by the things around. Therefore, it is a sin also against others, for to satisfy the desire, others are wronged. Thus, finally, it is self-destructive, for these wrong conceptions and activities always react upon the soul to its own undoing. And yet what ecclesiastical court ever yet arraigned a church-member for covetousness? Perhaps, the principle that qualification for throwing stones is freedom from the sin we would punish, is the reason of the reticence. At any rate, it may be well for us to allow our Lord to deal with us on the matter.

Remember my bonds.—Col. 4. 18.

That is the last word but one, in one of the most wonderful letters Paul wrote; certainly the letter which in conjunction with that to the Ephesians constitutes the crowning height of all his teaching. It is not quite the last word. That follows, and in consonance with all his life and teaching turns back to God, and out towards others, in the parting wish "Grace be with you." Yet it is very suggestive that there should come the cry which reveals his consciousness of limitation and suffering. The whole letter had been written in prison, and surely during the writing the place had flamed with light. Paul had been seated in the heavenlies. The most wonderful visions of the glories of his Lord had passed before him, and he had seen himself and all Christian souls filled to the full, complete in the fulness the completeness, of this Lord of surpassing glory. Having finished, he took the pen in his own hand to write the salutation; and as he did so, the weight of the chain which bound him was felt, and perhaps its pain also. Then his heart went out toward his comrades, and he craved their sympathy and help: "Remember my bonds." How close that human touch brings him to all of us, and how much more powerful becomes all his high spiritual teaching because of it! It is always so. The great things of spiritual interpretation are ever made more powerful to others when they are reinforced by the touch that reveals our fellowship with those whom we serve in the sense of need. And yet in spite of the chain, he wrote his salutation: "Grace be with you!"

FIRST THESSALONIANS

Ye turned . . . to serve . . . and to wait.—1 *Thess.* 1. 9, 10.

This letter is full of interest because it is certainly among the first of those which have been preserved for us from the pen of Paul. It was the first he wrote to European Christians, and in it the fundamental things of the Christian life are very clearly set forth. The words we have taken necessarily need their context for full interpretation, but taken out in this way they help us to see, in sharp outline, what it means to be a Christian. This is especially so if they are read in connection with an earlier description, that in which the Apostle spoke of their "work of faith, and labour of love, and patience of hope." The first thing in Christian life is that of turning to God: that is the "work of faith." The whole course of that life is that of serving the living God: that is "the labour of love." The persistent attitude of those who, thus turned to God, are serving Him, is that of waiting for His Son; that is "the patience of hope." It follows that here we have standards by which we may test ourselves constantly. To turn back to idols, such for instance as "covetousness which is idolatry," is to turn from God. To do that, is inevitably to slacken in service; therefore slackness in service should ever give us serious concern. To cease to wait for the Son is to lose the most powerful inspiration to loyalty, and the most urgent reason for service. Notice that the true expression of our having turned to God is that of our serving Him; and so also is service the true way in which to wait for the Son from heaven.

But we were babes in the midst of you, as when a nurse cherisheth her own children.—1 *Thess.* 2. 7.

I have resolutely adopted the marginal reading of the Revised, substituting the word "babes" for "gentle." Most of the ancient authorities have this word "babes." The word "gentle" has been preferred because it has been thought to suit the context better. Personally I do not think it does. The statement as it stands is very full of beauty. Perhaps no word of Paul anywhere more vividly sets forth his tender solicitude for his spiritual children. Observe the latter part of the figure first. It is not that of a mother. It is that of a nurse and mother. The Revised helps us here by the rendering, "a nurse cherisheth her own children." The conception is that of the merging of trained intelligent skill with natural mother-love. That is perfect care. A nurse may have real skill, and even be scientifically devoted to her charges, but all this leaves something lacking which is found in motherhood. On the other hand, mothers whose love and devotion are undoubted, have often wronged their children through ignorance. Given a nurse with her own children, and the ideal is realized. Paul said that this was his attitude toward his spiritual children, and he gives a beautiful description of it as he writes: "We were babes in the midst of you." Origen interpreted this to mean that Paul had talked to them in baby-language. Immediately the nurse-mother among her bairns is seen and heard, and there is nothing more to be said. Such was Paul's method with his babes in Christ; and such should ever be the way of those who have the oversight of the new-born children of God.

Hereunto we are appointed.—1 *Thess.* 3. 3.

The "hereunto" refers to "afflictions." These Thessalonian Christians were in circumstances of actual suffering, resulting from persecution by their own countrymen. Through these trials they had stood fast. Paul was full of joy because this was so, but was desiring to hearten and strengthen them in their loyalty. This he did, first, by reminding them that the churches in Judaea had suffered in the same way at the hands of their kinsmen. Then he made this declaration; "Hereunto we are appointed." Surveying the whole Christian movement, he saw suffering everywhere as the result of loyalty to the faith; and he did not conceive of it merely as something to be endured. He saw God ruling over all, and knew that this pathway of pain was a Divinely-arranged one. Therefore he realized that the sufferings of all Christian souls were not only within His knowledge; they were in His plan for His people. They were appointed to affliction. The word "appointed" here is the emphatic word. In affliction the saints are where God has put them, and they are there for purposes within the counsel of His will. It is patent that Paul was thinking in the realm of the Cross. As the sufferings of Christ were all by the determinate counsel and foreknowledge of God, and that in order to the accomplishment of His redemptive purpose, so all the affliction of those who followed Christ were of the same fellowship, and those enduring them were workers together with God.

That ye be ambitious to be quiet, and to do your own business, and to work with your hands.—1 *Thess.* 4. 11.

Here again we have adopted the marginal reading, because that is the exact meaning of the Greek word rendered "study." Here then is a revelation of proper ambition, and it is remarkable as contrasting with worldly ambition. Three things the Apostle exhorted these young Christians to be ambitious about. The first was to be quiet, and the word describes that which stands in sharp contrast to the passion for notoriety, the desire to be seen and known. He urges them to be ambitious to be secluded, hidden, quiet. The next was to attend to their own affairs, instead of interfering in the affairs of others. The last was to work with their own hands, rather than live by the exertions of others. As we have thus endeavoured to state the ideas, we have seen the contrary and unworthy ambitions which so constantly master human life. The first is that for distinction, for the conspicuous position. The second is for the power and opportunity to meddle with the business of other people. The last is for freedom from the necessity for personal toil, gained through imposing work on others. How revolutionary Christianity is! How it cuts clean across popular conceptions, and runs counter to the mean desires of the human heart! And yet how great it is in all its constructive purposes! Think of the life which is described here by implication. The life of quiet strength and repose; the life that is arranged and orderly; the life that is honourably independent. Surely it is good to be ambitious for such a life.

Rejoice alway; pray without ceasing; in everything give thanks.— 1 Thess. 5. 16, 17.

These three injunctions stand out in clear light upon this last page of the letter. Probably without design on the part of the writer they are closely related to the threefold description of the Christian experience with which the letter opens. In a work of faith they had turned to God; in all that such a revolution meant let them "rejoice always." In a labour of love they were serving the living God; let them maintain that service by remembering to "pray without ceasing." In patience of hope they were waiting for the Son from heaven; let them, therefore, "in everything give thanks." The one secret of true and constant joy is that of our right relation with God. To be reconciled to Him, to have access to Him, to stand in His favour—these are the results of turning to Him; and these are the things that make for perpetual joy. The one reason for prayer which is at once acceptable to God and of prevailing power, is that of a maintained service. To practise our fellowship thus, is to prevail in whatever labour He appoints. The one cause for perpetual thanksgiving is that upon all the shadowed pathway there shines the light of the glory that is to be revealed when the Son shall come again. Concerning all these injunctions the Apostle said: "This is the will of God in Christ Jesus to you-ward." That is our strength—God's will, and the enablement of Christ Jesus!

SECOND THESSALONIANS

He shall come to be glorified in His saints, and to be marvelled at in all them that believed . . . in that day.— 2 Thess. 1. 10.

The coming of the Lord to which the Apostle was referring in these words, is that which he had already described as "the revelation of the Lord Jesus from heaven, with the angels of His power in flaming fire" (see verses 7 and 8). This is the Apocalypse or Unveiling aspect of that Parousia or Presence of the Lord, which is to consummate the age commenced by His first Advent. It will be the Day of he Lord, in all the fulness of the great prophetic phrase. One aspect of it he has already described, that, namely, of punitive judgment. In these words another aspect is named, that, namely, of His vindication in His saints, that is, in those who have believed. In them He will be glorified; in them He will be marvelled at. While this implicates the fact of their close identification with Him in that great day of His triumph, its chief value is that it reveals how absolutely perfect His

work will be in them. Then they will be "without blemish in exceeding joy"; then their spiritual being will be perfected, their minds completely conformed to His mind; the very bodies of their humiliation will be "fashioned anew and conformed to the body of His glory." The wondrous perfection of the saints will be the central glory of the unveiled One, the Lord Jesus Himself; and their very glory will be such as to direct attention to Him rather than to themselves, for it is He Who will "be marvelled at in that day." While that is a radiantly beautiful description of the goal toward which we travel, should it not also be the ideal for our present life: that we should so live that He may be glorified in us daily; and He be marvelled at as the One to Whom we owe everything?

The mystery of lawlessness doth already work; only there is One that restraineth now.—2 Thess. 2. 7.

Many opinions have been held concerning what Paul meant here by "the mystery of lawlessness," and to whom he referred when he wrote of "One that restraineth." The difficulty has been largely created by the view that he was thinking of something and someone peculiar to the times in which he wrote. The context shows that he was looking forward to the day of the Lord at the consummation of the present age, to the Parousia, or Presence of Christ, and especially to the Apocalypse aspect of it, in which the "Man of sin" having been also revealed, should be slain. With that in view, he wrote these words, and they naturally apply to the whole age to be so consummated. During that age—this age in which we live, "the mystery of lawlessness," the principle of evil, which at last will be unveiled in the person of the Man of Sin, is already working. But it is also true that, during the same age, there is One Who restrains that working, holds it in check, prevents its final development, and He will continue to do so, until He is taken out of the way. The reference unquestionably is to the Holy Spirit, Who by His work of convincing the world of sin, of righteousness, of judgment, makes impossible the outworking of lawlessness to its final issues. The time will come when the restraining influence will be removed, so that the mystery of lawlessness may be wrought out to its final expression, and that, in order that it may be destroyed by the unveiling of the Lord.

The Lord direct your hearts into the love of God, and into the patience of Christ.—2 Thess. 3. 5.

That is the true attitude toward life, both with regard to its trials, and its one blessed hope. Our trials are ever likely to produce restlessness; and unless we are careful our very watching for our absent Lord may degenerate into impatience. Therefore it was that Paul expressed this desire for the sorely tried Thessalonians, to whom he had been writing in this letter very specially about future things, and the Lord's Return. I think the very method he adopted in stating his desire is in itself instructive. Let us glance at the desire, beginning where the Apostle ended. What a wonderful thing "the patience of Christ" was, and may we not say *is*, as He still waits in long-suffering love for the final victory! How He bore with men! How He still bears with them! That we may have His patience, is surely one of the greatest needs of life. What, then, was the secret of their patience? Surely "the love of God." Christ wrought and waited, secure in His knowledge of His Father's love for Him, and in His love for His Father. That is still the secret of patience. The measure in which we are sure of the love of God is the measure in which, amid all the afflictions of the little while, we shall rejoice in His tarrying, as surely as in the hope of His Coming. Finally, for our meditation, notice the Apostle's first words: "The Lord direct your hearts." This also must be His work. Only let us not hinder Him.

FIRST TIMOTHY

According to the Gospel of the glory of the blessed God.—1 Tim. 1. 11.

This is another instance where the Revision has added greatly to the understanding and beauty of a phrase. In a previous note we observed the difference between "the might of His glory" and "His glorious might" (Col. 1. 11). Here we have the same kind of change. Instead of reading "the glorious Gospel," we have "the Gospel of the Glory." That the Gospel is glorious we know, but the Apostolic phrase draws our attention to the fact that the good news is that of "the Glory of the blessed God." Knowing that it is the Gospel of His Grace, we are thus reminded that Grace and Glory in God are one. That which is the very essence of His splendour and beauty is the infinite love of His heart. Also we may, with perfect accuracy, render the description of God as "the happy God." What unfathomable depths of suggestiveness there are in the words: "The Gospel of the Glory of the happy God!" But now observe how the words are introduced. Immediately before them are the words "according to." When we go back to see what this Gospel is the standard of, we find a remarkable denunciation of evil things, some of the most fearful being named, and, all others being included in the words "and if there be any other thing." All these things are "contrary to the sound doctrine, according to the Gospel of the glory of the happy God." Thus again, as so constantly in the New Testament, we are reminded that the Gospel makes no excuse for sin, makes no terms with it.

Supplications, prayers, intercessions, thanksgivings.—1 Tim. 2. 1.

These four words are not synonymous They all describe activities of the soul in the presence of God, and so are synthetic. Each has its own peculiar value and suggestion. In the first and last, activities are described in which all unite out of a common experience. In the second, an activity which largely leaves behind the sense of human need. In the third, an activity which excludes personal need, and includes the needs of others. Supplications are requests which express a need in which all those offering them share. In my own view they refer to the deepest spiritual needs, for cleansing, for spiritual enablement, of which all worshippers are conscious as they approach the Holy Place. Prayers here are the distinct acts of worship, in which the saints offer pure praise to God. The sense of need is for the moment forgotten, and the sense of the majesty and mercy of God call forth adoration. Intercessions are those requests for others which are the expression of love for them, begotten of love for God, and in which those offering them are entirely forgetful of their own personal needs. Thanksgivings are those glad outpourings of grateful hearts in which they remember the Giver of all gifts, and render to Him the returns of expressed gratitude which are ever acceptable to Him. As we said, they are all exercises of the soul in the presence of God, and the variety of their suggestion helps us to realize how rich and glorious is the privilege of our access to God through Christ.

If a man knoweth not how to rule his own house, how shall he take care of the Church of God?—1 *Tim.* **3. 5.**

These words were used by the Apostle when he was giving Timothy instructions as to the orderly government of the Church; and their first application was to those who were to exercise oversight, that is, to be bishops or overseers. They contain a principle which applies to the whole field of Christian service. It may be said that every Christian witness is a centre around whom concentric circles are drawn in which his or her witness will operate. We may illustrate by saying that in the ordinary life of every Christian believer, the circles are those of home, church, city, nation, race. While the influence of a life may not seem to affect all these, it certainly does so in a measure. Necessarily it is more evident in the first circles. Now the principle involved in this statement is that we are only able to exert the true influence in the wider circles as we do so in the first. The question of the Apostle has a self-evident answer. If a man is not able to regulate the affairs of his own household, if his own children are unruly, he cannot guide and guard the Church of God so as to ensure its orderliness and power. That is so for two reasons. First, that he lacks the power to rule. If he possessed it, he could rule his own house. Second, that his failure in his own house must negative any attempt he may make in the Church, for men will only obey an authority which is evidenced by results. We may pass back to the central fact, and

say that fitness for the guidance of others, in home or Church, or anywhere, is created by the control of one's own life as it is wholly under the sway of the Lord.

Let no man despise thy youth.— 1 *Tim.* **4. 12.**

These were the words of Paul who in a yet earlier letter (Philemon) had described himself as "Paul the aged," to Timothy, a young man; and they constituted his counsel to him. This is self-evident, and yet it may be interpreted as a warning to others not to despise the youth of this servant of Christ. If that were its meaning, then Paul would have intended to say to Timothy that he must maintain the dignity of his office. Now ultimately that also is involved; but the first meaning of the injunction was that Timothy should so deport himself as to make it impossible for others to despise him. We might render it thus:—"See to it that, thy youth notwithstanding, thou art not despicable!" It may be that there is a tendency among older people to hold youth in contempt, but it is often as much the fault of youth as of age. When a young man, placed in the position of responsible oversight, so lives as to be "an ensample . . . in word, in manner of life, in love, in faith, in purity," he is not despised. This injunction to Timothy is of perpetual application, and not alone to the young. A man enamoured of the dignity of his office, and seeking to impress other people with that dignity, is always despicable and is invariably despised. A man concerned about his character, and seeking to realize in his life the ideals of his Lord, gives a weight and dignity to his office which is recognized and yielded to without any reference to his age.

If any provideth not for his own, and specially his own household, he hath denied the faith, and is worse than an unbeliever.—1 *Tim.* **5. 8.**

Paul was instructing Timothy as to the duty of the Church in the matter of caring for the poor of the flock, especially in the case of such as were widows. That the Church has such a responsibility he made perfectly clear, but he also showed with care how it ought to be safeguarded. Throughout the whole teaching, it is evident that the Apostle considered that in all such matters responsibility first lay with the family (see verses 4 and 16). In our verse this conception finds central and general expression, and nothing could be clearer or more positive. The statement is characterized by that sane, practical commonsense which is everywhere discoverable in Paul's outlook on life. A man's very first responsibility is that of his own, his own household. No call on him must be allowed to take precedence of that, not even that of the work of the

Church, and certainly not that of his own pleasures. To neglect to make such provision is to deny the faith, for the faith is that of the way of love in all its most practical bearings. The believer who does so, is worse than an unbeliever, for common human instincts, apart from the teaching of Christ, will prompt a pagan to care for his own flesh and blood. All this is very commonplace, but it is of the utmost importance; for Christianity is the transfiguration of the commonplace, and in proportion as it enables a man to realize all human obligations on the highest level, he is thereby recommending it to others. In a word like this, there is serious rebuke for some, and there is much of comfort for others. The family is God's first circle of society, and it is man's first sphere of responsibility.

The love of money is a root of all kinds of evil.—1 Tim. 6. 10.

Not money, but the love of it. Money is not a root of evil. Neither is it a root of good. It is non-moral. It may be the greatest curse that can come into a human life. It may be the instrument of untold good. Much depends upon the use of it. Everything depends ultimately upon the attitude of the soul toward it. Where we have three words in this statement, "love of money," the Greek has but one, and perhaps the word in our common speech which best conveys the thought is the word "avarice." It is not covetousness. That is also a root of evil, but it is not the same thing exactly as avarice! Covetousness is a desire to gain possession of money, or indeed anything. Avarice is love-of-money, for itself. It is often the low motive of covetousness from other motives. Love of money is just that, the love of it, that hoards and holds. It is indeed a root of all kinds of evil. It dries up the springs of compassion in the soul. It lowers the whole standard of morality. It is the inspiration of all the basest things, even covetousness; for if there may be covetousness without love-of-money, there is never love-of-money without covetousness. Yet how insidious a peril this is! It is sometimes created by prosperity and the consequent possession of money. It is often powerfully present in lives which are devoid of wealth. It is wholly material, the result of a wrong conception of life, due to forgetfulness of the fact that "a man's life consisteth not in the abundance of the things which he possesseth."

SECOND TIMOTHY

The unfeigned faith that is in thee; which dwelt first in thy grandmother Lois, and thy mother Eunice.—2 Tim. 1. 5.

Two matters arrest our attention in these words: first, the description of faith, and second, the transmission of faith. The description of the faith of Timothy as "unfeigned" is very striking. Unfeigned faith is faith that is not pretended; that is, it is true, it is real, and therefore it is trustworthy. So long as there lurks a suspicion of doubt in faith; or so long as a man's faith is for outward confession, and does not carry the man with it, it is faulty and weak, and not to be depended on. A man can live a better life, and do a better work, on a genuine faith in a small thing, than a pretended faith in a big thing. In Paul's first letter to Timothy, he had placed "unfeigned faith" in company with "a pure conscience"; and said that out of these love proceeds (1 Tim. 1. 5). It is good to seek after such a faith. Then we notice that Paul said that this quality of faith was found in Timothy's mother, Eunice, and in his grandmother Lois. There is a sense in which faith cannot be transmitted by parents to their children. Every individual must exercise faith for himself or herself. But it is also true that it is very difficult for some children not to believe, because of what they have seen of the power of faith in their parents. We cannot bequeath faith to our children, but we can make it much easier for them to believe by our own faith. And that is specially true of "unfeigned faith."

No soldier on service entangleth himself in the affairs of this life.—2 Tim. 2. 4.

This word of Paul took on new meaning for many of us during the years of the Great War. Indeed, to-day it seems to some of us as though we had never seen it at all before. Of course, we had seen it, and we had given it a certain conventional interpretation. Our thinking, however, of what was included in the phrase "the affairs of this life," was very superficial in many cases. We thought of certain liberties and comforts, which the soldier is denied; and, of course, that thinking was correct so far as it went. We needed the stern and awe-inspiring experiences of those dread years to enable us to apprehend the full content of the phrase. Now we know that nothing is left out. The soldier on active service breaks with everything except the War. We saw them go in millions, leaving father, mother, brother, sister, wife, and lover; we saw them march away from promising careers, loved occupations, high ambitions, and the finest things of responsibility. Nothing was permitted to entangle them, to hinder them, or in any way to interfere with the one thing. This new understanding has brought a new revelation of the claims which our Lord's campaign makes upon us. He only asks His people to do what the sons of the commonwealth did, ungrudgingly. Does not the consideration bring a sense of shame with it? How often those who should constitute the sacramental host of God have *played* at war! May God forgive us, and give us another chance! And if in His grace He will, may we be worthy of it!

Out of them all the Lord delivered me.—*2 Tim.* 3. 11.

The reference of the Apostle was to "things which befell" him, to "persecutions" he "endured"; for they were specific references, for he named the places —Antioch, Iconium, Lystra. What were his experiences then in these places? The story is told in the thirteenth and fourteenth chapters of the Book of the Acts. The men of Antioch "cast them out of their borders." From Iconium they "fled," knowing that there was an intention to "stone" them. At Lystra Paul was "stoned," and his enemies "dragged him out of the city supposing that he was dead." Such were the things that befell him; such the persecutions he endured. Now, looking back, Paul referred to them only to place on record his sense of the deliverances of the Lord. This is always the experience of the servants of the Master as they look back over the pathway. They do not forget the disappointment of being cast out, the bitterness of having to fly, the pain and exhaustion of the stoning; but they are more impressed with the fact of the governance of the Lord, and of how He has always delivered His own. His ways of deliverance are very varied. Sometimes He saves His servants from stoning by causing their enemies to cast them out. Sometimes He saves them from

stoning by making known to them the intentions of their foes, and so enabling them to escape. Sometimes He does not deliver them from stoning, but delivers them beyond the stoning, and sends them on their way enriched with new visions, and a new sense of the sufficiency of His grace. Whether in this way, or in that, He never fails to deliver.

Fulfil thy ministry.—*2 Tim.* 4. 5.

That was the very last word of Paul in the nature of a charge to Timothy concerning his responsibilities as a minister of Christ. He emphasized it by some great words concerning his own ministry. Afterwards, he gave him certain charges of a personal nature, but on that high note he ended so far as Timothy's responsibilities to his Lord concerning the Truth and the Church were concerned. It was a call to make full proof of his service; that is, so to discharge it that there could be no question as to its authenticity. It is a great word, and all those called to serve Christ, in whatever capacity, do well to take heed of it. How often our service is unequal! Sometimes it begins well, and then it wilts, it slackens, it evaporates. Sometimes it is characterized by irregularities occasioned by yielding to the insidious forces that are ever the enemies of constant and consistent endeavour. Paul dared to refer to his own example. He was nearing the end, but looking back he could say, "I have fought the good fight; I have finished the course; I have kept the faith." What a glorious ending to a life of service. Well may we earnestly desire so to finish. But the finishing depends upon the way of the going. In words immediately preceding this final injunction, the Apostle had revealed the secrets of obedience: "Be thou sober in all things; suffer hardship; do the work of an evangelist." These words need no interpretation, but they demand careful thought. The last charge: "Do the work of an evangelist," may not be for us all; but the former two: "Be sober in all things," and "Suffer hardship," are for everyone.

TITUS

To the pure all things are pure; but to them that are defiled and unbelieving nothing is pure.—*Titus* 1. 15.

These words closely follow a reference to "Jewish fables, and commandments of men," and this fact helps us to understand them. The whole system of living by tradition was unutterably evil; and our Lord Himself and His Apostles protested against it. Such traditions constantly led men to a burdensome life, in that they

made actions to be sins which were no sins, and left the truly sinful things of the inner life untouched. It is so even to-day. Man-made regulations as to what men may do or not do, are the greatest enemies to real spiritual life that it is possible to conceive. These words, then, touch the true deep note about life. The "all things" refers to everything which is non-moral; such as appetite and food, desire and marriage, exchange and commerce, weariness and recreation, and so on through all the varied realm of life. To the pure all these things are pure, and they will be maintained in purity. To the impure, every one of them may be made the vehicle and occasion of impurity. No traditions, no commandments of men, no rules and regulations, can save the ordinary things of human life from positive obscenity, if the man handling them is himself an impure man. On the other hand, the man who is pure may enter into them all; and not only will he not be defiled by them, but will not defile them; he will hold them in pureness. To all of which the words of Jesus testify, that not what goeth into a man defileth, but that which cometh out of him.

That they may adorn the doctrine of God our Saviour in all things.—*Titus 2. 10.*

Here are two ideas which flash with a surprising brilliance. The first is that the doctrine of God our Saviour can be adorned; and the second is that those who are spoken of as able to do it are slaves. Perhaps we shall understand the first better, if we begin with the second. The word servants here is distinctly the word for slaves, and it may well be conceived that the conditions of slaves in Crete, where Titus was labouring, were of the worst. Paul had already said that the testimony of one of their own prophets was true that the Cretans were liars, evil beasts, gluttons. Slavery in a society of such must have been a terrible thing. Among these slaves there were some who were saints, and these were declared able in the very life of slavery, to "adorn the doctrine." Moreover, the Apostle had declared how they would do it. It would be done by subjection to their masters; by seeking to be well-pleasing, by not gainsaying; by honesty, by faithfulness; in short, by such action in difficult circumstances as to win from their very masters a recognition of their goodness. Thus we see how "the doctrine of God our Saviour" may "be adorned." It is adorned when its effects on life and character are expressed in conduct. To be true and gentle and faithful in circumstances that are hard and unfair, and even unjust, is only possible in the power of some great spiritual conviction; and the value of such spiritual conviction is revealed in such conduct.

They which have believed God may be careful to maintain good works.—*Titus 3. 8.*

The alternative reading suggested in the Revised Version, "careful to profess honest occupations," helps us to understand what was in the mind of the Apostle when he wrote these words. The whole chapter reveals the kind of world in the midst of which these Cretan Christians were living. It was characterized by insubordination to authority, by laziness, by disaffection and contention, and by every form of evil excess. Moreover, it was intellectually a world of wrangling and disputes over all sorts of things. In the midst of such conditions the Christians stood fundamentally as those who believed God. To believe God is to believe His Word, His revelation of the true order of life. Those who stood on that belief could testify to the power of it in no better way than that of good works, that is, by following a quiet and diligent life of devotion to duty, in callings which in themselves were honest. And that is always so. There is no more powerful force for rebuking all evil things, whether of conduct or of opinion, than that of the quiet, strong, persistent life of man or woman who goes on from day to day doing the duties of the day well, cheerfully, and with joy. It is not easy; and that is recognized in the very verb employed. They are "to be careful"; that is, they are to make it a study, to take thought about it. It is not easy, but it is worth while.

PHILEMON

That the fellowship of thy faith may become effectual.—*Philemon 6.*

That was the burden of Paul's prayer for Philemon; and in sending Onesimus back to him, he was creating a new opportunity for his realization of that very thing. Philemon had faith, as Paul had already said; and it was a double faith, "toward the Lord Jesus, and toward all the saints." That faith necessarily placed him in the realm of fellowship, and that was also two-sided: fellowship with the Lord Jesus, and fellowship with all the saints. Such was his faith, his conviction, that to which he had yielded himself. Such was his fellowship, his vital relationship, the good thing which was in him. Paul's prayer for him was that it might be effectual; that is, effective. Faith and fellowship are at once made valuable and vindicated as they are active. While a number of names are found in this letter, three stand out prominently, those of Paul, Philemon, and Onesimus. They share a common faith; they are members of one fellowship. The circumstances were such as to give the fellowship of their faith an opportunity for action; that is, to become effectual. It was so in the case of Paul, as he sent Onesimus back to his master, even though he would have been serviceable to himself in his prison. It was so in the case of Onesimus, in that he went back to the master whom he had wronged in running away from him. The letter was written that it might be so in the case of Philemon as he received Onesimus, "no longer as a servant . . . but a brother beloved."

HEBREWS

God, having . . . spoken . . ., hath . . . spoken.—*Heb.* 1. 1, 2.

From the introductory sentences of this great writing, we have taken out the principal words. They need, of course, all the qualifying words by which they are surrounded in order to the full understanding of their meaning, but in themselves they reveal the fundamental truths with which the writing deals. The first fact is God. Without definition, or argument, or apology of any kind, the writer names God. The fact that the writing was for Hebrews shows that he accepted the Hebrew conception of God. All that had been revealed by the names and titles, the Law, the Prophets, and the history, was included. The second fact is that God does reveal Himself. He speaks to men; He makes known His will. These are the foundation truths of our religion. If we are not sure of these, we are sure of nothing. In the process of His dealings with men, He has proved Himself, by revealing Himself; and the nature of the revelation has proved it to be of God. Then the statement shows us the interrelationship between the past and the present. He did speak in the past, particularly, progressively, in divers portions and manners, as men were prepared to receive. He has now spoken fully, finally, in His Son; and men will progressively apprehend the meaning of this final speech, but they will never exhaust it. Moreover, the interrelation is part of one whole. Having spoken as He did in the past, it was necessary and possible for Him to speak in His Son. It was necessary, for all that He had said was incomplete. It was possible, and apart from the first partial messages, the full and final message would have been incomprehensible. Thus we see the wisdom and perfection of the Divine Revelation.

Therefore we ought to give the more earnest heed to the things that were heard, lest haply we drift away.—*Heb.* 2. 1.

The "therefore" of these words carries us back to the arguments of the previous chapter, and on to those of this chapter. The Hebrew people maintained, and rightly, that their whole religious and national economy had been ministered by angels. The writer agreed, but proceeded to show the superiority of the Son of God to the angels, and the consequently greater authority of the speech of the Son, to that of the word spoken by angels. That superiority being granted, it follows irresistibly that we should give the more earnest heed to what He has to say. The conclusion is so self-evident that we are almost inclined to wonder that there was any need for so solemn a warning. We shall find an answer to that wonder in the writer's description of the peril, and in the contrast which he makes between the word of angels and the message of the Son. Note this contrast first. The word spoken by angels was steadfast, and disobedience brought a just recompense. The word of angels was the word of law, stern, inflexible. The message of the Son is that which can be summarized in one word, "Salvation." It is the word of grace, compassionate, unfailing. That in itself is one reason why the foolish heart of men may fail to give earnest heed to it. Then again the peril is that of drifting. The figure is that of a boat, which caught by unseen currents, may be carried out of its course. This is so easy a thing to do. But it ought not to be. The message of Salvation, spoken by the Son, should make an even stronger appeal than that of law uttered by angels.

Wherefore, holy brethren, partakers of a heavenly calling, consider the Apostle and High Priest of our confession, even Jesus.—*Heb.* 3. 1.

Again we have an appeal based upon what has already been written. Having dealt with the humiliation of the Son, and shown that it had not detracted from His superiority to the angels, but rather enhanced it, in that such humiliation was in order to the doing of His saving, priestly work, the writer urged his readers to consider Him. We may link this appeal with the previous one. The sure way in which to "give earnest heed" to the message of the Son, and to be saved from "drifting," is to consider Him. That consideration is to be of Him in two ways, as Apostle and High Priest. Along these lines we are led in what follows. Jesus is "the Apostle . . . of our confession." That marks the Divine authority of His message. He is the Sent of God. His pre-eminence in this matter is shown by comparing Him with Moses and Joshua. Moses was faithful as a servant *in* the house, but Jesus as a Son *over* the house. Moses led the people out, but could not lead them in. Jesus leads out of bondage and into the promised possessions. Joshua léd the people in, but could not give them rest. Jesus gives rest. Jesus is also "the High Priest of our confession," and that is very fully developed. The whole emphasis of this verse is upon the necessity for considering Him. The idea is that of careful contemplation, attentive thinking. How sadly we often fail here. The holy exercise demands time, method, diligence, and wherever it is practised we are saved from drifting.

A great High Priest, Who hath passed through the heavens.—*Heb.* 4. 14.

With these words the writer began his more careful consideration of Jesus as the High Priest of our confession; and as he did so, he employed the word "great." To the Hebrew mind the phrase "High Priest" in itself expressed the highest form of priestly service; it was the ultimate word. This phrase is still further strengthened by the word "great." Jesus is not merely a priest; He is the High Priest, and in that He is great. His priestly work and position are characterized by the utmost finality. This greatness is here described in one way. He has "passed *through* the heavens." The statement is far stronger than it would be if it read "passed *into* the heavens." It helps us to think of Him as entering into the place of closest nearness to God in His priestly position. No lower heaven, however exalted, is the place of His work. Through all heavens He passed to that which in some sense is beyond the heavens, to the very place and being of God Himself. Moreover, the phrase is inclusive of His coming to us as well as to His going to God. He passed through the heavens to come to man, into closest identification; and having accomplished His purposes there, He passed through the heavens to go to God, into closest identification. The same thought is found in Paul's letter to the Ephesians: "Now this, He ascended, what is it but that He also descended into the lower parts of the earth? He that descended is the same also that ascended far . . . that He might fill all things."

**Thou art a priest for ever
After the order of Melchizedek.**
—*Heb.* 5. 6.

In considering the "High Priest of our confession," the writer had made clear His superiority to the Aaronic order. He now quoted this couplet from a psalm, and thus introduced the name Melchizedek, to which he presently returned. The really emphatic words of the couplet are "for ever." Aaron was called of God, and rendered his appointed service; but the period of that service was necessarily limited to his earthly lifetime, and he was succeeded by others. Our High Priest is the Son of God, and therefore there is no

end to the period of His priesthood, and there can be no successors. While that is so, the quotation also suggests the nature of His priesthood. It is not merely that of dealing with sin; it is that also of sustaining life amid service and conflict. Melchizedek appears once on the page of Hebrew history, and the appearance is full of suggestiveness in the matter of what he did. Abram had been forth to war in the interest of righteousness. His service was wholly on behalf of others. He was victorious. The king of Sodom went out to meet him. Then Melchizedek appeared, and "brought forth bread and wine"; also he blessed Abram; also he received a "tenth of all." Thus he appeared, these things he did, and then he passed out of sight. There is no further reference to him until David in a Messianic psalm wrote this couplet. There is no other reference to him till this letter. Thus we see him at once king of righteousness and peace, and his priestly function is that of sustaining and blessing those who serve the Kingdom of righteousness and peace.

Not sluggish, but imitators of them who through faith and patience inherit the promises.—*Heb.* 6. 12.

Having introduced the name of Melchizedek, and so also the idea of an order of priesthood higher than that of Aaron, before dealing with that subject more particularly the writer turned aside to exhort his hearers to diligence, and to warn them against the deadly peril of apostasy. In the course of this teaching, he thus put two attitudes toward all these great matters into contrast: the attitude of the sluggish, and that of imitators of those of faith and patience. Or we may say a contrast between "sluggishness" and "faith and patience." This calls us up again to "take heed," and to diligence in "considering." What, then, is sluggishness? The King James' Version rendered the word "slothful," but that left the emphasis too much on the failure to act. The word "sluggish" employed by the Revisers emphasizes a condition, which results in slothfulness. The Greek word means lazy, stupid. It is a condition of soul into which we inevitably pass if we fail in the utmost diligence. Great as is the glory of our High Priest, unless we resolutely maintain our attitude of mental alertness, we shall lose the power to see, to realize, and so to profit by, His greatness. In order to this diligence, we need "faith in patience": that is, faith reinforced and kept operative by patience. Here the word translated patience means more than endurance. It is the word elsewhere rendered long-suffering. It is active rather than passive. The cure for sluggishness is ever the activity which persists in conforming the life and its habits to the faith which is professed.

He is able to save to the uttermost them that draw near unto God through Him.—*Heb. 7. 25.*

This ability is based upon two things, His priesthood, and our availing ourselves of it. No other priest is equal to such complete saving of men. He, however, is only able to complete the work of saving, when men draw near to God through Him. There are very remarkable truths involved in this glorious declaration. Let us note two of them. First, the assumption of the statement is that it is only when men are near to God that the priesthood of Jesus is operative in all those continuous activities of intercession through which the saving of men can be carried out to its consummation. Not being perfect, not yet having attained, we may yet remain near to God, Who is the God of all patience. As that nearness is maintained, our High Priest is the Mediator through Whom all the resources of the Divine Wisdom, Strength, and Grace are communicated to us; that, growing up into Him in all things, our saving to the uttermost is completed. Departure from nearness to God separates us from the operation of our High Priest. That is a truth that we must never forget. Standing alone, it is liable to discourage us. But that brings us to the second truth, and that is that our nearness to God is through Him. It is through Him we draw near, and it is through Him we abide in nearness. Thus the two phases of His priestly work are in view. The first is atoning. Through that we draw near, and abide in nearness. The second is intercessory and perfecting. That operates as we are near to God through His atoning work.

He is the Mediator of a better covenant.—*Heb. 8. 6.*

The outstanding word here is the word "covenant," for it includes everything which accrues to the believer through the priesthood of Jesus. The writer had employed it once before (7. 22). Now he turned back to it, and from this point it constantly recurs to the end of the letter. It is well that we should recognize its real value. The Latin Vulgate invariably renders the word *testamentum*, and our Revisers always marginally suggest *testament* as an alternative rendering. This is suggestive, and indeed important. When we employ the word covenant, we think of a contract, into which two parties have entered, and which involves obligations and responsibilities on both sides; and all this is true in the use of the word in this connection. But the idea is not that of a covenant made after discussion, or by mutual concession and arrangement. A covenant is literally a testament, or disposition made by one, in the making of which the other is not consulted, but the benefits of which that other can only appropriate as he fulfils the terms laid down by the one. Our modern word *Will* exactly conveys the idea. The covenant between God and man which Christ Jesus has mediated is the disposition of God on behalf of man, the benefits of which man can only appropriate as he obeys the terms of that testament or disposition. To put the truth somewhat roughly, and perhaps, therefore, all the more forcefully—the better covenant is not one arrived at after bargaining with God. It is all of His grace.

Christ entered . . . into heaven itself, now to appear before the face of God for us.—*Heb. 9. 24.*

This is the fact which made possible the covenant. This was the supreme act of His priesthood, and it is continuous. In a former note we considered the statement that our great High Priest has "passed through the heavens" (4. 14). Here it is said that He has entered into heaven. This is not a contradiction, but an interpretation. The heavens *through* which He passed are the created heavens. The Heaven which He entered is the uncreated abode of God Himself, the very Holiest of all. Thither He went "to appear before the face of God." The statement is apprehended in all its fulness of meaning when we put it into contrast with the greatest hour in the life and ministry of Moses. In an hour of supreme need and highest communion Moses asked to see the glory of God; that is, to behold His face. The answer was, "Thou canst not see My face"; but in grace he was given to see the back of God. The Son of God, in His glorified manhood, entered into Heaven to be manifested before the face of God! There, as man, God beheld Him, and He beheld God. And this was for us. In His humanity ours was represented, our sin covered by His completed atonement, our imperfections cancelled in His perfection, our weakness ended in His strength. Henceforth we are accepted in the Beloved, and all the wisdom and might and love of God are given to us through Him in the covenant which God makes with us.

Let us draw near.—*Heb. 10. 22.*

In a previous note (7. 25) we considered the fact that the intercessory work of our High Priest is only operative on behalf of those who draw near to God through Him. In these words we are called upon to avail ourselves of the privilege He has created of access to God. It is that possibility of approach and access which is the supreme and glorious fact resulting from the work of our Priest. The very nature of this appeal emphasizes this. The one thing we are called upon to do is to draw near. In God, and the eternal order, there is no reason why we should not do so. Everything which excluded men from God has been put away. The rending of the Temple veil at the death of Jesus was symbolic. That which, in its wholeness, had been the symbol of man's exclusion from God through sin, in its rent condition was the symbol of the open way to God. The life of Jesus in its final perfection was a perpetual message to men concerning their unfitness to enter the Divine Presence. Because He lived a life of unbroken fellowship with God, I know that I cannot do so; His fellowship resulted from His being well-pleasing to God. Nothing ever has separated between man and God, save sin. He was sinless, and so lived with God. But the death of Jesus has dealt with my sin, and so has made possible my return to God, my access to Him at all times and under all circumstances. Therefore the appeal to me is not a call to prepare myself, or to make a way for myself to God. It is simply to come, to draw near, to enter in. This I do only through my great High Priest, but this I may do through Him without faltering and without fear.

These all . . . received not the promise.—*Heb.* 11. 39.

These words are full of encouragement for us in hours when we are tempted to discouragement because the victories of faith seem as though they never would be won. After the wonderful passage in which the writer reminded his readers of the heroes and heroines who had lived and suffered and died in faith, he declared that all of them died without seeing the full victory toward which they had been looking. It is an interesting study to follow this word *promise* through the Letter. It can easily be done by the aid of a good concordance, for the A.V. and R.V. uniformly render the Greek word by this word "promise." Such an examination will show that the word is always used with reference to declarations of God as to what He will do. These promises of God were what men heard and believed, and such belief was the sustaining power in all their service and suffering. In the course of the Letter it is said that Abraham "obtained the promise" (6. 15); that through the mediation of our High Priest we "may receive the promise" (9. 15); that we need patience that we "may receive the promise" (10. 36); that the patriarchs "died in faith, not having received the promises" (11. 13); that Abraham "had gladly received the promises" (11. 17); that Samuel and the prophets "obtained promises" (11. 33); and now that "these all . . . received not the promise." This grouping shows a distinction between the receiving the promise as a promise, and receiving the fulfilment. Faith has received the promise, and acts accordingly.

Therefore let us also . . . run . . . looking unto Jesus.—*Heb.* 12. 1, 2.

These words catch up and apply all that had been said as to the service rendered in the past by those who had "received the promises," and had died, not having "received the promise." If they so endured with courage and cheerfulness, we also should be prepared to endure with patience, and run the race toward the glorious goal without wavering, however hopeless the enterprise may seem, when judged by the circumstances of the hour. The ultimate strength of this appeal, however, lies in the contrast which it suggests between these men of the past and ourselves. They had the promises; we have Jesus. They look for the City; we look off unto Jesus. This means that in Him we have a clearer revelation of the glory of the City, and of the travail through which alone it can be built. Through Him our understanding of what the tabernacling of God with men means, is more perfect. In Him the call is to yet profounder suffering and to greater patience. But He is Himself the File-leader of the Faithful; that is, in His own life and service He takes precedence of all others. And so He is supremely the Vindicator of faith in the promises of God, as the one principle which moves toward the fulfilment of those very promises. He also is waiting for the consummation, waiting till His enemies shall be made the footstool of His feet, but waiting in the perfect assurance of the final victory. Then we are called upon to rest in His assurance, to have fellowship with His sufferings, and so to hasten the coming of the Day of God.

Now the God of peace . . . make you perfect.—*Heb.* 13. 20, 21.

This is the ultimate prayer of the writer of this wonderful letter, on behalf of those for whom he had been setting forth the glories and perfections of God's speech, to men through the Son. The verb, *to make perfect*, here, is not the one employed usually in reference to the perfecting of the saints. It is one that suggests the bestowment of complete equipment, the making fit; and here, as so constantly, the reason for the fitness, the purpose of the equipment, is the doing of His will, which includes "every good thing" as a means of rendering service. It is to that end that God ever speaks to men. In times past He had spoken to the fathers through the prophets, and by His Word they had received the promises; and believing them, they had served their generation by the will of God. Now He speaks through the Son more completely, yea finally, and that still in order that in Him the message may prevail in making those who hear it fit for all life and service. In this connection, therefore, He refers to God as "the God of Peace." He is in Himself the God of Peace. It is only as men hear His word and live by it, that they can know peace. His final word to men came through His Son, Who is the Lord Jesus, the great Shepherd, Who gathers the sheep into the fold, and leads them in the way of peace. This He does through the blood of the eternal covenant, and by God's raising of Him from the dead. In Him the God of Peace perfectly equips all believing souls, so that each may confidently say—

I nothing lack if I am His,
And He is mine for ever.

JAMES

Be ye doers of the Word, and not hearers only.—*James* 1. 22.

This letter of James is pre-eminently ethical, practical, forceful. In it there are more references to sayings in the Sermon on the Mount than in all the other letters of the New Testament. All this is of great interest when we accept the view, which is almost beyond dispute, that the man who wrote the letter was a brother of the Lord. He had lived with Jesus in all the early years in Nazareth. While it would seem that he did not join himself outwardly to the disciples till after the Resurrection, there are evidences that in the company of Mary, these brethren were much with Jesus in the central period of His ministry. All this would suggest that looking back, and thinking of all those years, this man was impressed with the harmony there had ever been in the Lord, between His teaching and His life. Thus he argued, and rightly, that a faith which was not expressed in deeds was of no value at all. This does not mean that he was in any way ignorant of the deep spiritual mysteries of Christian life. If in these words he urges us to be doers of the Word, we must remember that the Word he refers to is that which he has just described as "the inborn word" (verse 21, *mrg*.). He was referring, not merely to any written Word, nor to his Lord as the Word incarnate alone; but to the Word of God received into the soul through the written Word, and by the Word incarnate. That Word is only of real value as it is obeyed, as what it enjoins is done. There is no profit, but rather the reverse, in hearing, if there be no doing.

So speak ye, and so do, as men that are to be judged by a law of liberty.—*James* 2. 12.

Again the purpose of James is practical, but the arresting word here is the description of the standard of speech and action as "a law of liberty." The phrase had already been used, as a definition of "the perfect law" (1. 25). Its repetition shows that it suggests an aspect of law which impressed the writer, and it is interesting to remember that the phrase is peculiar to James. He had referred a little before to the "royal law"—"Thou shalt love thy neighbour as thyself"—words taken from the law of Moses, and emphasized in the teaching of Jesus. Was it not the sumtotal of the conception of life as implicated in that "royal law" that he described as a "law of liberty"? To keep that law is only possible when that which the Lord had connected with it is obeyed: "Thou shalt love the Lord thy God." When that law is kept, the soul is set free from all the bondage which results from the breaking of any of the enactments of the moral law. The law of liberty is the law which defines our relationship to God and man as love-mastered. To speak and do under that impulse, is to be free indeed. If that law be disobeyed, if no mercy be shown, then judgment based upon that law will show no mercy. Love is the most vigilant and severe sentinel that watches words and works. If it be obeyed, then is life a life of liberty. If it be disobeyed, then are we in bondage every way.

The fruit of righteousness is sown in peace for them that make peace.—*James* 3. 18.

The marginal reading of the Revised Version suggests the substitution of the word "by" for "for," and that would seem to be the real thought of the writer. He had been contrasting the wisdom from beneath with that from above. The first produces jealousy, faction, confusion. The second is first pure and then peaceable. Now carefully observe that he says much more than that peace is the fruit of righteousness. That is true, and it had already been said in the declaration that heavenly wisdom is first pure, then peaceable. But here the thought is that of the propagative power of life according to heavenly wisdom. Righteousness bears fruit after its kind, and that is peace. When this is sown, still in peace, it produces righteousness again, wherein is the further fruitage; and so ever on. Those who make peace had been declared by the Lord to be blessed, the sons of God. Here the blessedness is shown in its effect. The peacemakers are those who live by the heavenly wisdom, which is first pure and then peaceable, that is, by righteousness. These are the men who make peace. To compromise with wrong, to seek for quietness by the sacrifice of righteousness, is not to secure peace, but to make it impossible. On the other hand, to stand for righteousness, even though there must be conflict and suffering, is to sow the fruit wherefrom peace will come. The ways of God are all severe, but they are the only ways of goodness. To do right at the cost of ease, is to make peace. To seek ease at the cost of righteousness, is to make peace for ever impossible.

One only is the Lawgiver and Judge, even He Who is able to save and to destroy.—*James* 4. 12.

These words were written in connection with a warning against speaking against or judging a brother. They are clear and sharp and incisive, as they show the wrong of all such action. It is impossible for any man to find a final verdict against his brother. One only is able to do that, and that is the One Who makes the laws for the government of human lives. This is so because He alone knows those whom He governs, and because His laws are the result of that perfect knowledge. Therefore His laws are just, and so will His judgments be also. He only, therefore, can pass sentence of salvation or destruction. If these words thus warn us off from all judgment of our brother, what a glorious truth they reveal as to the rights of the individual soul! Every man is to be governed and judged by God. Every man has the right of final appeal from all the findings of men to the just judgment of God. To recognize that fact in all things, is to be lifted to the highest realm of life. If my judgment is to come from the Lord, then with what care I should live! But it is also true that I shall be judged with the strictest justice. Not by the seeing of the eyes, nor by the hearing of the ears, does He judge, but with righteous judgment. If that fact fills the soul with a perpetual sense of awe, it also gives it much comfort

and courage; for righteous judgment passes beyond all the actions, to the underlying motives and aspirations. These can only be known to God, Who is the Lawgiver, and the Creator of that which He governs.

Be patient therefore, brethren, until the coming of the Lord.—*James* 5. 7.

These words follow a stern denunciation of those prosperous men who have gained their prosperity by wronging their fellows. The ultimate in all such action had been reached when such men had "killed the Righteous One." Thinking of the sufferings of many to whom he wrote, sufferings resulting from the oppression of such men as he had denounced—James first reminded them that this Righteous One did not resist, and then called them to be patient, that is, long-suffering, until the Coming of the Lord. In that word his outlook on life shines out. The day of redress, when all wrongs will be righted and all oppressions cease, will be the day when the Righteous One will come again. For that day His suffering ones are to wait, and in their waiting, to be long-suffering even towards those who oppress them. The word of exhortation he then enforces by declaring that this is the attitude of God Himself, and that the reason of His patience is that He is waiting for the precious fruit of the earth. Is not this injunction to patience much needed? Too often we are inclined to become impatient as we wait. Sometimes, indeed, the very hope of the coming of the Lord has seemed to increase impatience rather than patience. To the true child of God, the Coming of the Lord is always at hand, and the glory of it sheds unceasing light upon the way. The true way of walking in that glorious light is ever that of thanking God at every morning's dawn, and evening's shadows, that He has not come, because He is still waiting for the precious fruit of the earth. Oh, to be patient in fellowship with God!

FIRST PETER

Which things angels desire to look into.—*1 Pet.* 1. 12.

What a wonderful chapter this is! After the introduction, it opens with a doxology, and then proceeds exultantly to deal with the wonders of Christian experience and privilege, resulting from the "great mercy" of "the God and Father of our Lord Jesus Christ." The whole theme is that of "the sufferings of Christ, and the glories which should follow them," or inclusively, that of "Salvation." Of this the prophets of the past had written having "sought and searched diligently,"

and that under the direction of the Holy Spirit, Whom the Apostle here describes as "the Spirit of Christ." These are the things into which angels desire to look. It is a revealing word, helping us to realize the depths and glories of our salvation. The angels are the unfallen ones, the high intelligences who serve God in holiness, and dwell in the light. So great is human salvation, that they desire to consider it. The word for "desire" is the simplest and strongest, showing us that they realize the amazing wonder, and earnestly wish to apprehend it. The word for "look," too, is a strong one, suggesting the closest attention and inspection, the bending over and careful examination of the matter. While prophets sought and searched diligently, and angels desire to look, those of us who are the objects of this mercy which is so full of wonder should surely be content with nothing less than the utmost diligence in our endeavour to apprehend the deep things of our "inheritance incorruptible, and undefiled, and that fadeth not away."

For you therefore which believe is the preciousness.—1 Pet. 2. 7.

This change in the Revised Version, from the "unto you therefore that believe He is precious" of the Authorized, gives a far better interpretation of the Apostle's words. The declaration is not that believers know the preciousness of Christ; it is rather that they share it. The idea of preciousness is that of honour, and therefore of honourableness, that is, of the qualities that are worthy of honour. This is the thought of the statement, then. The qualities of Christ that create His preciousness, His honour, are placed at the disposal of the believer. Twice already had the Apostle described the Lord as "precious" (see verses 4 and 6). In both cases the description was a declaration of God's estimate of Him. He was the rejected of men, but with God He was elect, precious. We know the things in Christ which made Him precious, honourable, in the sight of God. They were the things of His purity, His love, His conformity to all the perfect will of God. Here, then, is the wonder of this declaration. All these things are communicated to those who believe in Him. His very life and nature are given to the believer, and, by the might of their working, make that believer precious with His preciousness. He is the living Stone, and those who come to Him, who believe in Him, receive that very quality of life which is His, and so they become living stones. It is in the power of that preciousness that they become "an elect race, a royal priesthood, a holy nation, a people for God's own possession," and so are enabled "to show forth the excellencies" of God.

Sanctify in your hearts Christ as Lord.—1 Pet. 3. 15.

The simple meaning of the injunction is that at the very centre of life there is to be but one Lord, and that is Christ. To do this is to ensure the unification of being, consistency of conduct, and accomplishment of purpose. We are divided in our own life, inconsistent in our conduct, and ineffective in our service, when our loyalty is divided. This is so self-evident a truth that it hardly seems necessary to argue it. Nevertheless, while holding the truth theoretically, how constantly we are in danger of failing to live by it! Other lords are permitted to invade the sanctuary of the heart, and to exercise dominion over us. Our own selfish desires, the opinion of others, worldly wisdom, the pressure of circumstances, these and many other lords command us, and we turn from our simple and complete allegiance to our one Lord, and give ourselves up to the false mastery of these things. The results are always disastrous. We become storm-tossed and feverish; our conduct is not consistent; our work is spasmodic and devoid of power. Therefore the urgency of the injunction. To hallow the heart by excluding all other lords save Christ Himself, is to be strong, true, and effective. His knowledge is perfect, of the heart, of the circumstances, of the true way of life. To be governed by many lords is to be in bondage to them all, and to be desolated by their conflicting ways. To be in bondage to Christ, is to be released from all other captivity.

If a man suffer as a Christian, let him not be ashamed; but let him glorify God in this name.—1 Pet. 4. 16.

This is one of the very few places in the New Testament where this description of believers is employed. There are only three. In the first, we are told where it originated: "The disciples were called Christians first in Antioch" (Acts 11. 26). It would seem that it was given to them by the men of Antioch, and it was not necessarily a term of reproach, but one used to mark the fact that they were followers of Christ. The second is where Agrippa said to Paul, "With but little persuasion thou wouldst fain make me a Christian" (Acts 26. 28). This shows that by this time it had probably become a general term. The third and last time is here, where Peter employed it in a sense that shows that in some cases it brought suffering to be known as a Christian. The Apostle says two things in view of that fact. The first is that no shame is attached to such suffering. As he wrote this he was probably remembering the time when he and his fellow-apostles left the council of the Jews, in actual physical agony from the stripes which had been laid on them, but rejoicing "that they were counted worthy to suffer dishonour for the Name" (Acts 5. 41). The second word is an injunction: "Let him glorify God in this name." That is more than glorying in the name. It is so living worthily of all it means as to glorify God. If a man is known as a Christian, and does not live as one, he dishonours God. To bear the name is to take a responsibility, a great and glorious one, but none the less a very solemn one.

Knowing that the same sufferings are being accomplished in your brethren who are in the world.—1 Pet. 5. 9.

These words constitute the gounds of the Apostle's appeal to Christians to withstand the adversary who is ever "seeking whom he may devour"; and, rightly apprehended, they are full of power and of comfort. The outlook is on the whole conflict of the saints. It is seen as one. No soul is fighting alone. Each one is at once supporting, and supported by, all the rest. Therefore it follows that to cease to withstand is to weaken all the line of battle, and to create a vantage ground for the enemy; while to continue to withstand is to strengthen that line, and to make it difficult for the foe to break through the plan of the great Captain of salvation. This means that in order to help me to withstand, all the saints are fighting. The resources of the enemy are not limitless.

The greater the number of loyal soldiers opposed to him, the greater the difficulty he has in breaking through upon one soul. The resources of our Lord are limitless, and in proportion as we avail ourselves of them we are invincible. How it will help us if we remember this in hours of temptation! If we yield, we weaken the whole battle-line. If we withstand steadfast in our faith, the strength of our victory is a contribution of power to all the ranks. And moreover, we need not yield, not only because our Lord is on our side—that is enough—but also because all the saints who resist are helping us. We never fight alone.

SECOND PETER

Blind, seeing only what is near, having forgotten the cleansing from his old sins.—2 Pet. 1. 9.

That is a graphic description of the spiritual condition of a Christian who fails to make advance in Christian experience. It is because of that condition that there is arrest in development. The description moves in two stages. The first describes the condition in itself; the second gives the reason of the condition. The condition is that of blindness. This is immediately qualified by the words, "seeing only what is near." It is near-sightedness rather than total blindness. Such a man sees the things of time, and fails to discern those of eternity; he sees the material facts, but not the facts of which they are but passing expressions; in short, he sees himself and his fellowmen, but not God. This near-sightedness is destructive of a true Christian experience, and therefore makes advance impossible. The reason is that he has "forgotten the cleansing from his old sins." That is to say, he has failed to respond to all the enlargement of life and vision which came to him when he received the cleansing of his nature at the very beginning of his Christian life. What a revelation or reminder this is of the greatness of the blessing which comes to the soul when it is accepted, pardoned, justified, cleansed! That wondrous experience always means the relating of the life to the eternal, the opening of the eyes to God. In order to the maintenance of that relationship, and the continuity of that clear spiritual vision, it is necessary to abide at the Cross, never to forget the awe and wonder of forgiveness. In proportion as we wander from that solemn sense of grace, we become near-sighted, and all our Christian life is arrested.

Of whom a man is overcome, of the same is he also brought into bondage. —2 Pet. 2. 19.

This is a truth which is insisted upon in all the Biblical revelation. Paul had given it equally clear expression when in writing to the Romans he had said: "Know ye not, that to whom ye present yourselves as servants unto obedience, his servants ye are whom ye obey; whether of sin unto death, or of obedience unto righteousness" (6. 16). It is nevertheless a truth which man is slow to believe. It simply means that the freedom of the will is strictly limited. I am free to choose my master. I am not free when I have chosen. I become the servant of that master. It is possible for a man to yield to sin, but in such yielding he becomes the servant of that sin. It is impossible for any man to treat sin as completely under his control, to be indulged in at his will, and to be laid aside at his will. Yielding is yielding, and that means submission, bending of the neck, being compelled to obey the commands of sin. The only way of freedom from the mastery of sin, is that of escape therefrom through submission to Christ; and that submission must be more than an act, it must be an attitude maintained, or else we shall be "entangled" again in "the defilements of the world," and so our last state will become worse than the first. This is a truth which humbles the soul and leaves no room for pride of will. But it is the truth which, being recognized and obeyed, makes us free from the dominion of sin. In the uttermost abandonment of ourselves to the Lord, there is perfect deliverance from the power of sin; but in no other way shall we ever be any other than slaves of sin.

Forget not this one thing, beloved, that one day is with the Lord as a thousand years, and a thousand years as one day.—2 *Pet.* 3. 8.

Thus the Apostle charges all Christian souls in their thinking of the ways and works of God to cancel the time element. Time is as nothing either way to God. We become hurried and flustered because we have only a day in which to do something. God has no such unrest, for in our small one day He is able to accomplish the things which men could only hope to do in a thousand years. On the other hand, we look on down the vista of the coming years, and the long time that must elapse before things can happen which we earnestly desire oppresses us. God has no such depression, for the thousand years are in His sight but as a day. The application of the truth which is of greatest importance to us is that of its bearings on the activities of God. Men either declare that the promise of the coming of the Lord is false because nigh two thousand years have passed since it was made; or they are tempted to think that He Who made the promise is in some way slack, that He is not acting as speedily as He might. It is only to state these things thus, to see how false the views are. It is well, then, thus to be charged not to forget this great truth. The purposes of God are so vast and so wonderful, that their working out in human experience must take, what for lack of a better term, we call time. On the other hand, His power is such that if and when He will, things can be done in a "twinkling of an eye," which will revolutionize all life, and bring in the final order.

FIRST JOHN

Our fellowship is with the Father, and with His Son Jesus Christ.— 1 *John* 1. 3.

This is one of the greatest statements of the New Testament, and it may safely be said that its greatness is created by the richness of the word which is the emphatic word, viz. *fellowship.* This is a word which was actually used by Paul more often than any other New Testament writer, but the conception is most perfectly interpreted by John. The marvel of this particular statement will best be apprehended if we accurately apprehend the significance of the word. The Greek word *koinonia* is derived from the word *koinos,* which very literally means common, in the sense of being shared by all. The use of that word *koinos,* or common, in our New Testament, which will help us most in this consideration, is that made of it by Luke when he declared that "All that believed were together, and had all things common" (Acts 2. 44). Fellowship then is that community of relationship which expresses itself in community of resource and responsibility. Those who have a fellowship one with another, are those who share the same resources, and are bound by the same responsibilities. The idea becomes almost overwhelming when it is thus applied to the relationship which believing souls bear to the Father, and to His Son Jesus Christ. It is a subject which can be meditated in silence better than interpreted by words. The whole of this letter helps us in such meditation. We may reverently attempt to summarize by repeating what is already said. The Father, His Son Jesus Christ, and all believers have all things in common. All the resources of each in the wondrous relationship are at the disposal of the others. Such is the grace of our God, and of His Son.

If any man love the world, the love of the Father is not in him.—1 *John* 2. 15.

Frederick Maurice said of this text: "St. John is never afraid of an apparent contradiction, when it saves his readers from a real contradiction." The importance of remembering this, is recognized when we place these words, by the side of those with which we so constantly comfort and assure our hearts, that "God so loved the world that He gave His only-begotten Son." It is always necessary to distinguish clearly what the term "the world" connotes in the particular sentence in which it is used. The world which God so loved as to give His only-begotten Son, is the whole order of His creation, at the summit of which, under Himself, is man. He gave His Son to redeem and reinstate man; and through him, thus redeemed and reinstated, to redeem and reinstate the whole creation. The world which we are not to love, is that same totality which to use a later statement of John, "lieth in the wicked one" (1 John 5. 19). When that is recognized, this statement is seen to be, not a contradiction to the one we have quoted, but in strict harmony with it. To love this world as it is, alienated from God, and in rebellion against His government, is impossible to the man who loves it with the love of the Father, which is a love that seeks its highest good, and therefore can make no terms with evil, but is willing to die in order that it may live. Herein is the radical difference between the man of the world and the child of God.

Let us not love in word, neither with the tongue; but in deed and truth.—1 John 3. 18.

This is really a very practical application of the thought concerning the love of God which has been already considered. John had first written the words: "Hereby know we love, because He laid down His life for us." Whatever other men may mean by love, the child of God has had a final interpretation of it in that supreme and awe-inspiring manifestation. That being so, the Apostle here pertinently asked: "But whoso hath the world's goods, and beholdeth his brother in need, and shutteth up his compassion from him, how doth the love of God abide in him?" The enquiry admits of only one answer, that such a man is devoid of the love of God. Therefore the words of appeal follow. In them the Apostle puts two kinds of love into contrast, with a double description in each case. On the one hand is love in word and with the tongue; and on the other is love in deed and in truth. The contrast becomes more powerful when the different parts of each are placed over against each other. Opposed to love in word is love in deed. Opposed to love with the tongue is love in truth. Love in word may possibly be sincere, but it is of no real value if it stops short of the deed. Love in deed is always of value, even though it speak no word. Love with the tongue is evidently insincere, for it is placed over against love in truth. Thus it is finally seen that the first love is not love at all. Love that professes, while it does not act, is not true love. Love which acts is love in truth.

We love, because He first loved us.—1 John 4. 19.

The omission of the pronoun "Him" from this sentence by the Revisers is unquestionably warranted. So far from robbing the statement of point and power, it leaves it in all its fulness of meaning. It remains true that we love God because He first loved us; but it is also true that we love one another, that we love all men, because God first loved us. When John wrote this, he was true to his whole conception of love. He had come to realize that much which is called love is not love at all. He had already declared: "Hereby know we love, because He laid down His life for us" (3. 16); and "Love is of God" (4. 7); and superlatively, "God is love" (4. 8). To him, then, nothing was worthy

of the name which was not of that nature. Therefore when he wrote "We love," he was not thinking of any mere human affection or emotion, in which there may lurk much of selfishness; but of that pure, disinterested love, which pours itself out in the uttermost giving. How true, then, the declaration that "We love because He first loved us." We only come to the knowledge of love, when we find it redeeming us at infinite cost. We only come to the experience of love as that love is shed abroad within us, and begins to lead us out in activities of the same nature. But the statement is positive. When we know that love, when that love is shed abroad within us, then we do truly love. We love God in an utter abandonment of all we are and have to Him. Nothing is withheld from Him. We love men with the same abandonment. Like the early disciples, we do not say that anything we have is our own. Everything is valuable in proportion as it may be given for the enrichment of others.

Little children, guard yourselves from idols.—1 John 5. 21.

Thus the great epistle of fellowship with God, startlingly and yet fittingly ends. The cry of the heart that truly knows God is surely ever that of ransomed Ephraim: "What have I to do any more with idols?" (Hos. 14. 8). And yet the warning is necessary. There can be no perfect fellowship if devotion is divided. The one and only peril that threatens us in the life of fellowship is that we admit any person or passion which seeks to share the supreme place in our lives with our Lord through Whom we have fellowship with our Father. And by saying that we have defined the word "idols." Anything which divides the heart in its loyalty to the Lord, is an idol. It may be a very vulgar thing; or it may be that which in itself is perfectly right, so long as it is subservient to the final sanctions of His control. If its influence in the life is that of alienating us from Him, in thought, or in love, or in will, it is an idol. The urgency of the word is found in the fact that John has employed the strongest possible word to describe our attitude toward idols. We are to keep ourselves in isolation from them. That is the real force of the word. We are not to go near them, nor to allow them to come near us. Anything which has the remotest chance of interfering with our fellowship, is to be put away, to be kept away. We are to live lives of isolation from everything which threatens our devotion to our Lord.

SECOND JOHN

Whosoever goeth onward and abideth not in the teaching of Christ, hath not God.—2 John 9.

Dr. Findlay has pointed out in his wonderful volume on the letters of John, that both the second and the third have to do with the subject of Christian hospitality. In this one, addressed to "the elect lady," perhaps a church, and perhaps a person, the persons to whom no Christian hospitality is to be extended are dealt with. These are described as "deceivers . . . even they that confess not that Jesus Christ cometh in the flesh." It is with reference to such that this declaration is made. They were persons who claimed to be leaders; they were advanced thinkers, they were progressive. The Gnostic teachers of the time were claiming that while the Gospel of the historic Jesus might be all very well for unenlightened people, they had a profounder knowledge. Such were to receive no hospitality. In this warning, we find a principle of perpetual application. There is always room for advanced thinking, for progressive interpretation, for the things of Christ are as profound as God and life. We never ought to be content to tarry with the first principles of truth. We should in knowledge go on unto perfection. But there is one infallible test for such advanced thinking, for such progressive interpretation. It is that the advanced thinking do not contradict the first principles, or deny the fundamental facts of our faith —those of the historic Jesus, that of the fact that He came in the flesh. Such advanced thinking as denies these things, is not progress, but retrogression and apostasy.

THIRD JOHN

Worthily of God.—3 John 6.

If in his second letter John dealt specially with the subject of those to whom no hospitality should be extended, in this he commends hospitality, and shows what its nature should be. There were those who "for the sake of the Name went forth, taking nothing of the Gentiles." These were to be received and welcomed, and "set forward on their journey worthily of God." Two interpretations have been given of this phrase. One is that these men were to be treated as the very messengers of God, and so *worthily of that fact.* The other is that those who tendered them hospitality were to do it as God would do it, "worthily of God." Most probably both views are correct, both ideas being involved. In harmony with the whole spirit of the letter the second is the more patent. What a pattern and test is here of hospitality! What kind of a host is God? How does He treat His guests? When we have answered those questions, we shall have discovered the nature of the hospitality we ought to extend to all those who go forth for the sake of the Name. To those who receive the hospitality of God, He gives of His best, He gives lavishly, He gives of pure delight. His concern is ever for the highest wellbeing of His guests. He opens His home to them; He spreads His table before them; He admits them to familiar converse with Himself; He places at their disposal all His knowledge, and all the riches of His grace. If we are to entertain "worthily of God" these are the lines upon which our hospitality must proceed. It is one of the things which constantly cheer and help those who go forth for the sake of the Name.

JUDE

Unto Him that is able.—Jude 24.

These are words full of comfort, and they are pre-eminently fitted as the last to be considered in these New Testament letters. They introduce a great doxology, and suggest the inspiration of it. The whole value of this letter of Jude is that it warns us against apostasy, as it shows the perils thereof. Through all these writings we have been considering, in many ways and in various applications, "the faith which was once for all delivered to the saints." To deny that faith is to perish. That faith is denied most definitely, not by intellectual dissent, but by practical disobedience. What can be more important than this should be brought home to us, as it is in this vivid writing. And yet the peril is very real, and withal it is most insidious. How shall we guard against it? How shall we be true to the faith, in face of the forces which seek to destroy it? The answer is here at the end. There is One Who is "able to guard us from stumbling." And He is "the only God our Saviour." He is the One in Whom our faith is centred. He is our faith. Then the final responsibility is the initial activity. We must still live by confidence in Him. We must keep ourselves in the love of God, by building up ourselves on our most holy faith, and by praying in the Holy Spirit. As we do so, He is able to guard us.

REVELATION

The Revelation of Jesus Christ.— *Rev.* 1. 1.

This is the very key-note of this book. The phrase refers, not only to the opening section, but to the entire treatise. The wonder of the book is proved by the variety of interpretations which it has received. No wise expositor will be over-confident that his is the one and only correct interpretation. The possibility is that there are elements of truth in all. Whereas there may be, and almost certainly will be, difficulties in every reading of it, we shall be greatly helped and guided if we remember that its real value is that it is "the Revelation of Jesus Christ." Quite evidently the arresting word here is the word Revelation, which is a translation of the Greek word *Apokalupsis*, which literally means to take off the covering, that is, to uncover, to unveil, to disclose. It is a word with which we have become very familiar. It is found only eighteen times in the New Testament. Thirteen of these occur in the writings of Paul; three in Peter's first letter; one in the Gospel of Luke; and one in the writings of John. This is the only place in his writings where it is found. Thus it stands in all its suggestiveness at the opening of this book, giving us at once the supreme value of the whole. As we read, we see: The Church and the world; the hosts of witnesses to the living God, and the massed and mighty forces in opposition to His government, and these in conflict; but the supreme matter is that of the disclosure to us of Jesus Christ—first in His own glory, then in the grace of His dealing with the Church, and then in the wisdom and might of His government, whereby He establishes the Kingdom of God on earth.

Repent, and do the first works.— *Rev.* 2. 5.

In the first chapter of this book the Lord was unveiled before our eyes in all the glory of His Person. He was disclosed as to the eternity of His Being; as to the wonders of His official position; and as to the infinite grace and tenderness of His attitude toward men. In this chapter and the next He passes before us in the wisdom,

grace, strength, and august majesty of His relationship to His Church, as it is composed of different churches. To each one He says "I know," and on the basis of His knowledge He commends or condemns. He is the faithful and true Witness. To each one also He reveals the way of escape from those things which He condemns. To each one He speaks of the possibility of overcoming, and promises fitting rewards to such as do so. The words we have chosen constitute His call to the first of these churches, that at Ephesus. There was much in this church which gained His commendation, but it had one serious failing. It had lost its first love. It had lost the freshness and enthusiasm of its early devotion. It was still loyal and true, but the loyalty lacked passion, and the truth was devoid of flame. This is always a grave condition, because it so easily passes on into other phases. How was it to be remedied? By a return to the very starting-point, that of repentance and faith.

Behold, I stand at the door and knock.—*Rev.* 3. 20.

These words, of which such constant use has been made in evangelistic work, had their first application to a church; and while the other use may not be wholly unjustified, this is their true one. The words suggest two things full of solemnity. The first is that they show that it is possible for a Christian church still to exist in outward form, while yet it has excluded the Lord from its very life. Moreover, such a church may be perfectly satisfied with itself, for it may be saying: "I am rich, and have gotten riches, and have need of nothing." It is more than probable also that other churches might consider it to be an influential church, if we are to judge by the way that word influential is often used to-day. Can anything be more ghastly? A church organized and busy, but Christless! The condition of such a church is that of tepidity, a condition so loathsome to the Lord that of it He says: "I will spew thee out of My mouth." All that leads to and emphasizes the second suggestion of these words. It is that, even in the case of such a church, He is still the patient and compassionate

One. He waits at the door, and knocking, seeks re-admission, able and willing to bring to the church again all the true wealth. He stands waiting, offering such a church the hospitality of His love, and seeking that of her welcome. Oh, the poverty of the church from which He is excluded, whatever her worldly wealth and position may be; and oh, the wealth of the church where He is present and rules, whatever her material poverty may be!

A throne set in heaven, and One sitting upon the throne.—*Rev. 4. 2.*

This book is now about to pass on to matters of the earth, of its kingdoms, and forces, and behaviour. Jesus Christ is to be unveiled in His government. He is to be disclosed in the processes by which He battles against the destructive forces of evil, and finally establishes the Kingdom of God on earth. This chapter and the next are occupied with the established order, rather than with the executive activity. In this one, the central revelation is that of the Throne, and the One Who occupies it. The first fact is that of the Throne and the One. It is an unveiling. The Throne is not seen as now being set in Heaven, but as having been for ever set there. It is, in the words of the old Hebrew prophet, the Throne set on high from the beginning. It has always been there. Whatever the attitudes of men may have been toward it—whether that of forgetfulness, or indifference, or rebellion, or submission—they have never escaped from its power and authority. Moreover, the One Who is unveiled is not One Who has recently come to the Throne. He has ever occupied it. This is the Throne that Isaiah saw when Uzziah died, the Throne that has never been vacant, and that has never trembled. The imagery of the chapter is wonderful, as it helps us to apprehend the glory and majesty of that centre of authority in the universe. Perhaps, however, nothing in all the chapter is more impressive than the reverent reticence of the description of the One upon the Throne. No form is described, but only the effect produced by looking, that of the translucent light and beauty of jasper and sardius. When we attempt interpretation, we fail, because we are not sure about the stones. The impression is everything. Light, glory, beauty; and all that, living, and enthroned.

Worthy art Thou to take the book, and to open the seals thereof.—*Rev. 5. 9.*

Still dealing with the established order, this chapter takes us a step further than the former one. There we saw the Throne, and were made conscious of the One Who occupied it. In this chapter the first vision is of that same Throne, and that same One; but of that One holding in His right hand a Book, sealed with seven seals. As events prove, that Book is the Divine programme for dealing with evil and establishing the Kingdom of God. But more than a programme is needed. There must be One Who is qualified to carry it out; One Who will be able to administer the affairs of the Throne; and accomplish the purposes of the One Who sitteth thereupon. And none is found "in the heaven, or on the earth, or under the earth." There are those "in the heaven", fitted for government— "dominions, thrones, principalities" suggest that; but they cannot deal with this complex condition of good and evil in conflict. There may be those "on the earth" capable of governing; but they are themselves involved in evil, and cannot cope with it. There are those "under the earth," who are "rulers of the darkness," but they are in rebellion against the One Throne. Therefore none is "able to open the Book, or to look thereon." But there is One Who is able. He has overcome in order to do it. He is the Lion of the tribe of Judah, a Lamb as though it had been slain. He is in His nature of the heaven, and of the earth; and by conquest He is over the underworld. He now takes the Book out of the right hand of Him that sitteth upon the Throne, in order to carry out the Divine programme, to administer the affairs of the Throne, and to accomplish the purpose of the One that sitteth thereupon.

The Lamb opened one of the seven seals.—*Rev. 6. 1.*

Having seen the unveiling of Jesus Christ as the Executive of the Throne, in the right created by the fact that He is "the Lamb that hath been slain," we now proceed to His unveiling in actual government. Nothing takes place apart from His administration. He opens every seal, the story of which continues to the end of chapter 18, for the seven seals, the seven trumpets, and the seven bowls reveal different aspects of the same governmental procedure. Beyond that, He it is Who reigns for the thousand years, conquers the final manifestation of evil, and reigns over the final, perfected Kingdom. The words which we have selected refer to the first of the seals, but they are equally true of all of them. It is always the Lamb Who opens them. In this chapter we have the account of the opening of six seals. As they are opened, we first see forces commanded to come forth, and manifest and express themselves. After the opening of the first, the King is manifested; after the second, the Lord of War; after the third, the Prince of Commerce; after the fourth, Death with Hades. Under all these, souls suffer and die in fellowship with the suffering and death of the One Who opens the seals, and the opening of the fifth reveals them as calling for the ending of false rule on earth, and comforted, and commanded to wait until the process should be completed. The opening of the sixth gives the signs of the approach of the end. Amid the convulsions of the world-order, kings, princes, captains, the rich, the strong, bondmen, and freemen, are made conscious of the One Who sitteth upon the Throne, and of the wrath of the Lamb. All things are proceeding by the administration of the Lamb, Who opens every seal.

Hurt not the earth, neither the sea, nor the trees, till we shall have sealed the servants of our God on their foreheads.—*Rev.* 7. 3.

These words, uttered by one angel to four others, indicate a halt in the processes under the opening of the seals. Six have been opened; the seventh and last is about to be opened; but there is delay, during which an elect remnant of Israel is sealed. This is the spiritual realization of Israel. At this point John was also granted a vision of a multitude in heaven, so great that no man could number them. They are seen surrounding the Throne and the Lamb, worshipping and praising Him, as it is given to them to see the processes of the government of the earth, and to understand whereunto all these things are moving. This is the first of a series of interludes during these processes, and the fact of them is full of importance, proving as it does that God is not bound by times and dates and seasons. As six seals have been opened, there has been a steady development toward a climax of judgment. That climax is at hand, but it is halted in order that the justice of God's mercy may have full opportunity to accomplish its purpose also. The storm is ready to break, but that also is under the control of the angels who are the servants of the Throne; and until He has completed His work of securing loyal souls from the disaster, these angels must hold the winds in check.

A silence in heaven about the space of half-an-hour.—*Rev.* 8. 1.

And now the seventh seal is about to be opened. When it is opened, a sequence of seven trumpets will initiate the movements leading up to the manifestation of the King. At last it is opened, and there is "a silence in heaven about the space of half-an-hour." Before looking at the events on earth, we are thus taken again to the heaven, where is the Throne, and where is the One, and where is the Lamb, and where are the angels, all of them, and where is the great multitude. There, in contemplation of the events to transpire on earth, all is silence. There is no voice from the Throne, no song of angel or of saint. Everything is hushed. Eternity breathes the sense of time, for the silence in its duration is measured by the hours of men. It lasted half-an-hour. Surely no statement

could possibly be more arresting as a revelation of the dread and august solemnity of the things to follow. After the silence the angels were given the trumpets. And then followed another pause, in which incense was added to the prayers of all the saints. All the intercessions of the saints have been preserved. They are about to receive their final answer in the coming of the Kingdom. Then those prayers, mingled with fire, are cast upon the earth. So the Kingdom is coming by the fire which destroys the base and purifies the noble. At last the movement begins, and four angels sound their trumpets.

And they repented not of their murders, nor of their sorceries, nor of their fornication, nor of their thefts. —*Rev.* 9. 21.

The statement is an appalling revelation of the fearful nature of evil, and a vindication of those awful methods by which, and by which alone, God can deal with it so as to deliver men from its power. In this chapter the fifth and sixth angels have sounded, and so the first and second of the last three woes have fallen upon the earth. These have been of a new nature from those following the sounding of the first four trumpets. Those were physical. These have been terrible spiritual visitations, producing bodily sufferings and death. Nevertheless, men who had escaped actual death repented not. As the story is read, it seems almost incredible; and yet when we turn from these visions to the actual facts of human history, and most notably to the things in the midst of which we have lived recently, is not this view of the power of evil vindicated? How often have we seen men fear death, but, if they escape it, still persistent in evil, and indeed sometimes rush back to it with an abandonment and intensity that is utterly appalling. These methods of severe judgment are necessary in order to stamp out evil, but they will not save men. If men will not yield themselves to the grace and mercy of God, they will be destroyed, not saved, by His wrath. It is a solemn·and searching truth, the meaning of which we do well to ponder.

There shall be delay no longer.— Rev. 10. 6.

Everything was now moving up to the sounding of the seventh trumpet, and the seer was prepared for what he was to see. First, there was given to him the vision of a strong angel, vested with authority, and declaring that there should be no further delay. The whole method of God with men through ages had been that of mystery and apparent delay. Now both would cease. Its ceasing would be according to the good tidings which He had declared to His servants the prophets;

that is, it would issue in complete victory for all His purposes. But the processes would be those of further suffering, and the seer was symbolically prepared for this under the figure of the book which he was commanded to eat. It was the book of the Divine Word concerning these very things, containing unquestionably the messages which he would be called upon to deliver concerning many peoples and nations and tongues and kings. To a man called to such ministry there would be joy and bitterness. It is always so to those who deliver the messages of Divine judgment in true fellowship with the Lord Himself. All His delays are the result of His patience. When the hour strikes in which "delay shall be no more," God proceeds with the processes of His judgment, but never with delight. If He curse Jerusalem, it is always with a voice tremulous with the sorrow of His heart. The Lord delighteth in mercy, and judgment is His strange act; but when, in spite of grace and chastisement, man refuses to repent, then for the welfare of the race, and the fulfilment of His purposes of love, He will smite to destruction.

The kingdom of the world is become the kingdom of our Lord, and of His Christ; and He shall reign for ever and ever.—Rev. 11. 15.

The early part of this chapter is occupied with a continuation of the account of the preparation of the seer for what he was to witness after the sounding of the last of the seven trumpets. It is almost certainly an interpretation of the things which at that period in the Divine procedure had then already transpired, during the period of the opening of the seals until that moment. At last the seventh angel sounded, and the final stage under the seventh seal is ushered in. Directly the angel sounded, great voices followed in heaven, and these were the words they uttered. Much remained to be done; the last stages of the Divine judgment would be more terrible than any that had preceded; but the heavenly Intelligences knew whereunto it would all lead, and they rejoiced and worshipped, that the time had come when all false authority over the world would be abolished, and God and His Christ would firmly establish Their rule and authority over it. This, then, is heaven's perpetual song, even amid the conflict between Jerusalem and Babylon, between faith and rebellion, between good and evil; and it is the privilege of the heavenly people, of those whose names are written in heaven, to sing the same song. They know the Throne that is set; the One Who sits upon it, and the Lamb Who opens the seals. For them, there never can be any doubt as to the issue. The world must become actually and experimentally the Kingdom of God. Knowing this, they rejoice in tribulation also, and rest in the Divine justice as it proceeds to deal with evil in judgment.

And there was war in heaven.— Rev. 12. 7.

In these three chapters, 12, 13, and 14, we certainly have an interlude upon the account of the actual procedure. A series of visions were granted to the seer, setting forth the fact and conditions leading up to the things actually following the soundings of the trumpet. There is no doubt that here we reach the section of this book about which it is least possible to be dogmatic. I believe that the first section of this chapter looks back to the birth of the Man-child Jesus of ideal Israel. He is caught up unto God and to His Throne, while she is driven into the wilderness. For the purpose of this vision her time is dated as from the moment when that Man-child takes the book from the right hand of God, and begins to open its seals. At the end of 1,260 days, or three and a-half years, there is war in heaven. Our only conception of war is material, and therefore we cannot visualize this conflict. Enough for us to know that it is an actual conflict between principalities and powers, fallen and unfallen, and that the result is that the whole of the fallen ones are cast out of the heavenly places to which they have had access, and now exercise all their awful power on the earth. But terrible as is the manifestation of the power of evil thus centralized on earth, it is that of foes already defeated in the heavenlies, and everything proceeds under the government of the Lamb.

And the whole earth wondered after the beast.—Rev. 13. 3.

There was now given to the seer a vision of the method of Satan when thus cast down to the earth. It is that of a beast to whom power is given. It is certainly the portrayal of Antichrist, who is the counterfeit of Christ. He appears with all the signs and symbols of kingship. He, moreover, has supernatural signs, coming up out of the abyss, having a death wound which has been healed. He is characterized by great personal attractiveness, for the whole earth wonders at him. Moreover, he is followed by another beast, who makes men worship the first, and employs signs of fire and of occult wonders, and creates a fellowship of material things, in which men may buy and sell of each other if they have the mark of the beast. Upon the head of the first are "names of blasphemy"; and in this symbolic portraiture we see that the final method of evil will be that of attempting to seduce men by these false representations of the things of Christ and His Holy Spirit. Antichrist has surely not yet appeared in human history. Many tyrants, many despots, the world has had, but the last will surpass them all in subtlety, and in seductive influence. It is for us to remember that these are the true unveilings of godlessness, this is the true inwardness of evil. And further, it is for us to keep in mind most clearly the vision granted to us at the beginning, of the Throne, and the One, and the Lamb opening the seals. As we do so, we shall know that evil is being thus compelled to express itself by that Throne; and that, in order to its final overthrow. There is no moment in which that Throne is in danger.

And I saw, and behold, the Lamb standing on the Mount Zion.—Rev. 14. 1.

Having thus seen evil working itself out to its final manifestation on the earth, the attention of the seer is turned again to the heavenly order. The Lamb is seen on Mount Zion, associated with the elect remnant whose sealing had taken place before the opening of the seventh seal. Under His rule a threefold angel testimony is borne to the earth. The first declares the eternal Gospel, that is, the abiding truth of the Kingship of God. The second declares Babylon to be fallen, that is, the mystery of evil to be doomed. The third warns men against yielding to the beast, declaring that all who do, will drink of the wine of the wrath of God. Because during this period death will be the portion of many who remain true to God, a voice declares all such to be blessed. The last of these preparatory and interpretative visions granted to John was that of the Son of Man, having on His head the golden crown of absolute monarchy, and in His hand the sharp sickle of retributive justice. The words, "And He that sat on the cloud cast in His sickle upon the earth; and the earth was reaped," constitute a tremendous declaration, the full force of which will be apprehended more perfectly in the descriptions which follow. Suffice it now to say that it is a declaration of the final and all-inclusive judgment. The vintage is not that of the vine of heaven, but that of the earth, of the terrible counterfeit which we have seen under the figure of the beasts. In the final description here, the figurative merges into fact. The wine is blood.

Seven angels having seven plagues, which are the last, for in them is finished the wrath of God.—Rev. 15. 1.

The vision of the heavenly order is continued, as preliminary to that of the final stage in the processes of judgment leading on to the setting up of the Kingdom of God on earth. Seven angels are seen having seven plagues. Then, before they proceeded to the pouring out of the vials of wrath, the seer beheld a glassy sea, mingled with fire, and standing by that sea the victorious host who had overcome the beast. They were probably such as had sealed their testimony with their blood, and had overcome through death. Their song is a perfect ascription of praise to the Lord God, the Almighty, for His works, His ways, His holiness, and His righteous acts. He is referred to in this song as King of the ages, and thus the fact of all ages being under His government is recognized, the ages of tribulation, as well as those of triumph. Next in order John saw the opening of the Temple in heaven, and from thence the seven angels appeared. To these were given seven bowls full of the wrath of God. The introductory words of all this declare that these "are the last, for in them is finished the wrath of God." So that in the things that are to follow, we are to observe the final activities of the Lamb in judgment before the setting up of the Kingdom for the thousand years. The wrath of God can be finished. His love is never finished. His wrath moves forward ever to the accomplishment of that which is necessary to the full activity of His love. When that is done, His wrath is finished.

Babylon the great was remembered in the sight of God, to give unto her the cup of the wine of the fierceness of His wrath.—Rev. 16. 19.

In this chapter we have the account of the last activity of the Divine wrath in the pouring out of the seven bowls. Evil has wrought itself out to its most terrible expression. As men have made material things supreme, the first movements of the judgment are in the realm of the physical. The depth of the depravity of man is revealed in the fact that out of the experiences of pain, they still blaspheme and refuse to repent. After the sixth bowl, John heard a word of Christ, which he inserts parenthetically. It is a word announcing His coming, and proclaiming a blessing upon those who watch. When the seventh bowl is emptied, the voice out of the Temple declares: It is done. Then the interpreting word is written which we have selected. It declares the reason of all this method of wrath. God has never been unmindful of Babylon. She has ever been in His sight, and He has purposed always that she should drink the cup of the wine of the fierceness of His wrath. Let us never forget this. In what seem to us to be the long ages of the conflict, Babylon has seemed to be in the ascendant, she has acted as though there were no God, and in her appalling power has seemed to escape retribution; and more, she has trampled upon those who have believed in God and wrought for the building of His City. But God has never forgotten; He has never allowed Babylon to escape, and at last she must drink the wine of His wrath, which will be the vintage of her own wickedness.

Mystery, Babylon the great, the Mother of the harlots, and of the abominations of the earth.—*Rev.* 17. 5.

This chapter and the next constitute an interlude of interpretation dealing with the mystery of Babylon. It is represented under the figure of a woman upon whose forehead these revealing words are branded. The first word, Mystery, suggests the subtlety and spiritual nature of that which is in mind. Babylon stands for the whole system of organized godlessness in the history of the human race. It emerged into manifested activity as Babel when men organized to defeat the purposes of God. It is a spirit of evil, the mystery of lawlessness, which has been at work through every age. It has had countless manifestations, but its genius has been ever the same. It is described as the mother of harlots, in harmony with the unvarying method of Scripture, which ever refers to the departure of men from the true God to the worship of every form of idols, under that figure. This evil spirit, this mystery of iniquity, has been constantly garbed in the things of material splendour; "arrayed in purple and scarlet, and decked with gold and precious stones and pearls." This has been the method by which it has deceived the hearts of men. But she is the mother "of the abominations of the earth." All the things of vileness, of corruption, of cruelty, of tyranny, are her spawn. John saw her "drunken with the blood of the saints, and with the blood of the martyrs of Jesus." This is the evil thing against which God, through the Lamb, proceeds in wrath.

Fallen, fallen is Babylon the great. —*Rev.* 18. 2.

This word John heard proclaimed with a mighty voice by an angel who came out of heaven having great authority. It is rather a description of Babylon as she is seen from the height of the heavenly order, than a pronouncement of her doom. It is necessarily a pronouncement of doom, but it reveals the reason of the doom. She is fallen. Her condition is that of being a habitation of demons, the prison-house of unclean spirits. As the carcase of a bird with broken wings, fallen to earth, becomes infested with the life of corruption which is in itself death, Babylon is declared to be the place in which all violence and spiritual corruption of the worst type abides. Therefore is she fallen, and Heaven always sees her as fallen, even in hours when she seems to be triumphant. The words of Jesus inevitably recur to the mind: "I beheld Satan as lightning fallen from heaven." The fall of Babylon outwardly and manifestly will produce entirely opposite effects on earth and in heaven. The whole earth is plunged into mourning. Kings and merchants and masses will bewail the unutterable over-throw, for all the investments of ungodliness will be destroyed. But in that fall Heaven will rejoice, for in it, saints, apostles, prophets are vindicated and crowned. The last paragraph in this chapter declares the reason of the Divine wrath against Babylon. Her princes are "of the earth," that is, godless in their rule. Her sorceries have deceived the nations. She is full of the blood of those whom she has slain. Therefore, and because of the Throne, and the One Who sitteth upon it, and of the Lamb Who exercises His power and authority—Babylon is fallen.

After these things I heard as it were a great voice of a great multitude in heaven, saying, Hallelujah; Salvation, and glory, and power, belong to our God.—*Rev.* 19. 1.

The unveiling of Jesus Christ now presents Him coming into His Kingdom on the earth. In this chapter, and the first three verses of the next, we have the account of the inauguration of the reign of a thousand years. In this inauguration there are four distinct and august movements. The first is that of the heavenly rejoicing. The second is that of the marriage of the Lamb. The third is that of the actual manifestation of Jesus to the world. The last is that of the binding of Satan. The words we now consider constitute the key-note to everything. They are the words of a song, the expression of adoring gladness. There are three movements in the praise. First, it is the song of a great multitude. Then that of the elders and the living ones, in a great Amen. Finally, in response to a voice proceeding from the Throne, a mighty chorus breaks forth, which is as "the voice of a great multitude, and as the voice of many waters, and as the voice of mighty thunders." It is the music which celebrates the fall of the false, and 'the triumph of the true. Let us carefully observe that this music is heard "after these things." This is the vindication of all the terror of the things of wrath. That awful wrath has been working ever towards this song. The only way to the full realization of salvation is that of compelling the mystery of lawlessness to express itself to the fullest extent, in order that so it may be completely overcome.

They lived and reigned with Christ a thousand years.—*Rev.* 20. 4.

That is the brief but perfect account of the thousand years which we have come to describe as " the millennium." It is an arresting fact that in this wonderful book so little is said about that period. At the most only three verses deal with it. At the seventh verse we are at once beyond it. The glorious pictures of the last chapters are not those of the millennium, but of events following it, and a still more glorious age which is to succeed it. This is not to undervalue that period of a thousand years, but it is to draw attention to the fact that it is neither final nor complete. John was only given one version of it. He saw it as a period in which Satan would be bound, and Christ would reign in association with those who had suffered for His name, and had refused the mark of the beast. For any further interpretation of that period, we have to consult the writings of the old Hebrew prophets. The brief description, however, is sufficient to enable us to realize how wonderful a time it will be. Evil will not be absent from the earth, but it will no longer be in the ascendant, even to outward appearance. Its fountain head and centre, described here fully by John as "the dragon, the old serpent, which is the Devil, and Satan," will be bound, denied access to men. Men will be left to make their choice between good and evil apart from the seductions of evil spirits. What an age it will be for the preaching of the Gospel, and surely the preachers will be God's ancient people Israel! It will be the final period of preparation for the ultimate and perfected Kingdom.

I saw the holy city, new Jerusalem, coming down out of heaven from God. —Rev. 21. 2.

At last the city of God is seen, coming. It is the city which was in the counsel of God when He gave man a garden containing all its potentialities; the city which was in His purpose for man when He confused his Babel project; the city to reach which, Abraham left Ur of the Chaldees; the city whose walls have ever been before Him. It is the metropolis of the realized ideals of God for humanity, the centre of the true social order. Let us observe carefully the time of its coming. After the thousand years, Satan is to be loosed. Even the millennial reign will not have finally overcome evil in humanity. It will have held it in check, reigned over it. And so the master-spirit of evil is loosed to gather together to himself all those in whom this principle of evil still remains. The last earthly expression of it will be the futile gathering of these to war against the saints and the city of the Divine purpose. They are only gathered that they may be cast, with Satan, from the earth. So evil passes from the world for ever. Then follows the great assize, a period of august and awful silence, in which the records reveal the righteousness of the Divine government. It should be remembered that the purpose of everything in these visions is such unveilings of Jesus Christ as show Him in His relation to this earth. Evil is cast into the lake of fire. Then the new heaven and the new earth. Then the City of God, and the nations walking in the light thereof. Then the full answer to the prayers of the saints: "Thy name be hallowed, Thy Kingdom come, Thy will be done: As in heaven so on earth"!

He which testifieth these things saith, Yea, I come quickly. Amen; come, Lord Jesus.—Rev. 22. 20.

These are the last words before the benediction. They are the words of the Lord Jesus; and the words of those who bear His name, and wear His sign. The words of the Lord Jesus are the words of His confidence, and of His strength. To that glorious consummation He is coming, and that all the time. The word "quickly" must be interpreted, not by our finite lives, and our small almanacs, but by His age-abiding life, and our age-abiding life in Him. By our reckoning of the years, well nigh two millenniums have gone since John heard these words, and certainly another millennuim will pass ere the City of God shall come. But to Him to Whom a thousand years are but as a day, surely He cometh quickly. The haste of God may seem slow to men if they measure by the small span of an earthly sojourning. To them also it will be great haste, if they measure it by the eternal life. The one sure thing is that He cometh! Through patience, through wrath! through all the processes, He cometh! Nothing can prevent His coming. That very assurance gives urgency to the answering cry of His own: "Amen; come Lord Jesus!" That coming is the only hope of the world, and there is no desire so pure, so strong, so influential in all Highest ways, as that He should come indeed.